REVOLUTIONS AND
REVOLUTIONARY MOVEMENTS

Revolutions

and

Revolutionary Movements

FIFTH EDITION

James DeFronzo

University of Connecticut

WESTVIEW
PRESS

A MEMBER OF THE PERSEUS BOOKS GROUP

Westview Press was founded in 1975 in Boulder, Colorado, by notable publisher and intellectual Fred Praeger. Westview Press continues to publish scholarly titles and high-quality undergraduate- and graduate-level textbooks in core social science disciplines. With books developed, written, and edited with the needs of serious nonfiction readers, professors, and students in mind, Westview Press honors its long history of publishing books that matter.

Find us on the World Wide Web at www.westviewpress.com.

Every effort has been made to secure required permissions for all text, images, maps, and other art reprinted in this volume.

Westview Press books are available at special discounts for bulk purchases in the United States by corporations, institutions, and other organizations. For more information, please contact the Special Markets Department at the Perseus Books Group, 2300 Chestnut Street, Suite 200, Philadelphia, PA 19103, or call (800) 810-4145, ext. 5000, or e-mail special. markets@perseusbooks.com.

Designed by Jack Lenzo

Library of Congress Cataloging-in-Publication Data
DeFronzo, James.
Revolutions and revolutionary movements / James DeFronzo.—Fifth edition.
pages cm
Includes bibliographical references and index.
ISBN 978-0-8133-4924-4 (paperback)—ISBN 978-0-8133-4925-1 (e-book) 1. Revolutions. 2. Social movements. 3. Revolutions—Case studies. 4. World politics—20th century. 5. World politics—21st century. I. Title.
HM876.D44 2015
303.6'4—dc23
2014016782

10 9 8 7 6 5 4 3 2 1

CONTENTS

MAPS

PREFACE

A public that knows little about the political history and socioeconomic characteristics of other societies may permit its government to control how citizens perceive its actions in foreign lands. It is possible, for example, that US involvement in Vietnam would not have occurred or at least would not have progressed as far as it did if the American people had been fully aware of the Vietnamese revolution against French colonial rule, the loss of popular support for France's Indochina war effort, and the terms of the resulting Geneva peace settlement of 1954. Similarly, if the profound differences and conflicts between Iraq's Baath Party and the Islamic fundamentalist movement Al Qaeda had been more widely known in the United States, the American people would have been less likely to believe that Iraq was involved in the terrorist attacks of September 11, 2001, or to support the 2003 invasion of Iraq. New revolutionary movements and related conflicts have emerged in the Middle East, North Africa, and other places around the globe that once again tempt other countries, including the US, to consider intervention.

Although the US public was too poorly informed to prevent the tragedy in Vietnam, the collective memory of the Vietnam experience probably helped prevent direct US military intervention in several countries. But key elements of the Vietnam experience were apparently not passed on to post-Vietnam generations. This became clear to me through the responses I received to a question I asked students in several large sociology classes. The question was, "How many of you have had any treatment of the Vietnam conflict in high school?" In each case, less than 5 percent raised their hands! Most of them also indicated on anonymous questionnaires that they knew very little about social movements and political conflicts in other parts of the world. I found this disturbing because most of them were college juniors and seniors preparing to embark on their careers and take on their future political and social responsibilities.

There are probably several reasons why many Americans lack political knowledge of other societies. As citizens of the richest and most technologically advanced nation in the world, many of us feel little need to concern ourselves with the politics of less developed countries or to become familiar with the traditions of other cultures. Many people shy away from political topics because they want to avoid controversy. The fear of conflict over how to deal with the subject of Vietnam would have been especially acute in a high school faculty, with some faculty members being war veterans and others antiwar activists. In such a scenario this potentially explosive topic would have been avoided in history and social science classes. The same thing may be occurring with regard to the Iraq War.

The mass media, like the educational system, have often failed to provide information about foreign societies to the vast majority of the American people. Television networks, in the competition for advertising dollars, are intent on maximizing viewer ratings. Programs dealing with political topics in other lands cannot usually command a respectable percentage of the viewing public (except in times of war or other international emergencies such as the period immediately following the September 11, 2001, terrorist attacks, or during the Iraq War that began on March 20, 2003, or during the threat of US military intervention in Syria in 2013).

Yet when they are given a chance, many people display a strong interest in learning about political events and conflicts in other parts of the world. I have noted this in a course I have taught, Revolutionary Social Movements Around the World. Using lectures and documentaries, I attempt to explain the development and significance of important twentieth- and twenty-first-century revolutionary movements and associated political conflicts in Russia, China, Vietnam, Cuba, Central American nations, Iran, South Africa, Venezuela, nations of the Middle East, and other countries. Beginning in the mid-1980s class size often exceeded two hundred students, with about one-third of the enrollment drawn from outside the University of Connecticut's College of Liberal Arts and Sciences (i.e., from the colleges of business, engineering, nursing, education, and others; engineering and nursing students were often the best students in the course). According to surveys of class enrollees, the course attracted so much interest because it provided students an opportunity to learn about a significant number of political conflicts (and the societies in which they occur) in a single course. I hope to provide a similar opportunity to a wider audience through the fifth edition of this book.

In the first chapter, the reader is introduced to factors important for the discussion of modern revolutions, such as the development of revolutionary conditions, relevant theoretical perspectives, the roles of leaders, the functions of ideology, and the meaning of important concepts such as socialism, communism, nationalism, ideology, people's war, guerrilla warfare, and counterinsurgency, which are employed in specific contexts throughout the book. The revolutions, revolutionary movements, and conflicts covered include those of greatest world significance and those of central importance to the development of revolutionary ideology, strategy, and tactics in the twentieth and twenty-first centuries.

The chapters include references to books and articles that readers may wish to consult to broaden their knowledge of a particular topic as well as a list of relevant documentary DVDs, videos, and films. Information about obtaining these documentaries is provided at the end of the book. If a documentary was available online at the time of this writing, the web address is provided.

This volume is intended to fulfill several purposes. First, I hope it will serve as an instrument that students and other interested persons can use to expand their knowledge of the countries covered and of world politics in general. Second, faculty members can utilize the book or parts of it as well as the suggested documentary DVDs, videos, and films in sociology, political science, and history courses relating to social movements or political conflicts or to organize a course dealing specifically with revolutionary movements. Finally, this book can also be useful as a reference source for student or civic groups interested in stimulating greater public awareness of, interest in, and knowledge of world developments.

The list of those who played a significant role in the origin of this book includes my inspirational high school history teacher at St. Thomas Aquinas (New Britain, CT), Laurette Laramie; my sociology and history teachers at Fairfield University; and my instructors, fellow faculty members, and thousands of students at the University of Connecticut and Indiana University who inspired both the creation of my revolutions course and the concept of a manuscript on the subject. The reviews and advice of the experts in sociology, political science, anthropology, history, and economics who read individual chapters or the manuscript in its entirety have been of immense value. In particular, for kindly consenting to comment on various parts of this manuscript, I would like to thank Juan del Aguila, Robert Denemark, Susan Eckstein, Julie Feinsilver, Darrell Hammer, Peter Klaren, Mohsen Milani, Mark Selden, Thomas Shapiro, William Turley, Kamyar Vala, Mary Vanderlaan, John Walton, Claude Welch, and Ernest Zirakzadeh. I am also appreciative of the fine work done by Raymond Blanchette, who drew the maps used in the first three editions of this book. I would like to express my gratitude to the staff of Westview Press, in particular to Jennifer Knerr for the administrative guidance she provided (for the first two editions), to senior editor Steve Catalano of Westview and Perseus Books for his help with the third edition, to Evan Carver, Brooke Kush, Erica Lawrence, and Alex Masulis of Westview for their valuable suggestions and assistance on the fourth edition, and to Toby Wahl, Kelli Fillingim, and Sandra Beris of Perseus Books for their important advice and help in preparing this fifth edition.

Finally, I am deeply indebted to family members and friends: my mother, Mary Pavano DeFronzo, and father, Armand DeFronzo, Aunt Doris Pavano Pitts, Aunt Angie Pavano DiFronzo, Uncle Francis and Aunt Lenneye DiFronzo; my wonderful wife, Jungyun, and her parents, Sang-Deuk Gil and Bok-Dan Kim; her sister, Jungha Gil, and brother-in-law, Namho Kang; our nephews Jimin, Jihyun, and Doeun and our niece Yunsil; Jungyun's brothers, Chunghoon and Woongchan, and her sisters-in-law, Bo-na Gong and Kyungim Choi; my brother, Donald DeFronzo, and sister-in-law, Diane Bracha DeFronzo; Anthony Bracha of the United Auto Workers; my sister, Margaret Pastore, and her friend David Timm; David DeFronzo, Monica and Grace Hermanowski DeFronzo, Larry and Teresa Hermanowski, Victoria and Karen DeFronzo, Michael Pastore; my cousins Connie Manafort, Carl Tata, Sal and Lynne Romano, and my goddaughter Joy Anello; David and Randi Manafort, Michael and Ginny O'Connor, Jimmy and Jolyn Manafort, Tom and Lil Pitts, Vinnie and Jeanette Pitts, Nancy DiCaprio, Raffaele and Lucy Gironda, Javier and Dori Rathbun, Paul and Elaine Puzzo, Diane DiFronzo Hughes, Patrick and Frances Gallagher, and my friends Walter Ellis (whom I met when we were graduate students at Indiana University and who has used this book for his course on revolutions at Hillsborough College and has invited me to discuss revolution with his students), Deanna, Mathew, and Evan Levanti, Al Cohen, Gerianne Cohen, Jane Prochnow, Bill Tunmer, Lance Hannon and Monica Cuddy, John McVarish, Heather McVarish Benner, Billy and William Benner, Roger Gocking, Thomas and Sue Ryan, Walter and Elizabeth Clebowicz, Dave Fowler and Wendy Kimsey, Ted and Joni Rhodes, Sue Cook and Ken Ringle, Andy, Linda, and Mike Kissell, Jason and Sarah Jakubowski, and other good friends for their inspiration and encouragement in fulfilling this project.

—JIM DEFRONZO

ACRONYMS

AD	Acción Democrática
AIDS	Acquired Immune Deficiency Syndrome
ALBA	Bolivarian Alternative for the Americas (renamed the Bolivarian Alliance for the Americas)
ANC	African National Congress
ARDE	Democratic Revolutionary Alliance
ARVN	Army of the Republic of Vietnam
BBC	British Broadcasting Corporation
BCM	Black Consciousness Movement
CAFTA	Central American Free Trade Agreement
CANTV	National Telephone Corporation (Venezuela)
CDRs	Committees for the Defense of the Revolution
CDSs	Sandinista Defense Committees
CIA	Central Intelligence Agency
CNN	Cable News Network
COB	Bolivian Workers Central
COPE	Congress of the People
COPEI	Venezuela's Christian Democratic Party
COSATU	Congress of South African Trade Unions
COSEP	Superior Council of Private Enterprise
DR	Revolutionary Directorate
FDN	Nicaraguan Democratic Force

FMLN   Farabundo Martí National Liberation Front

FSLN   Sandinista Front for National Liberation

FTAA   Free Trade Area of the Americas

GCC   Gulf Cooperation Council

GDP   Gross Domestic Product

GMD   Guomindang

GNP   Gross National Product

HAMAS   Islamic Resistance Movement

HAPCs   Higher-Stage Agricultural Producers Cooperatives

HIV   Human Immunodeficiency Virus

ICP   Indochinese Communist Party

IDF   Israeli Defense Forces

IMF   International Monetary Fund

IPSP   Political Instrument for the Sovereignty of the Peoples

IRC   Islamic Revolutionary Council

IRG   Islamic Revolutionary Guard

IRP   Islamic Republic Party

ISCOR   Iron and Steel Corporation

LAPCs   Lower-Stage Agricultural Producers Cooperatives

MAK   Services Office

MAS   Movement Toward Socialism

MBR-200   Movimiento Bolivariano Revolucionario-200

MDN   Nicaraguan Democratic Movement

MIA   Missing in Action

MNR   National Revolutionary Movement

MPLA   Popular Movement for the Liberation of Angola

MRS   Sandinista Renewal Movement

MSR   Socialist Revolutionary Movement

MVR   Fifth Republic Movement

M-26-7   26th of July Movement

NACLA   North American Congress on Latin America

NATO   North Atlantic Treaty Organization

NLF   National Liberation Front

OAS   Organization of American States

OPEC   Organization of the Petroleum Exporting Countries

OSS   Office of Strategic Services

PAC   Pan-Africanist Congress

PCD   Democratic Conservative Party

PDVSA   Petroleum of Venezuela Company

PLC   Liberal Constitutionalist Party

PLO   Palestine Liberation Organization

PRC   People's Republic of China

PSUV   United Socialist Party of Venezuela

RCD   Constitutional Democratic Rally Party

SACP   South African Communist Party

SADF   South African Defense Force

SAIC   South African Indian Congress

SAVAK   Organization of National Security and Intelligence

SCAF   Supreme Council of the Armed Forces

SCIRI   Supreme Council for Islamic Revolution in Iraq (renamed the Islamic Supreme Council of Iraq, ISCI, after May 2007)

SEZs   Special Economic Zones

SIDOR   Orinoco Steel Company

SLA   South Lebanon Army

SOFA   Status of Forces Agreement

Soweto   South Western Townships

UAE   United Arab Emirates

UDD   United Front for Democracy Against Dictatorship

UDF   United Democratic Front

UIR   Insurrectional Revolutionary Union

UN	United Nations
UNEFA	National Experimental University of the Armed Forces
UNO	National Opposition Union
USSR	Union of Soviet Socialist Republics
VENIROGC	Joint Venezuelan and Iranian International Development Program for Projects in Third World Countries
VNQDD	Vietnamese Nationalist Party
ZANU	Zimbabwe African National Union

Introduction

The twentieth century was one of world revolution, characterized first by the Marxist-inspired revolution in czarist Russia, then fascist revolutions in Italy and Germany between the world wars, and later anti-imperialist nationalist revolutions in countries such as China, Vietnam, and Cuba. The Iranian revolution (1979) resulted in the victory of an Islamic fundamentalist movement, which, like several earlier major revolutions, significantly affected the course of world history. Later in the century, as Islamic fundamentalist movements grew strong in several nations, revolutions for democracy succeeded in Eastern Europe, Russia, and South Africa.

The beginning of the twenty-first century witnessed the devastating September 11, 2001, attacks on the United States, followed by the US overthrow of the extremist Islamic fundamentalist Taliban regime in Afghanistan in late 2001 and the March 2003 invasion and occupation of Iraq. During the same period, leftist revolutionary-oriented governments were elected in a number of Latin American nations, including Venezuela, Bolivia, and Ecuador. In Asia, Nepal's two major communist parties together won the majority of seats in the Constituent Assembly elected in 2008. The previous (fourth) edition of this book anticipated that the dictatorships of the Middle East were likely to experience revolutionary movements. Starting on December 18, 2010, in Tunisia, a revolutionary wave of protests for democracy began sweeping across the region. The age of revolution and revolutionary conflict continues in the twenty-first century. This book describes and analyzes the development of several major revolutions in an effort to discover their essential features (shared or unique), their individual contributions to revolutionary strategies and practice, and their interactions with and reciprocal effects on the larger world environment.

The revolutions in Russia and China, two of the world's largest and most populous countries, not only had tremendous impacts on their own populations but also affected how other nations and peoples would react to future revolutionary movements. Both the Russian and the Chinese cases constituted models of revolutionary strategy and alerted antirevolutionary ruling elites and governments throughout the world to the need to develop effective counterrevolutionary policies. The Russian Revolution was the first that resulted in the achievement of state power by revolutionists who aimed to create a socialist society. They succeeded first in urban areas with the support of the nation's industrial working class. Their ideal goal was to reorganize the country so that major resources and industries would be socially owned (i.e., collectively owned by all the people) and citizens would be guaranteed equality of opportunity and provision of basic needs for food, shelter, clothing, medical services, and education. What was to happen in Russia would serve for some revolutionaries as an inspiration but for others as the prime example of how a revolution could in many ways go wrong.

Many critics of the Russian Revolution viewed the installation of a one-party political system as a perversion of revolutionary ideals. After being imposed on several politically disorganized Eastern European countries at the end of World War II, the one-party system frustrated aspirations for national independence and unfettered democracy. Thus a number of Eastern European nations were ready for revolution from the moment Communist Party domination was established. When Soviet leaders reversed past Union of Soviet Socialist Republics (USSR) policy in 1989, and publicly proclaimed their willingness to allow political self-determination in Eastern Europe, they set off revolutionary transformations in a half dozen countries and set the stage for the disintegration of the USSR itself.

The Chinese revolution provided a model for revolutionaries in less developed, largely agrarian societies. Mao Zedong, who eventually emerged as the revolution's central leader, organized a movement based on rural rather than urban warfare. Through the promise of redistribution of land to poor peasants and, more generally, because Mao's revolutionaries directed effective resistance efforts against the 1937 Japanese invasion, Mao's movement attracted massive support.

The military victory of the communist-led revolution in 1949 was followed in later years by several social movements in China, including the Great Proletarian Cultural Revolution (1966–1968), which aimed to bring about greater equality, and the more recent democracy movement, whose leaders called for greater freedom of political expression and participation. Although it received significant mass support and was encouraged by powerful countries such as the US, the USSR, and Japan, the democracy movement was at least temporarily suppressed.

The Vietnamese revolution, apart from being a major movement in Asia for political and economic transformation, became a central cold war test case for US opposition to communist-led revolutions. The Vietnamese, whose homeland had often been attacked and controlled by foreign powers, waged a mainly rural revolution and eventually adopted a strategy of placing the nationalist aim (of freeing Vietnam from foreign domination) foremost among revolutionary goals. In so doing, Vietnamese revolutionary leaders not only inspired the maximum possible number of people to work for the revolutionary struggle but also, once the foreign presence was eliminated, had an easier task in defeating domestic opponents of their goal of economic transformation and redistribution of opportunity.

The revolution in Vietnam, however, met with strong resistance from the French and later from the US government, in great part because of the intense hostility between the Western nations on the one hand and the USSR and China on the other. In the context of the cold war US government officials were not prepared to tolerate communist-led revolutions. They erroneously (especially in the case of Vietnam) regarded the revolutionaries as puppets or agents of the Soviet Union or China rather than as the organizers of independent, nationalistic movements. The tendencies of both the United States and the USSR to be intolerant of defiance from smaller countries during the cold war and to interfere in their internal political affairs explain why several revolutions in less developed countries resulted, at least temporarily, in strongly anti-US governments and why revolutions in Eastern Europe in 1989 and 1990 had, in most cases, a distinctly anti-Soviet dimension.

The Cuban, Nicaraguan, and Iranian revolutions were also, in part, reactions to foreign intervention. They illustrate how outside interference in a country can provide revolutionaries an opportunity to make legitimate claims to be protecting national interests. The Cuban revolution was the first in the Western Hemisphere and Latin America to result in a government committed to building a socialist society. Both the Cuban and the Nicaraguan revolutions, although twenty years apart, were directed against regimes notorious for subservience to foreign interests, internal corruption, greed, and unjust economic conditions. The Nicaraguan revolution, like the Cuban, resulted in a new government committed to a redistribution of wealth and expansion of basic services toward the poor. It differed from the Cuban case in that Nicaraguan leaders formally pledged to develop and maintain a multiparty political democracy rather than implement a Leninist-style, one-party system. Although the sincerity of this commitment was often questioned by internal and external critics during the 1980s, United Nations (UN) and Organization of American States (OAS) observers certified Nicaragua's 1989–1990 national election campaign and vote as free and democratic.

The Iranian revolution was one of the major events in the Middle East during the cold war period. As in Cuba and Nicaragua, revolutionaries in Iran, an oil-rich and relatively populous nation, rose up against a regime they viewed as a tool of foreign exploitation and a conduit of moral corruption. The anti-imperialist and moralist aspects of the Iranian revolution, themes present to some extent in other revolutions, contributed to an exceptional outcome, the establishment of the religiously dominated Islamic Republic. As a consequence of this revolution, one of the largest and most powerful countries in the Middle East shifted rapidly from being a reliable ally and implementer of US policies in the region to one whose new government viewed the US, as well as the USSR, as a "great Satan." The victory of Islamic fundamentalists in Iran against a US-supported monarchy helped encourage Islamic resistance to the Soviet occupation of Afghanistan during the 1980s. The Soviet inability to defeat Islamic forces in Afghanistan is thought to have played a significant role in undermining the legitimacy of Communist Party rule and in contributing to the democratization of Russia and other Soviet republics and ultimately to the disintegration of the USSR at the end of 1991. The successful Islamic struggle in Afghanistan also gave birth to Al Qaeda, which repeatedly attacked the United States, including the September 11, 2001, mass killings and destruction. In turn, the September 11 events prompted the United States to invade and occupy both Afghanistan and Iraq, where Al Qaeda played a role in resisting the US presence.

Another major social movement is the revolutionary struggle to create a nonracial democracy in South Africa. That country's mineral wealth (gold, platinum, uranium, etc.) and industrial infrastructure are important to the world and potentially critical for the future development of the African continent. The struggle against white minority rule led to the 1994 election of the country's first nonwhite president, Nelson Mandela. He led a transitional government of national unity in the hope of carrying out a political, social, and economic revolution that is far from finished.

Many people around the world are now striving to achieve revolutionary transformation through democratic elections. Chapter 10 focuses on Venezuela and Bolivia, where leaders and political parties committed to socialist revolution in the twenty-first century repeatedly won elections, created new constitutions, and encouraged similar movements in other nations.

But to have this opportunity, revolutions to democratic political systems must take place where dictatorships currently control people's lives. Starting in December 2010, valiant uprisings for democracy occurred in a number of Arab countries. Chapter 11 describes this transnational revolutionary movement and the counterrevolution that severely limited its achievements.

Although many have attempted to formulate universal theories that explain how revolutions develop and predict their success or failure, such efforts have yielded disappointing results (Coleman 1995; Collins 1995; Foran 2005; 2006; Goldstone 1980; 1982; 1991; 1994; 2001a; 2001b; 2003; Goodwin 2001b; Greene 1990; Kiser 1995; Kuran 1995; McAdam, Tarrow, and Tilly 2001; Portes 1995; Selbin 1999; Skocpol 1979; Skocpol and Trimberger 1978; Smelser 1962; Sztompka 1993; Tilly 1978; 1995; Walton 1984; Wickham-Crowley 1992; Wolf 1969). However, several key factors that must be simultaneously present for a revolution to succeed have been identified. The central flaws of the so-called universal, or general, theories of revolution include their inability to recognize the importance of all the empirically demonstrated factors essential to a revolution's success, their resulting inadequacy in predicting a revolution's development or outcome, and their lack of appreciation for important elements that may be unique to specific revolutions. In this volume I will explore the significance of factors that appear necessary to the success of all revolutions. I will then analyze the development of individual revolutionary conflicts, devoting special attention to the history and unique social characteristics generating the essential revolution-promoting factors. Embedded in the presentations at appropriate points are references to these factors. Readers can anticipate the "summary and analysis" section of each chapter by being alert to these references and trying to relate the specific historical and social context to the general revolutionary factors at work. Finally, in the concluding chapter I will analyze the shortcomings of the general theories of revolution and identify the reasons why they fail to predict the development of all the key revolution-promoting elements and consequently fail to predict the success of specific revolutions.

References and Further Readings

Brook, Daniel. 2005. *Modern Revolution: Social Change and Cultural Continuity in Czechoslovakia and China*. Lanham, MD: University Press of America.

Coleman, James S. 1995. "Comment on Kuran and Collins." *American Journal of Sociology* 100:1616–1619.

Collins, Randall. 1995. "Prediction in Macrosociology: The Case of the Soviet Collapse." *American Journal of Sociology* 100:1552–1593.

DeFronzo, James. 2006a. Introduction. In DeFronzo, ed., *Revolutionary Movements in World History*, 1: xix–xxii.

———, ed. 2006b. *Revolutionary Movements in World History: From 1750 to the Present*. 3 vols. Santa Barbara, CA: ABC-CLIO.

Ellner, Steve. 2010. "Hugo Chavez's First Decade in Office: Breakthroughs and Shortcomings." *Latin American Perspectives* 37 (1): 77–96.

Foran, John. 2005. *Taking Power: On the Origins of Third World Revolutions*. Cambridge, UK: Cambridge University Press.

———. 2006. "Theories of Revolution." In DeFronzo, ed., *Revolutionary Movements in World History*, 3:868–872.

Gelvin, James L. 2012. *The Arab Uprisings*. New York: Oxford University Press.

Gill, Jungyun, and James DeFronzo. 2009. "A Comparative Framework for the Analysis of International Student Movements." *Social Movement Studies* 8 (3): 203–224.

Goldfrank, Walter L. 1994. "The Mexican Revolution." In Goldstone, ed., *Revolutions*.

Goldstone, Jack A. 1980. "Theories of Revolution: The Third Generation." *World Politics* 32 (3): 425–453.

———. 1982. "The Comparative and Historical Study Revolutions." *Annual Review of Sociology* 8:187–207.

———. 1991. "An Analytical Framework." In Jack A. Goldstone, Ted R. Gurr, and Farrokh Moshiri, eds., *Revolutions of the Late Twentieth Century*. Boulder: Westview.

———, ed. 1994. *Revolutions: Theoretical, Comparative, and Historical Studies*. 2nd ed. Fort Worth: Harcourt Brace College Publishers.

———. 2001a. "An Analytical Framework." In Katz, ed., *Revolutions*, 9–29.

———. 2001b. "Toward a Fourth Generation of Revolutionary Theory." *Annual Review of Political Science* 4 (June): 139–187.

———, ed. 2002. *Revolutions: Theoretical, Comparative, and Historical Studies*. 3rd ed. Belmont, CA: Wadsworth/Thomson Learning.

———. 2010. "The New Population Bomb: Four Megatrends That Will Change the World." *Foreign Affairs* 89 (January/February): 31–43.

Goodwin, Jeff. 2001a. "Is the Age of Revolution Over?" In Katz, ed., *Revolutions*, 272–283.

———. 2001b. *No Other Way Out: States and Revolutionary Movements, 1945–1991*. Cambridge, UK: Cambridge University Press.

Greene, Thomas H. 1990. *Comparative Revolutionary Movements*. Englewood Cliffs, NJ: Prentice-Hall.

Katz, Mark N., ed. 2001. *Revolutions: International Dimensions*. Washington, DC: Congressional Quarterly Press.

Kiser, Edgar. 1995. "What Can Sociological Theories Predict?" *American Journal of Sociology* 100:1611–1615.

Kohl, Benjamin. 2010. "Bolivia Under Morales: A Work in Progress." *Latin American Perspectives* 37 (3): 107–122.

Kohl, Benjamin, and Rosalind Bresnahan. 2010. "Bolivia Under Morales: Consolidating Power, Initiating Decolonization." *Latin American Perspectives* 37 (3): 5–17.

Kozloff, Nikolas. 2008. *Revolution: South America and the Rise of the New Left*. New York: Palgrave Macmillan.

Kuran, Timer. 1995. "The Inevitability of Future Revolutionary Surprises." *American Journal of Sociology* 100:1528–1551.

Lieven, Dominic. 1994. "Western Scholarship on the Rise and Fall of the Soviet Regime." *Journal of Contemporary History* 29:195–227.

Lynch, Marc. 2012. *The Arab Uprising*. New York: Public Affairs.

McAdam, Doug, Sidney Tarrow, and Charles Tilly. 2001. *Dynamics of Contention*. Cambridge, UK: Cambridge University Press.

Portes, Alejandro. 1995. "On Grand Surprises and Modest Certainties." *American Journal of Sociology* 100: 1620–1626.

Selbin, Eric. 1999. *Modern Latin American Social Revolutions*. 2nd ed. Boulder: Westview.

———. 2001. "Same as It Ever Was: The Future of Revolutions at the End of the Century." In Katz, ed., *Revolutions*.

Skocpol, Theda. 1979. *States and Social Revolutions: A Comparison of France, Russia, and China*. Cambridge, UK: Cambridge University Press.

Skocpol, Theda, and Ellen Kay Trimberger. 1978. "Revolutions and the World Historical Development of Capitalism." *Berkeley Journal of Sociology* 22:101–113.

Smelser, Neil. 1962. *Theory of Collective Behavior.* New York: Free Press.

Sztompka, Piotr. 1993. *The Sociology of Social Change.* Cambridge, MA: Blackwell.

Tilly, Charles. 1978. *From Mobilization to Revolution.* Reading, MA: Addison-Wesley.

———. 1995. "To Explain Political Process." *American Journal of Sociology* 100: 1594–1610.

Walton, John. 1984. *Reluctant Rebels: Comparative Studies of Revolution and Underdevelopment.* New York: Columbia University Press.

Wickham-Crowley, Timothy P. 1992. *Guerrillas and Revolution in Latin America: A Comparative Study of Insurgents and Regimes Since 1956.* Princeton, NJ: Princeton University Press.

Wolf, Eric. 1969. *Peasant Wars of the Twentieth Century.* New York: Harper & Row.

1

Social Movements and Revolutions

_____

A social movement can be defined as a persistent, organized effort by a relatively large number of people either to bring about social change or to resist it. Some examples of the many social movements in the history of the United States include the antislavery movement, antiwar movements (such as the movements against US involvement in the Vietnam conflict and the US invasion of Iraq), the antipoverty movement, the civil rights movement (the movement for equal treatment of minorities), the women's rights movement, and the occupy movement (the movement to reduce economic inequality and establish a morally just economic system). These liberal social movements advocated change from existing government policies or traditional patterns of behavior. Other social movements were organized to resist social change and reassert or restore particular traditional institutions, patterns of behavior, norms, or values. These conservative movements have included the prayer in public schools movement, the pro-life (anti-abortion) movement, the anti-pornography movement, and the Tea Party movement that emerged in 2009. Many Tea Party supporters claim that the movement's mission includes defending the US Constitution, demanding constitutionally limited government and laws, and supporting a free market as an inherent aspect of constitutionally protected personal liberty.

Although classifying movements as primarily change-oriented/liberal or change-resistant/conservative can be useful in conceptualizing their central goals, in reality few movements fit perfectly into these categories. For example, although the women's rights movement can be viewed as change-oriented in the sense of advocating a shift from patterns of male dominance toward greater equality of the genders in the economic and political spheres, it also has qualities that can be perceived as conservative (e.g., opposition to the sexual exploitation of women, an element of traditional religious morality). Similarly, the antislavery movement of the nineteenth century and the antipoverty and civil rights movements of the twentieth century, which were change-oriented in the sense of fighting for greater equality for minorities, attacked economic and political oppression in part because of their detrimental impacts on family life and child rearing.

The goal of creating optimal economic and political conditions for the maintenance of strong family units and positive family emotional relations can be viewed as conservative. This type of family environment has been an ideal of traditional culture and morality.

Regardless of whether a movement is publicly perceived as predominantly change-oriented or change-resistant in terms of the direction of its goals, it can be further classified as either a reform or a revolutionary movement on the basis of the scope or magnitude of its goals. A reform movement attempts to change limited aspects of a society but does not aim at drastically altering or replacing major social, economic, or political institutions. For example, the civil rights movement of the 1960s did not call for changing major US institutions such as the economic system (capitalism) or the political system (representative two-party democracy). The movement instead advocated limited change: opening up existing institutions to full and equal participation by members of minority groups. Thus the civil rights movement was a reform rather than a revolutionary movement. Similarly, the anti–Vietnam War movement was a reform movement because its goal was to change government policy rather than the structure of government itself or any other major institution.

A revolutionary movement, in comparison, is a social movement in which participants strive to drastically alter or totally replace existing social, economic, or political institutions. For example, the communist-led Chinese revolution transformed China's economy by giving ownership of the country's basic industries to the state rather than private individuals. Besides targeting different aspects of society for change, revolutionary movements also differ from reform movements by using a wider range of means to accomplish change (from legal protest demonstrations to nonviolent civil disobedience to acts of violence). Although revolutionary social change (change in the structure of basic institutions) can be brought about through nonviolent means such as peaceful labor strikes or democratic elections, most successful revolutionary movements have been accompanied by some level of violence emanating from both movement participants and governments and groups opposing revolution (DeFronzo 2006a; 2006b; Goldstone 1998; 2001b; 2003; Greene 1990).

Such violence may be branded terrorism by the ruling power being threatened (Cohen 2006; Combs 2005; Howard and Sawyer 2002), but terrorism—the use of force to intimidate for political purposes—is often in the eye of the beholder, and one person's terrorist can be another person's freedom fighter. Forms of revolutionary violence include people's war (Giap 1962; Mackerras and Knight 1985; Mao [1938] 1965; Wolf 1969)—characterized by widespread support for the goals of the revolution, so that the established government is fighting an entire people—and guerrilla warfare (Guevara 1985; Mao [1938] 1965; White 1984; Wickham-Crowley 1992; 2006), a form of mobile warfare involving small units of combatants operating even behind enemy lines. Forms of antirevolutionary violence may be generally described as counterinsurgency techniques (Calvert 1984; White 1984) and range from arrests and temporary detention to extremes such as the death squads in El Salvador and Guatemala in the 1980s (Binford 2006; Montgomery 1982; Streeter 2000; 2006; White 1984). In several instances since the mid-twentieth century, antirevolutionary forces have overturned electoral systems, for example, in Cuba in 1952 (Gott 2004; Szulc 1986), Guatemala in 1954 (Gleijeses 1991; Schlesinger and Kinzer 1982; Streeter 2000; 2006), Chile in 1973 (Sigmund 2006; Valenzuela 1978), and Egypt in 2013 (Norton 2013) in order to prevent sweeping institutional change or even progressive reforms from being carried out through democratic means.

Sociologists and other social scientists have often attempted to classify revolutions into one of two ideal types: leftist or rightist. In a left-wing revolution, the central goal is widely perceived as changing major social and political institutions in order to alter the dominant economic, social, or political relationships within a society (Greene 1990). This usually involves redistributing valuable resources between the rich and the poor, with more equal access to educational opportunities, medical services, higher wages, or in the case of a predominantly agricultural society, land, a stated goal. In a right-wing revolution, the primary aim is to restore traditional institutions. Right-wing revolutionary movements also generally emphasize the goal of maintaining social order and traditional authority over the goal of achieving greater social equality through institutional change.

Just as social movements in general are difficult to categorize as either totally liberal or totally conservative, many revolutions include both leftist and rightist characteristics. For example, the leaders of a revolutionary movement aimed at achieving greater social equality by radically transforming a society's economic and political systems (leftist characteristics) might attempt to appeal for mass support by arguing that the redistribution of wealth they propose would help reinforce traditional morality (a rightist element) by eliminating extreme poverty as a cause of social evils, such as prostitution, drug abuse, and predatory crime. A number of revolutions can be placed into one of the two categories on the basis of changes they brought about. Of the revolutions covered in this book, the first Russian and the Chinese, Vietnamese, and Cuban have been widely interpreted as primarily leftist. On the basis of the dominant ideological orientations and policies of the revolutionary leaderships of the two nations that experienced revolutions in 1979, the Iranian revolution can be classified as a predominantly right-wing revolution and the Nicaraguan as mainly leftist. The South African struggle for revolutionary change was oriented toward achieving greater equality by dismantling the nation's system of white racial domination and by greatly expanding political rights and roles for nonwhite South Africans and can—at least in that sense—be categorized as leftist. The post–Iranian revolution Islamic movements appeared primarily rightist in terms of their cultural goals. In comparison, the "revolutions through democracy" of the twenty-first century in Venezuela and Bolivia were generally viewed as primarily leftist in orientation. The Arab revolution is leftist in countries where the goal is to replace a conservative authoritarian regime, such as a monarchy, with a democratic political system. But within the revolution, some Islamist groups have the rightist goal of creating an Islamic state.

REVOLUTIONARY MOVEMENTS: CRITICAL FACTORS

Factors that can influence the development of revolutionary movements include the extent of inequality and impoverishment within a society, degree to which the population is divided along ethnic lines, perceived corruption of governmental officials, level of armament and degree of loyalty of a government's military forces, cultural traditions of violence or nonviolence as means of protesting social injustice, physical size of a country and nature of its terrain, and proximity and level of involvement of other countries that either support or oppose the development and success of a revolutionary movement. But of all possible factors, five stand out as critical and, if they occur simultaneously, appear to constitute necessary and sufficient conditions for the success of a revolutionary movement, according to the appraisals of leading academic scholars on the phenomenon of revolution (Foran 2005; 2006; Goldfrank 1994; Goldstone 1994; 2001a; Greene 1990). The order of development and relative importance of these elements differ from one revolution to another.

1 Mass frustration resulting in popular uprisings among urban or rural populations: A large proportion of a society's population becomes extremely discontented, which leads to mass-participation protests and rebellions against state authority. In technologically limited agricultural societies, the occurrence of rural (peasant) rebellion or at least rural support for revolution has often been essential (Foran 2005; 2006; Goldfrank 1994; Goldstone 1991; 1994; 2001a; Greene 1990).

2 Dissident elite political movements: Divisions among elites (groups that have access to wealth or power of various types or are highly educated and possess important technical or managerial skills) pit some elite members against the existing government (Foran 2005; 2006; Goldfrank 1994; Goldstone 1991; 1994; 2001a; Greene 1990).

3 Unifying motivations: Powerful motivations for revolution cut across major classes and unify the majority of a society's population behind the goal of revolution (Foran 2005; 2006; Goldstone 1994; 2001a; Greene 1990).

4 A severe political crisis paralyzing the administrative and coercive capabilities of the state: A state crisis occurs in the nation experiencing or about to experience a revolutionary movement. The crisis, which may be caused by a catastrophic defeat in war, a natural disaster, an economic depression, or the loss of critical economic or military support from other nations, or by any combination of these factors, may deplete the state of loyal personnel, legitimacy in the eyes of the public, and other resources. The state then becomes incapable of carrying out its normal functions and cannot cope effectively with an opposition revolutionary movement (Foran 2005; 2006; Goldfrank 1994; Goldstone 1991; 1994; 2001a; Greene 1990).

5 A permissive or tolerant world context: The governments of other nations do not intervene effectively to prevent a revolutionary movement from developing and succeeding in a given nation (Foran 2005; 2006; Goldfrank 1994; Goldstone 2001a).

Mass Frustration and Popular Uprisings

Revolution involves a tremendous increase in mass participation in political activity, motivated by widespread opposition to existing conditions. Such popular discontent can result when a gap develops between people's expectations (regarding the lifestyle they feel they should be able to achieve) and their ability to satisfy those expectations. Social scientists have referred to this phenomenon as relative deprivation (Fullerton 2006; Greene 1990; Gurr 1970).

There are several historical processes that can lead to relative deprivation. Among them is rapid deterioration in material living conditions, which may occur for the whole population of a country during an economic depression or for only some population groups during periods of transition in the economic system. A wide breach opens between the way people expect to live and their ability to meet those expectations—not because of changed expectations, but because their ability to attain them declines. This type of relative deprivation may also result when one country is invaded and conquered by another. The victor nation may exploit the resources and labor power of the defeated people, who then experience a drastically declining standard of living. People in the defeated nation may try to resist occupation forces with violence. During World War II many nations that were invaded by Nazi German or Japanese forces organized resistance groups, which, in some instances, grew into revolutionary movements; the latter not only helped expel the invaders but also brought about drastic changes in social, economic, and political institutions after the war.

A gap between people's expectations and capabilities can also result when expectations increase but capabilities do not change. Expectations are essentially a function of people's beliefs about what is possible and what is "right." Experiences that alter these conceptions can strongly influence people's expectations, for example, communication with people from other societies with a higher level of material existence or where a past revolution has resulted in a redistribution of wealth. Contact with other societies or with fellow citizens who have been exposed to other ways of life can lead people to believe that improvements are possible. Communication with foreigners can also influence what people consider to be morally acceptable.

A people's conception of what is morally right is most likely to shift if the message is communicated by recognized moral authorities. The upsurge in revolutionary movements in parts of Latin America during the 1970s and 1980s came about partly because religious leaders worked to change the conceptions of millions of poor farmers and workers about the moral acceptability of existing social conditions. Many young men and women of the clergy and religious orders began to embrace the idea of an expanded role for the Catholic Church in the lives of the poor. Rather than simply catering to spiritual needs through administering the sacraments and saying Mass, they felt it was their religious duty to work for social justice and a redistribution of wealth. This application of Christian values has been called liberation theology (Berryman 1985; 1987; White 1984). As these ideas were widely communicated, the poor came to see the poverty and misery they endured as being not God's will but rather the will of some individuals and the systems these people defended. The extreme inequality that characterized their societies was now considered wrong, even sinful. Peasants and workers began to desire, demand, and expect change. A situation of mass frustration had been created.

Historically a third process has operated to generate mass discontent. Davies (1962) found that for each of the major revolutions he analyzed, the period of revolutionary upheaval was preceded by several years of economic improvement. The associated rise in material living conditions likely raised people's expectations because they actually experienced improvement. After the interval of prosperity, living conditions suddenly declined due to war or natural or economic catastrophes, opening a wide gap between expectations and capabilities. Consequently mass frustration and support for revolutionary movements grew dramatically.

Dissident Elite Political Movements

Many who have explored the processes involved in the development of revolutionary movements (Goldfrank 1994; Goldstone 1994; 2001a; Gurr 1970; Selbin 2006; Skocpol 1979; Trimberger 1978) have argued that divisions among social elites can help a revolutionary movement succeed in a number of ways. First, conflict among elite members, if nothing else, contributes to confusion and disorganization in efforts to suppress a revolutionary movement. Second, if some elite members feel threatened by the actions of other elite members who control their society's government and if these alienated elites possess resources required by the state, their decision to withhold or withdraw support from the state can render it too weak and ineffective to cope with revolutionary forces. And finally, some of the nation's elite families may directly participate in a revolution by providing leadership or other resources to help transform popular discontent and uprisings into an organized, purposeful revolutionary movement. In this role, elites usually participate in formulating an ideology for the revolutionary movement: an indictment and criticism of the existing power structure, a set of justifications for the necessity of a revolutionary movement to bring about social change, and a long-range plan and strategy of action (Greene 1990).

Ideologies may range along a spectrum from those informed by socialism—the public ownership of land and capital administered for the community good—to capitalism—the private ownership of resources to produce commodities for profit and reinvestment. Ideologies often couple economic aims with powerful unifying goals, such as nationalist resistance to foreign domination or reaffirmation of traditional moral or religious principles, capable of facilitating alliances among a society's major social classes. The primary function of revolutionary ideology is to provide as many people as possible with the same or at least compatible viewpoints on the need to change society so that they will be motivated to cooperate in the revolutionary struggle.

Social theorists and researchers have hypothesized several ways elite conflict can develop. Marx and Engels ([1848] 1972; Engels [1880] 1972) argued that technological and economic changes result in one type of economic activity (e.g., the manufacture and sale of industrial products) replacing another (e.g., farming and the sale of agricultural products) as the major source of wealth in a society. The elites involved in the newly dominant economic activity eventually wrest control of the political system from elites representing the previously dominant economic activity. Goldstone (1994), Skocpol and Trimberger (1978), and others, in describing another process for the development of elite conflict, have argued that as a technologically and economically inferior state attempts to compete with more advanced states, some members of its national elite enact reforms. Other elite members interpret these reforms as a threat to their interests and privileges. Intra-elite conflict and elite opposition to government policies can result.

Huntington (1968), in addition, suggested that as technologically backward societies begin to modernize by expanding educational systems and introducing technologies and learning from the more advanced countries, they tend to create new, educated, and politically conscious elites that demand to participate in government. When traditional elites, such as the royal family and much of the nobility in czarist Russia, resist democratization of the political system, some members of the new elites come to favor revolution. Eisenstadt (1978) further observed that economic downturns or other disasters can cause elite conflict in societies with dictatorships based on a patronage system of personal rewards to elite members. When the benefits stop coming or are threatened by a particular dictator's continuation in power, the loyalty of elite members to the regime is greatly reduced. In other situations, some elites may feel threatened by the economic and political power of a dictatorship and turn against it. Both these factors were involved when some of Nicaragua's economic elite defected from the Somoza dictatorship (Booth 1985; Walker 1986).

Direct participation of elite elements in the leadership and organizational structure of dissident political movements has often been critical for the successful development of a leftist revolutionary movement (Greene 1990; Gurr 1970). Such individuals, who may represent only a small minority of elite members, bring crucial organizational and intellectual skills to a movement. According to Greene (1990), Gill (2006), Gill and DeFronzo (2009), and my own work (DeFronzo 1970), many of the young people from elite families who directly participate in left-wing revolutionary movements experienced a moral alienation from their society's economic and political systems, often developed or enhanced while attending their nation's colleges and universities. They turn against the very economic and political institutions that benefited their families and find it unconscionable that some people live in affluence while the majority of their fellow citizens live in abject poverty.

If revolutionaries of upper- and middle-class origin live at a time when the majority of their society's population experiences little or no political discontent, they may perish in violent but futile attacks on the armed forces of the government they oppose. But when their frustrations coincide with the aroused discontent of the poor, they may play vital roles in revolutionary movements that have widespread support and consequently may succeed. There are many examples of revolutionary leaders from relatively privileged families who emerged to lead leftist revolutions that proceeded to dispossess the very classes from which the leaders originated. For example, the Russian revolutionary V. I. Lenin, the Chinese revolutionary Mao Zedong, and the Cuban revolutionary Fidel Castro all came from well-to-do backgrounds.

Unifying Motivations for Revolution

Greene (1990), in his review of various revolutionary movements throughout history, noted that it is extremely rare for a revolution to succeed without backing from most major social classes in a society. For a revolution to triumph, several classes must join forces; thus there must be a shared motivation for revolution that cuts across class lines and possibly additional differing but simultaneous and at least temporarily compatible motivations. Although the concept of redistributing wealth in favor of the poor, often manifested in some form of socialist ideology, has motivated many leftist revolutions, the mass appeal of such a goal is usually limited to the lower classes of a society. Only a minority of the more affluent classes are likely to support a revolution intended solely to benefit the poor.

Broad cross-class participation in revolutionary movements has generally been the product of nationalism (Chirot 1986; Greene 1990) or widespread hatred toward a particular dictatorship (Greene 1990). Regardless of class or ideological orientation, people sharing the same language and culture who perceive that their ethnic or national group has been exploited by another group or country can join together to end their domination (Adleman 2006; Braveboy-Wagner 1985; Breuilly 1982; Sathyamurthy 1983; Smith 1983).

Nationalism as a motivating factor that unifies diverse social classes behind revolution is most likely to emerge as a reaction to direct colonial rule or indirect colonial domination (a local regime perceived to be operating on behalf of foreign rather than national interests). The controlling alien power is called imperialistic because of specific political actions (gaining control over a society and its resources), economic transactions (shaping and developing the society's economy on behalf of the colonizing power), and cultural transformations (inculcating the society with outside religious, educational, linguistic, and aesthetic values based on the foreign culture).

Sometimes the effects of colonization are so thoroughgoing that the overtaken society ends up with a native ruling class not only culturally similar to the imperialist power but also politically loyal to it and economically dependent on it. Neocolonialism is the continuing state of political and cultural dependency and economic exploitation that persists in a former colony after formal political independence has been declared (Calvert 1984; Cavatorta 2006; Chirot 1986).

Revolutionary movements organized with the stated goal of overthrowing either direct colonial rule or neocolonial governments have been called national liberation movements (Calvert 1984; Miller and Aya 1971). Revolutions in five of the countries covered in this book sprang in great part from such anti-imperialist impulses: China, Vietnam, Cuba, and Nicaragua—all organized mainly around socialist goals—and Iran—organized primarily around religious goals. The revolutionary movements in Venezuela and Bolivia, described in Chapter 10, "Revolution Through Democracy," also have strong anti-imperialism themes.

Beyond nationalism and national liberation, abhorrence of an especially unjust, brutal, or incompetent regime can bring several classes together in a movement to oust the detested government. The czar's dictatorial rule coupled with his personal arrogance, incompetence, and disregard for human life in conducting Russia's disastrous war effort eventually brought about a near-universal demand for his abdication and an end to the autocratic monarchy system. Similarly, multiclass aversion to the Batista government in Cuba and Somoza family rule in Nicaragua developed not only because of the widespread belief that these regimes allowed foreign interests to exploit their people and resources but also because of perceived crimes and acts of brutality committed by these dictatorships.

Severe State Crisis

A revolutionary movement may come into being and yet have no reasonable chance for success so long as the government maintains strong administrative capabilities and armed forces to coerce the dissidents into submission. But conditions and events beyond the control of either government or revolutionary forces may destroy the state's capabilities to function effectively and permit revolutionary elements to overcome its repressive powers (Goldstone 2001b). Dunn (1972) argued that several successful revolutionary movements of the twentieth century arose from crises caused by either war or the process of decolonization. Mobilization for war can strain a society's economic resources. And if the war effort is unsuccessful, the perceived futility of loss of life and national wealth can destroy the government's legitimacy in the eyes of its population. The shattering defeats suffered by the czar's army during World War I helped generate the state crisis that gave revolutionaries in Russia an opportunity to seize power.

Decolonization involves one country withdrawing its official administrative personnel and military forces from another country (the former colony). The resulting postcolonial government may include individuals who previously served the occupying country. Thus during the period immediately following decolonization, many citizens may perceive the government as a mechanism that the past occupying country uses to control their nation's economy and resources. Consequently a postcolonial or neocolonial government may lack the support of its own people and the loyalty of its armed forces. In this case, a postcolonial state can collapse in the face of a revolutionary movement that the population perceives to represent its true national interests.

A state collapse may also occur if an economically less developed state attempts to compete with more advanced states in the world economic system or to cope with pressure on food supplies or other resources caused by significant population increase (Goldstone 1994; Skocpol 1979). As a government attempts to achieve these goals through modernizing reforms (e.g., expanding the educational system, recruiting administrators and business and military leaders on the basis of talent and achievement rather than nobility or some other traditional factor, distributing land from large estates to the rural poor, and imposing higher taxes on the upper classes), some groups may resist, feeling the new policies threaten their wealth, power, or other privileges, even to the point of withdrawing support from the national government. The weakened state may then present revolutionary forces with an opportunity to develop unstoppable momentum. For example, Chinese rulers who attempted to modernize their country in the late nineteenth century were frustrated by wealthy landowners and other conservative forces that prevented sufficient reforms, weakened the power of the central government, and presented revolutionary forces with a divided, conflict-ridden, and consequently vulnerable national leadership (Skocpol 1979).

Another type of fragile state structure is the neo-patrimonial regime (Eisenstadt 1978). (This concept is similar to what Foran referred to as a "repressive, exclusionary, personalist state"; 2005, 20.) It is structured around a particular individual whose rule is based on control of resources that are dispensed as rewards to supporters (such as governmental administrative positions, profitable business monopolies, or high salaries and bonuses to military leaders). Important government supporters are loyal to the leader and to the system that rewards them. Such a state is vulnerable to several types of problems: economic depression, which reduces the resources available to the chief executive to parcel out to supporters; military defeat, which can create economic difficulties and tarnish the leader; and events such as illness, accidents, or assassinations, which remove a leader from power and thus endanger or destroy the state-supporting patronage system.

Permissive World Context

Any society exists in a world populated by other societies, including some with greater or equal military and economic power. Consequently a revolutionary movement that appears to be overcoming a national government may be suppressed, at least temporarily, by nations that oppose it (Goldfrank 1994). Foran (2005; 2006) and Goldstone (2001b) also recognize the importance of this factor. The US involvement in Vietnam and El Salvador exemplifies foreign intervention in domestic revolutionary situations. Similarly, in the past the USSR intervened in Hungary, Czechoslovakia, and Afghanistan to prevent the growth or success of movements it opposed. Another significant intervention occurred when several nations, including Britain, the United States, and Japan, sent military forces into the Soviet Union in an effort to help White Russian forces overturn the Bolshevik Revolution during the Russian civil war.

In some situations, outside nations have not intervened or have not intervened vigorously enough to prevent a revolution or defeat a revolutionary movement. This permissiveness may be attributable to fear of disapproval, economic sanctions, or even military attack from nations that support a given revolutionary movement; concern about provoking a hostile reaction from the potential interventionist country's own citizens; or displeasure with the government a revolutionary movement seeks to overthrow. Even if motivation to intervene exists, economic or military hardships or internal political turmoil may so physically or psychologically exhaust a nation that it is unable to intervene effectively.

Several examples of unsuccessful or nonexistent intervention by outside powers against revolutionary movements illustrate the concept of permissive world context. Following World War I, the European capitalist nations and the United States were too battered by years of conflict to mount a large-scale assault on revolutionary Russia, especially given the huge population and vast territory of the country and the level of popular support the revolution enjoyed. During the Cuban revolution of 1956–1958 and the Nicaraguan and Iranian revolutions of 1978–1979, no nations sent military forces to save the internationally despised regimes of Batista, Somoza, and the shah of Iran. And despite massive intervention in Vietnam and other parts of Southeast Asia between 1963 and 1973, the United States might have used even greater military power were it not for significant domestic opposition to the Vietnam involvement and the threat of direct military confrontation with the USSR or China over Vietnam. Finally, the USSR's 1989 renunciation of the right to intervene in Eastern Europe permitted the swift success of political revolutions in Poland, Hungary, East Germany, Czechoslovakia, Bulgaria, and Romania.

THEORIES OF REVOLUTION

Because the five factors—mass frustration, elite dissidence, unifying motivation, state crisis, and permissive world context—appear crucial to the success of revolutionary movements, it is important to evaluate existing theories of revolution in terms of their ability or inability to account for the simultaneous occurrence of these conditions.

Researchers have attempted to formulate theories of revolution. Edwards ([1927] 1970), Brinton ([1938] 1952), and Pettee (1938) identify what Goldstone (1982) and Foran (2006) describe as a natural history of revolutions by specifying the phases that a successful revolution includes.

1 A society's intellectuals, most of whom once supported the existing regime, turn against it.
2 The old regime tries to save itself from revolution by attempting reforms that ultimately fail to protect the old order.
3 The revolutionary alliance that eventually takes power from the old government is soon torn by internal conflict.

4   At first the post-revolutionary government is moderate.

5   When moderate revolutionaries fail to fulfill expectations, more radical revolutionaries gain control.

6   Radicals take more extreme actions to fulfill revolutionary aims, employing
coercive methods against those who resist or threaten the fulfillment of revolutionary goals.

7   Eventually pragmatic, moderate revolutionaries replace the radicals.

While the discovery of sequences of events during revolutions is interesting and
important, it only describes what must be explained by a theory of revolution. Similarly, the five factors described above as necessary and sufficient for a successful
revolution do not constitute a complete theory of revolution; instead, they represent factors that must be explained by a theory. Greene (1990), in reviewing theories of revolution and studies on participants, ideologies, organizational structures,
tactics, and settings for numerous revolutions, identified several major theoretical
perspectives, including Marxist, frustration-aggression, systems, and modernization approaches.

Marxist theory is too complex to cover here in its entirety and too important
to gloss over. Elements of Marxism will be presented here and in several of the
following chapters, but for solid overviews, see Robert Tucker's edition of *The
Marx-Engels Reader* (1972) and Richard Schmitt's *Introduction to Marx and Engels*
(1987). According to Marxist theory, revolution is likely to occur when existing social and political structures and leadership interfere with economic development.
Karl Marx traced such economic development through various stages from feudalism to capitalism to socialism and eventually to communism. As technological
and economic change occurs during capitalist industrialization, a conflict develops
between the new urban industrial working class—the proletariat—and the ruling
capitalist class. According to Marx, the importance of labor, such as the operating
of manufacturing technology, will inevitably supersede that of the ownership of
capital (wealth in the form of money, resources, investments, or the physical means
of production) in the industrialized economic system. While the capitalist class
attempts to maintain its control of the government, the working class is driven by
frustration and exploitation to revolution. What Marx posited as the dictatorship
of the proletariat ensues, with the working class taking over governmental power.
Many varieties of Marxist theory have developed over the years, but all of them assume the need for revolution at certain critical stages in economic history.

According to Foran (2005; 2006) and Goldstone (2001b), during the 1960s attempts to explain revolution resulted in two additional types of theories. The
frustration-aggression theory of revolution (Greene 1990) focused on mass frustration as a cause of mass mobilization for revolution. This theory included the relative

deprivation theories of popular discontent described by Davies (1962) and Gurr (1970), discussed above (see "Mass Frustration and Popular Uprisings"). The structural functionalist approach to explaining revolution, exemplified by the work of Smelser (1962) and Johnson (1964), is what Greene (1990) referred to as the systems theory of revolution.

Systems theory of revolution, unlike Marxist theory, is a more general perspective that does not view revolution primarily in terms of progressive historical changes in technology and forms of economic organization. Systems assumes that revolution is likely to occur when pre-revolutionary social structures fail to perform essential functions, no matter what the cause of the failure. Essential functions include not only economic and administrative tasks but also socializing the members of society to a culture (set of beliefs and attitudes) that supports existing social structures.

A fourth approach, modernization theory, is similar to Marxist theory in that it associates revolution with technological and economic change. But unlike Marxist theory, modernization does not hypothesize a set sequence of stages in economic development and does not specify which economic group would be the major proponent of revolutionary transformation. Rather, modernization theory holds that the experience of technological and economic change tends to mobilize new or previously apathetic groups by raising their economic aspirations and their demands for political participation. Revolution is likely to occur when those holding state power are unable or unwilling to meet the demands of groups mobilized by modernization.

The second half of the 1960s and the 1970s saw the rise of a fifth major contemporary theory of revolution, structural theory. Like the Marxist perspective, it emphasizes the importance of structural aspects of society. Barrington Moore's comparative study (1966) indicated that rebellious movements in peasant societies were most likely to develop when a traditional farming economy was beginning to undergo "transition to capitalist agriculture" (Foran 2006, 869). Wolf (1969, 276–302), in analyzing six peasant societies that experienced revolutionary conflicts, also found that increasing commercialization of agriculture, threatening "peasants' access to land," was a major factor in mobilizing support for rebellion (Foran 2006, 869).

Skocpol and Trimberger (1978; Skocpol 1979) developed the most influential and theoretically comprehensive modern structural theory. It agrees with Marx's view that a revolution is not exclusively the product of the subjective characteristics of a society, such as shared cultural values or social or economic expectations, but depends on specific objective conditions involving political and economic aspects of social structure. The Skocpol and Trimberger formulation, however, departs from Marx's original perspective in several ways. First, it viewed the state as a form of social organization that combines administrative and military functions and draws resources from society to use in maintaining social order and in competing against other nations economically and militarily. Second, in contrast to the original Marxist analysis, which saw revolution as the outcome of internal technological and economic factors, this new structural approach was oriented to the larger world environment and perceived revolution as the result of conflict among nations at different levels of technological and economic development.

The Skocpol and Trimberger structural theory specified that the key objective conditions for revolution have occurred in primarily agrarian, technologically inferior states that were confronted with overpowering military and economic pressure from more advanced nations. Inability to resist foreign aggression damaged the perceived legitimacy of the pre-revolutionary regimes, which were also undermined by divisions within elite population segments regarding how to deal with external threats. Government attempts to cope with foreign pressure, such as increasing state resources by raising taxes on an already impoverished population, and the economic effects of foreign exploitation generated mass discontent. The resulting popular support for revolutionary movements overwhelmed the severely weakened pre-revolutionary regimes. From the structural point of view, the purpose and outcome of such revolutions was primarily political: the establishment of a new governmental system in a less developed society, a system that would better utilize available resources to counter external threats from advanced nations.

These general theories of revolution all recognize, explicitly or implicitly, mass frustration as an essential element of revolutionary movements. Marxist, modernization, systems, and structural theories also suggest that when the state fails to meet mass expectations or carry out important economic or social functions, government legitimacy and coercive capacity are weakened, which heightens the probability of revolution. Modernization, Marxist, and structural theories identify processes by which social elites become discontented and withdraw their support for the government or even lead a revolutionary effort.

A major inadequacy of the Marxist, frustration-aggression, systems, and modernization theories is that they neglect two essential elements of successful revolutionary movements: a unifying motivation that brings together diverse groups to support a common revolutionary goal and the existence of an international environment that permits revolution. The Skocpol and Trimberger structural theory, at least implicitly, confronts the issue of unifying motivation by asserting the primacy of the population-bonding aim of creating a new, stronger government that can protect national interests. But like the other theories, it tends to ignore the world permissiveness factor. These omissions limit the ability of the major theories of revolution to predict either the development of revolutionary movements or a revolution's chance for success. The unifying motivation factor and the role of a permissive international environment will be highlighted in the chapters on individual revolutions. Together with mass frustration, elite dissidence, and state crisis, these factors surpass general theories in explaining and predicting revolutionary action and success.

ARE REVOLUTIONS DEVELOPING OR OCCURRING NOW?

Revolutionary movements are under way in several nations around the world. And in other countries there are conditions that appear conducive to revolution. Elected leaders like Hugo Chávez and Nicolas Maduro of Venezuela and President Evo Morales of Bolivia claimed they were leading their nations though revolutionary transformations. Venezuela and Bolivia will be discussed in Chapter 10, "Revolution Through Democracy." Nepal is another country where elections may lead to revolutionary economic change through democratic means. A peace agreement was negotiated in 2006, after a ten-year civil war between the monarchy and Maoist-oriented, communist-led guerrillas. Under a new temporary constitution a nationwide election for a constituent assembly was held in April 2008. Seats in the assembly were won mainly by three parties: the Communist Party of Nepal (Maoist), which received 38 percent of the vote; the Communist Party of Nepal–United Marxist-Leninist, 19 percent; and the Nepali Congress, 19 percent. At its first meeting in May 2008, the assembly changed the structure of Nepalese government by abolishing the monarchy and declaring Nepal a federal democratic republic (CIA 2014). In the 2013 election, two of the countries' four communist parties were again among the top three vote getters, along with the Nepali Congress party. The voting tendencies of the majority of Nepalese suggested that future elected governments would continue carrying out significant change.

In other countries, military actions have removed elected leaders committed to helping the poor. In 2009 a Honduran military coup ended the presidency of Manuel Zelaya (Main 2010), who had been elected in 2005 as a center-right politician but shifted significantly to the left, established ties with Hugo Chávez of Venezuela, and promised to combat poverty. Deposing a democratically elected president committed to aiding the poor in a country with one of the highest levels of income inequality in the world sparked mass protests and seemed to increase the potential for a revolutionary movement.

A few years earlier, the Thai military had ousted Prime Minister Thaksin Shinawatra, a former policeman who became a telecommunications billionaire and was "the first prime minister in Thailand's history to lead an elected government through a full term in office" ("Profile" 2010). He was very popular, especially among the country's rural poor in north and northeast Thailand, who benefited during Thaksin's five years in power from his education, health, and debt relief programs. He was also supported by pro-democracy urban intellectuals. But Thaksin was opposed by many among Bangkok's rich, accused of abuse of power and corruption, and removed from office in September 2006. In response a massive movement developed, the United Front for Democracy Against Dictatorship (UDD), also called the Red Shirt movement, for its trademark attire. The movement aimed not only to restore Thaksin Shinawatra to office but, more broadly, to establish a true democracy in Thailand ("Thailand Protests" 2010). For weeks during the spring of 2010, thousands of Red Shirts held demonstrations in Bangkok demanding fully democratic elections and protesting what they charged was an unfair system in which the wealthy and top military leaders were free to break laws without fear of punishment (Fuller 2010). At least eighty-eight persons were killed in a series of confrontations (Mydans 2010). The military dispersed the Red Shirt encampment in a commercial area of Bangkok on May 19. The Thai government claimed that several dozen people and some companies financed the Red Shirt protests and accused Thaksin Shinawatra and thirty-nine others of terrorism. Red Shirt supporters, though, claimed that financing came from thousands of small contributors who believed in the revolutionary potential of a real democratic political system.

The Arab revolution that began in December 2010 achieved some successes (as described in Chapter 11), but was repressed by a powerful international counterrevolution. Nevertheless, the Arab revolution for democracy continues. And in 2014, mass protests in Kiev, the capital of the Ukraine, forced the president who had been elected in 2010 to flee (as described in Chapter 2). But in eastern and southern Ukraine, many people protested against the new government in Kiev. The majority of the residents of the Crimea region then voted to secede from the Ukraine and unite with the Russian Federation.

Summary

This chapter provided an overview of concepts, theoretical perspectives, and research findings important to the discussion of revolutionary social movements. A revolutionary movement, in contrast to a reform movement, aims to change the basic institutions of a society. Five elements are crucially important to the success of a revolutionary movement: (1) the growth of frustration among the majority of a population; (2) the existence of elite elements who are alienated from the current government and, more specifically, of elite elements who support the concept of revolution; (3) unifying motivations that bring together the members of different social classes in support of a revolution; (4) a crisis that severely weakens government administrative and coercive capabilities in a society experiencing a revolutionary movement; and (5) the choice of other countries not to intervene or their inability to do so to prevent the success of a revolutionary movement.

Some of the reasons individuals support a revolutionary movement are highly personal, such as a desire to improve their own material well-being or a desire to take revenge on their opponents, or because they have loved ones or friends who support revolution. But as Greene (1990) pointed out, the participants in a revolution, often drawn from different economic backgrounds, also have shared motivations that unite them in a common effort. In several revolutions an adherence to cross-class religious beliefs or a desire to throw off foreign control or a despised dictatorship has acted in this way.

Nationalism, often spurred by reaction to imperialist exploitation, has been a powerful unifying sentiment. And although the redistribution of wealth is not necessarily synonymous with socialism, various forms of socialist ideology have figured prominently in the belief systems of many leftist revolutionary movements. Combining the nationalist goal of liberation from foreign domination and the goal of redistributing wealth to achieve a more egalitarian society has rallied otherwise diverse social groups to revolutions in Russia, China, Vietnam, and other societies. Nationalism, as a spur to unified action, and economic redistribution, as an antidote to mass frustration, combine with the other major revolutionary factors—elite dissidence, state crisis, and world permissiveness—to explain many sociopolitical upheavals. In the late twentieth century and early twenty-first century, the goal of achieving democracy became a powerful motivation uniting people of different social classes in revolutionary movements.

References and Further Readings

Adleman, David E. 2006. "Nationalism and Revolution." In DeFronzo, ed., *Revolutionary Movements in World History*, 2:589–594.

Alexander, George M. 1981. "The Demobilization Crisis of November 1944." In Iatrides, ed., *Greece in the 1940s*.

Anderson, Thomas P. 1971. *Matanza: El Salvador's Communist Revolt of 1932*. Lincoln: University of Nebraska Press.

Baerentzen, Lars, and David H. Close. 1993. "The British Defeat of EAM, 1944–5." In Close, ed., *The Greek Civil War*.

Berecz, Janos. 1986. *1956 Counter-Revolution in Hungary*. Budapest: Akadamiai Kiado.

Berryman, Phillip. 1985. *Inside Central America: The Essential Facts Past and Present on El Salvador, Nicaragua, Honduras, Guatemala, and Costa Rica*. New York: Pantheon.

———. 1987. *Liberation Theology: Essential Facts about the Revolutionary Movement in Latin America—and Beyond*. Philadelphia: Temple University Press.

Binford, Leigh. 2006. "The Salvadoran Revolution." In DeFronzo, ed., *Revolutionary Movements in World History*, 3:763–773.

Booth, John A. 1985. *The End and the Beginning: The Nicaraguan Revolution*. Boulder: Westview.

Braveboy-Wagner, Jacqueline A. 1985. *Interpreting the Third World: Politics, Economics, and Social Issues*. New York: Praeger.

Breuilly, John. 1982. *Nationalism and the State.* New York: St. Martin's.

Brinton, Crane. [1938] 1952. *The Anatomy of Revolution.* New York: Prentice-Hall.

Brook, Daniel. 2005. *Modern Revolution: Social Change and Cultural Continuity in Czecho-slovakia and China.* Lanham, MD: University Press of America.

Byrne, Malcolm. 2006. "The Hungarian Revolution of 1956." In DeFronzo, ed., *Revolutionary Movements in World History,* 2:370–378.

Calvert, Peter. 1984. *Revolution and International Politics.* New York: St. Martin's.

Cavatorta, Francesco. 2006. "Colonialism, Anti-Colonialism, and Neo-Colonialism." In DeFronzo, ed., *Revolutionary Movements in World History,* 1:163–168.

Central Intelligence Agency (CIA). 2014. "Nepal." In *World Factbook.* https://www.cia .gov/library/publications/the-world-factbook/geos/np.html.

Chalmers, Rhoderick. 2007. "Toward a New Nepal?" *Current History* 106 (April): 161–167.

Chirot, Daniel. 1986. *Social Change in the Modern Era.* San Diego: Harcourt Brace Jovanovich.

Close, David H., ed. 1993. *The Greek Civil War: Studies of Polarization.* London: Routledge.

Close, David H., and Thanos Veremis. 1993. "The Military Struggle." In Close, ed., *The Greek Civil War.*

Cockcroft, James D. 1989. *Neighbors in Turmoil: Latin America.* New York: Harper & Row.

Cohen, Albert K. 2006. "Terrorism." In DeFronzo, ed., *Revolutionary Movements in World History,* 3:862–868.

Combs, Cindy C. 2005. *Terrorism in the Twenty-First Century.* 4th ed. Upper Saddle River, NJ: Prentice-Hall.

Davies, James C. 1962. "Toward a Theory of Revolution." *American Sociological Review* 27:5–19.

DeFronzo, James V. 1970. "Revolution in the Twentieth Century." In Arnold O. Olson and Sushil K. Usman, eds., *Focus on Sociology: A Book of Sociological Readings,* 317–338. Dubuque, IA: Kendall/Hunt.

———. 2006a. Introduction. In DeFronzo, ed., *Revolutionary Movements in World History,* 1:xix–xxii.

———, ed. 2006b. *Revolutionary Movements in World History: From 1750 to the Present.* 3 vols. Santa Barbara, CA: ABC-CLIO.

Dix, Robert. 1983. "Varieties of Revolution." *Comparative Politics* 15:281–293.

Dunn, John. 1972. *Modern Revolutions: An Introduction to the Analysis of a Political Phe-nomenon.* Cambridge, UK: Cambridge University Press.

Edwards, Lyford P. [1927] 1970. *The Natural History of Revolution.* Chicago: University of Chicago Press.

Eisenstadt, S. N. 1978. *Revolution and the Transformation of Societies: A Comparative Study of Civilizations.* New York: Free Press.

Ellner, Steve. 2009. "A New Model with Rough Edges: Venezuela's Community Coun-cils." *NACLA Report on the Americas* 42 (May/June): 11–14.

———. 2010. "Hugo Chavez's First Decade in Office: Breakthroughs and Shortcomings." *Latin American Perspectives* 37 (1): 77–96.

Engels, Friedrich. [1880] 1972. "Socialism: Utopian and Scientific." In Tucker, ed., *The Marx-Engels Reader*.

Ewell, Judith. 2006. "Venezuelan Bolivarian Revolution of Hugo Chavez." In DeFronzo, ed., *Revolutionary Movements in World History*, 3:903–912.

Farhi, Farideh. 1990. *States and Urban-Based Revolutions: Iran and Nicaragua*. Urbana: University of Illinois Press.

Foran, John. 2005. *Taking Power: On the Origins of Third World Revolutions*. Cambridge, UK: Cambridge University Press.

———. 2006. "Theories of Revolution." In DeFronzo, ed., *Revolutionary Movements in World History*, 3:868–372.

Fuller, Thomas. 2010. "Rebellious Mood Takes Root in Rural Thailand." *New York Times*, April 23. www.nytimes.com/2010/04/24/world/asia/24reds.html.

Fullerton, Andrew. 2006. "Inequality, Class, and Revolution." In DeFronzo, ed., *Revolutionary Movements in World History*, 2:408–412.

Giap, Vo Nguyen. 1962. *People's War, People's Army: The Viet Công Insurrection Manual for Underdeveloped Countries*. London: Praeger.

Gill, Jungyun. 2006. "Student and Youth Movements, Activism and Revolution." In DeFronzo, ed., *Revolutionary Movements in World History*, 3:848–854.

Gill, Jungyun, and James DeFronzo. 2009. "A Comparative Framework for the Analysis of International Student Movements." *Social Movement Studies* 8 (3): 203–224.

Gleijeses, Piero. 1991. *Shattered Hope: The Guatemalan Revolution and the United States, 1944–1954*. Princeton, NJ: Princeton University Press.

Goldfrank, Walter L. 1994. "The Mexican Revolution." In Goldstone, ed., *Revolutions*.

Goldstone, Jack A. 1980. "Theories of Revolution: The Third Generation." *World Politics* 32 (3): 425–453.

———. 1982. "The Comparative and Historical Study Revolutions." *Annual Review of Sociology* 8:187–207.

———. 1991. "An Analytical Framework." In Jack A. Goldstone, Ted R. Gurr, and Farrokh Moshiri, eds., *Revolutions of the Late Twentieth Century*. Boulder: Westview.

———, ed. 1994. *Revolutions: Theoretical, Comparative, and Historical Studies*. 2nd ed. Fort Worth: Harcourt Brace College Publishers.

———, ed. 1998. *Encyclopedia of Political Revolutions*. Washington, DC: Congressional Quarterly Press.

———. 2001a. "An Analytical Framework." In Katz, ed., *Revolutions*, 9–29.

———. 2001b. "Toward a Fourth Generation of Revolutionary Theory." *Annual Review of Political Science* 4 (June):139–187.

———, ed. 2002. *Revolutions: Theoretical, Comparative, and Historical Studies*. 3rd ed. Belmont, CA: Wadsworth/Thomson Learning.

———. 2010. "The New Population Bomb: Four Megatrends That Will Change the World." *Foreign Affairs* 89 (January/February): 31–43.

Goodwin, Jeff. 2001a. "Is the Age of Revolution Over?" In Katz, ed., *Revolutions*, 272–283.

———. 2001b. *No Other Way Out: States and Revolutionary Movements, 1945–1991.* Cambridge, UK: Cambridge University Press.

Gott, Richard. 2004. *Cuba: A New History.* New Haven, CT: Yale University Press.

Greene, Thomas H. 1990. *Comparative Revolutionary Movements: Search for Theory and Justice.* Prentice-Hall Contemporary Comparative Politics. 3rd ed. Englewood Cliffs, NJ: Prentice-Hall.

Guevara, Che. 1985. In *Guerrilla Warfare: Selected Case Studies.* Ed. Brian Loveman and Thomas M. Davies Jr. Lincoln: University of Nebraska Press.

Gurr, Ted Robert. 1970. *Why Men Rebel.* Princeton, NJ: Princeton University Press.

Hoensch, Jorg K. 1988. *A History of Modern Hungary, 1867–1986.* New York: Longman.

Hondros, John L. 1981. "The Greek Resistance, 1941–44." In Iatrides, ed., *Greece in the 1940s.*

Howard, Russell D., and Reid L. Sawyer, eds. 2002. *Terrorism and Counterterrorism: Understanding the New Security Environment.* Guilford, CT: McGraw-Hill/Dushkin.

Huntington, Samuel P. 1968. *Political Order in Changing Societies.* New Haven, CT: Yale University Press.

Iatrides, John O., ed. 1981. *Greece in the 1940s: A Nation in Crisis.* Modern Greek Studies Association 4. Hanover, MA: University of New England Press.

———. 1993. "Britain, the United States, and Greece, 1945–1949." In Close, ed., *The Greek Civil War.*

Irazábal, Clara, and John Foley. 2010. "Reflections on the Venezuelan Transition from a Capitalist Representative to a Socialist Participatory Democracy." *Latin American Perspectives* 37 (1): 97–122.

Johnson, Chalmers. 1964. *Revolution and the Social System.* Hoover Institution Studies 3. Stanford, CA: Hoover Institution on War, Revolution, and Peace, Stanford University.

Kalyvas, Stathis. 2006. "The Greek Civil War." In DeFronzo, ed., *Revolutionary Movements in World History*, 1:316–325.

Katz, Mark. N. 1997. *Revolutions and Revolutionary Waves.* New York: St. Martin's.

———, ed. 2001. *Revolutions: International Dimensions.* Washington, DC: Congressional Quarterly Press.

———. 2006. "Transnational Revolutionary Movements." In DeFronzo, ed., *Revolutionary Movements in World History*, 3:872–876.

Kohl, Benjamin. 2010. "Bolivia under Morales: A Work in Progress." *Latin American Perspectives* 37 (3):107–122.

Kohl, Benjamin, and Rosalind Bresnahan. 2010. "Bolivia Under Morales: Consolidating Power, Initiating Decolonization." *Latin American Perspectives* 37 (3): 5–17.

Kozloff, Nikolas. 2008. *Revolution: South America and the Rise of the New Left.* New York: Palgrave Macmillan.

Lomax, Bill. 1976. *Hungary, 1956*. New York: St. Martin's.

Mackerras, Collin, and Nick Knight, eds. 1985. *Marxism in Asia*. New York: St. Martin's.

Main, Alexander. 2010. "'A New Chapter of Engagement': Obama and the Honduran Coup." *NACLA Report on the Americas* 43 (January/February): 15–21.

Mao Tse-Tung. [1938] 1965. "Problems of Strategy in the Guerrilla War Against Japan." In *Selected Works of Mao Tse-Tung*, vol. 2. Beijing: Foreign Languages Press.

Marx, Karl, and Friedrich Engels. [1848] 1972. "The Communist Manifesto." In Tucker, ed., *The Marx-Engels Reader*.

McAdam, Doug, Sidney Tarrow, and Charles Tilly. 2001. *Dynamics of Contention*. Cambridge, UK: Cambridge University Press.

Meckler, Mark. 2010. "Mission Statement and Core Values." Tea Party Patriots. docs .google.com/View?id=dhsxmzm7_19fcdzskg5.

Miller, Norman, and Roderick Aya, eds. 1971. *National Liberation: Revolution in the Third World*. New York: Free Press.

Montgomery, Evan Braden, and Stacie L. Pettyjohn. 2006. "Ideology, Propaganda, and Revolution." In DeFronzo, ed., *Revolutionary Movements in World History*, 2:379–383.

Montgomery, Tommie Sue. 1982. *Revolution in El Salvador: Origins and Evolution*. Boulder: Westview.

Moore, Barrington, Jr. 1966. *Social Origins of Dictatorship and Democracy: Lord and Peasant in the Making of the Modern World*. Boston: Beacon.

Mydans, Seth. 2010. "Thailand Acts Against Suspected Red Shirt Backers." *New York Times*, June 21. www.nytimes.com/2010/06/22/world/asia/22thai.html.

Norton, Augustus Richard. 2013. "The Return of Egypt's Deep State." *Current History*, December, 338–344.

Paige, Jeffery M. 1975. *Agrarian Revolution: Social Movements and Export Agriculture in the Underdeveloped World*. New York: Free Press.

Papastratis, Procopis. 1987. "The Purge of the Greek Civil Service on the Eve of the Civil War." In Lars Baerentzen, John O. Iatrides, and Ole L. Smith, eds., *Studies in the History of the Greek Civil War, 1945–1949*. Copenhagen: Museum Tusculanum Press.

Parsa, Misagh. 2000. *States, Ideologies, and Social Revolutions: A Comparative Analysis of Iran, Nicaragua, and the Philippines*. Cambridge, UK: Cambridge University Press.

Pettee, George Sawyer. 1938. *The Process of Revolution*. Studies in Systematic Political Science and Comparative Government 5. New York: Harper.

"Profile: Thaksin Shinawatra." 2010. BBC News, February 26. news.bbc.co.uk/2/hi /asia-pacific/1108114.stm.

Reed, Jean-Pierre, and John Foran. 2002. "Political Cultures of Opposition: Exploring Idioms, Ideologies, and Revolutionary Agency in the Case of Nicaragua." *Critical Sociology* 28 (3): 335–70.

Regalsky, Pablo. 2010. "Political Processes and the Reconfiguration of the State in Bolivia." *Latin American Perspectives* 37 (3): 35–50.

Richter, Heinz. 1981. "The Varkiza Agreement and the Origins of the Civil War." In Iatrides, ed., *Greece in the 1940s.*

———. 1986. *British Intervention in Greece: From Varkiza to Civil War, February 1945 to August 1946.* Trans. Marion Sarafis. London: Merlin.

Sathyamurthy, T. V. 1983. *Nationalism in the Contemporary World: Political and Sociological Perspectives.* London: Frances Pinter.

Schlesinger, Stephen, and Stephen Kinzer. 1982. *Bitter Fruit: The Untold Story of the American Coup in Guatemala.* Garden City, NY: Doubleday.

Schmitt, Richard. 1987. *Introduction to Marx and Engels: A Critical Reconstruction.* Boulder: Westview.

Scott, James C. 1976. *The Moral Economy of the Peasant: Rebellion and Subsistence in Southeast Asia.* New Haven, CT: Yale University Press.

Selbin, Eric. 1999. *Modern Latin American Revolutions.* 2nd ed. Boulder: Westview.

———. 2001. "Same as It Ever Was: The Future of Revolutions at the End of the Century." In Katz, ed., *Revolutions.*

———. 2006. "Elites, Intellectuals, and Revolutionary Leadership." In DeFronzo, ed., *Revolutionary Movements in World History,* 1:253–258.

Sigmund, Paul. 2006. "The Chilean Socialist Revolution, Counter-Revolution, and Restoration of Democracy." In DeFronzo, ed., *Revolutionary Movements in World History,* 1:107–116.

Sivak, Martin. 2010. *Evo Morales: The Extraordinary Rise of the First Indigenous President of Bolivia.* New York: Palgrave Macmillan.

Skocpol, Theda. 1979. *States and Social Revolutions: A Comparison of France, Russia, and China.* Cambridge, UK: Cambridge University Press.

Skocpol, Theda, and Ellen Kay Trimberger. 1978. "Revolutions and the World Historical Development of Capitalism." *Berkeley Journal of Sociology* 22:101–113.

Smelser, Neil. 1962. *Theory of Collective Behavior.* New York: Free Press.

Smith, Anthony D. 1983. *Theories of Nationalism.* 2nd ed. New York: Holmes & Meier.

Smith, Ole L. 1993. "The Greek Communist Party, 1945–9." In Close, ed., *The Greek Civil War.*

Streeter, Stephen M. 2000. *Managing the Counterrevolution: The United States and Guatemala, 1954–1961.* Athens: Ohio University Press.

———. 2006. "Guatemalan Democratic Revolution, Counter-Revolution, and Restoration of Democracy." In DeFronzo, ed., *Revolutionary Movements in World History,* 1:325–335.

Szulc, Tad. 1986. *Fidel: A Critical Portrait.* New York: Morrow.

"Thailand Protests." 2010. BBC News, May 24. news.bbc.co.uk/2/hi/asia-pacific/7584005.stm.

Thaxton, Ralph. 1983. *China Turned Rightside Up: Revolutionary Legitimacy in the Peasant World.* New Haven, CT: Yale University Press.

Tilly, Charles. 1978. *From Mobilization to Revolution*. Reading, MA: Addison-Wesley.

Trimberger, Ellen Kay. 1978. *Revolution from Above: Military Bureaucrats and Development in Japan, Turkey, Egypt, and Peru*. New Brunswick, NJ: Transaction.

Tucker, Robert, ed. 1972. *The Marx-Engels Reader*. New York: Norton.

Valenzuela, Arturo. 1978. *Chile: The Breakdown of Democratic Regimes*. Baltimore: Johns Hopkins University Press.

Vilas, Carlos M. 1995. "A Painful Peace: El Salvador After the Accords." *NACLA Report on the Americas* 28 (May/June): 6–11.

Walker, Thomas W. 1986. *Nicaragua: The Land of Sandino*. 2nd ed. Boulder: Westview.

Walton, John. 1984. *Reluctant Rebels: Comparative Studies of Revolution and Underdevelopment*. New York: Columbia University Press.

White, Alastair. [1973] 1982. *El Salvador*. Boulder: Westview.

White, Richard. 1984. *The Morass: United States Intervention in Central America*. New York: Harper & Row.

Wickham-Crowley, Timothy P. 1992. *Guerrillas and Revolution in Latin America: A Comparative Study of Insurgents and Regimes Since 1956*. Princeton, NJ: Princeton University Press.

———. 2006. "Guerrilla Warfare and Revolution." In DeFronzo, ed., *Revolutionary Movements in World History*, 1:336–340.

Wolf, Eric. 1969. *Peasant Wars of the Twentieth Century*. New York: Harper & Row.

———. 1971. "Peasant Rebellion and Revolution." In Miller and Aya, eds., *National Liberation*.

2

The Russian Revolutions
and Eastern Europe

———

The 1917 October Revolution was the first ever won by revolutionaries advocating a socialist society. By the beginning of 1917 the majority of the Russian people were extremely discontented with the czar's regime. Various revolutionary groups sought to mobilize this popular frustration to transform Russian society. When the coercive power of the czarist state collapsed in early 1917, revolutionary leaders had an opportunity to seize control of their nation's destiny. Soldiers and sailors refused orders to repress rebellious street demonstrations and instead went over to the revolutionaries. As the institutions of the czarist government deteriorated, workers, military personnel, and peasants elected revolutionary administrative councils, or soviets, from among their own numbers, to exercise power. In fall 1917 soldiers, sailors, and workers loyal to the Bolshevik-led citywide soviet of the capital, Petrograd (later Leningrad and after 1991, St. Petersburg), established a new national revolutionary government.

GEOGRAPHY AND POPULATION

The USSR, at 8,649,489 square miles (22,402,200 square kilometers) and comprising ethnically diverse states, succeeded the czar's vast empire. The largest country in the world until its dissolution in December 1991, most of the USSR's territory was a vast plain extending from Eastern Europe to the Pacific Ocean, interrupted occasionally by low mountain ranges. This huge plain is characterized by three distinctive sectors running east and west. The Arctic section is a frozen marshy tundra, the middle band of the country is heavily forested, and the southernmost area is composed of extensive arid grassy plains that in the far south become sandy deserts.

The population of the Soviet Union, which was about 150 million at the time of the revolutions in 1917, exceeded 287 million during the last year of its existence. The USSR was composed of fifteen union republics, the largest of which was Russia (now an independent nation), which was home to 52 percent of the USSR's population and included 76 percent of the land area. The second most populous republic was the (now independent) Ukraine, which had about 18 percent of the USSR's citizens. Each remaining republic included less than 6 percent of the USSR's population.

In 2014 the Russian Federation, at 6,601,638 square miles (17,098,242 square kilometers), had a population of 142,500,482 (CIA 2014b). The country's people were ethnically about 80 percent Russian, with small minorities of Tatars, Ukrainians, Chechens, and others.

THE SETTING FOR REVOLUTION

Before the Bolshevik Revolution, Russia was a vast empire ruled by a hereditary emperor, the czar, who governed the Russian people as well as many other nationalities and lands that later were incorporated into the USSR. At the time of the revolution, only about 15 percent of the population lived in cities. Russian industrialization had begun later than other European societies, but the process was well under way by 1917.

Large factories were mainly concentrated in eight industrial regions, including Petrograd (which was the capital at the time of the revolution) and Moscow (the old capital, which the revolutionary government established as the capital of the USSR). Approximately half the industrial plants were owned by foreign companies from the more technologically advanced nations. In 1917 at least one-half of Russia's industrial workers had peasant parents or had been peasants or rural laborers before migrating to urban areas.

Most peasants had reason to be discontented. Before the seventeenth century many had lived a nomadic existence, traveling about the countryside seeking optimal conditions, such as the highest possible wages or more fertile land, or simply enjoying new environments. But their freedom of movement was intolerable to many large landowners, who desired a more reliable labor force. Thus in 1649 serfdom, which bound individuals and their families to particular landowners or, in some cases, to the state, under penalty of law, was established. By the 1760s about 52 percent of those living in rural Russia were serfs (Wolf 1969).

After Russia was defeated in the 1854–1856 Crimean War, Czar Alexander II decided to strengthen the nation through a modernization program, which included

MAP 2.1 European USSR

reforms in the countryside. In 1861 serfdom was abolished, and parcels of land were distributed to former serfs. However, in many instances emancipation from serfdom generated more economic hardship than it alleviated. Most had to pay redemption fees, which stretched out over decades, for their land. Many former serfs awaited a second emancipation that would free them from the burden of redemption payments. Peasants also suffered from heavy taxes. Especially during the tenure of finance minister Sergei Witte (1882–1903), a primary architect of the nation's industrial drive, these taxes were a major source of government investment capital (Von Laue 1971). Many fell further and further into debt because they could not produce enough to feed their families, meet their redemption payments, and pay taxes simultaneously (Wolf 1969). Intense peasant discontent constituted one of the essential elements of the revolutionary situation.

Many peasants did not own their land independently but belonged to rural collectives called mirs. The mir assigned parcels of land to particular peasants and established taxation rates for households. This experience helped prepare much of the rural population to participate in a socialist revolution as well as the collectivization of agriculture that occurred during the late 1920s and early 1930s.

Achieving the goal of industrialization required that thousands of upper-class and upper-middle-class Russians receive a modern education. But since the source of advanced technological learning was Western Europe (by attending a university there or being instructed by a Western European or someone who had been educated there), education inevitably meant exposure to political and economic concepts that were alien to the autocratic Russian system.

By favoring more democratic forms of government and a redistribution of wealth and opportunity, many young people came to constitute a dissident element within Russia's educated elite. During the mid-nineteenth century some proponents of social change, influenced by the Russian revolutionary activist Mikhail Bakunin, who advocated anarchism, organized the populist movement. Anarchism included the concept that workers and peasants in collective associations should own all productive wealth. Economic inequality was to be minimized and people's basic needs satisfied. Since in this system participants would, ideally, accomplish important tasks on a cooperative basis, society would have no need to employ force through the police or the military. In other words, there would be no need for a centralized formal government. This was important, according to anarchists, because government had always functioned as an instrument of oppression used by the rich to exploit the labor of the majority of the population.

Many populist activists went into the countryside to educate the rural masses about the possibility and desirability of revolutionary change, but many villagers viewed them as outsiders and meddlers. Other populists, concluding that violent attacks on the czar's government would help topple the dictatorship, secretly organized Narodnaia Volia (People's Will) to carry out assassinations and acts of antigovernment terrorism (Dmytryshyn 1984, 25). People's Will, along with other branches of the populist movement, supported the creation of national and local elected assemblies; economic and administrative freedom of action for the village communes; bestowing ownership of all land on those who worked it; workers' control of industrial plants; complete freedom of speech, press, and political activity; granting all adults, regardless of gender, wealth, or landownership, the right to vote; and replacing the existing professional army with a people's militia (Dmytryshyn 1984). The major victim of People's Will terrorist activity was Czar Alexander II, who was assassinated on March 13, 1881. After the assassination, the government increased police repression, effectively destroyed People's Will, and clamped down on other revolutionary groups in Russia.

The populist movement helped formulate the concept of the dedicated revolutionist. Anarchists Sergei Nechaev and Mikhail Bakunin, in *Catechism of the Revolutionary* (1869), described the ideal revolutionary as a person with no inhibiting personal bonds or emotional concerns. His or her only passion was to accomplish the revolution (Wolf 1969). Populists also believed that traditional communal institutions among Russian peasants, such as the mir, could serve as the basis for a direct transition in Russia from rural collectivism to modern socialism without undergoing the brutalizing and dehumanizing experience of capitalist industrialization. The Russian revolutionaries who eventually succeeded, the Marxist Bolsheviks led by Lenin, incorporated some populist concepts, including an organization of dedicated professional revolutionaries and the possibility of industrializing under a socialist system without a period of capitalist development. Versions of the populist movement grew and faded away repeatedly over several decades. At the time of the 1917 revolutions, populism was manifested in the countryside through the Socialist Revolutionary Party, the most popular political party among the peasants.

THE RUSSIAN SOCIAL DEMOCRATIC PARTY

Some among the educated elite who advocated sweeping social change in Russia rejected terrorist methods. Such actions, they argued, not only intensified police repression but also alienated large numbers of citizens and led them to summarily reject the message of the revolutionaries. One organization that condemned terrorism, Osvobozhdhenie Truda (Liberation of Labor), was founded in 1883 in Geneva, Switzerland, by Russian exiles who were interested in the ideas of Karl Marx. This group included Georgi Plekhanov, the man who translated Marx's works into Russian.

Marx's analysis of history had led him to conclude that capitalism (the period of social development during which private ownership of resources, industry, and commerce characterizes the economic system and the owners of industrial and commercial enterprises control the government) would inevitably be succeeded by socialism (the phase of society characterized by public ownership of resources and productive institutions and by working-class control of government). In Marx's view, socialism would eventually lead to the final and highest developmental stage of history, communism, which was to be characterized by material abundance, cooperative social relations, and the end of the need for suppressive governmental institutions such as armies or police forces.

Marx predicted that capitalist society would create both the political means and the motivation for the exploited and toiling masses of the world finally, for the first time in history, to seize control and redirect the resources of society toward benefiting the needs of the great majority rather than catering to the interests of a numerically small ruling element (Marx and Engels [1848] 1998). According to Marx, capitalism provided the political means for the working class to seize power by physically concentrating working people in large cities where they could interact, organize, and develop a shared consciousness concerning the cause of their economic exploitation and the desirability of replacing capitalism with socialism. The motivation for the urban industrial working class, or proletariat, to strive for revolutionary change would be what Marx thought was a continuous characteristic of capitalism—the impoverishment and miserable living conditions of the working class. Once capitalism had been overcome, the new socialist society, as described by Marx ([1875] 1994) and later, Lenin ([1917] 1975), would be characterized by collective rather than private ownership of the economy, greater economic and social equality, an attempt to provide employment for all people able to work, and the provision of basic foods, medical services, education, and other necessities of life either free or at low cost to the entire population.

Russian Marxists, although advocating many populist goals, such as a democratic political system, did not initially feel that the peasant village commune could form the basis of a socialist Russia. They argued, strictly adhering to Marx's concepts, that the transformation to socialism could occur only after capitalism had transformed much of the peasantry into an urban industrial working class.

During the 1890s Liberation of Labor evolved into the critically important Russian Social Democratic Party, whose full name was Russian Social Democratic Labor Party. At its 1903 meeting, a split developed. An important party leader, Lenin (born Vladimir Ilich Ulyanov in 1870), tried to persuade other delegates that only hard-core party activists—lifelong committed revolutionaries and dedicated participants in the underground revolutionary organizations—should have a voice in governing the party. Lenin, whose older brother Alexander, a brilliant university science student, was executed at age twenty-one for involvement in a plot to assassinate Czar Alexander III when Lenin was seventeen (Volkogonov 1994), claimed that a fully open and democratic party system would be hopelessly vulnerable to infiltration and manipulation by the czar's secret police and easily repressed in autocratic Russia (Wilson 1972). He was defeated 28 to 23 on this issue (Dmytryshyn 1984). But Lenin's candidates won the election for control of the party's central committees and the editorial board of its newspaper, *Iskra* (The Spark). From that point on, his supporters called themselves Bolsheviks (the majority), and Lenin's opponents in the Social Democratic Party were known as Mensheviks (the minority).

The division within the Russian Social Democratic Party became permanent after the 1912 party conference in Prague. The Mensheviks continued to support the notion that the transition to socialism would occur gradually and in stages in Russia. First the monarchy would be destroyed and replaced by a political democracy with a capitalist economic system. As the capitalist business investors transformed the economy of Russia through industrialization, the Mensheviks would take advantage of the open democratic political system to educate the members of the industrial working class to the desirability of the fairer, more efficient economic system and society that the Mensheviks (as well as the Bolsheviks) felt socialism represented.

In contrast, the Bolsheviks, under Lenin's influence, concluded that once the monarchy had been overthrown, the post-revolutionary political system should immediately become a dictatorship of the proletariat, in which the government would be in the hands of leaders truly committed to the interests of the worker-peasant majority of the population and the rapid implementation of socialism (Fitzpatrick 1982; Rabinowitch 1976; Von Laue 1971).

Marx had asserted that socialist society would be characterized by the dictatorship of the proletariat—the political domination of the working class over the government. However, he never clearly defined how the working-class majority would control the political system and the institutions of governmental coercion, such as the army and the police. Lenin, in contrast, provided his own operational definition of the concept. He argued that the expanding Bolshevik organization should seize power in order to effect change rapidly and defend the revolution and the working class from opponents (Bottomore 1983; Fitzpatrick 1982). Thus for Lenin the dictatorship of the proletariat meant the rule of the revolutionary party in a one-party political system.

Lenin believed that although the industrial workers formed the basis of the revolution, on their own they could develop only what was called "trade union consciousness" (a concern about limited job-related objectives, such as wages, benefits, working hours, and working conditions). He argued that the workers required the leadership and inspiration of revolutionary intellectuals (whether they came from the working class or from middle- or upper-class backgrounds) to achieve

revolutionary consciousness (the commitment to socialist transformation of society). The Bolsheviks (known before the 1917 revolutions as the Russian Social
Democratic Labor Party and beginning in 1918 as the Communist Party) would,
according to Lenin, lead the masses through the stage of socialist development to
communist society (Lenin [1902] 1975; [1917] 1975). Whether Lenin would have
modified his concept of government after the threats to the revolution had subsided
will never be known: He died soon after the end of the Russian Revolution.

THE ATTEMPTED REVOLUTION OF 1905

At the turn of the century, discontent was manifested through the growth of political parties dedicated to the overthrow of the monarchy, industrial strikes for better wages and working conditions, protests and riots among peasants, university
demonstrations, and the assassinations of government officials, often by socialist
revolutionaries (the Bolsheviks and the Mensheviks opposed terrorist violence).
When in 1904 hostilities broke out between Russia and Japan in the Far East, Russian officials tried to reduce domestic tensions by rallying the country for a war they
were confident Russia would win. Instead, the Japanese inflicted one military disaster after another on Russian forces until the United States mediated a settlement.

Hardships caused by the war intensified discontent. In January 1905 a peaceful procession of thousands of workers, led by an activist priest, George Gapon,
attempted to present the czar a petition listing grievances and calling on him for
assistance. But soldiers fired on the demonstrators, killing many. Following the
massacre, known as Bloody Sunday, strikes and peasant uprisings spread. Even
some units of the army and navy rebelled. These events are known collectively as
the Revolution of 1905. Industrial workers in Petrograd elected a workers' governing parliament called the Soviet (council) of Workers' Deputies (representatives).

Fearing that the revolution might succeed, Czar Nicholas II promised reforms.
He pledged to allow (1) freedom of conscience, speech, and assembly; (2) the creation of a national parliament, or state Duma, which would have the power to confirm or block the implementation of any law; and (3) the right of men who did not
own property to participate in the election of the Duma (Dmytryshyn 1984; Salisbury 1981). These reforms caused great celebration among liberal aristocrats, businessmen, and many professionals. Workers and peasants who supported revolution
consequently lost the support of upper- and middle-class elements who had opposed the czar's dictatorial style of government. The czar then sent military units to
towns and villages still in rebellion. Thousands were executed and many thousands
more were forced to leave Russia.

In order to pacify the growing industrial working class, the government legalized labor unions and introduced health and accident insurance for some workers.

Plans were developed to provide free elementary education. The government also encouraged peasants to own parcels of land individually rather than participate in village communes. One purpose of this policy, named the Stolypin Land Reform, after its director, Premier Peter Stolypin, was to eliminate the mir, which had been a source of revolutionary organization during the 1905 Revolution, and to institute capitalist business relationships among farmers in place of the cooperative relationships of the village commune. This was intended to expand the class of landowning peasants, especially the number of rich peasants (kulaks), in order to use them as a protection against revolution in the countryside. The regime claimed that half of the peasants were private landowners by 1915.

The czar later refused to honor some promised reforms. Election laws were structured to prevent most of the adult population (including those most prone to revolutionary ideas, such as many of the industrial workers) from voting (Dmytryshyn 1984; Von Laue 1971). When those permitted to vote still elected a Duma that the czar could not totally control, he responded to its measures and demands by ignoring them or periodically disbanding the legislature. Thus the czar continued to exercise dictatorial power.

The attempted revolution in 1905 failed for a number of reasons. Most revolutionary leaders were surprised by the uprisings and were not in a position to coordinate the individual rebellions throughout the Russian Empire, making them easier to suppress. Furthermore, the creation of a national elected parliament persuaded upper- and middle-class liberals to desert the revolutionary cause. And the majority of army and naval units remained loyal to the czar's government. Each of these factors would be reversed in 1917.

THE REVOLUTIONS OF 1917
The February Revolution

During the early twentieth century, tensions among European nations intensified over competition for the resources of less developed parts of the world and worsening ethnic hostilities. When Archduke Ferdinand of Austria was assassinated by a Serb and the Austro-Hungarian army attacked Serbia, Russia, declaring its readiness to aid the Serbians, a fellow Slavic people, plunged into war against the Austro-Hungarian Empire and its powerful ally, Germany. Despite earlier commitments not to obey if ordered by capitalist governments to take up arms against working-class brothers in neighboring countries, most socialist leaders, apparently swept away on tides of nationalist fervor, pledged support for national war efforts. Among Russian socialists, Lenin and his fellow Bolsheviks were virtually alone in condemning the war as a capitalist atrocity perpetrated by the ruling classes of Europe that would result in the mass slaughter of millions of peasants and workers.

Although he opposed the war, Lenin recognized it as a potential opportunity for a new and successful revolution. He argued that Russia's defeat would be the best possible outcome because such a catastrophe would deprive the czarist state of its remaining aura of legitimacy and the loyalty of its armed forces and generate the level of mass discontent necessary to topple the regime (Fitzpatrick 1982).

Russian armies soon suffered devastating defeats by the better armed German forces. Millions of Russian soldiers perished; the call-up of 15 million men into military service caused serious industrial and agricultural labor shortages, which disrupted not only army supplies but food supplies for the entire population. In Petrograd, extreme shortages led to accelerated inflation. Between the start of World War I and 1917, the real (inflation-adjusted) wages of Petrograd workers declined to about one-third of prewar levels, owing largely to the rising price of necessities (Rabinowitch 1976). As conditions worsened, hundreds of thousands of soldiers, sailors, workers, and peasants elected soviets to demand change and to provide organization for a building revolutionary upsurge. By early March 1917 (late February according to the Julian calendar Russia followed at the time), mass industrial strikes had broken out in major urban centers. The czar, who was at the front, sent troops to Petrograd to subdue the strikers. However, most of the soldiers refused to fire on the demonstrators, and many joined the protests.

As the coercive power of the czarist state rapidly disintegrated, it became clear that not only the civilian workers and peasants but also the bulk of the armed forces (drawn from those classes), as well as most of the middle class and some in the upper class, were now united in opposition to the czar's continuation in power. Units of the Petrograd garrison mutinied, and soldiers, under the direction of the Petrograd Soviet of Soldiers' and Workers' Deputies, took control of the capital on March 12 (February 27 on the Julian calendar). On March 16 the czar was forced to abdicate, and Russia became a republic. The czar's parliament, the Duma, then drew from its numbers individuals to serve in a new provisional government, which was at first headed by an aristocrat, Prince Lvov, and eventually by the moderate socialist Alexander Kerensky (Katov 1967; Rabinowitch 1976).

But the immediate post-czarist national government suffered from critical weaknesses. Members of the provisional government reflected the social-class composition of the Duma: they were largely wealthy businessmen, aristocrats, or employed in the professions. Although moderate socialists served in the provisional government along with conservatives and liberals, it represented primarily upper-income interests and was viewed with some suspicion by workers and peasants, many of whom in the capital recognized only the authority of their Petrograd soviet. Despite the fact that the Petrograd soviet initially supported the right of the provisional government to exercise the power of the state, a system of dual power actually existed, with the provisional government and the Petrograd soviet as the two centers of authority. The Petrograd soviet agreed to share power with the pro-visional government and support it until national political power could be handed over to a Constituent Assembly elected by all male citizens.

Class hostility intensified all over the country. Soldiers no longer automatically obeyed their officers, who typically had higher-class backgrounds. Rather, soldiers and sailors debated issues and continued to elect self-governing soviets from their own numbers. Initially, the Petrograd soviet was dominated by Mensheviks and Socialist Revolutionaries. But from spring 1917 on, the Bolsheviks gained members—including many Mensheviks and Socialist Revolutionaries who defected—faster than any other group (Dmytryshyn 1984; Fitzpatrick 1982; Greene 1990; Rabinowitch 1976). The Bolsheviks achieved majorities in both the Petrograd and the Moscow soviets by early fall.

The October Revolution

The provisional government made several crucial decisions that rapidly dissipated its initially limited coercive capability, which had been based on the willingness of military personnel and the Petrograd soviet to accept its authority. First, it de-cided to continue the war against Germany. Those in favor, including the Menshe-viks and the more conservative of the Socialist Revolutionaries in the Petrograd soviet, were motivated by several factors: patriotism, hatred of Germany, and the perceived need for future economic and technical aid from England and France, Russia's allies against Germany. The Bolsheviks and the pro-Bolshevik Socialist Revolutionaries (called Left Socialist Revolutionaries) opposed the war. Crucially, the provisional government also delayed major economic reforms, including the redistribution of land to poor peasants, until after the war, and postponed the elec-tion of the national Constituent Assembly. The decision to delay land reform out-raged many peasants, who suspected the upper-class members of the provisional government were not going to carry out land reform at all. But the provisional gov-ernment feared mass desertions if land redistribution occurred during war time. Peasant soldiers would not want to miss out on the opportunity to obtain distrib-uted land. So once the provisional government decided to continue the war, it was forced to make the extremely unpopular decision to delay land reform.

When the czar was overthrown, two important revolutionaries were out of Russia. Lenin was in exile in Geneva, and Leon Trotsky (born Lyov Davidovich Bronstein in the Ukraine in 1879), who had participated in the Petrograd soviet during its brief 1905 existence, was in New York. Lenin realized the opportunity for a sweeping socioeconomic revolution was developing in his homeland and deter-mined to get to Petrograd as soon as possible. Assistance came from a remarkable source: the imperial German government. German capitalist leaders detested the revolutionary ideas of the Bolsheviks. But Germany was fighting on two fronts. If Russia were to give up the war, Germany could concentrate on the western front and perhaps deliver a knockout blow. German leaders correctly concluded that the chances of Russia leaving the conflict would be much greater if the charismatic Lenin, long an opponent of the war, were to return to Petrograd. The German government transported him in a railroad car through Germany. He boarded a ferry to Sweden and then Lenin made his way to Petrograd in April.

Trotsky arrived in Petrograd in May and declared that he supported Lenin and the Bolshevik program rather than the Mensheviks, who continued to support Russian involvement in the war and the concept of a gradual evolution toward socialist transformation. Trotsky, Lenin, and other Bolshevik leaders argued, in contrast, that there must be a second revolution, in which the workers and peasants take power from the upper class. Throughout Russia, Bolshevik speakers proclaimed, "End the war"; "All land to the peasants"; and "All power to the soviets" (Dmytryshyn 1984; Fitzpatrick 1982; Rabinowitch 1976).

In early July the provisional government launched a new offensive against the Germans, which ended in disaster. Then the Germans launched a successful counterattack. Thousands of deserting Russian soldiers flocked to Petrograd. These events encouraged some Bolshevik leaders to attempt an uprising. Lenin apparently was uncertain whether conditions were yet right for a Bolshevik seizure of power and may have opposed an insurrection at that point. In any case, the uprising failed, and Trotsky and several other Bolsheviks were jailed by soldiers loyal to the provisional government. Lenin went into hiding as Kerensky became head of the provisional government.

In September a conservative general, Lavr Kornilov, attempted to seize power. Expecting the attack, the provisional government released Trotsky and other imprisoned Bolshevik leaders and called on the growing ranks of the Bolsheviks to defend Petrograd. But Kornilov's attempted takeover failed, since most of his forces refused to carry out their orders and many joined the Bolsheviks. Growing numbers of workers, soldiers, and sailors concluded that any further counterrevolutionary attempts to crush the revolution and working-class power must be prevented. Therefore, the popularly elected soviets, led by those committed to establishing a socialist economic system, demanded total power.

By the end of September, Bolshevik majorities had been elected in the Petrograd and the Moscow soviets. Lenin concluded that the time had come for the Bolsheviks to seize power on behalf of the workers and peasants and decisively commit the country to socialism. On November 7 (October 25 according to the Julian calendar), soldiers, sailors, and armed workers of the Petrograd soviet, under Trotsky's command, occupied transportation and communication centers, government buildings, and the czar's winter palace. There was little bloodshed, since few military personnel in the capital still recognized the authority of the provisional government. Kerensky fled and the provisional government collapsed. Soviet workers and soldiers under Bolshevik leadership also took control in Moscow and other large cities. The Bolshevik-led revolutionary government instructed local village soviets to seize large private estates and church-owned land, abolished private ownership of industry, and announced its intention to end the war with Germany.

The Constituent Assembly was elected shortly after the Bolsheviks overthrew the provisional government. Bolshevik popularity had been increasing, but the party was still not well-known to most people in the countryside or in the southern part of the country. Votes of the 5 million soldiers and sailors were counted separately. The Bolsheviks won absolute majorities in the armies in the north and west and among the sailors of the Baltic Fleet, but the Socialist Revolutionaries and the Ukrainian ethnic parties won among the armies of the south and the Black Sea Fleet (Fitzpatrick 1982). The Bolsheviks also won majorities in Petrograd and Moscow and probably took most of the country's urban vote. The Bolsheviks received 24 percent of the total (9.8 million votes), placing them second to the loosely organized revolutionary party popular among the peasants, the Socialist Revolutionaries, which received 41 percent (17.1 million votes) (Dmytryshyn 1984). Other political parties won lower percentages. For example, the Constitutional Democrats (Cadets), who favored a parliamentary constitutional monarchy system and moderate economic reforms, received 5 percent (2 million), and the Mensheviks' vote was 3 percent (1.36 million).

At the time of the election, the Bolsheviks and the Socialist Revolutionaries took basically identical positions on the issue of central concern to the peasants— redistribution of land. Consequently, in the minority of villages that were close enough to cities, towns, military bases, or rail depots for the inhabitants to know the Bolshevik program, the peasants voted in about equal numbers for the Bolsheviks and the Socialist Revolutionaries. But in villages where people were not familiar with the Bolsheviks or their land policy, the rural-based Socialist Revolutionaries achieved majorities (Fitzpatrick 1982). When the assembly convened in January 1918, many of the delegates began criticizing the Bolsheviks. Before the assembly had been in existence for twenty-four hours, soldiers loyal to the Bolshevik-controlled Petrograd soviet forced it to disband.

In the following months, power shifted from the elected soviets to the Bolshevik Party (Daniels 1988; Dmytryshyn 1984; Fitzpatrick 1982; Rabinowitch 1976). Some revolutionaries objected to Bolshevik domination and demanded that major power be returned to the soviets. Most notably, in 1921 many of the sailors at the Kronstadt naval base rebelled and demanded a "true soviet republic of workers and peasants." The Kronstadt rebellion was quickly crushed by Bolshevik-led military units. The soviets assumed a role in influencing local community affairs. Not until the democratization reforms in 1989 and 1990 would a legislature exercise effective power at the national level.

Assessing the Bolshevik Seizure of Power

According to most interpretations of Marx's theories, the Bolsheviks were wrong to seize power in 1917. Marx felt that the transformation to socialism would first occur in the most advanced countries because they had the large urban industrial working classes that would constitute the basis of support for socialism. The Russian industrial working class in 1917 was revolutionary but included only a small fraction of the total population. Lenin believed, however, that an extraordinary political situation provided a unique opportunity: the Russian state collapsed in the face of rebellious armed forces and revolutionary peasants and workers desperate for relief from the miseries of war and economic exploitation. Most competing political groups had ineffectual leaders and confused or unappealing ideologies. Lenin believed that the Bolsheviks had a scientifically based understanding of human history and a realistic plan to create the first truly just human society. He and other Bolshevik leaders felt that history would not excuse a failure to take advantage of such remarkable circumstances.

But Lenin and his associates also realized their premature seizure of power would result in several problems. For example, the revolutionary leadership was attempting to carry out a socialist revolution in a primarily agrarian society. Marxist theory assumed that socialist revolution was impossible without the support of the majority. But in Russia the majority was the rural peasantry. Lenin, incorporating some concepts from the old populist movement, argued that the majority of peasants could be convinced to support the revolution. Mobilization of the peasants would proceed, Lenin argued, in the following sequence. The Bolsheviks, originally composed mainly of revolutionary intellectuals, would awaken and recruit the Russian industrial working class to the revolution. Then the revolutionary working class, hundreds of thousands of whom would join the Bolshevik organization (Communist Party after 1918) and many of whom had relatives who were peasants or had once been peasants themselves, would provide leadership and inspiration to the discontented peasant majority, many of whom would soon also join the party. Most peasants, according to Lenin, could be won over for several reasons. First, the lands of big private owners and the church were to be given to the peasants. Second, the Bolsheviks anticipated that the peasant communes (mirs), with their traditions of collectivism and cooperation, could provide the basis for peasant incorporation into the socialist revolution. Thus Lenin thought that whereas the industrial workers would constitute the core of the revolution in Russia, most peasants would also support the revolution (Fitzpatrick 1982).

Another major concern was the question of how to industrialize without capitalism. Industry and modern technology were necessary to produce the wealth needed to provide a materially satisfying life for all. But according to Marx, industrialization was to be accomplished under the system of private ownership, investment, and profit making. If the revolution preceded complete industrialization, the latter would have to be accomplished under socialism. But this would seem to mean that improving the material well-being of the population would have to be postponed while the system accumulated enough wealth (capital) to bring about industrialization.

Could a harsh transition to industrial society under socialism be avoided? Remarkably, Lenin, Trotsky, and some of their associates initially anticipated that once the Bolshevik Revolution succeeded, revolutionary Russia would provide inspiration and perhaps assistance to the working classes of the advanced industrial nations to accomplish their own socialist revolutions (Rabinowitch 1976). Then the revolutionary advanced societies could use wealth produced by their industries to assist Russia and other less developed countries so that they could industrialize without imposing harsh austerity or repressive measures on their populations. Although industrial workers in several nations that lost World War I, including Germany and Hungary, tried to organize revolutions, they failed because the armed forces suppressed the uprisings. Furthermore, peasants in other European societies were more conservative than those in Russia and generally opposed revolution (Greene 1990).

When no advanced nations of the World War I era experienced a socialist revolution, the leaders of revolutionary Russia confronted serious problems. Industrialization would have to be achieved through the Soviet Union's own resources. The Soviet state would have to take extreme austerity measures in order to accumulate the capital necessary to transform the economy.

Hostility from the industrialized societies intensified the motivation to industrialize as quickly as possible. In the event of military attacks from capitalist nations, heavy industry would be crucial for producing the weapons needed for defense (Von Laue 1971).

THE CIVIL WAR

The Bolshevik Revolution of November 7, 1917, did not win immediate victory throughout the czar's vast empire. Various forces gathered on the periphery of European Russia, some to overthrow the revolution and some to establish different versions of revolutionary society. Former czarist generals rallied anti-Bolshevik officers and soldiers and organized so-called White Armies. The more conservative elements of the Socialist Revolutionary Party attempted to set up a separate revolutionary government. An anarchist group that opposed any strong central state government, czarist or Bolshevik, attempted to maintain control of southern Ukraine (Palij 1976). Several capitalist countries, including Britain, the United States, and Japan, sent troops to Russia and provided military assistance to anti-Bolshevik armies.

The Bolshevik leadership responded by organizing the Red Army, which first was made up of volunteers; later a draft was imposed. The core of the army included hundreds of thousands of industrial workers and Communist Party members, led by the energetic, charismatic Trotsky. Eventually numbering more than 5 million, the Red Army defeated all the White Armies and other anti-Bolshevik forces by 1923.

The years of civil war and foreign capitalist military intervention instilled a siege mentality in Bolshevik supporters and helped militarize the Communist Party (Daniels 1988; Fitzpatrick 1982). In 1918 Fanya Kaplan, a member of the Socialist Revolutionary Party, shot and wounded Lenin in an attempted assassination. Kaplan objected to disbanding the Constituent Assembly and feared that Lenin's approach would be self-defeating for the cause of socialism. The assassination attempt and the killing of thousands of Communist Party members and supporters by anti-Bolshevik forces, were accompanied by the growth of the Bolshevik internal security forces (secret police) which executed thousands of people without trial during the civil war (Fitzpatrick 1982; Volkogonov 1994).

Anti-Bolshevik forces failed for several reasons, principally because the Whites' political and economic goals were far less appealing to the vast majority of Russia's population than those of the Bolsheviks. For example, most of the White Army leaders proposed returning land distributed to peasants to the big landowners and the church. The peasants were further alienated when White soldiers abused the civilian population, to a degree worse than the Red Army (Dmytryshyn 1984; Fitzpatrick 1982). Moreover, the anti-Bolshevik forces were not unified, nor were their efforts, for the most part, coordinated (Von Laue 1971). Receiving aid from foreign nations made them agents of imperialism to many. The Red Army, in contrast, was usually perceived as defending the country against the rich and their foreign allies. Finally, the assistance provided to White Armies and other anti-Bolshevik forces was limited both by the vast size of the country and by the fact that capitalist countries were still recovering from the devastation of World War I.

LEADERSHIP STRUGGLE

The death in 1924 of Lenin, who had been ill for some time, prompted a struggle for control of the revolution. The future of the Russian Communist Party and the Soviet Union was at stake. Lenin had evaluated in writing some of the top Bolshevik leaders and had at one time singled out Trotsky and Stalin as outstanding. Trotsky, the educated son of a rich peasant, was a brilliant organizer and leader; he had engineered the Bolshevik overthrow of the provisional government in 1917 and then led the Red Army to victory in the civil war.

Stalin (born Iosif Vissarionovich Dzhugashvili in 1879) was the son of a cobbler (who reportedly used alcohol heavily and was prone to violence) and a washerwoman, former serfs in Georgia, a small mountainous state that had been conquered by the czar's army and then incorporated into the Russian Empire. Stalin was one of the few top Bolshevik leaders to come from the lowest classes of pre-revolutionary czarist society. Although he had trained for the priesthood, Stalin left the seminary to become a revolutionary activist among oil industry workers. The czar's government exiled him to Siberia. Although neither a charismatic speaker nor a war hero, Stalin became a top-level Communist Party organizer. After the civil war, much of the Red Army was demobilized, but the Communist Party continued to grow. Controlling party leaders, bureaucracy, and newspapers was a more significant source of power than past military glory. In 1922 leading party officials appointed Stalin to the new position of general secretary of the Communist Party to oversee the rapidly expanding membership. This was crucially important to Stalin's later rise to dictator because, while other party leaders held top government posts, Stalin provided their staff personnel, who often felt more loyal to him than to the heads of their ministries. In his final days, Lenin wrote a letter to the Communist Party suggesting that party members "find a way to remove Stalin," whom he now considered too prone to violence and "too rude" to be party leader (*New York Times*, May 10, 1987). But Lenin's final disapproval came too late to block Stalin's ascent to power.

Trotsky and Stalin agreed on some important issues, such as rapid industrialization and the dominant political role of the Communist Party. However, they disagreed on two major points (Dmytryshyn 1984; Fitzpatrick 1982; Von Laue 1971). First, Trotsky, a former Menshevik, claimed that Stalin was imposing a type of dictatorial control over the Communist Party. Trotsky argued that there should be more freedom of expression and open, democratic methods of leader selection and policy development within the party. Stalin and his associates could assert that Lenin was responsible for or accepted some of the limitations on democracy within the party, such as the 1922 party congress resolution that permitted the central committee to expel by a two-thirds vote any party members involved in an organized faction opposing the policies of the governing majority (Von Laue 1971). But Trotsky and his supporters argued that Lenin's restrictions were a reaction first to the police state repression of the czar's regime and later to the threat posed by the civil war, the accompanying foreign military intervention, and other serious post-revolution problems and that they were not meant to be permanent, let alone tightened.

The second major disagreement had to do with Russia's role in regard to revolutionary movements in other countries. Trotsky argued that Russia should provide them all possible encouragement and physical assistance. His supporters used the slogan "World revolution now!" to express this point of view. According to Trotsky, true socialism would be impossible to achieve, particularly in a primarily agricultural society like Russia in the 1920s, without revolutions throughout the world, including in the advanced capitalist nations. An isolated, revolutionary but economically backward society without substantial assistance from advanced countries and, on the other hand, facing military opposition from them would, Trotsky predicted, tend to develop a repressive government for defensive reasons. And instead of improving the material well-being of the people, the state would be forced to limit political freedom and consumption in order to ensure a disciplined and reliable labor force and accumulate the capital needed for industrialization. These hardships could be avoided if worldwide revolution occurred. Fostering international revolution was an element of Trotsky's general theory of permanent revolution, a worldwide series of revolutionary upheavals, which together would bring about the conditions necessary for the achievement of socialism throughout the world (Bottomore 1983).

Stalin, in contrast, argued that events had proven that political circumstances were not right for socialist revolutions in most other countries. In light of these realities, Soviet aid to revolutionary movements in the more technologically advanced societies would not bring about more revolutions but provoke renewed military intervention against the Soviet Union. Rather, the Soviet Union should devote its energies toward rapidly industrializing and increasing the efficiency of agricultural production. Then, once the Soviet Union was a mighty industrial power, it could produce the weaponry necessary to defend its own revolution against capitalist intervention and supply aid to foreign revolutionary movements. Stalin's supporters represented this position by the slogan "Build socialism in one country first!" That made sense to many in the Soviet Union.

Trotsky suffered from several disadvantages in the power struggle. First, many people associated the limitations on party democracy with Lenin rather than Stalin, even though Stalin extended them. Also, many Bolsheviks were students of past revolutions and feared that, as happened after the French Revolution, a successful army officer could seize power and become a "Russian Napoleon." Even though it was Stalin who eventually assumed dictatorial power, in the 1920s many Bolsheviks feared that Trotsky, charismatic leader of the Red Army, represented the real danger of a one-man dictatorship. As noted earlier, Stalin's position as general secretary of the Communist Party provided him with a major organizational advantage over Trotsky. Also, as the Communist Party expanded, it included more workers and peasants than the earlier, smaller Communist Party, which was dominated by intellectuals. Stalin, from a peasant background, was able to communicate with the vast new membership better than highly educated members like Trotsky. Finally, although Stalin himself was Georgian rather than Russian, many Bolsheviks and other Soviet citizens were not certain about Trotsky's nationalist commitment to the Soviet Union because he had spent considerable time abroad and because he was Jewish. Some feared that Trotsky's commitment to world revolution might mean sacrificing the well-being or even the existence of the Soviet Union. In the struggle for control of the Communist Party, Stalin's supporters often portrayed Trotsky as an elitist cosmopolitan intellectual with only a weak loyalty to the Soviet Union (Fitzpatrick 1982). In 1929 Trotsky, after losing several political confrontations with Stalin's supporters, was expelled from the Soviet Union. He continued to write and critically evaluate developments in the Soviet Union until he was assassinated in Mexico City in 1940 by a supporter of Stalin.

THE SOVIET UNION UNDER STALIN

Stalin and the Communist Party confronted the task of industrializing the Soviet Union as rapidly as possible. Because the Soviet Union was on its own, industrialization was going to be a painful experience under socialism as it would have been under capitalism. The only advantages, hypothetically, would be a more equal distribution of the burden under socialism, and a more organized, centrally directed process. Unfortunately for the peasants, the Soviet Union would rely on agricultural productivity to finance industrialization.

During the late 1920s and the early 1930s virtually all agriculture was collectivized. Collectivization, by increasing efficiency, would theoretically make much of the agricultural labor force available for the growing needs of industry. More machinery, better management, and scientific farming methods were also supposed to raise productivity. But according to Von Laue (1971, 198–199), "the transition from private to collective farming was pushed forward with utter recklessness in 1929 and early 1930. For the countryside it meant a far more brutal upheaval than any previous agrarian measure since the imposition of serfdom." Vast rural areas experienced class warfare as poorer peasants and party activists forced affluent peasants (the kulaks), often the hardest working and most productive, to surrender their land, livestock, and costly farm equipment to the collectives. But many rich peasants killed their animals or sold them for slaughter rather than contribute them to the collective farms. Subsequently the number of farm animals declined significantly (Dmytryshyn 1984). In retaliation, the government arrested and deported perhaps a million kulak families to Siberia (Fitzpatrick 1982). Hundreds of thousands of others who resisted collectivization were separated from their families and sent as forced labor to new industrial centers (Von Laue 1971).

The government demanded a large part of peasant production for export in or-der to earn the capital needed to purchase technology and machinery for industri-alization. The loss of farm animals, the large percentage of agricultural production taken to finance industrialization, poor weather conditions, and the disruption caused by collectivization combined to generate a famine in some areas during the early 1930s. Several million people starved to death (Dmytryshyn 1984; Fitzpatrick 1982; Von Laue 1971).

The push for rapid industrialization also meant hardships for industrial workers. Trade union freedoms were restricted so that labor discipline could be maintained and industrial productivity raised as quickly as possible. Living standards im-proved at a slow pace because the state stressed investment in heavy industry rather than consumer goods. The Communist Party inspired a cultural revolution that generated literary works, cultural events, and art supportive of the revolution, col-lectivization of agriculture, and the crash industrialization program (Dmytryshyn 1984; Fitzpatrick 1982). The state's control over education, labor unions, peasant collectives, and the mass media as well as the government's marshalling of the arts and literature in support of its economic and political goals within the context of a one-party political system, has been characterized as a form of totalitarianism (to-tal government domination of all major social institutions) both by international critics of the Soviet regime and by later generations of Soviet and Russian citizens.

Stalin continued to lead the Soviet Union until his death in 1953. His fear of counterrevolutionary or anti-Stalinist plots led him to purge many government and party officials and army officers in the mid- and late 1930s. Thousands of people were executed, and millions were deported to remote regions of the country, often to labor camps, where many died. After Stalin's death, Soviet leaders condemned his excesses and brutally repressive tactics. Yet Stalin's leadership did accomplish rapid industrialization. And the Soviet Union's heavy industry enabled the Soviet people to repel the Nazi German invasion launched in 1941.

THE RUSSIAN REVOLUTION: LONG-TERM CONSEQUENCES

During a revolution, individuals and groups with differing philosophies and plans for the future join forces. Once the old order has been overthrown, disagreements among former allies are likely to resurface. During the Russian revolutions of 1917 some of the most popular slogans were "All power to the soviets," "Soviet democ-racy," "All land to the peasants," and "Power to the working class." When the Com-munist Party emerged victorious among the contending revolutionary groups, its leaders determined what these slogans were to mean in practice. "All power" went to the Communist Party, not the soviets. "Soviet democracy" was relegated mainly to local community concerns. Elections for party officials gave party members a role in political power, but ordinary citizens only voted yes or no for individuals nominated by the party for government positions. "All land to the peasants" meant land to peasant collectives and state farms, rather than to individuals. And "Power to the working class" did not mean the direct exercise of political power by all industrial workers and peasants but only those belonging to the Communist Party.

The Communist Party recruited millions of workers and peasants, provided them with an education and ideological instruction, and gave them access to political and economic power both through Communist Party membership and through managerial and technical occupations and positions in government. The victory of Marxism in Russia brought an extraordinary increase in social and economic mobility for industrial workers and peasants (Fitzpatrick 1982).

In later years, critics noted that the causes of economic and scientific shortcomings in the USSR included a political system that restricted freedom of expression and creativity and an economic system that was overly constrained by bureaucracy and central planning and did not provide enough incentive for productive individuals. By the mid-1980s, Soviet leaders acknowledged such problems and launched a series of reforms (*New York Times*, January 28, 1987, A1; June 26, 1987, A1) that ultimately led to the dissolution of the USSR.

There were additional reasons for the technological differences between the USSR and the United States. Czarist Russia began industrial development later, and the process was disrupted by the attempted revolution in 1905, the devastation of World War I, and the revolutions of 1917 and the accompanying 1918–1922 civil war. The economic achievements of the 1920s and 1930s were devastated by the Nazi German invasion. An estimated 28 million Soviet citizens were killed and hundreds of cities and towns destroyed. Then in response to the atomic bombs dropped on Japan, the Soviet Union diverted resources into developing its own nuclear weapons. All these elements retarded the growth of the Soviet economy.

The lack of political freedom in the USSR had multiple causes. First, the Soviet people had never experienced a stable democratic political system. The country went almost directly from the dictatorship of the czar to the dictatorship of the proletariat. Moreover, the authoritarian government that developed, especially during the Stalinist era (1927–1953), was in part a reaction to the threats and hostilities directed against socialist movements and against the first self-proclaimed socialist state. During the Russian civil war, the White Armies were financed and armed by the great capitalist powers and assisted by troops from these nations. Twenty years later, capitalist Germany under a fascist government invaded the Soviet Union to destroy Bolshevism and exterminate Russian Jews, colonize the Ukraine, and enslave the Slavic peoples, whom the Nazis considered racial inferiors.

Following World War II, the Soviet Union experienced rekindled hostility from capitalist powers, which introduced new devastating weapons: the hydrogen bomb, long-range jet bombers, missile-firing submarines, and so forth. The people of the Soviet Union from 1917 until relatively recent times experienced a series of events and hardships that promoted a siege mentality. That in turn helped justify restrictions on political freedom as well as the domination of Eastern Europe.

THE SOVIET UNION AND REVOLUTION IN EASTERN EUROPE

At the conclusion of World War II, Soviet armies occupied most of Eastern Europe. Their presence strengthened the position of local communist parties, many of whom had played significant roles in resisting the German Nazis and other fascists. Some anticommunists in these countries had disgraced themselves by assisting Nazis in the mass murder of Jews and political leftists during the war.

After the war left-wing coalitions, usually involving communist and socialist parties and sometimes peasant and liberal parties, dominated the governments of Eastern Europe. With the onset of the cold war between the United States and the USSR in 1947, the Soviet Union encouraged local communist parties to seize control and establish regimes similar to the system in the USSR. In the process many skilled persons were denied positions of authority, which were instead filled by less qualified individuals loyal to local pro-Moscow communist leaders. Stalinist-type governments subservient to Moscow were undermined when Stalin died in 1953 and when the new Soviet leader Nikita Khrushchev denounced Stalin's repressive policies in February 1956. Some Stalinist regimes in Eastern Europe were replaced by Communist Party governments that were less repressive and more independent of the USSR.

In 1956 the Soviet Union invaded Hungary after Hungarians attempted to withdraw from Moscow's influence. In 1968 it occupied Czechoslovakia after liberal communist leaders acted to increase political freedom. Soviet leaders rationalized these interventions by comparing them to the combined British, French, and Israeli invasion of Egypt in 1956 and US interventions in Latin America and Vietnam. The Soviet leader at the time of the 1968 occupation of Czechoslovakia, Leonid Brezhnev, proclaimed the right of other socialist countries (in his meaning those whose governments were controlled by the Communist Party) to intervene militarily elsewhere to protect socialism (i.e., Communist Party control of the state). The Brezhnev doctrine inhibited the democratization of Eastern European until it was abandoned in 1989.

In 1985 Mikhail Gorbachev became general secretary of the Communist Party and in 1988 president of the Soviet Union, possibly the most important factor leading to a new permissive orientation toward Eastern Europe. Gorbachev and large sectors of the Soviet population viewed their repressive political system, inefficient bureaucracies, and overly centralized economy as obsolete relics of a more hostile era. Many felt that economic progress would require a market-oriented economy, trade with and technological assistance from advanced capitalist nations, reduced military expenditures, and a democratic political system. President Gorbachev called for perestroika (restructuring) of the USSR's economic and political systems and increased glasnost (public openness). The perceived advantages of more positive relations with the United States and Western Europe, the incentive to decrease military spending, and the growing view that political control over Eastern Europe was no longer necessary for the security of the USSR contributed to the decision to allow the nations of Eastern Europe to select their own forms of government.

Many in Eastern European countries considered Communist Party rule an aspect of Russian domination and a suppression of both nationalist aspirations and democratic ideals. Although Communist Party–led governments accomplished some popular reforms such as land redistribution and improved access to education and medical care, frustrated nationalism, lack of democratic political systems, and, especially after 1980, stagnant economies were significant causes of mass discontent.

In the summer of 1989 Poland became the first Eastern European nation to end Communist Party domination of its government. It had experienced steady economic deterioration and huge increases in foreign debt since 1975. This was viewed as resulting from a combination of poor planning, lack of sufficient market incentives, and the devastating impact of the 1973 Arab oil embargo, which drastically increased the cost of Western technology and machinery. Clearly economic austerity measures would be necessary to rescue Poland. But in return for sacrifices (such as higher food prices and higher risk of unemployment), many Poles demanded the right to participate in governmental decision making. In 1980 workers' protests at Gdansk and Szczecin led to the formation of the Solidarity Labor Union, an organization independent of Communist Party control (Ascherson 1982; Kunicki 2006).

The Solidarity movement, an expression of nationalist, democratic, and economic aspirations, spread rapidly and enlisted more than 9 million people, including one-third of the members of the Polish Communist Party (called the Polish United Workers Party). Although an implied threat of Soviet intervention kept Solidarity suppressed during most of the 1980s, the continued inability of Polish communist leaders to solve the nation's economic crisis led the party to accept Solidarity's demand for revoking Communist Party control of government. Solidarity, in transforming the Polish government, had a powerful impact elsewhere in Eastern Europe and on the USSR itself.

In 1989, in the face of massive support for the Solidarity movement and the Polish Communist Party's agreement to give up control of the government if defeated in free elections, Soviet leaders announced their decision to abandon the Brezhnev doctrine and allow all Eastern European nations to select their own form of government. This constituted the advent of the only remaining necessary condition for the success of political transformations in Eastern Europe—the existence of a permissive world context for revolution. When the Communist Party was defeated in elections held in summer 1989, the Soviet Union allowed the establishment of the first noncommunist (Solidarity) government in Eastern Europe since the late 1940s (*New York Times*, August 25, 1989, A8).

The populations of Hungary, Czechoslovakia, East Germany, Bulgaria, and Romania, encouraged by Poland's achievement and the USSR's permissiveness, rapidly disposed of their own Communist Party–dominated governmental systems (Chirot 1994; *New York Times*, February 18, 1990, E2). A number of Soviet republics also initiated multiparty political systems, and newly elected governments in Lithuania, Estonia, and Latvia, which had been forcibly incorporated into the USSR at the beginning of World War II, resolved to secede from the Soviet Union (*New York Times*, October 26, 1990, A6; January 11, 1991, A1). Then in February 1990, Soviet leaders agreed to surrender the Communist Party's monopoly on power and construct a Western-style form of government in which parties would compete for popular support and a president would be elected directly by the people (*New York Times*, February 8, 1990, A1). The USSR and Eastern European nations moved toward a greater market orientation and private ownership of many businesses and industries (*New York Times*, October 17, 1990, A1).

THE SOLIDARITY MOVEMENT AND THE ROOTS OF CONFLICT IN POST–COMMUNIST PARTY STATES

In August 1980 thousands of striking workers at Poland's Gdansk Shipyard formulated a list of twenty-one demands for the Communist Party–dominated government. An analysis of this document, a major factor in the political revolution in Eastern Europe, illustrates the range of aspirations that motivated the opponents of the old one-party system and provides important insights into reasons for conflict in post–Communist Party states.

Among the twenty-one items was a demand to eliminate the Stalinist-era practice of appointing administrators of economic enterprises on the basis of party loyalty. Instead, workers wanted executives chosen on the basis of proven expertise and technical knowledge. The first six demands called for more political democracy, including the right to form labor unions independent of the government or the Communist Party, legalization of the right to strike, and freedom of information, expression, and communication. (In 1980, when the Soviet Union still supported the one-party system and claimed the right to intervene in Eastern Europe to maintain Communist Party control, Solidarity did not dare demand a totally democratic, multiparty political system.)

Virtually all of the other fourteen Solidarity items, however, were demands for increased economic security, social welfare measures, and government-provided economic benefits, including guarantees of automatic increases in wages parallel to rises in prices, lowering the retirement age, complete medical care, availability of day care facilities for all working families, and guarantees of longer maternity leaves. After the Solidarity Party won the 1989 parliamentary election, major disagreements arose within the movement concerning which goals should have priority and even whether workers aspirations for greater economic security should be abandoned. Solidarity figures who assumed government leadership roles began to implement pro-capitalist economic policies. These involved privatizing much of the economic system, closing down unprofitable enterprises, and limiting funding for social services and health care.

Although some people significantly increased their incomes, many of the workers and their families who had provided mass support for the pro-democracy movement suffered. Divisions developed in Solidarity. A large group of workers, apparently hoping their fate would improve if a fellow worker became head of state, pressed Lech Walesa, the former electrician and leader of Solidarity, to run for the presidency, which he won in 1990. But the pervasive disillusionment surfaced in the 1991 parliamentary election. Only 40 percent of the electorate voted, Solidarity split into five factions, and twenty-nine parties won seats in the parliament, none receiving more than 12 percent of the vote. And in 1993 the successor to Poland's Communist Party and its allied leftist Peasant Party, promising more concern for the welfare of the working class, won control of parliament. In November 1995, Aleksander Kwasniewski, a former member of the old Communist Party and the candidate of Poland's leftist parties, defeated Lech Walesa in the presidential election (*New York Times*, November 12, 1995, 10; November 21, 1995, A1) and was reelected president in 2000. Poland joined the North Atlantic Treaty Organization (NATO) in 1999 and the European Union in 2004. In 2005, an alliance of center-right parties won control of the parliament from the Democratic Left Alliance, which had been unable to reduce the country's 18 percent unemployment rate. Lech Kaczyñski was elected president but killed on April 10, 2010, with his wife and several other Polish leaders, in an airplane crash. He was replaced by acting president Bronislaw Komorowski, who was elected president in July 2010 as the candidate of the center-right Civic Platform party. In 2011, the Civil Platform Party finished first (with about 39 percent of the popular vote) among the five parties that won seats in the lower house of the Polish national legislature, the Sejm, and won sixty-three of the hundred seats in the upper house, the Senate (CIA 2014a).

The Disintegration of the Soviet Union

In February 1990 the USSR abandoned the one-party system and from then on the Communist Party would compete with other political parties in multiparty elections. Democratization led to the first free, multicandidate election for president of the Russian Republic (Russian Federation) of the USSR in June 1991. Boris Yeltsin, a former regional Communist Party leader who had resigned from the party, became the first democratically elected leader in Russia's history. This created a remarkable political incongruity: the president of the USSR's largest component republic could claim a higher level of political legitimacy than could Gorbachev, the president of the entire Soviet Union, who held power by virtue of the old Communist Party–dominated political process. Gorbachev envisioned not only democratizing the USSR but also preserving it in a looser form, which would gratify its constituent republics' demands for more local control of their resources and economies. But the reform movement surged beyond his control, resulting in the destruction of the USSR. The catalyst for this outcome was an attempted coup by Communist Party hard-liners in August 1991.

Gorbachev had held a referendum in Russia and eight other USSR republics (Rutland 2006) on the issue of preserving the USSR, in which 76 percent expressed support for maintaining a reformed Soviet Union. He apparently reached agreements with leaders of a number of USSR republics to ratify a modified, more decentralized constitution. Days before the scheduled signing of the new constitution, while Gorbachev was vacationing in the Crimea, several top Soviet leaders staged a coup, including the head of the KGB (the Soviet Union's national intelligence and security agency), a high-ranking army general, and the Soviet Union's vice president. Apparently fearing that the new constitution would lead to the destruction of the USSR, further economic disorganization, continued growth of crime and other social problems, and loss of their own power, these men placed Gorbachev under house arrest and announced that he had taken ill, requiring their assuming control of the nation.

But Yeltsin and the parliament of the Russian Republic refused to recognize the coup plotters, condemned them as criminals, and called on Russian citizens to defend the government of the Russian Republic at its parliament building, the so-called Russian White House. There, Russian president Yeltsin, many parliamentarians, and tens of thousands of citizens resisted the coup and the tanks, which were mostly manned by confused soldiers who had been ordered to Moscow to seize the White House. The coup plotters, in the face of massive peaceful popular resistance and the refusal of most military commanders to acknowledge their authority, gave up after three days and were arrested.

Gorbachev returned to Moscow only to see his dream of a new, democratic USSR destroyed. The parliaments of all of the Soviet republics, fearing that some future coup could lead to a new totalitarian Soviet government, rapidly announced

MAP 2.2 Russia, Eastern Europe, and Neighboring States (After 1991)

plans to secede from the USSR. On December 31, 1991, the USSR formally went out
of existence, replaced by fifteen independent countries. The collapse of the USSR
caused problems, as it disrupted economic relations among the republics. The surge
of nationalism among the former republics led to ethnically based wars between
and within several of the new nations, including Russia itself, where Chechens attempted to secede (Colarusso 1995; Goldman 1995; Lieven 2006; *New York Times*,
September 25, 1995, A1).

Hostility developed between Yeltsin and the Russian parliament in the face of
mounting ethnic strife, Yeltsin's authoritarian tendencies and alcohol use, rising
crime rates, organized crime, and the seemingly uncontrolled transfer of valuable
state property, including mineral resource companies, to well connected Yeltsin
supporters (crony capitalism), contributing to the creation of wealthy, powerful
oligarchs. Many parliament members blamed Yeltsin for creating these problems
or making them worse. Some expressed concern that Yeltsin's administration was
allowing foreign-based corporations to gain control over Russia's enormous natural resources. Parliament attempted to impeach Yeltsin and replace him with the
Russian vice president, Rutskoi, who sided with the parliament. In October 1993,
supporters of parliament seized several government buildings, including the Moscow mayor's office, and then attacked the main TV broadcasting center, which was
controlled by Yeltsin supporters. A number of people were killed in the battle for
the television building, which Yeltsin supporters successfully defended.

After the initial violence both Yeltsin and parliamentary leaders ordered the military to intervene against the other side. The army decided to obey Yeltsin, who
claimed that his election was more democratic than his opponents'. The military
may have supported Yeltsin because parliament supporters were the first to resort to
violence and because Yeltsin enjoyed the support of the US president, Bill Clinton.
On orders from Yeltsin, army troops and tanks assaulted the Russian White House,
from which Yeltsin and the parliament had resisted the August 1991 attempted coup.
After a day of fighting, with more than one hundred people killed and the building
bombarded by tanks, the remaining parliamentarians surrendered. After crushing
the parliament, Yeltsin held a national referendum on a new Russian constitution,
which put enormous power in the hands of the president. On December 12, 1993, a
majority of those participating voted to accept it. The constitution allows the president to appoint or remove the prime minister, disband the national legislature and
call for new elections, and call a referendum on a particular issue (Constitution of
the Russian Federation 1993). It also permits the president to issue binding executive orders as long as they do not violate the constitution or federal laws.

The newly elected parliament, dominated by anti-Yeltsin Russian nationalists
and leftists, forced Yeltsin to take action against governmental corruption. Over his
protests, the new parliament pardoned all who participated in the rebellion against

Yeltsin and also those who had participated in the attempted 1991 coup. By 1996 several parliamentarians had been assassinated, as was the head of the nation's major television network, with suspicion falling on organized crime. Many businesspeople and bankers, thought either to have been resisting extortion or corruption or to have had disputes with organized criminals, were also murdered (Handelman 1994; *New York Times*, December 11, 1994, E1; February 19, 1995, 1; March 2, 1995, A10; March 3, 1995, A8; March 10, 1995, A10; April 11, 1995, A3; May 23, 1995, A1; June 7, 1995, A10). Amid all this, the health and life expectancy of many Russians underwent a rapid and drastic decline (CBS 1996).

With the assistance of wealthy oligarchs and the media outlets they controlled, Yeltsin won reelection in 1996, defeating Communist Party candidate Gennady Zyuganov. Yeltsin was succeeded as president by the then prime minister, Vladimir Putin, a onetime member of the KGB.

Putin served two four-year presidential terms, during which his United Russia Party became the dominant political party, bolstered by his high public approval ratings (70 percent, Stoner-Weiss 2008, 316). The Communist Party fell to a very distant second-place position in national elections. Putin's ability to implement his policies benefited from the strong presidential powers provided by Yeltsin's 1993 constitution (Finan 2008). He expanded the power of the federal government in the economy and its influence over the mass media. Since the constitution prevented Putin from running for a third consecutive presidential term, in March 2008 Dimitri Medvedev, Putin's hand-picked successor, was elected president and took office in May. Medvedev immediately appointed Putin prime minister.

Four years later Putin was again eligible to run for president with the presidential term extended to six years. Putin, backed by the United Russia Party, won the March 4, 2012, election with almost 64 percent of the popular vote. Gennady Zyuganov, candidate of the Communist Party, finished second with about 17 percent (CIA 2014b). The United Russia Party won almost 50 percent of the popular vote and 53 percent of the seats for Russia's national legislature, the Duma, with the second-place communists getting 19 percent of the popular vote and 20 percent of the seats. Medvedev replaced Putin as prime minister (Treisman 2013).

Economic and Political Trends

Yeltsin aimed to transform Russia's economy as quickly as possible from state owned and centrally planned to privately owned and shaped by market forces. Supporters of the shock therapy changeover thought that privately owned competing businesses would increase efficiency and productivity and lead to rapid economic development (Goldman 2003, 320; Thompson 2004, 304). The privatization process, however, was very flawed.

According to Goldman (2003), there were three main types of owners of the new private businesses. One group was former factory directors or members of their staffs who together received about 50 percent of the stock in the newly privatized companies. Many of these, after accumulating stock inexpensively from poorly informed workers, became affluent participants in the new Russian economy. But a number of persons in the second and third categories became enormously wealthy. One group was composed of former government and Communist Party officials who were powerful and/or politically well connected, especially to President Yeltsin. Some of these obtained hugely valuable, previously state-owned energy resources for far below their real value and became billionaires in a short time. For example, Yukos Oil, estimated to be worth about $20 billion or more in 2003, was obtained for about $300 million; Sibneft Oil, worth about $10 billion in 2003, was obtained for about $100 million. The third major group of new business owners came from those who participated in illegal, highly profitable private business activity under the old soviet system. With the sudden change in laws regulating economic activity, many of these persons found that their previous illegal business activity was now legal. And their years of experience in locating and bringing together resources, products, and customers gave them a huge advantage over others in the new legal market economy. Some of these individuals reportedly became extremely wealthy by intimidating or physically eliminating rivals.

Although privatization helped create a small group of affluent persons, the Russian economy deteriorated dramatically, and millions became impoverished. According to President Vladimir Putin (Millar 2000, 330), during the 1990s Russian gross domestic product (GDP) plunged 45 percent, resulting in GDP per capita that was about one-tenth of that in the United States. In comparison, the decline in per capita GDP in the United States during the Great Depression, 1929–1933, was a little less than 25 percent (Millar 1999, 323). Much of the new business activity was monopolistic. The new monopolies were controlled by private individuals dedicated to maximizing their profits, not by the state as in the Soviet era. Prices rose dramatically in the early 1990s, and by 1999 an estimated 40 percent of Russians were living in poverty (World Bank 2004). The economy was further impaired by the expensive war in Chechnya. The privatization of major resources was considered legalized theft on a scale unheard of in human history by many millions of Russians. Some businessmen shipped billions of dollars to secure investments in other countries instead of investing in developing their own nation's economic infrastructure. They used their wealth to influence government officials and fund their favored politicians.

When Vladimir Putin succeeded Yeltsin as president in 1999, besides launching a new invasion of Chechnya to suppress terrorist attacks thought to be originating there, he reined in the oligarchs, renationalized some of the most valuable energy resources, and attempted to restore public faith in the economic system. Because so many of those benefiting from the post-Soviet economic reforms evaded paying the 35 percent tax rate, Putin instituted a universal 13 percent tax rate that seemed more effective (Goldman 2003). Russia benefited enormously from surging oil prices after 1999. Growth in energy export revenue appeared to account for half of Russia's 6–7 percent annual GDP growth during the early 2000s. By 2011 the poverty rate was less than 13 percent (CIA 2014b). Income inequality, which had risen during the 1990s, declined between 2000 and 2009 (Treisman 2012).

Putin's government used revenue from the export of energy resources to increase pensions by nearly 60 percent (adjusted for inflation) (Triesman 2013). Russia is the biggest oil producer in the world, and oil and gas account for two-thirds of its exports (Kelly and Nikolaeva 2013). However, heavy dependence on oil and gas makes the economy vulnerable to falling prices when the international supply increases or demand declines. In 2013 the economy grew by only 1.4 percent (Kelly and Nikolaeva 2013).

Economic growth, Putin's actions against oligarchs, and his war on terrorism helped maintain his personal popularity (Goldman 2003, 324; Goldman 2007, 320). As noted earlier, a pro-Putin political party, United Russia, was created, and Putin's supporters began to dominate parliament. Putin also reduced the power of regional Russian authorities—in part, according to Putin, to prevent local interference with central government efforts to diversify the economy from heavy reliance on energy exports, improve the country's industrial and communications infrastructure, reduce corruption, increase agricultural production, and create a fairer legal system. While some nations charged that Putin reversed his predecessor's market and democratic reforms, many Russians, viewing Yeltsin's policies as badly flawed, supported Putin's actions (Goldman 2007, 315–316). There was wide public approval when Putin renationalized companies, and the state-controlled production of crude oil climbed from under 20 percent of total production in 2000 to approximately 50 percent in 2007 (Goldman 2007, 316). The Putin administration also renationalized major television networks, arguing that they had been privatized too cheaply in the 1990s and also that their owners were using them to pursue personal or corporate business goals rather than provide fair news coverage.

By 2010, however, some believed that Putin and Medvedev were limiting democracy. In 2005 Putin eliminated directly elected governors in many regions, instead making the governorships presidential appointments subject to confirmation by local legislatures (which many critics regarded as a rubber stamp formality). Putin argued that this measure would prevent wealthy people from corrupting elections with their money, help reduce the number of corrupt or incompetent officials, and enhance the chain of command from the president to regional authorities to more effectively deal with emergencies such as terrorist attacks. While a majority of Russians seemed to favor this change at the time, a survey in 2010 indicated that more than half of the respondents now supported elections for governors (Whitmore 2010).

Beginning with the 2007 legislative election all Duma seats were awarded to political parties in proportion to the vote each party obtained, as long as it received at least 7 percent of the popular vote. In December 2008 President Medvedev approved changing the presidential term from four to six years (CNN, December 22, 2008), taking effect in the 2012 presidential election.

According to Thompson (2004) the Russian revolution of 1991 was a quadruple change: a shift from a state-controlled and state-owned economy to one that was in great part privately owned and governed by market forces; the replacement of a one-party state with a multiparty democracy; the shift from Marxist-Leninist ideology to a political culture stressing democratic freedoms and emphasizing individual rights over collective responsibilities; and replacement of a conflict-oriented stance toward many other nations with a more cooperative international approach. But, as noted, Putin renationalized much of the economy with the approval of most Russians. And his United Russia Party became so dominant that one-party rule seemed to have been reestablished. Russia reduced its cooperation with the United States when the George W. Bush administration used the war on terrorism to justify invading Iraq, an action opposed by Russia and carried out without the support of the United Nations, and maintained a hostile orientation toward Iran and nations with leftist governments in Latin America.

In 2011, when Britain and France, with US support, put forward Resolution 1973 requesting UN permission to intervene in the Libyan civil war to protect the well-being of civilians, Russia, like China, abstained rather than using its veto. Russia, however, viewed the actual military intervention as going way beyond what the resolution authorized. This was one reason the Russian government offered for its unwillingness to allow the UN Security Council to authorize sanctions against Assad's government in the Syrian civil war (Katz 2013). Russia instead assisted the Syrian government in opposition to US, British, and Saudi Arabian policy on Syria.

CORRUPTION

As Goldman (2005) observed, bribery was common during the czarist era, and forms of graft characterized Communist Party rule. But post-Soviet Russia became one of the world's most corrupt nations, allowing politically well connected persons to acquire billions of dollars of state property at little cost to themselves. According to Sun (2005, 259), Yeltsin depended on the oligarchs for help in his 1996 reelection, "rendering the government vulnerable to the group's demand for economic and political concessions." The willingness of public officials to accept bribes was related to the rampant inflation during 1992, which wiped out many people's savings. Government pay did not keep pace with price increases, and many officials, including traffic cops, began to demand bribes to supplement inadequate government salaries. Judges were accused of selling court decisions and university officials of accepting bribes to admit certain students. Some claimed that Putin's strengthening of central government power weakened regional governments' local anticorruption capabilities. And by intimidating the press, he may have reduced its ability to function as an independent watch dog against corruption. Yet Sun noted that in China many people supported strengthening central government power as a necessary anticorruption measure. But Russia was widely viewed as having a very corrupt business environment (Stott 2010). President Putin in April 2013 issued a decree requiring that state officials sell or otherwise liquidate any assets they had in foreign countries within three months or face being removed from their positions (Treisman 2013). This included closing foreign bank accounts and selling foreign stock.

HEALTH AND RELATED ISSUES

By 2002 the Russian death rate exceeded the birth rate by 70 percent (Powell 2002, 344). The birth rate decline occurred during a time when many people felt they lacked the resources to raise children in Russia's new economic environment.

Increasing inequality, drug use, deteriorating health care and welfare systems, and rising criminal activity contributed to a rapid reduction in life span, particularly for men. Researchers believed that a dramatic rise in alcoholism, perhaps caused by economic hardship, dismal expectations for the future, and/or moral or ideological disillusionment, led to a surge in disorders linked to alcohol use. Homicides, 80 percent of which were associated with alcohol use, rose (Chervyakov, Shkolnikov, Pridemore, and McKee 2002). By 1999, the homicide rate (age standardized) was 81 percent higher than it was in 1990, about double the rate of increase for other causes of death. Between 1993 and 1998 six members of parliament were murdered, nineteen journalists, ninety-five bankers, and hundreds of businessmen. These crimes were thought related to the fact that half of private businesses were controlled by criminals or were the victims of extortion. In the first decade of the twenty-first century the risk of becoming a homicide victim in Russia was about three times that in the United States. Russia experienced numerous terrorist attacks against trains, airplanes, government buildings, as well as a theater, a hospital, and a school (*Guardian*, March 29, 2010). Although the Russian government declared the end of the second Chechen war (or counterterrorist operation) in April 2009, officials also disclosed that "terrorist crime in the North Caucasus region, which includes Kabardino-Balkaria, Ingushetia, Chechnya and Dagestan, had increased 60 percent in 2009 over the 2008 level" (King and Menon 2010).

A dramatic surge in injection drug use contributed to the spread of the HIV virus and AIDS deaths. In 2006, the average life span among women was 74.1 years, while for men it was only 60.5 years (it had been 64.9 years in 1987). In the decades before the USSR collapse, the male-female differential had been about ten years (Powell 2002, 345), but in 2006, the gap had widened to over thirteen years. Belarus, Ukraine, and Kazakhstan—former soviet republics—also had gender mortality gaps of about eleven years. In contrast, the United States, United Kingdom, and Australia had gender differentials in mortality of five to six years. Two of the remaining Communist Party–dominated states had even smaller differences. For Cuba, with an average life expectancy nearly identical to that of the United States, the men's life span in 2006 averaged only 4.74 years less than women, and in China, with an average life span about five years less than the United States, the difference between women's and men's longevity was only 3.57 years. In 2013 the Russian gender difference was still about twelve years (CIA 2014b).

The rapid decline in the male life span in Russia, virtually unprecedented in history, and the other enormous social problems afflicting large sections of the population under the new economic and political systems had international impacts. To many in lesser developed countries, the negative developments in Russia confirmed their hostility toward neoliberal economic policies. And the Russian experience undoubtedly caused many people in China and Cuba to be cautious about changing their political system. In May 2006, Putin called on parliament to address the drastic population decline in Russia—a loss of almost 700,000 annually—by offering subsidies and financial incentives to Russian women who have more children (Chivers 2006). The steady loss of population and the widespread health problems constituted strategic challenges for Russia regarding its ability to maintain an adequate population for its vast territory, as well as a skilled labor force and military (Feshbach 2008, 336–341). By 2013 the annual population loss had dropped to about 29,000 (CIA 2014b).

THE UKRAINIAN REVOLUTIONS
The Orange Revolution

The Orange Revolution occurred during the 2004 presidential election in the Ukraine, the second most populous, after Russia, of the former Soviet republics. Leonid Kuchma, who had been president since 1994 (serving the maximum two consecutive five-year presidential terms), was accused by opponents of corruption, condoning the intimidation or elimination of critical journalists and opposition leaders, and allowing Russia to exercise too much influence, including on certain Ukrainian industries (Kramer 2008). Kuchma favored the country's prime minister, Viktor Yanukovych, to succeed him as president. Yanukovych, also widely seen as pro-Russian, appeared to enjoy disproportionate support among Russian-speaking residents of the Ukraine, who tended to live mainly in the eastern and southern parts of the country, and was the preferred candidate of the Russian government, which feared that his opponent would seek NATO membership for the Ukraine.

The main opposition candidate was Viktor Yushchenko, a former prime minister who had orchestrated market-oriented reforms and was seen as favored by the United States and some Western European nations. Support for Yushchenko was strongest in the western part of the country. After an initial round of voting in October 2004 failed to give any candidate more than 50 percent of the vote, a runoff election was held on November 21 between the top two vote getters, Yushchenko and Yanukovych. Official results gave the victory to Yanukovych, despite opinion polls suggesting Yushchenko won and reports indicating election fraud in favor of Yanukovych. Subsequently hundreds of thousands of Yushchenko supporters began a series of mass protests. Many protestors carried orange banners, the color of Yushchenko's campaign, giving rise to the expression Orange Revolution. Ultimately the Ukrainian Supreme Court ruled the election had been fraudulent and called for a new election in December. This time Yushchenko was declared the winner and became president in January 2005. In the United States the success of the Orange Revolution was viewed as a great victory for democracy.

Yushchenko soon ran into problems, however. Although he appointed another leader of the Orange Revolution, Yulia Tymoshenko, as prime minister, significant conflicts developed between them that shattered the unity of the Orange coalition. Disagreements with Russia brought interruptions to the flow of natural gas, and the country, which had borrowed heavily from other nations, suffered serious problems, including a 50 percent devaluation of its currency as a result of the international economic recession of 2008 (Marson 2010). And the Ukraine continued to be viewed internationally as characterized by a very high level of corruption. When the first round of voting for the 2010 presidential election was held in January, Yushchenko received only 5 percent. In the runoff in February, Viktor Yanukovych defeated Yulia Tymoshenko, in effect reversing the political outcome of the Orange Revolution.

The Ukrainian Revolution of 2014

Actions taken by the Ukrainian government provoked opposition from right-wing Ukrainian nationalists and the European Union. In April 2010, the Ukrainian parliament agreed to extend Russia's lease on the Black Sea Fleet base at Sevastopol, Crimea, for twenty-five years, in exchange for reductions in the price of Russian natural gas. In June, the parliament voted to not apply for NATO membership.

In October 2011, a court imprisoned former prime minister Yulia Tymoshenko after finding her guilty of abuse of power in 2009. The European Union strongly objected to this action. In July 2012, police dispersed hundreds of people protesting a new law that gave the Russian language official status in the thirteen of the Ukraine's twenty-seven administrative divisions that had at least a 10 percent Russian-speaking population. Despite the protest, President Yanukovych's Party of Regions won the October parliamentary elections, while the far-right Freedom Party gained increased electoral support. The key event that set off the wave of protests in Kiev that ultimately overthrew President Yanukovych was his November 2013 decision to abandon plans to sign an association agreement with the European Union (BBC 2014b). Protestors took to the streets accusing the Yanukovych government of siding with Russia and of being corrupt. As the economy continued to deteriorate, in December Russia agreed to reduce the price of the natural gas it sold to the Ukraine and lend the country $15 billion to help it avoid bankruptcy. But protests continued and intensified. Although protesters came from diverse political groups, the government claimed that right-wing anti-Russian Ukrainian nationalists played a prominent role and were among those who engaged in violent attacks on the police. There was some indication that the United States was siding with those seeking to overthrow Yanukovych (Cohen 2014).

When the police attempted to push protestors out of central Kiev during the third week in February, violence escalated. Yanukovych agreed to move elections up to December as part of a compromise with opposition leaders. But many protesters, particularly far right Ukrainian nationalists, refused to accept the agreement. In the violent clashes, eighty-eight people were killed according to the Ukrainian health ministry, mostly antigovernment protestors, but also some police officers. As conditions deteriorated, President Yanukovych, several of his aides, and many police officers and security personnel left the capital on February 21.The parliament then voted to remove Yanukovych from office and the interim interior minister issued an arrest order for him for murder (Stout 2014). The parliament also freed Yulia Tymoshenko from detention and declared that Ukrainian was the only official language in the country (BBC 2014a). The parliament also abolished changes to the Ukrainian political system that had occurred after 2004 that were viewed as giving more power to the president. Yanukovych reportedly traveled south to the Crimea region of the Ukraine, which has a large Russian population, and then to Russia. Crimea had been a part of Russia before it was joined to the Ukraine in 1954. Government security forces that had attempted to protect the Yanukovych government in Kiev also arrived in Crimea and were greeted as heroes for trying to, as a Crimean official stated, prevent a "fascist rebellion prepared by Western instructors" (Schuster 2014). Those in eastern and southern Ukraine who opposed the overthrow of the Yanukovych government called for militias to, as one volunteer put it, reject "the rule of that fascist scum running around in Kiev." Many people in Crimea and the eastern Ukraine were convinced that the revolt in Kiev was carried out by Ukrainian fascists financed by the United States, as suggested by certain Russian media.

On March 16, 2014, a large majority of Crimeans voted to secede from the Ukraine and join the Russian Federation (Collett-White and Popenski 2014). Then on March 20, the lower house of the Russian parliament voted overwhelmingly to accept Crimea into the Russian Federation (Gumuchian, Butenko, and Smith-Spark 2014). In retaliation, the US and its allies expelled Russia from the G-8 group of nations (Smale and Shear 2014). Can the rest of the Ukraine stay united? Would the Russians provide military assistance to other parts of the Ukraine if they move to secede as they did to the South Ossetia and Abkhazia regions that separated from Georgia in 2008? The future of the Ukraine remains unclear.

Summary and Analysis

For several decades before the revolutions of 1917, thousands of young, educated Russians had joined revolutionary movements or engaged in terrorist violence to topple the czar's government. Elite radicalism eventually led to the formation of the Russian Social Democratic Party and its Bolshevik faction under Lenin's leadership. The Bolsheviks condemned Russia's participation in World War I but perceived a great opportunity for revolution in Russia's likely defeat.

Inadequate land reforms fostered peasant frustration. Industrial development led to the growth of a large urban working class dissatisfied with its working and living conditions. Nationalism inflamed by the onset of World War I temporarily suppressed interclass hostilities, but catastrophic military losses and economic hardship resulted in widespread, intense discontent among both peasants and workers.

In the latter half of the nineteenth century, the monarchy was steadily undermined by government efforts to spur industrialization and modernization. Many young Russians schooled in the technology of more advanced societies learned of the relatively democratic political systems in Western Europe. As increasing numbers of educated Russians rejected autocracy in favor of a freer and more participatory government, the pre-revolutionary state was progressively weakened. Russia's military defeat in World War I and the accompanying social unrest finally forced the czar's abdication. Soldiers ordered to put down the protests of their fellow workers refused or openly joined the demonstrators. Faced with massive popular opposition and mutinies in the army and navy, and deserted by middle- and upper-class elites, the czarist state collapsed, providing a historic opportunity for revolutionaries to establish new political, social, and economic institutions.

A number of groups cooperated to overthrow the monarchy. Although the contending revolutionary movements and most members of the major social classes were temporarily united in the effort to oust the czar, they were divided over other issues. Various political movements favored divergent programs, ranging from instituting moderate social reforms to abolishing private ownership of major industries. The Bolsheviks demanded the changes most people yearned for, including a quick end to the war, an immediate redistribution of land to the peasants, and workers' control of industry. When the provisional government continued the war and delayed land redistribution, popular support swung to the Bolsheviks in the large urban areas, permitting them to seize control of the national government in fall 1917.

The czar's capitalist allies were unable to repress the revolutionaries as long as they were fighting World War I. In 1918 several nations sent troops and military supplies into the Soviet Union to aid White Armies attempting to reverse the Bolshevik Revolution. The White Armies, however, lacked unity, engaged in brutality toward civilians, and alienated popular opinion by offering peasants dissatisfied with Bolshevik policies the even less appealing alternative of a return to czarist landownership patterns. The fact that the capitalist nations were either unwilling or unable to launch major invasions of the Soviet Union in support of White forces facilitated the Bolshevik defeat of counterrevolutionaries. After the Russian civil war ended, Stalin and his supporters established an authoritarian governmental structure, which characterized the USSR until the democratizing reforms of the late 1980s.

At the end of 1991 the USSR disintegrated into fifteen independent nations. Russia's president, Boris Yeltsin, launched economic reforms that privatized much of the economy but in the process allowed politically connected cronies to acquire vast wealth from what was once state property. The economy spiraled downward and by 1999, 40 percent of Russians were living in poverty. Rates of drug use, crime, and corruption rose, while health care deteriorated and life span declined. Russia's population fell by more than 500,000 people each year, as death rates far exceeded birth rates. President Vladimir Putin, who took office in 1999, attempted to reduce corruption and the power of the economic oligarchs. With majority public support, Putin renationalized a number of major energy companies. He was accused of shifting government back toward authoritarianism, but some observers thought his actions were necessitated by the nature and scope of the problems his nation faced.

Dimitri Medvedev, a close associate of Putin, was elected president in 2008 and Putin became prime minister. In 2012, Putin was again elected president by a wide margin and Medvedev took over as prime minister.

The percentage of Russians living in poverty steadily declined as the economy continued to grow and the government significantly increased the size of pensions.

By 2013 the annual population loss had declined to a small fraction of what it had been in 2006. In 2014, the overthrow of the pro-Russian government in the Ukraine was followed by Crimeans voting to secede and join Russia.

RUSSIAN REVOLUTIONS: CHRONOLOGY OF MAJOR EVENTS

1898	The Russian Social Democratic Party is formed
1903	The Russian Social Democratic Party splits into the Bolshevik and Menshevik factions
1904–1905	Russia is defeated by Japan; attempted revolution
1914	Russia enters World War I
1917	March (February by Julian calendar) Revolution establishes the provisional government
	November (October by Julian calendar) Revolution: Bolsheviks seize power
1918–1922	Civil war and foreign intervention
1924	Lenin dies
1927–1929	Trotsky expelled from the Communist Party and then exiled from the Soviet Union; Stalin becomes the dominant Soviet leader
1929–1940	Forced collectivization of agriculture and rapid industrialization; development of Stalin's repressive regime
1941–1945	Nazi German invasion devastates USSR but Soviets win ultimate victory
1953	Stalin dies
1991	First democratically elected president of Russia; USSR divides into separate nations
1991–1999	Much of the Russian economy is privatized; some Russians prosper while many sink into poverty; mortality rates climb while birth rates decline, resulting in huge annual population losses
1993	In October, President Yeltsin orders the military to attack and arrest members of the Russian parliament for opposing him and certain of his policies
1994	War against rebellious Chechnya begins
1996	With help from the oligarchs, Yeltsin is reelected president
1999–2000	At the end of 1999, Yeltsin resigns, making Prime Minister Vladimir Putin acting president; Putin elected president in 2000
2004	Putin elected to a second term as president of Russia
2008	May—Dimitri Medvedev becomes president, and Putin becomes prime minister

            August—Russia occupies the separatist-oriented sections of Georgia, South Ossetia, and Abkhazia, and soon recognizes them as independent nations

2009 April—Russia announces the end of its counterterrorism operation in Chechnya

            September—President Medvedev applauds US decision to cancel construction of missile defense systems in Poland and the Czech Republic

2010 April—Presidents Medvedev and Obama sign an agreement to reduce Russian- and US-deployed nuclear warheads by 30 percent

2011 The percentage of Russians living in poverty falls below 13

2012 Putin again elected president of Russia

2013 President Putin requires state officials to liquidate foreign assets they may have, including stocks and bank accounts

2014 February—Russia hosts Winter Olympics in Sochi

            February—Mass protests in Kiev oust pro-Russian Ukrainian president

            March—Crimea secedes from the Ukraine and joins the Russian Federation

References and Further Readings

Ascherson, Neal. 1982. *The Polish August: The Self-Limiting Revolution*. New York: Viking.

BBC. 2014a. "Ukraine: Speaker Oleksandr Turchynov Named Interim President." February 23. www.bbc.co.uk/news/world-europe-26312008.

———. 2014b. "Ukraine Profile." February 25. www.bbc.co.uk/news/world-europe-18010123.

Beissinger, Mark. 2002. *Nationalist Mobilization and the Collapse of the Soviet State*. New York: Cambridge University Press.

Bottomore, Tom, ed. 1983. *A Dictionary of Marxist Thought*. Cambridge: Harvard.

CBS. 1996. "Facts of Life in Russia." *60 Minutes*, May 19.

Central Intelligence Agency (CIA). 2014a. "Poland." In *World Factbook*. www.cia.gov/library/publications/the-world-factbook/geos/pl.html.

———. 2014b. "Russia." In *World Factbook*. www.cia.gov/library/publications/the-world-factbook/geos/rs.html.

Chervyakov, V. V., V. M. Shkolnikov, W. A. Pridemore, and M. McKee. 2002. "The Changing Nature of Murder in Russia." *Social Science and Medicine* 55 (November): 1713–1724.

Chirot, David. 1994. "The Eastern European Revolutions of 1989." In Goldstone, ed., *Revolutions*.

Chivers, C. J. 2006. "Putin Urges Plan to Reverse Slide in the Birth Rate." *New York Times*, May 11.

Cohen, Stephen F. 2014. "Media Malpractice: Putin, Sochi and Ukraine." *The Nation*, March 3.

Collett-White and Ronald Popeski. 2014. "Crimeans Vote over 90 Percent to Quit Ukraine for Russia." Reuters, March 16. www.reuters.com/article/2014/03/16/us-ukraine-crisis-idUSBREA1Q1E820140316.

CNN. December 22, 2008. "Russian Presidential Term Extended to Six Years." edition.cnn.com/2008/WORLD/europe/12/30/russia.presidential.term.extension/index.html.

Colarusso, John. 1995. "Chechnya: The War Without Winners." *Current History* 94 (October): 329–336.

The Constitution of the Russian Federation. 1993. www.departments.bucknell.edu/russian/const/constit.html.

Daniels, Robert V. 1988. *Is Russia Reformable? Change and Resistance from Stalin to Gorbachev*. Boulder: Westview.

DeFronzo, James, ed. 2006. *Revolutionary Movements in World History: From 1750 to the Present*. 3 vols. Santa Barbara, CA: ABC-CLIO.

Dmytryshyn, Basil. 1984. *The USSR: A Concise History*. New York: Scribner.

Finan, William W., Jr. 2008. "Yeltsin's Uncertain Legacy." *Current History* 107 (October): 348–349.

Fitzpatrick, Sheila. 1982. *The Russian Revolution: 1917–1932*. New York: Oxford University Press.

Ganev, Venelin G. 2006. "Eastern European Revolutions of 1989." In DeFronzo, ed., *Revolutionary Movements in World History*, 1:217–235.

Getty, J. Arch, and Oleg Naumov. 1999. *The Road to Terror: Stalin and the Self-Destruction of the Bolsheviks, 1932–1939*. New Haven, CT: Yale University Press.

Goldman, Marshall I. 1995. "Is This Any Way to Create a Market Economy?" *Current History* 94 (October): 305–310.

———. 2003. "Render Unto Caesar: Putin and the Oligarchs." *Current History* 102 (October): 320–326.

———. 2005. "Political Graft: The Russian Way." *Current History* 104 (October): 313–318.

———. 2007. "Russia and the West: Mutually Assured Distrust." *Current History* 106 (October): 314–320.

Goldstone, Jack A., ed. 1998. *Encyclopedia of Political Revolutions*. Washington, DC: Congressional Quarterly Press.

Greene, Thomas H. 1990. *Comparative Revolutionary Movements: Search for Theory and Justice*. Prentice-Hall Contemporary Comparative Politics. 3rd ed. Englewood Cliffs, NJ: Prentice-Hall.

Guardian. March 29, 2010. "Russian Terror Attacks Timeline." www.guardian.co.uk/world/2010/mar/29/russian-terror-attacks-timeline.

Gumuchian, Marie-Louise, Victoria Butenko, and Laura Smith-Spark. 2014. "Russian Lawmakers Vote to Annex Crimea; U.S. Steps Up Sanctions." CNN, March 21. www .cnn.com/2014/03/20/world/europe/ukraine-crisis.

Handelman, Stephen. 1994. "The Russian Mafiya." *Foreign Affairs,* March/April, 83–96.

Katov, George. 1967. *Russia 1917: The February Revolution.* New York: Harper & Row.

Katz, Mark N. 2013. "Is Assad's Syria a 'Win' for Moscow?" *Current History,* October, 283–284.

Kelly, Lidia, and Maya Nikolaeva. 2013. "Russia's Stagnation Raises Pressure for New Growth Model." Reuters, December 3. http://www.reuters.com/article/2013/12/03/russia -economy-forecast-idUSL5N0JI1QG20131203.

King, Charles, and Rajan Menon. 2010. "Prisoners of the Caucus: Russia's Invisible Civil War." *Foreign Affairs* 89 (4): 20–34.

Kramer, Andrew E. 2013. "Behind Scenes, Ukraine's Rich and Powerful Battle over the Future." *New York Times,* December 6. www.nytimes.com/2013/12/07/world/europe /oligarchs-ukraine.html?pagewanted=all&_r=0.

Kramer, Mark. 2008. "Ukraine's Orange Evolution." *Current History* 107 (March): 112–118.

Kunicki, Mikolaj Stanislaw. 2006. "The Polish Solidarity Movement." In DeFronzo, ed., *Revolutionary Movements in World History,* 2:698–711.

Lenin, V. I. [1902] 1975. "What Is to Be Done?" In Tucker, ed., *Lenin Anthology.*

———. [1917] 1975. "The State and Revolution." In Tucker, ed., *Lenin Anthology.*

Lieven, Anatol. 2006. "Chechen Revolt Against Russia." In DeFronzo, ed., *Revolutionary Movements in World History,* 1:99–107.

Marson, James. 2010. "In Ukraine, the Death of the Orange Revolution." *Time,* February 3. www.time.com/time/world/article/0,8599,1954112,00.html.

Marx, Karl. [1875] 1994. "Critique of the Gotha Program." In Lawrence H. Simon, ed., *Karl Marx: Selected Writings,* 315–332. Indianapolis: Hackett.

Marx, Karl, and Friedrich Engels. [1848] 1998. *The Communist Manifesto.* New York: Signet Classics.

Millar, James R. 1999. "The De-development of Russia." *Current History* 98 (October): 322–327.

———. 2000. "Can Putin Jump-Start Russia's Stalled Economy?" *Current History* 99 (October): 329–333.

New York Times. January 28, 1987. "Gorbachev, Citing Party's Failures, Demands Changes, Asks Secret Votes, a Choice of Candidates," A1.

———. May 10, 1987. "Kremlin Reinterprets and Re-emphasizes the Legacy of Lenin," E3.

———. June 26, 1987. "Gorbachev Urges 'Radical' Changes to Spur Economy," A1.

———. August 25, 1989. "Soviet Congratulations Sent to New Premier of Poland," A8.

———. February 8, 1990. "Soviet Leaders Agree to Surrender Communist Party Monopoly on Power," A1.

———. February 18, 1990. "Up-to-the-Minute Scores from the Revolution in the East Bloc," E2.

———. October 17, 1990. "Gorbachev Offers His Plan to Remake Soviet Economy but Includes No Timetable," A1.

———. October 26, 1990. "In Soviet Union, Dizzying Disunion," A6.

———. January 11, 1991. "Gorbachev Warns the Lithuanians to Halt Defiance," A1.

———. December 11, 1994. "The Long Shadow of the Russian Mob," E1.

———. February 19, 1995. "Russia's Declining Health: Rising Illness, Shorter Lives," 1.

———. March 2, 1995. "Russian Journalist Is Slain; Profits May Be the Motive," A10.

———. March 3, 1995. "Celebrity's Killing Stirs Talk of Intrigue in Russia," A8.

———. March 10, 1995. "Yeltsin Vows Crackdown on Gangsters," A10.

———. April 11, 1995. "Latest Films for $2: Video Piracy Boom in Russia," A3.

———. May 23, 1995. "Russia's New Rulers Govern, and Live, in Neo-Soviet Style," A1.

———. June 7, 1995. "Images of Lawlessness Twist Russian Reality," A10.

———. September 25, 1995. "After Long Slide, Russia's Economy Nearing Stability," A1.

———. November 12, 1995. "Young Poles View Walesa as Passé: Generation X Votes for Ex-Communist," 10.

———. November 21, 1995. "Walesa's Nemesis: Aleksander Kwasniewski," A1.

Palij, Michael. 1976. *The Anarchism of Hector Makhno, 1918–1921*. Seattle: University of Washington Press.

Powell, David E. 2002. "Death as a Way of Life: Russia's Demographic Decline." *Current History* 101 (October): 344–348.

Rabinowitch, Alexander. 1976. *The Bolsheviks Come to Power: The Revolution of 1917 in Petrograd*. New York: Norton.

Rutland, Peter. 2006. "The Russian Revolution of 1991 and the Dissolution of the U.S.S.R." In DeFronzo, ed., *Revolutionary Movements in World History*, 3:739–752.

Salisbury, Harrison E. 1981. *Black Night, White Snow: Russia's Revolutions, 1905–1917*. New York: Da Capo.

Schuster, Simon. 2014. "The Russian Stronghold in Ukraine Preparing to Fight the Revolution." *World Time*, February 23. http://world.time.com/2014/02/23/the-russian-stronghold-in-ukraine-preparing-to-fight-the-revolution/print.

Smale, Alison, and Michael D. Shear. 2014. "Russia Is Ousted from Group of 8 by U.S. and Allies." *New York Times*, March 24. www.nytimes.com/2014/03/25/world/europe/obama-russia-crimea.html?emc=edit_th_20140325&nl=todaysheadlines&nlid=38763373&_r=0.

Stoner-Weiss, Kathryn. 2008. "It Is Still Putin's Russia." *Current History* 107 (October): 315–321.

Stott, Michael. 2010. "Russia Corruption May Force Western Firms to Quit." *International Business Times*, July 6. www.ibtimes.com/articles/20100316/russia-corruption-may-force-western-firms-quit.htm.

Stout, David. 2014. "Arrest Warrant Issued for Deposed Ukrainian President Yanukovych." *Time*, February 24. http://time.com/9237/ukraine-viktor-yanukovych-arrest-warrant.

Sun, Yan. 2005. "Corruption, Growth, and Reform: The Chinese Enigma." *Current History*, September, 257–263.

Thompson, John M. 2004. *Russia and the Soviet Union: An Historical Introduction from the Kievan State to the Present*. 5th ed. Boulder: Westview.

Treisman, Daniel. 2012. "Inequality: The Russian Experience." *Current History*, October, 264–269.

———. 2013. "Can Putin Keep His Grip on Power?" *Current History*, October, 251–258.

Tucker, Robert C., ed. 1975. *The Lenin Anthology*. New York: Norton.

Volkogonov, Dmitri. 1991. *Stalin: Triumph and Tragedy*. London: Weidenfeld & Nicolson.

———. 1994. *Lenin: A New Biography*. New York: Free Press.

———. 1996. *Trotsky: The Eternal Revolutionary*. New York: Free Press.

———. 1998. *Autopsy for an Empire: The Seven Leaders Who Built the Soviet Regime*. New York: Free Press.

Von Laue, Theodore H. 1971. *Why Lenin? Why Stalin?* New York: Lippincott.

Whitmore, Brian. 2010. "Kremlin Puts Its Interests First." *Asia Times*, February 26. www.atimes.com/atimes/Central_Asia/LB26Ag01.html.

Wilson, Edmund. 1972. *To the Finland Station: A Study in the Writing and Acting of History*. New York: Farrar Straus Giroux.

Wolf, Eric. 1969. *Peasant Wars of the Twentieth Century*. New York: Harper & Row.

World Bank. 2004. *Poverty Assessment Report on Russia*. www.worldbank.org.

Selected DVD, Film, and Videocassette Documentaries

See "Purchase and Rental Sources" at the end of this volume for information on how to obtain the following resources and for full names of media companies and other organizations listed here as abbreviations.

After Stalin. 1998. CNN Cold War Series Episode 7. 46 min. Eastern European resistance to Soviet domination, including the 1956 Hungarian Revolution.

Boris Yeltsin. 50 min. BIO. Russia's first elected president.

Forgotten Wars. 50 min. Video. AETV, HC. Includes US military intervention in the Russian civil war along with interventions in other countries.

History 1917–67, Unit II, No. 5: Lenin's Revolution. 1970. 20 min. Black-and-white film. KSU, UI, UMONT, UWASH.

History 1917–67, Unit II, No. 6: Stalin's Revolution. 1971. 22 min. Black-and-white film. KSU, UI, UMONT, UWASH. Explains how Stalin shunned Lenin's goal of world revolution but built the Soviet Union into a great industrial power.

Lech Walesa. 50 min. Video, DVD. BIO. Solidarity leader and president of Poland.

Lenin and Trotsky. 1964. 16 min. Black-and-white film. KSU, SYRU, UI, UWY. Traces the roles of Lenin and Trotsky in the Bolshevik Revolution.

Mikhail Gorbachev: A Man Who Changed the World. 50 min. DVD. BIO. Russian reformer.

The Putin System. 2009. Interesting but highly critical documentary of Vladimir Putin. Canadian Broadcasting Corporation. 89 min. http://topdocumentaryfilms.com/the -putin-system.

Pope John Paul II: Statesman of Faith. 50 min. DVD. BIO. The Polish pope and his impact.

Rasputin. 50 min. Video. BIO. Monk blamed for helping to destroy the Romanov dynasty.

The Rise and Fall of the Soviet Union. 124 min. SEG.

The Romanovs. 50 min. DVD. AETV. Last years of the Romanov dynasty.

The Russian Revolution: Czar to Lenin. 1966. 33 min. Black-and-white film. PSU. Outstanding documentary of the Russian Revolution.

The Soviet Union: Gorbachev's Reforms and the Eastern Block. 30 min. Video. PBS. Political and economic reforms in Eastern Europe.

Stalin and the Modernization of Russia. 1982. 29 min. Color film or video. Films, Inc. Covers Stalin's rise to power, the industrialization drive, and the collectivization of agriculture.

Stalin: Man of Steel. 100 min. DVD. BIO.

Stalin vs. Trotsky: Struggle for Power. 1964. 16 min. Black-and-white film. KSU, UARIZ, UI. The conflict between Stalin and Trotsky.

Struggle for Russia. 1994. 120 min. Video. AFSC. Problems of "shock economic therapy," economic and social chaos, and political conflict in Russia.

Trotsky: Rise and Fall of a Revolutionary. 2008. 60 min. DVD. Amazon.com. Black-and-white and color.

Vladimir Lenin: Voice of Revolution. 2005. 50 min. DVD. BIO.

Vladimir Putin. 50 min. DVD. BIO. Russia's second elected president.

3

Revolution in China[*]

———————

The world was shaken in 1917, when a socialist revolution swept through czarist Russia, the largest nation in the world. In 1949 another revolution triumphed, this one in the world's most populous country. Just as the success of the Russian revolution owed much to Lenin's ideas, the Chinese revolution resulted, in part, from innovations introduced by Mao Zedong (Mao Tse-Tung).

Mao realized that the sudden collapse of pre-revolutionary governmental authority and coercive capability that provided a unique opportunity for Russian revolutionaries at the close of World War 1 was unlikely to occur in China. He correctly predicted that in his nation the major cities would remain under antirevolutionary control almost until the conclusion of the revolution. According to Mao's analysis, the accomplishment of sweeping social change in China depended on wedding the frustration of the country's huge rural majority to a genuinely revolutionary ideology. Thus during the 1927–1949 period the peasant rebellion, the traditional mechanism for the expression of rural discontent, became a revolution that, more than simply replacing national government leaders, radically transformed the basic structure of China's economic, political, and social systems.

———————

[*] Chinese terms used in this chapter are written according to the pinyin (combination of sounds) procedure, the official system introduced by Chinese authorities in the late 1970s. In pinyin most letters are pronounced approximately the same as in those languages using the Latin alphabet, including English. Exceptions include c, which is pronounced as "ts" (as in "its"); x, as "sh" (as in "show"); zh, as "j" (as in "jump"); e, as "e" (as in "her"); and q, as "ch" (as in "cheese") (Chance 1985, xix). Each time a Chinese term first appears in the text, the Wade-Giles spelling follows in parentheses. The latter system was widely used in Western academic books on China before 1979 (Domes 1985).

Geography and Population

The People's Republic of China (PRC) has a land area of 3,705,390 square miles (9,596,961 square kilometers), making it the fourth largest country in the world after Russia, Canada, and the United States. Most of the country is mountainous, and only about 15 percent of the land is arable. In 2013 the population was 1.35 billion (CIA 2014a), with approximately 51 percent living in urban areas in 2011. About 91.5 percent were Han Chinese. The remaining 8.5 percent included fifty-five ethnic groups, such as Koreans, Manchus, Mongols, Tibetans, and Zhuang. China's relative ethnic homogeneity facilitated the mobilization of large numbers into periodic peasant rebellions and later into the peasant-based revolution of the twentieth century.

Social and Historical Settings for Revolution

When China entered the twentieth century, 90 percent or more of its people were in agriculture. The 10 percent who did not work the land included servants, urban laborers, soldiers, craftsmen, merchants, government administrators, and members of the economic elite. In rural China the top level of the class system was occupied by the landlord gentry. Families in this class gained wealth primarily through renting parcels of land to poor peasants and landless peasants and collecting interest on loans. The landlord gentry families constituted from 2 to 4 percent of the population and owned from 30 to 50 percent of all cultivated land until 1949 (Blecher 1986; Clubb 1978; Wolf 1969). China's landlords were usually in close contact with the peasants, typically living in or near the market towns, which served surrounding villages and hamlets.

Four economic categories—rich, middle, poor, and landless—were distinguishable among peasants. In general, rich peasants owned enough land not only to provide for their families but also to rent to others. Middle peasants owned enough land to satisfy their own families' needs but lacked any significant surplus to rent. Poor peasants did not have sufficient land to grow the food or generate the income needed to feed their families. Whereas a rich or middle peasant might choose to engage in work activity in addition to cultivating his or her own land, such extra labor was a necessity for poor peasants. Supplementary labor might involve renting land from a rich peasant or a landlord, hiring out as a farmhand to work on someone else's land, or engaging in handicrafts to make articles for sale to other peasants, merchants, or landlords. A fourth group of peasants owned no land at all and rented land or worked as farmhands for others. The percentage of rural families in each category varied from one part of China to another. It also varied over time owing to factors such as land fertility, rainfall or irrigation, land availability relative to population size, and external economic burdens such as government taxation.

During the late nineteenth and early twentieth centuries, according to anthropologists' estimates, nationally about 10 percent were rich peasants, 30 percent middle peasants, 50 percent poor peasants, and 10 percent landless peasants (Bianco 1971; Thaxton 1983; Wolf 1969).

Unequal distribution of land and other resources meant that wars and natural calamities, such as floods or droughts that disrupted agricultural production, could have negative effects on the majority of peasants who lived near or at the level of subsistence. Famines occasionally killed millions. To prevent an entire family from starving, poor and landless peasants sometimes resorted to selling children, prostitution, or some form of predatory criminal activity, such as banditry. Poverty and natural hardships in the countryside constituted a continuing source of mass frustration that would eventually combine with other critical factors to bring about a sweeping peasant-based socioeconomic revolution.

Pre-Revolutionary China

The official political-religious culture of China, Confucianism, functioned, in conjunction with the Chinese state and its military apparatus, to help maintain the traditional social structure in the face of periodic surges of peasant discontent. Confucius (551–479 BCE) was a philosopher who believed that respect for one's ancestors and obedience to one's parents constituted the foundations of society and formal authority (the state) and fostered social harmony. Confucianism promoted a sense of fatalism, or accepting one's lot in life as heaven's will, and obedience to authority figures. The Confucian stress on the individual's obligations to family and state provided a cultural and psychological receptiveness among many Chinese to the later communist emphasis on a collective rather than self-centered orientation.

The emperor, who exercised absolute authority over his subjects, merited the "mandate of heaven" as long as his rule embodied justice and goodness. Throughout its recorded history, China had twenty-four imperial dynasties. Replacement of a corrupt or incompetent regime was consistent with the Confucian doctrine that unworthy rulers lose their mandate and should be overthrown.

Although the emperor was divinely selected to rule, his governmental administrators were chosen on the basis of examinations that tested knowledge of the classical Confucian writings as well as administrative skills. The theory was that thorough comprehension of Confucian wisdom would result in officials who were morally good men and, consequently, government that was fair and effective in maintaining social harmony. It was estimated that during the late nineteenth century the national government comprised approximately 40,000 imperial officials, or mandarins (Skocpol 1979). Although entrance into the mandarinate was theoretically open to all, in the vast majority of cases only relatively wealthy families could afford the tutors and years of study required to prepare for the examinations and the loss of a son's labor and potential income during the educational period.

Mandarins delegated authority at the local level to members of the landlord gentry class. Landlords assumed leading roles in extended family networks, or clans. Poor peasants might refuse to join a protest against a landlord or government official from their own clan in order to avoid dishonoring the family. Furthermore, prestige rivalries among clans often meant that peasants of different clans who had similar economic interests might not readily cooperate with one another (Wolf 1969).

Traditional Forms of Peasant Resistance

Peasant and working-class hardships and consciousness of subordinate social status fostered opposition to the dominant Confucian system. Anti-Confucian secret societies, such as White Lotus, Red Spear, and Big Knives, were characterized by distinctive belief systems, oaths of allegiance, and other rituals. These organizations were generally polytheistic and often combined elements of several religious traditions, for example, the Buddhist concept of reincarnation and the Taoist emphasis on individual happiness and rejection of the value of Confucian scholarship (Chesneaux 1971; 1972b). Chinese scholars noted distinctions between the folk sects, which were older and primarily religious in purpose, and secret brotherhoods and protection societies, both of which functioned mainly to provide members with mutual assistance (Eastman 1988).

Secret societies were usually more egalitarian than the dominant social order, and often members took an oath to help the poor. Most members of these illegal organizations were poor peasants in the countryside and "marginal and destitute elements of the towns and villages," such as porters, laborers, peddlers, boatmen, poor artisans, and smugglers (Chesneaux 1972b, 8). In the countryside secret societies often carried out a peasant self-defense function against marauding imperial forces, bandits, or even attacks by rival societies (Bianco 1971). In the cities some societies, such as the Green Gang in Shanghai, capitalized on their group network and members' loyalty to develop into mafia-style organized crime associations involved in drug trafficking, smuggling, control of prostitution, and similar activities (Lust 1972; Posner 1988).

Unusually high levels of peasant unrest occasionally resulted in a peasant rebellion. These uprisings were sometimes preceded by the development of widespread banditry, with the mass of the peasantry finally driven to rebellion by the same conditions that earlier had provoked the poorest into banditry. In some instances rebellions were in part inspired by charismatic or visionary leaders. But often natural calamities played a precipitating role. When an earthquake, flood, or drought killed large numbers and endangered many more by significantly reducing agricultural productivity, many peasants interpreted the disaster as a sign that heaven had withdrawn its support for the governing regime.

Whatever the causes, peasant uprisings were rarely successful in overthrowing a ruling dynasty. And on the few occasions when a peasant rebellion played a role in actually toppling an emperor (in these cases, elements of the national elite, military and administrative, were known to desert a crippled dynasty to assume leadership roles in a popular rebellion), post-rebellion changes tended to be limited to establishing a new ruling dynasty and temporary improvements in the efficiency and fairness of government; meanwhile, the Confucian system was maintained. Although peasant rebels often fought for social justice within the Confucian framework, they almost never had the goal of transforming the traditional structure (political, economic, and social institutions) or the supporting cultural system of Chinese society (Blecher 1986; Wolf 1969). Participants felt that their goals could be achieved mainly by getting rid of bad or incompetent leaders and replacing them with virtuous men who would bring back the good old days of some real or mythical period of China's past. Since the basic economic and political relationships remained unchanged, the factors that caused the rebellion would eventually surface again and result in further peasant uprisings (Thaxton 1983; Wolf 1969).

The Manchu Dynasty

In 1644 the Manchus, a Sinified tribal people from beyond the Great Wall in northeastern China (constituting less than 0.5 percent of China's population), took advantage of incompetence among the Ming dynasty rulers and disunity and rivalries among provincial administrators and military leaders to sweep down and seize Beijing, China's capital. The Manchus established their own Qing (Ch'ing) dynasty, which would be China's last (1644–1911). Since, according to the Confucian belief system, a dynasty could not be overthrown and replaced by another unless heaven had removed the mandate from the defeated and bestowed it on the victorious, many Chinese accepted the rule of the Manchus, although resistance continued for years in southern China. Many of China's secret societies took upon themselves the defense of Chinese ethnic honor by opposing Manchu authority and advocating a return to Ming dynasty rule.

Several Manchu emperors, however, proved to be effective rulers, and two had exceptionally long reigns (covering 1683–1796), during which social stability returned to much of the country, Chinese military and political power achieved high levels, agricultural productivity increased, and there was peace. The latter two factors contributed to a doubling of the population between 1700 and 1900 to more than 400 million (Blecher 1986; Clubb 1978).

During the nineteenth century, various factors heightened peasant discontent and undermined the traditional Chinese state. Among these were increased strain on agricultural resources because of decades of population growth; military defeats by European nations and later Japan, which humiliated the Chinese, inflamed Chinese nationalism, and burdened China with huge war indemnities and unfavorable trade relationships; and massive, though unsuccessful, peasant rebellions, which resulted in millions of deaths and further depleted the resources of the central government (Bianco 1971; Blecher 1986; Eastman 1988; Skocpol 1979; Wolf 1969).

Foreign Involvement in China

The Opium War of 1839–1842 severely weakened China's ability to resist foreign imports. During the 1830s Great Britain's leaders were appalled by the flow of their hard currency into China to purchase tea, silk, porcelains, and other exports. They proposed to pay for Chinese goods by increasing sales in China of a product of their Burma and India colonies, opium. China's government feared an increase in drug dependency if the British were allowed to sell opium freely. After the Chinese destroyed an opium shipment, Britain sent military expeditions, whose advanced weaponry devastated the Chinese. As a result, China was forced to agree to (1) allow the British to sell opium and other products in China; (2) allow European missionaries to preach Christianity; (3) pay war indemnities to the British; (4) provide the British with certain cities or sections of cities as treaty ports or concessions, where they could establish economic enterprises, deploy military personnel, and provide exclusively European living quarters. Later other European nations and Japan forced similar concessions and war-indemnity payments and eventually carved China into spheres of influence, often making specific deals for cooperation with local governmental and military leaders. The six nations that developed a significant economic interest and military presence in China by the end of the nineteenth century were Great Britain, France, Germany, Japan, czarist Russia, and the United States.

Foreign victories over China had negative economic consequences. The Chinese government was forced to raise taxes to pay war indemnities and to cope with debts that stemmed from the country's unfavorable economic relationship with Europe. The burden fell disproportionately on the relatively powerless mass of poor peasants because, in order to pay taxes, the landlords and rich peasants increased rents they charged for land use as well as interest rates on loans. The poor were further victimized by the fact that sources of supplemental income needed to make ends meet, such as handicrafts, were undermined by the influx of manufactured articles from the industrialized countries. Many Chinese blamed the Manchu dynasty (and soon the Confucian system itself) for China's inability to resist foreign domination and for conditions in the countryside.

Nineteenth-Century Rebellions

Economic deprivation and hostility toward Manchu rulers led to major but ultimately unsuccessful peasant rebellions, the Nian (Nien) Rebellion (1853–1868) in central China and the Taiping (T'aip'ing) Rebellion (1851–1864), which began in south China and spread northward, establishing the Taiping capital at Nanjing (Nanking). Both rebellions advocated a redistribution of wealth in favor of the poor and at times the Taiping units advancing northward allied with Nian forces in battles against the Manchu army.

The Nian were members of a secret society devoted to overthrowing the Manchu dynasty. They were defeated in part because their decentralized military effort permitted the Manchus to concentrate large forces against isolated rebel towns (Wolf 1969). Nevertheless, the Nian Rebellion provided the peasants of central China with a tradition that helped prepare them culturally to support and participate in the communist-led peasant revolution of the twentieth century.

The Taiping (Great Peace) Rebellion was ideologically unique and more massive than the Nian. The Taiping Rebellion and its repression by the Manchus resulted in an estimated twenty million deaths. The movement was led by a man from the Hakka minority group, Hong (Hung) (1814–1864), who was born near the city of Guangzhou (Canton), a major site of early foreign influence. The culture of the Hakka people was more gender and income equalitarian than the dominant Confucian system. Hong's peasant family made sacrifices for his education, but he failed to pass exams for a state position. In Guangzhou, however, Hong received Christian religious instruction from an American missionary.

During a serious illness Hong dreamed that he was the younger brother of Jesus Christ and was to organize an army that would "destroy the demons on earth in order to create a new Kingdom of God" (Wolf 1969, 120). The landlord gentry class was to be eliminated. Land parcels would be assigned to peasants to farm, but ownership would be retained by the Taiping state. Production beyond individual families' needs would become a collective resource. Advancement in Taiping society was to be based on meritorious performance, not heredity, family wealth, or Confucian scholarship.

The Taipings granted extensive rights to women and forbade foot binding of female children and prostitution. Marriage was to be monogamous and based on mutual attraction rather than arranged by parents for financial gain. Women were allowed to serve as soldiers and occupy leadership positions. But Taiping attacks on all three of China's main religions (Confucianism, Buddhism, and Taoism) provoked opposition from many. Furthermore, Taiping land reforms did little to improve the lot of most peasants, who soon resented the heavy tax burden placed on them by the Taiping regime (Wolf 1969).

Moreover, foreign interests in China, having used force of arms to win favorable treaties, concessions, and trade relations from the Manchu dynasty, saw their privileges endangered by the possible countrywide victory of the Taipings. Consequently, industrialized nations provided the anti-Taiping Manchu (Ever-Victorious) army with weapons, technical assistance, and mercenary officers and advisers, which contributed significantly to the defeat of the Taiping movement and execution of its leaders in 1864 (Bohr 2006; Payne 1969).

The Taiping Rebellion and the later communist-led peasant revolution had important parallels. Both enjoyed support from intensely frustrated rural populations, and both were characterized by ideologies that incorporated ideas from the West and called for sweeping changes in major economic, social, political, and cultural institutions. The Taiping plans for wealth redistribution and collective ownership as well as for liberating women were remarkably similar to several of the basic goals proclaimed by communist revolutionaries sixty years later (Bohr 2006). And the twentieth-century peasant revolutionaries succeeded in establishing their first rural bases in areas of south China formerly supportive of the Taipings (Skocpol 1979; Wolf 1969).

THE DEVELOPMENT OF THE REPUBLICAN MOVEMENT

By the latter part of the nineteenth century, many Chinese realized that to regain its independence their country would have to modernize its political and social systems and industrialize. But the Confucian culture and political system constituted powerful barriers to social change. Since a rationalized and technologically advancing society would have little use for leaders whose authority was based on antiquated and nonutilitarian scholarship, most mandarins resisted modernization.

Large landholders throughout the country were also not inclined to support modernization because it would likely shift China's economy toward industry and commerce (Moore 1966; Skocpol 1976). Confucian culture assigned maximum prestige to agriculture as an economic activity, ideally coupled with training in the Confucian classics, and bestowed less honor on merchants or others involved in nonagricultural or nonscholarly endeavors (Blecher 1986). Many Chinese businessmen had turned to commerce or industry as a means of developing wealth because they did not possess large landholdings. But instead of using their profits to expand commercial or industrial operations, they often purchased land in order to gain entrance to the most time-honored status recognized in Confucian culture (Blecher 1986). This was an important reason why China did not develop a strong, independent national business class, which might have constituted the leadership element to bring about rapid modernization. Consequently, much of the major industry of pre-revolutionary China was foreign owned, and many of the smaller industrial enterprises were owned by westernized Chinese often shunned by their country folk as cultural apostates or lackeys of foreign interests.

Any modernization attempted by the central government also had to confront the woeful inadequacy of imperial finances. The government had spent enormous sums suppressing the Taiping and Nian rebellions and paying indemnities to victorious foreign powers. Because of their role in raising the resources and forces to crush the Taipings, provincial authorities won greatly enhanced power. Few provincial leaders were willing to support national modernization efforts that might threaten their new political and economic prerogatives.

When war broke out between China and Japan in 1894–1895, China's navy was easily defeated, a traumatic event for many Chinese, who had previously viewed Japan as almost a vassal state. Japan had been able to accomplish this feat largely because of its reaction to its own humiliation in 1853, when it was militarily unable to resist being opened to world trade by a US naval force. The event disgraced a traditionalist, isolationist dynasty and precipitated its fall and replacement by a dynasty committed to rapid technological modernization (Gurley 1983). The new regime succeeded in freeing the Japanese in a few decades from cultural impediments to industrialization, commercial development, and military modernization. Many Chinese began to look to Japan as a model.

In 1898 the Chinese emperor Guangxu (Kuang Hsu), then in his late twenties, and a small group of advisers attempted to introduce sweeping reforms that included abolishing Confucian exams for administrative posts and adopting a parliamentary form of government (a constitutional monarchy). All towns were to create free schools for the poor, and all existing governmental and military officeholders were to be reevaluated. However, the One Hundred Days Reform movement was abruptly halted by a palace coup in which the traditionalist majority of government ministers, along with the conservative and exceptionally ruthless dowager empress, Ci Xi (Tz'u Hsi), placed the emperor under house arrest and ordered the execution of his reform-oriented advisers (Payne 1969; Skocpol 1979).

In 1900 the antiforeign Fists of Harmony and Justice Society (called Boxers by the Europeans because of their clenched fist symbol), encouraged by the dowager empress, murdered several missionaries and hundreds of Christian Chinese and besieged the foreign embassies in Beijing. After several months, the siege was lifted by an international relief force. Once again, victorious foreigners imposed new reparation payments. After this humiliation, the central government finally decided that major reforms were necessary to facilitate modernization. Among the changes was the establishment of provincial parliaments in 1908. The legislators were selected through elections in which the economic elite voted. A national parliament was to be elected in 1917. Traditional Confucian examinations for admittance to the government bureaucracy were ended in 1905. Another reform established technical training centers for young army officers, who were to constitute the leadership of China's new army (Eastman 1988; Skocpol 1979).

Sun and the Republican Revolution

Much of the ideology for the revolution to establish a Chinese republic was developed by Sun Yixian (Sun Yat Sen), eventually honored as the Father of the Chinese Republic. Sun, whose father was a poor peasant, was born in a village forty miles from Guangzhou in 1866. He, like Hong, the leader of the Taiping Rebellion whom he came to admire, was of Hakka ancestry. Sun told friends that as a child he was deeply impressed by the stories he heard from a village teacher who was a surviving soldier of the Taiping rebel armies (Schiffrin 1989). Sun's older brother left the family for Hawaii when Sun was six and, using savings from his wages, bought a farm and later established a store. Sun traveled to Hawaii, where he worked for his brother and attended the English-language Anglican College of Honolulu. When Sun, after converting to Christianity, returned to China, he made his way to Xianggang (Hong Kong) and spent the years 1884–1892 obtaining a medical degree at Queen's College (Payne 1969).

Sun, like many young Chinese of his era, was outraged by China's backwardness and became determined to play a role in ridding China of the ineffective Manchu dynasty and in revitalizing and modernizing the nation. In 1905 Sun combined an organization he had helped found with another republican revolutionary group and formed the United Revolutionary Society, initially established among Chinese exiles in Japan. Thousands secretly joined inside China, along with many Chinese throughout the world. Thus, within China's educated minority profoundly intense divisions developed. Depriving the state of many of its most capable and skilled citizens, these divisions also provided leadership for the growing revolutionary movements aimed at overthrowing the monarchy and establishing a republic.

Sun and most of his associates either had professional careers or were students. Since they lacked a mechanism for directly incorporating the mass of China's population into the republican movement, they allied themselves with the anti-Manchu secret societies (Lust 1972). But Sun viewed these groups as backward-looking and a possible impediment to social, economic, and political modernization. He asserted that he supported alliances with secret societies only as a temporary method of extending mass involvement in the republican movement (Borokh 1972).

In 1908 the dynasty was weakened by the deaths of both Empress Dowager Ci Xi and her nephew, the deposed former emperor Guangxu. The monarchy fell into the hands of Prince Chun, who ruled as regent on behalf of the three-year-old Emperor Fu Yi (Pu Yi). As anti-Manchu riots broke out in south China, Prince Chun called on General Yuan Shikai (Yuan Shih-K'ai) to restore order.

On October 10, 1911, several thousand soldiers, fearing exposure and execution for their secret membership in republican revolutionary groups, staged a rebellion in Hubei (Hupei) Province in central China. The uprising was soon followed by similar mutinies against imperial rule in more than a dozen southern and central provinces. Local military commanders (or their successors) declared the independence of their provinces from Manchu rule. The insurrections resulted in part from the successful efforts of Sun and his associates in forging a powerful coalition that included their revolutionary organization; "southern Chinese secret societies; regional interest groups in Hunan, Hubei, Guangdong, Sichuan; and some of the modern crack military units" (Domes 1985, 29).

Yuan Shikai seized the opportunity to advance his ambition to be China's new leader by convincing the members of the royal family that they faced the possibility of execution if they failed to compromise with the republican forces. The Manchu rulers abdicated on February 12, 1912. At Nanjing, Sun was declared provisional president of the Republic of China. But in an effort to prevent a civil war, Sun resigned after fifteen days and agreed to accept Yuan Shikai as president if Yuan would declare support for the republic. Yuan consented and became president on March 10, 1912.

Sun's United Society was transformed into the Guomindang (GMD) (Koumin tang, KMT), National Party, in fall 1912. But in the new parliament the GMD members soon fell into conflict with Yuan Shikai's supporters over issues such as Yuan's assertion that his authority was above that of the parliament. The GMD's parliamentary leader was assassinated by Yuan's agents, and Sun temporarily fled the country. Yuan outlawed the Guomindang Party and then dismissed parliament in 1914. The following year he installed himself as China's new emperor, only to die in 1916. After Yuan's death, central state authority effectively ceased to exist, and most of the nation disintegrated into its component provinces. Each of these was ruled by local landowning elites in combination with the general in charge of the provincial armed forces, the local warlord.

Sun returned to south China and began to reorganize the republican movement. He appealed to the United States and other nations for financial assistance, weapons, and military advisers to train a republican army that could subdue the warlords. But these countries, some having made trade arrangements with warlords and perhaps fearful of the power of a unified China and the potential radical or antiforeign tendencies of the republican revolutionaries, declined to provide aid. Only the new revolutionary government in the Soviet Union agreed to send weapons and advisers (Jordan 1976; Wolf 1969).

Sun dispatched a republican officer, Jiang Jieshi (Chiang Kaishek), to Moscow to report on the Soviet political and military systems. He returned impressed by the Bolsheviks' success in carrying out and defending their revolution and in unifying the Soviet Union. But Jiang, son of a merchant in a family with claims to royal ancestry (Ming dynasty) and schooled in Confucian traditions, disagreed with the social revolution occurring in the Soviet Union. Sun, however, proceeded to pattern the Guomindang's organizational structure after that of the Russian Communist Party (Bianco 1971).

The ideological foundation of the Guomindang was Sun's Three Principles of the People. The first principle was independence, or nationalism, which meant freeing China from foreign domination and exploitation. Although it can be argued that this was the most clearly defined of the three principles, in reality Chinese political factions disagreed over which types and what degrees of economic and political association with other nations constituted manifestations of imperialism.

The second principle was democracy. Sun called for a strong central government but, by the early 1920s, was disillusioned with the representative (parliamentary) democracies of Europe. He felt that these governments were dominated by capitalist ruling classes willing to tolerate poverty in their own countries as well as exploit the people in less developed societies. Sun favored the direct election of the nation's leaders by its citizens, who would also have the right to recall public officials and the right to propose laws and vote on proposals through referendums. But Sun also advocated a period of tutelage, during which the Guomindang would be the only political party able to exercise state power. When China had achieved independence and political stability and had a powerful post-revolutionary central state government structure, full democracy would be established (Cheng 1989).

The third principle, people's livelihood, was even less completely defined than the first two, and its interpretation was a main point of contention among China's rightists and leftists in the years after Sun's death. In his earliest formulations of the third principle, Sun seemed to disagree with the Marxist concept that redistribution of wealth would be achieved through class conflict and instead proposed that it could be accomplished peacefully through cooperation among the classes. People's livelihood would include the provision of employment and the necessities of life for all. The government was to bring about an equalization of rural landownership gradually. How this could occur without the resistance of the landlords and, consequently, class conflict, was not adequately explained. Sun appeared to become more and more influenced by policies in the Soviet Union, his revolution's only source of external military assistance, and at one point confounded conservative members of the Guomindang by responding to a question about people's livelihood with the puzzling statement, "It is communism and it is socialism" (Ch'ien 1964, 75). With the republican revolution still in progress, Sun died of cancer in March 1925.

China's Communist Party

Despite Sun's attempts to develop a unified movement, the republican revolutionary elite was deeply divided. Rightist figures in the GMD typically came from the upper-income families of China's coastal provinces and had little interest in redistributing the nation's wealth to the poor. Rather, they favored retaining capitalist property relations along with much of the Confucian cultural system. In contrast, leftists in the GMD, particularly Communist Party members, viewed the revolution as both nationalistic and socioeconomic. Thus the emergent republican state was immediately characterized by a dissident elite movement of leftists favoring a further profound socioeconomic revolution.

China's Communist Party originated in the New Youth movement, in which many of the nation's Western-educated students participated between 1915 and 1919 (Meisner 1986). The movement's leaders had become convinced that the future development and independence of China depended on a near-total rejection of traditional culture and the rapid substitution of Western norms and values. New Youth advocates called for a radical shift in education. Schools should teach methods of rational inquiry and scientific research and convey information about modern technologies. The movement also called for a democratically elected parliament.

The apogee of the New Youth movement occurred after the disclosure of the terms of the Versailles Treaty ending World War I, which transferred German colonial holdings in China to Japan instead of returning them to the Chinese. To many it appeared that the victorious Western nations were bribing the Japanese to collaborate in the mutual exploitation of China and betraying the often stated promise that the defeat of Germany in World War I would bring democracy and the right of national self-determination to the entire world. On May 4, 1919, 3,000 students, proclaiming Democracy and Science, the slogan inspired by the New Youth movement, demonstrated in Beijing to protest both the treaty provisions and their nation's inability to resist foreign domination.

Many in the movement abruptly altered their perceptions of Western nations. "The intellectuals' views of the West underwent a rapid and dramatic transformation. The bitter nationalist resentments aroused by the fateful decision at Versailles coupled with growing nationalist political activism at home, led to a rapid erosion of faith that the 'advanced' Western nations would instruct China in the principles of democracy and science" (Meisner 1986, 17). Former leaders of the New Youth movement proclaimed a new movement, the May Fourth movement, whose participants continued to look to the West for inspiration but less to the dominant ideologies that justified capitalist economic systems and the perceived imperialism of the Western nations and Japan toward China. Instead, movement activists began to turn to Marxism, which some viewed "as the most advanced intellectual product of the modern West, but one that rejected the Western world in its capitalist form and its imperialist relationship with China. The latter was most forcefully demonstrated through the nationalist appeal of the Leninist theory of imperialism (which offered the colonial and semicolonial lands a crucial international revolutionary role) and the new Soviet government's renunciation of old czarist imperialist privileges in China" (Meisner 1986, 18).

Lenin, in his analysis of the international function of modern imperialism, attempted to explain the failure of Marx's prediction that the industrialized capitalist societies would be the first in the world to experience transformations to socialism. Imperialism involved the efforts over several hundred years of the technologically advanced societies to establish political, economic, and cultural control over less developed parts of the world. Lenin noted that through imperialism several capitalist countries gained access to huge land areas with vast agricultural and mineral resources as well as the labor power of much of the world's population. The countries dominated by foreign imperialism, especially the more affluent classes among the indigenous populations, also constituted significant new markets for products manufactured in the advanced countries. Lenin argued that the capitalist ruling classes of the advanced nations used some of the superprofits from their investments in less developed parts of the world to improve the living conditions of their own working classes, thus reducing the workers' inclination to join political movements advocating revolution and socialism (Lenin [1916] 1975). As a result, Lenin concluded, in reality revolutions would tend to occur first in less developed, economically exploited societies and would involve not only the relatively small industrial working class but also the participation of peasants (Bottomore 1983).

As such revolutions occurred, new leaders would demand more wealth in return for their countries' mineral, agricultural, and labor resources and limit the profits foreign capital could generate through business activity in their lands. Thus the exploitive relationships between the advanced capitalist nations and underdeveloped societies would gradually come to an end. As this change in international economic relationships began to cause shortages in the advanced capitalist societies, the capitalist ruling classes would try to force their working classes to bear most of the economic hardships. Then, according to Lenin, the people of the advanced societies would want to change from capitalism to socialism. Thus revolution in China could conceivably play a major role in causing revolution eventually in the more technologically advanced countries.

In 1920 young Marxists established political organizations in major cities, and in July 1921 twelve delegates from the various groups met in Shanghai to found China's Communist Party. The party initially attempted to recruit members of the country's small urban working class, following Marx's theory that this class would constitute the social basis for a socialist transformation (Bianco 1971). The Russian Communist Party pressured the Chinese communists into uniting with the Guomindang and collaborating with its landlord and capitalist elements. Sun, enamored of the Bolsheviks' achievements, accepted the growing communist movement into the GMD in January 1924 despite the objections of Jiang and other conservatives. The purpose of the alliance was to achieve the common goals of unifying the

3: Revolution in China

country, freeing it from foreign control, and, at least in terms of formal proclama-tions, eventually establishing a Western-style parliamentary democracy.

CIVIL WAR IN CHINA

In summer 1926 Jiang, who had become a prominent GMD general, launched the Northern Expedition (1926–1928), through which the Guomindang intended to defeat the provincial warlords and unite China under its rule. The Northern Ex-pedition involved an unstable coalition among conservative landlords and coastal merchants who helped finance the enterprise, the Communist Party and allied left-ist activists, and military forces led by Jiang and other mostly rightist officers. In this situation, as in the later revolutionary struggle, nationalism in the sense of the desire to construct a unified and powerful China free of foreign domination consti-tuted the main unifying motivation bringing different groups together on behalf of the revolutionary effort.

Young GMD activists, many of them communists, attempted to mobilize work-ers and peasants in cities and territories as the republican armies approached with the hopeful message that republican victory would result in relief from both polit-ical and economic oppression. Workers showed support by striking and shutting down factories and services, thereby hastening warlord surrender. But Jiang was also able to subdue warlords by offers of money and/or senior positions in the re-publican army (Jordan 1976; Wei 1985).

By the time Jiang's forces moved on Shanghai in 1927, he had decided to begin an all-out repression of the communist movement. Jiang first secured promises of funding from Shanghai financiers and businessmen who were eager to see the mil-itant workers' movement eliminated (Bianco 1971; Eastman 1988; Meisner 1986). He also negotiated with Shanghai's Mafia-like Green Gang secret society. Green Gang members were knowledgeable of the city's working-class sections and could help in the identification and liquidation of labor groups and communist workers who, only days before their annihilation, had played a substantial role in helping the GMD forces capture the city (Clubb 1978). Before dawn on April 12, GMD sol-diers and the Green Gang attacked the headquarters of communist-oriented labor unions and proceeded to destroy the workers' militia (Jordan 1976). In addition to the workers killed in the day-long battle, hundreds more were executed after capture.

Surviving communist activists went into hiding. Jiang's forces soon repeated these measures in other major cities. The left-leaning GMD civilian government was appalled at the murders of workers and the spreading persecution of the com-munists. But Jiang, because he controlled the armed forces, was soon able to assume governmental as well as military control. Some civilians in the GMD government

MAP 3.1 China (1927–1949)

also supported Jiang's seizure of power because they were alarmed at reports that the communists planned to take land from large landholders and factories from Chinese and foreign capitalists and turn these over to poor peasants and workers. Despite the reverses, most surviving communist leaders still dogmatically held to the belief that the communist movement must establish control of the cities and base the revolution on China's relatively minute urban working class. Some communist leaders, however, felt that in China a revolution could be based on the rural population. The most important of these was Mao Zedong.

Mao and People's War in the Countryside

Mao (1893–1976) was born in Hunan Province, the son of a rich peasant. At seventeen, he left school to join republican revolutionary forces attempting to overthrow the Manchu dynasty. In 1912 Mao resumed his education, earning a teaching degree, and then briefly joined the library staff at the University of Beijing. Later in 1920, the same year that he became a Marxist, Mao got a position as an elementary school principal in Changsha, Hunan Province. In 1921 he traveled secretly to Shanghai to participate with eleven other delegates from other locations in the founding congress of the Chinese Communist Party (Short 2000, 119). Unlike many other early members of the Chinese Communist Party, Mao, influenced by his knowledge of peasant support for the Taiping Rebellion and its popularity in his home province, favored a peasant-based socialist revolution. But after the 1927 Shanghai massacre, Mao and others were ordered by party leaders to assemble communist forces (which included armed workers and peasants and GMD regiments that had sided with the communists) and attack and seize several cities. These efforts, as well as attempts of communist-led workers to stage urban uprisings or resist GMD military takeovers, failed. Mao's forces retreated to heavily forested areas of Jiangxi (Kiangsi) Province in southeast China. There they recruited several hundred rural bandits to their cause and soon began to make inroads with local peasants (Wei 1985).

Mao developed the theory—a modification of earlier Marxist revolutionary thought—that in China, where the vast majority of the population was rural and where relatively strong anticommunist military forces, GMD or warlord, held the cities, the revolution would be based on the peasants (Bianco 1971; Mackerras and Knight 1985; Skocpol 1979). Marx had concluded that most peasants would not be receptive to revolutionary goals because of their relative ignorance of the world beyond their villages, their sense of powerlessness, and their ties to tradition. He anticipated that only after capitalist industrial economies had brought about the migration of millions of peasants to urban areas (and in the process caused tremendous adaptive changes in their cultural values and norms) would conditions be right for the transformation to socialism. The masses of urban-industrial workers

would hypothetically be much more willing than their rural ancestors to participate in a revolutionary movement to improve their economic condition. This would
be true not only because of their ability to interact in large numbers in urban areas
and carry out unified political actions but also because their recent alteration in
livelihood and living environment would provide them with a sense of the possibility of further sweeping social changes, which the pre-industrialization rural population was supposedly incapable of comprehending.

But Mao put faith in the power of ideas to transform the consciousness of peasants. Aware of how receptive the peasants of south and central China had been to
the untraditional ideology of the mid-nineteenth-century Taipings, Mao was certain that the similar but more scientific concepts of Marxism could transform China's historically rebellious peasants into a massive revolutionary force. The key, as
Mao saw it, was to fuse the tradition of peasant rebellion with the ideology of Marxism, which proposed a new plan for society in which major sources of wealth would
be collectively owned and in which socioeconomic inequality would be greatly reduced. Mao's innovation, referred to as the "Sinification of Marxism," proved to be
a major reason for the revolutionary victory in China.

Mao also extracted from his knowledge of past military conflicts the concept of
people's war and adapted it to the revolutionary struggle in China. The most essential aspect of people's war was the goal of achieving widespread popular support for
the revolutionary effort. Antirevolutionary forces would then confront not just the
revolutionary army but also the hostility of large numbers of noncombatants rendering whatever assistance possible to the revolutionary fighters. Another central
element of people's war was to create politicized armed forces that would manifest
the ideals of the revolution in their interaction with and treatment of noncombatants. The revolutionary soldier was to be motivated by the belief that he or she was
fighting for the creation of a morally just society and against the oppression of the
landlords, exploitive capitalists, and their instrument of violence, the GMD army.
The intended result of politicization of combatants was an armed revolutionary
force driven by high ideals to courageous acts and to waging a determined struggle.

The people were to be educated to the goals of the revolution through both word
(speeches and political instruction) and deed, such as land reform and the exemplary conduct of revolutionary leaders and soldiers. If the people supported the
revolution, the revolutionaries could overcome their disadvantages in armament.
This concept was expressed in a slogan: "The people are the water, the (revolutionary) army are the fish; without the water, the fish will die" (Fairbairn 1974, 99). The
revolutionary forces were to be nourished, hidden, informed about enemy troop
dispositions, and in other ways aided by the people.

The GMD waged five successive military campaigns against the communists'
main base area (called the Jiangxi soviet). During the fifth campaign in 1934,

700,000 GMD troops under Jiang's command, following a plan conceived by a German military adviser, closed in on the communist-controlled areas, constructing stone forts, or blockhouses, along roadways to reduce the revolutionaries' freedom of movement. The main communist forces in the province, numbering about 100,000, were forced to abandon Jiangxi. They slipped out of the encirclement and began a long and tortuous retreat, first toward the west, then north, and then northeast to the remote north-central town of Yan'an (Yennan). The journey covered about 6,000 miles and lasted over a year. Communist units were pursued by GMD forces and attacked by hostile warlord armies along the way. Fewer than 20,000 completed the Long March and made it to Yan'an in late 1935 (Blecher 1986; Domes 1985; Salisbury 1985).

The reform program at the new rural base differed from the Jiangxi soviet and came to be known as the Yan'an Way. At Jiangxi Mao had advocated a land reform in which the rich peasants, who were often the most productive, would retain an amount of land at least equal to the size of the farms of the poor peasants after land redistribution. He hoped to minimize resistance and maximize agricultural output by having the rich peasants make major contributions to production (Wei 1985). Mao had also favored providing dispossessed landlords with land to work. But at Jiangxi more vengeful thinking prevailed. Although rich peasants received some land of poor quality, landlords were transformed into landless laborers. These measures not only decreased agricultural production but also drove outraged landlords and rich peasants to provide important assistance to GMD forces in the successful encirclement campaign (Wei 1985). But in the Yan'an program both the rich peasants and the landlords were allowed to retain much of their land under conditions that restricted profit levels and the exploitation of poor and landless peasants (Thaxton 1983).

The mass-line approach to revolutionary leadership was also established at Yan'an. This method, while leaving ultimate decision making to the Communist Party, reflected Mao's conviction that party policy and its mode of implementation must stem from the people and be based on popular support. According to Mao, "All correct leadership is necessarily 'from the masses, to the masses.' This means: take the ideas of the masses (scattered and unsystematic ideas) and 'concentrate' them (through study turn them into concentrated and systematic ideas), then go to the masses and propagate and explain these ideas until the masses embrace them as their own" (Mao 1967, 117–119).

Japanese Invasion and Revolutionary Victory

The establishment of the Yan'an base coincided with Japanese attacks on China south of the Great Wall in 1937. The communists proposed an end to the civil war and the formation of a coalition with Jiang's GMD army in order to fight Japan jointly. Jiang, having long ignored the Japanese occupation of Manchuria and other parts of China to devote his attention to crushing the communists, was coerced by his associates into stopping the civil war and agreeing to a United Front of communist and GMD forces against the Japanese.

The land reform program during the United Front struggle against the Japanese (1937–1945) in communist-controlled areas was relatively mild. Landlords who were not collaborating with the Japanese generally did not experience land expropriation but rather were subject to a rent control program for the land they rented to poor or landless peasants and were limited in the amount of interest they could charge on loans.

During the war nationalist sentiment swung increasingly in favor of the communists (Blecher 1986). Jiang, anticipating that the United States and its allies would defeat Japan, held some of his best divisions out of the conflict so that they could be employed after the war against the communists. There was widespread corruption in the GMD officer corps and low morale among many enlisted men. The latter were subject to abuse and exploitation by their often profiteering officers (Blecher 1986). The GMD military's efforts and successes against the Japanese were far less than those of the communist-led army, and many members of the classes most supportive of Jiang's regime (the landlords and the merchants) collaborated with the Japanese in occupied areas in order to preserve their assets and comfortable lifestyles. Because of those factors, more and more people recognized Mao's forces (which expanded from 80,000 in 1937 to 900,000 in 1945) as the real army of China (Bianco 1971). GMD army abuse also alienated many peasants. Consequently, when the war ended, the legitimacy of the GMD state was severely weakened, and nationalist sympathy was more on the side of the communists.

Other factors reduced the moral authority of the GMD state. It seemed clear to many that the GMD under Jiang had effectively abandoned Sun's Three Principles of the People. As for fighting for independence and against imperialism, Jiang, who had been a cadet at a military academy in Japan, seemed so convinced that his forces could not effectively combat the Japanese that he preferred to leave the fight to the United States and the communists. His regime became heavily influenced by foreign advisers. Western-educated Chinese played major roles in the GMD, and Jiang's wife, Song Meiling (Soong Meiling), the daughter of a wealthy family, grew up in the United States and often seemed to manifest more allegiance to US culture than to Chinese. As a condition of marriage, Jiang became a Methodist; soon he was a great exponent of the church's teachings. His New Life movement, launched in 1934 to rejuvenate the Chinese, was a mixture of Confucian tenets and Methodist doctrine (Payne 1969). Thus the goal that had acted to unify various groups in the republican revolution of the early twentieth century, that of ridding China of foreign domination, united increasing numbers behind the communist-led revolution, which appeared capable of and likely to establish a genuinely Chinese-controlled national government.

Jiang's conception of advancing the second of Sun's principles, democracy, was apparently to crush the communists. But his own government became essentially a conservative military dictatorship with Jiang in control of the single party, the Guomindang, still patterned after the Russian Communist Party organizationally but, unlike the communists, functioning to preserve rather than reduce basic inequalities in the socioeconomic system.

The GMD regime attempted to maintain the support of rural landlords by protecting their landholdings. Consequently, the GMD did little to bring about a redistribution of wealth to fulfill Sun's third principle, people's livelihood. Because inequalities and oppressive conditions persisted or even worsened in GMD-controlled areas, discontent among the rural population found its expression in the communist-led, peasant revolutionary army (Bianco 1971; Blecher 1986; Moore 1966; Skocpol 1979).

After World War II and the failure of US-mediated attempts to forestall the renewal of the civil war, the conflict between the immensely strengthened communist movement and Jiang's huge but largely demoralized and incompetently led army resumed in 1947. Popular support in the countryside and massive defections from the GMD military helped the communist forces achieve a relatively quick victory. Other nations, awed by the gigantic proportions of the conflict and recovering from the devastation of war, chose not to intervene militarily to try to prevent or reverse the outcome of China's civil war. On October 1, 1949, Mao proclaimed the establishment of the People's Republic of China in Beijing.

Jiang and remnants of the GMD armies fled to Taiwan. There, protected by US naval forces, Jiang claimed to represent the legitimate government of China. With US support, the Taiwanese state, calling itself the Republic of China, held China's seat at the United Nations until 1971. At that point President Richard Nixon visited China—probably in an attempt to gain Chinese support in the US international competition with the USSR and to obtain Chinese assistance in pressuring the Vietnamese into agreeing to a peace settlement acceptable to US leaders. The Nixon administration decided to accept admission of the People's Republic into the United Nations and to agree that Taiwan is a part of China and must someday be reunited with the mainland.

THE PEOPLE'S REPUBLIC OF CHINA: 1949–1990

A revolutionary government was established, dominated by the Communist Party but including many noncommunists, such as Madame Song Qing Ling (Soong Ghing-ling) (1891–1981), the widow of Sun. Counterrevolutionary efforts and serious nonpolitical criminal acts were harshly dealt with. This was especially true after China began to fight in Korea against the United States in 1950. More than 100,000 official executions occurred in the first half of 1951, and many people were sent to forced labor camps.

In 1949 China had a gigantic urban drug problem in part as a result of GMD use of "secret societies and gangster organizations which profited from the drug trade" for the political purpose of repressing revolutionaries (Meisner 1986, 90). Revolutionary authorities quickly launched anticrime and antivice campaigns, which over a two-year period reportedly significantly reduced opium use, prostitution, gambling, and alcohol abuse. The antidrug drive "employed a combination of drastic criminal penalties (including execution) for major suppliers and dealers, amnesty for petty traffickers, rehabilitation for addicts, and a massive nationwide campaign of education and public 'ban opium' rallies appealing to patriotic sentiments by stressing the nineteenth century imperialistic origins of the drug problem" (Meisner 1986, 90–91). The revolution's redistribution of resources toward the poor, provision of jobs to the unemployed, assertion of Chinese nationalism in defiance of former imperialist powers, and exaltation of the roles of peasant and worker in society tended to elevate the self-esteem of many Chinese and reduce several psychological and economic causes of drug abuse.

Land redistribution reinforced support for the revolution among most poor peasants, and successful anticrime measures appealed to many urban residents. The confrontation with the United States in Korea beginning in November 1950 also strengthened the revolutionary government. "For over a century, China had been humiliated repeatedly by Western military forces, but now, for the first time, a Chinese army had defeated a Western army—and then fought the strongest military power in the world to a stalemate in a major conventional war. This event, perhaps more than any other in China's modern history, served to stimulate intense feelings of national pride and confidence among the Chinese people" (Meisner 1986, 79).

Rural Change

Mao asserted that "political power grows out of the barrel of a gun" (Mao 1965, 224). He meant that for the poor majority of the people to pursue their aspirations, the instruments of institutionalized force (army, police) must support their right to political power rather than protect the dominance of China's wealthy classes, as they had in the past. Once people no longer feared repression by warlord or GMD armies, they would feel secure in carrying out the redistribution of land they longed for (Blecher 1986; Meisner 1986).

Between 1950 and 1953 land was taken from landlords and rich peasants and distributed to the poor. But both landlords and rich peasants retained land to cultivate in approximate proportion to their percentage in the population. After land redistribution, 80 percent of the rural population were classified as middle peasants (average 2.3 acres), 5 percent as rich peasants (average 3 acres), and 15 percent as poor peasants (average 2.1 acres) (Domes 1985, 44). The continued existence of poor peasants was partly due to the lack of sufficient arable land in certain areas to permit each household a parcel large enough to provide minimum income requirements.

The land reform was economically, politically, socially, culturally, and psychologically transforming and, at times, violent. Throughout rural China villagers participated in confiscating and redistributing land. The poor were encouraged to confront landlords and express their feelings about past injustices. The process provided the poor, previously conditioned to accept subordinate status, an experience of successful use of power against the landlords who had formerly controlled their lives (Blecher 1986). Confrontations were typically explosive, with peasants "speaking bitterness" in recounting the deaths from starvation of children or other loved ones or the loss of friends or relatives in the struggles against the Japanese and the Guomindang.

Although Mao called for an end to the landlord class as an economic and political entity, he argued that landlords should not be physically eliminated, and the majority survived the land reform. But poor peasants often vented their outrage through violence. The number of landlords killed is estimated at between 0.5 and 1 million. China's 1950 population was approximately 600 million (Blecher 1986).

Many peasants could not significantly increase agricultural productivity since they lacked the resources to purchase machinery or improve irrigation systems. This led to the formation of local mutual assistance organizations (mutual aid teams) and then in the mid-1950s to the movement to combine land, livestock, and equipment to form lower-stage agricultural producers' cooperatives (LAPCs), which averaged about thirty households. In the LAPCs peasants received wages in proportion to their group-evaluated work contribution to farm production and in proportion to the amount of land and livestock and the value of equipment they contributed to the cooperative. Membership in the LAPCs was voluntary. In the late 1950s the government, encouraged by increased agricultural productivity, decreed the transition to the fully socialist, or higher-stage agricultural producers' cooperatives (HAPCs), in which all property was equally owned by participants and individuals received shares of produce and profits only in proportion to their labor as evaluated by their coworkers. Membership in the HAPCs seems to have been voluntary for many but coerced for some who had contributed the most property to the LAPCs (Blecher 1986).

Urban Change

In 1953, after the Korean conflict—in which China suffered approximately a million persons killed or wounded, including the death of one of Mao's sons—government leaders prepared to launch a rapid industrialization program. Because intense hostility existed at the time between China and the United States and most capitalist nations, the Chinese had no alternative but to rely on the Soviet Union.

The Chinese were encouraged by Russian advisers to adopt the model for industrialization that had worked for the USSR. This approach called for powerful bureaucracies to control industrialization through comprehensive central planning; for concentration of investment in heavy industry, such as steel production, rather than in the agricultural sector or consumer goods; and for obtaining financing through selling agricultural surpluses from the anticipated greater efficiency of cooperative over individual farms. The system placed economic authority primarily in the hands of technicians rather than having workers share in decision making.

During the years 1953–1957 China graduated 130,000 engineers and achieved a healthy annual growth rate of 8 percent. But Mao and others were not satisfied with this pace or with the de-emphasis on political education in favor of technical training and the low priority assigned to agricultural development. Furthermore, many of the revolutionaries whose concepts of political authority had been shaped by the popular input characteristics of the mass-line approach to leadership objected to the bureaucratic elite's monopoly on decision making. Mao and like-minded leaders decided to depart from the Stalinist model and launch a new program, the Great Leap Forward, intended to achieve more rapid growth and more worker and peasant participation in decision-making processes.

The Great Leap: 1958–1960

The new policy involved several components. First, heavy industry, light industry, and agriculture were to be developed simultaneously. Second, the distinction between urban and rural was to be minimized by locating industrial enterprises in the countryside and recruiting urban workers for periodic agricultural work. Dispersing industry to rural locations was also a way to ensure that a significant amount of industrial capacity could survive a nuclear attack on China's major cities. Third, to make up for China's deficiency in industry-building capital and equipment, the Great Leap was to substitute the resource of its vast population. It would provide jobs in new projects for the unemployed, and large numbers of women would be recruited into the labor force. Fourth, central planning was to give way to decentralization of authority to release the forces of creativity and to provide greater adaptability to local conditions and greater popular participation in policymaking.

The Great Leap also involved the shift in many rural areas from the fully socialist cooperative farms (HAPCs), which averaged about 160 households, to communes, which included several thousand households. Communes, unlike LAPCs and HAPCs, were much more than agricultural economic institutions. Many communes constructed their own industrial plants and functioned politically as local government units. The communes also provided social services such as child care, medical treatment, education, and food services (Blecher 1986).

The Great Leap registered some positive achievements. Many unemployed men, as well as many women never before in the labor force, gained jobs and a new sense of purpose. Massive improvements were made to the agricultural infrastructure, including dams and irrigation systems, and many rural industrial plants were established.

However, the negative consequences of the Great Leap seem to have outweighed the gains. The quality of the output of the rural factories was often too low to be useful. And agricultural productivity fell in part because of the reduction of material incentives. Food and important services were free in the commune system, and farming private plots for individual profit was discontinued. Moreover, the years 1959, 1960, and 1961 experienced the worst weather conditions in the century. During 1960 and 1961 food shortages contributed to a net loss in population of 20–25 million people, including deaths and deferred pregnancies (Blecher 1986; Meisner 1986). The crisis in agriculture affected industrial productivity, which decreased by 38 percent in 1961 and 17 percent in 1962.

Economic deterioration also resulted from the cutoff of Soviet economic and technical assistance ordered by Premier Krushchev. This signaled the beginning of more than two decades of hostility between the USSR and China. The antagonisms preceding the break included Soviet displeasure with Chinese abandonment of the Russian model of development and with the disruptive policies of the Great Leap, and Chinese criticisms of the elite Soviet political system and aspects of Soviet foreign policy. The suspension of Soviet aid not only halted dozens of industrial construction projects but also forced the shutdown of several existing power and industrial plants because of the lack of replacement parts for Russian-made machinery.

Retreat from the Great Leap: 1961–1965

To bring about economic recovery, the government increased centralized economic planning, canceled costly construction projects, and reduced the size of communes. Peasants were again allowed to cultivate their own private plots in addition to farming collectively. In both agriculture and industry, material incentives were increased. Worker participation in management was curtailed, and power was restored to factory managers (Blecher 1986; Meisner 1986).

The shift toward concentrating power in government and party bureaucracies and the emphasis on material incentives versus revolutionary idealism provoked Mao and other leftists. Prior to the 1960s Mao seemed to hold that any resurgence of capitalist traits was due to lingering feudalistic and capitalistic cultural values and that these would gradually erode as collective ownership strengthened socialist culture.

But in the early 1960s Mao formulated a new theory about the reemergence of capitalist traits. He said that in any social system that allowed one population element to become specialized in the function of exercising power, "capitalist tendencies" would begin to emerge. Greater power would lead to feelings of superiority, the desire for and rationalization of having a higher standard of living than others, and the development of mechanisms, such as elitist schools for the children of power holders, to perpetuate the concentration of power in the hands of certain groups and families, which could come to constitute a new ruling class. Unlike traditional Marxist thinking, Mao was arguing that changing the nature of the economic system did not preclude, even after some lengthy period of time, the reemergence of capitalism because such a phenomenon would be fostered whenever power differentiation occurred. In other words, he located the material basis for capitalist tendencies "not in *property* relations . . . but in *political* relations between leaders and masses" (Blecher 1986, 78; emphasis in original). He stated, therefore, that the people must be constantly ready to mount mass movements to prevent the domination of new privileged classes and to redistribute power.

These propositions constituted Mao's theory of the need for permanent revolution (Blecher 1986; Mackerras and Knight 1985). Such mass movements would, like China's communist revolution, involve the combination of leftist revolutionary intellectuals and the masses. In the mid-1960s Mao and others attempted to rally the masses against those perceived to be seeking power and privilege, including much of the bureaucratic elite of the government and the Communist Party. The occurrence of a mass movement inspired by the leader of a communist revolution against the party elite in the post-revolutionary period was unique. The Chinese refer to it as the Great Proletarian Cultural Revolution.

THE GREAT PROLETARIAN CULTURAL REVOLUTION: 1966–1968

A stated objective of the Cultural Revolution was to redistribute power to the people. Concentration of power in institutional elites was viewed as characteristic of both US capitalist society and the Soviet system. The worst offenders were to be removed from their positions and assigned employment at manual labor jobs. All persons in nonmanual occupations were in the future expected to also perform manual labor part of the time in order to maintain an appreciation of that form of work and to identify with workers and peasants. Wage differentials were to be reduced and rural development projects reemphasized lest China develop parasitic urban centers exploiting the surrounding countryside.

In early 1965 Mao began explaining the need for a cultural revolution in which leftist intellectuals would work through literature and the arts to erode the harmful residue of bourgeois culture and more rapidly develop cultural elements congruent with socialism and the future communist stage of society (Blecher 1986). The new culture was to generate a new psychology, or consciousness, favorable to the development of communist economic and social relations even before the advanced technology and material wealth assumed by Marx to be necessary conditions for communism existed (Meisner 1986).

The movement developed after a series of exchanges among leftist and rightist intellectuals over a play that focused on domineering officials and victimized peasants in a much earlier era in Chinese history. Many viewed this play as criticizing Mao's Great Leap for rearranging the lives of the rural population. "A radical Beijing University philosophy instructor . . . denounced the university president" for attempting to suppress leftist criticism and called "upon students and intellectuals to join the battle" against rightists (Blecher 1986, 82). Students and faculty entered the conflict. Mao sided with the philosophy instructor and had his arguments broadcast throughout the nation. Inspired students organized Red Guard committees to begin movements in their cities against rightists in positions of authority.

Often Red Guards would lead huge crowds in a march to a particular site, for example, the local Communist Party headquarters, and demand the presence of guilty officials, who would then be subjected to public criticism. The charges might include self-enrichment, acting in "antidemocratic" ways, advocating material incentives, or other practices that reflected the "capitalist road" to economic development. Between 700,000 and 800,000 officials reportedly lost their positions during 1966–1968.

In late 1966 factions developed among Red Guard members over issues such as whether particular sets of officials should be attacked or defended. And in 1967 violent conflicts broke out in a number of locales between movement supporters and opponents, and in some places among rival Red Guard factions. Mao called on the People's Liberation Army to restore order. He stated that "capitalist roaders" constituted only a minority among the Communist Party's leadership. Estimates of deaths in the turbulent 1966–1968 period as a result of fighting, Red Guard persecution, and army actions range from 40,000 to 400,000 (Blecher 1986; Meisner 1986).

After 1968, the turmoil subsided, but the movement had widespread influence until the mid-1970s. Several top Chinese leaders died around then, including Mao, on September 8, 1976. A month later, on October 6, Hua Guofeng (Hua Kuo-feng), premier and party chairman, while professing support for the Cultural Revolution, had four top leftist leaders (the so-called Gang of Four), including Mao's wife, arrested on charges of "trying to foment civil war by allegedly arming the Shanghai militia and planning an attack on the organs of state" (Blecher 1986, 90). Hua's efforts to work out a compromise between left (Maoist) and right factions in the Communist Party failed, and the right wing won control of the party central committee in December 1978. The leader of the right-wing faction, Deng Xiaoping (Teng Hsiao-p'ing), became vice premier and head of the party committee that oversaw the armed forces (Blecher 1986; Domes 1985).

POST-1978 REFORMS

Prominent Maoists were demoted, and many persons removed from their positions during the Cultural Revolution were rehabilitated. Mao was accused of errors, such as unsound plans during the Great Leap and his role in the Great Proletarian Cultural Revolution. But he was still officially recognized as "a great Marxist and a great proletarian revolutionary" whose "contributions to the Chinese Revolution far outweigh his mistakes" (Blecher 1986, 92).

The Cultural Revolution was interpreted by the new leadership as largely a catastrophe. Although the movement brought some redistribution of education, health care, and industrial resources to rural areas, lasting democratization of political and workplace authority structures was not achieved (Meisner 1986). Economic development stagnated because of conflict, interruption of the educational system that reduced output of new engineers and other skilled professionals, and the large number of incompetent administrators recruited when emphasis was on loyalty to Mao's ideas rather than on expertise (Blecher 1986; Domes 1985).

Changes in the 1980s to increase productivity included greater reliance on material incentives and legalizing small-scale private businesses such as restaurants, clothing manufacture and sales, and transport services. Decollectivization permitted individuals to withdraw from cooperative farming by leasing land parcels from the cooperatives. The leasing party would then farm independently, being allowed to keep profits (the farmer had to sell a quota of crops to the state at a fixed price but could sell the surplus beyond the quota at market prices).

Reforms to state-owned industries included allowing them to "produce for the market demand as long as they fulfilled the assigned state quota . . . purchase needed raw material through the market, rather than remaining dependent on central allocation . . . [and allowing that] prices for the products . . . be set by the supply and demand mechanism" (Theen and Wilson 1986, 448). Another important innovation involved allowing foreign corporations to build plants in specific restricted-access sites inside China called special economic zones (SEZs). In 1989, 450 US corporations were involved in joint ventures with the Chinese government, including projects such as aircraft assembly, nuclear power plants, and coal mining (CNN, May 24, 1989). Renewed emphasis was placed on higher education and technical training and on obtaining technology and scientific knowledge from advanced industrial nations. To this end, tens of thousands of Chinese students were allowed to go to the United States, Japan, and other nations for graduate school.

China's politics were reshaped by the 1982 constitution, which shifted citizen political participation away from mass movements (viewed by the post-Mao leadership as potentially too disruptive) and toward representative governmental mechanisms. Although the Communist Party remained dominant, under the new constitution citizens voted for representatives to local assemblies in multicandidate elections. Those elected voted in turn for the next level of officials. This process continued up to the national level. China's post-Mao leadership hoped that under the reforms "some will get rich faster so that all may get rich" (Schell 1985, 16) and that individual initiative and effort would be maximized within an essentially socialist framework (Blecher 1986; Mackerras and Knight 1985; Meisner 1986).

THE 1989 PRO-DEMOCRACY DEMONSTRATIONS

Changes in China's political system were insufficient to satisfy demands for greater democracy in the late 1980s. Among factors leading to the movement for more political freedom were the historic desire of Chinese intellectuals for a genuinely democratic political system, the increase in freedom of initiative in the economic system, higher levels of cultural contact with societies that have relatively open political expression, and the example of Gorbachev's democratizing reforms in the USSR. Economic progress and relaxation of international tensions also reduced public perception of the need for an authoritarian regime. The Communist Party had lost prestige because of the failure of a number of its pre-1980s programs and allegations of corruption of some party and government officials (Kristof 1989). And many people believed greater freedom and political participation were necessary for technological modernization.

Pro-democracy protests began in April 1989 (*New York Times*, May 20, 1989, 6). On April 15 Hu Yaobang, the ousted Communist Party leader who had advocated reforms to bring about greater freedom of expression, died. Beijing University students put up posters praising him and criticizing party and government officials who had forced his resignation after blaming him for fomenting student demonstrations in 1986 and 1987. On April 17 thousands of students marched in Beijing and Shanghai, chanting the slogan "Long live Hu Yaobang! Long live democracy!" Students began a boycott of classes at Beijing universities and demanded a dialogue with government officials concerning further democratization.

On May 4 tens of thousands marched in Beijing and other cities to commemorate the anniversary of China's first modern student demonstration in 1919. On May 13, 2,000 students began a hunger strike in Tiananmen Square in Beijing, asking for increased political and media freedom. Within a few days, hundreds of thousands, including journalists, intellectuals, and workers, joined the protestors, who appeared to enjoy widespread sympathy in urban areas and even some support among party, government, and military leaders.

The majority of China's leaders, however, were unwilling to grant all demands. After unarmed police and soldiers failed to clear Tiananmen Square, heavily armed troops, untrained for dealing with civilian protests, brutally repressed the demonstrators. At a minimum, hundreds were killed, mainly nonstudent residents of the city attempting to block the advance of troops in the streets leading to Tiananmen Square. In the weeks following the June 3 crackdown, thousands were arrested. Several high-ranking officials accused of encouraging pro-democracy activism were demoted. The government also enacted measures intended to heighten political loyalty and intensify student social bonds with the working class, peasants, and the People's Liberation Army. These included more political education in the universities and the requirement that students spend at least one year working at manual labor jobs. Egalitarian ideals championed by Mao were again emphasized.

The suppression of pro-democracy activists was in part a reaction to the dangers many Communist Party leaders perceived in the movement. They feared that the conflicts and uncertainties resulting from a rapid transition to full democracy could lead to a Chinese government too weak and divided to defend against economic exploitation by other nations, resulting in a new era of subservience and humiliation by imperialist powers. Some party officials complained that many student activists were overly concerned with personal gain and with attaining lifestyles like the affluent classes of Western nations at the expense of the peasant and worker majority. Finally, government and party leaders who had been victims of the Great Proletarian Cultural Revolution feared the spread of a new, uncontrolled mass social movement that might cost them their positions and again plunge the nation into social chaos, conflict, and economic disruption.

The weaknesses of the pro-democracy movement were the opposite of several strengths of the earlier communist-led revolution. Although in 1989 over 70 percent of China's people lived in the rural areas where Mao's revolution had thrived, the pro-democracy movement was mainly urban based. Its core constituency was highly educated young persons, an elite sector of the population whose goals movement opponents could portray to the larger public as reforms that would mainly benefit an already advantaged minority to the detriment of the majority's well-being. Furthermore, nationalism was employed to mobilize public opinion against pro-democracy activists instead of operating in support of the movement as had been the case in the communist-led revolution. Antimovement government officials depicted the most radical activists as foreign inspired and argued that rapid, unconditional democratization would leave the country, while still relatively underdeveloped economically, too divided politically to resist domination by Western nations and Japan.

China's Economic and Political Systems in the 1990s

Between 1982 and the mid-1990s real wages in China approximately doubled (Yabuki 1995). Economic progress was greater in coastal areas than in inland provinces, which tended to increase regional inequalities and promote migration to certain urban areas. Observers noted that China's development policies of fostering private enterprise, maintaining a leading role for the state in economic planning and coordination, and a disciplined, one-party political system characterized by a gradual democratization process seemed to resemble past development programs pursued by US-supported Asian success stories such as Taiwan, Hong Kong, Singapore, South Korea, and post–World War II Japan (Overholt 1993; Ross 1994; Yabuki 1995).

Since the creation of non-state-owned economic enterprises, the share of China's gross national product (GNP) generated by the state sector declined between 1978 and 1992 from 56 percent to less than 40 percent. The share of collectively owned enterprises (those owned by town or village residents or by groups of people in urban areas) climbed from 42 percent to 50 percent. The share contributed by private businesses and joint ventures (corporations with stock owned partly by the Chinese government and partly by foreign companies) rose from 2 percent to 10 percent (Yabuki 1995; Zhang 1994). By the mid-1990s, the prices of most consumer goods (with exceptions such as medicines and salt) were set by market forces. And from the late 1970s to the early 1990s the percentage of self-employed and private businesspeople rose from .04 percent to 3.7 percent (Zhang 1994). The Chinese government appeared committed to revitalizing rather than privatizing major state industries (*New York Times*, June 18, 1995, 8; Ross 1994).

China's Economic Success Relative to the Former USSR

China's economy made impressive gains during the 1990s. In contrast, Russia was plagued by economic difficulties, organized crime in thousands of supposedly legitimate businesses, and gigantic levels of corruption. Differences in both political and economic policies between China and Russia apparently contributed to the divergent outcomes. In terms of economic policies, social and economic scientists (Overholt 1993; Yabuki 1995; Zhang 1994) concluded that China's decisions were superior in terms of timing, order, and perhaps dimension of reforms in comparison to Russia's. China determined to change economic policies gradually and piece by piece and to reflect cautiously on past performance before deciding on where, when, and how to make the next change. Russia's initial postcommunist leaders, in contrast, allegedly advised by US professors (Overholt 1993), attempted to employ economic shock therapy characterized by multiple, near-simultaneous changes, often with catastrophic results.

Another major difference was the order of changes. Chinese policy involved first altering areas of the economy where simple and relatively inexpensive changes were likely to produce large, rapid gains, leaving more complex, difficult issues for later evaluation. In China, the private enterprise option was first introduced in agriculture, thereby allowing farmers to cultivate for private profit. This quickly improved productivity, income, and lifestyle for hundreds of millions of farmers. Next, profit-oriented, small- and medium-size enterprises in the areas of service and light industry were permitted, again resulting in rapid productivity and income gains. The Chinese also developed infrastructures for a privatized economy, in particular stock markets where investors could purchase shares of ownership of companies, a seemingly logical step before considering the sale of state-owned industries.

Whereas there were fewer than 5,000 foreign-affiliated businesses in China in 1987, there were almost 50,000 by 1992. Just over 16 percent were totally foreign owned, compared to near zero in 1987 (Yabuki 1995).

Russia, in contrast, tended to avoid agricultural reforms, waffled over large-scale foreign investments (nationalists in the Russian parliament opposed increased foreign control over the economy), and rapidly privatized a number of large state-owned industries, which often required significant infusions of capital for technological updating, with any substantial economic gains years off. In the meantime, tens of thousands of workers faced layoffs, contributing to declining social morale, growing inequality, drug use, and street and organized crime. Furthermore, the disrupted supply and rising prices of critical materials produced by newly privatized industries contributed to the failure of many other businesses and to the deterioration of Russia's agricultural sector, which suffered substantially from the loss of machinery and fertilizers previously provided by the state.

Politically, a major difference was the level and point in time of democratization relative to economic reform. Gorbachev attempted to fully democratize the political system in the USSR and Russia before economic reforms. Some believed this was necessary for economic reforms to succeed, a somewhat dubious notion given the impressive economic performance of capitalist Singapore, Taiwan, and South Korea, which developed under authoritarian political systems.

In Russia, democracy allowed nationalistic tensions to destroy the USSR and its system of economic integration of industries and resources. This caused massive disruption in new nations that had been republics of the USSR and provided huge opportunities for organized crime smuggling operations to satisfy supply demands across borders and avoid arrest by taking advantage of new international boundaries and divisions in police jurisdiction.

China, however, opted to maintain a one-party state. Or as Deng, a leader of China's economic reform program put it, to achieve economic development by adhering to the Four Cardinal Principles: (1) maintain the political system that puts the interests of the worker-peasant majority first—the people's democratic dicta-torship; (2) maintain the political leadership of the Communist Party; (3) adhere to Marxist-Leninist-Maoist thought; and (4) pursue the socialist road to develop-ment (Fewsmith 1994). The potential advantages of a one-party system, assuming a party leadership genuinely committed to the welfare of the majority of China's people, theoretically include: maintaining a strong, united state capable of prevent-ing the type of social chaos that ensued from Russia's economic reforms; planning and carrying out economic change in a cautious, integrated way; and countering economic, diplomatic, or covert measures by foreign powers aimed at weakening China or generating internal conflict.

Another major political strategy of Deng and his associates was to carry out economic and other reforms in ways that built or reinforced popular support for reform policies (Overholt 1993). This meant a process of modernization and change through consensus building rather than one that, in trying to do many things at once, risked alienating large population segments from the government. Thus, once agricultural reforms had succeeded in substantially raising income for almost 800 million rural Chinese, the government, enjoying their support, could move se-curely to the next phase of reform.

Deng and associates viewed economic failure as the central cause of the collapse of the European Communist Party states, and they believed that economic growth was necessary to the survival of a socialist system, at least during periods when citizens feel free from major external threats. An implication is that, following suc-cessful economic development, popular support might sustain the Chinese Com-munist Party, even in a more democratic political system.

China's Progress, Problems, Policies, and Plans for the Future
Economic Growth, Population Structure, and Energy Needs

Since the start of major economic reforms, China's gross domestic product (GDP) growth averaged about 9–10 percent per year, though by 2012 this had slowed to around 7.8 percent (CIA 2014a). China is now the third largest economy in the world in terms of purchasing power parity after the European Union and the United States. GDP per capita rose from about $1,071 in 1978 to $9,300 in 2012. One aspect of China's development program was to limit population growth through requiring couples to have only one child. But now the country's total fertility rate is falling be-low that required to maintain its population. This means that the percentage of the population made up of older, retired persons who need disproportionate levels of medical care will increase, while the proportion of active workers and primary tax-payers will decrease, thus putting a drain on the economy and government funds unless the trend is reversed (Menon 2009). At the third plenary session of the Communist Party of China's central committee in November of 2013, it was decided that the policy would be changed by allowing couples to have two children if one of the parents is an only child (Qiang 2013).

China's spectacular economic progress has been based primarily on its expanding "vast and diverse manufacturing sector" (Sharma 2006, 170). By 2006, China was consuming about one-third of the world's steel and close to half of the world's cement. China's growth drastically increased its demand for energy. The projected increase in use of its abundant coal resources poses the threat of environmental hazards unless technologies for reducing pollutants from coal are widely employed (Klare 2006). In 2008 China surpassed the United States as the biggest emitter of carbon dioxide, although "on a per capita basis, US power-sector emissions are still nearly four times those of China" (Center for Global Development 2008). In 2013, only 1 percent of people living in urban areas breathed air that met European Union standards (Shapiro 2013), and several major Chinese cities such as Beijing and Harbin experienced dangerously high levels of air pollution (Reuters 2013). Shapiro (2013) reported that 500 million Chinese did not have access to safe drinking water. In response to the enormous environmental problems, Chinese citizens have organized thousands of groups that investigate the level and causes environmental damage, identify companies responsible (including foreign corporations), and provide this and related information to the Chinese people and the world. In some cases, these efforts have led to government action or international consumer protests that prompted domestic and foreign companies to reduce the release of toxins into the environment.

In 2006, 70 percent of China's energy needs were met by coal, 20 percent by oil, and the rest from other sources (US Energy Administration Information 2009). But oil consumption was dramatically increasing. Until 1993 China produced enough to satisfy its needs. By 2010 it was importing about half the oil it consumed (*People's Daily Online*, April 20, 2010). China obtained oil from Indonesia, Yemen, Oman, Angola, Sudan, Republic of the Congo (Vines 2007), Iraq (*China Digital Times*, June 10, 2010), Saudi Arabia, Iran, and Russia, and has entered into agreements to explore for and extract oil reserves in Venezuela and coastal Cuba (Hennock 2005).

In return for oil and other resources from African countries, such as uranium from Niger, copper from Zambia, and raw wood from the Republic of the Congo, China has provided long-term loans, becoming in 2006 a bigger lender to Africa than the World Bank (Vines 2007, 218), and infrastructure construction such as apartment buildings, highways, water systems, sports facilities, and airports (Finan 2010). In Latin America, China or its companies loaned Argentina $10 billion and invested $8 billion in Bolivia for highway and rail construction (Gallagher 2010, 50–51). In 2008 Brazil and Argentina sent, respectively, about 50 percent and

75 percent of their soy exports to China. And in 2010 Venezuela began shipping 600,000 barrels of oil per day to China in exchange for Chinese investment in energy resources production and mining (Gallagher 2010, 50). Although China has become an important market for Latin American energy, mineral, and agricultural exports, it has damaged the industrial sector by providing manufactured products that out-compete with the region's companies (Gallagher 2010, 52). Gallagher argues that Latin America would benefit more from its relationship with China if trade agreements involved China sharing technology and collaborating on research and technological development.

Corruption

China's economic liberalization was accompanied by a surge in corruption afflicting almost all transitions to market economies (Sun 2005, 257). Corruption interfered with development, infuriated millions, and "cast doubt on the neoliberal logic" (Sun 2005, 257). Corruption-related losses to state revenue may have amounted to 4 percent of GDP and capital flight to about 2 percent of GDP in the early twenty-first century (Sun 2005, 258). Yet China "has avoided the most destructive kinds of corruption at the national level": kleptocracy, in which a national leader uses his power for personal material gain, and bilateral monopoly, in which the ruler and "a few private interests share in the spoils" (Sun 2005, 259). According to Sun, bilateral monopoly corruption characterized the Yeltsin government in Russia and a number of Yeltsin's associates became economic oligarchs. In contrast, China's leadership at the national level has been relatively free from this type of corruption.

The most serious corruption generally occurred at the lower level of provincial government, especially in remote areas less closely monitored by the central government. A number of corrupt officials were imprisoned and some executed. The dominant form of corruption was what Sun called competitive corruption, in which a businessman offers someone, often a lower-level state official, a bribe to secure a business contract, a loan, access to markets, tax breaks, or regulatory influence (Sun 2005, 259–260). But extortion, common in post-Soviet Russia, appeared rare in China. New Left intellectuals and political leaders in China believe that strengthening the power of the central state is the best way to combat corruption spawned by neoliberal economic policies. Besides corruption, China's New Left is concerned with growing economic inequality, the erosion of socialist values (Fewsmith 2012), and an unacceptable social gap between the people and the political leadership.

One astounding corruption case involved Bo Xilai, a charismatic former head of the Communist Party in the southwestern city of Chongqing and a member of the country's twenty-five-member politburo (BBC 2013). After Bo led an impressive campaign against organized crime in the city, the city's police chief revealed evidence that Bo's wife, Gu Kailai, had murdered a British businessman over a financial dispute. The following investigations reportedly indicated that Bo, while not accused of involvement in the murder, was guilty of accepting bribes and abusing his power by trying to cover up his wife's crime.

One form of organized crime in China is human trafficking. In September 2013, for example, Chinese police rescued 92 abducted children and detained 301 persons in eleven provinces (Al Jazeera 2013). Police stated that they rescued over 13,000 abducted children in 2011 and about 23,000 women between 2011 and 2013.

Inequality, Poverty, the Nature of Protests, and Government Response
China's economic growth was accompanied by rising inequality between cities and rural areas, among regions, and among citizens. In 2012, urban households had incomes on average three to four times those of rural households (Whyte 2012). As many as 251 Chinese had become billionaires (in US$) by 2012 (Bloomberg News 2012), and one million or more millionaires (Whyte 2012). And many of the richest people in the country were or became members of the Communist Party. Whyte (2012) stated that in 1976, the year Mao died, the Gini coefficient of income inequality for China (ranging from 0 for total equality of income to 1 for total inequality: one person has all the income) was about .30. But the Gini coefficient rose to around .47 in 2012 (CIA 2014a), slightly higher than the Gini coefficient of .45 for the United States in 2007 (CIA 2014b). Yet Whyte (2012) reported that many Chinese view contemporary Chinese society as fairer than before the 1978 economic reforms because individuals have much greater freedom of movement geographically (e.g., increased freedom to leave their village of birth) and economically.

But as inequality increased, absolute poverty—in terms of people lacking basic minimum physical and service requirements—declined. According to Sharma (2006, 172), the proportion of China's population living in poverty in 1981 was 53 percent. But in 2011, less than 14 percent of the population was below the poverty income line (CIA 2014a). And China's middle class has been growing both because of the country's economic growth and because of greatly expanded opportunities for higher education (Whyte 2012). Whyte reported that social surveys conducted nationally in China indicate that a majority of Chinese believe that hard work, talent, and education can bring success in today's China and feel optimistic about their futures.

Walder (2009, 262–263) notes that protest movements in China in the 1980s involved mainly students, educated young people, and some intellectuals. They targeted the national leadership with demands for liberalization of the political system and freedom of the press.

In contrast, since around 1995, apart from student demonstrations against the actions of foreign powers, many protests have involved farmers and blue-collar workers. Their grievances were linked to the shift to a profit-driven economy, including the collusion of bribed local officials and business persons. Complaints included the confiscation of land or homes with inadequate compensation to make way for development projects, nonpayment of pensions or compensatory funds to workers laid off from downsized or privatized state companies, excessive local taxes, and pollution. The protestors typically appealed to the national government for help, justice, and enforcement of laws in dealing with the incompetence, unfairness, and/ or corruption of local officials or businesses. This wave of worker and farmer protests, nearly 80,000 events in 2005 alone (Walder 2009, 262), prompted comprehensive central government responses (Dickson, Gilley, Goldman, and Yang 2007). These included efforts to crack down on corruption, ensure adequate compensation for confiscated property, and provide help for laid-off workers. In rural areas local school system debts were eradicated and children guaranteed nine years of free schooling. An income subsidy was provided for rural workers and the agricultural tax was abolished (except for tobacco), measures intended to slow migration to the cities. However, there were still over 100,000 protests with more than 100 participants annually in recent years (Li and McElveen 2013).

Li and McElveen's (2013) analysis of the 85 million member Communist Party of China (Bloomberg News 2013) indicates that there are two broad coalitions within the party referred to as the elitists and the populists. They describe the top leaders of the elitist coalition as including persons who are the children of veterans of the Chinese revolution or high-ranking party or government officials. Many began their political careers in the developing coastal cities. Politically and economically, the elitist coalition tends to champion the interests of business leaders, especially those involved in state-owned enterprises, and the majority in the growing middle class. The populist coalition, in comparison, includes leaders from less prestigious families who started their careers in less developed inland areas. Many of these persons had once been leaders in the Communist Youth League and are also known as the League Faction. The populist coalition tends to represent the interests of less powerful social categories such as the poor, farmers, and migrant workers. Li and McElveen (2013) claim that there is a balance of power between these two coalitions. Party policy reflects competition and compromise between the elitists and populists.

Party leaders in 2013 stated that freedom of movement from the countryside will increase because restrictions on rural migration to many towns and smaller cities would be abolished and be eased for medium size cities (Qiang 2013). This will make it much easier for rural migrants to get health care and educational services in urban areas (Schiavenzadec 2013). But the population size of large cities will still be strictly controlled. Party leaders also decided that state-owned companies would allow private investors to acquire up to 15 percent ownership and use more of company profits to fund social welfare programs.

Democracy and Human Rights

Since 1988 China has mandated that individual villages hold direct elections every three years for village committees, which have the power to determine local issues such as land rights (Luard 2005). But direct voting for officials was not extended to higher levels of government. The government censored the Internet, even forcing US Internet service providers to assist in filtering material (Dickson, Gilley, Goldman, and Yang 2007, 249). In 2010 Google rebelled against this process (Barboza and Helft 2010). The political system lacks the level of freedom identified as a human right in Western capitalist democracies. But Chinese leaders emphasize benefits they view as essential economic human rights that they accuse capitalist-oriented governments of relegating to market forces, both domestically and internationally. Charles Tang, head of the Brazil-China Chamber of Commerce, stated: "The Chinese government has achieved the greatest victory in the history of human rights. It has removed 400 million Chinese people from poverty and enabled them to live with dignity and take part in economic life. That is the true measure of human rights" (Hawksley 2006, 4).

As Jeffrey Wasserstrom (2001) notes, people's view of human rights is shaped by their experience and their knowledge (or ignorance) of history. When Western leaders discuss human rights abuses in China, they generally refer to restrictions on political activities. But from the official Chinese point of view, the massive human rights abuses by foreign powers dwarf limitations on politics. The British victory in the Opium Wars is blamed for the spread of opium addiction to tens of millions. The multinational Boxer Protocol, the military mop-up campaign that followed the defeat of the Boxer Rebellion in 1901, reportedly involved many killings, rapes, and lootings. And the Japanese invasion and occupation during the 1930s and the first half of the 1940s inflicted massive atrocities. Chinese leaders credit the revolution and its communist leadership with freeing people from the abuses of foreign aggression and exploitation and, despite sometimes disastrous mistakes, eventually lifting the large majority out of dire poverty. Thus Wasserstrom suggests a history-driven human rights policy (2001, 267). Such an approach might advance human rights by acknowledging all past human rights abuses, including those by Western and other foreign powers, and by recognizing China's achievements in dealing with certain human rights issues, such as the harmful aspects of imperialism. Then the quest for human rights could proceed in an atmosphere of historical integrity and be more effective than a Western-biased approach that might be viewed as hypocritical and/or racist.

Future Political Change: Conditioning Factors

According to Tim Luard (2005, 5), "former Chinese leader Deng Xiaoping was quoted as saying there would be national elections in 50 years—by 2037." Wasserstrom (2002) identified several factors that affect the pace of political change and the forms it may take. China's immense size makes the organization of a nationwide antigovernment movement difficult as long as "factional disputes within the top leadership are kept under control," relatively good cooperation exists between civilian and military leadership and between the central and provincial governments, and "the flow of information through systems of mass communication is tightly held" by the central government (2002, 258). Wasserstrom stated that the Chinese government has been relatively tolerant of local protests but has "been ruthless toward anything that seems to have the potential to provide an organizational framework for collective action by people from different regions and walks of life."

One reason for the legitimacy of Communist Party rule among wide sectors of the population is the relatively strong link between patriotism and communism in that "the Chinese Communist Party has a historical record of anti-imperialist accomplishment" and national liberation (Wasserstrom 2002, 258).

Another reason for the preservation of Communist Party rule in China is that Chinese leaders learned from the failed East European communist states the importance of increasing consumer goods, reducing government intrusiveness, and launching high-profile anticorruption campaigns (Wasserstrom 2002, 258).

Political change in China is also inhibited by an awareness of the serious problems that have afflicted a number of postcommunist countries: declining life span, rising rates of organized crime and homicide, drug use, prostitution, damaging forms of corruption, ethnic strife, and terrorism, along with deteriorating health care and social services—all while a tiny minority grows enormously wealthy. Some postcommunist states became "harsh dictatorships or deeply corrupt and illiberal regimes" (Walder 2009, 260). Some experienced brutal civil wars. The Soviet Union and Yugoslavia disintegrated. These events demonstrated negative consequences of shifting rapidly to an alternate political system and diminished the appeal of multiparty democracy as a form of government to cope with China's problems and ensure continued economic development. Gilley's study of perceived state legitimacy between 1998 and 2002 in seventy-two countries—based on factors such as opinion surveys, political violence, voting, and paying taxes—indicated that China had an overall ranking of thirteenth, ahead of France and Australia (Dickson, Gilley, Goldman, and Yang 2007, 245–246).

Walder (2009, 257–258) notes the current generation "feels China's rise and the national pride that comes with it." And the leaders of China's Communist Party "are fundamentally united about the direction the country should take," namely, continue the blend of Communist Party rule, strong state guidance of the economy, market reform, international economic activity, and limited political liberalization (Walder 2009, 258, 260, 262).

Dickson (Dickson, Gilley, Goldman, and Yang 2007) states that the growing Chinese middle class and business entrepreneurs, among the main beneficiaries of the Communist Party's economic policies, do not seem to be pushing hard for democracy. Walder (2009, 263) concludes that the Chinese government has more popular support and stability now than during the first ten years of economic reform. He believes that at present "popular protest is mostly creating pressure on China's government to create new institutions that fairly adjudicate the conflicts" and that political change will be gradual.

Summary and Analysis

Several factors contributed to rising discontent among China's peasants during the late nineteenth and early twentieth centuries, including massive population growth, intense poverty, and humiliating military defeats and exploitation by foreign powers. Impoverished millions, culturally inclined to rebellion as a means of expressing outrage, were attracted to communist plans for land redistribution and formed the basis of the peasant revolution.

Two types of revolutionary elites created the republican movements of the early twentieth century: the relatively conservative leadership of the GMD and the more radical leadership of the Communist Party. Most of these individuals came from the upper 10 percent of China's population and had achieved a relatively high degree of education. GMD leaders were drawn largely from the business classes of the coastal cities and often had considerable contact with Western culture and economic interests. The leadership of the Communist Party tended to emerge from the radicalized children of rich peasants and landlords. Ideologically, these two sets of leaders developed strikingly different interpretations of Sun's Three Principles of the People. The main point of contention was the meaning of the third principle, people's livelihood. For GMD leaders who relied on the backing of merchants, foreign business interests, and rural landlords, people's livelihood could not mean a substantial redistribution of wealth toward the poor.

The GMD's failure to implement meaningful economic reform after the death of Sun not only alienated the impoverished majority but also affected its ability to fulfill the first and second of Sun's principles, independence and democracy. Failing to carry out significant land reform and consequently forced to repress popular aspirations, the GMD became a conservative military dictatorship exercising power through force of arms and a one-party government. The GMD reliance on weapons and other assistance from Western nations compromised its claims to nationalism.

After the Manchus abdicated in 1911 and the military dictator Yuan died in 1916, China dissolved into separate provinces ruled by warlords. Although China had no central government control until 1927, conservative province-level governments and armed forces remained. Jiang and the GMD unified most of China through military force as well as financial, political, and military favors to warlords, landlords, and urban merchants and other businessmen, domestic and foreign. The primary limitations on state power were a lack of sufficient resources and a lack of coordination among anti-revolutionary military commanders to crush insurgency in the countryside and later the inability to resist the Japanese invaders. Because the GMD state, with its armed forces and allied provincial governments and warlord armies, was relatively strong in the 1920s and 1930s, communist revolutionaries were defeated in urban areas, unlike their Russian predecessors, and turned to organizing a peasant-based rural revolution.

Other nations did not directly intervene in China to stop the revolution. Their role was largely limited to providing weapons and advisers to Jiang's GMD forces. The Japanese invaded China to conquer it, but not specifically to prevent a revolution. After Japan was defeated, a war-weary world was loath to intervene in an internal conflict among 600 million Chinese.

By advocating the redistribution of landlord property, communists took advantage of the lack of GMD land reform to attract peasants to their cause. Although this policy received an enthusiastic response from many, an additional powerful cause for peasant support and a more general unifying motivation for the participation of other groups in the revolution was the nationalism inspired by the Japanese invasion. The Japanese attack reduced Jiang's ability to combat communist rebels and provided an opportunity for communist forces to display their nationalist commitment. Jiang's armies generally performed poorly against the Japanese and often retreated. In contrast, the communist forces in north China organized an effective peasant-based guerrilla war against the Japanese and Chinese collaborators, often pro-GMD landlords and merchants, and largely isolated them in cities. After the Japanese withdrew, the combination of the communists' proven nationalist fervor and their program for wealth redistribution resulted in a mounting tide of popular support. This support facilitated the relatively quick defeat of the GMD, and the People's Republic of China was established on October 1, 1949.

Subsequently China collectivized its agricultural, industrial, and commercial systems. After Mao died in 1976, China's new leaders embarked on a policy of economic reform, including the personal responsibility system and market socialism. Innovations involved allowing farmers to cultivate land for personal profit at prices set by market demand (once state quotas were met), permitting privately owned businesses, and allowing state-controlled foreign investment.

The economic reforms and related government policies unleashed spectacular economic growth. As China's economy rapidly expanded, so did its need for energy, and after 1993 China dramatically increased oil imports. The booming economy permitted some citizens to become enormously rich while drastically reducing the percentage of the country's people living in poverty. It also led to major environmental problems.

Partly because China has made enormous economic progress and has improved the lives of the large majority of its people, the government appears to enjoy significantly more popular support currently than it did in the late 1980s. Contemporary public protests center on issues that have arisen from economic reforms or have resulted from the accompanying excesses and corruption. Many demonstrators appeal to national officials for help in combating local problems, and in recent years the central government has responded with policies to address some of their major concerns, like improving conditions for people migrating from rural areas to cities and reducing air and water pollution. Political change in China, including democratization, appears to be an ongoing but long-term process.

CHINESE REVOLUTION: CHRONOLOGY OF MAJOR EVENTS

1839–1842 Opium War, resulting in British victory; beginning of Chinese subjugation to foreign economic and political interests

1851–1864 Taiping Rebellion

1911 Republican revolution, led by Sun

1912 Sun organizes republican revolutionary groups into the Guomindang (GMD) Party

1921 Formation of the Chinese Communist Party

1925 Sun dies

1926 Guomindang armies under General Jiang launch campaign to subdue warlords and unify China

1927 Jiang attacks communists, precipitating a new civil war

1934–1935 Communist forces retreat in the Long March; Mao, advocate of a peasant-based revolution, becomes the dominant communist leader

1937–1945 The Guomindang and the communists halt civil war and form an alliance to fight Japanese invaders

1947–1949 Civil war resumes; communists win

1958–1960 Great Leap Forward

1966–1968 Great Proletarian Cultural Revolution

1976 Mao dies

1978 Shift in Communist Party leadership followed by major changes in economic policy

1989 Pro-democracy movement develops and is suppressed

1994 China's dramatic economic growth drastically increases its demand for energy; China begins to import oil

2003 China becomes the third nation to launch an astronaut into earth orbit and recover him

2004 China imports 48 percent of the oil it consumes

2006 China's economy, depending on the method used, is rated from fourth to second largest in the world; poverty, according to international standards, has been greatly reduced

2008 August—China hosts the Summer Olympics

2009 China celebrates the sixtieth anniversary of the revolution

2010 January—China becomes the world's largest exporter
March–July—Google rebels against China's Internet censorship
October—Imprisoned pro-democracy advocate Liu Xiaobo awarded Nobel Peace Prize

2011 The percentage of poor people in China falls below 14

2013 Many of China's cities suffer severe air pollution
One child per family policy significantly relaxed
Restrictions on rural to urban migration eased

REFERENCES AND FURTHER READINGS

Al Jazeera. 2013. "Chinese Police Rescue 92 Abducted Children." September 28. www.aljazeera.com/news/asia-pacific/2013/09/92-abducted-kids-rescued-by-police-china-201392844259676177.html.

Barboza, David, and Miguel Helft. 2010. "China Renews Google's License." *New York Times*, July 9. www.nytimes.com/2010/07/10/technology/10google.html.

BBC News. 2005. "Chinese Billionaires on the Rise." November 4. news.bbc.co.uk/2/hi/business/4406922.stm.

———. 2013. "Chinese Court Rejects Bo Xilai Appeal and Upholds Life Sentence." October 25, www.bbc.co.uk/news/world-asia-china-24652525.

Bianco, Lucien. 1971. *Origins of the Chinese Revolution, 1915–1949*. Trans. Muriel Bell. Stanford, CA: Stanford University Press.

Blecher, Marc. 1986. *China, Politics, Economics, and Society: Iconoclasm and Innovation in a Revolutionary Socialist Country*. Marxist Regimes Series. London: Pinter.

Bloomberg News. 2012. "China's Wealthiest Discreetly Stay Away at Party Congress." October 1. http://www.bloomberg.com/news/2012-09-30/absent-china-billionaires-show-wealth-limited-at-party-congress.html.

———. 2013. "China's Communist Party Meets to Map Out Economic Changes." No-
    vember 8. www.bloomberg.com/news/2013-11-08/china-s-communist-party-meets
    -in-beijing-to-map-economic-changes.html.
Bohr, Richard. 2006. "The Taiping Revolution." In DeFronzo, ed., *Revolutionary Move-
    ments in World History*, 3:855–862.
Borokh, Lila. 1972. "Notes on the Early Role of Secret Societies in Sun Yatsen's Republi-
    can Movement." In Chesneaux, ed., *Popular Movements and Secret Societies in China*.
Bottomore, Tom, ed. 1983. *A Dictionary of Marxist Thought*. Cambridge: Harvard Univer-
    sity Press.
Center for Global Development. 2008. "China Passes U.S., Leads World in Power Sector
    Carbon Emissions." August 27. www.cgdev.org/content/article/detail/16578.
Central Intelligence Agency (CIA). 2014a. "China." In *World Factbook*. www.cia.gov
    /library/publications/the-world-factbook/geos/ch.ht.
———. 2014b. "United States." In *World Factbook*. www.cia.gov/library/publications
    /the-world-factbook/geos/us.html.
Chance, Norman. 1985. *China's Urban Villagers: Life in a Beijing Commune*. New York:
    Holt, Rinehart & Winston.
Cheng, Chu-yuan, ed. 1989. *Sun Yat-sen's Doctrine in the Modern World*. Boulder:
    Westview.
Chesneaux, Jean. 1971. *Secret Societies in China in the Nineteenth and Twentieth Centuries*.
    Trans. Gillian Nettle. Ann Arbor: University of Michigan Press.
———, ed. 1972a. *Popular Movements and Secret Societies in China, 1840–1950*. Stanford,
    CA: Stanford University Press.
———. 1972b. "Secret Societies in China's Historical Evolution." In Chesneaux, ed., *Pop-
    ular Movements and Secret Societies in China*.
China Digital Times. June 10, 2010. "China Reaps Benefits of Iraq War with Oil Deals."
    chinadigitaltimes.net/2010/06/china-reaps-benefits-of-iraq-war-with-oil-deals.
Clubb, O. Edmund. 1978. *20th Century China*. 3rd ed. New York: Columbia University
    Press.
CNN. May 24, 1989. "U.S.-China Joint Economic Ventures."
DeFronzo, James. 2006. *Revolutionary Movements in World History: From 1750 to the Pres-
    ent*. 3 vols. Santa Barbara, CA: ABC-CLIO.
Dickson, Bruce J., Bruce Gilley, Merle Goldman, and Dali L. Yang. 2007. "The Future of
    China's Party-State." *Current History*, September, 243–251.
Domes, Jürgen. 1985. *The Government and Politics of the PRC: A Time of Transition*. Boul-
    der: Westview.
Eastman, Lloyd E. 1988. *Family, Fields, and Ancestors: Constancy and Change in China's
    Social and Economic History, 1550–1949*. New York: Oxford University Press.
Fairbairn, Geoffrey. 1974. *Revolutionary Guerrilla Warfare: The Countryside Version*. Mid-
    dlesex, UK: Penguin.

Fewsmith, Joseph. 1994. "Reform, Resistance, and the Politics of Succession." In William A. Joseph, ed., *China Briefing*. Boulder: Westview.

———. 2012. "China's 18th Party Congress: What's at Stake?" *Current History*, September, 203–208.

Finan, William W., Jr. 2010. "Behind China's Rise in Africa." *Current History*, May, 213–214.

Gallagher, Kevin P. 2010. "What's Left for Latin America to Do with China?" *NACLA* 43 (3): 50–52.

Gurley, John G. 1983. *Challenges to Communism*. San Francisco: Freeman.

Hawksley, Humphrey. 2006. "Chinese Influence in Brazil Worries US." BBC News, April 3. news.bbc.co.uk/2/hi/americas/4872522.stm.

Hennock, Mary. 2005. "China's Global Hunt for Oil." BBC News, March 9. news.bbc. co.uk/2/hi/business/4191683.stm.

Jordan, Donald A. 1976. *The Northern Expedition: China's National Revolution of 1926–1928*. Honolulu: University Press of Hawaii.

Klare, Michael T. 2006. "Fueling the Dragon: China's Strategic Energy Dilemma." *Current History*, April, 180–185.

Kristof, Nicholas D. 1989. "China Erupts." *New York Times Magazine*, June 4.

Lenin, V. I. [1916] 1975. "Imperialism: The Highest Stage of Capitalism." In Robert C. Tucker, ed., *The Lenin Anthology*. New York: Norton.

Luard, Tim. 2005. "China's Village Democracy Skin Deep." BBC News, October 10. news. bbc.co.uk/1/hi/world/asia-pacific/4319954.stm.

Lust, John. 1972. "Secret Societies, Popular Movements and the 1911 Revolution." In Chesneaux, ed., *Popular Movements and Secret Societies in China*.

Mackerras, Collin, and Nick Knight, ed. 1985. *Marxism in Asia*. New York: St. Martin's.

Mao Zedong. 1965. *Selected Works of Mao Tse-Tung*. Vol. 2. Beijing: Foreign Languages Press.

———. 1967. *Selected Readings from the Work of Mao*. Beijing: Foreign Languages Press.

Meisner, Maurice. 1986. *Mao's China and After: A History of the People's Republic. The Transformation of Modern China*. New York: Free Press.

Menon, Rajan. 2009. "Pax Americana and the Rising Powers." *Current History*, November, 353–360.

Moore, Barrington, Jr. 1966. *Social Origins of Dictatorship and Democracy: Lord and Peasant in the Making of the Modern World*. Boston: Beacon.

Overholt, William. 1993. *The Rise of China: How Economic Reform Is Creating a New Superpower*. New York: Norton.

Payne, Robert. 1969. *Chiang Kai-shek*. New York: Weybright & Talley.

People's Daily Online. April 20, 2010. "China, Thirsty for Oil, Looks to Central Asian Neighbors." english.peopledaily.com.cn/90001/90776/90883/6957402.html.

Posner, Gerald L. 1988. *Warlords of Crime: Chinese Secret Societies—The New Mafia*. New York: McGraw-Hill.

Qiang, Liu. 2013. "How the Third Plenum Will Change People's Lives." China.org,cn, November 29. www.china.org.cn/china/third_plenary_session/2013-11/29/content _30746484.htm.

Reuters. 2013. "China Smog Emergency Shuts City of 11 Million People." December 7. http://photoblog.nbcnews.com/_news/2013/10/21/21061668-china-smog-emergency -shuts-city-of-11-million-people?chromedomain=behindthewall&lite.

Ross, John. 1994. "Economic Reform: Success in China and Failure in Eastern Europe." *Monthly Review,* May, 19–28.

Salisbury, Harrison E. 1985. *The Long March: The Untold Story.* New York: McGraw-Hill.

Schell, Orville. 1985. *To Get Rich Is Glorious: China in the 1980s.* New York: Mentor.

Schiffrin, Harold Z. 1989. "Sun Yat-sen: His Life and Times." In Cheng, ed., *Sun Yat-sen's Doctrine in the Modern World.*

Shapiro, Judith. 2013. "The Evolving Tactics of China's Green Movement." *Current History,* September, 224–229.

Sharma, Shalendra. 2006. "Asia's Challenged Giants." *Current History,* April, 170–175.

Short, Philip. 2000. *Mao: A Life.* New York: Henry Holt.

Skocpol, Theda. 1976. "Old Regime Legacies and the Communist Revolutions in Russia and China." *Social Forces* 55 (2): 284–315.

———. 1979. *States and Social Revolutions: A Comparison of France, Russia, and China.* Cambridge, UK: Cambridge University Press.

Sun, Yan. 2005. "Corruption, Growth, and Reform: The Chinese Enigma." *Current History,* September, 257–263.

Thaxton, Ralph. 1983. *China Turned Rightside Up: Revolutionary Legitimacy in the Peasant World.* New Haven, CT: Yale University Press.

Theen, Rolf H. W., and Frank L. Wilson. 1986. *Comparative Politics: An Introduction to Six Countries.* Englewood Cliffs, NJ: Prentice-Hall.

Thompson, Clive. 2006. "Google in China: The Big Disconnect." *New York Times Magazine,* April 23.

Vines, Alex. 2007. "China in Africa: A Mixed Blessing?" *Current History,* May, 213–219.

Walder, Andrew G. 2009. "Unruly Stability: Why China's Regime Has Staying Power." *Current History,* September, 257–260, 262–263.

Wasserstrom, Jeffrey N. 2001. "Human Rights and the Lessons of History." *Current History,* September, 263–268.

———. 2002. "Waiting for China's Lech Walesa." *Current History,* September, 256–258.

Wei, William. 1985. *Counterrevolution in China: The Nationalists in Jianxi During the Soviet Period.* Michigan Studies on China. Ann Arbor: University of Michigan Press.

Whyte, Martin King. 2012. "China's Post-Socialist Inequality." *Current History,* September, 229–234.

Wolf, Eric. 1969. *Peasant Wars of the Twentieth Century.* New York: Harper & Row.

Yabuki, Susumu. 1995. *China's New Political Economy: The Giant Awakes.* Trans. Stephen M. Harner. Boulder: Westview.

Zhang, Jialin. 1994. "Guiding China's Market Economy." *Current History,* September, 276–280.

SELECTED DVD, FILM, AND VIDEOCASSETTE DOCUMENTARIES

See "Purchase and Rental Sources" at the end of this volume for information on how to obtain the following resources and for full names of media companies and other organizations listed here as abbreviations.

The Boxer Rebellion. 50 min. HC.

Chiang Kai Shek. 50 min. HC, BIO.

China: 1949–1972. 1998. 46 min. CNN Cold War, Episode 15. Truman Library.

China: A Century of Revolution. 1989–1997. 1: *China in Revolution, 1911–1949.* 2: *The Mao Years, 1949–1976.* 3: *Born Under the Red Flag, 1976–1996.* AEMS.

China: A Century of Revolution. 2007. 360 min. 3 DVD set. Amazon.com.

China: Century of Revolution, Part 1: Agonies of Nationalism, 1800–1927. 1972. 24 min. Film. UC-B, UI, ISU, KSU, UMISSOURI, SUNY-B, PSU, PU, UT-A, WSU. Impact of foreign interventions in China, the republican movement, and the Communist Party.

China: Century of Revolution, Part 2: Enemies Within and Without, 1927–1944. 1972. 26 min. Film. UC-B, UI, ISU, KSU, UMISSOURI, SUNY-B, PSU, PU, UT-A, WSU. Chinese civil war and Japanese invasion.

China: Century of Revolution, Part 3: Communist Triumph and Consolidation, 1945–1971. 1972. 20 min. Film. US-B, ISU, KSU, UMISSOURI, SUNY-B, PSU, PU, WSU. Communist victory in the late 1940s.

China from the Inside. 2006. 220 min. DVD. Amazon.com. Also http://topdocumentary films.com/china-from-the-inside.

China Rises: A Documentary in Four Parts. 2008. 264 min. DVD. Amazon.com.

China Rising. 150 min. HC. Modern Chinese history.

Democracy Crushed: Tiananmen Square. 50 min. HC.

The Gate of Heavenly Peace. 1995. 50 min. NAATA. Demonstrations at Tiananmen Square and repression.

Korea. 1998. 47 min. CNN. Cold War Series Episode 5. DVD. Amazon.com.

Made in China: The People's Republic of Profit. 2008. 45 min. CNBC. http://video.us.msn. com/watch/video/made-in-china-the-peoples-republic-of-profit/17wk66v3g.

Mao Tse Tung. 50 min. BIO.

Small Happiness: Women of a Chinese Village. 1984. 58 min. Video. Highly acclaimed unrestricted investigation of changes in rural women's lives after the revolution as well as the persistence of traditional views.

Through the Consul's Eyes. 1999. 50 min. FRIF. China 1896–1905.

4

The Vietnamese Revolution

While Mao and his associates were building rural bases in south-central China, revolutionary ideas were taking root in Vietnam. In 1930, several groups of Marxist-inspired Vietnamese nationalists formed the Indochinese Communist Party (ICP). Party members vowed to accomplish a social revolution in Vietnam, then under French colonial control. After years of organizational efforts, localized rebellions, and repression, the ICP focused on achieving independence from foreign rule and united many Vietnamese behind this nationalist goal. The party established a network of mass organizations, the Viet Minh (League for Vietnamese Independence), which it led. In 1941 the party launched a war of resistance against the French and Japanese armed forces then jointly occupying Vietnam. The Vietnamese were to be involved in armed conflict almost continuously for more than three decades.

Geography and Population

Vietnam, which has a land area of 127,246 square miles (329,566 square kilometers), is a long, narrow country situated along the eastern side of the Indochinese peninsula in Southeast Asia. China lies to the north and Laos and Cambodia to the west. The South China Sea borders Vietnam's entire coastline. Heavily forested mountain and plateau regions constitute most of the country's territory. Two fertile river delta areas are located at opposite ends of Vietnam, the Red River delta (about 5,800 square miles, or 15,000 square kilometers) in the north and the Mekong River delta (about 14,000 square miles, or 36,250 square kilometers) in the south. The population, which numbered 92 million in 2012, is about 86 percent ethnic Vietnamese (CIA 2014). The remaining 14 percent comprises other groups such as residents of Thai ancestry and tribal peoples in the lightly populated highland areas.

Most ethnic Vietnamese live in the fertile lowlands below three hundred feet in altitude and are concentrated in the two large river deltas as well as smaller river deltas and coastal plains along the length of the country. Those areas constitute 20 percent of the land area but contain 85 percent of the population. About 31 percent of the population lived in urban areas in 2011.

Early Cultural and Political Characteristics

The Vietnamese are apparently of Mongol ancestry and originated as a distinct ethnic group thousands of years ago. They gradually moved south from the Red River delta, assimilating the local residents (or forcing them to seek refuge in the mountains). The Chinese attacked and defeated the Vietnamese in 111 BCE and occupied the country, despite repeated rebellions, until 939 CE. In that year, Viet forces finally defeated the Chinese and ended direct Chinese control (except for a twenty-year Chinese reoccupation of Vietnam in 1407–1427). The Vietnamese occupied the southernmost region of the country, which had been Cambodian territory, in 1780.

Often afflicted by dynastic wars and other conflicts, the country was finally united within its current borders under Emperor Gia Long in 1802. The Vietnamese repelled subsequent Chinese invasions and retained their independence until conquered by the French during the nineteenth century. The Chinese referred to Vietnam as Annam (the pacified south), a term most Vietnamese detested. Later the French referred to the Vietnamese as Annamites and outlawed the use of "Vietnam."

Prior to Chinese conquest the Vietnamese were a tribal people whose king was one of the most powerful tribal chiefs to whom other chiefs owed feudal obligations. They practiced a form of animism that venerated spirits thought to control natural phenomena, such as the soil and water. During a thousand years of Chinese domination, the Vietnamese adopted a Confucian political system (see Chapter 3), along with the Chinese writing system, clothing styles, and technology. But they retained their own language (related to the Mon-Khmer and Thai linguistic families) and refused to relinquish their separate ethnic identity or their desire for independence. Throughout the period of Chinese rule, Viet leaders (such as the Trung sisters in 39–43 CE) mounted heroic rebellions.

The peasant culture that evolved under Chinese domination combined earlier rural customs and beliefs with ideologies brought by the Chinese, including Confucianism (with its emphasis on obedience and social order), Buddhism (stressing morally right behavior and denial of self-importance in order to achieve nirvana and escape the cycle of reincarnation), and Taoism (emphasizing the individual's search for the Tao, the path or way, to happiness and enlightenment in this world and the hereafter). Although these belief systems contained conflicting elements (e.g., Taoism rejected the importance of Confucian scholarship in favor of seeking harmony with nature), the Vietnamese selected and blended compatible aspects of the imported doctrines with indigenous folkways (Bain 1967).

French Conquest

In 1516 Portuguese explorers visited Vietnam. They referred to the country as Cauchichina, deriving this term from the Chinese characters for Vietnam, *giao chi*, and adding "china" to distinguish it from their "Cochin" colony located in India. Later the French came to play the dominant European role in Vietnam after it became clear that Portugal was simply too weak to master the task of Christianizing and colonizing Asia. The French, who portrayed Vietnam to the world as three separate countries, modified the Portuguese misnomer and referred to the southernmost part of Vietnam, including the Mekong delta and Saigon, as "Cochinchina." They labeled the long middle section of the country, with the old imperial capital Hue, "Annam," and called the northernmost part of Vietnam, including the Red River delta and the cities of Hanoi and Haiphong, "Tonkin."

French missionaries, originally entering Vietnam under Portuguese auspices, enthusiastically embraced the goal of converting the Vietnamese and returned to France with stories of immense wealth and excellent harbors to entice support from French businessmen and military leaders. Eventually a mutually supportive relationship evolved among French missionaries and merchants, as well as the navy, which developed an interest in the potential usefulness of Vietnamese ports for extending its operational range. Some Vietnamese monarchs craved the modern weapons and other technology and products the Europeans could provide and periodically tolerated missionary work in order to obtain benefits or avoid French displeasure. But Vietnamese officials became alarmed that the spread of Christianity heralded the threat of a massive expansion of French imperial presence in Vietnam.

In 1847, outraged by Vietnamese campaigns against Christian missionaries and envious of Britain's gains in its successful Opium War against the Chinese, the French defeated Vietnamese naval forces and obtained concessions from the emperor. Further disputes led to a French assault in 1858 and the seizure of Saigon and its surrounding provinces in 1861. The Vietnamese ceded control of Cambodia to the French in 1863, and the emperor surrendered the provinces west of Saigon in 1867. The French soon established Cochinchina as a colony, displacing Vietnamese administrators with French officials. Later, a series of military conflicts resulted in French protectorates over Annam and Tonkin. In these areas many Vietnamese mandarins (those willing to collaborate) maintained their positions under the authority of French civil and military officials. By the end of 1883 the French conquest of Vietnam was complete.

The French Impact on Vietnam
Economic Effects

Few Frenchmen had as great an impact on Vietnam as Paul Doumer, who arrived in Vietnam as governor-general of Indochina in 1897. The measures that Doumer instituted, although harmful to the welfare of many Vietnamese, transformed Vietnam into a colony that not only paid for the cost of its own military occupation but also generated great wealth for France and many of its citizens.

In addition to accelerating French colonial programs begun earlier, Doumer introduced innovations. Confronted with a country of basically self-sufficient agricultural communities, the French resolved to exploit Vietnamese resources in such a way as to generate products for the world market and construct a regionally complementary economic infrastructure. Because mineral deposits were discovered in the north and labor could be readily obtained from the densely populated Red River delta, mining and industry were developed primarily in the northern third of Vietnam. Recognizing the potential of the much larger Mekong delta, the French government constructed hydraulic projects there to control water levels, opened huge tracts to cultivation, and sold large sections cheaply to French and Vietnamese investors in order to pay for the water control program and bring the new land under cultivation quickly. As a consequence, landownership was highly concentrated in Cochinchina. Of 6,530 landholders in all of French Indochina (Vietnam, Cambodia, and Laos) with more than 125 acres, 6,300 resided in this southernmost part of Vietnam: There 2.5 percent of the population owned 45 percent of the cultivated land (Duong 1985; McAlister 1969). Tenant farmers and landless agricultural laborers made up more than half of the rural population in Cochinchina (many had migrated from the overpopulated Red River delta in search of employment).

The French increased the amount of rice exported from Vietnam from about 57,000 tons in 1860 to more than 1.5 million tons in 1937 (Wolf 1969). They also developed rubber plantations (over 1,000 in Cochinchina and Cambodia), which employed tens of thousands under generally harsh conditions. The colonial authorities introduced heavy taxes. Since many peasants could not make ends meet, they fell into debt and were forced to sell their land. By 1930, 70 percent of the country's rural population either were landless or lacked sufficient land to meet minimal living requirements. They had to rent land or engage in other work to survive (Duong 1985; Karnow 1983; Popkin 1979).

To expand produce for export, the amount of land and grain that had traditionally been held communally to assist peasants in times of hardship was reduced, depriving rural Vietnamese of their state-sponsored aid system (Duong 1985; Popkin 1979). Doumer's agents recruited the landless to work in mines, on rubber plantations, or in the construction of roads and railways, sometimes using laws against vagrancy or "vagabondism" to coerce laborers. As the majority could no longer maintain a

MAP 4.1 French Indochina

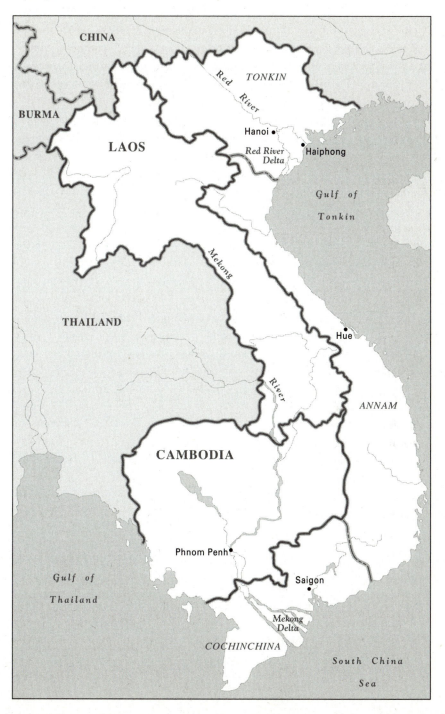

self-sufficient existence, their material well-being became dependent on international market prices for Vietnam's exports. The affected wages of landless workers, farm income, and consumer prices for food and other necessities. Thus the export-oriented economy developed under colonialism benefited French and Vietnamese landholders and the industrial and commercial elite by providing them with high incomes. But it had negative consequences for the larger population, particularly when international prices for Vietnam's products fell (McAlister 1969; Wolf 1969).

When Doumer reached Vietnam, generally only Chinese residents smoked opium. He proceeded to build an opium refinery that produced a quick-burning mixture. It proved popular, and opium addiction spread extensively among the Vietnamese. Eventually profits from drug sales accounted for one-third of the colonial administration's income (Karnow 1983). Doumer's success in generating large profits for France and its agricultural, industrial, and commercial enterprises helped reduce criticism of imperial policy. Wealthy Vietnamese visited Paris and expressed gratitude for France's role in their nation, thus contributing to the self-serving illusion that most Vietnamese were happy with colonial status.

By 1931 some 0.3 percent of Vietnamese received five or more years of schooling in the French colonial educational system. (French education was a key to social mobility in colonial Vietnam.) But their economic and political opportunities were limited. The French dominated the colonial bureaucracy and commerce, along with Vietnam's Chinese minority (McAlister 1969). Lack of social mobility may have motivated some in Vietnam's French-educated elite to work for independence.

By 1929 the colonial process had generated an industrial, mining, and commercial working class of about 140,000 (probably under 5 percent of the working population). A 1931 analysis of income in Vietnam showed that the top 1 percent (composed of French administrators, large landholders, and well-to-do Vietnamese) enjoyed an annual income that was about eight times the average income of the 9 percent who were largely urban, nonpeasant employees and twenty-four times the income of the 90 percent who were peasants. Although landowning peasants were usually able to raise part of their food, the money they earned reflected their ability to pay taxes and purchase equipment and other commodities (McAlister 1969).

Cultural and Social Changes

French colonialism undermined the Confucian system, which was blamed for Vietnam's inability to resist French conquest. Many of the Vietnamese elite, schooled in the Confucian scholarship that had in the past constituted the means to governmental and economic opportunity, now sought a French education for their children. French culture soon enveloped the upper levels of Vietnamese society and, in varying ways, affected the larger population.

The colonial educational system was intended to propagate admiration for French culture and achievements and to recruit a French-educated Vietnamese elite that would collaborate with colonial authorities and businesspeople. But many Vietnamese took their lessons on French history and politics to heart. The French Revolution and concepts of political democracy and socialism eventually would help inspire an effective revolutionary movement in Vietnam. Prominent among future revolutionary figures was a brilliant history teacher, Vo Nguyen Giap, who enthralled his students with accounts of the French Revolution and the unjust society it overthrew. In the late 1930s he left the classroom to organize and lead the revolutionary armies that would drive the French from Vietnam.

As a result of French economic policy, large numbers of landless Vietnamese left their home villages for mining areas, industrial centers, plantations, and the newly developed agricultural land in the Mekong delta. Migration had great emotional and moral consequences for many of the uprooted poor because traditional culture provided few satisfactory interpretations of their new experiences and because they were isolated from their extended family networks. Many succumbed to opium addiction or became involved in prostitution, both promoted by the French colonial presence. Others turned to new religions. In the Mekong delta, where many migrants established villages, new religions provided a feeling of community and a sense of prestige and personal worth through membership in the "true faith." Cao Dai, a syncretic (eclectic) cult founded by a mystic in 1926, and a Buddhist reformist sect, Hoa Hao, formally established in 1939, gained many adherents.

Cao Dai, named for a spirit who communed with its founder, was based on the concept of combining the best elements of all faiths and secular philosophies and included among its saints Jesus, Buddha, Joan of Arc, and Sun Yixian (Sun Yat Sen) (Karnow 1983). While incorporating beneficial elements of Western cultures, Cao Dai strongly emphasized Vietnamese nationalism. The religion integrated Buddhism, Confucianism, and Taoism to present a sort of united religious-cultural front to French imperialism (Tai 1983; Werner 1981; Woodside 1976). Hoa Hao (named after the Mekong town where it was invented by a prophetic faith healer) was a kind of Buddhist Protestantism; the poor were attracted to its simplicity and rejection of expensive rituals or religious artifacts. Hoa Hao was strongly nationalistic. It stressed traditional Vietnamese Buddhist doctrine and customs and opposed Western values and technology (Tai 1983).

Both Cao Dai and Hoa Hao developed into political-religious organizations with their own armed militias. The leadership of these two religions (both of which eventually fragmented into feuding subdivisions) strove for autonomous political control over districts in the Mekong delta. At times they allied with communist-led independence forces and at other times with the French, depending on which seemed to maximize their goal of localized political authority. By the mid-1950s the

Cao Dai and the Hoa Hao each numbered over a million (together about 6–8 percent of the population), while 10 percent of the Vietnamese embraced Catholicism,
and 80 percent claimed varying degrees of association with one of the dozen or so
other Buddhist sects.

Political Consequences

As noted earlier, the French ruled the southernmost part of Vietnam, Cochinchina,
which the Vietnamese called Nam Bo (south territory, also called Nam Ky) as a
directly administered colony. This part of Vietnam was controlled the longest by
France and was most influenced by French rule. In contrast, the middle section of
Vietnam, Annam (Trung Bo or Trung Ky), and the northernmost region, Tonkin
(Bac Bo or Bac Ky), were technically French protectorates. The Vietnamese emperor, with his court at Hue, served primarily as a figurehead, and scholarly mandarins exercised political authority on the condition of serving French interests.
But as the French-educated elite gradually replaced the Confucian mandarins in
Tonkin and Annam, the distinction between direct rule (in Cochinchina) and
indirect rule (in Tonkin and Annam) became virtually meaningless by the early
1940s (McAlister 1969, 43).

The French also changed local government. Traditionally a village had been
governed by a council of notables including local Confucian scholars and village
elders. Under the new system a council was elected with a strong executive who had
to be approved by the province governor and was directly responsible for carrying
out colonial policy (McAlister 1969; Wolf 1969). Many Vietnamese did not accept
the new arrangement and viewed it as a mechanism of colonial control; thus the
French destroyed the popularly supported form of local government without replacing it with one that was accepted by the majority of the population. A political
vacuum developed and persisted until it was filled by the new forms of political and
social organization developed by Vietnamese revolutionaries (McAlister 1969).

The French received their strongest support in Cochinchina from the wealthy
French settlers and Francophile Vietnamese large landholders. This group organized the pro-French Constitutionalist Party, which ran candidates for the Saigon
city council and other local government posts. In 1937, of the 2,555 largely affluent
Vietnamese who had received French citizenship, 1,474 resided in Cochinchina,
which had only about 20 percent of Vietnam's population (McAlister 1969).

A major mechanism of French control was the colonial militia, composed of
Vietnamese in service to the French. This institution became a channel of social
mobility for those willing to improve their lot at the probable expense of their country folk. It also served as the nucleus of the antirevolutionary Vietnamese armies

that fought first alongside the French and later alongside US forces in attempts to crush the Vietnamese revolution.

A final but critically important political consequence of colonial policy was the development of a Vietnamese revolutionary elite from among the French-educated fraction of the population. This group would make use of concepts derived from their Western educations, fuse them with Vietnamese nationalism, and organize the successful movement to oust the French.

RESISTANCE TO FRENCH RULE

McAlister (1969), Wolf (1969), and Khanh (1982) suggest four phases of Vietnamese resistance: a period of tradition-based rebellion, a transitional phase involving integration of traditional goals with new concepts, the creation of modern but unsuccessful nationalist movements, and development of a successful revolutionary effort, the Viet Minh.

Tradition-Based Rebellion: 1883–1900

During the period of tradition-based rebellion, many Confucian scholars refused to collaborate with the French and organized rebellions against colonial rule. But they were localized and easily suppressed. Furthermore, these traditional leaders attempted to rally Vietnamese nationalism through the Confucian system of the past, which had proven to be oppressive and ineffective.

Transition: 1900–1925

After 1900 several Vietnamese scholars, originally educated in Confucian classics, attempted to organize independence movements that incorporated concepts from technologically advanced societies. Most important were Phan Boi Chau (1867–1940) and Phan Chu Trinh (1872–1926), who represented a transitional generation between the tradition-oriented pre-1900 rebellions and the modern nationalist movements, which began in the 1920s. Although both believed that traditional Confucian learning had failed to provide Vietnam the ability to resist Western colonialism, they advocated different methods.

Phan Boi Chau favored a Vietnamese state that would integrate useful modern concepts into traditional culture. Over time he advocated traditional monarchy, then a constitutional monarchy, then a totally republican form of government. Only the best-educated Vietnamese understood his ideas, and they often viewed his proposals as ill suited to Vietnam. In the end Phan Boi Chau was valued as a fervent nationalist who exalted the intellectual capabilities, resourcefulness, and stubborn determination of the Vietnamese people and supported violent resistance to colonialism (Duiker 1976; Marr 1971; Woodside 1976).

Phan Chu Trinh, in contrast, refused to support armed rebellion, which, given Vietnam's technological inferiority, he viewed as a senseless waste of life. He held that modernization of Vietnam's technology, culture, and political and social systems was an absolute necessity even if this required an extended period of colonialism. He optimistically called on the French to modernize Vietnam rapidly and assist in building self-government leading to full independence. Although ultimately colonialism was thrown off not through a reformist process but through armed revolution, Phan Chu Trinh was credited with encouraging young Vietnamese to learn from Western societies those concepts that could one day make Vietnam a strong and independent nation.

Phan Chu Trinh, whom the French treated leniently because his nonviolence and his advocacy of French-Vietnamese harmony, died of natural causes in March 1926. Phan Boi Chau was arrested by the French secret police in 1925. He spent the rest of his life under detention and died in 1940.

Modern Nationalist Attempts: 1925–1940

By the late 1920s a significant number of educated young Vietnamese had traveled abroad, some hoping to discover new methods for bringing independence to Vietnam. Several groups coalesced to form two nationalist organizations, the Vietnamese Nationalist Party (VNQDD) in 1927 and the Indochinese Communist Party in 1930.

The VNQDD, loosely patterned after the Chinese GMD (Guomindang), incorporated several of Sun Yat Sen's ideas. Its platform proclaimed the goals of national liberation and social revolution. But it never clearly defined the meaning of social revolution, and members held differing interpretations (Khanh 1982). The party recruited mainly students and urban, middle-income workers, such as teachers, clerks, and journalists. The VNQDD also gained the support of many Vietnamese soldiers in the French-organized and French-controlled colonial militia. Among the limitations of the VNQDD was its being primarily urban based; consequently, it had almost no organized support among the 90 percent of Vietnam's population who were peasants. Instead of developing a program for redistribution of resources that would appeal to peasants and patiently building revolutionary support and organizational structures in the countryside, the VNQDD created special units to carry out attacks and assassinations against French officials. VNQDD leaders apparently thought that violence against colonial agents would arouse Vietnamese patriotism and win mass support.

The VNQDD was crushed after the failure of the Yen Bay mutiny in February 1930. In Yen Bay, VNQDD-organized Vietnamese colonial militia soldiers mutinied and killed their French officers. But they were overwhelmed in one day. More than a thousand VNQDD members were arrested. About one hundred were given life sentences, and eighty sentenced to death. The VNQDD lost most of its best leaders and ceased to be a credible nationalist movement. Following the destruction of the VNQDD, some of its members joined Marxist-led movements, and others escaped to China or Japan, where they reorganized under foreign sponsorship and entered Vietnam during or immediately after World War II. But many Vietnamese viewed the resurrected versions of the VNQDD as extensions of foreign imperialism (Khanh 1982).

During the latter half of the 1920s several Marxist-inspired groups, including Thanh Nien (Youth) and Tan Viet (New Vietnam), were organized by students and young, educated Vietnamese employed in nonmanual professions, such as teaching or office work. These Marxist-oriented nationalists called for both anti-imperialism (independence for Vietnam) and antifeudalism (social revolution). When these groups, along with peasant activists, united in 1930 to form a Communist Party, the membership was mostly a combination of middle-class and peasant revolutionaries with only a small representation of urban industrial workers.

At first the party prioritized the goal of independence, as reflected in the title Vietnamese Communist Party. But during the same year, the international congress of communist parties (the Communist International, or Comintern) decided that communist parties should emphasize class conflict and social revolution rather than nationalism and criticized the communist parties in less developed countries for cooperating in nationalist alliances with parties that opposed social revolution. The Comintern encouraged communist parties to break off relations with other parties, including socialists, in order to communicate party concepts more effectively to the masses and organize them for the class conflict viewed as necessary to achieve a social revolution.

This shift influenced the Vietnamese Communist Party to change its name to the Indochinese Communist Party within a few months of its founding. The name change also reflected party members' acceptance of the Comintern's policy of matching Communist Party organizations to colonial jurisdictions (in this case French Indochina) rather than to ethnic divisions. The ICP was at least nominally given the task of bringing social revolution to Cambodia and Laos as well as Vietnam, although there were only a few Cambodians and Laotians in the party during its early years. As the ICP energetically mobilized peasants and workers for class conflict and social revolution, neglecting the independence struggle, the party lost much of its appeal to educated Vietnamese in urban nonmanual occupations (who had previously rallied to fight against foreign domination, even if the movement was led by communist revolutionaries).

In 1930 and 1931 many Vietnamese suffered because of the worldwide depression, which lowered prices for Vietnam's exports. ICP agitation led to strikes and protests in many parts of Vietnam. There was a peasant insurrection in Nghe An, a province that traditionally rebelled against foreign rule, and the neighboring province, Ha Tinh, in north-central Vietnam. Peasants staged demonstrations demanding the abolition or deferment of taxes and higher prices for their produce from the colonial government. Soon peasants began electing local revolutionary councils (soviets) to take the place of collaborationist and French authorities and to enact reforms. The national ICP leadership had little role in planning the insurrection and considered it premature because outside of Nghe An and Ha Tinh, most peasants were not yet committed to revolution.

Repression of the rural soviets was carried out in summer 1931. Hundreds lost their lives in the rebelling provinces, and thousands of ICP supporters were incarcerated throughout Vietnam. But the commitment demonstrated by the ICP to social revolution in the countryside and the examples of heroism on the part of individual ICP members (important to public perception in a land inspired by myths of heroic resistance to foreign oppression) won further support from many peasants and workers (Karnow 1983; Khanh 1982; McAlister 1969; Wolf 1969). The concept of communism itself, *cong san* in Vietnamese, was popularly defined as taking all property and equally dividing it among the population (Khanh 1982), a notion well received by Vietnam's impoverished classes.

Developments in the international communist movement and in France improved the ICP's situation. The leaders of the world's communist parties became alarmed at the success of fascist movements, which espoused extreme nationalism and racial and cultural superiority. The election of the Nazi Party in Germany in 1933 was blamed in part on the hostility between the German communist and socialist parties. Consequently, in the mid-1930s communist parties advocated formation of popular fronts involving leftist and other anti-Fascist parties. In France a popular front coalition including the French socialist and communist parties was elected and ordered the release from Vietnamese prisons of many ICP members. The period of 1936–1939 was one of growth for the ICP throughout Vietnam. In Saigon, members of the Communist Party were even elected to the city council.

But in 1939 the French government, in response to shifts in policy by both the USSR and the French Communist Party, made a new attempt to crush the ICP. The Soviets had been outraged when Western democracies failed to help the elected leftist Spanish government prevent the victory of conservative forces and fascist armies (Italian and German) in the 1936–1939 Spanish Civil War and when the British and the French decided to grant Nazi Germany effective control of Czechoslovakia at Munich in 1938. The Soviets suspected that the capitalist democracies were attempting to appease Hitler so that he would turn east and launch an invasion of the USSR; he could then seize and colonize Soviet territory as he had advocated years earlier in *Mein Kampf*. To forestall an expected attack, the Soviet leader, Stalin, signed a nonaggression pact with Germany, which greatly increased the probability of a German attack on France. After Germany invaded Poland in September 1939 and France and Britain declared war, the new French government outlawed the pro-Moscow, temporarily antiwar French Communist Party and ordered the repression of the ICP in Vietnam. But by then many ICP members had gone into hiding (Khanh 1982).

Ho Chi Minh and the Formation of the Viet Minh

No person contributed as much to the development of the revolution in Vietnam as Ho Chi Minh. According to official accounts, he was born on May 19, 1890, the third child in an anticolonial family in northern Annam. His scholar father was dismissed from his government position for punishing a prominent person too harshly (Duiker 2000, 41), although his action was consistent with his belief that the law should be administered fairly for the rich as well as the poor. Ho's parents named him Nguyen Sinh Cung at birth. Following a common tradition, his father chose a new name for him, Nguyen Tat Thanh, when he was eleven (Duiker 2000, 22–23). His mother died soon after giving birth to another son.

Both at home and abroad, Ho used as many as seventy-six aliases in writing hundreds of articles and political analysis. However, he became famous under two names. During 1919–1945, the world knew him as Nguyen Ai Quoc (Nguyen who loves his country), energetic Vietnamese nationalist and most prominent organizer of the Vietnamese communist movement. After the Viet Minh–led revolution in August 1945, when he became the first president of the Democratic Republic of Vietnam, he was known as Ho Chi Minh (he who enlightens) (Duiker 2000, 248–249).

Ho became involved in anticolonial activities at age fifteen, working as a courier for pro-independence scholars. He later told friends that after he learned the French slogan "Liberty, equality, and fraternity," he was confused by the lack of application of these ideals in Vietnam, and he yearned to understand better the civilization behind both the concepts and the imperialism Vietnam experienced. His interest in traveling to France and other advanced nations reflected a Vietnamese saying popular with the youth of the period, "Go abroad to study to come home to help the country" (Khanh 1982, 59). After acting as an interpreter for a group of peasants protesting to French authorities about high taxes and forced labor in May 1908, shortly before his eighteenth birthday, Ho was expelled from the National Academy (Duiker 2000, 36–37). In December 1911 he left Vietnam for France, earning his way as a laborer on the SS *Latouche-Treville*. He would not return to Vietnam for thirty years.

Ho traveled to many ports and learned that Vietnam was only one of many European colonies. Sensing that many Europeans did not regard Asians and Africans as equals, he began to understand imperialism and racism as worldwide phenomena.

Ho also visited the United States, living and working in Boston and New York for several months. Ho was favorably impressed that Asian immigrants to the US enjoyed political rights that the Vietnamese did not have in their own country, and he viewed the United States as a nation born from a successful revolution against British imperialism. Later he patterned Vietnam's September 1945 declaration of independence after the corresponding American Revolutionary War document. Ho left the United States in 1913. In England he worked as a dishwasher and then a chef at the Carlton Hotel (Duiker 2000, 52).

In 1917 Ho arrived in France, where 80,000 Vietnamese were serving in the armed forces or working in defense industries as part of the war effort. He remained there until 1923. Ho was surprised to find that most of the French at home were good people, while "the French in the colonies were cruel and inhuman" (Khanh 1982, 60). This observation, along with similar conclusions regarding Americans and the British, led him to assume that the Western democracies would honor President Wilson's commitment to national self-determination around the globe.

Ho attempted to present a list of moderate proposals for Vietnamese self-government to the world leaders attending the 1919 Paris Peace Conference. This effort made him an instant national hero among many Vietnamese (Khanh 1982; Lacouture 1968). But when the proposals were not even granted a hearing, he became disillusioned with the concept of reforming colonialism peacefully from within. Ho instead concluded that independence would probably come only as the result of an autonomous effort in Vietnam, without reliance on a change of heart on the part of the colonial power, and that decolonization, like colonial enslavement, would likely be a violent process (Khanh 1982).

In December 1920 Ho, who was affiliated with France's Socialist Party, as its program seemed most beneficial toward the colonized peoples, voted with the majority of its members to form the French Communist Party. Ho's decision was reportedly because the Socialists inclined to follow Lenin had the greatest concern with freeing the colonial peoples. Once Ho read Lenin's works on imperialism and colonialism, he was reportedly overcome with emotion and the feeling that Lenin had formulated conceptually the reality that he and all the colonial peoples he had encountered actually experienced. For Ho, the path to independence for Vietnam was through the international communist movement.

In 1924 Ho went to Moscow to study revolutionary theory and organizational methods and to prepare to build a revolution in Vietnam. In December he left for China to act as a translator for the Soviet advisory mission under Mikhail Borodin. In southern China in 1925 Ho introduced the members of a Vietnamese anti-colonial organization to Marxist thinking and Leninist concepts. Together they organized the Marxist-oriented group Thanh Nien (Youth), which would be the primary forerunner of the ICP. During 1925–1927 Ho gave lectures covering world history, colonial history, Marxist theory, Lenin's analysis of imperialism, and rev-olutionary theory and method to about three hundred Vietnamese exiles (Khanh 1982). Many of them returned to Vietnam to create local Thanh Nien organizations.

After the Chinese civil war broke out between Chiang Kai-shek's (Jiang Jieshi's) wing of the GMD and the Chinese communists in 1927, Thanh Nien members fled from Canton to Hong Kong. There Ho and others founded the Vietnamese Com-munist Party in 1930, which, as we have seen, in a few months became the Indochi-nese Communist Party. But on June 5, 1931, Ho was arrested by Hong Kong police and incarcerated. His health deteriorated, and he was hospitalized. He evidently convinced hospital personnel to allow him to leave. A story spread that he had died from tuberculosis. Memorial services were held for him in Paris and Moscow. With the help of friends, including a visiting French communist in Shanghai and, accord-ing to Duiker (2000, 210), Sun Yat Sen's wife, Soong Qingling, who secretly had a close relationship with the Chinese Communist Party, Ho eventually made his way to Moscow, where he spent 1934 to 1939 recuperating, studying, writing, and teach-ing history and political theory to Vietnamese students being educated in the So-viet Union. During these years Ho seems to have played no direct role in the ICP in Vietnam. The party, at the time, was pursuing the goal of social revolution through class warfare over the nationalistic, independence-first strategy Ho favored.

Ho returned to China in 1939, during the period the GMD and the Communist Party halted the civil war in order to fight the invading Japanese; in 1941 he reen-tered Vietnam. In a mountain cave in a northern province of Tonkin, Ho and sev-eral other ICP members established the League for Vietnamese Independence, the Viet Minh. The formation of the Viet Minh represented the shift in ICP strategy back to an emphasis on the primacy of national liberation and the reestablishment of Ho's leadership.

Ho emphasized that the "elimination of imperialism" in Vietnam, or indepen-dence, had to take precedence over the "elimination of feudalism" (breaking the hold of the landlord class and redistributing wealth, largely land, to the popula-tion). He argued for this on two major grounds. First, since many peasants and workers already supported the social revolution program of the ICP, advocacy of nationalism would appeal not only to them but also to other patriotic Vietnamese of all classes who wanted to free their country from foreign domination. Second, Ho's analysis indicated that foreign imperialism was the main source of strength for the feudalistic system in Vietnam and that a major step toward accomplishing social revolution had to be first severing the old social and economic order from its powerful outside support. Consequently, the Viet Minh gave priority to achieving independence and delayed sweeping land reform until 1953.

The Viet Minh combined mass-membership organizations, whose participants were committed to an independent Vietnam and generally also to social revolution, under the leadership of the ICP, which would act as a coordinating mechanism. The ranks of the ICP were filled by members of mass organizations willing to devote all their time to working for revolution and developing an understanding of Marxist and Leninist concepts. Actually, the ICP had been linked with mass-membership organizations even before the independence-oriented Viet Minh was formulated. Through the mass organizations, the ICP had provided an opportunity for large-scale political participation and mobilization. Thus in many areas the ICP not only filled the vacuum created by the French destruction of traditional village political mechanisms but also brought more people than ever before into the political process (McAlister 1969).

Many rural people considered the revolutionary village councils and mass-membership organizations to be truly Vietnamese rather than serving the interests of a foreign occupying power. The mass organizations were based on social categories easily understood by peasants and workers. These included national women's, youths', peasants', and workers' associations and other groups with local chapters and national leadership; they were linked at all levels to the ICP. Many of the nationalists who joined the Viet Minh were not interested in working their way into ICP membership. Some opposed communism or expressed little support for wealth redistribution. But they joined the Viet Minh and accepted ICP leadership because they recognized the ICP, especially under Ho Chi Minh, as a truly nationalist organization and the only viable means for establishing an independent Vietnam (Khanh 1982; McAlister 1969).

THE IMPACT OF WORLD WAR II

World War II had profound effects on the Vietnamese revolution. In June 1940 Germany defeated France, and in the unoccupied sector of the country an extremely conservative government based in the town of Vichy assumed power. The Vichy regime collaborated with the Nazi Germans and their allies, the Japanese, when the latter became interested in occupying Indochina to exploit its agricultural and mineral resources and to use it as a staging area for troop deployments elsewhere. The Vichy government allowed Japan to occupy Indochina in September 1940. But the Japanese left the French colonial administration, armed forces, and French-controlled Vietnamese colonial militia intact. Thus the French were able to maintain a repressive stance toward Vietnamese rebels, smashing a communist organized uprising in Cochinchina in late 1940 (Khanh 1982).

The Japanese presence did, however, gradually weaken French control. And on March 9, 1945, for specific political and military reasons, the Japanese attacked French colonial forces, and most French units surrendered within twenty-four hours. The ability of the Japanese, an Asian people, to dictate to the previously all-powerful French and cast them aside at will had a significant effect on many Vietnamese. Just as the French conquest had destroyed the concept of a heavenly mandated, immutable Confucian system, the Japanese victory annihilated the myth of European racial superiority. Many more Vietnamese were thereafter encouraged to resist the French.

While some Vietnamese supported the Japanese, and others, mostly among the 10 percent Catholic minority and the wealthy landowners, supported the French, the Viet Minh opposed both imperialist intruders. Under the military leadership of Vo Nguyen Giap, the Viet Minh began to educate peasants politically and organize them in the northern highlands of Vietnam. Giap and other Viet Minh leaders, who had been exposed to Chinese communist concepts of "people's war" and had repeatedly witnessed the defeat of urban or lowland insurrections against the French, realized that a key element in gaining independence would be the establishment of secure base camps in the northern mountains, where tanks and heavy weapons would be of little use to the enemy. Giap's plan for a people's war called for obtaining the support of the people in base area regions and developing intensely motivated revolutionary soldiers before fighting began. According to this approach, revolutionary combatants, highly committed to the goal of establishing a more just moral, social, economic, and political order, would constitute the fighting arm of a mobilized supportive population. Such a combination could conceivably overcome the imperialist's advantage in weaponry (Giap 1962; Karnow 1983).

ICP activists won the support of many Tay and Nung tribal people, who lived in a mountainous region extending from northern Vietnam to southern China. Leaders of these groups were hostile toward the French, who had intervened in their affairs, and many were favorable to the ICP because relatives in China, having been in contact with Chinese communist activists, had told them of benefits for most peasants of communist-led revolution. Support from the Tay and Nung, several of whom became prominent generals in the Viet Minh army, and from other minority groups in the northern Tonkin highlands was a key factor in constructing secure base areas where the Viet Minh could organize and train a revolutionary army (Khanh 1982; McAlister 1969).

As World War II continued, the Viet Minh network expanded throughout most of Vietnam. Groups tolerated by the Japanese or the French—such as the Advanced Guard Youth militia in Cochinchina (transformed by the Japanese from the French-sponsored Sports and Youth movement into a paramilitary group [McAlister 1969]) and the University of Hanoi Student Association in Tonkin—affiliated with the Viet Minh. The wide support the Viet Minh enjoyed soon became obvious to the nations fighting Japan. GMD leaders in China recognized the Viet Minh as the only effective countrywide anti-Japanese intelligence and resistance network in Vietnam and worked with the Viet Minh despite its communist leadership. US military forces air-dropped weapons, along with Office of Strategic Services (OSS, CIA predecessor) advisers, to Giap's forces (Karnow 1983; Khanh 1982). When Ho became seriously ill, medicine provided by a US agent possibly saved his life. The presence of US advisers suggested the US supported the Viet Minh, further enhancing the movement's appeal to Western-educated Vietnamese.

INSURRECTION

The conditions for revolutionary insurrection improved dramatically in March 1945, when Japanese forces, anticipating a possible Allied invasion, imprisoned French administrators and captured or routed French military forces. The advantage for the Viet Minh was that the repressive French colonial apparatus in the countryside was destroyed without being replaced by Japanese forces. For the next five months, "the most important period in the history of the ICP" (Khanh 1982, 309), the Viet Minh were relatively unimpeded in their organizational and mobilization efforts. Viet Minh military forces expanded rapidly. In the northern provinces of Tonkin, local authorities who had previously served the colonial administration threw their support to the Viet Minh, fled to areas under Japanese control, or, in some cases, were assassinated as collaborators of foreign imperialists. By August 1945 the Viet Minh controlled six northern provinces in Tonkin and had as many as 5,000 men and women under arms (to increase to 75,000 within a year and more than 350,000 by the early 1950s). A countrywide network of 200,000 Viet Minh activists was led by the ICP, which had 5,000 members (it was also rapidly expanding). The Viet Minh's membership was many times greater than the 5,000 to 10,000 estimated for the largely elite urban, foreign-sponsored, alternate nationalist groups of the period (Khanh 1982; McAlister 1969; Wolf 1969).

The Viet Minh and opposing groups committed assassinations against one another. The Viet Minh targeted identified agents of the colonial regime or colonial military personnel. The violence was intended to win popular support from the majority of the population who had suffered under French and Japanese imperial policies and longed to strike back and win a truly independent Vietnam (Dunn 1972).

As the Japanese overthrew the French administration, a terrible famine reached its height in Tonkin and northern Annam. From several hundred thousand to over 1 million of Tonkin's 1945 population of 8 million perished (Karnow 1983; Khanh 1982). The food shortage was in part due to heavy rainfall, which caused flooding of cultivated areas, and to Allied bombing, which reduced rice shipments sent from the Mekong delta to relieve the starving north. But the famine was blamed primarily on the French and the Japanese. The Japanese demanded a rice quota from the French, who then demanded the rice from the northern peasants (who barely produced enough for their own needs). The Japanese also demanded that industrial-use crops, such as peanuts, other oilseed crops, and cotton, be planted in place of some food crops (Khanh 1982; McAlister 1969). The Viet Minh organized peasants and attacked landlord and Japanese grain storage buildings, rationing out what they found. The famine greatly intensified hostility toward the French and Japanese and increased support for the Viet Minh.

By summer 1945 the Viet Minh were immensely more powerful and had more popular support than any of the other Vietnamese groups who labeled themselves nationalists despite their foreign sponsorship. Anti–Viet Minh groups generally lacked charismatic leadership and put forth ideologies that were narrow in scope and unappealing. They basically offered a partially independent Vietnam run by a foreign-educated urban elite under the sponsorship of China, Japan, or France (depending on the particular clique). Furthermore, their programs contained virtually no proposals for improving the social and economic conditions of the majority of Vietnamese (largely because to do so would endanger the interests of the wealthy classes they represented, the interests of the foreign countries that sponsored them, or both). The Viet Minh, in contrast, offered not only an independent Vietnam controlled by Vietnamese but also a plan for redistribution of resources to the nation's majority.

Maximally favorable conditions for a revolutionary uprising developed suddenly on August 15, 1945, when Japan surrendered shortly after two of its cities were destroyed by atomic bombs. With French troops still incarcerated and the Japanese demoralized and unlikely to resist the efforts of another Asian people to seize their independence before the return of European imperialists, the likelihood that the insurrection would succeed was high. By mid-August many villages surrounding Hanoi were under Viet Minh control. The stage was set for the "August Revolution." In major cities leaflets urging preparations for insurrection were circulated, movies and plays were interrupted for announcements concerning the national liberation struggle, and the flag of the Viet Minh with its gold star and red background suddenly appeared flying from prominent buildings throughout the country (McAlister 1969). On August 18 the insurrection began. For the next ten days uprisings swept the Viet Minh and allied groups into power in sixty-four major cities, including Hanoi on August 19, Hue on August 23, and Saigon on August 25 (Khanh 1982). In essence, the Japanese turned Vietnam over to the Viet Minh without armed resistance (Karnow 1983).

In the Tonkin and Annam regions, the Viet Minh met little organized opposition from other Vietnamese political groups. The situation was more complicated in Cochinchina. The Viet Minh won the support of the Japanese-armed youth militias. But armed political-religious sects had popular support in the Mekong delta, and Trotskyite communists also enjoyed some popular support (Khanh 1982). Consequently, the insurrection in Saigon involved an alliance that included the Viet Minh as the most prominent group. But participants soon began to feud among themselves. The well organized pro-French party, the Constitutionalists, desired to maintain close ties with France (McAlister 1969). In the weeks that followed the August Revolution, scores of Vietnamese were assassinated, usually by fanatical members of rival groups. Groups with limited membership and little popular appeal could not survive the loss of a few prominent figures. But the Viet Minh did survive terrorist attacks because it had thousands of members, a resilient organizational structure, and widespread popular support.

On August 30, after the pro–Viet Minh Students Association of the University of Hanoi petitioned the figurehead emperor, Bao Dai, to support the revolution, the latter abdicated in favor of the Viet Minh provisional government. Two days later, on September 2, Ho Chi Minh addressed several hundred thousand people at a Hanoi rally to proclaim Vietnam's declaration of independence and announce the establishment of the Democratic Republic of Vietnam. No other nation at that point recognized Vietnam's independence.

The victorious Allied powers instead decided to occupy Vietnam. British and Indian troops (under British control) entered the southern half of Vietnam, while approximately 125,000 anti-Communist Chinese GMD troops were sent into the northern half of the country. In late September 1945 the British commander in Saigon rearmed the 1,400 French soldiers the Japanese had arrested there in March. In a surprise move the French troops quickly seized the city's government buildings and with British assistance drove the Viet Minh from Saigon. In October an additional 25,000 French troops arrived and reoccupied all the major cities in Cochinchina. In the northern part of Vietnam, the Viet Minh bribed Chinese commanders (with gold from rings and other jewelry donated by thousands of Vietnamese) to prevent repression of their new government. And in December 1945 elections were held for a national assembly in Tonkin and Annam; the Viet Minh appeared to receive about 90 percent of the vote (Khanh 1982; McAlister 1969). French authorities refused to allow elections in Cochinchina, where almost 25 percent of Vietnam's 1945 population of 22 million resided. The national assembly elected Ho Chi Minh president. Ho, asserting his intention to create a government of national unity, included socialist and Catholic politicians as well as communists among his cabinet ministers (Karnow 1983).

To Ho the Chinese presence in the north represented a greater danger than the French reoccupation in the south. China had long threatened Vietnam with its immensity and power. Ho, lacking international support for immediate independence, would have to make a deal with the French, the more distant imperialist power, to get the Chinese out. As Ho put it, "Better to sniff a bit of French shit briefly than eat Chinese shit for the rest of our lives" (Karnow 1983, 100). In a move to gain acceptance of the Viet Minh–led government from the GMD Chinese and the French, the ICP publicly dissolved in October 1945. The party continued to function covertly through its extensive social network and was formally reestablished in 1951 as the Vietnamese Communist Party (officially labeled the Vietnam Labor Party).

Early in 1946 the Chinese decided to withdraw and allow the French to reenter northern Vietnam, provided the French relinquish their colonial claims to territory within China. The Viet Minh government allowed the French to station military forces in northern Vietnam on the condition that these units be withdrawn in five years. According to this proposal, the French would then grant Vietnam independence within the framework of the French Union, which would keep Vietnam economically associated with France (Karnow 1983; Lacouture 1968; McAlister 1969). The future status of southernmost Vietnam, Cochinchina, was a major point of contention. Neither the French nor the wealthy Vietnamese wanted unification with the other parts of Vietnam, whereas the Viet Minh demanded that Cochinchina be joined with Annam and Tonkin into one independent Vietnamese state. As a compromise, a referendum would be held in which the people of Cochinchina would vote to join the other parts or to remain separate. The Viet Minh were certain the majority would vote for unification. But the Cochinchina colonial administration, ignoring the pledge of the French government, refused to hold the referendum.

Tensions continued to rise. The government of France, despite its leftist slant, was staunchly nationalistic and wished to restore French pride by reclaiming imperial territory. On November 23, 1946, a dispute over who controlled customs collections in the port of Haiphong precipitated skirmishes between Viet Minh and French units. French naval forces opened an artillery bombardment on the city, resulting in hundreds, perhaps thousands, of deaths.

THE FRENCH INDOCHINA WAR: 1946–1954

The French seized major cities and towns and built a colonial Vietnamese militia of more than 300,000 to help fight the Viet Minh. French allies included the most Europeanized Vietnamese, some anti-Vietnamese members of minority groups, the political-religious sects in the south, and the Binh Xuyen criminal mafia, which controlled much of the drug trade and organized prostitution in the Saigon area. France's military leaders anticipated that their professional army and superior firepower would bring victory in a few weeks. But the Viet Minh chose to fight on terrain that reduced the effectiveness of the French advantage in weaponry. Throughout the war with the French (and later with the United States) Vietnamese revolutionary forces, in addition to the small-unit harassment tactics characteristic of guerrilla warfare, often employed the technique of attacking many widely dispersed targets simultaneously, forcing the enemy to scatter its forces. Then, when possible, revolutionary forces would use large units to attack individual positions that had been drained of manpower to meet attacks elsewhere. The Viet Minh usually enjoyed popular support in the areas of military operation and were more highly motivated than the Vietnamese who fought alongside the French, often as mercenaries.

At the beginning of the war the Viet Minh emphasized the popular goal of winning independence. Rather than alienate potentially patriotic landlords and rich peasants, until 1953 the Viet Minh left landownership patterns intact while easing the economic burdens of the poor by reducing the rent that tenant farmers had to pay for the land they cultivated.

But in the later stage of the war, demands of the poor for land and the need for their increased involvement as revolutionary combatants and in transporting by foot large quantities of equipment prompted the Viet Minh in 1953 to begin significant land redistribution in much of the countryside (Moise 1983).

The French invited Bao Dai to resume the role of emperor in a partially independent French-sponsored Vietnamese state. They continued to control the country's economy and army. The men willing to serve the French in Bao Dai's cabinet were characterized by a US diplomat in Hanoi in 1952 as "opportunists, nonentities, extreme reactionaries, assassins, hirelings, and, finally, men of faded mental powers" (Karnow 1983, 180). As communist-led rebellions began to develop in Laos and Cambodia with Viet Minh assistance, the French allowed noncommunist governments in these countries to declare independence in 1953.

By the 1950s the French were experiencing extreme difficulty in Indochina. After the end of its revolution in 1949, China began giving valuable assistance to the Viet Minh, including artillery. The French economy could not support the war, and subsequently the United States, determined to help the French defeat the communist-led Viet Minh, was paying 78 percent of the cost of the war near its end, including Bao Dai's $4 million yearly stipend (Karnow 1983; Turley 1986). The French military started losing more officers in combat than were graduating from the main French military academy. And army morale deteriorated, not only because of battlefield losses, but also because much of the French public turned against the war.

In 1953 both the French and the Viet Minh were considering negotiations to end the fighting. But each side sought a final battlefield triumph that would give it the stronger bargaining position. General Giap, commander of the Viet Minh forces, sent three divisions toward Laos, taking the village of Dienbienphu on the Vietnamese-Laotian border. French commanders, eager to protect the pro-French Laotian government from the Viet Minh, decided to recapture the town and then use it as a base to attack Viet Minh camps. Despite its remote location, the French were confident it could be supplied by aircraft if necessary.

The first of 12,000 French paratroopers entered Dienbienphu in November 1953. Simultaneously, 50,000 Viet Minh, including artillery, antiaircraft, and engineering units, encircled them. In March 1954 Viet Minh forces attacked and quickly destroyed French artillery bases and the airfield. The Viet Minh then closed in by digging tunnels and trenches ever closer to French positions. The desperate French appealed unsuccessfully to the United States for heavy bomber attacks to break the siege. On May 7, 1954, the day the Geneva negotiations to end the fighting convened, the Viet Minh banner was raised over the French command center at Dienbienphu.

THE 1954 GENEVA ACCORDS ON INDOCHINA

As the Geneva Conference opened, the Viet Minh controlled most of the countryside in the northern two-thirds of Vietnam, with base camps, sizable liberated areas, and large forces in the southern third of the country (Karnow 1983; Turley 1986). The Viet Minh concluded they had won the war and expected to negotiate terms for the French departure. But they did not anticipate the compromise stance that would be taken by the two communist giants. The USSR leadership was attempting to establish better relations with the West after the death of Stalin in 1953 and avoided pushing for a settlement favorable to the Viet Minh. The Chinese had suffered a million casualties in the Korean War and were determined not to risk another violent confrontation with the United States. Both the USSR and China pressured the Viet Minh to settle for a partial victory (Karnow 1983; 1990; Turley 1986).

The key provisions of the Geneva settlement included a temporary division of Vietnam at latitude 17 degrees north—the 17th parallel—which explicitly was not to be a national boundary. French units were to be withdrawn south of this line and Viet Minh forces to the north. No foreign military forces were to be introduced into Vietnam. And the settlement stipulated that elections would be held throughout Vietnam in 1956 to unify the country under one government (Bergerud 1991; Duiker 1995, 2000; Karnow 1983; Lacouture 1968; McAlister 1969; Turley 1986; Wolf 1969).

The fulfillment of the Geneva Accords was to be supervised by observers from Canada, India, and Poland. During a three-hundred-day regroupment period, about 900,000 Vietnamese moved south of the 17th parallel (about two-thirds were Catholics fearing communist persecution and encouraged by CIA leaflets stating, "Christ has gone to the South," while the rest were largely businessmen and employees of the French); approximately 87,000 Viet Minh combatants and 47,000 civilians headed north (Turley 1986, 11).

US INVOLVEMENT IN VIETNAM: 1954–1975

The US decision to provide aid to the French in Indochina was based, in part, on the conception of a monolithic communist movement expanding outward from its origin in European Russia. In this formulation, communist China represented the success of communist aggression against China, and Ho Chi Minh and the Viet Minh represented communist aggression against Vietnam (supposedly directed from China). Ignoring the nationalistic character of the Viet Minh movement and the fact that Vietnam's unique history and political and economic characteristics had brought about an essentially nonexportable revolution (except, in a sense, to the two other countries of French Indochina), the Eisenhower administration resolved to stop the spread of communism.

President Diem: An Anticommunist Leader

An important aspect of the plan to prevent southern Vietnam from reuniting with the north was the selection of a leader for the south who was both anticommunist and recognized as a nationalist. The anticommunist chosen for South Vietnam was Ngo Dinh Diem. Diem was born to a wealthy Catholic family at Hue in 1901 and attended the French School of Administration in Hanoi, where he finished first in his class. He rose rapidly through governmental ranks and in 1933 was appointed minister of the interior to Emperor Bao Dai. He resigned because of French interference in his official duties. This earned him the reputation of being a Vietnamese patriot among Vietnam's middle- and upper-class anticommunist nationalists. Diem, who at one time considered becoming a priest, was a religious ascetic. His conception of exercising political authority was akin to the absolute power of Vietnam's ancient emperors, and "concepts of compromise, power-sharing and popular participation" were alien to him (Turley 1986, 13).

The Viet Minh captured Diem in 1945. In 1946 Ho Chi Minh offered him a governmental position, but he refused to work with communists. He blamed the Viet Minh for the death of a brother and a nephew. In 1950, after residing in seclusion at Hue, he left Vietnam and settled at the Maryknoll Seminary in Lakewood, New Jersey. Diem came to the attention of the influential Catholic leader Cardinal Spellman and was later accepted by the Eisenhower administration as an anticommunist leader for southern Vietnam.

In July 1954 Diem was appointed prime minister of South Vietnam by Emperor Bao Dai. By 1955 the Eisenhower administration was pouring economic and military aid into South Vietnam. It organized the soldiers who had served in the French colonial armed forces into what was called the Army of the Republic of Vietnam (ARVN). The weapons and military advisers the US sent to Vietnam violated the Geneva Accords. During the same year, Diem consolidated his power by intimidating and bribing the leaders of the political-religious sects and pursuing military action against the French-supported Binh Xuyen crime group. He also turned on Bao Dai, eliminating the position of emperor through a rigged referendum in October 1955 (Karnow 1983).

MAP 4.2 Vietnam (1954–1975)

CHINA

NORTH
VIETNAM

Red River

BURMA

•Dienbienphu

LAOS

Hanoi•

•Haiphong

Gulf of

Tonkin

Mekong

"Demilitarized Zone"
(July 22, 1954)

THAILAND

Hue•

River

SOUTH
VIETNAM

CAMBODIA

Phnom Penh•

•Saigon

Gulf of

Thailand

South China

Sea

Diem refused to hold the reunification elections scheduled for 1956, anticipating that Ho Chi Minh and the Viet Minh would win (Karnow 1983; Turley 1986; Wolf 1969). He launched the fierce Denunciation of Communists Campaign, in which thousands of Viet Minh supporters, relatively unprotected since most of the revolutionary soldiers had gone north as called for by the Geneva Accords, were imprisoned. Many were tortured to obtain information about their compatriots, and some were killed. Morale among Viet Minh sympathizers in the south deteriorated because the government in the north would not immediately give consent for armed resistance to Diem's repression.

Ho Chi Minh and the government of the Democratic Republic of Vietnam in the north hoped international pressure would force the Diem regime to hold the reunification elections and clung to this increasingly remote possibility because they anticipated the devastation a war with the United States would bring. And they were unsure of what assistance the USSR and China would be willing to provide in the event of large-scale US intervention.

The North Vietnamese government also became preoccupied in the mid-1950s with the mishandled land reform program, which had created chaos in parts of the north. The planners selected mainly poor, semiliterate rural youth to implement the reform. These young zealots, often recruited from the revolutionary army, had thrown the countryside into an uproar by organizing other poor peasants to denounce landlords for past crimes, such as collaborating with the French. Seized lands were distributed to 75 percent of the region's peasants. But 5,000 to 15,000 landlords and collaborators were killed by peasants who blamed them for the deaths of loved ones and other past hardships (Moise 1983).

Distressed by disruptions, protests, and injustices resulting from the poorly executed land reform, the North Vietnamese government initiated a period of self-criticism and reassessment. Eventually many of North Vietnam's peasants were organized into lower-stage, or semisocialist, cooperatives. Participants retained individual ownership of their pooled land, livestock, and equipment. The cooperative paid them rent in proportion to their contributed assets as well as a share of the profits in proportion to their labor (Duiker 1983; Moise 1983). During the 1960s most cooperatives became higher-stage, or fully socialist, in that land and productive agricultural property were owned collectively by all members of the cooperative, with an individual paid only in proportion to the amount of work he or she performed.

In the south the Saigon regime repressed Viet Minh activists and suspected communists, seriously damaging the revolutionary social network. Surviving Communist Party members demanded that the government north of the 17th parallel consent to their launching all-out armed resistance against Saigon forces (Bergerud 1991; Race 1972; Turley 1986).

The call for violent opposition to the South Vietnamese government was well received by large numbers of peasants. Since 1954 they had been outraged by Saigon's policies, particularly reversal of the land reform that the Viet Minh had carried out in much of the countryside. Saigon forced poor peasants to return their land to former landlords and then pay rent for its use. The Saigon regime, in attempting to assert control over the countryside, allied itself with the rural landlord class, which had fled to the cities during the war. The Saigon government returned the landlords to the villages, some as village administrators, protected by armed guards, and largely reinstituted the economic and political domination of the traditional rural elite (Bergerud 1991; Race 1972).

Formation of the National Liberation Front

On December 20, 1960, resistance forces proclaimed the formation of the National Liberation Front (NLF) of South Vietnam, an organization of southern nationalists united under the leadership of the southern branch of Vietnam's Communist Party for the purpose of bringing about the reunification of Vietnam (Turley 1986). The Diem government quickly branded the NLF the "Viet Cong" (Viet Communists). The leaders of the Communist Party evidently hoped that the actions of the NLF, together with expected mass uprisings against Diem, would precipitate the formation of a coalition government in the south that would include representatives of the NLF. The new government would then hold negotiations with the north to reunify Vietnam. The decision to mobilize the southern nationalists for armed resistance to the Diem regime under the banner of the NLF resulted in a rapid revitalization of both the revolutionary effort and Communist Party membership in the south, which reached 70,000 by 1963 (Turley 1986). NLF armed forces grew at a dramatic pace, and attacks on Saigon forces multiplied.

As the NLF expanded, the Diem regime, with US support, launched the so-called strategic hamlet program, which relocated peasants from their homes to fortified sites or fortified existing hamlets (Bergerud 1991; Duiker 1983; Turley 1986). According to Saigon authorities, the peasants in their new living environments would be safe from Viet Cong terrorism. They would also be inhibited from supporting or joining the NLF, if they were so inclined. The policy was a counterinsurgency technique intended to deprive revolutionary forces of their popular support by physically removing its source—the peasants—from the open countryside (an attempt to starve the guerrilla "fish" by drying up the popular "sea" that nourished them). However, many peasants resented being displaced from their ancestral villages and compelled to build hamlets and fortifications so that they could reside under the surveillance of the Saigon regime and be subjected to its coercive measures. The strategic hamlet program was so unpopular with most peasants that it influenced many to join the NLF. In fact, the ARVN colonel in charge of implementing the program for the Saigon regime secretly belonged to the National Liberation Front (Karnow 1983). It is likely that he helped carry out the policy precisely because of its positive impact on NLF recruitment.

Diem favored the Catholic minority, of which he was a member. This prompted opposition from some Buddhists, and Diem responded with violent repression. After several Buddhist monks set fire to themselves in protests in June 1963, Diem's special forces, commanded by his brother, donned regular army uniforms and raided several Buddhist pagodas. These counterproductive actions outraged many ARVN officers, mostly Buddhists. Saigon's top military leaders also resented Diem's interference in the war against the NLF. Fearing a possible military plot against his government, Diem regularly rotated officers around the country. Consequently, they were unable to adapt to one command situation before they were shifted to another. Moreover, military incompetence was reinforced by Diem's tendency to promote loyalists rather than those most able (Karnow 1983; Turley 1986).

Most important, Diem's regime was clearly losing the war. Both Washington and the Saigon general staff decided that Diem had to go. On November 1, 1963, most of Diem's generals, assured of support or at least noninterference by US officials, rebelled (Karnow 1983). Diem and his brother were executed the next day. President John F. Kennedy, although anticipating that Diem would be forced out, was shocked by his killing. On November 22, 1963, Kennedy, who had reportedly decided to begin withdrawing US forces from Vietnam, was himself assassinated in Dallas.

At the end of 1963 some 15,000 US military advisers were in South Vietnam. Several thousand former Viet Minh had moved south to help organize the growing NLF ranks, but these were almost all individuals born in the south who had gone north in line with the 1954 peace accords (Karnow 1983; Turley 1986). In Saigon a council of generals replaced Diem. Leadership changed hands seven times in 1964, as Saigon military figures struggled for power. According to Turley (1986, 52), Saigon's military leaders were "mostly products of French education and bourgeois families, holdovers of the colonial system who made up the South's anti-Communist elite" and were usually unconcerned with the economic hardships experienced by the majority of the population. After Diem, corruption in the military appeared to increase. And the NLF continued to expand the area it controlled. US advisers concluded that only large-scale US military action could save the Saigon regime (Karnow 1983; Turley 1986).

Massive US Military Intervention

On August 2, 1964, an American destroyer, the *Maddox*, engaged in close surveillance in the Gulf of Tonkin off the coast of North Vietnam, was attacked by North

Vietnamese patrol boats. ARVN units had earlier raided several positions in the area. The patrol boat incident, which inflicted no damage on the US vessel, and a second alleged but unconfirmed incident involving another destroyer two days later, were represented to Congress and the US public as unprovoked Communist aggression. On August 7, 1964, the US Congress passed the Gulf of Tonkin Resolution (unanimously in the House of Representatives and with only two dissenting votes in the Senate), giving President Lyndon Johnson the power to take any military action necessary to defend US forces. This vote constituted congressional authorization for the war in Southeast Asia, and until 1973 Congress would continue to vote appropriations for various aspects of the conflict (Karnow 1983; McNamara 1995).

In February 1965 the United States initiated continuous bombing raids over North Vietnam, and by December US troop strength reached 200,000. Regular North Vietnamese army (People's Army of Vietnam) units were entering the south along the Ho Chi Minh Trail (a network of mountain and jungle paths extending through Laos into Vietnam's central highlands as well as into its southern regions) to assist several hundred thousand NLF (Viet Cong) fighters organized into village militia, regional defense units, and main combat units. US force levels continued to rise, approaching 500,000 by the end of 1967. The Soviet Union provided the north with weapons, including anti-aircraft missiles, and China contributed weapons and rice.

In a 1967 South Vietnamese election without NLF participation—but with eleven slates of candidates—General Thieu, a former major in the French army who had married into a wealthy Catholic family and converted from Buddhism to Catholicism, and his running mate, General Ky, won with 34.5 percent of the vote (Karnow 1983; Kolko 1985). Toward the end of that year, US military leaders assured President Johnson and the US public that the war was being won and that enemy forces would be hard-pressed to mount any significant attacks. This assessment was highly inaccurate. Communist Party leaders planned an offensive that would significantly affect the course of the war. It was set for the Vietnamese new year, Tet, January 31, 1968.

The Tet offensive had several goals. The main ones were to disrupt Saigon's efforts to expand control over the countryside by forcing its forces to fall back toward the cities into defensive positions; to destroy the confidence and sense of security of the Saigon government's urban supporters, who had been sheltered from the violence of the war; and to disrupt any US or Saigon plans to invade the north. The organizers also hoped that Tet would disillusion the US government and public and demonstrate that the conflict would last indefinitely if US troops were not withdrawn. The most optimistic potential outcome, which few planners expected, was to provoke widespread uprisings throughout the south to end the war and reunify the country before the death of Ho Chi Minh (who was ill and would die in 1969) (Karnow 1990; Kolko 1985; Turley 1986).

On January 31 approximately 80,000 National Liberation Front soldiers simultaneously attacked about one hundred cities and towns (North Vietnamese units took part in assaults in the northernmost sections of South Vietnam) (Duiker 1995; Karnow 1983; Turley 1986). Four thousand NLF fighters invaded Saigon, and one unit seized the grounds of the US embassy before being annihilated. Hue, the old imperial capital, was captured and held for weeks against a tremendous counterattack organized by US and Saigon forces. In the end, all the major cities and towns captured by the NLF were retaken.

The NLF suffered as many as 40,000 casualties, a devastation that would take years of recovery. The offensive, however, did weaken Saigon's control over areas of the countryside previously thought to have been secured from the NLF. But probably the most important consequence of Tet was the powerful demoralizing effect it had on the US public and government. Top military leaders who had previously claimed the war was being won now appeared incompetent or deceitful. The war itself seemed destined to go on without end. While Vietnamese revolutionaries were prepared to keep fighting for decades, the US public was willing to endure the sacrifices of warfare only if a limit could be set and victory assured (Karnow 1983).

Although virtually all observable military targets in North Vietnam had been repeatedly bombed, some US political figures called for greater armed might, such as a US invasion of North Vietnam or even tactical nuclear weapons. However, this demand ignored important realities. The publicly asserted purpose for the US presence in Vietnam was to promote democracy. But the massive resistance to US intervention by millions of Vietnamese suggested that the high level of military violence used was necessary precisely because US policy ran counter to the aspirations of the majority of Vietnamese. Since many of the people of other nations not directly involved in the conflict interpreted the situation in this manner, the US government received little support from its major allies for its actions in Vietnam. Greater levels of military force might have further isolated the US. Of critical importance, moreover, all the presidents and Congresses of the Vietnam era feared the possibility of direct military intervention by the USSR and China. That could have forced the United States to choose between accepting an enormous military catastrophe for its forces in Vietnam or using nuclear weapons in an attempt to protect them, possibly precipitating a world war.

Public opinion in the United States turned decisively against the war after the Tet offensive. Some who voted for peace candidates in the 1968 presidential primary campaign (Eugene McCarthy and Robert Kennedy, who was assassinated after winning the California Democratic primary) felt the war was immoral. Others believed US forces were not allowed to use all their destructive might to win the war (Karnow 1983). But clearly, after 1968 the majority of Americans demanded an end to the conflict.

Richard Nixon, inaugurated president in January 1969, pledged to end the war with honor. Before he took office, 30,000 Americans had died in Southeast Asia, and over 26,000 more would perish before the final US departure in 1975. Nixon's approach involved greatly increasing the size and level of armament of the Saigon armed forces while gradually withdrawing US units. This process was referred to as Vietnamization. Nixon also threatened massive bombing attacks against the North Vietnamese to pressure concessions during negotiations (Karnow 1983).

1973 Peace Agreement

The peace agreement between the Nixon administration and North Vietnam permitted North Vietnamese troops to remain in place in South Vietnam. The Saigon government was to enter into negotiations with the NLF's provisional revolutionary government to form a coalition government in South Vietnam. The new coalition government would then negotiate the issue of reunification with the north. US prisoners of war would be returned, and the US would provide economic assistance to Vietnam. In essence, the peace agreement was much like what the National Liberation Front had hoped to achieve when taking up arms in the early 1960s. Thieu and many in his Saigon government were outraged by the peace accords (Kolko 1985).

Nixon promised Thieu that any communist offensive in violation of the treaty would be countered with massive US air attacks. Saigon's air force was, at the time, the fourth largest in the world (Karnow 1983). Thieu ignored the cease-fire in certain areas and ordered his army to attack NLF units and seize territory. His plan was evidently to expand the land (and population) under his control until that held by the NLF was insignificant, thereby making the formation of a coalition government appear unnecessary (Karnow 1983).

Communist-led forces, however, poured equipment and soldiers into the south in preparation for the final campaign to reunify Vietnam. The offensive was launched in March 1975. Since Nixon had been forced to resign in August 1974 over the Watergate affair, and Congress had banned any further US military action in Southeast Asia, Saigon's forces were on their own. Initial communist victories in Vietnam's central highlands precipitated an ARVN retreat, which turned into a rout. As some ARVN generals and other officers fled Vietnam, enlisted soldiers surrendered or changed into civilian clothes and simply went home (Karnow 1983; Kolko 1985; Turley 1986). With the exception of a few South Vietnamese army and air units, the startlingly sudden collapse of Saigon's forces appeared to testify to the inherent weakness and moral shallowness of the Saigon government. Communist-led forces accepted the surrender of Saigon on April 30, 1975, and renamed it Ho Chi Minh City. Vietnam reunited into a single nation. In retaliation for the communist offensive, the US canceled its assistance and enforced a trade embargo on Vietnam, which was not lifted until 1994. The United States and Vietnam finally established formal ties in August 1995 (*New York Times*, August 6, 1995, 3).

AFTERMATH AND RELATED DEVELOPMENTS

At least 200,000 former South Vietnamese government officials and military officers were sent to reeducation camps for a few months to several years. Upon release, many of these men and their families joined the more than 1 million people who emigrated from Vietnam after the war.

Vietnam was left to repair war damage, clear mines and bombs, and cope with the medical and ecological catastrophe caused by thousands of tons of herbicides spread over the countryside (the US military had attempted to defoliate large areas to inhibit the movement of enemy forces). The country also had to care for hundreds of thousands of injured soldiers and civilians and thousands of war orphans. Population growth of 3 percent per year put additional strains on resources.

US conditions for establishing diplomatic and commercial relations with Vietnam included assistance in resolving questions concerning more than 2,200 US personnel missing in action (MIA). Most Vietnamese had little hope of finding the remains of their estimated 300,000 MIAs (*New York Times*, October 10, 2002, A1).

The constitution of the Socialist Republic of Vietnam specified that the nationally elected legislature, the National Assembly, was Vietnam's supreme governing body. But the legislature tended to be subservient to the executive branch (Duiker 1995), which initially consisted of a presidency with strong powers. The 1980 constitution created an executive committee headed by the prime minister, which replaced the position of president. A new constitution was enacted in 1992 and then amended in 2001 (Socialist Republic of Vietnam 2013).

The constitution stipulated that the Communist Party was the leading political force. The party maintained its political dominance due to several factors. Duiker (1995) suggested that one reason was the "paternalistic character of Vietnamese political culture," which "idealizes benevolent despotism and a hierarchal view of social relationships" (Duiker 1995, 122, 123). Duiker's second reason was that the Communist Party enjoys its dominant position since the party played a "historically central role in the creation of an independent and united Vietnam" (Duiker 1995, 123).

Inadequate economic progress caused the country's leaders to implement renovation (*doi moi*) reforms in 1986. Similar to reforms adopted earlier in China, these policies gave farmers greater control over their crops and permitted direct foreign investment. Economic growth accelerated. Vietnam became the second largest exporter of rice, as its agricultural production increased by 100 percent. By 2001 privately owned enterprises produced about 20 percent of industrial output, foreign investment about 30 percent, and state-owned companies approximately 50 percent (Manyin 2003, 12–13). Poverty in rural areas declined from 66 percent in 1993 (World Bank 2005) to 11 percent in 2012 (CIA 2014). In 2012 GDP growth was about 5 percent. Vietnam achieved major advances in the exploration and extraction of energy resources, such as oil and natural gas, and development of hydroelectric power (Index Mundi 2013).

The significance of business enterprise for the welfare of the Vietnamese people and the continued leadership of the Communist Partly led the party's central committee to allow private businessmen to be considered for Communist Party membership in 2005 (BBC News, July 18, 2005). Like other countries shifting from central planning to market economies with private business ownership and large-scale foreign investment, Vietnam experienced expanded corruption. The reasons appeared to be new opportunities for corruption inherent in competition among enterprises, as the proprietors of some attempted to gain unfair advantages through bribery, and a decrease in the state's ability to deter corruption through effective detection and punishment in the decentralizing economy.

In 2004 a major organized crime figure, Troung Nam Cam, charged with murder, assault, extortion, drug trafficking, bribery, and other offenses, was executed by firing squad along with four of his gang members (BBC News, July 16, 2002; June 3, 2004a; June 3, 2004b). Some 150 people stood trial in connection with the case, including two expelled members of the 150-member Communist Party central committee, the former head of the state radio system, and the former director of police in Troung Nam Cam's base of operation, Ho Chi Minh City. He was accused of allowing the gang to operate without fear of police interference. Corruption continued to be a major problem and global surveys have given Vietnam a poor rating on this issue (Thanh Nien News 2013). Top Communist Party leaders have repeatedly committed themselves to fighting corruption. In November, 2013, a court in Ho Chi Minh City handed down a death sentence to the former director general of the Vietnam Bank for Agricultural and Development's Financial Leasing Company No. 2 for embezzlement, fraud, and other offenses in a loan scam that cost over $25 million. The head of a construction company was also sentenced to death for allegedly taking $3 million in the scam. Three other businessmen and nine other bank officials received prison terms for three to fourteen years.

Many Vietnamese are aware of the social devastation that occurred in several postcommunist regimes. Despite the shortcomings of Vietnam's political system, fear of similar disasters may inhibit sweeping political change. Since Vietnam has repeatedly been invaded by foreign powers, the US invasion of oil-rich Iraq on a false WMD allegation undoubtedly reminded Vietnamese of the Gulf of Tonkin incident that a previous US administration used to justify its catastrophic intervention in Vietnam. The perception of international lawlessness and unjustified resort to violence by the world's most powerful nation strengthens governments that use the threat of foreign imperialism to block political change. One implication is that democratization in Vietnam and elsewhere is partially dependent on the choices of voters in the United States.

Some officials were concerned that the tendency to criticize government policy was greater among Vietnamese who attended foreign universities. In 2013, 16,098 Vietnamese were attending US colleges and universities (Consulate General of the United States, Ho Chi Minh, Vietnam 2013). Public controversy developed over a plan to allow a Chinese company to mine bauxite in the central highlands (Mydans 2009). Critics raised concerns over potential environmental damage, displacement of thousands of ethnic minority people, and Chinese influence over the economy. The country's greatest war hero, General Vo Nguyen Giap, who would die in 2013 at age 102 (Gregory 2013), joined the protest against the project. Government leaders responded by providing more information and assuring the public that the environment and minority groups would be protected and that Chinese involvement would be limited. These events indicated a willingness to respond positively to popular protests. But the government still imprisoned citizens who called for multiparty democracy, including US-educated human rights lawyer Le Cong Dinh, charged with violating Article 79 of the criminal code, which forbids "carrying out activities aimed at overthrowing the people's administration" (Mydans 2010). Limits were reportedly imposed on blogs and other Internet discussion sites and access to Facebook. The government punished activists for publicly protesting certain policies of the Chinese government (Lai 2013). Yet on November 12, 2013, Vietnam was elected to the United Nations Human Rights Council for the 2014–2016 period, receiving 184 favorable votes out of 193, the highest number among the fourteen countries elected to the forty-seven-member council in that year (Vietnam News 2013). On the social front, Vietnamese lawmakers in 2013 proposed to decriminalize, but not officially recognize, gay marriage (Than Nien News 2013b).

Summary and Analysis

The prime unifying motivation for revolution in Vietnam was the goal of throwing off foreign subjugation. For hundreds of years the Vietnamese fought against a multitude of enemies, taking on and often defeating Chinese armies, the forces of Kubla Khan, and numerous other foes before the twentieth century. Vietnamese nationalism, although temporarily checked by the modern weaponry of Western nations, experienced a rapid resurgence in the 1920s and, heightened further by colonial repression, contributed greatly to the development of the revolution.

Frustrated nationalism and widespread economic hardship led to mass discontent and popular participation in revolution. Traditional inequalities of Vietnamese society had occasionally spurred rebellions against landlords and exploitation by the mandarin elite. In many ways the French colonization of Vietnam, while elevating a small percentage of Vietnamese to great wealth and extending the benefits of Western education and technology to a larger minority, brought dislocation, loss of self-sufficiency, and dependence on the world market to much of the peasantry. Many rural residents were transformed into tenant farmers, plantation workers, or mine or factory laborers. Downturns in the world economy meant lower prices for exports and hardships for those at the bottom of Vietnam's economic pyramid. Mass starvation occurred in northern Vietnam during World War II when the occupying powers disrupted agriculture. This disaster intensified hostility against the French, the Japanese, and those Vietnamese who supported the foreigners.

A small percentage of Vietnamese obtained access to the French colonial educational system, and some even studied in France. After the 1920s three major divisions existed among the educated. First, French colonization had generated a small but significant Francophile elite among the Vietnamese, including large landowners, some in the Catholic minority, officers in the French-trained Vietnamese colonial army, and some businessmen. These individuals supported close ties with France, if not outright colonial status, and hundreds were granted French as well as Vietnamese citizenship. Most in this group shifted their allegiance to the United States after the French defeat in the 1946–1954 war.

A second elite element claimed to be nationalists (i.e., neither front men for a foreign power nor communists) but were anticommunists, such as Ngo Dinh Diem. But Diem and his supporters manifested little interest in the welfare of the population. The Diem regime did little to redistribute resources to the masses. Lack of commitment to social revolution reduced the appeal of noncommunist nationalists to peasants, and sponsorship by foreign powers undermined their claims to nationalism.

The third elite element to develop in Vietnam during the 1920s was composed of Marxist-oriented, largely middle-class, educated individuals who came together as the Indochinese Communist Party in 1930. Ho Chi Minh did more than anyone else to organize the ICP and develop its revolutionary program. The ICP fused traditionally fierce and resilient Vietnamese nationalism with Marxist-Leninist concepts. The result was an ideology that called for both the defeat of imperialism (attainment of true independence) and the defeat of feudalism (social revolution involving redistribution of resources). The party's program won broad support. Eventually the ICP, accepting Ho Chi Minh's view, put primary emphasis on achieving independence from foreign domination.

During the revolutionary conflict, the antirevolutionary state was always flawed in terms of its legitimacy to govern the Vietnamese people because it was either the creation of some foreign power or dependent on foreign support. From the early

1930s to 1955, the playboy emperor, Bao Dai, occupied the role of puppet for which-
ever outside power was paying the bills. Diem, dependent on US economic and military aid, which was used to suppress revolutionaries and Buddhist religious leaders
alike, also failed to gain the support of most Vietnamese. The succession of generals
who followed Diem included General Thieu during 1967–1975; he had previously
served in the French colonial army.

The coercive capability of the antirevolutionary state fluctuated over time. On
paper it was high at the time of the victorious communist offensive in 1975. Saigon had 1 million soldiers and outnumbered its adversaries in the south by about
three to one. But South Vietnam's army was riddled with corruption. After US
combat troops departed in 1973, the South Vietnamese economy went into decline,
deprived of US service members shopping for goods, bars, drugs, and prostitutes.
Urban unemployment rose to 40 percent. Many Saigon officers embezzled army
funds and even charged tolls for other military units to cross through areas they
controlled. By 1975 the large majority of enlisted soldiers were not earning enough
to support their families, and morale was low (Karnow 1983; Kolko 1985; Turley
1986). Deprived of US support, the Saigon government and military could not with-
stand the onslaught of highly motivated revolutionary forces.

The Vietnamese revolution experienced periodic windows of permissiveness
regarding the larger world context. The 1936–1939 Popular Front government in
France released many ICP members from Vietnamese prisons and presented an
opportunity for the ICP to organize openly after earlier repression. The Japanese
overthrow of French colonial authority in March 1945 provided the Viet Minh with
five months of relative freedom of movement in the countryside, during which it established base areas and created the revolutionary armed forces. The several weeks
between the mid-August surrender of the Japanese and the arrival of Chinese and
British (and later French) occupation forces provided favorable conditions for
revolutionary insurrections. These occurred with virtually no resistance from the
demoralized Japanese in more than sixty Vietnamese cities. After that, the coercive power of the French (400,000 Vietnamese killed during 1946–1954) and the
massive military strength of the United States (about 3 million Vietnamese dead
between 1956 and 1975) were inadequate to reverse a revolution that long before had
succeeded in achieving widespread popular support. Steadily declining US interest
in supporting the Saigon regime after 1973 resulted in nonintervention during the
1975 communist offensive and a relatively quick end to the military conflict.

The US lifted its economic embargo against Vietnam in 1994, and in 1995 the
two nations established diplomatic relations. Like China, Vietnam enacted market-
oriented reforms and permitted foreign investment. Vietnam's development
of its energy resources soared. As its economy grew at a strong pace in the early
twenty-first century and poverty declined, Vietnam experienced new forms of

corruption, increased criticism of government and Communist Party officials, and popular demands for greater political democratization.

The Vietnam conflict had long-term impacts on the United States and its policies. The wars in Afghanistan and Iraq under the administrations of George W. Bush and Barack Obama elicited comparisons to the US involvement in Vietnam (Bai 2009; Barry 2009). And the memory of the Vietnam War, along with the deceptions and the difficulties of America's more recent wars, continues to influence decisions regarding whether and how to get involved in new international conflicts.

VIETNAMESE REVOLUTION: CHRONOLOGY OF MAJOR EVENTS

1847–1883	In a series of wars, French forces defeat the Vietnamese and establish control over Vietnam, Cambodia, and Laos, which they call "French Indochina"
1919	Ho Chi Minh's proposal for Vietnamese autonomy rejected at Paris Peace Conference
1930	French suppress noncommunist Vietnamese nationalists; Vietnamese Communist Party (called the Indochinese Communist Party) founded
1940	France defeated by Germany; Vietnam occupied by Japanese forces
1941	Communist-led nationalist movement, Viet Minh, established
1945	August Revolution results in Vietnamese declaration of independence
1946–1954	French Indochina War; victory for the Viet Minh
1954	Geneva Peace Conference temporarily divides Vietnam
1954–1959	Diem becomes leader of South Vietnam and uses US support to suppress opponents and prevent reunification
1960	National Liberation Front (NLF) formed
1963	Diem assassinated; Johnson becomes US president after Kennedy assassination
1964	Gulf of Tonkin Resolution passed by US Congress
1965–1973	Major commitment of US armed forces to conflict in Vietnam
1968	Tet offensive increases antiwar sentiment in the United States
1975	Vietnam reunified
1994	United States lifts trade embargo
1995	United States and Vietnam establish full diplomatic relations
2000	Bill Clinton becomes the first US president to visit Vietnam since reunification
2005	Prime Minister Phan Van Khai becomes the first Vietnamese leader to visit the United States since the end of the war

2006 Vietnamese economy continues rapid growth as leaders promise intensified crackdown on corruption

2008 Prime Minister Nguyen Tan Dung makes official visit to Washington confirming normalization of relations

2010 Several pro–multiparty democracy activists sentenced to prison terms

2012 The percentage of persons below the poverty income line in Vietnam falls to 11

2013 General Vo Nguyen Giap, leader of the Vietnamese revolutionary military forces, dies; Vietnam's energy resources soar

References and Further Readings

Bai, Matt. 2009. "Escalations." *New York Times*, November 1. www.nytimes.com /2009/11/01/magazine/01fob-wwln-t.html.

Bain, Chester A. 1967. *Vietnam: The Roots of Conflict*. Englewood Cliffs, NJ: Prentice-Hall.

Barry, John. 2009. "Could Afghanistan Be Obama's Vietnam?" *Newsweek*, January 31. www.newsweek.com/2009/01/30/obama-s-vietnam.html.

BBC News. July 16, 2002. "Vietnam Officials Sacked for Mob Links." news.bbc.co.uk/2 /hi/asia-pacific/2129842.stm.

———. June 3, 2004a. "Nam Cam: Vietnam's Godfather." news.bbc.co.uk/2/hi/asia -pacific/2794607.stm.

———. June 3, 2004b. "Vietnam Executes Gang Leader." news.bbc.co.uk/2/hi/asia -pacific/3772037.stm.

———. July 18, 2005. "Vietnam Party Eying Capitalists." news.bbc.co.uk/2/hi/asia -pacific/4693449.stm.

———. March 2, 2006. "Communist Debate Grips Vietnam." news.bbc.co.uk/2/hi /asia-pacific/4766846.stm.

Bergerud, Eric M. 1991. *The Dynamics of Defeat: The Vietnam War in Hau Nghia Province*. Boulder: Westview.

Central Intelligence Agency (CIA). 2014. "Vietnam." In *World Factbook*. www.cia.gov /library/publications/the-world-factbook/geos/vm.html.

Consulate General of the United States, Ho Chi Minh, Vietnam. 2013. "16,098 Vietnamese Students Studying at United States Colleges and Universities." http://hochiminh. usconsulate.gov/pr-11132013.html. Accessed January 28, 2014.

Duiker, William J. 1976. *The Rise of Nationalism in Vietnam, 1900–1941*. Ithaca, NY: Cornell University Press.

———. 1983. *Vietnam: Nation in Revolution*. Boulder: Westview.

———. 1995. *Vietnam: Revolution in Transition*. Boulder: Westview.

———. 2000. *Ho Chi Minh*. New York: Hyperion.

Dunn, John D. 1972. *Modern Revolutions: An Introduction to the Analysis of a Political Phenomenon.* Cambridge, UK: Cambridge University Press.

Duong, Pham Cao. 1985. *Vietnamese Peasants Under French Domination, 1861–1945.* Monograph Series 24. Berkeley: Center for South and Southeast Asia Studies, University of California.

Giap, Vo Nguyen. 1962. *People's War, People's Army: The Viet Công Insurrection Manual for Underdeveloped Countries.* Praeger: New York.

Gregory, Joseph R. 2013. "Gen. Vo Nguyen Giap, Who Ousted US From Vietnam, Is Dead." *New York Times,* October 4. www.nytimes.com/2013/10/05/world/asia/gen-vo-nguyen-giap-dies.html?pagewanted=all&_r=0&pagewanted=printIndex.

Joshi, Pradnya. 2009. "Vietnam Is Refining Its Role on the Global Stage." *New York Times,* December 25. www.nytimes.com/2009/12/25/business/global/25export.html.

Karnow, Stanley. 1983. *Vietnam: A History.* New York: Viking.

———. 1990. "Hanoi's Legendary General Giap Remembers." *New York Times Magazine,* June 24.

Khanh, Huynh Kim. 1982. *Vietnamese Communism: 1925–1945.* Ithaca, NY: Cornell University Press.

Kolko, Gabriel. 1985. *Anatomy of a War: Vietnam, the United States, and the Modern Historical Experience.* New York: Pantheon.

Lacouture, Jean. 1968. *Ho Chi Minh: A Political Biography.* New York: Random House.

Lai, Tuong. 2013. "Vietnam's Angry Feet." *New York Times,* June 6. http://www.nytimes.com/2013/06/07/opinion/vietnams-angry-feet.html?_r=0.

Manyin, Mark E. 2003. *CRS Issue Brief for Congress: The Vietnam-US Normalization Process.* Washington, DC: Congressional Research Service.

Marr, David G. 1971. *Vietnamese Anticolonialism: 1885–1925.* Berkeley: University of California Press.

McAlister, John T., Jr. 1969. *Vietnam: The Origins of Revolution.* New York: Knopf.

McNamara, Robert S. 1995. *In Retrospect: The Tragedy and Lessons of Vietnam.* New York: Random House.

Moise, Edwin E. 1983. *Land Reform in China and North Vietnam: Consolidating the Revolution at the Village Level.* Chapel Hill: University of North Carolina Press.

Mundi. 2013. "Viet Nam." December 10. www.indexmundi.com/energy.aspx?country=vn&product=ethanol&graph=production.

Mydans, Seth. 2009. "War Hero in Vietnam Forces Government to Listen." *New York Times,* June 29. www.nytimes.com/2009/06/29/world/asia/29iht-viet.html.

———. 2010. "Vietnam, Quelling Dissent, Gives 4 Democracy Advocates Jail Terms." *New York Times,* January 21. www.nytimes.com/2010/01/21/world/asia/21vietnam.html.

New York Times. August 6, 1995. "In a War-Haunted Hanoi, US Opens Formal Ties," 3.

———. October 10, 2002. "Vietnam Seeking to Identify 300,000 MIAs from War," A1.

Popkin, Samuel L. 1979. *The Rational Peasant: The Political Economy of Rural Society in Vietnam*. Berkeley: University of California Press.

Race, Jeffrey. 1972. *War Comes to Long An: Revolutionary Conflict in a Vietnamese Province*. Berkeley: University of California Press.

Socialist Republic of Vietnam. 2013. *1992 Constitution of the Socialist Republic of Vietnam (As Amended 25 December 2001)*. www.vietnamlaws.com/freelaws/Constitution 92(aa01).pdf.

Tai, Hue-Tam Ho. 1983. *Millenarianism and Peasant Politics in Vietnam*. Harvard East Asian Series 99. Cambridge: Harvard University Press.

Than Nien News. 2013a. "How Tough Is Vietnam Actually Getting on Corruption?" November 18. www.thanhniennews.com/index/pages/20131114-how-tough-is-vietnam-actually-getting-on-corruption.aspx.

———. 2013b. "Vietnam Moves to Decriminalize, Not Recognize Gay Marriage." November 18. www.thanhniennews.com/index/pages/20131116-draft-law-shows-vietnam-undecided-about-gay-marriage.aspx.

Transparency International Global Coalition against Corruption. 2011. "Corruption Perceptions Index 2011." www.transparency.org/cpi2011/results.

Turley, William S. 1986. *The Second Indochina War: A Short Political and Military History, 1954–1975*. Boulder: Westview.

Vietnam News. December 10, 2013. "Vietnam Pursues Policy to Protect Human Rights." http://vietnamnews.vn/politics-laws/248753/vietnam-pursues-policy-to-protect-human-rights.html.

Werner, Jayne Susan. 1981. *Peasant Politics and Religious Sectarianism: Peasant and Priest in the Cao Dai in Viet Nam*. Monograph Series 23. New Haven, CT: Yale University Southeast Asia Studies.

Wolf, Eric. 1969. *Peasant Wars of the Twentieth Century*. New York: Harper & Row.

Woodside, Alexander B. 1976. *Community and Revolution in Modern Vietnam*. Boston: Houghton Mifflin.

World Bank. 2005. *Accelerating Rural Development in Vietnam*. siteresources.worldbank.org/vietnam/resources_vietnam_brochure18aug05.pdf.

Selected DVD, Film, and Videocassette Documentaries

See "Purchase and Rental Sources" at the end of this volume for information on how to obtain the following resources and for full names of media companies and other organizations listed here as abbreviations.

The Fog of War. 2004. 95 min. DVD. Amazon.com.

Guerrilla Warfare: Vietnam. 1997. 46 min. Amazon.com. Masters of War Series: General Vo Nguyen Giap Versus General William Westmoreland.

"Guns, Drugs, and the CIA." 1988. *Frontline.* Possible connections between the CIA and drug trafficking in Southeast Asia and Central America.

Hearts and Minds: Criterion Collection (1974). 2002. 112 min. Color film. Amazon.com. Award-winning documentary of the effects of the Vietnam War on both the Vietnamese and the American people. This film should be preceded by lecture or reading material on the factors that led to the Vietnam conflict.

Ho Chi Minh. 1998. 50 min. BIO. Life of the man who led the Vietnamese revolution.

Inside the Vietnam War. 2008. 150 min. Amazon.com.

LBJ and Vietnam. 100 min. BIO.

Most Dangerous Man in America: Daniel Ellsberg and the Pentagon Papers. 2009. 94 min. Amazon.com.

Passage: Journeys from War to Peace. 60 min. PBS. Impact of the war on the Vietnamese.

Viet Cong. 2008. 50 min. DVD. Amazon.com.

The Vietnam War. 45 min. History Channel.

Vietnam: An Historical Document. 1975. 56 min. Color film. UARIZ, UC-B, USF, UIOWA, KSU, PSU. CBS documentary history of US involvement in Vietnam.

Vietnam: A Television History. 1983. 60 min. per part. Color video. 13 parts. Amazon.com. Parts 1–12 available from UIOWA, PSU, Films Inc; Part 13 from PSU, Films Inc. This highly acclaimed series includes: 1: Roots of War; 2: First Vietnam War, 1946–1954; 3: America's Mandarin, 1954–1963; 4: LBJ Goes to War, 1964–1965; 5: America Takes Charge, 1965–1967; 6: America's Enemy, 1954–1967; 7: Tet, 1968; 8: Vietnamizing the War, 1969–1973; 9: No Neutral Ground: Laos and Cambodia; 10: Peace Is at Hand, 1968–1973; 11: Homefront USA; 12: End of the Tunnel; 13: Legacies.

Vietnam's Unseen War: Pictures from the Other Side. 2002. 60 min. DVD, VHS Tape, Amazon.com.

Vietnam: The Ten Thousand Day War. 1980. Color film. 26 parts. Part 1 available from UI, ISU; Parts 2–26 from IU. America in Vietnam. Part 1, 55 min.; Parts 2–26, 26 min. each. 1: America in Vietnam; 2: France in Vietnam; 3: Dien Bien Phu; 4: Early Hopes; 5: Assassination; 6: Days of Decision; 7: Westy's War; 8: Uneasy Allies; 9: Guerrilla Society; 10: Ho Chi Minh Trail; 11: Firepower; 12: Village War; 13: Airwar; 14: Siege; 15: TET!; 16: Frontline America; 17: Soldiering On; 18: Changing the Guard; 19: Wanting Out; 20: Bombing of Hanoi; 21: Peace; 22: Prisoners; 23: Unsung Soldiers; 24: Final Offensive; 25: Surrender; 26: Vietnam Recalled.

Vietnam: The Vietnam Conflict. 1998. CNN Cold War Series, Episode 11. 46 min. Truman Library.

The Vietnam War. 2008. 346 min. 4 parts. DVD. Amazon.com.

5

The Cuban Revolution

_____

In the 1950s, as the United States became increasingly involved in Vietnam, Cuba was torn by civil war. Many Cubans took up arms to win a fairer distribution of the island's wealth for the poor, while others aimed at establishing a truly democratic political system. Of critical significance for the success of the revolution, however, was the desire of all revolutionaries to overthrow the corrupt Batista dictatorship, widely viewed as protecting the economic status quo and, perhaps most important, serving as a mechanism that foreign interests used to dominate and exploit the Cuban people.

The Cuban revolution had important consequences for the Cuban people, the United States, other countries of the Americas, and other parts of the world. The success of the movement established the first socialist economy in the Western Hemisphere. Radical social change and the coercive measures used to accomplish it polarized Cuban society. A majority of Cubans, craving social justice, inflamed by nationalist fervor, and inspired by Fidel Castro's charismatic leadership, supported the revolution (Aguila 1988; 1994; Quirk 1993; Szulc 1986). A minority, disproportionately urban upper and middle class, objected to aspects of the revolutionary program and especially to the dominant role of the Communist Party. Since 1959 more than 1 million Cubans have left their homeland.

The revolution, however, succeeded in providing hundreds of thousands with educational opportunities, medical services, and other benefits they never would have enjoyed otherwise. These accomplishments contributed to consolidating the support of most of the island's working and peasant classes for the post-revolutionary government and the development of a relatively strong, resilient sociopolitical system (Aguila 1988; 1994).

Cuba's success in providing its population with essential needs contributed significantly to phenomenal achievements in sports, such as Cuba's fifth-place finish in total medals at the 1992 Summer Olympics in Barcelona (after Russia, the United States, Germany, and China, and with more than ten times as many medals as Brazil and Mexico; *Hartford Courant*, August 10, 1992, D6). Cuban dominance among Latin American countries in total medals continued until it was edged out by Brazil at the 2012 London Olympics (*Sports Illustrated* 2012).

The Cuban armed forces, including reservists, were estimated to number about 300,000 in the 1990s, with an additional 1.3 million men and women in militia units. But by 2005 the active forces had been reduced to an estimated 46,000, with "39,000 reservists and a militia of at least one million" (International Institute for Strategic Studies 2005). During the 1970s and 1980s more than 50,000 Cuban troops and military advisers were deployed around the world, most notably in Angola, where they helped turn back forces of the white minority government of South Africa (Aguila 1994; PBS 1985). Thousands of Cuban doctors, nurses, teachers, and engineers, whose expenses and salaries were paid by the Cuban government, served as volunteers in dozens of developing countries. This program, which began in 1963 when fifty-three Cuban health workers arrived in Algeria, provided much aid to African peoples (Gott 2004, 221).

In the early 1990s, the formerly communist governments in Eastern Europe ended most assistance to Cuba, and the island nation came under greater economic pressure than at any time since the 1960s. But in the second half of the 1990s, despite the US Helms-Burton Act of 1996, which was intended to discourage foreign companies from doing business with Cuba, its economy began to recover, benefiting from foreign investment, increased tourism, money sent by Cuban Americans to their relatives on the island, and, in the twenty-first century, Venezuelan oil.

Cuba has been the subject of world attention and controversy far out of proportion to its physical size or population. This chapter will address a number of important questions: Why did the revolution succeed in Cuba? Why did the revolution lead to the domination of the Communist Party? How has Cuba affected, assisted, or reacted to revolutionary movements in other societies? How has Cuba adapted to the changing world environment? What role is Cuba playing in the revolutionary movements of the twenty-first century?

Geography and Population

Cuba has a land area of 42,803 square miles (110,860 square kilometers—about the same size as Pennsylvania) and a population in 2013 of about 11.1 million. The island, 90 miles (145 kilometers) south of Key West, Florida, is 744 miles (1,197 kilometers) long, with an average width of 60 miles (97 kilometers). The nation's capital is Havana, which has about 2.1 million residents. According to the 2002 census, about 65 percent of Cubans were white, 25 percent mixed racial ancestry, and 10 percent black

(CIA 2014a). The health and educational levels of the Cuban population improved significantly after the revolution. By 2013, 99.8 percent of the population was literate, the infant mortality rate was about 4.8 per 1,000 live births (in the US it was 5.9, CIA 2014b), and life expectancy was about seventy-eight years (CIA 2014a). These statistics are comparable to those of the US and advanced European societies.

PRE-REVOLUTIONARY POLITICAL HISTORY

Columbus discovered Cuba in 1492 on his first voyage to the New World. Spanish settlers forcibly recruited thousands of Taino Arawak Indians, the indigenous people of Cuba, to mine gold and clear land for agriculture. As harsh conditions, poor nutrition, and imported diseases depleted the indigenous population, African slaves were brought to Cuba. Early agriculture involved tobacco and later coffee. After war and rebellion disrupted the economies of French colonies in the Caribbean, wealthy migrants established large sugar plantations in Cuba and imported large numbers of slaves. From 1792 to 1821, 250,000 slaves passed through Havana customs, and an estimated 60,000 were brought in illegally (Wolf 1969). Unsuccessful slave rebellions occurred in 1810, 1812, and 1844. The African heritage of the slaves blended with Spanish culture, so that later the Cuban government described the nation's overall culture as Afro-Latin.

When other Spanish colonies were gaining their independence in the 1820s, many Cubans preferred Spanish military occupation. Because at the time the majority of Cuba's population was black, members of the dominant European minority feared that without the Spanish army they would be overwhelmed in a slave rebellion. Cuba's independence movement did not gain support until the last third of the century, when Cubans of European ancestry were clearly a majority of the island's inhabitants. But Spain's loss of its major colonies strengthened its determination to retain control of Cuba as a valuable trade and military asset.

A reformist movement appeared in the early 1860s, when Creole planters (agriculturalists born in Cuba) desired greater economic influence. After negotiations with Spain failed, planters in Cuba's easternmost province, Oriente, demanded total independence for several reasons: Cuba's lack of effective representation in the Spanish parliament, limitations on freedom of speech and other civil rights, an unfair tariff system that put Cuban planters at a disadvantage, and discrimination against native-born Cubans in business and government. The rebels also called for an end to slavery, although the wealthiest planters, clustered in the western part of the country, depended on it for their prosperity. In 1868 a war of independence broke out and lasted ten years. But disagreement among rebel leaders, lack of US support, and strong resistance by Spanish forces led to stalemate. The conflict ended up costing more than 200,000 Cuban and Spanish lives (Aguila 1988).

Martí and the Struggle for Independence

After 1878, Spain introduced some reforms and abolished slavery. But many Cubans craved full independence. A second war (1895–1898) was inspired in part by the writer José Martí (1853–1895). Martí was born in Havana, the son of Spanish immigrants. He enthusiastically embraced the cause of Cuban independence and at seventeen was sentenced to six years at hard labor for writing pro-independence literature. After serving a few months, he was exiled to Spain, where he earned university degrees in law, philosophy, and literature. Martí returned to Cuba in 1878, after the Pact of Zanjón had ended ten years of warfare. When he resumed pro-independence activities, Spanish authorities again expelled him. Martí settled in New York and worked as an art critic for the *New York Sun* (Ruiz 1968).

In the US (1881–1895) Martí wrote prolifically and inspired many who later would lead the struggle for Cuban independence. At first he extolled capitalism. But after 1883 some of Martí's views changed. Witnessing the hardships of US workers and experiencing deprivation himself, he became critical of the capitalist society of his era and much more favorable toward labor unions. Martí supported some of Karl Marx's ideas and praised Marx's concern for the welfare of workers. Martí expressed the belief that poverty, racism, and other forms of oppression could and should be eliminated. One of his favorite sayings was "I will stake my fate on the poor of the earth" (Ruiz 1968, 67). Martí feared possible US economic imperialism toward Cuba. But according to most scholars, Martí never became a Marxist revolutionary. His first passion was to liberate Cuba. Whatever plans he had for social revolution would presumably have followed independence. Because Martí's views changed in reaction to his experiences, his writings contain contradictory concepts and attitudes. Consequently, later Cubans with diverse and even conflicting political and economic philosophies found support for their particular ideologies in Martí's works (Ruiz 1968; Szulc 1986).

Martí landed in eastern Cuba in 1895 in an effort to join rebel groups. He was soon killed in an ambush. Despite Martí's death, a new war for Cuban independence was under way. The Spanish army erected fortified barriers to seal off one part of the country from another and forcibly relocated the rural population to special camps or to the cities in an effort to separate independence fighters from civilian supporters (Wolf 1969). Rebel forces burned sugar plantations in western Cuba to deprive Spain and its supporters of revenues. Tens of thousands on both sides perished in the conflict. By 1898 the Spanish army had been driven from most of the rural areas. Many Cubans felt Spain had been defeated through their sacrifices and would be forced to withdraw.

At that point the United States, motivated by popular support for the rebels, reports of Spanish atrocities, a desire to protect US interests in Cuba, and, finally, the sinking of the battleship *Maine* while it was visiting Havana harbor, entered the

MAP 5.1 Cuba

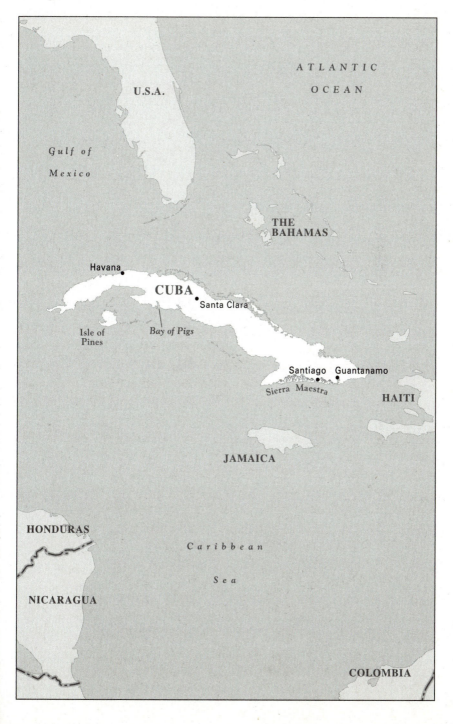

war. Once US naval forces destroyed the Spanish fleet, Spain's armies could not be resupplied and were forced to surrender. As a result of the Spanish-American War, the US assumed control of Cuba, the Philippines, and Puerto Rico.

When President William McKinley requested authority to "end the hostilities between the government of Spain and the people of Cuba," Congress approved the measure, but only after attaching the Teller Amendment, which asserted that the United States would not attempt to "exercise sovereignty, jurisdiction or control" over Cuba once peace was restored (Aguila 1994, 17). The occupation forces, however, established a military government that restructured Cuba's economic, administrative, and political systems. The United States also encouraged the rehabilitation and expansion of Cuba's sugar industry. A number of Cuban political figures argued that Cuba would be locked into a dependent status if a monoculture based on sugar was revived and extended. They advocated greater diversification in agriculture and in the economy generally so that Cuba would become economically self-sufficient instead of being tied to an external market for sale of a single crucially important crop. Through sugar, however, foreign investors in good times could obtain sizable returns on their capital, and Cuban growers could earn foreign currency with which to purchase luxury items from other nations.

After bringing about significant improvements in health, education, sanitation, public administration, and finance, US authorities turned over the reins of government. But before granting Cuba independence in 1902, the US Congress forced Cuban political leaders to incorporate the so-called Platt Amendment into their constitution. The amendment, drafted by Senator Orville Platt and Secretary of State Elihu Root as part of an army appropriations bill, declared that the United States could intervene to preserve Cuban independence and to maintain a government capable of protecting life, property, and individual liberty (Ruiz 1968; Szulc 1986). The Platt Amendment also prevented Cuba from contracting any foreign debt that could not be serviced from existing revenues, barred Cuba from entering into treaties with other governments that compromised its sovereignty, and gave the United States the right to buy or lease land for naval facilities (Wolf 1969). Although some Cubans supported US involvement in Cuba and even requested US military intervention, many others deeply resented the Platt Amendment and the growing US role in Cuba's economy and politics. Under the terms of the Platt Amendment, the United States intervened militarily in Cuba during the years 1906–1909, 1912, and 1917 to protect business interests or to reestablish order (Aguila 1988; 1994). Frustrated Cuban nationalism and widespread abhorrence of corrupt and authoritarian regimes perceived as prostituting the nation for the benefit of foreigners welded Cubans of diverse backgrounds into a powerful revolutionary coalition.

Discontent and the Emergence of Batista

Following several unstable governments, a Liberal Party candidate, Gerardo Machado, a popular veteran of the independence war, was elected president in 1924. Machado promised to work for the elimination of the Platt Amendment and fight corruption. But after his election Machado dropped his campaign to abolish the Platt Amendment, financed his corruption-plagued projects with loans from US financial institutions, and in general was compliant with US business interests (Ruiz 1968). In 1928 Machado had the Cuban congress he controlled change the constitution to permit him an additional six-year presidential term. Supported by the army and US business interests, he instituted a repressive and bloody dictatorship (Aguila 1988; 1994).

The Great Depression intensified protest against Machado's regime. Middle-class reformers, students, Havana University professors, and many workers, whose unions were often led by Cuban Communist Party members, joined forces against the dictatorship. As disorder and violence reached extraordinary levels, the Franklin D. Roosevelt administration convinced Machado to resign. Once Machado was out, frenzied mobs attacked and killed many of his supporters, who were accused of torture and murder. Machado's successor, Carlos Manuel de Céspedes, was quickly overthrown by a coup of noncommissioned officers led by a sergeant, Fulgencio Batista. Soldiers supporting Batista had been outraged by pay cuts, troop reductions, and other grievances.

Batista initially supported a five-man revolutionary government led by a professor of physiology at Havana University, Ramón Grau San Martín. The revolutionary government attempted to enact reforms, such as establishing the eight-hour work day, cutting utility rates, granting land to poor peasants, limiting land purchases by foreigners, taking control of some foreign-owned properties, and mandating that a minimum of 50 percent of a factory's employees be Cuban citizens (some employers imported foreign workers willing to work for less pay). These reforms were strongly opposed by the Cuban upper class and US business interests. Grau, an anticommunist, also faced opposition from the Communist Party. And the Roosevelt administration refused to recognize his government. After serving for four months, Grau, under pressure from Batista, who declined to continue supporting a government opposed by the United States, resigned on January 15, 1934.

Following Grau's resignation and the cancellation of certain reforms, the US government abolished the Platt Amendment, stating that political stability had returned to Cuba. But many Cubans came to feel that the 1933 rebellion, like that of 1895, had failed to achieve its most important goals of eliminating corruption, significantly redistributing wealth, and freeing Cuba from foreign control. This perception fostered further mass discontent and elite dissidence. Some of those craving significant reforms formed the Auténtico Party, which pledged to make an "authentic revolution," faithful to the concepts of José Martí.

With Batista holding real power through control over the army, Cuba was governed by a succession of puppet presidents until 1940. After a new constitution was enacted, Batista defeated Grau in what historians regard as a free election (Aguila 1988; 1994; Ruiz 1968; Szulc 1986). As the new constitution limited the presidency to a single four-year term, Batista could not succeed himself. He was followed by the Auténtico administrations of Ramón Grau (1944–1948) and Carlos Prío (1948–1952). These governments enacted some reforms in agriculture, education, and labor but avoided measures that challenged US business interests; these administrations were characterized by massive corruption, political patronage, and theft and abuse of public funds.

In protest, a leading charismatic Cuban senator, Eduardo Chibás, quit the Auténtico Party in 1947 to organize a new reform movement, the Orthodoxo Party, which Chibás claimed was dedicated to the true (orthodox) principles of the Cuban hero Martí. Chibás, who formulated the slogan "honor against money," exposed corruption through his popular weekly radio program. Despite the fact that many viewed him as the potential victor in the 1952 presidential election, Chibás, bitterly disappointed when colleagues failed to provide him with the evidence needed to prove a charge of corruption, as he had promised the public, shot himself during a broadcast in August 1951 (Ruiz 1968). The Orthodoxo Party continued to campaign for reform and still might have won the 1952 elections, including the congressional seat sought by a young activist lawyer, Fidel Castro. But before the elections could be held, the army, again under Batista's leadership, seized power. Batista installed an authoritarian regime that lasted until he fled Cuba on New Year's Day, 1959.

ECONOMY AND SOCIAL CLASSES

Sugar represented over 80 percent of Cuban exports, most of which went to the United States. In the 1950s US-owned companies controlled nine of the ten largest sugar mills and twelve of the next twenty in size and accounted for almost 40 percent of the island's sugar crop (Wolf 1969). US businesses also had hundreds of millions of dollars invested in utilities, manufacturing, mining, and oil refineries (Aguila 1988; 1994). US organized crime figures played a significant role in casinos and hotels in Havana, which was a major international gambling resort (PBS 1985).

Approximately 160,000 Cubans were employed by US-owned businesses, and 186,000 by the Cuban government. There were about 400,000 in the regularly employed nonagricultural working class. Another 250,000 worked as waiters, servants, entertainers, and gift shop proprietors and in other occupations serving tourists and well-to-do Cubans. The poorest urban stratum included several hundred thousand underemployed or part-time workers (Wolf 1969). Official statistics indicated that during the period 1943–1957, national unemployment averaged 20–30 percent (Amaro and Mesa-Lago 1971). Consumer price increases caused real per capita income to fall during much of the decade preceding the revolution (Ruiz 1968).

The Cuban economy ranked fifth among Latin American countries in per capita income. Other measures of development, such as life expectancy (about sixty years), infant mortality (32 per 1,000 live births), and literacy (between 75 and 80 percent), all placed Cuba among the top five Latin American societies (Aguila 1988; Ruiz 1968; Wolf 1969). But the island's wealth was unevenly distributed, fostering a feeling of social injustice. Although in 1956 per capita income for Cuba's 6 million people was 336 pesos, the majority of rural families (about 44 percent of the population) survived on 90 pesos. Eight percent of farms controlled 75 percent of farmland (and 0.5 percent, mostly large sugar concerns and cattle ranches, held one-third of the land). Eighty-five percent of the farms had only 20 percent of the land (Aguila 1988; 1994).

Medical personnel, hospitals, teachers, and schools were concentrated in urban areas. The illiteracy rate in the countryside was 42 percent versus 12 percent in the cities. In rural areas about 500,000 were employed as sugarcane cutters and 50,000 as sugar mill workers. Between sugar harvests, all the cane cutters were laid off, as were two-thirds of the mill workers. During periods of unemployment, many rural families subsisted in part on raw sugarcane. Sugar workers desiring to end the debilitating cycle of seasonal unemployment constituted a major source of support for the revolutionary government after the 1959 victory (Wolf 1969). Perception of foreign dominance and exploitation of the Cuban economy, high unemployment, declining real income, and the poverty of the rural population all contributed to the growth of mass discontent preceding the revolution.

Social scientists argue that Cuba never developed a large, independent native capitalist class because of the dominant role of US businesses and the dependency of Cuban capitalists on US financial institutions (Wolf 1969). Furthermore, both Cuba's upper class and middle class, which together constituted perhaps 25 percent of the population, were generally enamored of US lifestyles and culture. Members of Cuba's middle class were often unsatisfied with their status and yearned to be rich. Highly educated Cubans, trained mainly in the legal and medical professions, often turned to government for employment and enrichment. Some viewed political office, with its access to public money and opportunities for graft, as their only potential source of wealth (Ruiz 1968). So many politicians had failed the public trust that government officials received little respect from the population, a fact that constituted a critical flaw in the pre-revolutionary state.

Upper- and middle-class Cubans were disproportionately represented among practicing Catholics. The Catholic Church in Cuba was relatively weak and did not provide an effective bond among the island's classes and social groups. Although most Cubans were nominally Catholic, only about 10 percent practiced their religion (Ruiz 1968). Part of the reason for the church's limited influence was that the church in Cuba was Spanish-dominated and had opposed Cuban independence, which provoked harsh criticism by José Martí and alienated many Cubans. Martí accused the clergy of being unconcerned with the plight of Cuba's rural poor. Even in the 1950s the large majority of Cuba's eight hundred priests were Spaniards and very conservative (*New York Times*, May 15, 1987, A4). The Catholic Church was especially weak in rural Cuba, particularly among Afro-Cubans.

The subordinate status of multiracial and black people was a major reason why many nonwhite Cubans became prominent in two rather distinct institutions, the army and the Communist Party. The pre-revolutionary army had been organized by occupation authorities early in the century and was trained and equipped by the US. As with most armies in Latin America, it functioned not to defend Cuba from foreign enemies but to preserve order and protect traditional institutions and the interests of the privileged classes. The armed forces, numbering about 40,000 in 1958, provided employment, relative economic security, and social mobility for lower-income groups.

After Batista took over the army in 1933, 384 of its 500 officers resigned, in part because they were unwilling to accept a mixed-race commander (Batista was of Chinese, African, Amerindian, and European ancestry). Batista then granted commissions to 527 enlisted men, expanded the army, and increased military pay levels (Ruiz 1968). After 1933 one-third of the officers were Afro-Cuban. Under Batista, the army was not as directly responsive to conservative upper-class interests as in the past. Batista occasionally supported limited reforms that benefited the poor or organized labor but did not threaten the basic interests of the upper class. Consequently, many nonwhite Cubans identified positively with Batista before the late 1950s. The army, however, was generally unpopular with many Cubans (Ruiz 1968), because of its origin as a product of occupation, its hindering of major reforms proposed by leaders of the 1933 revolution against Machado, and its use of repressive measures, which greatly intensified during the 1950s.

In the 1860s, Spanish political refugees introduced socialist concepts in Cuba. After the 1917 Bolshevik Revolution, Leninist ideas began to spread among Cuban intellectuals and the working class. In 1925 several union activists joined militant students from Havana University to form the Cuban Communist Party. A popular university student leader, Julio Antonio Mella, became the party's first secretary-general. Although the Machado regime outlawed the Communist Party and apparently paid assassins to murder Mella, the party grew in membership and influence (Ruiz 1968). The party's success was due to worker frustration with exploitive labor conditions and corrupt business and government officials, and the fact that communist union leaders won improvements from management and government.

The communists gained thousands of members from Cuba's impoverished nonwhite population. Afro-Cuban communist leaders included Lázaro Peña, the most powerful labor leader in the island's history; Blás Roca Calderío, ideological spokesperson for the party; and Jesús Menéndez Larrondo, who headed the Sugar Workers Federation until assassinated in 1947 (Ruiz 1968). The communists obtained about 10 percent of the vote in the 1946 legislative elections. But membership and public support varied over time, stemming from factors such as periodic government repression and the occasional willingness of party leaders to compromise principles for short-term political gains. The Communist Party generally supported Batista during the 1930s and early 1940s and discredited itself by accepting Batista's military regime in the 1950s, with some party members serving in the dictator's government. Most communist leaders initially refused to support Fidel Castro's movement to get rid of Batista by force of arms, claiming it would result in useless bloodshed; those people did not endorse Castro until 1958, when the revolution was clearly gaining momentum (Aguila 1988; Ruiz 1968; Szulc 1986).

REVOLUTION
Fidel Castro and the M-26-7 Movement

Fidel Castro was born in 1926 in the town of Biran in eastern Cuba. His father, Angel Castro y Argiz, was a Spanish immigrant who sold lemonade and other items to sugar workers and their families. With his savings he obtained land to grow sugar. Eventually he had some 26,000 owned or permanently rented acres (Szulc 1986). Fidel's mother was his father's second wife, Lina Ruz González, who had been a maid or cook in the Castro household and was at least twenty-five years younger than her husband. Lina was illiterate until well into adulthood and, though religious and devoted to her five children (Fidel was the third), did not marry Angel until several years after Fidel's birth.

Fidel, competitive and physically active, studied and played with the children of the rural poor at the little country school near his home. He later recalled realizing that his barefoot classmates would soon leave school and that their parents' impoverishment would condemn them to lives of ignorance and abject poverty. Castro claimed this early experience set him on the path toward becoming a revolutionary. After a few years Fidel enrolled in a Jesuit-run private school in Santiago. Later he entered Cuba's best preparatory school, Belén College, in Havana. At Belén, Jesuit instructors, usually conservative politically, considered Castro perhaps the most intelligent student and certainly the best all-around athlete in his class. Although prone to rebelliousness, Castro claims he knew little of political parties and their ideologies until he entered law school at Havana University (Szulc 1986).

At the university, political activity was intense. Activist organizations included the student branch of the Communist Party and two revolutionary but anticommunist groups, the MSR (Socialist Revolutionary Movement) and the UIR (Insurrectional Revolutionary Union). These organizations and others competed for control of the student government. Physical intimidation, beatings, and even assassinations occurred. Because the university was autonomous and self-governing, neither the army nor the police could enter the campus (Szulc 1986). The fact that so many children of Cuba's educated classes joined revolutionary groups devoted to radical change reflected acute elite discontent in the nation, a critical element in the development and success of the revolution. Once Castro became involved in politics, he, like other student activists, often carried a gun.

Not yet twenty-one years old but already recognized as an eloquent speaker, Castro was invited (the only university student asked), along with six senators, ten congressmen, and about eighty other government and business figures, to the May 15, 1947, founding of the Orthodoxo Reform Party. Although Castro became interested in Marxist and socialist concepts, he felt the Cuban Communist Party lacked sufficient popular support to bring about revolutionary change. He preferred to work with the Orthodoxos because of their potential for greater mass appeal and the greater freedom of action this allowed him. His younger brother Raúl, in contrast, joined the communists.

After passing law exams, Fidel handled cases for lower-income people in Havana. He built a base of support that appeared to ensure him election to congress on the Orthodoxo ticket in the scheduled 1952 election. Castro claimed he intended to work within the democratic system and campaign for high public office. He would then use his political and oratorical skills to prepare Cubans gradually for a socialist economic system, which he believed was necessary for the welfare of the large majority of the population (Quirk 1993; Szulc 1986).

Batista's seizure of power before the 1952 elections could be held changed Castro's plans. Fidel, Raúl, and others decided on armed insurrection. Over several months scores of young working-class people and university-educated activists met for training sessions to organize an uprising. The target was the Moncada army barracks in Santiago at the eastern end of the island, 533 miles from Havana. The participants hoped to surprise the four hundred soldiers based there and seize weapons. After distributing captured arms to supporters in Santiago, the rebels planned to take the city and call for a general uprising throughout the island.

On the morning of Sunday, July 26, 1953, about 125 men and women crowded into sixteen automobiles and drove to Moncada. But they immediately encountered an army patrol. When firing broke out, soldiers in the base were alerted. Several rebels were killed in the fighting, more were captured, and the rest fled. During the next few days almost all the rebels were caught, and about half were executed. The Castro brothers had the good fortune to be captured by a squad under the command of Afro-Cuban Lieutenant Pedro Manuel Sarria Tartabull, who refused on ethical grounds to kill the surrendering rebels, despite the demands of some of his men. (Years later Sarria was arrested for refusing to fight against Castro's new rebel band. After the revolution, Sarria was promoted to captain and proclaimed a Hero of the Revolution; Szulc 1986.)

Castro was brought to trial and delivered a stinging indictment of the dictatorship, governmental corruption, and social ills, ending with the words "History will absolve me." Fidel was sentenced to fifteen years. The Castro brothers were confined to the maximum-security prison on the Isle of Pines. Feeling secure in power and hoping to improve his public image, Batista declared an amnesty and freed the Moncada rebels after they had served one year and seven months (Szulc 1986). The Castro brothers and several associates, fearing assassination by Batista agents and impeded in efforts to organize a new rebel organization, left for Mexico, Raúl on June 24 and Fidel on July 7, 1955.

Shortly after arriving, Castro announced the formation of the 26th of July movement (M-26-7), which included Orthodoxo Party members, liberals, socialists, and communists (although Communist Party leaders condemned the Moncada attack and plans for armed revolution). Castro contacted the Cuban-born Alberto Bayo, a guerrilla warfare expert who had served in the Spanish Civil War with Republican forces against the conservative Spanish military and its Italian and German fascist allies. Castro convinced Bayo to help train members of M-26-7. While a training base was being established, Castro traveled to the US and addressed anti-Batista Cuban exiles in New York and Florida. He raised thousands of dollars for weapons, supplies, and an old yacht, the *Granma*, to transport his revolutionaries to Cuba.

Che Guevara and the Lesson of Guatemala

In Mexico the Castro brothers met a young Argentine physician, Ernesto (later nicknamed "Che") Guevara. After becoming an allergist (he suffered from asthma himself), Guevara had traveled from Argentina to several other Latin American countries. Before joining M-26-7, he had lived in Guatemala, where an elected government was attempting progressive reforms (Gott 2004). Mass protests followed by an army coup in 1944 had toppled a brutal military dictatorship. Genuinely free elections resulted in the election of President Juan José Arévalo, a former university professor dedicated to improving the life of the poor. Arévalo's reforms offended wealthy conservatives who repeatedly tried to overthrow him. He left office in March 1951 worried that fascism, though defeated in Europe in World War II, was

growing stronger in Latin America (Schlesinger and Kinzer 1982). Arévalo was succeeded by the second democratically elected president, Jacobo Arbenz Guzmán,
one of the officers who had overthrown the previous dictatorship.

President Arbenz enacted a sweeping land-redistribution program that involved
parceling out acreage to poor peasants. A major target for land appropriation was
the United Fruit Company, based in Boston. The Arbenz government confiscated
over 300,000 unused acres from United Fruit (which planted only 15–20 percent
of its approximately 600,000 acres annually), offering to pay compensation, which
the company considered inadequate. The Eisenhower administration became convinced that the Arbenz government was influenced by communists and threatened
US interests. The CIA proceeded to recruit several hundred conservative opponents of Arbenz, arm them, and provide them with a mercenary air force, flown
by US pilots, and a CIA-run radio station to broadcast false news reports to demoralize and disorganize Arbenz supporters. Some Guatemalan generals were
persuaded to support the 1954 CIA-sponsored invasion or at least not to resist it.
Arbenz was forced to resign and flee the country. The right-wing military governments that followed Arbenz murdered many of his supporters, reversed some of
the reforms, and engaged in repressive measures for decades to prevent the growth
of leftist revolutionary or reform movements (Gleijeses 1991; *New York Times*, April
9, 1994, E5; July 24, 1994, 3; Schlesinger and Kinzer 1982; Streeter 2000a; 2000b;
2006).

Guevara witnessed firsthand the overthrow of the elected progressive Guatemalan government. The tragedy of Guatemala convinced many who supported change
in Latin America that future US administrations would most likely again take
advantage of the vulnerabilities inherent in open democratic systems in poorer,
less powerful states and, through the CIA, frustrate disagreeable policies or even
destroy elected governments. Guatemala convinced Guevara of the necessity for
armed struggle. It also taught him a lesson about Latin American armies. He felt
that the Guatemalan army had deserted and betrayed Arbenz. Guevara concluded,
and emphasized to Castro, that a revolution could not be secure until the armed
forces were purged of conservative, corrupt, and unreliable officers and soldiers and
brought firmly under revolutionary control.

Revolutionary Struggle

On November 25, 1956, eighty-two men sailed on the *Granma* for a landing in Oriente Province in eastern Cuba. Bad weather and mechanical problems that delayed
arrival by two days until December 2 led to failure to reach a waiting supply party
on shore and inability to coordinate with a planned uprising by the M-26-7 underground in Santiago. Within a few days the rebel band was betrayed by a peasant

guide, who helped an army unit stage a successful ambush. Members of the land-ing party were killed or dispersed. About sixteen survivors, including the Castro brothers and Guevara, reassembled in the Sierra Maestra (mountain range). With help from friendly peasants and reinforcements from Santiago and the local rural population, the rebel army began to grow.

In the mountains many farmers were small landowners who settled there to avoid having to work as farmhands or seasonal employees for big landholders. Though economically more independent than sugarcane workers, they were sub-ject to bullying and other forms of exploitation by Batista military units (Szulc 1986; Wolf 1969). Many were inclined to support the rebels but were reluctant be-cause the army executed peasants who assisted Castro's guerrillas.

The rebels released captured soldiers who were only doing what they perceived to be their patriotic duty. The guerrillas, however, executed military personnel guilty of murder, rape, or torture, as well as civilians who informed on revolution-ary forces to the army (Szulc 1986; Wolf 1969). The rebels tended to fight harder than their opponents because they believed they would most likely be tortured and executed if captured, whereas the army's enlisted soldiers knew their lives would be spared if they surrendered. Guerrilla tactics involved high mobility, attacking vulnerable military outposts that could be looted for weapons, staging ambushes, and relying on peasant supporters for information regarding enemy movements. As farmers saw the dictator's army defeated and learned of the revolutionaries' plans for land reform, schools, and health care, more joined or assisted the rebels. Eventu-ally most Batista army units refused to venture into the hostile mountains.

Soon after the rebel landing, Batista announced that Fidel Castro had been killed. To expose this falsehood the rebels invited *New York Times* reporter Her-bert Matthews to interview Castro in February 1957. The interview brought Castro to the attention of the US media as a patriot fighting against a brutal and corrupt dictatorship. Castro appeared to be a non-Marxist moderate nationalist with dem-ocratic ideals. Although he displayed hostility to the US government for providing weapons to Batista, he claimed the rebels wanted friendship with the United States. Publicity from the interview provided hope and encouragement to rebel sympa-thizers throughout the country.

M-26-7 organized a national directorate with Castro as leader; it included rep-resentatives from urban movement units and rural guerrilla bands. Urban resis-tance appeared more moderate in plans for social change and was more middle and upper class in composition than the rebel guerrillas in the mountains. One of the anti-Batista revolutionary groups outside of Castro's M-26-7 was the urban-based Revolutionary Directorate (DR). The DR was anticommunist and drew members from university students and the middle class. On March 13, 1957, the DR launched an unsuccessful assault on the National Palace in Havana trying to kill Batista.

Thirty-five DR members died at the palace, and scores of others were hunted down, tortured, and killed.

Throughout 1957–1958 urban assaults against the dictatorship met with defeat, which probably both promoted the success of the revolution and increased the likelihood of a radical outcome. First, urban repression eliminated some of the moderate revolutionary leaders, making Fidel Castro an even more dominating figure. Second, defeats in the cities made the rural guerrilla strategy seem more effective and intelligent, bestowing greater prestige on this wing of the revolution. Third, torture and killing by Batista security forces provoked immense popular outrage and alienated much of the middle class from the Batista government, since the victims were often from this class. The carnage, coupled with perception of Batista's unpopularity and a lack of appreciation for Castro's plans for sweeping social change, resulted in the Eisenhower administration's stopping arms shipments to Batista's military in March 1958, although Batista's planes were still allowed to refuel at the US naval base at Guantanamo while on bombing missions against the rebels (Szulc 1986, 438–39). Eisenhower's action not only contributed to creating a severe state crisis for Batista's regime through accelerating the deterioration of army and government morale but also essentially constituted the advent of a permissive stance of the US government toward the developing revolution.

M-26-7 urban units planned to precipitate Batista's fall by a general strike set for April 9, 1958. When large-scale participation failed to materialize, partly because organizers kept the strike date secret until the last moment, the urban moderates in M-26-7 lost much of their remaining influence (Szulc 1986). Meanwhile, the rebels in the mountains were scoring repeated successes. Cuban army morale was sinking because of defeats in the Sierra Maestra and the US weapons cutoff. Other demoralizing factors included growing popular opposition to the army, the sympathy of some soldiers for the revolution, the disgust of many at the brutality of fellow soldiers, and the knowledge that many officers were corrupt. Several officers refused to combat the rebels and even organized mutinies against Batista. Partly as a result of the army's deteriorating confidence, Batista's 1958 summer offensive against the rebels failed miserably.

In the fall Castro ordered two guerrilla units, with 230 combatants, under the command, respectively, of Che Guevara and Camilo Cienfuegos, to advance into the lowlands. Remarkably, the army withdrew in the face of the oncoming rebels. At the end of December Guevara was victorious at Santa Clara, 168 miles east of Havana, the first major city taken by the rebels, while Castro's forces surrounded Santiago and negotiated a surrender of the city's garrison on December 31, with the troops placed under Castro's command (Szulc 1986). Batista fled the country on January 1, 1959.

REVOLUTIONARY CUBA

When Castro assumed control in January 1959, he enjoyed the enthusiastic support of the great majority of the Cuban people. He invited anti-Batista moderates and liberals to join with M-26-7 in organizing a provisional government under his leadership. Wage levels for workers and lower-middle-class employees were increased. In May an agricultural reform act limited farm holdings to a maximum of 966 acres, with sugar, rice, and cattle-raising enterprises allowed to be as large as 3,300 acres (Szulc 1986). This measure destroyed the large landholdings (latifundia), including US-owned sugar properties, several of which exceeded 400,000 acres. Land was distributed to tens of thousands of rural workers. Support for the revolution increased throughout the countryside. A literacy campaign sent an estimated 100,000 young volunteers to rural areas in 1961 to teach people to read and write (Gott 2004, 189). The government also began building hundreds of new schools and training thousands of additional teachers. New clinics and hospitals were constructed, many in rural areas where they had been almost nonexistent. Private beaches and resorts were opened to the public. These changes were immensely popular with most Cubans.

Szulc claims that Castro decided to develop Cuba into a Marxist-Leninist one-party state during 1959 or even earlier. Castro's reasons apparently included the belief that a centrally controlled government was necessary to counter anticipated US opposition to planned socioeconomic changes (Ruiz 1968; Szulc 1986). Castro viewed the US government as capitalist-dominated and was sure that it would not easily accept a socialist economic system in Cuba not only because of the negative impact on US investments there, but also out of fear that other Latin American countries might follow Cuba's example. Castro's experience with self-seeking and corrupt political figures and Cuba's shifts between elective politics and pro-US dictatorships probably convinced him that a multiparty democratic system would be too vulnerable to US economic and military pressure or to covert actions by the CIA, such as the bribery, intimidation, or assassination of key leaders ("The CIA Hit List" 1975). Castro also believed that Marxist-Leninist-style socialism could solve Cuba's socioeconomic problems, such as high inequality, unemployment, crime, and corruption (Ruiz 1968). Control of Cuba's government by a revolutionary party could bring about rapid structural change.

Castro and his associates felt that past revolutions had bitterly disappointed the economic and nationalist aspirations of most Cubans. In contrast, the new revolutionary government's rapid redistribution of wealth rallied enthusiastic support for the revolution among the majority of Cuba's rural and urban populations. Revolutionary leaders concluded that a nationally owned (rather than foreign-dominated) economic infrastructure would give Cuba the ability to resist economic control from other countries more effectively. The possibility that Cuba, having alienated the United States, might become economically dependent on the USSR seemed less onerous because the Soviet Union was distant and presumably could not exercise the same level of control over Cuba as the military and economic giant only ninety miles away.

By the end of 1959 Castro's M-26-7 had consolidated control over the armed forces. This involved removing conservative officers and soldiers and trying and executing 550 military and police personnel accused of murder and torture. The firing squads offended some North Americans but won the strong approval of thousands of Cubans whose families or friends had suffered Batista's repression (PBS 1985; Quirk 1993; Szulc 1986). In 1959 Castro held negotiations with leaders of the Communist Party; his goal was to fuse his M-26-7 movement and their organization to create a new Communist Party under his leadership.

Revolutionary instruction schools were established that trained young recruits to run revolutionary institutions and taught Marxist-Leninist concepts and interpretations of Cuban history (Szulc 1986). Castro concealed plans to transform Cuba into a Communist Party–dominated state in an attempt to delay expected furious opposition from the US and provide time to strengthen the revolutionaries' control over the army and prepare the Cuban people psychologically to accept the new system. Later Castro cited Martí's advice to revolutionaries that to achieve desired goals, deception must sometimes be used because to state those goals openly might provoke powerful opposition that revolutionaries might not yet be able to overcome. In April 1961 Castro revealed to the Cuban people that the revolution was going to result in socialism, and he used Martí's demands for social justice and the elimination of poverty and racism as the basis for the proclamation.

When moderates in the provisional government and M-26-7 realized that the revolution was moving toward a socialist economy and a political system dominated by a rejuvenated Communist Party, they began to resign in protest. Castro condemned such resignations as counterrevolutionary and called on supporters to stage mass demonstrations. Some who opposed Castro's plans launched a new guerrilla war in the Escambray Mountains in central Cuba. The counterrevolutionary guerrillas included former Batista soldiers, landowners opposed to agrarian reform, and even disillusioned former rebel army members, all loosely bound together under the banner of anticommunism (Szulc 1986). They numbered as many as 5,000 in the early 1960s, but Castro sent tens of thousands of revolutionary militia into the mountains, positioning one person every few hundred yards along trails and roads. This made movement of opposition forces extremely difficult, and most of the weapons and supplies the CIA air-dropped to them fell into the hands of Castro's people. In a few years, the counterrevolutionary guerrilla threat was eliminated.

In the cities, hundreds of thousands joined neighborhood committees for the defense of the revolution (CDRs) to carry on organized surveillance, which brought an end to violent attacks on the government in urban areas. In the 1980s over 80 percent of adults appeared to belong to CDRs (Aguila 1994; Szulc 1986). The revolutionary armed forces and the CDRs were aided by Castro's intelligence service, which had agents placed in virtually every counterrevolutionary group. Several hundred thousand Cubans, mostly upper and middle class, left Cuba in the first half of the 1960s. Exporting dissent reduced security problems but hurt the economy because many who left possessed important skills.

US REACTIONS TO THE REVOLUTION

In April 1959 Fidel Castro visited the United States and expressed a desire for friendship and continued trade. But by late 1959 the CIA began sending weapons to anti-Castro guerrillas. And by mid-1960 the Eisenhower administration decided to organize and arm an exile force to overthrow Castro's government (Quirk 1993; Szulc 1986; Wyden 1979). In September 1960 the CIA recruited several US Italian American organized crime figures, formerly involved in Havana casinos, to assassinate Castro. It is possible that Eisenhower and later presidents were not specifically informed of plans to kill Castro; the CIA often neglected to inform a president about a controversial operation in order to give him plausible deniability if the matter ever came to light (Szulc 1986).

In 1959 Cuba purchased 25,000 rifles, 50 million rounds of ammunition, 100,000 grenades from Belgium, and mortars, cannons, and heavy machine guns from Italy. The United States would not sell Cuba weapons and soon pressured Western European countries into refusing arms sales. Cuba then had to obtain military equipment from the Soviet Union and Eastern Europe. Weapons from Czechoslovakia and the USSR began reaching Cuba in late 1960, several months after President Eisenhower severed economic relations (Szulc 1986). Deliveries of jet military aircraft began in mid-1961, after the US-organized Bay of Pigs invasion had failed.

At first the Soviet Union was not very enthusiastic about Castro's government because for years Cuba's Communist Party had portrayed Castro as an irresponsible adventurer precipitating pointless bloodshed before objective conditions were right for revolution. But events during 1960 greatly increased Soviet interest in aiding Cuba (Szulc 1986). First, relations with the United States worsened following the downing of a US U-2 spy plane over the Soviet Union. As tensions increased, the Soviets quickly recognized that given their inferiority to the United States in nuclear weapons and delivery systems, Cuba could be a valuable strategic asset. Furthermore, in 1960 the ideological conflict between the USSR and the People's Republic of China became public knowledge. The Soviets and the Chinese were thereafter in competition for influence among less developed countries. Cuba provided the USSR an opportunity to demonstrate its concern with aiding a developing nation attempting to free itself from what its revolutionary leaders viewed as imperial domination.

As Cuba developed ties with the USSR, relations with the US worsened. In June 1960 oil refineries in Cuba owned by US citizens, under pressure from the US government, refused to refine crude oil from the Soviet Union. Cuba, in turn, nationalized the refineries and all remaining US properties. The United States then cut its purchase of Cuban sugar by 95 percent; it soon imposed an economic embargo and convinced all Latin American countries except Mexico to refuse trade with Cuba. Cuba responded by rationing to ensure that families with the greatest need, generally those with the most children, obtained basic commodities.

The Eisenhower administration initiated a major attempt to overthrow the revolutionary government, the Bay of Pigs invasion. By the latter half of 1960 the CIA had recruited hundreds of anti-Castro Cuban exiles and established bases for them in Guatemala (Gott 2004). The plan was modeled on the CIA's successful 1954 overthrow of the elected reform government in Guatemala. Some CIA instructors evidently promised exiles direct US military intervention, apparently assuming that Nixon, a strongly anticommunist conservative and Eisenhower's vice president, would be elected president instead of Kennedy in fall 1960 (Wyden 1979).

After Kennedy was elected, the CIA informed the new president of the invasion plan and attempted to convince him to approve it (Quirk 1993; Wyden 1979). The agency suggested that if Kennedy refused to let the invasion go forward, he would be seen as a weakling unwilling to confront a communist threat, perhaps encouraging more revolutions. Furthermore, the CIA misinformed the president, evidently through mistaken intelligence, that Castro was no longer popular and an invasion would spark mass uprisings against him. This error may have been caused by relying on the opinions of middle- and upper-class exiles, among whom Castro was unpopular. The revolution, however, was immensely popular with other sectors of the population, and Castro was strongly supported by a large majority (Quirk 1993; Szulc 1986; Wyden 1979). Besides 25,000 in the regular army, 200,000 had volunteered to join militia forces all over the island and trained day and night to learn how to use newly arriving weapons. When the invasion, preceded by the detentions of several thousand Cubans suspected of counterrevolutionary activity, occurred, no uprising materialized. Kennedy, also incorrectly informed that the Cuban air force would be destroyed before the assault, gave the go ahead, but on the condition that once the landing force was on Cuban soil, there would be no direct US military involvement.

The CIA recruited Cuban American–owned ships to transport the invasion force and assembled a secret air force of World War II–era B-26 twin-engine bombers, with Cuban-exile air crews, along with pilots on loan from the Alabama Air National Guard (four US pilots were killed in the assault). Cuban air force markings were put on the CIA planes to create an impression that Cuban pilots had mutinied and joined the counterrevolutionary attack. The CIA air force was to destroy the Cuban air force on the ground through bombing attacks and support the invasion. Two days before the invasion, eight CIA B-26s raided Cuban airfields. After the attack the CIA attempted to stage a false defection by having an anti-Castro Cuban impersonate a Cuban air force pilot. Wearing a Cuban uniform, he landed his B-26 in Florida and announced that he had defected and bombed his own air base. The charade was probably an attempt to persuade the US public that the loyalty of Castro's armed forces was disintegrating, and to demoralize Cubans. But the revolutionary government quickly pointed out that the front ends of its B-26s were Plexiglas, whereas on the falsely defecting plane the front end was metal, a detail the CIA had apparently overlooked (Quirk 1993; Szulc 1986; Wyden 1979).

After the CIA bombing raid destroyed five planes, the Cuban air force consisted of four British-made Sea Fury light attack bombers (propeller driven), one B-26, three T-33 jet trainers, and seven pilots. Unknown to the CIA, the Cubans had equipped the T-33 jets with two 50-caliber machine guns each and used them as interceptors during the invasion to destroy or drive off the CIA's B-26s. The Sea Fury bombers were directed against the invasion transport ships, sinking or disabling two and forcing the others to flee, thereby isolating more than 1,300 counterrevolutionaries on the beach (more than 100 would be killed, along with about 160 defenders; Gott 2004, 194).

On April 16, 1961, Castro publicly proclaimed for the first time that Cuba's revolution was a socialist one. He had planned to make the announcement on May 1, but realizing the invasion was about to occur, he made the statement just before the April 17 landing. Later Castro said that he felt those who were preparing to give their lives in defense of the revolution had the right to know what they were fighting for (Szulc 1986).

Immediately attacked by local militia forces and then surrounded by thousands of Cuban army and militia, cut off from resupply or evacuation and with its air force neutralized, the invasion brigade surrendered after about forty-eight hours. Later, more than 1,100 members of the brigade were sent back to the US in return for about $53 million worth of medicine and food. The Cuban victory at the Bay of Pigs further consolidated Castro's revolution by demonstrating that it had given Cuba the strength to defeat US intervention. Cuban nationalism soared, and Castro's popularity was greater than ever. On December 1, 1961, Castro went beyond his April speech to announce that Cuba would proceed along a Marxist-Leninist course of development (Szulc 1986).

The Soviet Union, taking advantage of Cuba's fear of a new invasion directly involving US forces, offered to station nuclear missiles in Cuba, precipitating the October 1962 Cuban missile crisis (Gott 2004). The Kennedy administration demanded that the missiles be removed and placed a naval blockade around the island. The USSR, at the time weaker than the United States in nuclear military capability and fearing world war, withdrew the nuclear missiles and the battlefield tactical nuclear warheads that the US apparently did not know were there and would possibly have been used against a US invasion force. The Kennedy administration, for its part, pledged that the United States would not invade Cuba. But the CIA recruited scores of brigade veterans and other Cuban exiles; they waged a secret war of infiltration and sabotage against Cuba through the early 1970s and continued efforts to assassinate Castro (Brenner 1988; "The CIA Hit List" 1975; PBS 1985; Szulc 1986).

Cuba and Revolution in Other Countries
The Quest for a Continental Revolution

The success of the Cuban revolution in resisting US economic and military pressures encouraged revolutionaries throughout Latin America. Many came to Cuba to train in guerrilla tactics. The United States, which had trained and armed thousands of soldiers for rightist governments in Latin America, intensified its efforts, adding specialized counterinsurgency instruction to its military aid programs.

The Kennedy administration also launched a major economic assistance project, the Alliance for Progress, intended to improve the life of the poor, increase the size of the middle class in Latin American societies, and support the efforts of anticommunist reform movements, especially Christian Democratic parties, to accomplish constructive social change. The Alliance contributed to significant improvements in education, health, and housing but failed to achieve most of its objectives. It did succeed in raising the expectations of millions of the disadvantaged, thereby helping to generate frustration when expectations were inadequately gratified, and it threatened the interests of ruling elites. These consequences contributed to the overthrow of democracies by conservative military leaders in Brazil (1964), Argentina (1966), Peru (1968), Chile (1973), and Uruguay (1973). The fear of Cuban-style revolutions motivated several US administrations to provide recognition and military and economic assistance to these conservative dictatorships despite their elimination of democratic systems and their human rights violations.

Several Cuban leaders called for a continental revolution to liberate all of Latin America from imperialism and social injustice. Che Guevara became the major public proponent of this concept through his speeches and his widely read works, *Guerrilla Warfare* (1960) and *Guerrilla Warfare: A Method* (1963) (Guevara 1985). Guevara, along with the French philosopher Regis Debray (1967), formulated the so-called theory of the guerrilla *foco*. The *foco* concept contradicted the policies of the established Marxist-Leninist leadership around the world regarding the justifiability and prospects for success of revolutionary violence to accomplish structural change. The leaders of the Soviet Union, China, and most communist parties took the position that violent revolution was not justifiable and could not be successful if the society in question had a democratic political system. In such a situation, in which there was at least a theoretical possibility that a revolutionary party or leaders could be elected to power, people would likely view individuals who resorted to violence as terrorists, and armed revolutionaries would be unable to achieve popular support and, therefore, unable to win.

Furthermore, traditional Marxist thinking held that political work among the population had to precede any armed revolutionary effort, even if a society was governed by a rightist dictatorship rather than an elected government. The people had to be educated about the desirability and possibility of revolutionary change and organized into mass-support networks before revolutionary war commenced. Only when revolutionaries enjoyed the support of a majority of their fellow citizens could they hope to overcome the superior weaponry of the ruling element's professional army. Finally, Russia's Lenin, China's Mao, and Vietnam's Giap all stated that the revolutionary armed forces must be under the leadership of the nation's revolutionary political party.

In contrast, Guevara argued that in a society where the majority of people suffered extreme economic inequality, the injection of an armed revolutionary band of as few as thirty combatants could, through violent attacks on the state's instruments of repression, create the objective conditions necessary for a successful revolution. Guevara and Debray claimed that even if the majority of a nation's population was apathetic and culturally conditioned to view deprivation as unavoidable, the actions of the guerrilla *foco* would gain people's attention and begin to make them aware that their rulers were not all-powerful but were vulnerable to popular resistance. Once awakened, many of the people would identify positively with the revolutionaries who were striking against the rich or hated army or police officials. Then the guerrillas would spread their concept of revolution. Eventually they would convert a majority of the people to the desirability of the revolution's goals. Popular support would constitute the necessary condition for revolutionary victory. Because virtually all the communist parties of Latin America criticized the guerrilla *foco* concept, revolutionaries following Guevara's strategy would have to proceed, at least in the beginning, without the support of their nation's revolutionary party.

In his 1960 work, *Guerrilla Warfare*, Guevara stated that his approach was applicable to Caribbean-style personalist dictatorships, which openly used violent repression and were not accepted by the people as democratic governments. But in his 1963 book, *Guerrilla Warfare: A Method*, he argued that the *foco* strategy could work in almost any Latin American country, even those that were formally (in Guevara's thinking, superficially) democracies but in reality dominated by wealthy oligar-chies. In November 1966 Guevara entered Bolivia under a false identity and formed a guerrilla *foco* with a number of Cubans, who had also infiltrated Bolivia, and Bo-livians. Guevara thought that Bolivia provided good physical terrain for guerrilla warfare and that, if he were successful, it could serve as a base of operations for sim-ilar efforts in several countries it borders. However, the Bolivian Communist Party refused to endorse his effort. And many Bolivian peasants his guerrillas encoun-tered were not inclined to support outsiders. After a few months Bolivian rangers, trained and assisted by US military and CIA advisers, wounded, captured, and ex-ecuted Guevara. A few of the Cubans escaped and eventually made it back to Cuba. In 1997 Guevara's remains were located, returned to Cuba, and reburied at Santa Clara, Cuba, the site of his greatest victory during the Cuban revolution.

The Attempt at Democratic Revolution in Chile

Cuba's support for leftist guerrilla movements, which according to Gott (2004, 231) reached a high tide at the January 1966 Havana Tricontinental Conference attended by revolutionaries from around the world, created a host of problems. Many Latin American governments used Cuba's aid to revolutionaries to justify their participa-tion in the US economic embargo. To demonstrate displeasure with some of Cas-tro's policies, both foreign and domestic, the Soviet Union slowed oil shipments to Cuba in the late 1960s. Possibly because of this pressure and Guevara's failure in Bo-livia, Castro declared in the early 1970s that Cuba recognized alternative paths to socialism. Local conditions could dictate methods other than armed revolution. In particular Castro expressed his willingness to support Salvador Allende's attempt to achieve a socialist revolution in Chile through democratic means.

Allende, leader of the Socialist Party, had won 36.3 percent of the vote for pres-ident on September 4, 1970, in a three-way race. He had been the candidate of the Popular Unity coalition involving the socialist, communist, and radical parties and was a self-avowed Marxist (though not a Marxist-Leninist in the sense that he did not advocate a one-party state). Since he had not received more than 50 percent of the popular vote, Allende was not formally elected until seven weeks later, when many Christian Democrats joined Popular Unity legislators in voting for Allende in a joint session of the Chilean Senate and Chamber of Deputies (Davis 1985; Op-penheim 1993; Petras and Leiva 1994). Allende's dream was to establish socialism in Chile through elections. He was committed to preserving the multiparty system and allowing opposition political forces to express their positions through the mass media. Allende and Popular Unity anticipated that the improvements and greater social equality they planned to bring to Chile would win the electoral support of most Chileans.

But President Allende faced enormous obstacles. The economy was dominated by domestic capitalists opposed to his government and by foreign corporations, which owned copper mines, 70 percent of the telephone company, and other significant investments (Davis 1985). The Nixon administration, outraged at Allende's election, waged economic warfare against Chile (greatly restricting aid, trade, and credit) to generate scarcities and hardships to increase discontent with the Allende government. The CIA engaged in covert operations, such as financing opposition media, political parties, and even violent right-wing groups that carried out terrorist acts such as the murder of army commander General René Schneider, who supported the democratic constitution and refused to block Allende's election ("The CIA Hit List" 1975; Davis 1985; Oppenheim 1993; Petras and Leiva 1994). The army, which continued to receive assistance and training from the Nixon administration, was generally under conservative leadership hostile to Allende. Those high-ranking officers who supported Allende or were firm defenders of the country's democratic constitution were gradually removed from positions of effective authority.

The Allende government enacted reforms that benefited working-class and poor Chileans and nationalized the foreign-owned copper mines, which won widespread approval. But many well-to-do Chileans opposed Allende's plans to extend the role of state-owned enterprises in the economy (Oppenheim 1993; Petras and Leiva 1994). And growing economic difficulties adversely affected the lifestyles of middle- and upper-class Chileans, many of whom rallied against Allende's government. In the 1971 municipal elections Popular Unity received slightly more votes than the combined Christian Democrat and National (conservative) party opposition, and in 1973 Popular Unity received about 44 percent of the vote in congressional elections. But a major weakness of Popular Unity was that it never achieved the clear and stable support of a majority of Chilean voters.

Allende never had an opportunity to use the second half of his six-year term to build support for Popular Unity. On September 11, 1973, the armed forces overthrew the government and Chile's democratic constitution, ending the longest continually functioning democratic political system in the history of South America. The presidential building was hit with bombs and rockets; as a result, Allende apparently committed suicide rather than surrender. Many other Chileans died resisting the military takeover.

Through the 1970s international human rights groups gave Chile's conservative military dictatorship one of the world's worst ratings. General Augusto Pinochet's regime carried out assassinations of critics in Argentina, Italy, and the United States (Dinges and Landau 1980; Freed and Landis 1980). Pinochet, perhaps overestimating his popularity, permitted a plebiscite on October 5, 1988 (*New York Times*, October 7, 1988, A1). By an official tally of 55 to 43 percent, Chilean voters rejected extending the general's presidency for another eight years. This led to a multicandidate presidential election in December 1989. The Socialist Party backed the nominee of the Christian Democratic Party, Patricio Aylwin. He defeated the candidate favored by the military and was inaugurated in 1990 as Chile's first civilian president since the 1973 armed forces takeover. But the constitution, drafted under Pinochet's dictatorship, granted the military a continued role in overseeing the Chilean government. Christian Democrat–Socialist Alliance candidates won the presidency through the 2006 election of Michelle Bachelet, a socialist medical doctor. Bachelet was Chile's first woman president. She was the daughter of an air force general who supported the Allende government and was tortured and died in prison under the right-wing military regime. Bachelet, who along with her mother, had also been imprisoned by the dictatorship, pledged to work to solve social problems. Amending the constitution, punishing human rights abusers, or challenging the economic power of domestic and foreign corporations proved difficult, however. In 2010 a center-right candidate Sebastián Piñera was elected president. But in December 2013, Michelle Bachelet again won the presidency with 62 percent of the vote.

The overthrow of Allende's government provided yet another bitter lesson to those who favored peaceful and democratic revolutionary change. And just as US economic pressure and CIA intervention in Guatemala had influenced Cuban revolutionaries in the early 1950s, similar actions against Chile's elected government had a significant impact on victorious revolutionaries in Nicaragua in 1979 (see Chapter 6).

Cuba and Revolutions in Latin America and Africa

During the 1970s and 1980s Cuba provided training and weapons to Sandinista revolutionaries, who achieved power in Nicaragua in summer 1979, to leftist rebels in El Salvador, and to anticolonial revolutionaries in Angola. The Popular Movement for the Liberation of Angola (MPLA) requested Cuban advisers and troops to assist in resisting invasions by South African forces (Quirk 1993; Szulc 1986). According to Gott (2004, 254), several hundred Cuban special forces soldiers played a major role in helping the MPLA turn back a South African invasion in November 1975. The defeat of the white South African army by Angolans and Cubans encouraged the 1976 Soweto uprising against apartheid by black schoolchildren. Cuba was estimated to have had about 45,000 troops in Angola by 1988, the year of another victory by Angolan and Cuban forces over invading South African troops at the Battle of Cuito Cuanavale. (Cuban troops were later withdrawn as part of a peace settlement.)

Cubans also assisted the anti-apartheid African National Congress (ANC), which in 1994 won the first post-apartheid elections in South Africa. Nelson Mandela, speaking in Cuba on July 26, 1991, on the anniversary of the 1953 Moncada attack, stated that the victory of Angolan and Cuban forces at Cuito Cuanavale protected Angolan independence, helped bring about the liberation of Namibia, showed again that white racist forces could be defeated, and encouraged the anti-apartheid struggle in South Africa (Gott 2004, 279). On Cuba's National Day, July 26, 1995, the ANC addressed the Cuban people with the following message (African National Congress 1995):

> The ANC . . . wishes to salute the Cuban people for the immense role they have played in the national liberation struggle both in South Africa and the Southern African region as a whole. Without the internationalism and sacrifice of the Cuban people and its government in supporting progressive national movements in our region, we possibly would not have reached the historic victory of April 27, 1994. . . . The Cuban government selflessly sacrificed their own precious physical, financial and human resources to ensure that our members in exile were fed, provided with basic necessities, as well as opportunities to further their education. The people and the government of Cuba remain a shining example of practical solidarity to oppressed peoples of our continent. . . . We call upon the USA to allow the people of Cuba to freely develop as a nation, and to immediately lift the blockade. The US government is maintaining this blockade despite the fact that it has been strongly condemned internationally. . . . We also wish to assure the government and the people of Cuba that in the ANC they have an unwavering ally in their struggle for self-determination without foreign interference.

International developments in the late 1980s and the 1990s had major implications for revolutionary movements in terms of ideological goals, methods, and any future Cuban role in revolutionary efforts in other countries. First, the cold war ended in a defeat for the authoritarian socialist model that characterized the pre-Gorbachev USSR. Following the disintegration of the USSR, revolutionary ideologies advocating one-party systems lost favor among discontented intellectuals.

Revolutionaries in countries such as El Salvador reformulated their ideologies to focus on achieving genuine political democracy and guarantees of basic human rights; an economic system including operation of market forces, individual initiatives, and substantial private ownership of economic enterprises; and increasing the economic security, opportunity, and welfare for the poor (Vilas 1995).

The shift in economic ideology can also be seen in Chile's Socialist Party (Oppenheim 1993; Petras and Leiva 1994). The Chilean Socialist Party had been driven from power by the brutal 1973 democracy-destroying military coup in part for attempting to expand the economic role of the state. In the 1990s, as a condition of being allowed to participate in electoral politics and also because of genuine changes in many of its leaders' points of view, the Chilean Socialist Party—along with its

new political ally, the Christian Democratic Party—adopted the following guidelines: (1) maintain a market economy and policies to ensure economic growth; (2)
in the context of capitalist domination of the world economy, maintain cooperative
relations with multinational corporations; (3) preserve a consensus-oriented approach to developing government policy, meaning avoiding conflict with either the
Chilean military or wealthy capitalist elites (Petras and Leiva 1994).

The changes in Chile's Socialist Party came in response to US administrations
intervening overtly or covertly against regimes or political movements that advocated revolutionary change (structural change) viewed as damaging to US economic or security interests, a Chilean military establishment virtually unpunished
for human rights abuses, and relatively high economic growth associated with market-oriented policies of the period of direct military rule (Oppenheim 1993; Petras
and Leiva 1994).

The positive achievements of the Cuban revolution helped inspire the Venezuelan Bolivarian revolution of Hugo Chávez (Gott 2000). Chávez, a leftist former
army paratroop lieutenant colonel, was able to resist an attempted coup in 2002
partly because of his strong support in a sector of the military coupled with his continued popularity with about 58 percent of voters (Ewell 2006). President Chávez
began supplying Cuba with large quantities of much needed oil. Under Chávez's
leadership Venezuela formed an alliance with Cuba to accomplish sweeping international economic and social goals (Azicri 2009).

CUBA AND VENEZUELA'S BOLIVARIAN REVOLUTION AND
THE DEMOCRATIC SHIFT TO THE LEFT IN LATIN AMERICA

For many years Cuba stood alone as the sole socialist revolution in the Western
Hemisphere. But in 1998 Hugo Chávez was elected president of Venezuela, pledging a Bolivarian revolution to aid the poor and resist imperialism (Ewell 2006; Gott
2000; Kozloff 2008). Chávez admired Fidel Castro for the benefits the Cuban revolution brought to Cuba's poor. Within a short time Venezuela was shipping oil to
Cuba, and Cuba was sending thousands of its doctors, nurses, and teachers to provide medical and educational services to Venezuela's people. The revolution-promoting efforts of Venezuela and Cuba, the Chávez government's use of Venezuelan
oil money to aid the poor in many countries, the devastating impact of neoliberal
economic policies on wide sections of Latin American populations, and the intense
unpopularity of the George W. Bush administration all contributed to the elections
of leftist governments in a number of Latin American nations during the twenty-first century (Carlson 2005).

In 2005 Bolivians elected their first indigenous president, Evo Morales, an admirer of Venezuela's Hugo Chávez. Morales pledged to pursue similar policies and

use the resources of his country to more effectively serve the interests of the Bolivian people. On May 1 Morales met with Chávez and Castro in Havana to make Bolivia a member of the Bolivarian Alternative for the Americas (ALBA, renamed the Bolivarian Alliance for the Americas in 2009), founded by Cuba and Venezuela in 2004 to counter the US-sponsored Free Trade Area of the Americas (FTAA) project (Salazar 2006). Critics of FTAA claim it benefits US multinational corporations but threatens economic development in Latin America (Williams 2006). In contrast, ALBA is described as promoting socially beneficial and constructive trade among nations. In 2006 Ecuadorians elected President Rafael Correa, a leftist with a PhD in economics from the University of Illinois. In 2009 Ecuador joined ALBA, and in May 2010 the Ecuadorian National Assembly awarded the nation's highest honor to Fidel Castro. Arriving in Cuba to make the presentation, the Speaker of the Assembly, Fernando Cordero Cueva, said, "Fidel is a constant light for our peoples . . . who has contributed to the new reality that we are experiencing today on our continent" (Moonze 2010). He also noted that 2,500 Ecuadorians were studying in Cuba along with thousands from other nations. President Correa was reelected in 2013.

In 2014, besides Venezuela, Cuba, Bolivia, and Ecuador, ALBA also included Antigua and Barbuda, Dominica, Nicaragua, Saint Lucia, and Saint Vincent and the Grenadines. Leftist presidents were also elected in Argentina in 2007, Paraguay in 2008, and El Salvador and Uruguay in 2009. Some observers predicted voters in Latin America would bring more left-wing governments to power, creating the continental social revolution dreamed of by Fidel Castro and Che Guevara—not by the guerrilla *foco*, but instead through mass participation movements and democratic elections. ALBA may become a new variety of transnational revolutionary movement to be added to those previously analyzed by Mark Katz (1999; 2002; 2006). Revolutionary movements in Venezuela and Bolivia are covered in more depth in Chapter 10.

A major dimension of Cuba's global presence has been its medical internationalism (Andaya 2009; Burnett 2010; Huish and Kirk 2007). Approximately 30,000 Cuban health workers, including 19,000 doctors, served in more than sixty countries (Huish and Kirk 2007, 78). Besides ideological or moral motivations, service abroad pays more than medical salaries in Cuba and also guarantees a boost in pay after returning to Cuba. Many people from developing countries receive free medical education on the island. Cuba was training about 30,000 foreigners in its medical schools. Cuba also developed a rapid response capability for major disasters. After Hurricane Mitch struck Central America in 1998, 1,300 Cuban medical volunteers arrived in the affected areas within twenty-four hours (Huish and Kirk 2007, 77). When Hurricane Katrina devastated New Orleans in August 2005, "Cuba offered to send, at no cost, some 1,586 medical personnel and 36 tons of emergency medical supplies to help the affected communities" (Huish and Kirk 2007, 77). But the Bush administration rejected the offer. And when a destructive earthquake hit Haiti in January 2010, Cubans were among the first foreign doctors to respond, since 380 Cuban medical personnel were already working in the country (Burnett 2010).

Cuban Economy and Political System

Cuba's economy suffered crippling losses during the early 1960s because of the cut-off of trade with the US and almost all Latin American countries as well as the flight of middle- and upper-class Cubans with valuable skills. Economic development was also impeded by idealistic but impractical reliance on moral appeals and revolutionary commitment rather than material incentives for good work performance. Castro's inadequately thought-out projects, such as the drive to harvest 10 million tons of sugar in 1970, also contributed to economic inefficiency.

Beginning in the early 1970s Cuban leaders employed greater material incentives. In 1976 Cuba introduced more autonomy for state enterprises, and markets in which farmers could sell some of their produce outside the state-controlled rationing structure. During 1970–1979 the nation's annual economic growth averaged over 5 percent.

President Castro and others, however, feared that profit-making activities would undermine revolutionary collectivism and idealism and promote excessively self-centered individualism. This concern and alleged business corruption led Cuba to launch the 1984 Campaign of Rectification of Errors and Negative Tendencies "to rectify vices and antisocialist attitudes spawned by the reforms of the 1970s. . . . Once again moral incentives are emphasized, private gain is chastised" (Aguila 1988, 108–109). But Cuba still experienced problems fulfilling its trade and foreign debt obligations (Brenner 1988).

The Soviet Union aided Cuba's economy (Eckstein 1986) by purchasing large quantities of sugar at stable prices usually well above world market prices, which benefited Cuba by billions of dollars. Cuba portrayed this arrangement as an example of how all technologically advanced powers should economically interact with developing nations.

In the 1990s Cuba lost favorable trade relations and military assistance from the former USSR and Eastern Europe and faced the continuing US economic embargo (Aguila 1994). Almost all nations, however, opposed the embargo. On October 29, 2013, the UN General Assembly voted—for the twenty-second year in a row—to condemn the US embargo against Cuba; 188 nations voted against the embargo, and only the United States and Israel supported it (Siegelbaum 2013). Cuba claimed that the fifty-year embargo has caused $1.126 trillion in damages.

Cuba was less able to pay for imported oil. Manufacturing declined and electricity was severely rationed. Farmers stored tractors and returned to animal and human power and to organic farming that avoided the need for scarce chemical fertilizers (Rosset 1994).

To spur production, Cuba again legalized small-scale capitalist activity and negotiated joint business ventures with companies in Spain, Mexico, Italy, Canada, and other nations (Fedarko 1995; *New York Times*, February 3, 1994, A4; September 7, 1995, A12). A major source of foreign currency was tourism. Other sources of revenue were the sale of crops and resources, including sugar, nickel, tobacco, citrus, seafood, and biotechnological, industrial, and medical-pharmaceutical products (Feinsilver 1993).

In March 1996 the US Congress passed the Helms-Burton Act (The Cuban Liberty and Solidarity Act), intended to increase pressure on Cuba by forcing businesspeople from other nations to stop doing business with Cuba. Title III of the act would allow US citizens or companies to use US courts to sue foreign companies using property in Cuba that once belonged to them. If victorious, US courts could provide compensation to the former owners by seizing US assets of the accused foreign companies. Many countries opposed the Helms-Burton Act, and warned of economic retaliation against the US if it was fully implemented. Apparently to avoid provoking international economic warfare, US presidents Bill Clinton, George W. Bush, and Barack Obama repeatedly delayed activation of Title III (*Buenos Aires Herald,* June 8, 2010; *New York Times*, February 21, 1997, A1; PBS, July 17, 2001).

US administrations continued the embargo against Cuba on the grounds that Cuba was not democratic. Important Cuba scholars, such as Juan del Aguila, expressed the view that "many of the reasons for Cuba's isolation stem from its refusal to grant ordinary civil and political rights" (Aguila 1994, 125). But this argument appears incomplete. Were Guatemala and Chile, states friendly to the US, "democratic" when their military personnel were neither under effective elected civilian control nor accountable for human rights abuses, including thousands of murders? Where did political dissidents have the greatest fear of being killed for their views in the 1980s, in Cuba or in the non-embargoed "democracies" of Guatemala and El Salvador? Further, undemocratic nations, such as oil-rich dictatorial monarchies, did not suffer US-orchestrated isolation and economic pressure but rather enjoyed US support because they assured the United States and its allies easy and affordable access to important resources. Cuba's isolation may have been due less to its lack of democracy than to its lack of submission.

The goal of a more democratic Cuba may be more quickly achieved by trade, investment, and cultural exchanges between the United States and Cuba. US administrations appear disinclined to employ this approach, fearing the anti-Castro Cuban American vote in Florida. Florida's electoral votes proved crucial in the 2000 election, when George W. Bush lost nationally by 543,895 votes but became president because he officially won Florida by 537 votes.

Some observers who have repeatedly predicted the fall of Cuba's government believe that the legitimacy of the Cuban regime is derived primarily from its ability to provide Cubans with social benefits, such as access to health care, education, and basic nutrition (McFadyen 1995). The implication is that Cuba's economic problems will erode its social welfare system, leading to the delegitimization of the government and its downfall. But this view neglects the public's perception of the reasons for hardships and whether it views the government as defending national interests and protecting its citizens from even worse consequences that could result from capitulation to foreign pressure.

In February 2008, Raúl Castro, who had been acting president since July 2006 as a result of Fidel's illness, was formally elected president by Cuba's National Assembly. Earlier Raúl, as minister of defense, had modified the military's range of activities, using troops to work on farms and in the resort industry. Some officers were sent to Europe to learn about business management (*New York Times*, March 4, 2009). Once president, Raúl made several economic changes, including purchasing thousands of air-conditioned, television-equipped, Chinese-made buses to improve mass transportation; allowing easier purchase of computers, cell phones, and other consumer electronics; and opening restaurants and hotels to Cubans that had previously been reserved for foreign tourists (Israel 2008; Valdes 2010). People were allowed to open transportation businesses by renting small buses from the government or using their cars as taxis. Farmers were permitted to lease unused state land and had more freedom in purchasing supplies (Frank 2010a; *New York Times*, March 4, 2009). In the wake of $10 billion damage by three 2008 hurricanes, Raúl aimed to make Cuba more self-sufficient in food production (Frank 2010a; Grogg 2010).

When Barack Obama became president in 2009, he ended restrictions on Cuban Americans' ability to travel to Cuba and send remittances to relatives there (Allen 2009; Shifter 2010, 71). These changes were supported by most Cuban Americans, especially young people and recent immigrants from the island (Adams 2009; Allen 2009). On the whole, Cuban Americans became more favorable toward improving US-Cuban relations. But the Obama administration was still inhibited by fear of alienating Florida's Cuban American voters and did not end all trade and travel restrictions. Several observers in Cuba believe that the younger generation may be less committed to the Cuban revolution than older Cubans (Chase 2008). Many young Cubans want to preserve the positive achievements of the revolution while exercising greater freedom.

In 2013, more economic changes were being considered. Some Cuban leaders believed that the key to economic progress was achieving greater efficiency in state-owned enterprises (Burbach 2013). Others focused on developing a socialist market economy with competition, private ownership of enterprises, and strong state oversight and prevention of corrupt practices. Cuba appeared to be moving toward the socialist market economy approach, favorably impressed by the examples of China and Vietnam. By late 2012, about 380,000 persons of Cuba's 5-million-member workforce were self-employed in many of the 181 occupations for which self-employment had become legal. In addition, 172,000 Cubans had taken advantage of the new program of ten-year renewable leases to farm previously uncultivated land. Earlier in 2010 the government had announced plans to gradually downsize the number of state employees by a million workers (Frank 2010b). So some former public employees are likely among those shifting to self-employment or farming. The productivity of the agricultural reform was initially below expectations (Cave 2012). Part of the problem appeared to be inadequate transportation for harvested crops (Cuba's scarcity of reliable trucks). And it's possible that a lease period longer than ten years would provide more motivation for farmers.

Foreign investment has played a limited but significant role in the Cuban economy (Feinberg 2013). However, foreign investment is lower in Cuba than in many similar-size nations. This may be due to several factors. One appears to be fear of US retaliation for doing business in Cuba. Another is lack of confidence that the Cuban government will maintain conditions favorable to foreign investment. Also, some potential investors may be concerned that Cuba's anticorruption rules and enforcement may be too difficult for them to deal with (Grogg 2013).

The sudden death of President Hugo Chávez of Venezuela, whose government provided Cuba with significant economic assistance in the form of low-cost oil, created concern over whether and to what degree aid would continue (Sweig 2013). This appears to have intensified Cuban efforts to increase trade with and investment from other nations. Sweig (2013) also notes that Cuba has decided to increase its digital infrastructure and online access, including Internet cafés. Another significant policy change is the Cuban government's 2013 decision to allow its athletes to sign professional contracts in other countries (Castillo and Oppmann 2013). This will eliminate the need for Cuban baseball players to defect in order to play for US teams and will generate income for Cuba through taxation of players' salaries.

The Cuban constitution of 1976—approved, according to the government, by an overwhelming majority of the population in secret ballot elections—institutionalized the dominant role of the Communist Party. The constitution was revised in 1992 to permit direct elections of the members of the National Assembly (from lists of candidates approved by the Communist Party). "At the same time, references in the constitution to Marxism-Leninism were quietly dropped and the ban on Christians joining the Party was also abandoned" (Gott 2004, 294). Cuba was further declared a secular rather than an atheist state (Gott 2004, 308). The executive branch is the twenty-eight-member Council of State (last elected in 2013), which includes the president (Raúl Castro in 2013), vice president (Miguel Díaz-Canel in 2013), and the heads of several major government agencies. Council members are elected by the National Assembly of People's Power, the country's national legislature (CIA 2014a). The 614 members of the National Assembly were directly elected by the voters in 2013 to serve a five-year term (all candidates were nominated by or acceptable to local branches of the Communist Party, which had about 820,000 members). The Communist Party's central committee had 118 members in 2013 (Associated Press 2013).

At the beginning of the twenty-first century Cuba's economy and its regional influence were reinvigorated through its alliance with Venezuela as well as the election of leftist governments in other Latin American nations. The creation of a supportive leftist political environment in Latin America, long a goal of the Cuban Communist Party, if accompanied by increased security and economic progress for the Cuban people, may speed the future democratization of Cuba. Shortly after South African revolutionary Nelson Mandela passed away, US President Barack Obama and Cuban President Raúl Castro exchanged a handshake at the memorial for Mandela on December 10, 2013, in Johannesburg (Valdes 2013). This event led many to wonder whether a historic reconciliation between the US and Cuba might be in process.

Summary and Analysis

Cubans repeatedly took up arms to win national independence during the nineteenth and twentieth centuries. In the 1950s a broad coalition developed to oppose the Batista government, a regime widely viewed as not only authoritarian but also corrupt and subservient to foreign interests. Pervasive hatred for the Batista dictatorship and its collaboration in the foreign domination and exploitation of the Cuban people was the key factor motivating a desperate and heroic revolutionary struggle.

Members of Cuba's educated elite historically initiated or joined revolutionary movements. José Martí led the generation that launched the 1895 fight for independence. The outcome of that costly struggle, a political and economic system dominated by the United States, alienated many intellectuals not only from the political leaders who ran the country but also from the entire corrupt political apparatus, especially after the betrayal of the major reform goals of the 1933 rebellion. During the 1950s other rebellious children of the elite, led by Fidel Castro, launched a violent revolution against the Batista dictatorship. Apart from those members of Cuba's privileged classes who were openly revolutionary, others withdrew support from Batista as a result of his regime's brutal, repressive tactics.

Popular discontent grew. Depending on a single export crop, sugar, meant both seasonal unemployment for hundreds of thousands of rural workers and cycles of prosperity and depression for much of the general population as world sugar prices rose and fell. During the 1950s, real income in Cuba declined. In addition to the discontent related to economic problems, nationalism was often inflamed when military, economic, and political figures displayed subservience to foreign interests.

Batista's state apparatus was inherently weak. First, many Cubans viewed Batista's regime as strongly influenced by foreign governmental, business, and even organized crime figures and, consequently, not truly representative of Cuban national interests. Second, since Batista had blocked an election and used military force to seize power, his government lacked legitimacy. Batista's government was weakened further by growing hostility from the island's middle class, in great part owing to the torture and murder of hundreds of young middle-class activists and revolutionaries by Batista's security forces. Finally, the army became increasingly demoralized by guerrilla successes, the growth of popular hostility toward the army, the defection of army personnel to the rebel cause, and other factors, such as the decision of the Eisenhower administration to stop sending weapons to the Cuban armed forces in March 1958.

Since the Spanish-American War the United States had played an active role in the Cuban economy and political system. In the early twentieth century the US government ordered troops into Cuba and later helped precipitate changes in the country's leadership by withholding, bestowing, or withdrawing support. The US supported Batista with arms, military advisers, and other assistance. But recognition of intense popular opposition to Batista and his regime's human rights violations, coupled with a belief that the revolutionary leadership was not dominated by Marxists, influenced President Eisenhower's decision to end arms shipments to Batista's army and not to intervene militarily to prevent the revolution.

Soon, however, the Eisenhower administration reversed its permissive stance toward the Cuban revolution, instituted an economic boycott, and engaged in efforts to alter the revolution's outcome. The defeat of the 1961 Bay of Pigs invasion, which the Kennedy administration allowed to go forward, generated increased nationalistic support for the revolutionary government.

Fear of future revolutions stimulated a new US economic aid program for Latin America as well as more military assistance and further covert CIA activities, such as those directed against the Popular Unity movement in Chile. In the 1960s and 1970s US administrations aided conservative military dictatorships that seized power in a number of Latin American countries. Measures taken by US administrations helped prevent the victory of Latin American revolutions until the Carter presidency. Carter's policy of making military assistance contingent on human rights behavior constituted a new period of permissiveness for change in Latin America and contributed to the success of the Nicaraguan revolution.

In the 1990s, after losing aid from Russia and Eastern Europe, Cuba faced a difficult economic situation. In response, the island's leaders moved to increase productivity and technological benefits by encouraging private enterprise and co-operating with foreign-owned capitalist corporations while maintaining Cuba's independence and impressive educational, health care, and social service systems. The US Congress attempted to inhibit Cuban economic recovery through the Helms-Burton Act of 1996, designed to prevent companies of other nations from doing business with Cuba. In contrast, the vast majority of countries voted repeatedly in the United Nations that the US should end its economic embargo against Cuba. Cuba's international influence grew in the early twenty-first century through its alliance with Venezuela and when leftist governments were elected in several Latin American countries.

In 2008, Raúl Castro replaced Fidel as president. Cuba benefited from low-cost oil from Venezuela in exchange for thousands of Cuban health care workers and teachers. Cuba was further bolstered by the addition of Bolivia, Nicaragua, Ecuador, and other nations to ALBA. President Obama eliminated restrictions on the travel and remittances of Cuban Americans to Cuba and allowed US companies to improve the island's telephone and Internet capabilities. Many Cubans looked forward to better relations with the US, a freer political system, and an economically improving future that would retain the best features of Cuban society.

In 2013, Cuba continued its shift toward a socialist market economy and permitted its athletes, including its highly sought after baseball players, to sign professional contracts in other countries. That same year two major supporters of Cuba, Venezuela's Hugo Chávez and South Africa's Nelson Mandela, passed away. A historic handshake between Presidents Barack Obama and Raúl Castro at the memorial for Mandela in Johannesburg raised hopes that relations between the US and Cuba may improve.

CUBAN REVOLUTION: CHRONOLOGY OF MAJOR EVENTS

1868–1878 First war of Cuban independence
1895–1898 Second war of Cuban independence
1902 Cuban independence limited by Platt Amendment
1933 Revolution ousts Machado; Batista gains control of Cuban armed forces
1947 Orthodoxo Party founded
1952 Batista military takeover
1953 Moncada attack fails
1954 Democratically elected reform government in Guatemala overthrown with CIA assistance, providing starkly different lessons for the CIA and Cuban revolutionaries

1955 Castro organizes M-26-7

1956–1958 Cuban revolution

1959 Castro assumes power in January

1961 Bay of Pigs invasion, patterned after the CIA's successful 1954 operation in Guatemala, is defeated; Castro declares Cuban revolution socialist

1962 Cuban missile crisis; US pledges not to invade Cuba

1966 Revolutionaries from many countries attend the Tricontinental Conference in Havana

1967 Che Guevara captured and executed in Bolivia

1970 Cuba recognizes alternate paths, such as democratic elections, to social revolution, including the election of Allende in Chile

1973 On September 11 Chilean military overthrows the elected government and establishes a right-wing dictatorship

1975–1989 Cuban troops aid Angolan revolutionaries to defeat repeated South African invasions of Angola

1980 More than 100,000 leave Cuba for the US during the Mariel boat lift

1988 At the battle of Cuito Cuanavale, Angolan and Cuban forces defeat South African invasion; Nelson Mandela describes this as a major victory over apartheid

1991 USSR disintegrates; Cuba loses valuable assistance

1992 Cuba's revised constitution permits direct popular election of members of the National Assembly and describes Cuba as a secular rather than atheist nation; the Communist Party allows practicing Christians to join

1993 Cuba allows some private business activity

1996 US Congress passes the Helms-Burton Act to try to prevent companies of other nations from doing business with Cuba

1997 Che Guevara's remains transported from Bolivia and reburied at Santa Clara, Cuba

1998 Pope John Paul II visits Cuba, sparking renewed interest in Catholicism, and calls for the US to end its economic embargo; leftist Hugo Chávez, an admirer of the achievements of the Cuban revolution, is elected president of Venezuela

2000 Venezuela provides oil to Cuba; Cuba provides thousands of doctors, nurses, and teachers to Venezuela

2004 Cuba and Venezuela create the Bolivarian Alternative for the Americas (ALBA), an economic alliance for socially beneficial trade

2006 Bolivia, under newly elected leftist president Evo Morales, joins ALBA

2008 Raúl Castro becomes president

2009   Ecuador joins ALBA; Organization of American States lifts 1962 ban
       on Cuban membership
2010   Cuba sends additional aid to Haiti after earthquake
2011   Cuba shifts toward socialist market economy
2012   Several hundred thousand Cubans are self-employed workers
2013   Cuba permits athletes to sign professional contracts abroad
       Two legendary supporters of Cuba, Hugo Chávez and Nelson
       Mandela, die
       Historic handshake between Presidents Barack Obama and Raúl
       Castro

References and Further Readings

Adams, David. 2009. "Cuban-American Generational Shift Brings New Attitudes To-ward Cuba." Federation of American Scientists, October 12. www.fas.org/sgp/crs/row/R40566.pdf.

African National Congress. 1995. "Statement on Cuba's National Day." July 26. www.hartford-hwp.com/archives/43b/025.html.

Aguila, Juan M. del. 1988. *Cuba: Dilemmas of a Revolution*. Westview Profiles: Nations of Contemporary Latin America. Rev. and updated ed. Boulder: Westview.

_____. 1994. *Cuba: Dilemmas of a Revolution*. Nations of Contemporary Latin America. 3rd ed. Boulder: Westview.

Allen, Greg. 2009. "Cuban-Americans Split Over New Cuba Rules." National Public Radio, April 14. www.npr.org/templates/story/story.php?storyId=103070179.

Amaro, Neson, and Carmelo Mesa-Lago. 1971. "Inequality and Classes." In Carmelo Mesa-Lago, ed., *Revolutionary Change in Cuba*. Pittsburgh: University of Pittsburgh Press.

Andaya, Elise. 2009. "Cuba: Health Care as Social Justice." *NACLA Report on the Americas* 42 (September/October): 42–44.

Anderson, Jon Lee. 2010. *Che*. New York: Grove Press.

Associated Press. 2013. "Cuba: Communist Party Leaders Ousted." *New Yorker*, July 3. www.nytimes.com/2013/07/04/world/americas/cuba-communist-party-leaders-ousted.html.

Azicri, Max. 2009. "The Castro-Chávez Alliance." *Latin American Perspectives* 36 (1): 99–110.

Brenner, Philip. 1988. *From Confrontation to Negotiation: US Relations with Cuba*. Boulder: Westview.

Buenos Aires Herald. June 8, 2010. "Obama Renews Waiver on Cuba-Property Lawsuits." www.buenosairesherald.com/BreakingNews/View/6478.

Burbach, Roger. 2013. "A Cuban Spring?" *NACLA*, Spring, 10–12.

Burnett, John. 2010. "Cuban Doctors Unsung Heroes of Haitian Earthquake." National Public Radio, January 24. www.npr.org/templates/story/story.php?storyId=122919202.

Carlson, Laura. 2005. "The Continental Drift of the Left." *NACLA Report on the Americas* 38 (May/June): 13–17.

Castillo, Mariano, and Patrick Oppmann. 2013. "Cuba to Allow Athletes to Seek Pro Contracts Abroad." CNN, September 29. www.cnn.com/2013/09/28/world/americas /cuba-athletes-abroad/index.html.

Cave, Damien. 2012. "Cuba's Free-Market Farm Experiment Yields a Meager Crop." *New York Times,* December 8. www.nytimes.com/2012/12/09/world/americas/changes -to-agriculture-highlight-cubas-problems.html?pagewanted=print.

Central Intelligence Agency (CIA). 2014a. "Cuba." In *World Factbook.* www.cia.gov /library/publications/the-world-factbook/geos/cu.html.

———. 2014b. "United States." In *World Factbook.* www.cia.gov/library/publications /the-world-factbook/geos/us.html.

Chase, Michelle. 2008. "Cuba's Generation Gap." *NACLA Report on the Americas* 41 (November/December): 9–13.

"The CIA Hit List." 1975. *Newsweek,* December 1, 28–35.

Davis, Nathaniel. 1985. *The Last Two Years of Salvador Allende.* Ithaca, NY: Cornell University Press.

Debray, Regis. 1967. *Revolution in the Revolution? Armed Struggle and Political Struggle in Latin America.* Trans. Bobbye Ortiz. New York: Monthly Review Press.

DeFronzo, James, ed. 2006. *Revolutionary Movements in World History: From 1750 to the Present.* 3 vols. Santa Barbara, CA: ABC-CLIO.

Dinges, John, and Saul Landau. 1980. *Assassination on Embassy Row.* New York: Pantheon.

Eckstein, Susan. 1986. "The Impact of the Cuban Revolution: A Comparative Perspective." *Comparative Studies in Society and History* 28 (July): 502–534.

Ewell, Judith. 2006. "Venezuelan Bolivarian Revolution of Hugo Chavez." In DeFronzo, ed., *Revolutionary Movements in World History,* 3:903–912.

Fedarko, Kevin. 1995. "Open For Business." *Time,* February 20, 51–53.

Feinberg, Richard. 2013. "Foreign Investment in the New Cuban Economy." *NACLA,* Spring, 13–18.

Feinsilver, Julie. 1993. "Can Biotechnology Save the Revolution?" *NACLA Report on the Americas* 26 (May): 7–10.

Frank, Marc. 2010a. "Cuba Cedes to Farmers Right to Purchase Supplies." Reuters, May 17. www.reuters.com/article/idUSTRE64G0RB20100517.

———. 2010b. "Cubans Brace for "Reorganization" of Labour Force." Reuters, July 10. http://uk.reuters.com/article/2010/07/20/uk-cuba-layoffs-idUKTRE66 J38O20100720.

Freed, Donald, and Fred Simon Landis. 1980. *Death in Washington: The Murder of Orlando Letelier.* Westport, CT: Lawrence Hill.

Gleijeses, Piero. 1991. *Shattered Hope: The Guatemalan Revolution and the United States, 1944–1954.* Princeton, NJ: Princeton University Press.

Gott, Richard. 2000. *In the Shadow of the Liberator: Hugo Chavez and the Transformation of Venezuela*. London: Verso.

_____. 2004. *Cuba: A New History*. New Haven, CT: Yale University Press.

Grogg, Patricia. 2010. "Quake Damage Begins at Home." Reuters, April 14. ipsnews.net /news.asp?idnews=51041.

_____. 2013. "Getting Tough on Corruption in Cuba." Inter Press Service, July 3. www .ipsnews.net/2013/07/getting-tough-on-corruption-in-cuba.

Guevara, Ernesto Che. 1968a. *The Diary of Che Guevara*. New York: Bantam.

_____. 1968b. *Episodes of the Revolutionary War*. New York: International Publishers.

_____. 1969a. *Che: Selected Works of Ernesto Guevara*. Ed. Roland E. Bonachea and Nelson P. Valdes. Cambridge: MIT Press.

_____. 1969b. *Guerrilla Warfare*. New York: Vintage.

_____. 1985. *Guerrilla Warfare: Selected Case Studies*. Ed. Brian Loveman and Thomas M. Davies Jr. Lincoln: University of Nebraska Press.

Hartford Courant. August 10, 1992. "Barcelona '92 Medals Table—All 257 Events Completed," D6.

Huish, Robert, and John M. Kirk. 2007. "Cuban Medical Internationalism and the Development of the Latin American School of Medicine." *Latin American Perspectives* 34 (6): 77–92.

International Institute for Strategic Studies. 2005. "Cuba's Military Celebrates 49 Years." December 2.

Israel, Esteban. 2008. "Chinese Buses Bring Welcome Change to Cuba." Reuters, March 13. www.reuters.com/article/idUSN1321778820080313.

Katz, Mark N. 1999. *Revolutions and Revolutionary Waves*. New York: St. Martin's.

_____. 2002. "Osama bin Laden as Transnational Revolutionary Leader." *Current History* 101 (February): 81–85.

_____. 2006. "Transnational Revolutionary Movements." In DeFronzo, ed., *Revolutionary Movements in World History*, 3:872–876.

Kozloff, Nikolas. 2008. *Revolution: South America and the Rise of the New Left*. New York: Palgrave Macmillan.

McFadyen, Deidre. 1995. "The Social Repercussions of the Crisis." *NACLA Report on the Americas* 29 (September/October): 20–22.

Moonze, Larry. 2010. "Ecuador Honors Fidel." *Post News Papers Zambia*, May 31. www .postzambia.com/post-print_article.php?articleId=9806.

New York Times. May 15, 1987. "Man and God in Cuba: A Castro-Church Detente?" A4.

_____. October 7, 1988. "Regime of Pinochet Accepts Defeat in Chile's Plebiscite," A1.

_____. February 3, 1994. "On the Street Cubans Fondly Embrace Capitalism," A4.

_____. April 9, 1994. "Guatemala's War: Ideology Is the Latest Excuse," E5.

_____. July 24, 1994. "Guatemalan Police Find 1,000 Bodies," 3.

_____. September 7, 1995. "Cuba Passes Law to Attract Greater Foreign Investment," A12.

_____. February 21, 1997. "US Rejects Role for World Court in Trade Dispute," A1.

_____. March 4, 2009. "Raul Castro." topics.nytimes.com/topics/reference/timestopics/people/c/raul_castro/index.html.

Oppenheim, Lois Hecht. 1993. *Politics in Chile: Democracy, Authoritarianism, and the Search for Development.* Boulder: Westview.

PBS. 1985. "Crisis in Central America: Castro's Challenge." *Frontline.*

_____. 2001. "Bush Renews Waiver of Helms-Burton Provision." *NewsHour Update,* July 17. www.pbs.org/newshour/updates/july01/cuba_7-17.html.

Petras, James, and Fernando Ignacio Leiva. 1994. *Democracy and Poverty in Chile: The Limits to Electoral Politics.* Series in Political Economy and Economic Development in Latin America. Boulder: Westview.

Quirk, Robert E. 1993. *Fidel Castro.* New York: Norton.

Reuters. 2008. "Fact Box: Facts About Cuba's Communist Party." February 24. www.reuters.com/article/topNews/idUSN2226406020080224.

Rosset, Peter. 1994. "The Greening of Cuba." *NACLA Report on the Americas* 28 (November/December): 37–41.

Ruiz, Ramon Eduardo. 1968. *Cuba: The Making of a Revolution.* Amherst: University of Massachusetts Press.

Salazar, Luis Suárez. 2006. "Cuba's Foreign Policy and the Promise of ALBA." *NACLA Report on the Americas* 39 (January/February): 27–32.

Schlesinger, Stephen, and Stephen Kinzer. 1982. *Bitter Fruit: The Untold Story of the American Coup in Guatemala.* Garden City, NY: Doubleday.

Shifter, Michael. 2010. "Obama and Latin America: New Beginnings, Old Frictions." *Current History* 109 (February): 67–73.

Siegelbaum, Portia. 2013. "U.N. General Assembly Votes Against US Cuba Embargo for the 22nd Year in a Row." CBS News, October 29. www.cbsnews.com/news/un-general-assembly-votes-against-us-cuba-embargo-for-the-22nd-year-in-a-row.

Sigmund, Paul. 2006. "Chilean Socialist Revolution, Counter-Revolution, and the Restoration of Democracy." In DeFronzo, ed., *Revolutionary Movements in World History,* 1:107–116.

Sports Illustrated. 2012. "2012 Medals." http://sportsillustrated.cnn.com/olympics/2012/medals/tracker/index.html.

Streeter, Stephen M. 2000a."Interpreting the 1954 US Intervention in Guatemala: Realist, Revisionist, and Postrevisionist Perspectives." *History Teacher* 34 (1): 61–74.

_____. 2000b. *Managing the Counterrevolution: The United States and Guatemala, 1954–1961.* Athens: Ohio University Press.

_____. 2006. "The Guatemalan Democratic Revolution, Counter-Revolution, and Restoration of Democracy." In DeFronzo, ed., *Revolutionary Movements in World History,* 2:325–335.

Szulc, Tad. 1986. *Fidel: A Critical Portrait.* New York: Morrow.

Valdes, Rosa Tania. 2010. "Cuba Letting Drivers Rent Buses, Make Money." Reuters, May 17. www.reuters.com/article/idUSTRE64G3RA20100517.

_____. 2013. "Obama-Castro Handshake: A Sign of Mandela-like Reconciliation?" Reuters, December 10. www.reuters.com/article/2013/12/10/us-cuba-usa-mandela-idUSBRE9B90YS20131210.

Vilas, Carlos M. 1995. "A Painful Peace: El Salvador After the Accords." *NACLA Report on the Americas* 28 (May/June): 6–11.

Williams, Howard. 2006. "Chavez, Castro Political Alliance Grows with Bolivian Entry." CNS News, May 1. www.cnsnews.com/viewforeignbureaus.asp?page=/foreign bureaus/archive/200605/for20060501d.html.

Wolf, Eric R. 1969. *Peasant Wars of the Twentieth Century.* New York: Harper & Row.

Wyden, Peter. 1979. *Bay of Pigs: The Untold Story.* New York: Simon & Schuster.

Selected DVD, Film, and Videocassette Documentaries

See "Purchase and Rental Sources" at the end of this volume for information on how to obtain the following resources and for full names of media companies and other organizations listed here as abbreviations.

*Battle for Chile.*1976. 184 min. Black-and-white film. FRIF. Parts 1–2. Efforts at peaceful democratic social revolution and the violent right-wing military seizure of power.

Bay of Pigs Declassified. 50 min. AETV (History Undercover). CIA-organized Bay of Pigs invasion of Cuba.

Castro's Challenge. 1985. 60 min. Video. Films Inc. PBS account of the Cuban revolution.

Chile: Hasta Cuando? 1987. 57 min. Color film or video. Filmmakers Library. Academy Award–nominated documentary of the overthrow of the Allende government in 1973 and Chile under the military dictatorship.

CIA Secret Files: Part 3, Executive Action. 1992. 50 min. Check www.worldcat.org for libraries with this item. Describes CIA actions regarding Cuba, Che Guevara, and the Allende government in Chile. Includes interviews with former CIA personnel.

Conflict in Cuba: The Bay of Pigs and the Cuban Missile Crisis. 50 min. AETV.

Controlling Interests. 1978. 40 min. Color film. AFSC. Classic on multinational corporations in less developed societies, with specific coverage of Latin America.

Cuba. 2012. 59 min. BBC. http://videosift.com/video/Cuba-2012-BBC-documentary.

Cuba. 1998. 47 min. Cold War Series. DVD. Amazon.com. http://www.youtube.com/watch?v=viGffhaoLDk&list=PL4FF5F03E7FE6342C.

Cuba! Africa! Revolution! 2007. 60 min. BBC.

The Cuban Missile Crisis of October 1962. 1998. 46 min. CNN Cold War Series, Episode 10. Truman Library.

Dirty Secrets: Jennifer, Evardo, and the CIA in Guatemala. 1998. 56 min. AFSC. Jennifer searches for her disappeared husband and makes discoveries about the CIA in Guatemala.

El Che: Investigating a Legend. 1998. 150 min. DVD. Amazon.com.

Fidel Castro. 2004. 120 min. DVD, video. PBS. Fidel Castro as leader of Cuba.

Fidel Castro: El Comandante. 2007. 50 min. DVD, video. BIO. Castro as revolutionary and president of Cuba.

Fidel: The Untold Story. 2002. 91 min. DVD. Amazon.com.

Inside Cuba. 2010. Two parts, 11 min. each. BBC. Part 1, http://www.youtube.com /watch?v=eNVTb9oyyNM. Part 2, http://www.youtube.com/watch?v=_5BGC jkU2Jo.

The Pinochet Case. 2001. 109 min. FRIF. General Pinochet, leader of the military government of Chile, 1973–1989.

Salud! 2006. 93 min. Cuban health care, domestic and international. www.saludthefilm .net/ns/order-now.html.

South of the Border. 2010. 78 min. DVD. Amazon.com. Oliver Stone documentary. Includes interviews with the leaders of Argentina, Bolivia, Brazil, Cuba, Ecuador, Paraguay, and Venezuela.

The True Story of Che Guevara. 2008. 91 min. DVD. Amazon.com.

Venezuela: Revolution in Progress. 2005. 50 min. DCTV. President Hugo Chávez and conflict over his policies.

The Yankee Years. 1985. 60 min. Video. Films, Inc. PBS documentary on Cuba, Guatemala, Nicaragua, and El Salvador during the first half of the twentieth century.

6

Revolution in Nicaragua

In the 1930s, as Batista assumed control of the Cuban army, Anastasio Somoza García used the Nicaraguan armed forces to seize the government of that Central American nation. After rebel nationalist leader Augusto César Sandino was murdered in 1934, the Somoza family and its primary mechanism of coercion, the National Guard, dominated Nicaragua for decades. The Somozas amassed a huge fortune while the gap between the nation's privileged and poor classes widened. By the mid-1970s many Nicaraguans, enraged by the greed and brutality of the regime, were willing to temporarily set aside their differences and unite in a revolution. During 1978 and 1979, 30,000–50,000 Nicaraguans perished in the conflict before the Somozas fled the country. Following the July 19, 1979, victory, the new Sandinista government became a major concern of successive US administrations. The Democratic majority in Congress repeatedly clashed with Presidents Reagan and Bush over issues such as CIA aid to counterrevolutionaries (contras) trying to overthrow Nicaragua's government and the question of how much, if any, danger the Nicaraguan revolution posed to the United States.

GEOGRAPHY AND POPULATION

Nicaragua (50,336 square miles, or 130,370 square kilometers) is about the size of New York State and had 5,788,531 residents in 2013 (CIA 2014; about 3 million at the time of the 1979 revolution). The population was estimated to be 69 percent mixed Amerindian and white ancestry, 17 percent white, 9 percent black, and 5 percent Amerindian. About 95.3 percent of Nicaraguans spoke Spanish, and the rest (mainly on the Atlantic coast) spoke Amerindian languages or English. Approximately 90 percent lived on the Pacific side of the country and shared a Spanish culture. Those among the 10 percent of the population on the Atlantic side were characterized by diverse cultural heritages. The largest indigenous group was the Miskito; about 1.7 percent of Nicaraguans spoke the Miskito language. Other inhabitants of the Atlantic coast included the descendants of former African slaves who fled to Nicaragua from other lands. Britain controlled the Atlantic side of Nicaragua until the 1890s, so many in the region spoke English and were Protestants. Overall, 58.5 percent of Nicaraguans were Roman Catholic, 21.6 percent Evangelical, 1.6 percent Moravian, 0.9 percent Jehovah's Witness, 1.6 percent other religions, and 15.7 percent none (CIA 2014 from the 2005 census). About 57 percent of the population lived in urban areas in 2010.

NICARAGUA BEFORE THE REVOLUTION

After obtaining its independence from Spain in the 1820s, Nicaragua was ruled by a small number of well-to-do families. Economic and regional conflicts and ideological disagreements often resulted in civil wars in which wealthy Nicaraguans hired small armies of a few hundred men each. One important early rivalry was that between the prominent families of the cities of León and Granada. The leading citizens of León supported greater personal liberty and an economic shift toward commerce, industrialization, and other modern business activities. Calling themselves liberals, in the classical sense of favoring increased freedom from church or state controls, they organized Nicaragua's Liberal Party. In contrast, the landowning families of Granada, who founded the Conservative Party, supported the values of traditional Spain and the dominance of the Catholic Church in social and political life and tended to favor an economy based on agriculture.

In the mid-nineteenth century US citizens became interested in Nicaragua as a route of travel from the eastern United States to California. North Americans sailed down the Atlantic to the Nicaraguan coast and then traveled up the San Juan River to Lake Nicaragua, where employees of the American industrialist Cornelius Vanderbilt operated a steamship. After the fifty-mile lake crossing, stagecoaches carried passengers approximately twenty miles to the Pacific and another sea voyage up to California.

During a civil war in 1855 the liberal faction recruited about sixty heavily armed North American mercenaries led by William Walker, an adventurer from Tennessee. After his men helped the liberals defeat the conservatives, Walker, who controlled the liberal army, declared himself president of Nicaragua. Walker decided to promote North American colonization of Nicaragua, establish slavery, and possibly later annex Nicaragua to the United States as a slave state to help increase the South's representation in the US Senate. In 1857, once Walker's plans became clear, Nicaraguans, aided by other Central Americans, drove him out of the country.

MAP 6.1 Nicaragua

MAP 6.1 Nicaragua

When Walker attempted to repeat his intervention in 1860, he was captured and executed in the neighboring country of Honduras.

After 1857 Nicaragua technically functioned as a republic with a president and a national legislature; many, however, did not consider Nicaragua a democracy but rather a society governed exclusively by wealthy families. As the Liberal Party had disgraced itself by inviting in North American mercenaries, the Conservative Party held the presidency during the years 1858–1893. A Conservative Party dictatorship enacted laws in 1877 intended to end indigenous ownership of communal lands and force peasants to work as laborers harvesting coffee crops and cutting mahogany trees for European and US markets. These measures provoked rebellions that were repressed in 1881, costing several thousand lives (Cockcroft 1989). In 1893 Liberal Party General José Santos Zelaya took over the government. Although many considered Zelaya a dictator, most felt he was also a staunch nationalist who attempted to reduce dependence on foreign business interests (Cockcroft 1989; Diederich 1981; Millett 1977).

The fact that a river and a lake cut through all but about twenty miles of the country inspired the idea that Nicaragua would be an ideal location for a canal to link the Atlantic and the Pacific. However, disagreements between Nicaragua and the United States, coupled with an exaggerated fear of volcanic eruptions and earthquakes, promoted by business interests favoring a canal through Panama, resulted in the US selecting Panama as the canal site. When President Zelaya considered negotiating with Britain and Japan about their building a Nicaraguan canal that would compete for interocean traffic with the upcoming Panama Canal, US officials encouraged conservatives to rebel. Military intervention by the US navy and marines helped force Zelaya to resign in 1909. After fighting resumed among liberal and conservative factions, the US again intervened militarily in 1912, and a pro-US conservative government was installed. A marine contingent stationed in Nicaragua from 1912 to 1925 helped maintain Conservatives from the Chamorro family in the presidency. In 1913 and 1914 new treaties gave the US the right to build a canal through Nicaragua and lease land for US army and naval bases.

Sandino, Somoza, and the Nicaraguan National Guard

US officials publicly supported establishment of a real democracy in Nicaragua. One measure instituted to achieve a democratic system was the organization of the Nicaraguan National Guard during the 1920s. The guard, trained and equipped by the US, was to take the place of the small personal armies and political party militias that had previously constituted Nicaragua's factionalized armed forces. The National Guard, it was hoped, would be loyal not to any one man or political party but to a democratic constitution. US advisers selected as leader for the new army Anastasio Somoza García (nicknamed "Tacho"). Somoza was the US-educated son of a coffee plantation owner. Although he had previously been accused of involvement in a counterfeiting scheme, he spoke English well (serving as a translator for US officials), was familiar with US customs and popular sports, and had an appealing personality (Macaulay 1967; Millett 1977).

In 1924 US officials helped supervise a national election that resulted in the victory of an anti-Chamorro conservative, Carlos Solorzano, for president and a liberal, Juan Bautista Sacasa, for vice president. In 1925 the marines withdrew. Within a few months a new civil war broke out when Chamorro conservatives rebelled and attempted to seize power. When US marines landed in 1926 to force a settlement of the conflict, a liberal general, Augusto César Sandino, a farm owner whose ancestry was half indigenous and half European, refused to lay down his arms as long as US troops occupied Nicaragua. He stated that the US was trying to impose terms that would benefit foreign, not Nicaraguan, interests and would result in the installation of another US puppet as president. Rejecting bribes, Sandino and about fifty supporters fought on. Between 1926 and 1933, Sandino's forces, which eventually grew to more than 3,000, battled several thousand marines and the Nicaraguan National Guard. Although newsreels shown in US movie theaters portrayed Sandino as a bandit leader, many Latin Americans viewed him as a nationalist fighting heroically against a foreign invasion.

Facing public pressure to end the intervention, whose cost during the Great Depression made it even more unpopular, as well as opposition from many Latin American countries, US marines withdrew in 1933. Sandino then agreed to a settlement of the war that involved allowing Juan Bautista Sacasa, a liberal, to serve as president. The agreement, which allowed Sandino's forces to control much of Nicaragua and compete for national political power, proved unacceptable to General Somoza. After having dinner with President Sacasa one evening in 1934, Sandino and two of his aides were kidnapped and executed by officers of Somoza's National Guard. President Sacasa was outraged at the murder of his friend Sandino and demanded that those guilty be punished. They never were. Two years later, in 1936, Somoza used the National Guard to install himself as president (Macaulay 1967; Millett 1977; Stahler-Sholk 2006). Anastasio Somoza García ("Tacho I") ruled Nicaragua until he was assassinated by a Nicaraguan poet in 1956; he was succeeded by his eldest son, Luis Somoza Debayle, who died of natural causes in 1967. The younger, West Point–educated son, Anastasio Somoza Debayle ("Tacho II" or "Tachito"), took over and ruled until the 1979 revolution forced him to flee, first to the United States and then to Paraguay, where he was assassinated in 1980 by Argentinean leftists.

Somoza Family Rule

The Somozas dominated Nicaragua through a number of methods. Most important was the National Guard. Men of lower-middle-class, working-class, and peasant background joined the guard seeking social and economic mobility in a land of limited opportunity. In return for loyal service, the guard provided steady pay, food, medical care, and a retirement pension. The retiree could often obtain a job in a Somoza-owned business or assistance in opening his own business (Millett 1977).

The Somozas were clever politicians who kept the opposition divided and ineffectual through bribery, intimidation, or even imprisonment and death (some dissidents were shot supposedly trying to escape). Vote buying, ballot box stuffing, or both reportedly occurred, and the Somozas rewrote the constitution to maintain power (Booth 1985; Diederich 1981; Walker 1986).

Anastasio Somoza García adapted to changing political conditions. Between 1936 and 1938, when upper-class groups sponsored a Nazi-style brown shirt organization, he adopted a pro-fascist position. In contrast, during World War II Somoza allied with the US against Germany, and as European fascism was going down to defeat in 1944, he convinced labor leaders to support his rule. His pro-labor policies (1944–1948) won him the temporary backing of Nicaragua's Communist Party (then called the Nicaraguan Socialist Party). But once Somoza had succeeded in co-opting leaders of his major upper-class opposition in the Conservative Party by giving them subordinate roles in his government, and once his major foreign sponsor, the United States, became hostile to the Soviet Union, he abandoned many of his previous labor reforms. Somoza then "violently purged former union leaders and forced many unionists and socialists into exile" (Booth 1985, 65).

The Somoza family accumulated great wealth through its control of the government. Foreign and domestic businesses were charged fees to exploit the nation's gold and timber. During World War II the government confiscated German estates, some of which the Somoza family obtained at little expense. The Somozas were accused of violating trade restriction laws that bound other business owners. By 1979 the family owned 10–20 percent of cultivated land, more than 150 factories, several banks, an airline, and port facilities (property valued in the hundreds of millions of dollars), and was thought to have $500 million in foreign investments (Booth 1985; Walker 1986).

The US supported the Somoza dynasty because of its friendliness toward North American business interests and strong anticommunist stance. Because the Somoza family's hold on power was in great part due to foreign intervention and sponsorship, and repression coupled with opportunistic political alliances and bribes, and because its continuous goal was to increase Somoza wealth, Somoza rule lacked moral legitimacy. The regime, consequently, was vulnerable to loss of US support.

The Nicaraguan Economy

When Sandino was murdered in 1934, Nicaragua was suffering from the worldwide depression and the drastic decline in international prices for the nation's major exports (coffee prices in 1933 were only one-third their 1929 level and did not recover fully until 1947). Many small farmers lost their land to wealthy landowners. As landownership became more concentrated, displaced peasants joined the ranks of landless agricultural laborers and urban workers. Many agricultural laborers were bound to plantations because laws prevented departure of any workers who owed money to the plantation stores. Since such stores usually sold food or tools at high prices and provided credit only at high interest rates, many rural workers remained mired in long-term debt and were forbidden from seeking alternate employment.

During World War II the economy improved as the US became more dependent on Central America's resources (e.g., rubber, metals, and wood). Following the war, the economy fluctuated in response to changing demand for Nicaragua's exports. In the early 1960s fear of further Cuban-style revolutions prompted the US to increase economic assistance to Nicaragua and to form the Central American Common Market to spur trade among nations within the region. Partly as a result, Nicaragua's GNP rose by 250 percent between 1960 and 1975. But benefits reaching the majority in the lower classes were limited by restrictions on labor unions, low wages for many workers, and lack of extensive agrarian reform. Because the population doubled between 1950 and 1970 and the economic system disproportionately benefited the upper- and middle-class minorities, inequality increased (Booth 1985).

By the start of the 1970s, 50 percent of economically active Nicaraguans were employed in agriculture, 10 percent in industry, and about 20 percent in other largely urban, blue-collar jobs such as construction, transportation, and domestic labor. The middle class included 15–20 percent of Nicaraguans working in management, sales, and clerical jobs, small businesses, and government. The lower half of income earners received 15 percent of all income, whereas the top 5 percent received 30 percent (Booth 1985). The largest 0.6 percent of farms had 31 percent of the farmland, and the bottom 58 percent had only 3.4 percent. The rural population was 75 percent illiterate (compared to 25 percent in urban areas).

In the 1960s the upper class prospered, and many in the middle class and urban working class enjoyed economic improvements. By the mid-1970s, however, there was an economic downturn. The devastating 1972 earthquake caused 5,000–10,000 deaths and destroyed thousands of homes, businesses, and manufacturing jobs. Within a few years the economy was damaged by lower international coffee prices, labor unrest, and intensified political repression that discouraged new investments in business and industry. Real wages dropped by 29 percent for industrial workers between 1968 and 1975, 15 percent for construction workers, and 26 percent for

communications and transportation workers (Booth 1985). Economically generated frustration increased in the years leading up to the revolution.

The Revolution
Formation of the FSLN

Widespread poverty, along with Somoza corruption, greed, subservience to foreign
interests, and repression, earned the regime many enemies. Survivors of Sandino's
army repeatedly attempted to launch guerrilla wars. In 1961 a small group of young
anti-Somoza militants, led by Carlos Fonseca Amador, Tomás Borge, and Silvio
Mayorga, created a new organization, the Sandinista Front for National Liberation
(FSLN) (Stahler-Sholk 2006). Only Borge survived to witness the overthrow of
the Somoza regime. FSLN leaders, viewing the Somoza dynasty as a creature of
US intervention and a corrupt instrument of foreign exploitation, were inspired
by national liberation movements around the world. Taking the name of the nationalist hero Sandino for their movement, FSLN organizers intended to rid the
country of the Somozas and launch a social revolution to redistribute resources
to the poor and create a society without extremes of wealth and poverty (Booth
1985; Cockcroft 1989; Walker 1986). The creation of the FSLN reflected not only the
development of dissident elements within Nicaragua's educated elite but also the
increasing commitment of young elite members to armed revolution as the only
feasible means of social transformation.

Although most FSLN leaders from 1961 to 1979 came from middle- and upper-
class families, Carlos Fonseca, widely recognized as the "prime mover" in the formation of the FSLN, was the illegitimate son of a poor single mother who worked
as a cook (Zimmermann 2000). Excelling as a student and leader at Matagalpa High
School, Fonseca was attracted to Marxist concepts such as the view that the flow of
history involved a struggle among economic classes, that the majority of Nicaragua's
people were the victims of greedy US corporations and an exploiting Nicaraguan
capitalist class, and that there was a need for a revolutionary redistribution of wealth
and power (Booth 1985; Pastor 1987; Reed and Foran 2002). Fonseca, who would
die in combat against Somoza's National Guard in 1976, became a leftist activist at
the National Autonomous University and joined the Nicaraguan Socialist Party
(the country's communist party).

Fonseca, Borge, and Daniel Ortega and Lidia Saavedra de Ortega—parents of
the Ortega brothers (one of whom, Camilo, was to die in the revolution; another,
Daniel, to become the first president of the revolutionary government; and a third,
Humberto, to become commander of the Sandinista army)—and thousands of
others suffered imprisonment and often torture for openly opposing the Somoza
regime (Booth 1985; Pastor 1987). Following the assassination of Anastasio Somoza

García in 1956, Fonseca was one of more than 2,000 arrested. In 1957 Fonseca was released from prison, and the Nicaraguan Socialist Party sent him to the Soviet Union. But in 1960 Fonseca quit the party, in part because it refused to support a violent revolution to oust Somoza. Fonseca and others in the FSLN received training in jungle warfare from Santos López, a veteran of Sandino's original army.

Mass discontent in the 1960s, however, had not yet reached the critical level. The Sandinistas had not widely communicated the purpose and desirability of the revolutionary movement before launching their guerrilla war. Therefore, another of the necessary conditions for revolutionary victory, a shared motivation for revolution capable of uniting the Sandinistas with the majority of workers and peasants, did not exist when the Sandinistas initiated armed struggle. Thus the FSLN in the 1960s lacked the enthusiastic support of the people, the only possible means of victory against the well equipped National Guard. Somoza's army, bolstered by US aid given in fear of another Cuban-style revolution, devastated the Sandinistas (Stahler-Sholk 2006; Zimmermann 2000).

Partly in reaction to initial failures, disagreements arose within the FSLN concerning which approach would be most effective in overthrowing the Somoza regime. Between 1975 and 1977 three distinct factions existed (Booth 1985; Pastor 1987). The Guerra Popular Prolongada (Prolonged People's War) faction, led by Tomás Borge and Henry Ruíz, held that rural warfare was the key to success. Members of this group, influenced by China's Mao and Vietnam's Giap, planned to build up peasant support gradually and to construct a large revolutionary army, which over a lengthy period would wear down, demoralize, and defeat Somoza's forces. The Proletarios (Proletarians), one of whose leaders was Jaime Wheelock, believed that mobilizing the urban working class would be the most effective way to achieve victory. They sought to organize labor unions and residents of urban neighborhoods for a campaign of workers' strikes and mass demonstrations that would bring down the regime. The Terceristas (Third Force), also called the Insurrecionales (Insurgents) and the Christian Wing, included Daniel and Humberto Ortega. This group differed from the others in two major ways. First, the Terceristas deemphasized the original FSLN Marxist point of view and rapidly expanded their ranks with non-Marxist socialists, Catholic and Protestant social activists (including priests), and other diverse anti-Somoza advocates of social reform and democracy. Second, they carried out much bolder attacks and were eventually successful in provoking widespread insurrection against the Somoza regime.

As the Terceristas' tactics proved effective and the majority of the population came to support the revolution, disagreements among the FSLN factions declined. This led to provisional reunification in December 1978 and formal reunification in March 1979, with each faction contributing three representatives to a nine-person FSLN governing directorate (Stahler-Sholk 2006; Zimmermann 2000). Following the success of the Terceristas and the growth of the FSLN by 1979 into a mass move-ment with philosophically diverse members, the ideology of the FSLN evolved in a moderate direction. FSLN policy after the victory was Marxist in the sense of pro-moting a "profound socioeconomic transformation to benefit the working classes but was also innovative in that it institutionalized political opposition, preserved a large private sector [in the economy], and established traditional civil liberties" (Booth 1985, 147).

Increased Popular Discontent

During the late 1960s and early 1970s, several developments drastically increased dissatisfaction with the Somoza dictatorship. One was the growth of social activism among younger priests and religious workers. As in other Latin American countries, liberation theology was taking hold. The clergy, often central to the cultural and emotional life of the poor, began to tell impoverished workers, peasants, and farm-hands that education, medical care, and decent wages were not unrealistic fantasies but rights to which they were morally entitled. The spread of these ideas helped gen-erate demand for change (Berryman 1987; Reed and Foran 2002; Walker 1986).

The 1972 earthquake that devastated Managua, a city of more than 600,000, fur-ther increased mass discontent. The Somozas and their friends reportedly siphoned off huge amounts of relief aid through real estate speculation, mortgage financing, and steering reconstruction projects to Somoza-owned land. Elements of the Na-tional Guard were accused of stealing and selling donated reconstruction supplies.

Real wages of many urban workers declined, and unemployment grew to almost 30 percent by 1979. Discontent was intensified by the luxuriant lifestyles pursued by the upper class. But even some wealthy individuals began to feel that Somoza's greed could simply not be satisfied. Using his enormous economic and political resources, Somoza was steadily absorbing more of the economy. The desire for self-preservation turned an increasing number of businesspeople against the dic-tatorship (Walker 1986). Thus diverse population segments, which had differing economic interests, became temporarily united by the motivation to end Somoza family rule.

State of Siege: 1974–1977

On December 27, 1974, thirteen armed Sandinistas seized hostages at the home of a wealthy cotton exporter, including the mayor of Managua, foreign minister, ambas-sador to the United States, and others, including Somoza family members. The FSLN released the hostages in exchange for eighteen Sandinista prisoners (including Dan-iel Ortega), $5 million, publication of a message from the FSLN to the Nicaraguan people, and safe passage to Cuba. Somoza, however, declared martial law under a state of siege, which lasted until September 1977. During this period the FSLN lost many personnel and leaders, including Fonseca (Stahler-Sholk 2006; Zimmermann 2000). Somoza's National Guard tortured and killed hundreds of peasants suspected of supporting the FSLN, greatly increasing hatred for the regime.

In 1977, however, several factors prompted Somoza to lift the state of siege. Most important was the election of President Jimmy Carter, who tied continuing military assistance to improvements in Nicaragua's human rights situation. On July 28, 1977, while Somoza was recovering in Miami from a heart attack, Amnesty International released a report condemning the behavior of his armed forces. To counter the negative publicity and prevent an aid cutoff by the Carter administration, and also because he apparently thought that his military had crushed the Sandinista threat, Somoza ended the state of siege on September 19, 1977.

With the cessation of martial law, the FSLN was able to organize more freely and extend its support network around the country. Since the relaxation of repression was in part a response to President Carter's human rights ultimatum, Somoza's regime was significantly weakened by the widespread impression that his government no longer enjoyed the unconditional support of the United States. It now appeared that the US might not intervene to prevent Somoza's overthrow. Thus Carter's human rights policy simultaneously meant a significant increase in the level of international permissiveness toward a revolution in Nicaragua and a substantial weakening of the pre-revolutionary state.

The Revolution Intensifies

Pedro Joaquín Chamorro, the Conservative Party editor of the newspaper La Prensa, was a leader of upper-class Somoza critics and attacked the regime in several articles. Chamorro's final assault exposed the activities of several Somoza supporters who ran a blood plasma–exporting business in Managua. Blood was purchased from poor Nicaraguans to sell at considerable profit to hospitals in the US. Evidence suggested that the owners of the business hired assassins to murder Chamorro on January 10, 1978 (Booth 1985; Christian 1985). Although perhaps not directly responsible, Somoza was blamed, and anti-Somoza businesspeople declared a strike in protest.

On August 22, 1978, an FSLN unit seized the National Palace and took more than 1,500 hostages, including most of the government's officials. The raid was led by Edén Pastora, who blamed Somoza's National Guard for the death of his father in a land dispute. In exchange for the hostages, the Sandinistas got the release of more than fifty FSLN members, $500,000, publication of FSLN proclamations, and safe passage out of the country (Christian 1985; Diederich 1981).

After the National Palace episode, excited teenagers in several towns grabbed what weapons they could and began spontaneous insurrections. Somoza reimposed martial law in early September and ordered his National Guard to attack with planes, tanks, and artillery. Perhaps 5,000 people were killed in fall 1978, many shot after capture by Somoza's soldiers. But many fled to Sandinista camps to organize and train for a coordinated revolutionary offensive.

Until 1978 the FSLN received only limited foreign assistance. Cuba was initially reluctant to send arms, fearing that the US would view this as a reason to intervene to crush the FSLN while it was still weak. But once mass uprisings demonstrated the real possibility of ousting the Somoza regime, Venezuela, Panama, Costa Rica, and Cuba provided aid to the Sandinistas. In 1979 Cuba commenced large-scale arms shipments to the FSLN.

The number of full-time FSLN soldiers averaged about 150 from the mid-1960s through 1976. In 1977 the number rose, reaching 500 to 1,000 in early 1978 and climbing to 3,000 by early 1979. In the climactic combat of summer 1979, the FSLN had about 5,000 regular soldiers, one-quarter women (Booth 1985; Kampwirth 2002; Reif 1986; Shayne 2006). FSLN forces at the combat fronts were typically increased several times over by local volunteers.

Since Somoza refused any compromise deemed acceptable by even moderate opponents to his government, the Carter administration restricted the flow of US weapons to Somoza's military in February 1979. Much of Somoza's ammunition and weapons were later provided by Argentina, Guatemala, and Israel (Pastor 1987).

On May 29, 1979, the Sandinistas launched the final offensive. After weeks of combat, several major towns and cities were under FSLN control, and fighting had commenced in Managua. Somoza's air force repeatedly bombed FSLN-held neighborhoods, killing many and destroying thousands of homes and many factories and businesses. After the June 20 videotaped murder of ABC news reporter Bill Stewart by Somoza's National Guard (guardsmen felt that press coverage was aiding the Sandinistas) was seen by millions of Americans on news programs, the Carter administration essentially ordered Somoza to leave Nicaragua. The Organization of American States (OAS) on June 23 voted 17 to 2 (Paraguay voted with Somoza) to demand Somoza's resignation. At that point, with the US withdrawing support for Somoza and several nations assisting the Sandinistas, a maximally permissive international environment existed for the revolution.

After Somoza fled Nicaragua on July 17, the National Guard rapidly disintegrated. On July 19, 1979, Sandinistas took control of Managua. Several thousand National Guardsmen were captured, and hundreds fled to Honduras. In the following months, the behavior of each captured guardsman was investigated. Those for whom there was no evidence of personal involvement in torture or murder were let go. Hundreds thought guilty of war crimes were kept in prison, but most were released before the end of 1989. Nicaragua did not have the death penalty.

Post-Revolutionary Government, Changes, and Conflicts

While the Sandinista front controlled the revolutionary armed forces, it joined with other anti-Somoza groups to establish a revolutionary executive committee of five persons to run the country until elections were held. The governing committee included three top Sandinista leaders (who favored a partially collectively owned economy rather than one based exclusively on private ownership) and two non-FSLN opponents of the Somoza regime: multimillionaire businessman Alfonso Robelo Callejas, a leader of the Nicaraguan Democratic Movement (MDN), and Violeta Barrios de Chamorro, widow of the assassinated *La Prensa* editor.

The revolutionary leadership faced immense problems. The struggle to oust Somoza had cost 30,000–50,000 killed and many more injured or homeless. Many industries and businesses had been destroyed or badly damaged. Somoza left Nicaragua approximately $1.6 billion in debt (Booth 1985; Walker 1986). Moreover, the revolution faced the task of reducing the vast inequalities in resources, education, and health care.

The revolution did, however, possess certain strengths. As Thomas Walker notes, the dictator's National Guard had been destroyed and replaced by a new armed force that was "explicitly sandinist—that is, revolutionary and popularly oriented" (1986, 43). This meant that conservative and counterrevolutionary elements, whether internal or external, would not be able to use Nicaragua's military to block progressive change. But Sandinista domination of the post-revolution military, ostensibly to ensure socioeconomic transformation to benefit the poor, was criticized by many outside the FSLN on the grounds that one political party's control over the armed forces interfered with the realization of the fully democratic political system also promised by the revolution.

Another strength was that "the mass organizations created in the struggle to overthrow the dictator gave the FSLN a grass-roots base that dwarfed the organized support of all potential rivals" (Walker 1986, 43). The pro-revolutionary mass organizations provided hundreds of thousands with their first experiences of direct political organization and participation. By 1984 almost half of all Nicaraguans over fifteen were members of pro-Sandinista voluntary membership mass organizations (Cockcroft 1989; Walker 1986). The knowledge and experience gained through involvement in these groups inspired feelings of political competency and empowerment. No longer was political participation limited to Nicaragua's wealthy minority or men only. Women constituted a large proportion of both the mass organizations and the revolutionary armed forces.

Revolutionary leaders moved quickly to help impoverished Nicaraguans. Somoza family land, along with that of several Somoza associates who had fled, was confiscated; some large holdings became state farms, and more than 6 million acres were distributed to poor peasants and landless rural workers (Cockcroft 1989). Somoza banks and industries were nationalized. But more than half of all farms, businesses, and industries continued to be privately owned. The revolutionary government stated it would (1) maintain a mixed economy and encourage investment by the private sector; (2) institutionalize political pluralism (a multiparty political democracy) and solicit feedback from all classes; and (3) establish diplomatic and economic relations with "as many nations as possible, regardless of ideology" (Walker 1986, 44).

Educated people were asked to volunteer to combat illiteracy. Tens of thousands, primarily urban high school and college students, spent months living with farm families teaching family members to read and write (Arnove 1986). With the aid of hundreds of doctors, nurses, and health care workers from many countries, including Western and Eastern European nations, Cuba, the US, and Canada, scores of health clinics were established all over the country, and several hospitals were built, primarily with international funding (Booth 1985; Donahue 1986; Walker 1986). In 1982 the World Health Organization declared revolutionary Nicaragua a model for primary health care.

Opposition to the FSLN

Despite these achievements, internal and external opposition developed to the leading role of the FSLN. The opposition included much of the business elite and middle class. Before the revolution, economic class was a major social division. About 20 percent of economically active persons were in nonmanual careers. The norms of interclass relations had required lower-class persons to address middle- and upper-class individuals by family name or with terms of respect such as don or doña (Walker 1986).

The FSLN, in contrast, encouraged Nicaraguans to treat one another as social equals. Private country clubs were confiscated and converted to public recreational centers, importation of luxuries was reduced, domestically produced luxury items were taxed, and new taxes were assessed on income and property. These actions upset many of the well-to-do. Some economically advantaged Nicaraguans, though, agreed with these policies and supported the goal of social revolution, even to the point of granting the necessary parental permission for their children to take part in the national literacy crusade of 1980.

Some businesspeople, however, began to liquidate their assets in order to free up capital for investment outside Nicaragua. Much of the opposition to the FSLN came from the Superior Council of Private Enterprise (COSEP). The leadership of COSEP objected to the literacy crusade (evidently fearing pro-revolutionary indoctrination of peasants), the participation of hundreds of thousands in pro-revolutionary mass organizations, and the fact that the new army was led by FSLN members dedicated to social revolution and was serving as an instrument of political indoctrination of recruits (Booth 1985; Christian 1985; Walker 1986).

The Nicaraguan Catholic Church was divided between conservatives and liberation theology proponents (O'Shaughnessy and Serra 1986). Some priests supported the FSLN. In the revolutionary leadership priests served as foreign minister, cultural affairs minister, and head of the literacy crusade (Booth 1985; Christian 1985; Walker 1986). A number of clergy formed the popular church movement, which explicitly advocated progressive social change, proclaiming that "between Christianity and revolution there is no contradiction" (Christian 1985, 221). But the nine-member Council of Bishops led by Archbishop (later Cardinal) Miguel Obando y Bravo, often criticized the FSLN. The archbishop objected to priests and Sandinista activists combining Christian values and Marxist concepts and voiced fear of Russian and Cuban "ideological imperialism" (Booth 1985, 214). He also objected to the draft, fearing that draftees would be exposed to Sandinista indoctrination. Catholic bishops were outraged at what they perceived as disrespectful treatment of the pope when he visited Nicaragua in 1983. After the pope had criticized priests holding government positions and refused—possibly wanting to avoid taking sides—to bless Nicaraguan soldiers killed by counterrevolutionaries, though entreated to do so by the soldiers' mothers, pro-Sandinista crowds at the pope's Managua Mass began chanting "we want peace" (Booth 1985, 213).

A split developed in *La Prensa*, the Chamorro-family-owned newspaper, over Sandinista leadership (Christian 1985). Carlos Fernando Chamorro, youngest son of the martyred Pedro Joaquín Chamorro and Violeta Chamorro, had joined the Sandinistas during the revolutionary war and became editor of the Sandinista newspaper *Barricada*. The editor of *La Prensa* after the revolution was Xavier Chamorro Cardenal, brother of the assassinated former editor, Pedro. By spring 1980 the majority of the Chamorro clan became convinced that Xavier was too favorable to the FSLN. Xavier, in turn, accused several relatives of slanting news coverage to slander the FSLN, promoting discontent by printing false rumors, exaggerating problems, and giving disproportionate coverage to government critics. On April 20, 1980, the family decided to replace Xavier. Subsequently he and much of the *La Prensa* staff established a new newspaper, *El Nuevo Diario* (Christian 1985).

In April 1980 Alfonso Robelo and Violeta Chamorro resigned from the revolutionary governing committee. Both opposed changes in the makeup of the Council of State, which acted as a legislature until elections were held. At first it appeared that the assembly would have a majority of delegates representing non-FSLN business and union groups that existed during the Somoza dictatorship. But the Sandinistas on the revolutionary governing committee decided to include representatives from the newly created revolutionary neighborhood committees, called CDSs (Sandinista Defense Committees), and from new labor unions and other groups created or expanded after the revolutionary victory. The Sandinistas argued that the people would be fairly represented only with the addition of delegates from new organizations (Booth 1985; Walker 1986). The resulting Council of State had forty-seven delegates with twenty-four seats held by pro-Sandinista groups. The ruling executive committee after the departure of Robelo and Violeta Chamorro was reduced from five to three members, with two from the FSLN and one from the Democratic Conservative Party (PCD).

The opposition accused the FSLN of postponing elections to use the time for rallying youth to its side and thus ensure an FSLN victory once elections were held. But Sandinista leaders claimed that the literacy crusade, land redistribution, and health care and other basic reforms took priority over quick elections (Booth 1985; Walker 1986).

Atlantic Coast Opposition

Perhaps the biggest error made by the revolutionary government was its flawed initial policy regarding integrating the Atlantic coast region with the more populous Spanish side of the country. Foreign-owned companies had reaped the mineral and timber resources of the area since the nineteenth century. The indigenous groups (Miskito, Sumu, Rama, and others, who resided largely in the northern section) and the English-speaking, Protestant blacks (largely in the southern section) historically viewed Spanish-speaking Nicaraguans as alien exploiters (Booth 1985, 234). After the revolution, scores of young, Spanish-speaking, pro-FSLN Nicaraguans arrived to take over nationalized mines, lumber operations, and fisheries, as well as to open new schools and health clinics.

Sandinista militants expected to find enthusiastic support for the revolution among the impoverished inhabitants. Instead, they found unfamiliar peoples and cultures isolated from Hispanic Nicaragua for generations (Dishkin 1987). Atlantic coast residents relished the freedom to live according to their own customs, even if in poverty. Although some indigenous people were friendly to the Sandinistas, others viewed the new schools, clinics, and public works projects as part of a plan by the central government to destroy local cultures. Disputes broke out in the early 1980s, and in the violent skirmishes that followed more than 150 local people and dozens of Sandinistas were killed (Walker 1986). The government tried and punished soldiers for violating the human rights of Atlantic coast residents. In 1987 the government approved limited autonomy for the Atlantic coast and in effect granted amnesty to the indigenous guerrillas who had fought against the Sandinista-led army. By spring 1987 fighting between Atlantic coast people and government forces had largely ended (Cockcroft 1989; *New York Times*, April 14, 1987, A12).

US AND WORLD REACTIONS TO THE REVOLUTION

President Carter provided over $100 million to Nicaragua after Somoza's departure, mostly to assist private businesses. Carter's administration believed that providing aid would allow the United States to influence the Nicaraguan revolution nonviolently. According to Robert Pastor, a member of Carter's National Security Council, the Carter administration objectives were:

(1) internal: to assist the revolution to fulfill its stated promises of political pluralism, elections, and a vigorous private sector, and conversely, to reduce the chances
that the revolution would become Communist [result in a Leninist-style one-party
state]; (2) strategic: to deny the Sandinistas an enemy and thus a reason for relying
on Cuban and Soviet military assistance; and (3) regional: to make clear that a
good relationship with the United States was contingent on Nicaraguan noninterference in the internal affairs of its neighbors. (1987, 194)

But when convinced that some Sandinistas were transporting arms to leftist rebels in nearby El Salvador, Carter suspended aid.

The Reagan administration, which took office in January 1981, was much more hostile. President Reagan permanently canceled aid and pressured all US busi-nesses to stop buying Nicaraguan coffee, cotton, sugar, and other goods and to stop selling US products to Nicaragua, eventually outlawing all trade in May 1985 (Con-roy 1987). As a result, from 1980 to 1986 the percentage of Nicaraguan trade (im-ports and exports combined) with the US fell from 30.4 percent to zero and with other Central American nations from 28.1 to 7.4 percent. In contrast, Nicaragua's trade with Western European countries (almost all opposed to the hostile mea-sures of the Reagan administration and the later Bush administration) rose from 17.6 to 37.7 percent. Trade with Eastern Europe increased from 1.0 to 27.2 percent and with Japan from 3.0 to 9.0 percent (Kornbluh 1987).

The Contras

The Reagan administration attempted to attack the revolutionary government and impede Nicaragua's development under FSLN leadership by sponsoring, recruit-ing, and arming the contras (counterrevolutionaries), who operated primarily out of bases in Honduras supplied by the CIA (Walker 1986; White 1984). The initial counterrevolutionary units were organized by former officers of Somoza's National Guard after they fled Nicaragua and were funded by wealthy Nicaraguan exiles (PBS 1987). Following past strategies designed to overturn "undesirable" govern-ments in Guatemala and Cuba, the CIA, bolstered by Reagan, provided funds, weapons, and advisers to expand the contras dramatically.

The contras drew recruits and supporters from several groups. First, most of the top military leadership consisted of former Somoza National Guard members. When Somoza was overthrown, their status, privileges, and careers were destroyed. Their goals were generally to eliminate the Sandinista government and restore their position in Nicaragua (Booth 1985; PBS 1986). Second, many affluent business-people opposed the Sandinista government because they viewed it as undemocratic and also probably because it prevented them from dominating Nicaragua politi-cally and economically. Often with reputations among US officials as moderates or conservatives, they provided the contras with a civilian political wing and a public image of respectability (PBS 1987). In August 1981, these elements joined to form the largest contra organization, the Nicaraguan Democratic Force (FDN), which in the latter half of the 1980s had between 6,000 and 12,000 soldiers. The FDN was assisted at times by mercenaries from Honduras, Chile, and Argentina paid by the CIA (Kornbluh 1987).

One prominent Sandinista, Edén Pastora, deserted the revolutionary govern-ment and started his own contra group in 1982, the Democratic Revolutionary Alliance (ARDE), in Costa Rica. He felt the Sandinistas had failed to establish a pluralist democracy. Pastora's background (his family had been involved in the Conservative Party) and past political associations indicated that he was more con-servative than other Sandinistas (Christian 1985). He had successively joined and quit several anti-Somoza movements and joined the FSLN when he perceived it capable of defeating the Somoza regime. His motives for turning against the FSLN might have been as much personal as ideological. After the revolution he appeared upset because he believed he was not accepted as a true Sandinista (PBS 1985) and did not receive a desired government appointment.

Pastora refused to ally with the contra army in Honduras because it was un-der CIA influence. As most of the popular support he had enjoyed as a Sandinista hero quickly evaporated once he took up arms against the revolution, and as his resources were limited without CIA support, his movement became insignificant by 1985 (*New York Times*, September 4, 1985, A3). In 1986 Pastora turned himself in to Costa Rican authorities and retired from the contra war. He told CNN that he believed the FDN counterrevolutionaries tried to assassinate him because he would not unite with them (CNN, May 22, 1987). In 1989 Pastora, benefiting from Nicaragua's amnesty, returned to Nicaragua.

By the mid-1980s while 90 percent of the top fifty FDN officers had been in So-moza's army, 80 percent of contra field officers and many young contra soldiers had not (Vanderlaan 1986). Some were relatives of National Guard soldiers or of former Somoza supporters. Others were religiously conservative peasants of northeast-ern Nicaragua who, largely because of contra misinformation, feared a Sandinista attack on their religion. Many independent farmers turned against the Sandinis-tas because of Managua's restrictions on marketing produce or because of harsh FSLN anti-contra measures, such as the forcible relocation of some peasants away from their farms. Salaries for contra soldiers were an incentive for some farmers to join—the pay levels were often far above their usual incomes.

Opposition to Reagan Administration Policy on Nicaragua

The conduct of contra forces provoked condemnation from international human rights organizations, which stated in 1986 and in 1987 that although the Sandinistas committed human rights violations, their offenses were generally of a lesser magnitude and far less frequent than those of the contras (Americas Watch Committee 1985; *New York Times*, February 10, 1987, A10; PBS 1986). CBS broadcast that as many as 125 citizens of Honduras (the site of contra bases) who opposed the contras were assassinated by contra death squads after being identified by the CIA as subversives (CBS, March 29, 1987).

Some US officials not only knew about contra atrocities, including the murders of mayors, teachers, doctors and nurses, and captured Nicaraguan soldiers, but actually prepared and distributed to the contras approximately 2,000 copies of an instructional booklet entitled *Psychological Techniques of Guerrilla Warfare*. This manual, among other things, provided instructions on how to carry out public executions of captured military or civilian leaders (Cockcroft 1989; *Providence Journal*, October 20, 1984, 1).

The behavior of contras caused the disillusionment and resignation of several individuals recruited by the CIA to serve as the civilian political leadership for the contras. They included Edgar Chamorro, who had been FDN public relations director in 1981–1984. In a letter to the *New York Times* (January 9, 1986, A22), Chamorro stated that the contras had a policy of terrorizing civilian noncombatants to discourage support for the FSLN-dominated government. He also noted that the Sandinistas, despite serious shortcomings, had created a national atmosphere of social equality for the first time in the country's history and had made huge improvements in health care, education, and housing, much of which was destroyed by the contra war. He concluded that the Nicaraguan economy had been devastated primarily by the contra war and the US economic embargo. According to Chamorro, the goals of the contra leaders were to recover their wealth and restore their previous dominant social status.

Western European US allies almost unanimously refused to cooperate with the Reagan administration's embargo and instead provided assistance to Nicaragua and increased trade with it. International opposition to the contra war was reflected in the overwhelming ruling of the United Nations World Court in 1984 to condemn the January–February CIA mining of Nicaragua's harbors. In 1986 the World Court, again by a large majority, found the Reagan administration's support for the contras in violation of international law and ruled that the US must cease its assault on Nicaragua and pay reparations to Nicaragua for loss of life, property, and other costs of the contra war (Cockcroft 1989; Sklar 1988).

A majority of US citizens consistently opposed aid to the contras. A 1986 ABC/ *Washington Post* national survey found that 62 percent opposed US efforts to overthrow the Nicaraguan government, while 28 percent supported, and 10 percent had no opinion (Kornbluh 1987).

Contra atrocities and the mining of Nicaragua's harbors outraged many members of the US House of Representatives as well as the leaders of most major religious denominations. Congressman Berkley Bedell (D-IA) asserted, "If the American people could have talked with the common people of Nicaragua whose women and children are being indiscriminately tortured and killed by terrorists (contras) financed by the American taxpayer, they would rise up in legitimate anger and demand that support for this criminal activity be ended at once" (New York Times, April 14, 1983, 1). In October 1984 the House of Representatives refused to approve further military aid to the contras (Booth 1985; Gutman 1988).

But in June 1986 a few members of the House, under administration pressure and angered by reports of Sandinista army incursions into Honduras in pursuit of contras, shifted their position, resulting in a 221 to 209 vote victory for the Reagan administration's proposal to provide $70 million in military assistance (and $30 million in nonmilitary aid) to the contras (Sklar 1988). The contras had received tens of millions during the two years Congress blocked US government funds (Cockburn 1987; Sklar 1988). It was disclosed in 1986, 1987, and 1988 that Reagan administration personnel had sold weapons to Iran (involved then in its war with Iraq) at two to three times the cost, diverting some of the profits to the contras (New York Times, November 26, 1986, 1). The Reagan administration had also convinced other governments, such as Saudi Arabia and Brunei, to contribute millions to the contras (New York Times, April 25, 1987, 1). Finally, a Senate investigative committee found evidence of a $10 million contribution to the contras from Colombian drug traffickers and other revenues derived from the transportation of drugs into the US on planes returning from delivering weapons to contras (Cockburn 1987; PBS 1988; Sklar 1988). Public knowledge of these disclosures, a larger Democratic majority in Congress following elections, and increased congressional sentiment for nonviolent resolution of Central American conflicts led Congress to vote again in February 1988 to ban US military assistance to the contras (Cockcroft 1989).

Impacts of the Contra War and the Economic Embargo

The contra war took at least 30,000 lives and strained the Nicaraguan economy. Over half of the national budget was shifted to defense, thus impeding development and social programs. Contras and non-Nicaraguan mercenaries damaged industrial installations and repeatedly interfered with harvests. Out of an adult (sixteen or over) population of approximately 1.5 million, Nicaragua had to mobilize an army of more than 60,000 and local militia units numbering more than 200,000 (PBS 1987; Walker 1986). The huge proportion of Nicaraguans under arms was one of the strongest indicators of popular support for the Sandinista government. But this also caused a labor shortage only partially offset by international volunteer workers. The low-intensity warfare waged by the Reagan administration through the contras, the CIA, and the economic embargo appeared intended to motivate an overthrow of the Sandinista-led government by a population exhausted and desperate for peace at any price (*New York Times,* March 23, 1987, A10; October 16, 1988, A1; PBS 1987).

Nicaraguan Defensive Measures and International Assistance

In November 1984 elections were held. In a seven-party, secret ballot competition, the Sandinista Party won about 62 percent of the vote, both for the presidency and for seats in the legislature (awarded in proportion to the popular vote). The Democratic Conservative Party received 13 percent, Independent Liberals about 10 percent, People's Social Christians 5 percent, and three parties to the left of the Sandinistas (the Socialist, Communist, and Marxist-Leninist parties) 4 percent. About 6 percent of the ballots were filled out incorrectly and declared invalid. Approximately 80 percent of those eligible to vote (those at least sixteen years old) did so. The political parties were given weekly radio and TV time and were able to post signs and distribute campaign literature. International observers from several democracies, although noting that conditions were not perfect, provided favorable evaluations of election procedures, especially in comparison to elections in other nations in the region that the Reagan administration viewed as acceptably democratic (*Manchester Guardian,* November 5, 1984, 6; November 6, 1984, 7; Walker 1986). The election was held just before the 1984 US presidential vote in order to ensure that Nicaragua would have an elected government before the reelection of President Reagan. There was fear that once Reagan no longer had to worry about running for a second term, he would intervene militarily if Nicaragua did not have an internationally recognized, popularly elected government.

Another defensive action was press censorship. Restrictions were suspended during the election campaign period but reinstituted shortly afterward. *La Prensa* was shut down temporarily in 1986 (in order to prevent, according to the Nicaraguan government, publication of militarily useful information or rumors that might incite panic hoarding of essential goods). Labor strikes were banned during the contra war. As the war continued, Sandinista activists attempted to mobilize the mass organizations on behalf of government policies. The increasing FSLN- and government-directed character of mass organizations reduced their popularity, and participation declined in the late 1980s (Vickers 1990).

The Sandinista government justified limitations on civil liberties by noting that during World War I and World War II the US restricted freedom of the press and freedom of speech, and imposed a ban on strikes, all to be more effective in a fight against enemies thousands of miles away. And the Sandinistas were aware of how the CIA and its conservative Chilean allies had made use of democracy during Allende's presidency to overthrow not only the Allende government but also the entire democratic system in Chile (see Chapter 5). The Sandinistas asserted that the true cause of limitations on civil liberties was the war being waged on Nicaragua by the Reagan administration.

Outside assistance bolstered Nicaragua. Western and Eastern Europe increased trade and economic and technical assistance. Cuba sent military advisers. The Soviet Union provided aid, including weapons, estimated at about $400 million annually in the late 1980s (Cockcroft 1989).

1989 PEACE AGREEMENT AND 1990 ELECTION

In 1989 Nicaragua won the support of the Organization of American States and the United Nations for a peace plan (*New York Times*, February 16, 1989, A14; August 8, 1989, A1; October 2, 1989, A10). The agreement called for dismantling the contra camps in Honduras, amnesty and repatriation for all those who wished to return to Nicaragua, and national and municipal elections by the end of February 1990. Voter registration, campaigning, and the election itself were to be supervised by observers from the UN and the OAS.

In the February 25, 1990, election, fourteen political parties formed a coalition, the National Opposition Union (UNO), to run against the FSLN. UNO included (in alphabetical order) the Central American Integrationist Party, the Communist Party, the Conservative National Action Party, the Conservative Popular Alliance, the Democratic Party of National Confidence, the Independent Liberal Party, the Liberal Constitutionalist Party (PLC), the Liberal Party, the National Action Party, the National Conservative Party, the Nicaraguan Democratic Movement, the Nicaraguan Socialist Party, the Popular Social Christian Party, and the Social Democratic Party (*New York Times*, March 1, 1990, A20). UNO was also supported by Yatama, a Miskito Indian organization. UNO selected Violeta Barrios de Chamorro as its presidential candidate. She did not belong to any of the parties in UNO.

An estimated 93 percent of those eligible voted. UNO received 55 percent, while the FSLN received 41 percent and other parties 4 percent. This outcome resulted in the election of Violeta Chamorro over the FSLN presidential candidate Daniel Ortega (*New York Times*, February 27, 1990, A1; February 28, 1990, A1). Seats in the new parliament were awarded in approximate proportion to the votes received by each slate of candidates.

Voter surveys identified reasons for the FSLN defeat. The most important appeared to be concern about the economy, which had 1,700 percent inflation in 1989 (following over 33,000 percent in 1988) along with 30 percent unemployed or underemployed (*New York Times*, March 4, 1990, A1). Austerity measures imposed by the FSLN-dominated government in 1988, designed to rescue the economy, appeared to hurt low-income workers and peasants more than the middle or upper classes (Vilas 1990). Since many FSLN leaders were insulated from economic hardships by virtue of their government jobs and privileges, such as cars and housing, resentment among the poor grew. As a result, support for UNO came not only from affluent people but also from the most impoverished. The poor desperately hoped for economic salvation under a new government (O'Kane 1990). As many as 150,000 voters were estimated to have shifted from their 1984 vote for the FSLN to UNO and Violeta Chamorro in 1990.

The contra war had taken an estimated 30,000 lives by 1990 and destroyed much of the early post-revolutionary educational and medical gains in the countryside. The military draft imposed to fight the contras became unpopular. Some voters felt that Sandinista policies and hostility toward the US government were responsible for economic problems and the war. Others opposed the Sandinistas because of their periodic repressive measures.

Many voters blamed the US embargo and contra war for Nicaragua's problems but concluded that the only way to save Nicaragua would be to replace the FSLN with a government more acceptable to the US and likely to receive immediate US economic aid. Finally, many voters admired Violeta Chamorro, whose husband had been martyred in the struggle against the Somoza dictatorship and whose own family, like others in Nicaragua, had divided over support or opposition to Sandinistas (one son and one daughter on each side).

President Ortega and other Sandinista leaders peacefully surrendered governmental power and control of the military to President Chamorro and the new parliament on April 25, 1990 (*New York Times*, April 26, 1990, A1). To the surprise of many, President Chamorro reappointed Humberto Ortega, brother of the former president, as head of the armed forces (*New York Times*, January 10, 1991, A6). Following the election, President Bush ended the US trade embargo against Nicaragua and announced plans to send $300 million in assistance to help restore Nicaragua's devastated economy (*New York Times*, March 14, 1990, A15). In accordance with the peace agreement, most contras turned in their weapons to UN peacekeeping troops (*New York Times*, June 11, 1990, A3).

The FSLN remained the country's best organized, most popular individual political party. Daniel Ortega, an FSLN member of parliament after the 1990 elections, and other Sandinista leaders vowed to defend the revolution's achievements in parliament and through the threat of labor strikes and demonstrations (*New York Times*, May 30, 1990, A1). President Chamorro pursued neoliberal economic policies that included downsizing government agencies and expenditures (including the country's armed forces), creating conditions favorable to business enterprises, attempting to privatize some government-owned enterprises, and seeking to compensate former owners of many properties confiscated by the previous Sandinista administration (*New York Times*, December 8, 1994, A17).

NICARAGUA AFTER THE VIOLETA CHAMORRO PRESIDENCY

Following Violeta Chamorro, conservative populist Arnoldo Alemán of the Liberal Constitutionalist Party (PLC) became president in 1997, after defeating FSLN candidate Daniel Ortega. This administration was accused of corruption, resulting in Alemán's arrest, conviction, and imprisonment. During the Alemán administration an agreement, opposed by many Nicaraguans, was made between the Liberal Constitutionalist Party and the FSLN, called "El Pacto" (Bendaña 2002, 14). The purpose of the pact seemed to be an attempt to ensure that future presidents would be candidates of either the PLC or the Sandinista Party. Since Nicaragua had a number of political parties, it was possible that in the first round of presidential elections, no candidate would get enough votes to win without having a second runoff election between the top two vote getters in the first round. But in order to have a chance to win, the remaining two candidates would be forced to make agreements with and likely promise positions or other benefits to members of the smaller parties to gather enough votes for victory in the second round. El Pacto greatly reduced the possibility that a runoff election for the presidency would be needed. Under El Pacto the election law was changed to allow the top vote getter in the first round to win with only 40 percent of the popular vote. Furthermore, it even permitted a top vote getter with as low as 35 percent of the popular vote to win the presidency, so long as that candidate's vote total was at least 5 percent of the total vote higher than the percentage for the next highest candidate. Many people viewed El Pacto as a partial betrayal of democratic principles by Alemán of the PLC and Ortega of the FSLN.

Polls indicated that FSLN candidate Daniel Ortega might win the presidential election in November 2001, despite the accusation by his stepdaughter that he sexually abused her as a child. But the September 11, 2001, terrorist attacks in the United States ensured that the FSLN would be defeated. President George W. Bush's post–9/11 speech stating that the US would deal harshly with any country that aided or harbored terrorists, terrified many Nicaraguans and played into the hands of PLC candidate, Enrique Bolaños, a former contra. Bolaños's presidential campaign proclaimed that an FSLN victory could provoke the Bush administration into punishing Nicaragua economically and perhaps even more harshly. The threat of new economic hardships and possible US military intervention likely helped to ensure the Bolaños victory.

President Bolaños allowed his party's outgoing president, Alemán, to be charged in 2002 with embezzlement while in office and money laundering. In 2003 Alemán was sentenced to twenty years' confinement. In January 2004 the World Bank wrote off 80 percent of the debt owed by Nicaragua, and in July Russia similarly forgave billions of dollars in loans (BBC News, April 21, 2006). In 2005 many PLC members of congress, angered at Bolaños over the imprisonment of Alemán, collaborated in an alliance with the Sandinista representatives against the president and attempted to limit his power. The congress in 2005 also approved the Central American Free Trade Agreement (CAFTA) with the US.

The World Bank (2004, 1) estimated that 45.8 percent of Nicaraguans lived in poverty. Apparently attempting to improve FSLN electoral prospects and help low-income Nicaraguans, leftist Venezuelan President Hugo Chávez's government agreed to supply oil to Nicaragua's municipalities on favorable payment terms (Rogers 2006).

Although the revolution failed to achieve the socioeconomic transformation goals of Carlos Fonseca and the other FSLN founders, it dramatically increased political participation and built a far more democratic political system. According to Richard Stahler-Sholk (2006, 618), "the Sandinista revolution began democratizing Nicaragua, ending an era when the US controlled client states by designating autocratic leaders who lacked popular support. The Nicaraguan revolution also helped shift the focus of revolution itself, from the seizure of state power to the longer-term process of social transformation. That shift continued with the rise of diverse social movements, confronting not so much the state as transnational capital in the era of globalization."

Daniel Ortega and the FSLN Regain the Presidency

In November 2006 Daniel Ortega again ran for the presidency. More than a year before the vote, Ortega and his companion of some twenty-seven years, Rosario Murillo, with whom he had six of his eight children, were married in the Catholic Church by Nicaraguan Cardinal Obando y Bravo, who had previously been a critic of the Sandinistas. Another politically charged event, supported by the leaders of both the Catholic and the Evangelical churches, was the October 2006 vote of the Nicaraguan legislature to end therapeutic abortion (Kampwirth 2008, 123). Although the Sandinista Party had formerly supported the right to abortion to protect a woman's health, all FSLN legislators voted for the ban. Many observers believe that Ortega's embrace of the Catholic religion, his Catholic marriage, and the FSLN's National Assembly vote against abortion, which was supported by a large antifeminist women's movement, were calculated actions intended to help Ortega win the presidential election. Furthermore, Ortega campaigned on the themes of

238

peace and reconciliation with former enemies. In fact, Ortega's vice presidential running mate, Jaime Morales Corazo, was a former contra leader (Kampwirth 2008, 124). Ortega said he "would maintain a market economy and peace while providing universal health care and ending unemployment" (McConnell 2007, 84).

In the November 5, 2006, election, Ortega received 38.1 percent (CIA 2010), about 9 percent more than his nearest rival, avoiding the need for a runoff. The next year Nicaragua joined ALBA, the trade alliance created by Venezuela and Cuba, and continued to receive low-cost Venezuelan oil. The Ortega administration launched new programs to expand the number of children in school and provide assistance to poor families. The government reinstituted free health care to great popular approval (Hoyt 2009; Siegel 2010). Ortega won the presidency again in 2011, receiving 62.5 percent of the vote (CIA 2014). And his Sandinista Party took sixty-three of the ninety seats in the national legislature. In 2013 the legislature voted to alter the constitution to remove term limits for the presidency. This would allow Ortega to run again in 2016 (Associated Press 2013). The constitutional changes would also give the president more authority and permit active military officers to hold civilian government positions. In addition, the legislation states that the winner of future presidential elections would be the candidate that gets the most votes, eliminating the previous requirement that winner get at least 35 percent. For the constitutional changes to actually go into effect, the legislature has to vote approval again in 2014.

Controversy over Ortega and the FSLN

Some among Nicaragua's economic elite believe Ortega plans to shift the economy in a socialist direction. They fear his friendships with Venezuelan socialists and Cuban leaders and his criticisms of "savage capitalism." But some former members of his party claim that Ortega's FSLN changed from an internally democratic to an authoritarian organization. They argue that the FSLN under Ortega abandoned socialism and became an instrument Ortega and his friends could use to expand their power and privileges. Many feminists believe that Ortega's support for banning therapeutic abortion cost the lives of dozens of women between 2006 and 2010. Ortega's supporters, however, argue that Ortega had to sacrifice some elements of social liberalism in order to win the presidency and have an opportunity to improve the well-being of the country's poor.

Economic Development

In 2012, gross domestic product growth was estimated at 5.2 percent (CIA 2014). The percentage of Nicaraguans living in poverty declined to 42.5 percent by 2009, and family income inequality appeared to drop significantly between 1998 and

2010. Economic development could benefit significantly from an interocean canal through Nicaragua linking the Atlantic and Pacific. The planned canal, approved by the Nicaraguan government, would be able to handle ships with much larger container capacity than the Panama Canal (Cave 2013; Randle 2013).

SUMMARY AND ANALYSIS

The major unifying motivation for the Nicaraguan revolution—the widespread desire to end Somoza family rule—joined diverse groups in the FSLN-led movement. Later, conflicting class interests and differing conceptions of a post-Somoza society fractured the revolutionary alliance.

The FSLN was formed by young, educated Nicaraguans who intended to oust the dictator and also accomplish a social revolution. Others in Nicaragua's elite had periodically mobilized against the dictatorship. The assassination of an outspoken critic of the Somozas, wealthy newspaper editor Pedro Chamorro, convinced more upper-class Nicaraguans that the family dictatorship must end. In 1978 and 1979 many business and church leaders helped weaken the Somoza government by withdrawing their support.

Popular discontent developed in response to vast inequality, as well as the avarice, corruption, and repression of the Somozas. Discontent was widened and intensified by liberation theology, the misuse of earthquake relief aid, human rights abuses, and the assassination of Pedro Chamorro.

For decades US administrations had supported Somoza control of Nicaragua and provided weapons and training to the dictatorship's armed forces. But President Carter's emphasis on human rights and his policy of making military aid contingent on improvements in the recipient nation's treatment of its citizens caused Anastasio Somoza Debayle to end a state of siege. This relaxation of repression allowed opposition forces greater freedom of movement. Later, as evidence of the regime's brutality increased, the Carter administration pressured Somoza to leave, thereby precipitating the final collapse of the National Guard and the remaining pre-revolutionary state structure. The Reagan administration later attempted to change the outcome of the revolution.

Somoza's regime disintegrated in stages. The withdrawal of unconditional US support in 1977 was a central factor, as Nicaraguans no longer viewed the strength of the dictatorship as identical to US economic and military power. Acts of repression by the regime further alienated Nicaraguans of all classes. Eventually, support for Somoza's government narrowed to some rightist Nicaraguans and the Nicaraguan National Guard, whose officers correctly anticipated its extinction in the advent of an FSLN victory. Loss of US support in summer 1979, coupled with the dictator's flight to Miami, caused the final destruction of the Somoza system.

The Republican administrations' strategy of low-intensity warfare appeared to involve inflicting hardship on the Nicaraguan people and provoking post-revolution authorities into enacting unpopular measures, such as the military draft and restrictions on civil liberties, in order to foster mass discontent with the revolutionary government. The military and economic pressures brought against Nicaragua had catastrophic effects on health care, education, social welfare, and general living standards, which contributed to the 1990 election defeat of the FSLN.

Following the inauguration of Violeta Chamorro as president in 1990, economic development remained difficult. The September 11, 2001, terrorist attacks in the US contributed to the electoral defeat of the FSLN that year, when Nicaraguan voters were warned that electing the FSLN might make Nicaragua a target in the US war on terrorism.

Finally, after moderating FSLN ideology and adopting more conservative views on some social issues, Daniel Ortega won the presidency in November 2006. His new administration enacted policies, such as free health care and more aid for low-income people, that significantly improved the lives of many. The FSLN hoped that the success of these policies would result in greater electoral support in coming elections, providing a more secure basis for future change. In 2011, Ortega and the FSLN won the presidency and control of the national legislature, receiving more than 62 percent of the popular vote. The Nicaraguan government in 2013 moved to fulfill the national dream of building an interocean canal that would significantly spur economic development.

NICARAGUAN REVOLUTION: CHRONOLOGY OF MAJOR EVENTS

1909 US helps oust President Zelaya

1912–1925 US troops stationed in Nicaragua

1926–1933 US troops return to Nicaragua during civil war to train and support the Nicaraguan National Guard in the conflict against forces led by nationalist rebel leader Sandino

1934 Sandino is murdered

1936 Somoza uses National Guard to seize Nicaraguan government

1956 Anastasio Somoza García assassinated

1961 Sandinista Front for National Liberation founded

1977 Carter makes US aid conditional on improved human rights situation; Anastasio Somoza Debayle ends state of siege

1978 Pedro Joaquín Chamorro murdered; Sandinista unit seizes National Palace; insurrections and strikes against Somoza regime

1979 Civil war intensifies; Somoza flees July 17; Sandinistas control
Managua and declare victory July 19
1980 Divisions occur in revolutionary coalition
1981 Reagan provides US support for counterrevolutionaries
1981–1989 Contra war
1990 Following peace agreements, internationally supervised vote results
in election of Violeta Chamorro as president of Nicaragua
1990–2005 FSLN repeatedly defeated in presidential elections while continuing
to hold about 40 percent of the seats in the Nicaraguan legislature
2006 Daniel Ortega of the FSLN elected president
2007 Nicaragua joins ALBA
2008 FSLN wins elections in a large majority of municipalities
2009 Nicaraguan constitutional court removes ban on president running
for reelection
2011 Daniel Ortega and the FSLN win the presidency and control
of the legislature; receive more than 62 percent of the popular
vote
2013 Interocean canal through Nicaragua, approved by the Nicaraguan
government, in the planning stage
Constitutional changes in process to remove term limits on the
presidency

REFERENCES AND FURTHER READINGS

Americas Watch Committee. 1985. *An Americas Watch Report: Violations of the Laws of War by Both Sides in Nicaragua, 1981–85.* New York: Americas Watch.

Arnove, Robert F. 1986. *Education and Revolution in Nicaragua.* New York: Praeger.

Associated Press. 2013. "Nicaragua Leader Moves Closer to Indefinite Power." *Washington Post*, December 10. www.washingtonpost.com/world/the_americas/nicaragua-leader-moves-closer-to-indefinite-power/2013/12/10/d592e564-6215-11e3-a7b4-4a75ebc432ab_print.html.

BBC News. April 21, 2006. "Country Profiles, Timeline: Nicaragua." news.bbc.co.uk/2/hi/americas/country_profiles/1225283.stm.

Bendaña, Alejandro. 2002. "Washington and the Caudillos: Calculation and Miscalculation in Managua." *NACLA: Report on the Americas*, January/February, 12–16.

Berryman, Phillip. 1987. *Liberation Theology: Essential Facts about the Revolutionary Movement in Latin America—and Beyond.* Philadelphia: Temple University Press.

Booth, John A. 1985. *The End and the Beginning: The Nicaraguan Revolution.* Special Studies on Latin America and the Caribbean. 2nd ed. Boulder: Westview.

Cave, Damien. 2013. "Nicaragua Approves Building Its Own Canal." *New York Times*, July 13. www.nytimes.com/2013/06/14/world/americas/nicaragua-approves-building-its -own-canal.html?_r=0.

CBS. March 29, 1987. "Contra Country." *60 Minutes.*

Central Intelligence Agency (CIA). 2010, 2014. "Nicaragua." In *World Factbook*. https:// www.cia.gov/library/publications/the-world-factbook/geos/nu.html.

Christian, Shirley. 1985. *Nicaragua: Revolution in the Family*. New York: Random House.

CNN. May 22, 1987. Interview with Edén Pastora.

Cockburn, Leslie. 1987. *Out of Control: The Story of the Reagan Administration's Secret War in Nicaragua, the Illegal Arms Pipeline, and the Contra Drug Connection*. New York: Atlantic Monthly Press.

Cockcroft, James D. 1989. *Neighbors in Turmoil: Latin America*. New York: Harper & Row.

Conroy, Michael E. 1987. "Economic Aggression as an Instrument of Low-Intensity Warfare." In Walker, ed., *Reagan Versus the Sandinistas.*

DeFronzo, James, ed. 2006. *Revolutionary Movements in World History: From 1750 to the Present*. 3 vols. Santa Barbara, CA: ABC-CLIO.

Diederich, Bernard. 1981. *Somoza and the Legacy of US Involvement in Central America*. New York: Dutton.

Dishkin, Martin. 1987. "The Manipulation of Indigenous Struggles." In Walker, ed., *Reagan Versus the Sandinistas.*

Donahue, John M. 1986. *The Nicaraguan Revolution in Health: From Somoza to the Sandinistas*. South Hadley, MA: Bergin & Garvey.

Eckstein, Susan. 1986. "The Impact of the Cuban Revolution: A Comparative Perspective." *Comparative Studies in Society and History* 28 (July): 502–534.

Hartford Courant. May 19, 1985. "US Churches Called Formidable Foe in Fighting Aid to Nicaraguan Contras," A12.

Hoyt, Katherine. 2009. "Report from a Fact-Finding Trip to Nicaragua: Anti-Poverty Programs Make a Difference." *NACLA*, December 12. https://nacla.org/node/6313.

Kampwirth, Karen. 2002. *Women and Guerrilla Movements: Nicaragua, El Salvador, Chiapas, Cuba*. University Park: Pennsylvania State University Press.

———. 2008. "Abortion, Anti-Feminism, and the Return of Daniel Ortega: In Nicaragua, Leftist Politics?" *Latin American Perspectives* 35 (6): 122–136.

Kaufman, Chuck. 2010. "Ortega's Anti-Poverty Campaign Is Real." *NACLA*, February 18. https://nacla.org/node/6421.

Kornbluh, Peter. 1987. *Nicaragua: The Price of Intervention*. Washington, DC: Institute of Policy Studies.

Macaulay, Neill. 1967. *The Sandino Affair*. Chicago: Quadrangle.

Manchester Guardian. November 5, 1984. "Nicaraguans Pack Polling Stations," 6.

———. November 6, 1984. "Huge Vote of Confidence for Sandinistas, But Conservatives' Showing a Surprise," 7.

McConnell, Shelly. 1993. "Rules of the Game: Nicaragua's Contentious Constitutional Debate." *NACLA Report on the Americas* 27 (September/October): 20–25.

———. 2007. "Nicaragua's Turning Point." *Current History* 106 (February): 83–88.

Millett, Richard. 1977. *Guardians of the Dynasty*. Maryknoll, NY: Orbis.

———. 1994. "Central America's Enduring Conflicts." *Current History* 93 (March): 124–128.

———. 1995. "An End to Militarism? Democracy and the Armed Forces in Central America." *Current History* 94 (February): 71–75.

New York Times. April 14, 1983. "Key House Member Fears US Breaks Law in Nicaragua," 1.

———. June 18, 1985. "Reagan's Untruths About Nicaragua," A27.

———. September 4, 1985. "Pastora Beleaguered," A3.

———. January 9, 1986. Letter to the Editor, by Edgar Chamorro, A22.

———. November 26, 1986. "Iran Payment Funds Diverted to Contras," 1.

———. February 10, 1987. "US Group Finds No Improvements in Contras' Human Rights Records," A10.

———. March 23, 1987. "Casualties in Nicaragua: Schools and Health Care," A10.

———. April 14, 1987. "Sandinistas Test Autonomy in East Province," A12.

———. April 25, 1987. "Contra Suppliers Reportedly Got US Military Help," 1.

———. October 16, 1988. "Nicaragua's Economic Crisis Seen as Worsening," A1.

———. February 16, 1989. "Text of Accord by Central American Presidents," A14.

———. August 8, 1989. "5 Latin Presidents Defy US and Urge Contras' Eviction," A1.

———. October 2, 1989. "In Nicaragua, the Election Observers Are Coming!" A10.

———. February 27, 1990. "Nicaraguan Opposition Routs Sandinistas: US Pledges Aid, Tied to Orderly Turnover," A1.

———. February 28, 1990. "Chamorro and Sandinista Rulers Begin Delicate Transition Talks," A1.

———. March 1, 1990. "The Parties That Beat the Sandinistas," A20.

———. March 4, 1990. "Message for Nicaraguan Victors: Things Must Get Better, and Fast," A1.

———. March 14, 1990. "Nicaraguans on Both Sides Praise Embargo's End," A15.

———. April 26, 1990. "Chamorro Takes Helm; Hails a New Era," A1.

———. May 30, 1990. "Ruling Nicaragua: Almost a Daily Battle with Foes," A1.

———. June 11, 1990. "Contras Continue to Surrender Arms," A3.

———. January 10, 1991. "Managua Defends Army Chief in Missile Uproar," A6.

———. December 8, 1994. "Confiscations by Leftists Still Embroil Nicaraguans," A17.

———. July 26, 1995. "Critics Question Nicaraguan Army's Makeover," 10.

O'Kane, Trish. 1990. "The New Old Order." *NACLA Report on the Americas* 24 (June): 28–36.

O'Shaughnessy, Laura Nuzzi, and Louis Serra. 1986. *The Church and Revolution in Nicaragua*. Monographs in International Studies, Latin America series, 11. Athens: Latin American Studies Program, Ohio University.

Pastor, Robert A. 1987. *Condemned to Repetition: The United States and Nicaragua.* Princeton, NJ: Princeton University Press.

PBS. 1985. "Crisis in Central America: Revolution in Nicaragua." *Frontline.*

———. 1986. "Who Runs the Contras." *Frontline.*

———. 1987. "War on Nicaragua." *Frontline.*

———. 1988. "Guns, Drugs, and the CIA." *Frontline.*

Providence Journal. October 20, 1984. "Top Aide in CIA Defended Killings in Nicaragua," 1.

Randle, Jim. 2013. "New Nicaragua Canal May Change Global Trade." Voice of America News, August 28. www.voanews.com/content/new-nicaragua-canal-may-change-global-trade/1739153.html.

Reed, Jean-Pierre, and John Foran. 2002. "Political Cultures of Opposition: Exploring Idioms, Ideologies, and Revolutionary Agency in the Case of Nicaragua." *Critical Sociology* 28 (3): 335–370.

Reif, Linda L. 1986. "Women in Latin American Guerrilla Movements: A Comparative Perspective." *Comparative Politics,* January, 147–169.

Rogers, Tim. 2001. "Silent War in Nicaragua: The New Politics of Violence." *NACLA Report on the Americas* 34 (January/February): 11–15.

———. 2006. "Chavez Plays Oil Card in Nicaragua." *Christian Science Monitor,* May 5.

Shayne, Julie. 2006. "Women and Revolution." In DeFronzo, ed., *Revolutionary Movements in World History,* 3:936–940.

Siegel, Robert. 2010. "In Defense of Daniel Ortega." *NACLA,* May 7. https://nacla.org/node/6421.

Sklar, Holly. 1988. *Washington's War on Nicaragua.* Boston: South End.

Stahler-Sholk, Richard. 2006. "Nicaraguan Revolution." In DeFronzo, ed., *Revolutionary Movements in World History,* 2:609–622.

Vanderlaan, Mary B. 1986. *Revolution and Foreign Policy in Nicaragua.* Westview Special Studies on Latin America and the Caribbean. Boulder: Westview.

Vickers, George R. 1990. "A Spider's Web." *NACLA Report on the Americas* 24 (June): 19–27.

Vilas, Carlos M. 1990. "What Went Wrong." *NACLA Report on the Americas* 24 (June): 28–36.

Walker, Thomas W. 1986. *Nicaragua: The Land of Sandino.* 2nd ed. Boulder: Westview.

———, ed. 1987. *Reagan Versus the Sandinistas: The Undeclared War on Nicaragua.* Boulder: Westview.

World Bank. 2004. *Nicaragua Poverty Assessment.*

Zimmermann, Matilde. 2000. *Sandinista: Carlos Fonseca and the Nicaraguan Revolution.* Durham, NC: Duke University Press.

Selected DVD, Film, and Videocassette Documentaries

See "Purchase and Rental Sources" at the end of this volume for information on how to obtain the following resources and for full names of media companies and other organizations listed here as abbreviations.

American/Sandinista. 2008. 30 min. Story of a group of US engineers working in Nicaraguan communities (English and Spanish with English subtitles). Cine Las Americas.

Dreaming Nicaragua. 2010. 60 min. IMDb.

Forgotten Wars. 50 min. AETV, HC. US military intervention in Nicaragua in the 1920s and 1930s and other US military interventions, including during the Russian civil war.

Guns, Drugs, and the CIA. 1988. 60 min. PBS Frontline. Possible connections between CIA activities and drug operations in Central America and Southeast Asia.

Revolution in Nicaragua. 1985. 60 min. Video. PBS, AFSC. Documentary of the revolution, produced by PBS.

The Secret Government: The Constitution in Crisis. 1987. 90 min. SUN. Investigation into secret government activities, including the Iran-contra operation.

War on Nicaragua. 1987. 55 min. Video. AFSC. PBS traces the development of the contra war.

7

The Iranian Revolution and Islamic Fundamentalism

———

As the Sandinistas battled to defeat the Somoza regime in Nicaragua, another revolutionary coalition mobilized to overthrow the shah of Iran. In the mid-1970s Iran's economy seemed to prosper from the high price that Europe, Japan, and the US paid for Iranian oil. But the oil-derived wealth disproportionately benefited a minority of Iran's people and contributed to increased inequality and disruptions of traditional social and economic patterns. Much of the expanded national income was channeled into grandiose military and economic development projects conceived by Muhammad Shah Pahlavi and his advisers. The repressive aspects of the shah's regime, its ties to foreign interests, and certain of its economic and cultural policies fostered a pervasive hatred of the monarch.

Animosity toward the shah and the intensification of Iranian nationalism, aroused by the perception of the shah's regime as an instrument of foreign imperialism and moral corruption, united otherwise incompatible groups into a powerful revolutionary alliance. In the course of one year, 1978, the monarchy was swept away. Among the contending revolutionary forces, religious leaders possessed a greater cultural affinity with Iran's masses and better access to extensive social networks for mobilizing large numbers of people than any other component of the anti-shah coalition. The result was a startling innovation in the history of world governments—the creation of the Islamic Republic.

GEOGRAPHY AND POPULATION

Iran is a Middle Eastern nation located south of the Caspian Sea and north of the Persian Gulf and the Gulf of Oman. It is bordered by Iraq, Turkey, Armenia, Azerbaijan, Turkmenistan, Afghanistan, and Pakistan. At 636,293 square miles (1,648,000 square kilometers), it is more than twice the size of Texas. Much of the country is a plateau averaging 4,000 feet (1,219 meters). A large desert stretches 800 miles (1,217 kilometers), but there are also many oases and forests. In 2013 Iran's population was approximately 81,000,000 (CIA 2014). The capital, Tehran, had an estimated 7.2 million residents in 2013. About 61 percent of Iran's people are Persian, in addition to Azeri (16 percent), Kurd (10 percent), Lur (6 percent), Arab (2 percent), Baloch (2 percent), Turkmen (2 percent), and others (1 percent).

NATIONAL CULTURE

Until 1934 Iran was known as Persia, the Greek word for Pars, a part of ancient Iran. In the sixth century BCE, Cyrus the Great established the Persian Empire, which reached its greatest extent around 525 BCE, spanning territory from the Indus to the Nile. Most of Iran's population converted from the Zoroastrian religion to Islam after the Arab conquest in 637 CE.

Islam, an Arabic word, means the state of submission to the one and only God (Allah), and *Muslim* refers to a person who has submitted to the will of Allah. Muslims share a faith in the teachings of the Prophet Muhammad, who was born in 571 CE in Mecca. When he was about forty years old, he began preaching to the local people that he had been given messages from God through the Archangel Gabriel. Muhammad's verbal expositions of God's revelations were recorded by the Prophet's followers in 114 chapters (of greatly varying length), which together constituted the Qur'an (Koran). By the time Muhammad died in 632, Islam was prevalent in much of contemporary Saudi Arabia.

Leaders of the Islamic community elected a successor to the Prophet, known as the caliph. The first caliph died after only two years, and the next two were assassinated. The fourth elected caliph was Ali, a cousin of the Prophet and husband of the Prophet's daughter Fatima. Ali, revered by many as a champion of the poor and exploited, was opposed by several powerful Muslims and was assassinated in 661. A belief developed among some Muslims, however, that Ali had originally been chosen as successor by Muhammad. According to this line of reasoning, only descendants of Ali and Fatima were to rule the community of Islam. Those who accepted this concept came to be known as Shiat Ali (Partisans of Ali), or Shia. The Shia Muslims referred to Ali and certain male descendants of Ali and Fatima, whom they recognized as having the right to rule on behalf of Allah, as "imams."

The imams were thought by the Shia to be infallible. Other Muslims rejected this notion and instead held the view that the faithful were to consider infallible only the Qur'an, the word of Allah and the most central element of the Sunna (tradition) of Islam. According to the Sunnis, no person after Muhammad was infallible. Religious leaders could only attempt to interpret the Qur'an to the faithful in the particular context of each historical era. In the twenty-first century the large majority within Islam were Sunni, and about one-sixth were Shia.

The Shia attached special significance to the martyrdom of Imam Hussein in 680. Hussein was the grandson of the Prophet and, according to the Shia, the third imam (the first being Hussein's father, Ali, and the second, Hussein's brother Hassan). Following the death of Ali, the caliphate was assumed by Muawiya Abi Sufian, governor of Syria and antagonist of Ali. During the course of his nineteen-year reign, Muawiya attempted to alter the basis for ascendancy to the caliphate from election by the Islamic community to that of heredity (the dynastic principle). However, Muawiya's plan was for the line of descent to follow from him rather than from the Prophet. Muawiya designated his son Yazid as the successor to the caliphate. Yazid demanded that Ali's son Hussein pledge his allegiance to him. When Hussein refused, Yazid's army surrounded and killed him and many of his seventy-two companions in the Karbala desert in Iraq. In subsequent years Hussein's death while resisting Yazid's tyranny came to symbolize the major example of jihad (a struggle conducted on behalf of the Islamic community) and martyrdom for the Shia (Hussain 1985). The concept of martyrdom thus became especially powerful among the Shia.

Despite the issue of what constituted the right to govern the Islamic community after the death of the Prophet, the Sunnis and the Shia otherwise had similar beliefs based on the Qur'an and the Sharia, Islamic law derived from the Qur'an. However, several divisions developed among the Shia concerning how many imams had actually followed Muhammad. The Twelver Shias hold that the last imam, the infant son of the eleventh Imam, vanished in 873. With his disappearance there was no longer an infallible interpreter of the Qur'an and Islamic law. This situation will only change when the twelfth imam—the hidden imam, or Mahdi—returns to the faithful. Twelver Shia adherents believe that in the absence of the infallible imams Islamic scholars (*mujtahid*) qualified to issue authoritative, though fallible, opinions in all matters relating to Islam were to govern the Islamic community (Hussain 1985).

Prior to the sixteenth century the people of Iran were mostly Sunni. The spread of Twelver Shiism was occasioned by the Safavid conquest of Iran at the beginning of that century. The Safavids decided to foster a distinct religious culture in order to maintain the population's loyalty in the conflict against the powerful Sunni Ottoman Empire expanding from Turkey. Consequently, the Safavid rulers adopted Twelver Shiism as Iran's state religion. They imported Shia religious experts on Islamic law (ulama) from southern Iraq, as well as from Syria and Lebanon, and provided them with wealth and status. In return the ulama accepted the Safavid dynasty and provided the new rulers with a Shia clerical infrastructure. By 1700 most Iranians were Shia. In 2013, 90–95 percent of Iran's population was Shia, 5–10 percent Sunni, and 1 percent other religions, such as Christian, Baha'i, Jewish, and Zoroastrian (CIA 2014).

THE QAJAR DYNASTY AND FOREIGN INFLUENCE

In 1779 Aga Muhammad Khan Qajar, leader of the Qajars (a Shia tribe), conquered most of Iran. In return for the support of Shia religious leaders, the Qajars confirmed the ulama's right (originally established during the Safavid dynasty) to accept and administer religious endowments, or *waqfs*, donated by wealthy Iranians. This provided the clergy with significant economic independence. They were also allowed to collect religious taxes.

The Qajar rulers cooperated with Britain and Russia. In 1859 the British began a thirteen-year project to put a telegraph system through Iran to link Britain with its colonial interests in India. And in 1879 Nasser al-Din Shah accepted Russian military aid to organize and train an elite Iranian military unit, the Iranian Cossack Brigade. Both Britain and Russia were granted economic privileges that many Iranians perceived as detrimental to their country.

Early in the twentieth century a number of Iranian intellectuals, thinking that a parliament could protect national interests from the foreign imperialists who exercised so much influence over the Qajar shahs, organized a movement for a constitutional monarchy. The first parliament, or Majlis, convened in October 1906 but was prevented from fully confronting the British and the Russians by internal strife and foreign military intervention. By World War I Great Britain's interest in Iran intensified; the British navy had begun to switch from coal to oil fuel, much of which was obtained from the British-owned Anglo Persian Oil Company's Iranian wells at secretly lowered prices (Hussain 1985). When the Bolshevik Revolution succeeded, Russian officers left the Iranian Cossack Brigade to return home. The British then took control of the brigade and the ministries of war and finance.

In 1921 the new Soviet government and Iran signed a treaty stating that neither the USSR nor Iran would allow its territory to be used as a platform for launching aggression against the other. The British, who had been aiding counterrevolutionaries trying to overthrow the Soviets, became alarmed that Bolshevism might spread to Iran and also to the huge British colonial possession of India. To counter the threat of socialist revolution, the British considered helping oust the ineffective, corrupt Qajar dynasty and supporting a new leader committed to modernization and the organization of a strong Iranian government with a military capable of defeating revolutionary movements (Abrahamian 1982; Milani 1988).

The British-backed candidate for post-Qajar leadership was forty-two-year-old Colonel Reza Khan of Iran's British-advised Cossack Brigade. On February 21, 1921,

Reza Khan led 3,000 soldiers to Tehran, forced the resignation of the Qajar government's prime minister, and soon became minister of war. For the next four years, Reza Khan manipulated the government and expanded the standing army he commanded to 40,000 men. Reza increased his support among the Persian-speaking majority by suppressing tribal rebellions and unifying the nation. Finally on October 25, 1925, the parliament voted (80 to 5 with 30 abstentions) to depose the Qajar dynasty. Reza adopted the name of a pre-Islamic Iranian language, Pahlavi, as the name for his dynasty and crowned himself *shah-en-shah* (king of kings) in 1926.

THE PAHLAVI DYNASTY

Reza Shah Pahlavi quickly enacted measures to modernize the economy and speed the development of a new middle class, including engineers, doctors, lawyers, businesspeople, civil servants, secular teachers, and other professional and technical workers. Because Reza Shah viewed traditional Shia influence in the social and political systems as an impediment to social change, he decided to reduce the power of the clergy. He minimized opposition to this policy by simultaneously carrying out popular economic reforms and pro-nationalist actions.

During the 1930s new laws restricted the number of seminaries, placed several theological centers under state supervision, and gave the state approval power over religious endowment expenditures. The shah ordered all state institutions to accept women, and he reversed the previous requirement that women appear in public wearing the veil. At the same time he gratified Iranian nationalism by renegotiating the British oil concession, resulting in more favorable terms for Iran. Although the shah restricted candidacy for the national legislature to individuals he approved, the basis of his political strength was his growing army and police and his development of an extensive patronage system (continued and expanded by his son), through which loyal military officers, businesspeople, and even some religious figures were rewarded for their allegiance. The shah's government built thousands of miles of roads, the trans-Iranian railroad, and 230 factories, providing opportunities for the shah and his associates to enrich themselves.

The concerns of vastly more powerful nations locked in the conflict of World War II and aware of Iran's strategic importance led to Reza Shah's loss of power. The shah had been favorably impressed by the German Nazi government, which came to power in 1933. Adolf Hitler had referred to Iran as an Aryan nation, inhabited by people racially related to Germans. In 1934 the shah proclaimed that the country should in the future be referred to by the rest of the world as Iran, "land of the Aryans" (the name used by most of Iran's people), rather than Persia. The shah also invited hundreds of German advisers to Iran to assist in construction projects and in the organization of an Iranian Youth Corps.

MAP 7.1 Iran and Neighboring States (During the Revolution and the Iran-Iraq War)

When the Germans invaded the Soviet Union in June 1941, both the Russians and the British feared the shah would side with Germany, possibly denying them Iran's oil and bestowing this resource on their enemy, and forbid the use of Iranian territory as a weapons supply route to the Soviets. On August 25, 1941, the Soviets occupied northern Iran, and the British seized sections in the south. Fearing that the Allied invaders would terminate the Pahlavi dynasty, Reza Shah abdicated in favor of his twenty-year-old son, Muhammad Reza, a course of action acceptable to the British, who were apparently concerned for the future stability of Iran and the possibility of expanded Russian influence if the monarchy was not preserved (Abrahamian 1982). Reza was transported to the British island colony of Mauritius and then to Johannesburg, South Africa, where he died in 1944. The first Pahlavi shah left behind an Iran with two distinct and antagonistic cultures. "The upper and new middle classes became increasingly westernized and scarcely understood the traditional or religious culture of most of their compatriots. On the other hand peasant and urban Bazaar classes [traditional middle-class merchants, craftsmen, and their employees] continued to follow the ulama, however politically cowed the ulama were.... These classes associated 'the way things should be' more with Islam than with the West" (Keddie 1981, 111).

Muhammad Reza Shah Pahlavi

The new shah was a Western-educated playboy who lacked his father's charisma, forcefulness, and physical stature; he ascended to the peacock throne under British sponsorship, his exercise of power limited by Allied occupation authorities. Following the end of the war, he desperately needed internal as well as external support. Leftist political parties had attempted to establish independent republics in the Kurdistan and Azerbaijan sections of Iran while Russian forces were present in those areas. In particular, Russian troops delayed their departure from Azerbaijan. The US government, fearing either Russian imperialism or the establishment of new nations in the region controlled by leftist governments, backed the shah's demand that the Russians withdraw. After their departure, the shah's army marched in and suppressed the separatist governments. The shah's actions not only rallied significant nationalist support for his leadership but also seemed to identify him as an effective anticommunist leader.

The shah appealed to the ulama by portraying himself as both a defender of Islam and a foe of communism. Eventually, divisions appeared within the ulama regarding the monarchy. The majority of the clergy prior to the revolutionary turmoil of the 1970s, the orthodox ulama, accepted the monarchy and rejected involvement in politics unless government actions threatened Islam or violated Islamic law. A significant minority, the fundamentalist ulama, held that Islam and the clergy must be involved in politics and government and that any concept of separating church and state was un-Islamic and a key element of foreign imperialist strategy against Muslim societies intended to subvert them morally, culturally, politically, and economically (Hussain 1985; Milani 1988). Until the 1970s this group sometimes supported the shah as a bulwark against the spread of Iran's communist movement. But after 1971 the fundamentalists, by then led by Ayatollah Khomeini, openly attacked the monarchy form of government.

Following World War II, the shah feared further growth of the Iranian Communist Party, called the Tudeh (Masses), which during the wartime period of Russian influence had increased its membership to more than 50,000, drawing recruits from both the modern middle class and industrial employees, particularly oil field workers (Abrahamian 1982). The shah repeatedly predicted that his government would be attacked by an alliance of Islamic fundamentalists and leftists, in effect anticipating that these otherwise mutually hostile groups could be united by their hatred of his regime. The unsuccessful attempt on the shah's life on February 4, 1949, in which he was shot and wounded, appeared to justify his concern. The attacker, immediately killed by the shah's bodyguards, was carrying identification papers indicating that he was a reporter for an Islamic newspaper and that he also belonged to a journalists union affiliated with a communist-led union federation (Abrahamian 1982). In reaction, the government temporarily imprisoned Ayatollah Kashani, then leader of the fundamentalists, and enacted repressive measures against the Iranian Communist Party.

The 1953 National Front Government

The ouster of Reza Shah during World War II revived the vitality of the national parliament and helped shift the balance of power toward it and away from the monarch. Smarting from the humiliating wartime foreign occupations, parliamentary leaders of the National Front coalition of political parties attempted to assert Iranian national interests through a proposed expropriation of the British-controlled Anglo Iranian Oil Company. In March 1951 the parliament voted 79 to 12 in favor of nationalization and the following month demanded that the shah name Muhammad Mossadeq, leader of the National Front, as premier.

The National Front was composed primarily of secular nationalists, drawn mainly from the urban, educated, new middle class, who favored an end to foreign political influence and economic exploitation. National Front leaders proclaimed that they were also dedicated to strengthening democracy by shifting control of the military from the shah to elected government leaders and by reducing other monarchal prerogatives and ending what they viewed as the Pahlavis' repeated autocratic violations of the 1906 constitution. But the National Front had little grassroots organization among either the industrial working class or the peasants. Mossadeq, in fact, attempted unsuccessfully to bar illiterate men from voting (women did not vote at all) because he thought they were easily manipulated by traditional authorities such as the heads of families with large landholdings (Abrahamian 1982). The support Mossadeq received from the masses was based primarily on the popularity of his nationalist appeals to the people and his charisma. When opposed by the shah or members of parliament, Mossadeq's solution was often to speak directly to the nation and provoke marches and demonstrations in support of his policies. The temporary ally of Mossadeq's National Front was Ayatollah Kashani's fundamentalist Islamic movement, which advocated anti-imperialism on behalf of removing un-Islamic foreign influences. The Tudeh, while not allied with the National Front, also wished to end foreign economic exploitation as well as achieve an extensive redistribution of wealth.

Mossadeq seized control of the military from the shah, confiscated royal lands, and reduced the palace budget, giving the savings to the country's Health Ministry. He also increased the peasants' share of agricultural produce by 15 percent and shifted the burden of taxation away from the poorer classes (Abrahamian 1982).

Great Britain was outraged when Iran seized its oil holdings (Kinzer 2008). And although Mossadeq looked to the United States for support, the British convinced the Eisenhower administration that the Mossadeq government was a threat to Western interests and had to be eliminated. The British got major Western oil companies to cooperate in a largely successful international boycott of Iranian oil, and subsequently Iran's economy deteriorated. The traditional middle class, whose businesses suffered from worsening economic conditions and Mossadeq's emergency regulatory measures, became increasingly dissatisfied. In January 1953 Ayatollah Kashani, troubled by the complaints of the strongly Islamic merchants and shopkeepers, and the increasing strength of the Tudeh and other leftists, ended his alliance with the National Front.

When Mossadeq's ability to control the parliament was impaired by opposition from conservative, pro-shah, and clerical legislators and the filibustering tactics (unending debates) they employed, National Front parliamentarians (thirty members of parliament) resigned their seats, which reduced the size of the legislative body below its necessary minimum and in effect disbanded it. Mossadeq then held a national referendum, a measure not in accordance with the country's constitution, in July 1953, to prove that the majority of Iran's people backed his actions (Abrahamian 1982; Diba 1986). The vote, which he won overwhelmingly, was interpreted as supporting both the dissolution of parliament and his continuation in power (although Mossadeq opponents criticized the referendum procedures as unfair).

Several groups conspired to eliminate the Mossadeq government. Most important were royalist military officers who had received benefits that might be threatened if anti-shah civilian authorities gained permanent control of the armed forces.

British agents and the US CIA worked with pro-shah officers during 1953 to organize and coordinate the overthrow of the National Front government. Other Mossadeq opponents included many in the upper class who had profited through their association with the shah or Western businesses and feared that future reforms might harm their interests. Finally, a number of high-ranking clerics, in addition to Kashani, began to look again to the monarchy as a mechanism for suppressing the communist movement (Abrahamian 1982; Keddie 1981).

On August 12, 1953, the shah dismissed Mossadeq as premier and appointed General Fazlollah Zahedi as his successor. Troops in the Imperial Guard moved to carry out the shah's order. However, soldiers loyal to the Mossadeq government surrounded and arrested the pro-shah unit. Subsequently the shah fled in his private plane to Rome. His departure sparked wild street celebrations, which deteriorated into three days of rioting, often with strong anti-British and anti-American aspects. Mossadeq's order for the army to end civil disorder provided the cover for General Zahedi to launch the coup. As troops suppressed pro-Mossadeq demonstrators, pro-shah civilians, including anti-left clerics and pro-shah merchants and their employees, marched into central Tehran and joined with pro-shah military units, which proceeded to attack the prime minister's residence. After nine hours and 164 deaths, the shah's forces prevailed.

The shah quickly returned to Iran to assume dictatorial power. Mossadeq and other members of his government were arrested and tried for crimes against the monarchy by a military court. In the next two years hundreds of the shah's opponents were executed, given long prison sentences, or driven into exile. Many of these were from among six hundred military personnel who had secretly belonged to the Tudeh (Milani 1988).

The shah lavishly rewarded businessmen and military officers who had organized or supported the coup. CIA assistance was instrumental in helping the shah create a new secret police force to gather information and harass or destroy political opposition groups. The Sazman-e Amniyat Va Ittilaat-e Keshvar (Organization of National Security and Intelligence, or SAVAK), formally organized in 1957, would be accused of torturing and killing thousands of Iranians. The shah decided to allow a degree of primarily elite political participation through a parliament with two controlled parties—both led by his own cronies. The new two-party system was apparently also meant to demonstrate to concerned members of the US government that the shah was "democratizing" his regime.

The White Revolution

In November 1961 the shah temporarily dispensed with parliament and ruled by decree to carry out a reform program rapidly. The so-called white revolution, or shah-people revolution, had six announced goals: (1) distributing large landhold-ings among former sharecroppers; (2) asserting government ownership of forests; (3) selling government-owned factories to private interests to raise the funds for compensating those who gave up land; (4) providing women the right to vote; (5) encouraging profit sharing between workers and management; and (6) creating a literacy corps to reduce illiteracy and promote acceptance of compulsory education (Graham 1979).

The purposes of the white revolution, apart from the six explicitly stated aims, were to promote modernization (e.g., by encouraging dispossessed large landhold-ers to use compensation money to invest in industry and commerce), to extend state control in the countryside in place of the political power previously held by landlords, and to set in motion changes, such as mechanization of farming, that would motivate much of the rural population to migrate to urban centers where labor was needed for construction projects and growing industry. The shah also hoped to win support for his regime from previously disadvantaged groups, mainly peasants and women; gratify middle-class progressives who advocated land redis-tribution and greater equality for women; and accommodate pressures for eco-nomic reform emanating from Iran's powerful ally, the United States, during the Kennedy administration.

Landowners were allowed to retain mechanized farms, as the productivity of these enterprises was considered too important to sacrifice by dividing them into less efficient small holdings. Recipients of distributed land were scheduled to pay for their parcels in annual installments over fifteen years (usually less than the pre-vious rent). The 40 percent of rural residents who lacked cultivation rights under the old system, most of whom had worked as farm laborers or in nonagricultural service jobs, were not eligible for the reform and, consequently, were permanently barred from acquiring land. Many of them abandoned the countryside to seek em-ployment in urban areas. To blunt opposition from the ulama, land held by reli-gious organizations was not sold but instead leased to peasants on a long-term basis (up to ninety-nine years), with rent paid to the clergy.

At the conclusion of the land reform program in the early 1970s, about half of the nation's cultivated land had been distributed to half of the rural families. However, most of the parcels owned or leased by peasants were actually below the minimum necessary for subsistence. Many new landowning families were forced to supplement their income through paid labor. But opportunities in the country-side were limited because manufactured goods eroded the market for traditional peasant handicrafts, and increasing mechanization of the large farms reduced the demand for part-time agricultural laborers (Hooglund 1982; Najmabadi 1987). Thus migration to cities accelerated. Social surveys indicated that 85 percent of mi-grants claimed their main reason for leaving the countryside was unsatisfactory employment opportunities there. Many were also drawn to cities by relatively high wage levels (Najmabadi 1987). In Tehran most of the hundreds of thousands of rural migrants lived on the south side of the capital in primitive conditions. Many of these would join the anti-shah revolutionary upsurge in 1978.

The 1963 Protest

The white revolution provoked serious opposition. Some secular opponents of the shah objected to the unconstitutional way the program was implemented. A number of religious leaders attacked the land reform as un-Islamic because it violated what they viewed as the landlord's right to maintain his private property and weakened the independent economic resources of the clergy and its staunchest contributors. Other clerics objected to the establishment of new rights for women. Ayatollah Khomeini, who in the early 1960s was emerging as the main spokesman for the fundamentalists, also found fault with the shah's program.

Ruhollah Khomeini, born September 24, 1902, the son and grandson of religious scholars, had been oriented toward a theological career from an early age. When he was only five months old, his father was murdered, possibly in revenge for enforcing a death penalty on a man who had publicly violated an Islamic fast. Khomeini's religious education was supported by members of his landowning extended family. As a member of the clergy, he became widely known for his integrity, scholarship, teaching ability, and charismatic personality (Bakhash 1984).

In his attack on the white revolution, Khomeini criticized the shah for carrying out the reforms by decree instead of calling for new parliamentary elections. Khomeini believed that a parliament would have at least partially represented the view of the Islamic clergy. By ignoring parliament and the religious leadership, the shah was governing in an un-Islamic manner—without the consent or guidance of the ulama (Hussain 1985). Khomeini also accused the shah and his wealthy supporters of corruption and of reaping huge, undeserved profits from the nation's oil income. In a courageous speech Khomeini asked:

> And those who have filled foreign banks with the wealth produced by our poverty-stricken people, who have built towering palaces but still will not leave the people in peace, wishing to fill their pockets . . . are they not parasites? Let the world judge, let the nation judge who the parasites are! Let me give you some advice, Mr. Shah! . . . Don't you know that if one day some uproar occurs and the tables are turned, none of those people around you will be your friends? They are friends of the dollar; they have no religion, no loyalty. They are hanging responsibility for everything around your miserable neck! (Khomeini 1981, 178, 180)

The shah had Khomeini arrested on June 5, 1963, provoking anti-shah demonstrations and rioting in Qom, Tehran, and other cities. The shah proclaimed martial law and temporarily jailed twenty-eight prominent clergymen. In crushing the protests, troops killed at least eighty-six.

Khomeini was released from prison to placate the public and other major religious leaders. By January 1964 "Khomeini had emerged as the most popular religious leader in Iran" (Milani 1988, 93). When a new pro-shah parliament voted to grant legal privileges to US citizens engaged in military projects in Iran, Khomeini proclaimed, "If some American's servant, some American's cook, assassinates your religious leader in the middle of the bazaar . . . the Iranian police do not have the right to apprehend him! Iranian courts do not have the right to judge him! The dossier must be sent to America, so that our masters there can decide what is to be done! . . . Americans . . . are to enjoy legal immunity, but the ulama of Islam, the preachers and servants of Islam, are to live banished or imprisoned" (Khomeini 1981, 181–182, 186).

In retaliation, Khomeini was exiled, and in 1965 he took up residence in the Shia holy city in Iraq.

Economic Development and Class Structure

After the white revolution, the government expanded subsidies for farm machinery and irrigation projects. But agricultural production increased by only 2.5 percent per year, which could not keep pace with the 3 percent population growth. Iran began to import food. Industrial productivity, however, rose dramatically from 5 percent per year in 1963, with 1,902 factories, to 20 percent in 1977, with 7,989 factories. During the same period the number of doctors tripled, and hospital capacity doubled. College enrollment increased by more than 700 percent.

The financing for Iran's rapid growth in industry and services came primarily from its rising oil income, which was $450 million in 1963 but $4.4 billion in 1973. After the October 1973 Arab-Israeli war, Arab nations imposed an oil blockade on the US and European nations aiding Israel. Consequently, the price of oil rose from $2.55 per barrel in September 1973 to $11.65 in December. As Iran was not cooperating in the boycott, its oil income climbed to $11.7 billion in 1974 (Hiro 1987). The shah and many of his advisers decided to expand both industrialization and the acquisition of military hardware. Much of the expertise needed to use advanced machinery and weapons was imported in the form of an estimated 60,000 foreign technicians and military advisers. The high salaries paid to these individuals, as well as to Iranians with technical expertise, contributed to rising inflation and a widening income gap between technical and professional workers and the rest of the population (Graham 1979).

Economic development had significant impacts on labor force and social class composition. At the top of the pre-revolutionary class system was the aristocratic core, including the shah and his brothers, sister, and cousins, totaling about sixty families. Several hundred other families were ranked in the nobility in terms of closeness of relationship to the monarch. These, as well as the nonaristocratic upper-class families, derived wealth from landholdings and investments in urban projects. The entire upper class was estimated to constitute less than 0.01 percent of the population (Abrahamian 1989).

Approximately 1 million families made up the traditional middle class (13 percent of the 1976 population). These were headed by individuals in the type of middle-income occupations that existed before modernization. About 500,000 were bazaaris, in that their occupations were associated with the bazaar system of trade and craft industries. The bazaar structure involved a network of guilds or associations for its participants. By 1926 there were more than one hundred guilds for craftsmen, about seventy for merchants, and forty for various types of unskilled bazaar employees. A guild-dominated district (bazaar) in a town or city typically contained one or more mosques, traditional religious schools, businesses, craft workshops, and several teahouses. The percentage of the labor force who were bazaaris declined slightly from 6.8 percent in 1966 to 6.4 percent in 1976 (Milani 1988, 107, 116). The other half of the traditional middle class included families that owned one or more of the nation's 420,000 village workshops that were not part of the bazaar guild system (many of these were carpet-weaving shops employing women workers) or one or more of the several hundred thousand moderate-size farms.

Both branches of the traditional middle class contributed money and sons (as theological students and future clergy) to Islam. Major categories among the Shia clergy included mullahs (preachers), who were thoroughly versed in the Qur'an and Islamic traditions and laws. Mullahs who memorized the entire Qur'an and the Islamic traditions merited the title *hojatolislam* (proof of Islam). Of these some were considered learned enough to qualify as *mujtahids* (interpreters) and were entitled to issue judgments and interpretations concerning both religious affairs and events occurring in other areas of life. Those *mujtahids* who achieved wide recognition and large popular followings were awarded the title "ayatollah" (sign of Allah) (Graham 1979; Hussain 1985). At the time of the modern Iranian revolution, Iran was estimated to have more than 5,000 mosques and at least 23,000 mullahs (and probably thousands more who were not officially certified as clergy by the shah's government), of whom as many as 5,000 were *hojatolislam* and 50 were ayatollahs (estimate of mullahs from Milani 1988; estimates of *hojatolislam* and ayatollahs from Abrahamian 1982).

The modern middle class included white-collar professionals, engineers, skilled technicians, bureaucrats, managers, teachers, other intellectuals, and the large

majority of students preparing for careers in these occupations. Iran's modernization resulted in a massive expansion, between 1966 and 1976, of the high school
population, from 158,798 to 482,042, and college enrollment, from 52,943 to 437,089.
The percentage of the labor force employed as professional workers, technicians,
administrators or managers, and teachers increased from 2.8 percent (201,577) in
1966 to 6.5 percent (571,068) in 1976 (Milani 1988, 107, 114).

The industrial working class (including workers in manufacturing, mining, oil
operations, and construction) climbed from 26.5 percent (1,886,988) of the labor
force in 1966 to 34.2 percent (3,012,300) in 1976. The fastest-growing component
was the lowest stratum of urban wage earners, primarily construction workers, who
were 7.2 percent (509,778) of the labor force in 1966 but 13.5 percent (1,188,720) in
1976 (Milani 1988). Most were relatively recent migrants to the cities, poorly educated but deeply imbued with religious values. They sought continuity with their
traditional culture through affiliation with the urban mosques and in 1978 became
disproportionately involved in the revolutionary street protests.

Corresponding to the increases in the modern middle class and industrial working class, the percentage in agricultural labor declined from 47.5 percent in 1966 to
34.0 percent in 1976 (Milani 1988).

Support for the Shah's Regime

Between 1963 and 1977, despite occasional attacks from small revolutionary groups,
the shah's regime was relatively stable. His patronage system rewarded loyal businesspeople, high-ranking state administrators (who by 1977 controlled a bureaucratic network of more than 300,000 civil servants), and military leaders. In the late
1970s the army had 285,000 men, the air force 100,000, and the navy 30,000. Many
officers owed their careers and salary levels to the vast sums the shah invested in
the military.

The secret police, SAVAK, with thousands of full-time agents, tens of thousands
of informants, and a fearsome reputation for torture and murder, deterred many
from attacking the regime. SAVAK focused mainly on threats from the modern
middle class through gathering data on anti-shah activists, attempting to weaken
nonviolent anti-shah groups, and crushing violent groups among college students
and professional workers (Abrahamian 1982; Milani 1988).

US involvement in preserving the Iranian monarchy was motivated by several
factors, including an interest in keeping Iran's oil resources under the control of a
friendly government. The shah's military buildup reduced the cost of oil to Western countries by returning much of Iran's oil profits to those nations in the form
of billions of dollars for advanced jet airplanes and other expensive military hardware. The shah used his armed forces to police the Persian Gulf area, intervening

in Oman in 1975 and 1976 to help suppress a leftist rebellion and intimidating other potential foes of pro-Western governments in the region. The belief that the shah enjoyed the unconditional support of the United States, a nation most Iranians viewed as enormously powerful and potentially ready to intervene again in Iran as it had in 1953, helped discourage open opposition. And the perception in the latter half of the 1970s that US support for the shah had weakened contributed significantly to the development of the Iranian revolution.

Increasing national wealth during the years 1963–1975 contributed to regime stability by benefiting large sectors of the population (Milani 1988). The state's growing resources allowed the shah to extend medical care, education, and social services.

Opposition to the Shah

The 1970s saw several major anti-shah movements. The secular nationalists were drawn largely from the modern middle class and included survivors of the National Front. Most demanded a return to strict adherence to the 1906 constitution and genuinely free elections. Another component of secular nationalism (in the sense of opposing Western control of Iran) was Iran's Communist Party. The Tudeh, however, was tainted by its strong pro-Soviet stance. Furthermore, both the National Front and the Tudeh had little support in the countryside or among recent migrants to the cities (Abrahamian 1982).

The fundamentalists among the religious leadership constituted a potentially powerful adversary to the shah's policies and eventually to the monarchy itself. The advantages the religious opposition enjoyed compared to the other anti-shah groups included the fact that the thousands of clergy constituted an organizational network permeating most classes and social groups, urban and rural. Furthermore, the masses shared a common religious value system with the clergy and did not need to be converted to a new revolutionary perspective under Islamic leadership; the fundamentalist ulama merely activated the potentially revolutionary concepts already present within Islamic ideology. A key factor in the process of mobilizing the faithful was the emergence of the charismatic, uncompromising, and widely admired anti-shah member of the religious leadership, Ayatollah Khomeini, as preeminent among the ulama (Green 1982; Hussain 1985).

The religious opposition enjoyed the support of many bazaaris, who were strongly religious and had been harmed by the shah's policies. The shah promoted Western-style shopping centers to the detriment of the bazaars, urban development projects that destroyed some bazaar districts, and government price inspection teams that, in combating inflation by suppressing excessive profiteering by bazaar merchants, precipitated many arrests. Many bazaaris shifted from seeing the shah as a bulwark against communism to viewing him as an un-Islamic agent of corrupting foreign cultural and economic interests.

The formation of anti-shah guerrilla movements occurred after the suppression of the 1963 protests. Many young activists became impatient with nonviolent resistance, such as election boycotts, strikes, and demonstrations. Some university students formed secret discussion groups and studied revolutions in countries like China, Vietnam, Cuba, and Algeria. By the early 1970s two groups developed the capacity to launch limited armed attacks against the shah's regime: the Fedayeen-e Khalq (Martyrs of the People), a secular, Marxist-oriented group, and the Mujahideen-e Khalq (Islamic Soldiers of the People), an Islamic leftist movement. The Fedayeen developed out of a union in 1970 of three Marxist groups initially organized by university students and writers in Tehran, Mashad, and Tabriz. Many of the Fedayeen were the children of modern middle-class parents who had been involved in either the Tudeh or the left wing of the National Front. Ideologically, the founders appeared to draw on the Debray-Guevara theory of the guerrilla *foco*. As one leader put it, "To inspire the people we must resort to a revolutionary armed struggle . . . to shatter the illusion that the people are powerless" (Abrahamian 1985, 156).

The Fedayeen-e Khalq initiated the guerrilla struggles of the 1970s with its February 1971 attack on security forces at the village of Seyahkal. The group robbed banks, assassinated the chief military prosecutor, and bombed foreign corporate offices. By 1977, 106 Fedayeen had died in combat and sixty-six others through execution, torture, murder, or suicide while in custody (Abrahamian 1985). Of those killed seventy-three were college students, and another fifty-four were in occupations requiring a college degree. These characteristics reflected the fact that the shah's regime succeeded, through both repression and publicly portraying them as atheistic terrorists, in limiting largely to college-educated individuals the Fedayeen-e Khalq's appeal.

The Mujahideen-e Khalq, like the Fedayeen, originated in the early 1960s. But many of its members were the children of parents in the highly religious, traditional middle class. The Mujahideen were a manifestation of modernist Shiism and were influenced by a number of prominent Iranian Islamic figures who never directly participated in the group and may not have approved of its violent actions (Abrahamian 1982; 1989).

Modernist Shiism developed as an alternative to orthodox Shiism and fundamentalism. The central themes of modernist Shiism were that Islam, if properly interpreted, could provide Iranians with a progressive ideology capable of modernizing Iran, achieving a more equitable distribution of wealth, and protecting the nation from foreign cultural domination and economic exploitation. Proponents of this view felt that their version of Islam could unify all major population groups, from those in modern occupations to the clergy, in a shared, indigenous

Shia belief system. Among its major proponents was Mehdi Bazargan, who attempted to demonstrate a compatibility between scientific knowledge and Shiism. He called for a future Islamic government run by highly educated lay administrators and technically trained individuals, not clergy. An associate of Bazargan whose ideas also influenced the Mujahideen was Ayatollah Taleqani, who, "unlike most ayatollahs, . . . came from a poor family, . . . openly criticized his colleagues for being fearful of the modern world," and had ties to leftist political groups that favored a redistribution of wealth to the poor (Abrahamian 1985, 161). Taleqani and Bazargan formed the nonviolent Islamic Liberation (Freedom) movement of Iran in 1961, which was often critical of the shah and foreign influence.

Another inspirational modernist figure for the Mujahideen was Ali Shariati, a famous Iranian sociologist and political activist who is regarded (along with Ayatollah Khomeini) as one of the "two most important persons whose writings exercised an all-pervading influence on the Iranian people" in the years leading up to the revolution (Hussain 1985, 66). Shariati, unlike several past revolutionary theorists who held that religious beliefs generally inhibited social revolution, argued that Islamic doctrine, properly interpreted, promoted and required revolution. Shariati believed that the Prophet Muhammad had intended to create a classless society but that his mission had been subverted. He asserted that "true Muslims had the duty to fight against despotic rulers, foreign exploiters, greedy capitalists, and false clergymen who use Islam as an opiate to lull masses into subservience" (Abrahamian 1985, 163).

After the 1963 repression, nine young members of Bazargan's and Taleqani's Islamic Liberation movement split off to form the Mujahideen. As one founder put it, "it was the duty of all Muslims to continue the struggle begun by the Shia Imams to create a classless society and destroy all forms of despotism and imperialism" (Abrahamian 1985, 163). The Mujahideen launched its first military actions in August 1971. In the next several months the organization lost almost all its original leadership through gun battles with the shah's forces and executions. But the group found many willing new recruits to replace losses and even expand membership, the large majority of whom were college educated, mainly within the physical sciences—unlike the Fedayeen, who were more often drawn from the humanities and the social sciences. After 1972 the Mujahideen developed an ideology more closely aligned with Marxist concepts. Many in the Tehran branch abandoned Islam as the basis of their revolutionary thought in favor of secular Marxist thinking, but most Mujahideen outside the capital continued to adhere to Islam. This division led to a split and two separate organizations after May 1975, with the secular Marxist offshoot adopting the name "Paykar."

By early 1976 both Mujahideen groups and the Fedayeen, which itself was divided over the effectiveness of violence, had suffered so many losses that most members decided to avoid violent combat until more favorable circumstances existed. Therefore, just prior to the mass revolutionary upsurge of 1978, there were four major guerrilla groups, two Fedayeen and two Mujahideen. "All four were well equipped to move into action and take advantage of the revolutionary situation" (Abrahamian 1985, 168).

THE SETTING FOR REVOLUTION

The Iranian revolution was in part precipitated by the fact that although the economy modernized rapidly during the 1960s and the 1970s, the country's political system failed to provide new avenues of effective political participation. In contrast, the shah and his advisers in 1975 decided to combine the previous two parties into the new Resurgence Party and establish a one-party government. The purpose of this shift was to strengthen the regime through creation of a single party whose branches and activists would permeate every aspect of Iranian society. In bringing religion and other major institutions under state control, it would transform Iran from a "somewhat old-fashioned military dictatorship into a totalitarian style one-party state" (Abrahamian 1982, 441). Resurgence leaders claimed their disciplined party would "break down traditional barriers and lead the way to a fully modern society" and, combining the best aspects of capitalism and socialism, develop a "great civilization" under the leadership of the shah, "the Light of the Aryan Race" who "guides the . . . hearts of his people" (Abrahamian 1982, 441, 442).

The shah's Resurgence Party government characterized much of the ulama as medieval reactionaries and sent a religious corps into the countryside to teach the rural masses the pro-shah version of Islam. The regime announced that in the future only state-controlled religious organizations could publish theological books and asserted state rather than clerical jurisdiction over family matters. These measures and the perception that moral evils (such as pornography, prostitution, and alcohol and drug abuse) were being spread by the shah's foreign advisers and other sources of what a large number of religious leaders viewed as contaminating Western culture pushed many of the previously passive orthodox ulama into openly opposing the shah.

Between the early 1950s and the 1970s various policies of the shah's regime alienated it from almost all numerically significant social groups. When the military destroyed the Mossadeq government in 1953, the shah enjoyed the backing of not only the majority of army officers but also many from the landowning upper class, the wealthy bazaar merchants, and the religious leadership. However, by the mid-1970s, the shah's white revolution had severely reduced the political influence of the landlords. Other economic measures and religious and cultural policies damaged the interests of the bazaar merchants and provoked opposition from much of the ulama. Deprived of the support of these important groups without really winning the loyalty of the intended beneficiaries of the reforms (such as the peasant recipients of land), the shah's government depended primarily on the allegiance of the military, the state bureaucracy, Iranian industrialists, foreign investors, and the United States (Milani 1988).

Whereas lack of meaningful opportunities for political participation generated discontent in the middle class, important economic changes promoted widespread frustration. Income from Iran's oil increased from about $1 billion in 1968–1969 to $5 billion in 1973–1974 to $20 billion in 1975–1976. The benefits went disproportionately to the upper and modern middle classes. Inequality increased significantly between these classes and the mass of the population. Many of the poor experienced some lifestyle improvements, but these were far outpaced by the wealth accruing to the upper class, whose "conspicuous consumption . . . gave rise to increasingly vocal discontent" (Keddie 1981, 174).

The shah's somewhat reckless acceleration of Iran's technical and military development after 1973 "created a host of national problems: constantly increased spending on imports; orientation of the economy toward dependence on foreigners; the huge population flow into the crowded cities; and a lack of urban low-cost housing" (Keddie 1981, 175). Because of energy conservation measures in the United States and Europe and the end of the Arab oil embargo, Iran's oil revenue fell behind the cost of its imports, and its foreign debt began to climb rapidly. In mid-1977, the shah's regime attempted to cut expenditures and reduce the inflation rate (which had reached 30 percent) by canceling or postponing construction projects and slowing economic development in other ways as well. As a result, unemployment increased and working-class wages fell, especially among semiskilled and unskilled urban workers. Because the shah's program of growth had raised expectations, the sudden worsening of conditions heightened mass discontent.

But the shah apparently still felt secure. The nation in general had been prospering, becoming more educated, more technologically advanced, and far better armed. The regime was backed by the world's most powerful nation. And the shah perceived his opposition to be largely fragmented and easily countered by his security forces. Only the Islamic clergy had a mass base in most classes and an extensive organizational network. But the religious leadership appeared divided, with only a few ayatollahs—such as the exiled Khomeini—openly attacking the shah and, after 1971, calling for an end to the monarchy. The shah's false evaluation of the weakness of the ulama and decline in fundamentalist Islamic views prompted an enormously damaging measure. The puppet parliament passed a law in 1976 officially shifting Iran from an Islamic calendar, with year 1 beginning at the time of the Prophet's *hijra* (journey) from Mecca to Medina, to a monarchal calendar, with year 1 set at the founding of the Persian monarchy by Cyrus the Great. Many of the faithful viewed this change as an outrageous anti-Islamic act (Graham 1979; Milani 1988).

The shah also felt confident enough to accommodate pressure from the Carter administration to improve the human rights situation and restrain the brutality of the SAVAK in return for the continued flow of US weapons. Relaxation of repression, which began in February 1977 with the freeing of 357 political prisoners, led to more demands for greater freedoms and reforms.

Thus by late 1977, after more than two decades of autocratic rule that had progressively narrowed the social base of support for the monarchy, a number of revolution-promoting conditions existed simultaneously. First, numerous discontented groups, several of which had major ideological differences among themselves, all shared an intense animosity toward the shah and the foreign imperialism they perceived he represented. This constituted the basis for the necessary degree of unity among developing revolutionary factions, none of which alone was capable of overthrowing the shah and establishing a revolutionary government. Second, mass discontent grew, arising from inequality, regime attacks on Islamic traditions, religious authority, and the bazaar, and soaring inflation coupled with rising unemployment and falling working-class wages. The intensification of mass frustration coincided with the shah's temporary relaxation of repression to gratify the Carter administration. This change, along with the perception that the shah's regime no longer enjoyed the unconditional support of the United States, precipitated the release of pent-up hostility through a series of ever larger protest demonstrations.

THE REVOLUTIONARY PROCESS

The release of political prisoners encouraged public criticism of the monarchy, mostly from discontented members of the modern middle class. On June 12, 1977, members of the National Front published 20,000 copies of an open letter calling for the shah to "desist from authoritarian rule . . . abandon . . . the single party system, permit freedom of the press and freedom of association, free all political prisoners," and establish a popularly elected government based on the 1906 constitution (Hiro 1987, 67). The following week the well-known Islamic leftist critic of the shah, Ali Shariati, died in England. Iranians widely believed that he had been poisoned by SAVAK.

By October 1977 the National Front, the liberation movement, and the Tudeh were all stronger than they had been in years and were committed to winning more reforms. From his exile in Iraq, Ayatollah Khomeini, through his taped sermons smuggled into Iran, called on the clergy to form *komitehs* (derived from the French word for "committees") at the mosques to organize and lead the Islamic faithful in the struggle against the shah. The suspicious October death of Khomeini's forty-five-year-old son, Mustapha, at Najaf, thought by many to have been caused by SAVAK agents, provoked grief and anger among millions. Those arrested during subsequent demonstrations benefited from the new liberalization policies. They were tried by civilian, rather than military, courts, where most received light sentences. The lenient treatment facilitated further protests.

Ayatollah Khomeini as Revolutionary Leader

The shah and his advisers soon realized their limited although significant reforms were allowing the increasingly turbulent release of previously suppressed resentment. They decided to promote disunity among the anti-shah groups by attempting to discredit and isolate Khomeini, the shah's most hostile and adamant critic. This tactic, however, had a serious drawback. By singling out Khomeini, the shah was enhancing the ayatollah's image as his most feared opposition figure. In effect, this helped hand leadership of the revolution over to religious fundamentalists instead of the more moderate middle-class opposition movements.

The politically suicidal assault on Khomeini was launched on January 7, 1978, through an unsigned newspaper article titled "Iran, and the Black and Red Reactionaries." The piece characterized Khomeini as "an adventurer, without faith, tied to the centers of colonialism" who was paid by the British to oppose the shah's reforms and policies. In addition to alleging that Khomeini was the son of a "dancing girl" and was characterized by "homosexual inclinations" (Hussain 1985, 129), the attack on Khomeini's well-known anti-imperialism appeared outrageous to most Iranians. Hundreds of theological students in the seminary city of Qom demonstrated in protest. At least ten were shot and killed. Khomeini immediately called for new demonstrations as part of the mourning procession to be held, as tradition stipulated, forty days after the deaths of the student martyrs. Many peaceful marches in commemoration of the victims took place throughout Iran on the designated day, February 18, but in Tabriz crowds attacked police stations, Resurgence Party offices, liquor stores, and large banks. Scores were killed and hundreds more wounded as troops suppressed the disorders.

Khomeini praised the uprising, and a new protest was organized for March 29, forty days after the killings in Tabriz, in order to mourn these new martyrs. On this occasion demonstrations were held in fifty-five cities and turned violent in five, with crowds attacking the same types of targets as in the earlier Tabriz rioting. Dozens of people died, prompting another set of mourning processions at which still more people lost their lives. Shaken by the repetitive and massive disorders, the shah sought to placate the opposition. On June 6 he removed the widely detested General Nemattollah Nassiri, chief of the SAVAK, and promised free elections. But whereas some religious leaders appeared willing to accept the word of the shah and permit him to remain with greatly restricted powers and controlled by a proposed new and supposedly freely elected parliament, Ayatollah Khomeini was adamant that the monarchy must be overthrown (Green 1982; Keddie 1981).

On September 6 Khomeini stated, "Pay no attention to the deceptive words of the shah, his government, and its supporters for their only aim is to gain another reprieve for their satanic selves," and he called on the armed forces to "renew your bonds with the people and refuse to go on slaughtering your children and brothers for the sake of the whims of this Pahlavi family of bandits" (Khomeini 1981, 236). On September 7, 500,000 people marched in Tehran to the parliament building, chanting "Death to the shah" and "Khomeini is our leader." Thousands wore the white shrouds of martyrdom, demonstrating their willingness to die.

The shah, deciding that his concessions were encouraging the opposition, reversed himself and imposed martial law in twelve cities. On the morning of September 8, 15,000 people gathered at Jaleh Square in Tehran unaware that on the previous night the regime had banned public assemblies. By 8:00 AM troops equipped with tanks surrounded the square and opened fire. According to the government, eighty-six people were killed, but the opposition put the figure at 3,000 (Milani 1988). To many the September 8 Black Friday Massacre proved that the shah and his regime were as brutal as ever, as Khomeini had vehemently asserted. Later that month staff members of Iran's Central Bank released information indicating that in the previous week 177 rich Iranians (including members of the royal family and top military figures) had sent $2 billion out of the country. This news further encouraged anti-shah forces by showing that as the people rose in rebellion, the shah's regime-supporting patronage system was collapsing, and his moneyed allies were "jumping ship."

In a counterproductive move the shah pressured neighboring Iraq to expel Khomeini so that the ayatollah would have no more contact with Iranians on pilgrimage to Iraq. On October 6 Khomeini flew to France, where, to the distress of the shah, he became the focus of attention of the international press. This greatly increased his ability to make his views known quickly to his followers inside Iran and function as the revolution's guiding force. Representatives of anti-shah groups such as the National Front and Bazargan's and Taleqani's liberation movement began flying to Paris to consult with Khomeini and draft coordinated policies, thereby acknowledging Khomeini as their leader (Green 1982; 1994; Keddie 1981; Milani 1988).

Disarming the Army

The ayatollah realized that to overthrow the shah, the armed forces must be neutralized. Although Khomeini beseeched soldiers and police not to obey orders to fire on demonstrators, he called on the faithful to confront the army fearlessly and demonstrate their willingness to sacrifice themselves. When troops refused to fire or even joined the protesters, their actions helped accelerate the deterioration of the shah's regime by showing that it was losing control of its armed forces. If some units fired on and killed marchers, Khomeini knew that many other soldiers would be ashamed of such action and become demoralized and ready to join the revolution.

Khomeini's strategy differed radically from the armed assaults on the military by the Fedayeen-e Khalq and the Mujahideen-e Khalq. He reasoned that attacking anyone in a uniform would increase solidarity within the military and delay the fall of the shah's regime. Khomeini chose to wage a moral attack on Iran's armed forces. He explained, "We must fight the soldiers from within the soldiers' hearts. Face the soldier with a flower. Fight through martyrdom because the martyr is the essence of history. Let the army kill as many as it wants until the soldiers are shaken to their hearts by the massacres they have committed. Then the army will collapse, and thus you will have disarmed the army" (Hiro 1987, 100).

In late October Ayatollah Khomeini called on oil workers to strike and cripple the regime economically. The resulting work stoppage, supported by the Tudeh, cost the shah's government $74 million a day. The shah imposed a military government on the entire nation on November 6, with the chief of staff, General Gholam Reza Azhari, as the new prime minister. During November the shah appeared to suffer from bouts of depression over his inability to stop the uprisings. His emotional status was probably also affected by the fact that he was terminally ill from cancer; this was not to be made public for many months.

In 1978 the shah vacillated between repression and concession. His decision to scapegoat several of his previously faithful military and government officials to save the monarchy dismayed and alienated many of his wealthy supporters. They fled Iran with millions in personal wealth, speeding the deterioration of the regime.

The Soviet government, anticipating the possibility of US military intervention to save the shah's regime, let it be known that such an event might result in the movement of Soviet troops into Iran in accordance with the 1921 Iran-USSR treaty, which permitted the Soviets to send forces into Iran if another nation had already carried out such an action. The Carter administration, however, made it clear that it had no intention of sending US forces to save the monarchy, further disheartening the shah (Hiro 1987).

On 10 Muharram (December 11), the anniversary of Imam Hussein's death in the seventh century, 2 million people, led by Ayatollah Taleqani of the liberation movement, religious leader of the capital's faithful, and Karim Sanjabi, a major figure in the National Front, marched in Tehran. During a successful strike on December 18, five hundred army troops with tanks defected to the revolution in Tabriz, and hundreds of others defected elsewhere.

Revolutionary Victory

Confronted with almost continuous insurrectionary conditions and December oil production falling to only 40 percent of domestic requirements, the shah made a last desperate attempt to save the monarchy. He persuaded Shah-pour Bakhtiyar, a leader of the National Front, to become premier on December 29. Bakhtiyar accepted on the condition that the shah leave the country on a "vacation" and that when he returned he would in the future act as a "constitutional monarch." But Bakhtiyar's collaboration with the doomed monarchy was so abhorrent to most anti-shah forces that he was not only condemned by Khomeini but also expelled from the National Front (Hiro 1987; Keddie 1981).

On January 16 the shah left Iran, initially for Egypt, but apparently expecting to return once conditions were right for his generals to seize power again and invite him back in a manner similar to the 1953 overthrow of the National Front government. Under mounting popular pressure Bakhtiyar reopened Tehran's airport, allowing the return of Ayatollah Khomeini on February 1. A reported 3 million people lined the streets of the capital to welcome him. The ayatollah quickly appointed a provisional government to exercise power in opposition to the Bakhtiyar regime (Keddie 1981). On February 7 delegates from lower-ranking air force personnel met with Khomeini and pledged their allegiance to him. In the following days representatives of much of the army and navy enlisted personnel and lower-level officers did the same.

Army generals sent units of the most pro-shah branch of the military, the Imperial Guards, to suppress air force personnel who had gone over to the revolution. The airmen resisted, and thousands of civilians, including Fedayeen and Mujahideen guerrillas, joined the battle, resulting in the defeat and rout of the pro-shah forces. Guerrillas and military defectors proceeded to take arms from captured arsenals and distribute them to tens of thousands of young people and pro-revolutionary army reservists who gathered at Tehran University and volunteered to fight elements of the military still loyal to the shah or the Bakhtiyar government. On February 10–11, revolutionary forces attacked and defeated one of the Imperial Guard's two armored units. The rest of the military declared its neutrality. As revolutionaries seized the capital's television station, its prisons, and its police stations, Bakhtiyar fled the country.

REVOLUTIONARY IRAN
Divisions Within the Revolutionary Coalition

The anti-shah groups differed on how Iran's new government should be structured and what policies it should pursue. Khomeini's fundamentalists wanted an Islamic republic led by clerics. Many lay Islamic revolutionaries in the liberation movement, such as Bazargan, favored an Islamic state headed by Shiite laymen. Liberals in the National Front intended to create a secular parliamentary government similar to those in Western Europe. The Mujahideen-e Khalq and other Islamic leftists hoped for a significant redistribution of wealth and the establishment of an egalitarian

Islamic state. The Marxist-Leninist Fedayeen-e Khalq and Tudeh saw the current revolution leading to a later secular socialist revolution. All these groups took advantage of the immediate post-shah period to express their views freely, recruit new members, stage demonstrations, and propagate their goals to the larger population.

The clerically organized pro-Khomeini movement raced to build a huge volunteer armed force, the Islamic Revolutionary Guard (IRG). Within two years this organization had expanded to 200,000. The IRG functioned to safeguard the emerging Islamic government from any potential royalist coup in the armed forces and from possible attacks by other revolutionary groups that did not agree with Khomeini's plans for Iran. Khomeini partisans purged the army of suspected pro-shah personnel. Hundreds of officers in the military and SAVAK were tried by clerical revolutionary courts controlled by Khomeini supporters; found guilty of crimes including torture, murder, and "fighting against God"; and quickly executed (Hiro 1987).

Significant disagreements existed within the ulama about the future development of the economy as well as the role of clergy in government. The economic views of the ayatollahs frequently reflected their class of origin and family ties. Those from landlord or wealthy merchant families manifested the preference of these classes for maintaining an economic system that would protect their interests, and ayatollahs from less affluent families generally expressed more concern for redistributing wealth toward the poor. The most important of the few ayatollahs from relatively poor families was Ayatollah Taleqani, the religious leader of Tehran. Taleqani, one of whose sons was a member of a Marxist-oriented guerrilla group, had ties to both the National Front and the Mujahideen-e Khalq and played an essential role in holding the revolutionary alliance together. Ayatollah Taleqani's sudden death in September 1979, apparently from natural causes, contributed to the breakdown of the revolutionary coalition.

Taleqani had also helped prevent a split between Ayatollah Khomeini and other top members of the ulama, particularly Ayatollah Shariatmadari, who had become one of the most influential clerical figures in Iran while Khomeini was in exile. Shariatmadari, representing the orthodox clerical view, did not agree with Khomeini that the Qur'an mandated that the clergy have control of the government. Rather, he held that the government was simply required not to pass laws or commit acts that violated Islamic law.

Groups that opposed Khomeini's version of an Islamic republic looked to Ayatollah Shariatmadari as their major ally within the religious leadership, especially after the death of Taleqani. Shariatmadari, however, suffered from tremendous disadvantages. First, his following tended to be limited ethnically because he was from an Azeri rather than a Persian-speaking family. Second, during the revolutionary turmoil of 1978 he had expressed a willingness to tolerate the continuation of the monarchy and to compromise with the shah and later Bakhtiyar. But Khomeini's analysis that the shah's regime could be abolished through continued protest and refusal to compromise was proven correct. In fact, Khomeini's success in guiding the revolution convinced many that he must have been specially chosen and empowered by God to defeat the shah's powerful army and his evil regime. Thus Ayatollah Khomeini's views overcame Shariatmadari's criticisms (Hussain 1985; Milani 1988).

Constitution of the Islamic Republic

After the shah fled and the Bakhtiyar government fell, a situation of dual power characterized Iran. A provisional government approved by Khomeini and headed by Bazargan technically exercised state authority. Its officials were overwhelmingly lay members of the National Front and the liberation movement with administrative skills. Real power, however, was held by Khomeini and his clerical associates, who enjoyed the loyalty of the large majority of poor and lower-middle-class Iranians who had served as the foot soldiers of the revolution. Khomeini's followers dominated the local revolutionary *komitehs* and militias, then coalescing into the huge Islamic Revolutionary Guard. In contrast, the National Front and the liberation movement lacked support outside the middle classes, and neither had a militia. Although the Mujahideen and Fedayeen groups had thousands of members under arms, they had much less grassroots support than Khomeini's fundamentalists did.

Khomeini selected a group of clergy and laymen, the Islamic Revolutionary Council (IRC), to oversee government policy until a totally new government system could be established. To hasten this event, he insisted on holding a referendum almost immediately. Voters would be given the option of declaring yes or no to the proposal to establish an Islamic Republic (as opposed to being allowed to select a preference from several clearly defined alternate forms of government). The referendum was held on April 1, 1979, with a reported 89 percent turnout (more than 20 million people) and a 98 percent approval for the creation of an Islamic Republic.

In early August an election was held for an Assembly of Experts to draft the new constitution. Khomeini's followers had organized their own political party, the Islamic Republic Party (IRP), to compete in the vote. All the candidates for the assembly, regardless of party, had to be approved by Khomeini. The IRP won the biggest bloc of seats. The resulting constitution called for an elected parliament, including clergy and laymen who were approved as good Muslims and supporters of the constitution before being allowed to run; a separately and popularly elected president; and a supreme court, the Council of Guardians, to be composed of six clerics and six laymen selected, respectively, by the clergy and the parliament, to serve six-year terms. The Council of Guardians was given authority to approve candidates for parliament and to rule on whether any act of government or law passed by parliament violated either the constitution or Islamic law (Abrahamian 1989).

The overriding theme of the constitution was the concept that ultimate sovereignty over the political system belonged to God. Any other basis for sovereignty, whether the people, a ruling dynasty, or conformity to some alternate ideology, was un-Islamic and unacceptable. In the Islamic Republic, God's will is expressed through the "rule of the just Islamic jurist," the *vilayat-e faqih*. He is to advise the parliament and the president and has the power, at the rare times he may deem it necessary, to overrule the government or any part of the government. The first *faqih* of the Islamic Republic was Ayatollah Khomeini. His successors were to be selected by the Assembly of Experts. If no single individual was perceived qualified for the position, a committee of three or five could be selected to fill the role (Bakhash 1984; Hussain 1985).

The Constitution of the Islamic Republic with the inclusion of the crucial *vilayat-e faqih* principle embodied the victory of the Shia fundamentalists over the other groups in the revolutionary alliance. The fundamentalists' triumph was due to a number of factors. Of primary importance was Ayatollah Khomeini's role as the dominant personality of the revolution. Because Khomeini and the fundamentalists enjoyed a much wider base of popular support than any of the other anti-shah groups, the fundamentalists controlled most of the revolutionary organizations (the *komitehs* and the revolutionary courts) and possessed by far the biggest militia, the Islamic Revolutionary Guard, to enforce their will.

The fundamentalists, however, were characterized by a potentially critical weakness: the division between much of the ulama, whose families' financial interests depended on the existing pattern of property and income relations, and the poor majority of Iranians, who tended to push for a socioeconomic revolution to distribute the nation's wealth more equally. In the short run, the fundamentalists were able to delay resolution of this issue and further strengthen their dominant position relative to former revolutionary allies by making themselves appear to be the true defenders of the revolution in the face of external threats during the American hostage crisis and the war with Iraq.

American Hostage Crisis

A major crisis developed on October 22, 1979, when the shah was allowed to fly to New York for cancer treatment. However, Iranian revolutionaries questioned whether the shah was really ill or why, if the affliction was real, he could not get treatment elsewhere.

Ayatollah Khomeini and other ulama viewed New York City as a world center of corruption and the home of enthusiastic shah supporters and agents of US imperialism, such as Henry Kissinger. Many Iranians believed that a conspiracy was being hatched to restore the shah to power, possibly involving US military intervention in conjunction with a coup by antirevolutionary military figures still in Iran. SAVAK agents confessed that certain personnel in the US embassy in Tehran were courting Iranian officers and several leaders of minority ethnic groups. Consequently, revolutionaries planned to seize the embassy in order to protest the presence of the shah in New York and capture documents relating to CIA activities in Iran (Bakhash 1984; Hiro 1987; Hussain 1985).

On November 4, a group of 450 young militants stormed the embassy and found many of the sought-after documents. In addition to the bonanza of information used to purge the military and discredit Khomeini critics, the embassy seizure, with fifty-three US officials held hostage, helped to demonstrate that Khomeini's supporters were just as anti-imperialist as the members of the leftist Fedayeen-e Khalq and Mujahideen-e Khalq.

Those holding the hostages refused to release them unless both the shah and his wealth (in foreign investments and bank accounts) were delivered to Iran. The US government refused to return the shah to stand trial, but that demand was resolved when he died on July 27, 1980.

Eventually the US and Iran worked out financial arrangements in which some frozen Iranian assets in the United States were used to pay US business and other foreign claims on Iran's revolutionary government, with the excess, over $2 billion, going to Iran. Resolution of the crisis may have been delayed by fundamentalist leaders, who used the confrontation with the US to weaken their internal opponents by portraying them as disloyal to the revolution or tools of foreign imperialists, until all the major institutions of the Islamic state were firmly established (Milani 1988). In the midst of the hostage crisis Iran experienced a violent rebellion by the Mujahideen-e Khalq, a major conflict between the president and parliament, and an invasion by neighboring Iraq.

Conflict Between the IRP and the Mujahideen-e Khalq

The conflict between Khomeini's Islamic Republic Party and the Mujahideen-e Khalq was based on differing interpretations of Islam. The Mujahideen held that the Qur'an supported the concept that ultimate control of government resides in the hands of the people, not the clergy, and that Muhammad had intended to create an economically egalitarian society, a notion that ran counter to the family financial interests of many of the ulama. Since the Mujahideen disagreed with clerical domination of the state, they refused to vote on the new constitution.

Khomeini used the Mujahideen referendum boycott as the reason for barring the Mujahideen leader Masoud Rajavi from running as a candidate in the February

1980 presidential election. The Mujahideen responded by throwing their support to Abol Hassan Bani-Sadr, who won the election. Bani-Sadr had studied economics, sociology, and Islamic law. He was the son of an ayatollah and had been an adviser to Khomeini and a member of Khomeini's pre-constitutional Islamic Revolutionary Council. The Mujahideen backed him in part because of his commitment to a redistribution of wealth and to fostering a relatively open democratic system.

The fundamentalist clergy feared the Mujahideen more than the solely Marxist groups (which, although also barred from running candidates in elections, generally supported Khomeini for pragmatic and anti-imperialist reasons). The Mujahideen were seen as especially dangerous because they espoused Islam, which gave them a basis of appeal to Iran's masses, and because much of their membership was drawn from the younger generation of the traditional middle class, the same class that provided most of the IRP leadership.

The growing hostility against the Mujahideen was paralleled by increasing IRP dissatisfaction with the president, Bani-Sadr, who had been elected with a 75 percent majority on February 4, 1980, over the IRP candidate (but with considerable public perception that Khomeini actually favored Bani-Sadr). When in fall 1980 President Bani-Sadr repeatedly challenged members of the IRP for their restrictive interpretation of the Qur'an and their harassment and repression of other political parties, he provoked the animosity of the IRP-dominated parliament and the Council of Guardians. These groups were further infuriated by the president's accusation that IRG personnel were torturing prisoners. Some IRP members of parliament accused President Bani-Sadr of being a traitor and of causing disunity. Khomeini tried to reimpose calm by banning all public speeches. But when Bani-Sadr violated the restriction and was declared incompetent by the parliament in June 1981, Khomeini removed him from office (Bakhash 1984; Milani 1988).

On June 28, 1981, after fundamentalists again attacked Mujahideen supporters, a massive explosion—caused by thirty kilograms of dynamite placed in a building adjoining an IRP conference hall—killed seventy-four top figures in the party. The Mujahideen were blamed.

The Mujahideen carried out scores of assassinations and bombing attacks and in turn suffered the execution of many leaders and hundreds of other members. But they appeared unable to convey their message sufficiently beyond the middle class to the poor, who were generally imbued with more traditional religious views. Thus the Mujahideen campaign of assassination failed because popular support for the IRP and the religious dedication of IRP members meant that murdered officeholders were rapidly replaced and regime stability was maintained. By the end of October 1981 the Islamic Republic had succeeded in containing internal rebellion, although air force sympathizers had managed to help both Bani-Sadr and Masoud Rajavi escape Iran.

The Iran-Iraq War

The ability of the IRP government to crush its opposition had much to do with the wave of nationalism that swept Iran after the Iraqi invasion on September 22, 1980. Animosity had long simmered between Iraq, at that time a nation of about 14 million, and its neighbor Iran, with about three times the population and close to four times the land area. Most Iraqis speak Arabic; the majority of Iranians, Persian. The religious composition of the two nations differs significantly, with about 63 percent of Iraqis being Shia and approximately 35 percent Sunni, whereas in Iran approximately 90–95 percent are Shia. A long-standing territorial controversy between Iraq and Iran concerned control over the river waterway to the Persian Gulf, the Shatt-al-Arab (the Arab River). Iran had previously forced Iraq to relinquish the east bank and had moved the international boundary between the two nations to the middle of the river. Another point of contention was the fact that Iraq was governed by the Baath Socialist Party, whose members were disproportionately secularly oriented Sunni Muslims. Khomeini viewed the government of Iraq as un-Islamic and called on Iraqi Muslims, both Shia and Sunni, to establish a second Islamic republic.

Iraqi President Saddam Hussein decided to attack Iran to reclaim the east bank of the Shatt-al-Arab and to overthrow Iran's Islamic republican form of government, the source of inspiration for fundamentalist Islamic rebels inside Iraq. Iraqi leaders estimated that Iran's military was in disarray following the revolution and would eventually run out of spare parts to maintain and repair its US military equipment, as the United States had banned arms shipments to Iran (*New York Times*, March 31, 1989, A5).

Most Iranians, however, rallied to meet the Iraqi assault. Masses of Iranian army troops and Islamic Revolutionary Guards, supported by the air force with more than four hundred combat planes, soon halted the Iraqi advance. Iran was able to obtain replacement parts and even some new weapons from diverse sources such as Vietnam (with its stores of abandoned US weaponry), the People's Republic of China, international arms dealers, US companies violating the arms embargo, and the Reagan administration's covert Iran-contra operation. The Islamic Republic, however, could not match the massive supplies of modern weapons Iraq purchased from France, the Soviet Union, and other nations with the aid of tens of billions in loans from Arab states such as Saudi Arabia and Kuwait, whose monarchs feared the spread of fundamentalism. Iran's larger population, though, permitted it to endure a two-to-one disadvantage in war casualties.

By mid-1982 Iraqi forces had been driven from much of the Iranian territory they had originally occupied. Iran launched a counterinvasion of Iraq in July, demanding the overthrow of Iraq's President Saddam Hussein and huge war reparations as the price of peace. As Iranian forces slowly advanced, despite terrible losses to superior Iraqi air power, artillery, and armor, Iraq resorted to desperate measures.

These included attacking Iranian civilian population centers with aircraft and missiles (Iran retaliated by firing missiles into the Iraqi capital, Baghdad), using internationally banned poison gas weapons, and in spring 1984 launching air attacks
on Iranian oil facilities and tankers in the northern Persian Gulf. Iran responded
by attacking the tankers of nations aiding Iraq—Saudi Arabia and Kuwait (Iraq
was transporting much of its oil by pipeline to the Mediterranean). As the threat
to Europe's oil or at least oil prices increased, the Reagan administration sent US
naval forces to the area to protect first Kuwaiti tankers (reflagged and renamed as
US ships) and then other supposedly neutral vessels. Some nations viewed these
actions as, in effect, US intervention in the war on Iraq's behalf. But according to
Milani (1994), Washington's objective seemed to be the "mutual destruction of
belligerents," similar to Great Britain's primarily sideline-observer orientation to
much of World War II while Germany and the Soviet Union waged massive land
warfare against each other between 1941 and 1944.

By mid-1988 hundreds of thousands had perished in the conflict, many more
had been wounded, and hundreds of billions of dollars lost or wasted as a result
of destruction, weapons purchases, and lost oil revenues. Faced with the apparent
impossibility of victory, Ayatollah Khomeini agreed to negotiate an end to the war
in summer 1988 (*New York Times*, June 6, 1988, A1; June 20, 1988, A8). Although
fighting largely halted after 1988, the first face-to-face talks between the two countries on a final peace agreement did not take place until July 1990 (*New York Times*,
July 6, 1990, A2). Iraq, faced with military and economic pressures from the US and
other nations because of its August invasion and occupation of Kuwait, suddenly
granted Iran most of its settlement terms, hoping for Iranian assistance or at least
neutrality in the confrontation with Western nations (*New York Times*, August 16,
1990, A1; January 6, 1991, A5).

IRAN AFTER KHOMEINI

Millions of Iranians wanted the government to do more to redistribute the nation's
wealth. However, the framers of the Constitution of the Islamic Republic had included a provision stating that individuals had a right to private ownership as long
as the property in question was the result of the owner's honest labor. High-ranking
ulama on the Council of Guardians used their interpretation of this principle to
block parliamentary proposals to transfer some privately owned wealth to the impoverished. Disagreement over this issue between top (generally anti-reform) and
lower-level personnel in the Islamic Republic Party was so great that to minimize
divisive confrontations, Khomeini dissolved the IRP in July 1987. In late March
1989, Khomeini forced the resignation of Ayatollah Montazeri, whom the Assembly
of Experts had previously designated as Khomeini's successor in the role of *faqih*

of the Islamic Republic. Montazeri, once Khomeini's prize student, had called for greater political tolerance, charged that the revolution had failed to fulfill important promises to the people, accused the Islamic Republic's security forces of prisoner abuse, and associated with critics of Khomeini's policies such as Mehdi Bazargan (*New York Times*, May 22, 1989, A1). Montazeri had also declined to support Khomeini's call for the death of author Salman Rushdie for writing *The Satanic Verses*, a book the ulama considered blasphemous.

After Khomeini died in June 1989, Iran's government was divided over adherence to extreme fundamentalist principles in the face of the pragmatic requirements of domestic and foreign policymaking. On June 4, the day after Khomeini's death, the assembly of religious experts selected Hojatolislam Ali Khamenei (later elevated to ayatollah), who had served for eight years as president of Iran, as Khomeini's successor in the role of supreme religious-political leader (*New York Times*, June 5, 1989, A1).

The constitution, revised in 1989, specified that it is the *faqih* who plays the dominant role in developing general policy interests of the Islamic Republic and appoints the heads of the TV and radio networks. It also stipulated that the *faqih*, not the elected president, is the head of the armed forces. The modified constitution eliminated the position of parliamentary prime minister and transferred all of the prime minister's powers to the president of the republic.

After years of fundamentalist rule, Iranian voters, especially women and lower-income people, selected a moderate cleric, Mohammad Khatami, as president in 1997, giving him almost 70 percent of the vote. Khatami was also reelected in 2001 to serve into the year 2005. President Khatami attempted to increase the level of democracy, enhance women's rights, and pursue friendlier relations with the US and its allies. However, his ability to carry out reforms or modify Iran's foreign policy was limited because fundamentalists continued to dominate the courts, armed forces, and police. Most importantly, President Khatami's power as head of government was superseded by Iran's head of state, the fundamentalist supreme religious leader, Ayatollah Ali Khamenei. Iran's moderate politicians were weakened by US President George W. Bush's hostile attitude toward Iran after the September 11, 2001, terrorist attacks. In response, voters in 2005 elected an Iranian president more openly critical of Bush administration policy, fundamentalist-supported Mahmoud Ahmadinejad.

IRAN AND THE 1991 GULF WAR

Iraq invaded Kuwait in 1990, prompted by several factors beyond its assertion that Kuwait was really a part of Iraq that had been split off by British imperialism. The Iraqis, as well as many Iranians, believed that the oil-rich monarchies were

puppets of Western imperialism. Despite stating their support for political democracy around the world, the US and Great Britain supplied the weapons, military
advisers, and other technological means to preserve monarchies threatened by
the democratic aspirations of their people. The royal families of nations such as
Saudi Arabia and Kuwait, beholden to Western nations for their continued existence, served the purpose of maintaining world oil prices lower than they might
otherwise be. They were also apparently available for supplying funds for projects
deemed desirable by Western intelligence services, which were to be kept secret or
were even banned by the Western nations' elected leaders (as in the case of the US
Iran-contra scandal; see Chapter 6).

Low oil prices buttressed the economies of Western Europe, Japan, and the US
and kept internal economic discontent in these countries lower than it otherwise
might have been. Furthermore, low oil prices, coupled with the arms race, ended
or reduced several perceived threats to capitalist nations. The Soviet Union ex-
pended huge financial resources to keep pace with the Reagan administration's
arms buildup and proposed Star Wars antimissile program. It could not simultaneously pay for arms expenditures and tend to urgent domestic needs, in part because
revenues from oil exports were lower than anticipated. Thus US influence over
the oil-rich monarchies of the Persian Gulf and their levels of oil production and
oil-pricing policies was a key element in the economic crisis that helped dismantle
the USSR and Communist Party leadership in Russia. Iraq's situation preceding its
invasion of Kuwait paralleled the economic distress that was simultaneously afflicting its Soviet ally.

Iraq had powerful economic reasons to seize Kuwait and its oil. Iraq perceived
itself as having fought off an aggressive, Iranian-based, fundamentalist Islamic
threat to the benefit of other Arab states. Several, including Saudi Arabia and Kuwait, had loaned Iraq billions of dollars to purchase weapons while hundreds of
thousands of Iraqis were killed or wounded in the conflict with Iran. Following the
war, Iraq had over $80 billion in foreign debt, much of this owed to rich Arab mon-
archies. Iraq hoped to win the cooperation of its OPEC partners to raise oil prices
and thereby increase Iraq's oil revenues to facilitate repayment of its loans. Instead,
Saudi Arabia, Kuwait, and the United Arab Emirates (UAE) opposed higher oil
prices (Milani 1994). And Kuwait and the UAE reportedly violated OPEC's quotas
and overproduced oil to depress world oil prices, cut Iraq's oil income, and reduce
Iraq's ability to pay off its foreign debts (Milani 1994).

The Iraqi leadership felt trapped by the oil-rich monarchies that Iraq's war
against Iran had helped protect. Since the monarchies were supported by the
United States and in turn supported the implementation of US foreign policies,
Iraqi leaders perceived the Arab monarchies' oil policies as another diabolical CIA
plot. Iraq attempted to use its military strength to seize Kuwait and save Iraq's

financial future. If successful, this would have permitted Iraq to continue its military buildup, pay its debts, improve domestic living standards, and increase its regional and world influence, since it would then control about 20 percent of the world's known oil reserves. Fearing a more powerful Iraq, Iran was among the first nations to condemn the invasion of Kuwait and demand an Iraqi withdrawal.

Iraq secured Iran's military neutrality by agreeing to many of Iran's demands for a final settlement of the Iran-Iraq War. As a result of Iraq's defeat by the US-led coalition during the 1991 Gulf War, Iran's historic enemy was severely weakened. By 1995 US oil companies were allowed to purchase Iranian oil, as long as they sold it outside the United States, paying billions for about one-fourth of Iran's production (*New York Times*, April 1, 1995, 5).

IRAN AND ISLAMIC REVOLUTION ELSEWHERE

The central themes of Islamic fundamentalism included the concept that Islamic religious rules and moral principles must be integrated with government and influence all aspects of society. Ayatollah Khomeini and other like-minded religious leaders asserted that Islamic fundamentalism must become the dominant political ideology among both Shia and Sunni Muslims and that Iran was to be only the first of many Islamic republics. By the end of the 1980s significant Islamic fundamentalist movements existed in Afghanistan, Algeria, Egypt, Jordan, Lebanon, Morocco, Sudan, Tunisia, Turkey, and the Arab-populated lands under Israeli control.

One powerful cause for the spread of fundamentalism was the quest for a genuinely homegrown culture capable of instilling a sense of pride, dignity, and self-worth. The process of modernization in Muslim countries had exposed many educated persons not only to advanced technologies and managerial skills but also to foreign values and norms and relatively nonreligious lifestyles. But the largely secular ideologies, whether pro-capitalist or pro-socialist, characteristic of the ruling elites and skilled-occupation classes of a number of Islamic societies, often appeared to offer little to the middle and lower classes except a perpetual sense of cultural and technological inferiority and the threat of the progressive erosion of cherished moral values. In contrast, the fundamentalists put forward the appealing notion of a value and belief system ordained by God and thus immeasurably superior to all other cultures.

A powerful Islamic fundamentalist movement grew among Palestinians in opposition to the Israeli-Palestinian peace proposals, which were viewed by many Palestinians as containing too many concessions to Israel. The Palestine Liberation Organization (PLO) had supported Iraq's effort to seize Kuwait in part because of Iraq's promise to utilize oil revenue to aid the millions of Arab poor, including Palestinians. But Iraq's defeat not only crippled its ability to assist the PLO and the

Palestinian people but also resulted in a retaliatory cutoff of aid to the Palestinians from the oil monarchies. Hamas, the Palestinian Islamic resistance movement, a fundamentalist organization that appeared to receive funding from international sources, some of whose members were accused of terrorism, provided much needed assistance to thousands of poor Palestinians who felt abandoned by both the PLO and the oil-rich Arab states. A number of young Palestinians, looking forward to a happier existence in the next life and hoping to serve both God and their people, proved willing to sacrifice their own lives and take many other lives in suicidal bombing attacks against Israeli soldiers and civilians (*New York Times*, November 8, 1994, A1; January 25, 1995, A8; March 5, 1996, A1). Terrorist activities by extremists in the Islamic fundamentalist movement also affected nations outside the Middle East. Bombings occurred in Great Britain, France, and Argentina.

Iran, Afghanistan, the War on Terror, and the US-Led Invasion and Occupation of Iraq

The triumph of Islamic fundamentalists in the Iranian revolution was widely viewed as a victory over the world's foremost superpower, the United States, which had backed the shah's regime. Islamic fundamentalists were in part inspired by the Islamic success in Iran to fight against the world's second greatest superpower. When the USSR invaded Afghanistan in 1979 to support a pro-Soviet regime against Islamic rebels, tens of thousands of Islamic volunteers from many countries headed for Pakistan to be armed and trained and then cross the border into Afghanistan to fight Soviet forces and their leftist Afghan allies. Among the volunteers was Osama bin Laden, a college graduate and son of a Saudi Arabian billionaire construction company owner. Bin Laden not only fought but used his money to aid other Islamic fighters and care for widows and war orphans. Islamic fighters, armed with US-supplied, shoulder-fired anti-aircraft missiles to shoot down Soviet helicopters and other low-flying aircraft, were ultimately successful, and Soviet forces withdrew in 1989. The long, brutal conflict in Afghanistan helped foster popular unrest in the Soviet Union and damaged the legitimacy of the communist government, contributing to its downfall.

The victory of Islamic forces over the Soviet Union in Afghanistan and the United States in Iran further encouraged Islamic fundamentalists to confront not only non-Islamic nations but also governments in Islamic countries that were allied with the United States or other non-Islamic states. In particular, Osama bin Laden and his associates organized a communication network, Al Qaeda ("the base" or "foundation"), among the tens of thousands of Arab and other Islamic volunteers who fought in Afghanistan. After Iraq invaded Kuwait in 1990 and posed a threat to Saudi Arabia, Osama bin Laden offered to recruit thousands of Al Qaeda members to defend Saudi Arabia against a possible Iraqi invasion. When instead the Saudi royal family decided to allow the US to deploy its armed forces within Saudi Arabia's borders, bin Laden and many other fundamentalists were outraged. Bin Laden claimed that the US was establishing a permanent imperialist occupation of both the religious-cultural core of Islamic nations and the oil resources of the Middle East. Al Qaeda's response, along with that of allied extremist fundamentalist groups, was to launch attacks against the United States and its interests. Among these were the 1993 truck bomb attack on the New York City World Trade Towers, the 1998 bombings of the US embassies in Kenya and Tanzania, the 2000 suicide bombing of the USS *Cole*, and the 2001 destruction of the World Trade Towers and attack on the Pentagon.

In retaliation the United States, Britain, and several allies invaded and occupied first Afghanistan, which had provided training sites for Al Qaeda, and later oil-rich Iraq, which had nothing to do with the 2001 attacks in the United States. During the US occupation of Iraq, internal conflict increased, especially between Iraqi Shiites and Sunnis; a major anti-US occupation insurgency developed among Arab Sunni Iraqis, and many young people from various Islamic countries, including persons affiliated with Al Qaeda, came to Iraq to resist the US occupation.

Following the September 11, 2001, attacks, President Bush in his January 2002 State of the Union message identified Iran, Iraq, and North Korea as members of an "axis of evil." Ironically, Iranian leaders had been cooperating with US officials against the Taliban regime in Afghanistan. The Sunni fundamentalist Taliban tended to be hostile toward the Shia minority in Afghanistan. Iran almost attacked Afghanistan after its diplomats were murdered in the Afghan city of Mazari Sharif in 1998. Iran reportedly provided aid to the Afghan forces resisting the Taliban, the Northern Alliance, who fought on the US side after the American invasion of Afghanistan. But President Bush's verbal attack on Iran undermined moderate Iranian politicians who had been enjoying significant popular support in the years before Bush's axis of evil speech. Combined with the March 2003 US-led invasion of neighboring Iraq, the Bush administration's threatening orientation toward Iran contributed to the election of Mahmoud Ahmadinejad, a relatively hard-line Islamic fundamentalist, in Iran's 2005 presidential election. Ahmadinejad defended Iran's nuclear energy program, which the US feared could lead to Iranian nuclear weapons. Other nations also suspected that Iran, following the US invasion of Iraq, might develop nuclear weapons to deter the United States from invading Iran.

DEVELOPMENTS AFTER THE ELECTION OF OBAMA

President Barack Obama attempted to shift the US approach to Iran from confrontation to diplomatic engagement. Obama delivered a video address on March

20, 2009, for the festival of Nowruz celebrating the 2009 Iranian New Year. He appealed directly to the people and leaders of Iran, stating, "We have serious differences that have grown over time. My administration is now committed to diplomacy that addresses the full range of issues before us, and to pursuing constructive ties among the United States, Iran and the international community. This process will not be advanced by threats. We seek instead engagement that is honest and grounded in mutual respect" (Obama 2009). But in his 2010 Nowruz address his words were more critical. "Faced with an extended hand, Iran's leaders have shown only a clenched fist" (Obama 2010). This appeared to be a reaction to Iran's rejection of US supported initiatives such as proposals for international supervision of and restrictions on Iran's nuclear program. Obama also noted the conflict surrounding Iran's national election in June 2009. "Last June, the world watched with admiration, as Iranians sought to exercise their universal right to be heard. But tragically, the aspirations of the Iranian people were also met with a clenched fist, as people marching silently were beaten with batons; political prisoners were rounded up and abused."

The 2009 Iranian Election and the Green Revolution

In 2009 President Mahmoud Ahmadinejad ran for reelection against Mir-Hossein Mousavi, who was considered to be more moderate and more supportive of women's rights, greater freedom of expression, and better relations with the US (Black 2009; New York Times, Jun. 18, 2009). The official results indicated that Ahmadinejad won with about 63 percent of the vote. However, many believed vote fraud had occurred and that Mousavi might have received the most votes. While the percentage of those eligible to vote who participated in the election in 2009 was reported as 84 percent, far higher than the 60 percent for the 2005 election, in some locations it appeared that voter turnout was mysteriously more than 100 percent (Ansari 2010, 6–7; Ansari, Berman, and Rintoul 2009, 2–3). Pre-election polls yielded contradictory results. However, a post-election telephone survey of about a thousand Iranians nationwide indicated that a majority of respondents said they voted for Ahmadinejad and a larger majority believed that he was the legitimate president (WorldPublic Opinion.org 2009, 8–9). It should be noted, though, that only 84 percent of Iranians have telephone land lines, and 52 percent of those contacted refused to participate in the survey (WorldPublicOpinion.org 2009, 2).

Massive street demonstrations in support of Mousavi commenced as soon as the results were announced. These lasted for weeks and constituted the largest public protests in Iran since the 1978–1979 Islamic revolution. Since the demonstrators adopted the Mousavi campaign color, green, for their banners and armbands, the wave of protests became known as the green movement or green revolution. Top

Iranian religious and political figures appeared divided over the existence and level of election irregularities and whether fraud actually altered the election outcome. Ahmadinejad supporters, police, and the fundamentalist Basij militia, created by Ayatollah Khomeini in 1979 as an auxiliary force for the Islamic Revolutionary Guard (Simone 2009), began to confront and then reportedly attack members of the pro-Mousavi crowds. Conflict on the streets resulted in many injuries and some deaths. Many leaders of the green movement were taken into custody and ultimately the demonstrations subsided.

We can analyze the green revolution in terms of the five factors necessary for the success of a revolution. The huge demonstrations protesting the election results indicated intense discontent among many people. It is difficult to estimate what proportion of the population they represented, however. Furthermore, unlike the successful 1978–1979 revolution, the 2009 protests did not include an economically devastating strike by oil workers, which would have put significantly more pressure on the government (Sadeghi 2010). The lack of a strike by oil workers also raises the question of the class composition of the green revolution. Namely, how far did it extend beyond the middle class? Elite dissidence was evident in the 2009 protests. Former Iranian president Mohammad Khatami, for example, supported Mousavi in the election, and prominent figures questioned the validity of the official results. The outside world certainly seemed permissive toward the green revolution. But the perception of foreign support for the demonstrators convinced some Iranians that the protests were serving the interests of imperialist powers. This meant that nationalism could not serve as a unifying factor to unite different classes and groups against the government. Instead, nationalism appeared to keep the population divided and bolster support for Ahmadinejad.

Finally, the Iranian state did not collapse, and its armed forces remained loyal to the regime. Ghadar (2009, 424) points out that the fundamentalist Islamic Revolutionary Guard, estimated around 120,000 in 2009, had taken over large sections of the Iranian economy. This means that the IRG combines major economic, military, and political assets into a powerful, state-supporting, internal structure and that thousands of leaders and members of the IRG are highly committed to preserving its powers on the basis of self-interest. Therefore, unlike the 1978–1979 revolution, the conditions characterizing the green movement did not satisfy all five of the factors necessary for a successful revolution.

Another issue is what an election victory for Mousavi might have meant. It almost certainly would not have constituted a revolution in terms of structural change. Since Mousavi supported the concept of the Islamic Republic, as polls suggest most Iranians do (Leverett and Leverett 2013), any changes he might have initiated would likely have been more in the nature of reforms. And it is unlikely that Mousavi would have significantly modified Iran's nuclear energy policy, since the vast majority of

Iranians believe that Iran has a sovereign right to enrich uranium (Kodmani 2008, 204). Iranians view international concerns about Iran's nuclear program as extremely hypocritical, since there is no comparable reaction to Israel, which is widely believed to possess nuclear weapons and the means to deliver them.

Nevertheless, the green revolution was a major antigovernment protest. Future efforts to modify Iran's political system appeared likely.

Iranian International Relations

Iran under President Ahmadinejad developed friendly relationships and economic and technological ties with other nations critical of the US such as Venezuela, Bolivia, Russia, and China. Venezuela and Iran agreed to work together to cooperate on energy related projects. The two nations established an entity called VENIROGC to develop joint projects in third world countries, such as an oil refinery in Syria (Southern Pulse 2010). Iran has provided aid to the Shia Hezbollah in Lebanon and the Sunni Islamist party Hamas among the Palestinians.

After civil war broke out in Syria in 2011 (see Chapter 11), Iran provided assistance to the Syrian regime (Evans 2013). This reportedly included billions of dollars of economic aid and Iranian military officers. In the Syrian civil war, the rebels fighting the Iranian backed government included people trying to establish a genuinely democratic government and also Syrians aiming to establish a Sunni fundamentalist Islamic state hostile to Shia Iran. The Islamist rebels received the support of thousands of Sunni volunteers from other countries (Maguire 2013). Sunni monarchies reportedly provided financial assistance to the opponents of the Syrian regime. So the Syrian civil war became in part a proxy war between Shia Iran and Sunni Saudi Arabia and other Arab monarchies.

Iran was disappointed when Russia and China supported UN Resolution 1929 (2010), which imposed new sanctions on Iran with the goal of preventing it from producing its own nuclear fuel (MacFarquhar 2010). The Security Council voted twelve in favor, with Brazil and Turkey opposing and Lebanon abstaining. The resolution restricted military- or nuclear-related commerce, including banning the sale to Iran of combat aircraft, attack helicopters, missiles, warships, large caliber artillery, and battle tanks. The resolution deterred international financial transactions with certain military- and technology-related organizations dominated by the Islamic Revolutionary Guard, which controls Iran's nuclear program. It also required nations to inspect planes and ships traveling to or from Iran suspected of carrying banned materials and to restrict the travel and freeze the assets of forty-one Iranians, including the head of the Isfahan Nuclear Technology Center (United Nations 2010). The European Union imposed new sanctions against Iran in July 2012 by refusing to purchase Iranian oil and by curtailing financial transactions (Torbat 2012).

Sanctions imposed on Iran had serious impacts. Iran was denied access to approximately $100 billion of its assets in foreign accounts, including payments for much of its exported oil (Weinberg and McClam 2013). Iran was limited to selling only about a million barrels of oil per day. This cost the Iranian economy about $4 billion a month, and unemployment was estimated at 24 percent in 2013 (Sayah, Yan, and Levs 2013). Without the oil income, Iran's government was running a $35 billion per year deficit. In addition, Iran's restricted access to the world banking system contributes to a 50 percent annual inflation rate, about twenty-five times that of the US in 2013.

The sanctions also had a significant negative impact on health and health care (International Institute for Peace, Justice and Human Rights 2013). While the sanctions do not ban the sale of medicines and medical devices to Iran, the economic impact of the sanctions makes it difficult for Iranians to afford medicines for diseases like cancer and asthma. Iranian hospitals often cannot afford to buy needed equipment. And many people lack the ability to pay for treatment not covered by their medical insurance, often as high as 20–30 percent of the costs.

THE 2013 IRANIAN ELECTION

In the June 2013 Iranian presidential election, President Mahmoud Ahmadinejad was legally barred from seeking a third consecutive term. The election pitted Hassan Rouhani, a politically moderate cleric, against five conservative candidates (Al Jazeera 2013). Rouhani stated the he favored commitment and growth over extremism. He also advocated a conciliatory rather than confrontational approach towards the US and other nations with which Iran has had disagreements. Rouhani won the election with about 51 percent of the vote compared to about 17 percent for the distant second-place finisher Bager Qalibaf, the mayor of Tehran (BBC 2013). Rouhani's electoral win set the stage for new efforts to bring an agreement between Iran and the US and its allies concerning Iran's nuclear program.

THE 2013 IRANIAN NUCLEAR AGREEMENT

After Rouhani assumed Iran's presidency in August, Iran and the US continued secret negotiations begun earlier to reach an agreement regarding Iran's nuclear energy program. The initial agreement, which was supposed to lead to a comprehensive settlement of the nuclear energy controversy and the complete lifting of sanctions against Iran, was announced on November 24, 2013 (Arkin 2013; Sayah, Yan and Levs 2013; Weinberg and McClam 2013). Iran agreed not to enrich uranium above 5 percent. This is far below the level of enrichment necessary for making a nuclear bomb. However, this compromise seems to implicitly confirm Iran's right to continue to enrich uranium as long as the 5 percent level is not exceeded. Iran also agreed to neutralize the uranium it has already enriched to almost 20 percent, stop expansion of enrichment capacity, cease work on its plutonium reactor, and permit inspection of its nuclear facilities. The agreement, which covers a six-month period of further negotiations, allows Iran to earn $4.2 billion dollars from the sale of its oil. During the six-month period Iran also gets to import airplane parts as well as equipment for its auto industry. The Iranians also get to trade in metals, including gold, and are allowed access to $400 million of Iran's invested funds to pay tuition and other costs for Iranian students in other countries. This includes about 8,700 Iranians attending colleges in the US (Weinberg and McClam 2013). The agreement was estimated to provide Iran with $7 billion in relief from sanctions over the six-month term.

SUMMARY AND ANALYSIS

The motivation temporarily unifying diverse pro-revolution groups was the desire to oust the shah and free Iran from foreign domination. Several distinct revolutionary elites developed. The fundamentalist branch of the Shia clergy believed that God, through the ulama, must govern society. This variety of elite opposition constituted potentially effective leadership for the masses because the clergy espoused an ideology and value system already shared by most Iranians. Furthermore, they constituted a network of tens of thousands with control over thousands of mosques and hundreds of bazaars as possible sites for community political organization. The fundamentalists viewed their belief system as God's creation and their plan as God's intention. This had great appeal. It provided poor Iranians with a sense of moral superiority to the humanly created cultures and ideologies of the technologically advanced societies. As the shah became progressively identified with foreign interests, the fundamentalist clergy appeared to many to be the true representatives of Iran's traditional culture and historical identity.

Whereas the fundamentalist clergy were recruited from Iran's traditional middle class, other revolutionary elites came from the nation's modern middle class. But when the opportunity for revolution arose, most of the relatively secular and Westernized anti-shah groups in this category were unable to effectively communicate with, much less mobilize, the Iranian masses.

Most important in determining the precise ideological direction of the antimonarchal revolution was the fact that the movement's primary leader was a fundamentalist, Ayatollah Khomeini. Khomeini's adamant refusal to compromise with the shah, despite the monarch's massive military and economic power, appealed to the Iranian Shia faithful, schooled in the legendary martyrdom of Imam Hussein. Khomeini rewarded their loyalty by developing a successful "technology of revolution" tailored to the culture and psychology of Shia Iran. The ayatollah instructed the faithful to use the forty-day-interval mourning processions for the martyrs of previous demonstrations and those religious holidays commemorating sacrifice or heroic deeds as opportunities for new and ever larger protests. He called on his followers to offer themselves in martyrdom before the shah's soldiers, knowing the shared religious significance of resulting deaths would gradually demoralize the armed forces and ultimately destroy the coercive capacity of the monarchal regime.

When Khomeini's tactics worked, many Iranians concluded that to defeat the shah's worldly might, the ayatollah must indeed be endowed with divine powers. Having witnessed or even participated in this fantastic achievement, many of the faithful were thereafter much inclined to seek out Khomeini's point of view on important post-revolutionary matters and follow his advice. Consequently, when conflicts developed among former revolutionary allies, Khomeini's advocacy of a political system in which both parties and candidates had to be approved by clerical leaders and in which final authority rested in the hands of the clergy ensured the defeat of alternative revolutionary elites.

The large majority of the rural population received either no land or not enough to constitute viable commercial farms through the shah's white revolution. Many of the poorest, who were generally strongly religious, migrated to the booming cities during the 1960s and 1970s; thus at the time of the revolution 45 percent of Iran's people lived in urban areas, which would constitute the battleground for the Iranian revolution.

Though the standard of living improved for the poor, it rose much faster for other classes, resulting in greater inequality and a sense of injustice among the urban working and lower classes. Discontent increased markedly after the mid-1970s as a result of high inflation, increased unemployment, and lowered wages. Hostility toward the shah's regime intensified because many of the shah's wealthy supporters displayed conspicuously expensive lifestyles and abandoned Islamic religious practices. The shah's attempt to control religion and reduce its traditional social and political influence was a cause of outrage for many, since Islam, more than providing a sense of identity, constituted the psycho-cultural mechanism through which most Iranians coped with and understood life. Once the wave of protests began in early 1978, the anger of the urban poor was heightened by the repeated slaughter of participants.

Inherent flaws as well as circumstantial factors contributed to the deterioration of the coercive capacity of the shah's regime. The National Front government's effort to reduce the shah's power ended in 1953, in part because of foreign intervention. This fact impaired the legitimacy of the shah's rule. Some of the shah's economic policies and attempts to modify or control religious institutions and traditions deprived his regime of the support of many landlords, bazaar merchants, and ulama who had backed his overthrow of Mossadeq's government. Without the loyalty of these groups, the existence of the shah's state depended largely on its ability to suppress opposition groups, its support from domestic and foreign business-people, the backing of the United States, and oil revenue, which paid for weapons, fed the shah's patronage system of military and industrial elites, and bought the temporary complacency of the masses. Thus the regime was seriously weakened after 1976, when oil income failed to keep pace with the level of expenditure and the regime lost the capacity to improve the physical well-being of its citizens.

One key factor in the deterioration of the shah's regime was his relaxation of restrictions on political activities in 1977 in reaction to pressure from the US; moreover, he was under the mistaken impression that his popular support was much greater and his opposition much weaker than they actually were. Reduction of repressive measures and the belief that the shah no longer had the unconditional support of the United States encouraged anti-shah forces to regroup, expand, and demand increasingly far-reaching concessions, which eventually could not be met without endangering the monarchy. The regime was shaken by the religiously oriented confrontation tactics orchestrated by Ayatollah Khomeini, which succeeded in crippling the shah's military.

Foreign powers influenced the development and the success of the revolution. The Carter administration's demands for the shah to improve the human rights situation by relaxing restrictions on dissent contributed to mounting revolutionary pressures in 1977 and 1978. But even three weeks after the Black Friday Massacre of September 8, 1978, a CIA report asserted that the shah would stay actively in power for at least another ten years (Hiro 1987, 312). President Carter's human rights pressures on the shah, his continued support for the shah (which infuriated Khomeini and many other Iranians), and his decision not to intervene militarily to preserve the monarchy may all have been influenced by the incorrect assessment of the shah's ability to stay in power. The Carter administration eventually accepted the shah's departure rather passively. But in September 1980 Iraq attacked Iran, with the goal of ending the Islamic Republic form of government. The Iraqi assault, rather than weakening the Islamic Republic, bolstered it by inflaming Iranian nationalism.

During the 1980s Iran endured civil war, confrontation with the US, eight years of devastating war with Iraq, and finally the death of the revolution's charismatic leader, Ayatollah Khomeini. The post-Khomeini leadership faced enormous economic problems and continued US hostility, ostensibly because Iran fostered fundamentalist terrorism. But the US also feared that Iran's revolution threatened the survival of the oil-rich monarchies and consequently effective US control over much of the region's vast energy resources.

Following Iraq's defeat in 1991 by the US-led coalition, Iran emerged as the most powerful Islamic power in the region. Iran, however, was confronted by Israel's suspected nuclear arsenal and by likely permanent facilities to accommodate any future US interventions in Saudi Arabia, Kuwait, or neighboring countries. The triumph of Iranian Islamic fundamentalists against the shah's regime was widely viewed as a victory over the world's number one superpower, the United States. Islamic fundamentalists were encouraged by Islamic success in Iran to fight against the Soviet Union in Afghanistan. The defeat of the USSR there contributed to the Communist Party's loss of power and the disintegration of the Soviet Union in 1991.

Osama bin Laden organized the Al Qaeda network among the tens of thousands of Islamic volunteers who fought in Afghanistan. When after the 1990 Iraqi invasion of Kuwait the Saudi royal family allowed US military forces to be stationed in Saudi Arabia, bin Laden and Al Qaeda launched attacks against the United States, including the September 11, 2001, destruction of the World Trade Towers.

Iran opposed the Sunni fundamentalist extremists who took over most of neighboring Afghanistan in 1996 and assisted the Northern Alliance, a group that resisted the Taliban and proved of great value to American forces when the US invaded Afghanistan in late 2001. But in the lead-up to the US invasion of Iraq, the Bush administration alienated Iran by referring to it as a member of the so-called axis of evil with North Korea and Saddam Hussein's Iraq. Bush's statement appeared to undermine the reform movement in Iran and contribute to the election of conservative Mahmoud Ahmadinejad as president in 2005.

President Barack Obama attempted a less confrontational approach but backed increased UN sanctions regarding Iran's nuclear energy program. In 2009 Mir-Hossein Mousavi's green presidential campaign challenged Ahmadinejad's bid for reelection. When Ahmadinejad was declared the winner, hundreds of thousands took to the streets in the biggest antigovernment mass mobilizations, the green revolution, since the 1978–1979 revolution. Although the protest movement failed to bring about a complete recount of the votes, it likely contributed to building a foundation for a more democratic Iran in the future.

The Arab uprisings that began in 2010–2011 led to civil war in Syria. Iran provided assistance to the regime in its fight against rebels. In 2012, the European Union, concerned about Iran's nuclear program, intensified economic sanctions. In June 2013, Iranians elected a new president, a moderate cleric Hassan Rouhani, who promised to try to ease tension with the US and Britain and promote international reconciliation. President Rouhani visited the United Nations General Assembly in New York and had a brief telephone conversation with President Obama, the first such contact between leaders of Iran and the US since the 1979 Iranian revolution. In November the US and Iran announced an initial agreement to end conflict over Iran's nuclear energy program and begin the process of easing economic sanctions against Iran.

IRANIAN REVOLUTION: CHRONOLOGY OF MAJOR EVENTS

1906 Iran's first constitution establishes a parliament

1926 Reza Khan founds Pahlavi dynasty

1941 Britain and the Soviet Union occupy Iran and force Reza Shah to abdicate in favor of his son, Muhammad

1951 Iran's legislature votes to nationalize the Anglo-Iranian Oil Company

1953 Mossadeq's National Front government overthrown; shah establishes dictatorship

1957 SAVAK organized

1963 Protests against the shah's white revolution; Ayatollah Khomeini jailed (expelled from Iran in 1964)

1971 Fedayeen and Mujahideen guerrilla groups are formed and launch attacks on the shah's regime

1973 Arab-Israeli war and oil price rise; much of Iran's oil income used for advanced weapons

1977 Carter makes US aid conditional on improved human rights situation; the shah eases repression but enacts economic austerity program

1978 Shah's government slanders Ayatollah Khomeini; protesters killed by shah's forces; series of growing massive protests against the shah's regime

1979 The shah flees Iran on January 16; Ayatollah Khomeini returns to Iran on February 1; militants seize US embassy and hostages; Constitution of the Islamic Republic ratified

1980 Iraq invades Iran in September

1981 US hostages freed in January; open conflict between the IRP and the Mujahideen; Mujahideen and most other opponents of the IRP suppressed over the next two years

1988 Iran-Iraq war ends

1989 Ayatollah Khomeini dies and is succeeded by Hojatolislam Khamenei as Iran's religious leader

1990 Iraq invades Kuwait

1991 First Gulf War; United States and its allies defeat Iraq

1997 Moderate Mohammad Khatami elected president of Iran, defeating fundamentalist candidate

2001 September 11—Al Qaeda terrorist attacks take place against the United States

2002 January 29—In State of the Union address President George W. Bush calls Iran a member of the "axis of evil" nations, angering many Iranians

2003 March—United States and its allies invade and occupy Iraq

2005 Iranians elect fundamentalist-supported Mahmoud Ahmadinejad their new president

2009 Ahmadinejad officially reelected; opponents charge vote fraud and launch sustained protests known as the green revolution, which the government attempts to suppress

2010 UN imposes new penalties on Iran because of its nuclear program

2011 Iran begins aiding the Syrian regime during the Syrian civil war

2012 European Union intensifies sanctions against Iran

2013 In June, moderate cleric Hassan Rouhani elected president of Iran

2013 In November, Iran, the US, and other nations reach an initial agreement on Iran's nuclear program

References and Further Readings

Abrahamian, Ervand. 1982. *Iran Between Two Revolutions*. Princeton Studies on the Near East. Princeton, NJ: Princeton University Press.

———. 1985. "The Guerrilla Movement in Iran, 1963–77." In Haleh Afshar, ed., *Iran: A Revolution in Turmoil*. Albany: State University of New York Press.

———. 1989. *The Iranian Mojahedin*. New Haven, CT: Yale University Press.

Al Jazeera. 2013. "Iran Celebrates Rouhani's Presidential Win." June 16. www.aljazeera.com/indepth/spotlight/iranelections.

Ansari, Ali M. 2003. *Modern Iran Since 1921: The Pahlavis and After*. Upper Saddle River, NJ: Pearson Education.

———. 2010. "Last Year's Iranian Presidential Election: Urban Myths Revisited." *World Today*, July. www.chathamhouse.org.uk/files/16737_july2010_iran.pdf.

Ansari, Ali, Daniel Berman, and Thomas Rintoul. 2009. *Preliminary Analysis of the Voting Figures in Iran's 2009 Presidential Election*. Chatham House, June 21. www.chathamhouse.org.uk/publications/papers/view/-/id/755.

Arkin, Daniel. 2013. "How Did That Happen? What You Need to Know About the Iran Nuclear Deal." NBC News, November 24. http://worldnews.nbcnews.com/_news/2013/11/24/21596267-how-did-that-happen-what-you-need-to-know-about-the-iran-nuclear-deal?lite.

Bakhash, Shaul. 1984. *The Reign of the Ayatollahs: Iran and the Islamic Revolution*. New York: Basic.

BBC News. June 15, 2013. "Hasan Rouhani Wins Iran Presidential Election." www.bbc.co.uk/news/world-middle-east-22916174.

Black, Ian. 2009. "A Devastating Defeat for Iran's Green Revolution." *Guardian*, June 14. www.guardian.co.uk/world/2009/jun/14/iran-tehran-election-results-riots.

Central Intelligence Agency (CIA). 2014. "Iran." In *World Factbook*. www.cia.gov/library/publications/the-world-factbook/geos/ir.html.

Diba, Farhad. 1986. *Mohammad Mossadegh: A Political Biography*. London: Croom Helm.

Ghadar, Fariborz. 2009. "Behind Iran's Crackdown, an Economic Coup." *Current History* 108 (December): 424–425, 427–428.

Graham, Robert. 1979. *Iran: The Illusion of Power*. New York: St. Martin's.

Green, Jerold D. 1982. *Revolution in Iran: The Politics of Countermobilization*. New York: Praeger.

Hiro, Dilip. 1987. *Iran Under the Ayatollahs*. London: Routledge & Kegan Paul.

Hooglund, Eric J. 1982. *Land and Revolution in Iran, 1960–1980*. Austin: University of Texas Press.

Hussain, Asaf. 1985. *Islamic Iran: Revolution and Counter-Revolution*. New York: St. Martin's.

International Institute for Peace, Justice, and Human Rights (IIPJHR). 2013. "The Impact of Sanctions on the Iranian People's Healthcare System." IIPJHR, October 18. www.globalresearch.ca/the-impact-of-sanctions-on-the-iranian-peoples-healthcare-system/5354773.

Keddie, Nikki R. 1981. *Roots of Revolution: An Interpretive History of Modern Iran*. New Haven, CT: Yale University Press.

Khomeini, Ruholla. 1981. *Islam and Revolution: Writings and Declarations of Imam Khomeini*. Trans. and annotated by Hamid Algar. Berkeley: Mizan.

Kinzer, Stephen. 2008. *All the Shah's Men*. New York: Wiley.

Kodmani, Bassma. 2008. "Clearing the Air in the Middle East." *Current History* 107 (May): 201–206.

Leverett, Flynt, and Hilary Mann Leverett. 2013." The Real Challenge from Iran." *The Nation*, February 25. www.globalresearch.ca/the-impact-of-sanctions-on-the-iranian-peoples-healthcare-system/5354773.

MacFarquhar, Neil. 2010. "UN Approves New Sanctions to Deter Iran." *New York Times*, June 9. www.nytimes.com/2010/06/10/world/middleeast/10sanctions.html.

Maguire, Mairead. 2013. "Report on Syria–Noble Prize Laureate Mairead Maguire: The Syrian State Is Under a Proxy War Led by Foreign Countries." *Global Research*, May 27. http://globalresearch.ca/report-on-syria-nobel-peace-laureate-mairead-maguire-the-syrian-state-is-under-a-proxy-war-led-by-foreign-countries/5336569?print=1.

Milani, Mohsen M. 1988. *The Making of Iran's Islamic Revolution: From Monarchy to Islamic Republic*. Boulder: Westview.

———. 1994. *The Making of Iran's Islamic Revolution: From Monarchy to Islamic Republic*. 2nd ed. Boulder: Westview.

Najmabadi, Afsaneh. 1987. *Land Reform and Social Change in Iran*. Salt Lake City: University of Utah Press.

New York Times. June 6, 1988. "Teheran Said to Reassess the Future of Its Dream," A1.

———. June 20, 1988. "Iraqi-Backed Army Attacks Iranian City," A8.

————. March 31, 1989. "The War Over, Iraq's Ruler Announces Plans for Liberalization," A5.

————. May 22, 1989. "Son of Khomeini Gains Authority," A1.

————. June 5, 1989. "Iran Quickly Appoints Successor to Khomeini," A1.

————. July 1, 1990. "Islamic Fundamentalism Is Winning Votes," E5.

————. July 6, 1990. "Iran's Chief Links Aid to Better Ties," A2.

————. August 16, 1990. "Iraq Seeks Peace with Iran, Turning Back Spoils of War in Move to End Its Isolation," A1.

————. January 6, 1991. "Kurds Routinely, and Easily, Smuggle Food from Iran to Iraq," A5.

————. November 8, 1994. "Palestinian Religious Militants: Why Their Ranks Are Gaining Strength," A1.

————. January 25, 1995. "Palestinian 'Martyrs,' All Too Willing," A8.

————. April 1, 1995. "Christopher Proposes Tighter Curbs on Trade with Iran," 5.

————. June 18, 2009. "A Different Iranian Revolution." www.nytimes.com/2009/06/19 /opinion/19shane.html.

Obama, Barack. 2009. Videotaped Remarks by the President in Celebration of Nowruz. White House, March 20. http://www.whitehouse.gov/the_press_office /videotaped-remarks-by-the-president-in-celebration-of-nowruz.

————. 2010. Remarks of President Obama Marking Nowruz. White House, March 20. www.whitehouse.gov/the-press-office/remarks-president-obama-marking-nowruz.

Sadeghi, Eskandar. 2010. "Iran's Greens Continue to Meander." *Guardian*, June 12. www. guardian.co.uk/commentisfree/2010/jun/12/iran-green-movement-weaknesses.

Sayah, Reza, Holly Yan, and Josh Levs. 2013. "Iran Reaches Nuclear Deal With World Leaders—Now What? CNN, November 25. http://www.cnn.com/2013/11/25/world /meast/iran-nuclear-deal/index.html.

Simone, Samira. 2009. "Feared Basij Militia Has Deep History in Iranian Conflict." CNN, June 22. www.cnn.com/2009/WORLD/meast/06/22/iran.basij.militia.profile /index.html.

Southern Pulse. 2010. "Energy Cooperation Drives a Murky Venezuela-Iran Relationship." OilPrice.com, June 6. oilprice.com/Geo-Politics/International/Energy -Cooperation-Drives-a-Murky-Venezuela-Iran-Relationship.html.

Torbat, Akbar E. 2012. "EU Embargoes Iran Over the Nuke Issue." World News Daily, July 8. www.informationclearinghouse.info/article31795.htm.

United Nations. 2010. Resolution 1929 (Non-Proliferation). daccess-dds-ny.un.org/doc /UNDOC/GEN/N10/396/79/PDF/N1039679.pdf.

Weinberg, Ali, and Erin McClam. 2013. "Easing of Iran Sanctions Will Do Little to Lift Crippled Economy, Experts Say." NBC News, November 25. http://worldnews.nbcnews .com/_news/2013/11/25/21611878-easing-of-iran-sanctions-will-do-little-to-lift-crippled -economy-experts-say?lite.

WorldPublicOpinion.org. 2009. "Iranian Public on Current Issues." September. www
.worldpublicopinion.org/pipa/pdf/sep09/IranUS_Sep09_rpt.pdf.

SELECTED DVD, FILM, AND VIDEOCASSETTE DOCUMENTARIES

See "Purchase and Rental Sources" at the end of this volume for information on how to
obtain the following resources and for full names of media companies and other organizations listed here as abbreviations.

Anatomy of a Coup: The CIA in Iran. 2000. 50 min. AETV (History Undercover). CIA in
    Iran during the 1953 coup in support of the monarchy.

Blood and Oil. 2008. 52 min. Amazon.com.

Bush's War. 2008. 270 min. DVD. Amazon.com. Bush administration invasion of Iraq.

A Death in Tehran. 2010. 60 min. PBS. Amazon.com. Iran's largest protests since the
    revolution.

Iran and the West. 2009. Three parts: 23 min., 23 min., and 26 min. BBC.

Mohammed Reza Pahlavi: Politics of Oil. 1980. 24 min. Color film. BU, UIOWA, IU,
    UMINN, PSU, SYRU, UNEV-R. Covers the rise and fall of the shah.

Oliver's Army with Eric Mendelson. 1987. 28 min. PTTV. Iran-contra operation.

Osama Bin Laden. 50 min. BIO.

Saddam Hussein. 50 min. Biography. BIO.

The Secret Government: The Constitution in Crisis. 1987. 90 min. SUN. Investigation into
    secret government activities, including the Iran-contra operation.

Soldiers of God. 1998. 46 min. CNN Cold War Series, Episode 20. Islamic revolutionaries
    and fighters in Iran and Afghanistan. Truman Library.

8

Islamic Revolutionary
Movements

By the late 1970s, after the appeal of Arab nationalist and Marxist-Leninist ideologies had declined, another transnational revolutionary movement, Islamic fundamentalism, began to spread rapidly and score political victories or pose serious threats to governments. One version emerged from the Shia branch of Islam largely through the religious interpretations of Iran's Ayatollah Ruhollah Khomeini. Khomeini's call for a government in which clerical leaders would play a leading role contributed to the elimination of the Iranian monarchy and the creation of the Iranian Islamic Republic. Shia fundamentalism had significant international effects: Its victory in Iran over a government backed by the United States, the world's most powerful nation, attracted many to conservative versions of Islam and encouraged Islamic fundamentalists, both Shia and Sunni, to aspire to achieving political goals.

Shia fundamentalism was limited to places where the Shia were a major component of the population, such as Iraq and Lebanon. But fundamentalist movements among the Sunni also began to have major political impacts from the early 1980s on, including the 1987 creation of Hamas among the Arab Palestinians, the 1988 formation of Al Qaeda among Islamic volunteers in the Afghan war against the Soviets, and the 1994 founding of the Taliban movement in Afghanistan. The victory of Islamic fundamentalism in Iran also alerted the secular republican and monarchal governments in the Middle East to the threat of fundamentalism. Non-Islamic nations either supported secular governments against the fundamentalists or fundamentalists against secular political leaders, depending on the self-interests of the non-Islamic nations.

HISTORICAL BACKGROUND OF ISLAMIC FUNDAMENTALISM

The term "fundamentalism" was first applied in the 1920s to US Christian groups who believed in a literal interpretation of the Bible (Halliday 1998; Joffé 2006). Christian fundamentalists, for example, denied the theory of evolution because the Bible said that God created the world and all its creatures in six days. Later the term was used to refer to religious conservatives in other faiths who also believed in a literal interpretation of their sacred texts and desired to bring government and society into greater alignment with their beliefs. In the case of Islam, it came to refer to movements that proposed replacing relatively secular governments with political systems integrating religion and state and transforming society by adopting characteristics of the original Islamic community.

One important Islamic fundamentalist (Islamist) movement was launched by Muhammad al Wahhab (1705–1791), a Sunni leader who held "that no doctrine or practice originating after the end of the third Islamic century would be acceptable" (Joffé 2006). Wahhab and his followers allied with the Saud family in 1744 and proved to be of great assistance in helping the family represent its military effort to conquer other groups and create what became known as the nation of Saudi Arabia as a crusade to purify Islam. The victory of the Saud family resulted in Wahhabi Islam becoming the major form of Islam in Saudi Arabia. Requiring the continued support of the very conservative Wahhabi clergy, especially problematic after Western interests established first a technical presence to exploit the country's great oil resource and later a military deployment, the Saudi royal family provided hundreds of millions for the building of impressive mosques in Saudi Arabia and in other Islamic nations and for Islamic religious schools around the world. In many of these schools a form of conservative Islam similar to Wahhabi Islam was taught to children who often would otherwise have received little or no education at all. Tens of thousands grew up to participate in later Islamist movements.

Napoleon's 1789 invasion and occupation of Egypt spurred the development of contemporary forms of Islamic fundamentalism by initiating the modern European domination of the Middle East and North Africa. The French victory shocked Muslims by demonstrating that Christian Europeans had achieved a marked advantage in technology and weapons. Some Islamic scholars concluded that Islamic societies had grown corrupt, and the solution to European imperialism was a return to the faith and practices of the Rashidun era, the time of the "rightly guided" caliphs. This was the period of the first four caliphs or leaders of the Islamic community, those who had personally known the Prophet Muhammad.

A leading proponent of a return to the early form of Islam was Jamal al Din al Afghani (1839–1897), who began the Salafist movement. *Salaf* here refers to the "ancestors" who lived during the Rashidun period. Jamal believed that returning to the Islam of the Rashidun period would revitalize and strengthen Islamic societies in the face of the European threat. This form of Islam contained the political and moral concepts that, if adopted, could help Islamic societies modernize and accomplish technological achievements similar to those of Europe while remaining true to Islamic values. Thus this movement was at once backward looking and forward looking, in that it sought solutions to the problem of Islamic modernization in an idealized distant past.

Further impetus to Islamic fundamentalist movements was provided by the British Balfour Declaration of 1917, which advocated establishing a homeland for the Jewish people in Palestine, whose residents at the time were overwhelmingly Islamic Arabs. This perceived assault of European imperialism was almost immediately followed in 1918, at the conclusion of World War I, by British and French occupation of Islamic Arab lands, which had previously been part of the Ottoman Empire. These events led to the development of another version of Islamic fundamentalism, Ikhwan Muslimin (the Muslim Brotherhood), described by some as the first explicitly political Islamic fundamentalist movement. The Muslim Brotherhood was founded by Hassan al-Banna (1906–1949) in Egypt in 1928. Its leaders advocated the nonviolent change of Islamic societies in a fundamentalist direction, but offshoots or associated movements, such as Gam'iyat Islamiyya (Islamic Groups), Islamic Jihad (Islamic Holy War), and Hamas (the Islamic Resistance Movement), sometimes turned to violence.

Joffé (2006, 456) states that the Muslim Brotherhood "became the model for all subsequent Islamist movements" among Sunni Muslims. In line with the Salafi approach, the leaders of Ikhwan Muslimin believed that the best way to strengthen Islamic societies against European domination was by resurrecting the earliest form of Islam. Once this transformation was achieved, Islamic societies could successfully modernize and compete with Western societies. Joffé argues against the Huntington (1993) and Lewis (2002) perspectives, which suggest the "doctrinal and cultural content of Islam" inherently necessitates a confrontation with Western societies (Joffé 2006, 454). Rather, Joffé asserts that the rise of Islamist revolutionary political movements followed a historical pattern in which the "profound asymmetries" between developed and developing countries were the real cause of revolutionary movements and resulting political conflict. According to this analysis, people react to domination and exploitation by the more powerful nations by seeking within their indigenous cultural patterns an ideology that can unite people of various social classes and backgrounds against the perceived external aggression.

Nationalism has served this purpose in a number of societies, for example, in the case of the Vietnamese and Cuban revolutions. But after the crushing defeat of several Arab nations by Israel in the 1967 Six Day War, Arab nationalism, which had once offered the promise of uniting into one nation the many states whose people spoke the Arab language, lost much of its appeal. Instead, revolutionary ideologies based on Islam began to grow in popularity for several reasons. First, while also drawn from indigenous culture, Islam in theory had the potential to unite an even greater number of people across class, racial, ethnic, and national boundaries than Arab nationalism. Second, the commitment and spirit of self-sacrifice so important in revolutionary soldiers and supporters as they confront initially overwhelming odds conceivably would be easier to generate with a religiously grounded ideology in which participants believe they are doing God's will and could also look forward to a glorious reward after death. Finally, as noted in Chapter 7 on the Iranian revolution, for those enduring oppression and deprivation, an Islamist-type ideology offers its adherents a level of psychological comfort that the more secularly oriented ideologies such as nationalism could not provide: a sense of pride, dignity, and self-worth deriving from the concept that they share a value and belief system created by God that is immeasurably superior to all other cultures, including those of the more technologically advantaged nations.

According to Joffé (2006):

> "Islamic fundamentalist revolution" is often a culturally determined political response to perceived external threat. It appears to be revolutionary because one of its objectives is a domestic transformation of the political scene on the grounds that only in that way can the external threat be effectively countered: it had been a domestic political failure that had allowed the threat to develop in the first place. Indeed, this, too, is nothing new. One of the justifications for extreme nationalism and Fascism in Europe was that this was the only way in which the resources of the nation could be mobilized to counter internationalist cultural and political threats, whether from communism or other foreign conspiracies.

Joffé's analysis is consistent with Skocpol and Trimberger's structural theory of revolution, discussed in Chapter 1, which specified that the most powerful conditions for revolution have occurred in technologically inferior states facing overpowering military and economic pressures from advanced nations. Inability to resist foreign aggression reduced the perceived legitimacy of the pre-revolutionary regimes, which in many cases had fallen under the influence of the external powers.

The purpose of such revolutions, according to Skocpol and Trimberger's structural theory, was primarily political: to establish a new political system that would make a less developed society more capable of resisting threats from advanced nations. An essential step in building such a revolution was identifying and propagating a motivational ideology for revolution, in this case Islamic fundamentalist ideology, with the capacity to unite diverse social groups in a common revolutionary effort.

Hassan al-Banna's Muslim Brotherhood was an Islamic movement intended for such a political purpose. Hassan was acting in response to foreign exploitation and to the lack of status and dignity that many Arabs and Muslims suffered. His approach emphasized personal psychological revitalization through embracing the elements of the original, pure form of Islam, which, through the exemplary behavior of Brotherhood members living morally upright lives and manifesting altruism, concern for others, and solidarity and promoting social justice among all Muslims, would help renew Islamic culture in the larger society. The cultural renewal would be a necessary step in the process of modernizing in a manner consistent with Islam and in throwing off the colonial yoke. This approach was in part meant to confront the problem that under colonial domination those Muslims who were educated in modern science and technology also typically underwent a process of secularization or conversion to the culture of the colonizing power. The Brotherhood also advocated reducing inequality and establishing a relatively equalitarian society that was perceived to be consistent with the religious culture of the earliest Muslims.

The Muslim Brotherhood publicly opposed the use of violence. Members of the Brotherhood became concerned with the situation of the Arab Palestinians, who, under British control after World War I, believed that they were being denied the right to self-determination and that their land was being inundated by Zionist settlers intent on establishing a homeland for the Jewish people, a goal supported by the British government in its 1917 Balfour Declaration. The Brotherhood tried to provide assistance to the Palestinians during their work strikes against the British during 1936–1939. War broke out in 1948 between the new state of Israel, which the United Nations had voted to create in 1947, and several Arab countries. Members of the Muslim Brotherhood, who by that time were estimated to number in the hundreds of thousands, and many other Egyptians believed that the Egyptian monarchy, under British influence, refused to mount an effective military effort, contributing to Israel's victory and the flight of hundreds of thousands of Arab Palestinians from their homes. In revenge, members of an extreme faction of the Brotherhood assassinated the Egyptian prime minister in 1948. Apparently in retaliation, secret agents of the government reportedly assassinated Hassan al-Banna in 1949. After 1948 the Egyptian government alternately banned or relegalized the Brotherhood, but several of the Brotherhood's members, splinter factions, and associated groups carried out acts of violence.

An Egyptian member of the Muslim Brotherhood, Sayyid Qutb (1906–1966), along with Pakistani Mawlana Abu al-Mawdudi (1903–1979), who formulated similar ideas, was considered one of the major Sunni fundamentalist theoreticians of the modern era. Qutb's innovations helped transform political Islam into an explicitly revolutionary ideology by providing the religious rationale for the removal of certain Muslim leaders or governments. Qutb (Berman 2003) concluded that by the time of Jesus, regarded by Muslims as a great prophet but not divine, the leaders of Judaism, the guardians of God's revelations to Moses, had distorted their faith into a system of rigid ritualism. This ritualism interfered with the realization of the purpose of the rules revealed to Moses, which was to provide humankind with the proper way to integrate religion and the physical world in a manner that would both fulfill the will of God and gratify the needs inherent in human nature.

Qutb believed the Christians "went too far in rejecting Jewish teachings" (Berman 2003), in particular the code of Moses, which governed aspects of daily life. He argued that the early Christians made what he viewed as the disastrous mistake of importing "into Christianity the philosophy of the Greeks—the belief in a spiritual existence completely separate from physical life, a zone of pure spirit" (Berman 2003). According to Qutb, this theological blunder, the splitting of the "sacred from the secular," led over time to the destructive concept of the separation of church and state. Qutb believed that not only was this opposed to God's intention but such a separation necessarily failed to fulfill the needs of human nature. The result was that, despite their wealth and technology, the people of Western societies were generally unhappy and prone to anxiety, abusing drugs, and exhibiting exploitive criminal behavior.

Fortunately, according to Qutb, God provided Muhammad in the seventh century with a new legal code intended to properly integrate religion and the physical world. The Sharia (Islamic law), therefore, could not be replaced by moral or legal codes developed by governments. Qutb pointed to the Muslim development of the scientific method of inquiry as evidence that early Islam fostered both intellectual and scientific advances. He claimed that attacks by Christian Crusaders from the west and Mongols from the east, as well as the deterioration of the Muslim faith over time, prevented the Muslim world from exploiting the very scientific method that it invented. Instead, Europeans adopted this approach, leading to their great scientific and technological breakthroughs, which eventually allowed European nations and the United States to dominate the world beginning in the nineteenth century.

This domination also permitted European nations and the US to begin contaminating the culture of Muslim societies, often with the collaboration of corrupt rulers, using the notion of separation of church and state. Qutb was, consequently, one of the first Muslim intellectuals to identify not only non-Islamic imperialist nations as the enemy of Islam but also supposedly Muslim rulers or governments that in reality collaborated with the imperialists.

According to Euben, "in contrast to classical doctrine . . . to endure unjust Muslim rule, Mawdudi and Qutb argue that jihad is an urgent imperative . . . between Muslims and so-called Muslims who aid and abet Western supremacy by betraying the precepts of Islamic sovereignty and opening the door to foreign corruption" (2002, 369–370). The radical theological change in this new formulation is that jihad (in the sense of holy war) can be carried out within the community of Islam, not just against aggressive foreign powers. Leaders or governments that serve un-Islamic foreign interests to the detriment of the Islamic faithful must be struggled against and removed from power. According to this perspective, which Qutb developed in his famous book *Milestones*, a Muslim leader "who had transgressed Muslim precepts could be considered non-Muslim," and Muslims had a duty to wage jihad against such a leader or government as well as against external enemies.

Though faced with enormously powerful forces attempting to destroy Islam, Qutb believed that the true Islam of early Muslim society was so inherently superior to other faiths and ideologies, including in its unmatched ability to fulfill human needs and deliver happiness, that it would ultimately triumph and spread to the entire world. In his book *Milestones* he called on young people to form an Islamic vanguard to lead the struggle against external threats and internal traitors to Islam. In response to his teachings, as well as to reported assassination attempts against government officials by members of the Muslim Brotherhood, Sayyid Qutb was imprisoned by Egyptian President Nasser's government from the mid-1950s to the mid-1960s, when he was briefly released. Although he was offered refuge in other Arab nations, Qutb refused to leave Egypt and apparently preferred to become a martyr, setting an example for his estimated 3,000 students when the government executed him in 1966 (Berman 2003). Sayyid's brother, Mohammad Qutb, escaped to Saudi Arabia, where he became a professor of Islamic studies. According to Berman, one of Mohammad Qutb's students was Osama bin Laden. It was probably no accident that bin Laden used Sayyid Qutb's term "vanguard" when he referred to the nineteen men who carried out the September 11, 2001, terrorist attacks in the United States as "a group of vanguard Muslims" (Crenshaw 2001, 432).

Following Qutb's death, some of his followers helped create Gam'iyat Islamiyya (Islamic Groups) and Islamic Jihad (Islamic Holy War), which turned to violence; some of its members later united with Al Qaeda. Others inspired by Qutb's views assassinated Egyptian President Sadat, who had made peace with Israel in 1981. Leaders of these Egyptian groups asserted that the United States must be attacked, since the rulers and governments they sought to overthrow were generally supported and protected by the US. Sayyid Qutb's work, including his enormous *In the Shade of the Qur'an*, written while he was in prison, is widely viewed as a central component of the intellectual foundation for virtually all politically violent Sunni Islamic groups, including Al Qaeda.

FUNDAMENTALISM, MILLENARIANISM, AND REVOLUTIONARY POTENTIAL IN SHIA ISLAM

After the death of Muhammad, the fourth elected caliph was the Prophet's cousin, Ali, the husband of the Prophet's daughter, Fatima. Ali, admired by many as a champion of the poor, was assassinated in 661. Some Muslims came to believe that the Prophet had chosen Ali as his successor and that only descendants of Ali and Fatima were to lead the Islamic faithful. Those who held this view were called Shiat Ali (Partisans of Ali), or Shia. The Shia Muslims called Ali and specific male descendants of Ali and Fatima whom they believed had the right to lead Islam "imams."

The Shia considered the imams to be infallible. Other Muslims rejected the concept that only biological descendants of Ali and Fatima were to lead Islam and that these persons were infallible. Instead, they held that only the Prophet Muhammad was infallible, along with the Word of Allah—the Qur'an—the most important component of the Sunna (tradition) of Islam. According to the Sunnis, since no one after Muhammad was infallible, religious leaders could only interpret the Qur'an to Muslims in the unique context of each historical era.

Most Shia held that there were twelve imams. Twelver Shias believed that the last infallible imam vanished in 873. After his disappearance, there was no longer an infallible leader of Islam. But this will change when the twelfth imam, the Mahdi (hidden imam), returns to lead Islam. In the meantime Islamic scholars (*mujtahid*) were to issue opinions, authoritative but fallible, in matters concerning Islam. Since the Shia believed that the twelfth imam would return to create a socially just Muslim society, various rebellions occurred in Iran over the years led by someone who claimed or was believed to be the Mahdi. Thus revolutionary potential was inherent in this millenarian aspect of Shiism.

According to Rinehart (2006) Shia millenarian rebellions had a recurring theme. All were led by a charismatic figure claiming that Muslims had strayed from the guidance and laws of the Prophet. The Mahdi would reestablish true Islam among the people. Thus Shia millenarian religious movements were generally conservative or fundamentalist in nature, in the sense of leading the people back to a divinely ordained religious and social system.

Ayatollah Khomeini, the main leader of the 1978–1979 Iranian revolution, who may have been influenced by the ideas of Mawdudi and Qutb, had a similar fundamentalist revolutionary message. He was viewed through the prism of Shia millenarianism as a divinely inspired holy man sent by God to liberate the people from the corruption of the shah's regime and from the un-Islamic imperialist masters the shah's government served. Khomeini proclaimed that political power came directly from God and that the new constitution of the Islamic Republic of Iran should give supreme power to a clerically selected Islamic religious leader who represented God in the political system. Another great attraction of Ayatollah Khomeini's message to many Iranians was the sense of psychological security and moral superiority it provided to people who had been exploited and humiliated by their own pre-revolutionary government and by Western imperialist powers. In the face of Western technological and military superiority, Islamic people could feel gratified that their culture was vastly morally superior to the secular, humanly created cultures of more technologically advanced societies. Khomeini's ideas and the example of the successful Iranian revolution helped inspire the creation of the Hezbollah (Party of God) movement among Shia Lebanese (discussed later in this chapter).

CONTEMPORARY REVOLUTIONARY FUNDAMENTALISM IN SUNNA ISLAM: HAMAS, AL QAEDA, TALIBAN

Sunni revolutionary fundamentalist movements had a greater potential to spread than Shia movements because many nations had majority Sunni populations. But there were important differences between Sunni fundamentalist movements and Khomeini's Shia revolution. Ayatollah Khomeini's innovation in the 1970s was to argue that the clergy should play a dominant political role in society as representatives of Allah among the people and as interpreters of the Qur'an. Khomeini's revolution changed the nature of the political system by making clergy the dominant participants in a new republican political system in place of the previous monarchy (Joffé 2006). Church and state would no longer be separated. Instead, under the guidance of the clergy, both the political leaders and the political system would be required to conform to Islamic law.

But some Sunni Islamic movements were even more radical than Khomeini's revolution. The Sunni Taliban movement, discussed below, imposed totalitarian conditions in Afghanistan and enforced a drastically more restrictive form of Islam, particularly with regard to women. And the Sunni Al Qaeda movement, instead of acting only within the context of one nation, attempted to wage a global jihad.

Hamas of Palestine

Hamas (the Islamic Resistance Movement) is one of the fundamentalist-oriented Islamic organizations inspired by the Egyptian Muslim Brotherhood. As Kifner (1996) notes, "Typically, the Brotherhood's strategy is to fight what it sees as Westernization and corruption of Arab governments by running its own schools, hospitals and other services in order to spread its beliefs."

Hamas was founded in 1987 by Sheikh Ahmed Yasin, a teacher who suffered a childhood accident that left him paralyzed and partially blind. Yasin had been supervising educational programs and social services in Gaza when the Palestine Liberation Organization (PLO) launched the first intifada (mass participation uprising) against Israeli occupation. As Palestinian youth flocked to participate in the uprising, Yasin and his associates created Hamas to lend support and to provide young people with an Islamic alternative to the PLO. Article 2 of the August 18, 1988, "Covenant of the Islamic Resistance Movement" (Hamas 1988) stated that "the Islamic Resistance Movement is one of the wings of Moslem Brotherhood in Palestine. Moslem Brotherhood is a universal organization which constitutes the largest Islamic Movement in modern times . . . characterized by its . . . accurate comprehension and its complete embrace of all Islamic concepts of all aspects of life, culture, creed, politics, economics, education." The slogan of Hamas, as stated in Article 8 of the Covenant, is, "Allah is its target, the Prophet is its model, the Koran its constitution: Jihad is its path and death for the sake of Allah is the loftiest of its wishes."

Leaders of Hamas believed that the Palestinian people would have to revitalize their faith in Islam in order to free themselves from Israeli control. First, each person would have to wage "the Greater Jihad . . . of the heart" (Euben 2002, 368), the internal jihad (the personal struggle against oneself to follow the path of God). Then each person would be able, if necessary, to engage in the lesser jihad, the jihad of the sword, the struggle against the enemies of Islam, which, according to Islamic fundamentalists, also includes the requirement to resist corrupt Muslim rulers or governments.

According to Kifner (1996), "in the 1970s and early in the Palestinian uprising, Israel allowed the surging Islamic movement to flourish and even covertly supported it, calculating that Muslim groups would undermine and draw support from Mr. Arafat's P.L.O., which was then the more immediate threat." But in 1989 Israel outlawed Hamas and incarcerated Sheikh Ahmed Yasin.

When the PLO supported the Iraqi invasion of Kuwait in 1990, several oil-rich Arab monarchies cut off their aid to the PLO and instead reportedly provided more assistance to Hamas, which used most of the funds to expand Islamic educational and social services to the huge number of poor Palestinians. By 2003 the Palestinian Ministry of Education estimated that about 65 percent of all schools in Gaza below the level of secondary education were Islamic (Roy 2003, 16). Hamas also received funds from supporters in Europe and the US. While the large majority of Hamas activities involved providing Palestinians with basic necessities of life and other services, Hamas also had a military wing, the Izzadin al-Qassam Brigades, named after a Muslim preacher in Haifa who in the 1930s had led rebellions against Zionist settlers and the British occupation and had died in battle in 1935. Members of the brigade reportedly conducted numerous attacks on Israeli soldiers and civilians, including suicide and bus bombings, during the 1990s and early twenty-first century. In response, some nations labeled Hamas a terrorist organization. Israel killed a number of Hamas leaders. After a failed Israeli attempt to assassinate an important Hamas leader, Khaled Meshal, in Jordan, Israel agreed to free Sheikh Ahmed Yasin in return for the release of its captured Mossad (Israeli Intelligence) agents (Westcott 2000). But in March 2004 an Israeli missile strike succeeded in killing Yasin.

Hamas opposed the US-negotiated attempts at peace agreements between the Palestinians and the Israelis and refused to accept the legitimacy of the existence of the state of Israel. According to Roy (2003), the Al Aqsa intifada, which began on September 28, 2000, provided a new opportunity for Hamas. In retaliation for both Hamas- and PLO-associated attacks, the Israelis disrupted much of the Palestinian Authority's governmental infrastructure, in part because Israel blamed the Palestinian Authority for not suppressing those Palestinians carrying out acts of violence. With the Palestinian Authority crippled, many Palestinians turned to Hamas for help. The new intifada, according to Roy (2003, 13), was in part a "response to seven years of a 'peace' process that not only deepened Palestinian dispossession and deprivation but strengthened Israel's occupation." The US war on terrorism after September 11, 2001, was perceived as further strengthening Israel's freedom to deal harshly with the Palestinians and sabotage the peace process.

Over the next few years, this view, coupled with the perception of corruption within the Palestinian Authority government and the persistent widespread poverty among the Palestinians in the Gaza Strip and the West Bank, which, according to Roy (2003, 19) approached 70 percent below the poverty line and 60 percent unemployment, seemed to increase popular support for Hamas. In January 2006 Hamas won control of the Palestinian parliament defeating Fatah, which had been the major component of the PLO, taking 74 of 132 seats, including 6 won by Hamas women candidates (Fisher 2006). But on June 30, 2006, in an attempt to win the release of a captured Israeli soldier, Israeli forces invaded Palestinian territory and captured a number of Hamas government and party officials, including approximately one-third of Palestinian cabinet members and twenty-three Hamas members of parliament (Erlanger 2006b).

The Bush administration was distressed that Hamas won the election and that Hamas continued to refuse international demands to reject violence, recognize the right of Israel to exist, and accept the terms of previous Israeli-Palestinian peace agreements (Rose 2008). Although several nations stopped or reduced funding to Gaza, Hamas reportedly received hundreds of millions from Iran. The Bush administration, which had previously pushed for the 2006 Palestinian parliamentary election, was now accused of plotting with leaders of Fatah, including Mahmoud Abbas, who had been elected president of the Palestinian Authority in 2005, to overthrow the elected Hamas-dominated government. The plan was reported to include training and weapons for new forces exclusively under Fatah control, President Abbas dismissing parliament and declaring a state of emergency with an emergency government committed to officially renouncing violence and recognizing Israel's right to exist, and a call for new parliamentary elections (Rose 2008).

The new, well equipped Fatah forces were expected to give Abbas the means to crush Hamas resistance. But after part of the plan was published in a Jordanian newspaper, fighting broke out between Hamas and Fatah units. Hamas seized control of Gaza in June 2007, while Abbas and Fatah seized the West Bank, resulting in two Palestinian governments. In the face of loud international condemnation, Israel proceeded to blockade Gaza, banning the importation of certain construction materials but allowing many food items on humanitarian grounds. In response to fighting between Hamas and Israeli forces, including rocket attacks into Israel, Israel launched a devastating three-week invasion of Gaza on December 27, 2008. Israel provoked further international outrage when its troops seized ships carrying relief supplies to Gaza on May 31, 2010, and killed nine civilians, mostly citizens of Turkey, which had been one of Israel's best friends in the region. In response to the resulting unrelenting criticism, Israel eased the blockade by lifting the ban on many consumer goods on July 5, 2010 (Sherwood 2010), but restrictions were maintained on certain construction materials and equipment which the Israeli government stated could also be used to make weapons.

Al Qaeda and Transnational Islamic Fundamentalist Revolution

After Islamic fundamentalists triumphed in the Iranian revolution, Salafi Sunni Islamists were encouraged to join the struggle against the Soviet occupation of Afghanistan, which began in 1979. The USSR had intervened to support a pro-Soviet leftist regime threatened by traditionalist Islamist Afghans. Thousands of volunteers from many countries traveled to Pakistan, where funds from Saudi Arabia and other nations helped pay for equipment and sustenance. The Pakistani intelligence service helped prepare the volunteers to cross the border into Afghanistan.

Abdallah Azzam (1941–1989) was a Palestinian-born professor who received a PhD in Islamic law from al-Azhar University in Egypt. He fought for the Palestinian cause before becoming dissatisfied with what he considered the overly secular orientation of some of its leaders. Subsequently he established a recruiting organization, al-Maktab al-Khidmat (MAK, the Services Office), for bringing young Islamic men to Pakistan to fight in neighboring Afghanistan. In Pakistan, Azzam taught and advised many of the volunteers, including Osama bin Laden, the son of a Saudi Arabian construction company owner, originally from Yemen, who had become a billionaire. Azzam proclaimed that Muslims had lost their former power because they no longer waged jihad against imperialist and culturally subversive nations. It was the personal responsibility of every Muslim to support or participate in jihad, including at the international level, to restore and defend true Islam. Bin Laden not only fought but used his money to aid Islamist fighters and care for war orphans and widows. Islamists won the war after receiving US-supplied, shoulder-fired anti-aircraft missiles to shoot down or drive off low-flying Soviet air-craft. Soviet forces withdrew in 1989. That same year Azzam was killed by a hidden bomb planted by unknown assassins.

During the Afghan conflict, an Egyptian volunteer, Ayman al-Zawahiri, became a close associate of bin Laden. Zawahiri was born to a prominent Egyptian family, some of whose members had been nationally known educators and physicians. Za-wahiri was a brilliant student who became a medical doctor. As a child he became interested in religion. At age fifteen he joined the Muslim Brotherhood. Later he joined the radical, violent Egyptian Islamic Jihad. When Egyptian President Sadat was assassinated by Muslim fundamentalists in 1981, Zawahiri was arrested, along with hundreds of others. Charismatic and fluent in English, he became a spokes-person for many of those imprisoned. While not proven to have participated in the assassination, he was convicted of illegal possession of weapons and sentenced to three years in prison, where he suffered torture. After his release, Zawahiri traveled to Peshawar, Pakistan, where he worked as a surgeon for Islamic fighters wounded in the holy war. There Zawahiri reportedly advocated to bin Laden that the US should be attacked directly, since it provided crucial support for corrupt regimes in Muslim countries, as well as for Israel.

The victory of Islamic forces in Afghanistan further encouraged Islamic funda-mentalists to confront non-Islamic nations and governments in Islamic countries, such as Egypt and Saudi Arabia, that they perceived to be US allies. In 1988 Osama bin Laden and his associates organized a database and communication network for thousands of foreign volunteers who had fought in Afghanistan. This network was later called Al Qaeda (the base or foundation). Soon after the Soviets withdrew from Afghanistan, bin Laden returned to Saudi Arabia, where he was initially wel-comed as a hero. But then Iraq invaded Kuwait in 1990 and appeared to threaten Saudi Arabia. Strongly opposed to the secular Baath Party government of Iraq and President Saddam Hussein, bin Laden offered to recruit as many as 35,000 Al Qaeda members to defend Saudi Arabia against a potential Iraqi invasion (Joffé 2006, 460). But the Saudi royal family declined bin Laden's offer and instead al-lowed the US to deploy large forces to Saudi Arabia and use the country as a base of operations.

The Saudi monarchy's decision was likely based on several factors. First, it is doubtful that bin Laden's forces could have made much difference against an Iraqi invasion. Second, Al Qaeda probably could not have aided significantly in forcing the Iraqis to leave Kuwait. Third, the Saudi royal family was highly dependent on the US for military equipment and training for its armed forces and for other types of assistance and was certainly reluctant to turn down the US request to use Saudi territory to wage war against Iraq. Fourth, neither the US nor the Saudi Arabian monarchy wanted to see Al Qaeda forces in oil-rich, strategically important Saudi

Arabia. The idea of tens of thousands of battle-hardened Islamic fundamentalist fighters, brimming with self-confidence after defeating the Soviets, on Saudi Arabian territory, undoubtedly terrified the royal family and its US and British allies. The Salafi-oriented Al Qaeda leadership favored replacing despotic monarchies with an Islamic government dominated by clerics. Once the Iraqi threat was neutralized, or even before, an Al Qaeda fundamentalist army in Saudi Arabia could have turned on the pro-US royal family.

Bin Laden and other fundamentalists were outraged. Having just fought a long, costly war to drive the Soviets from one Islamic nation, the fundamentalists were betrayed by the Saudi royal family, which allowed another infidel army to occupy the religiously sacred territory of Arabia. Bin Laden claimed the US was establishing a permanent military occupation of the Middle East and its oil resources. For opposing the Saudi monarchy's policies, he was forced to leave the country. He traveled to Sudan and established several businesses. In 1996 he left Sudan for Afghanistan. Al Qaeda and allied Salafi-led Islamist groups launched a series of attacks against the US, including the 1993 truck bombing of the World Trade Towers in New York City.

In February 1998 bin Laden, his second in command, Zawahiri, and leaders of other Islamist extremist organizations announced the formation of the Islamic World Front for the Struggle Against the Jews and the Crusaders, an international global jihad alliance. By this point members of Zawahiri's Egyptian Islamic Jihad had merged with Al Qaeda. In August 1998, Al Qaeda associates bombed the US embassies in Kenya and Tanzania. In 2000, suicide bombers, using a small boat, struck the USS *Cole*. And on September 11, 2001, Al Qaeda associates used hijacked airliners to destroy the New York World Trade Towers and to attack the Pentagon.

The US invaded Afghanistan in October 2001 and ousted the Taliban regime, which had provided training sites for bin Laden and Al Qaeda. In March 2003, the US, Britain, and other nations invaded Iraq, a country that had nothing to do with the 9/11 2001 attacks on the US, justifying the action on false information concerning nonexistent weapons of mass destruction. The war and related conflict took the lives of tens of thousands of Iraqis and more than 4,400 US military men and women. After 2007, the violence declined significantly, and by summer 2010 the US was experiencing more casualties in Afghanistan than Iraq.

By 2006 the structure of the Al Qaeda–led alliance was thought to be highly decentralized, involving groups with somewhat varying versions of Islam. Top leaders such as Osama bin Laden and Ayman al-Zawahiri were in hiding. It seemed that often bin Laden or Zawahiri relied on sending messages of encouragement to followers through the Internet or internationally broadcast video or audio recordings. This suggested that Al Qaeda, rather than being a tightly organized hierarchal organization, was a transnational social movement attempting to spread and popularize its ideas to millions of Muslims who were expected to organize and act with little or no direct Al Qaeda assistance.

One of the most notorious acts of violence attributed to Al Qaeda was the December 27, 2007, assassination of Benazir Bhutto, thought likely to become Pakistan's prime minister in 2008. But the organization regarded her as a major asset of the American government. After her assassination the US increased missile strikes, often from remotely piloted Predator or Reaper aircraft, to kill targets in Pakistan (Schmitt 2010). These strikes were intended to disrupt Al Qaeda efforts to organize attacks against US and allied forces in Afghanistan and Pakistan, such as the suicide bombing attack that killed seven CIA officers at a base in Khost, Afghanistan, on December 30, 2009 (Baer 2010). Individuals trained or inspired by Al Qaeda or allied groups repeatedly attacked US citizens. An Afghan immigrant attempted to bomb the New York City subway system in September 2009; a US army major killed thirteen soldiers at Fort Hood, Texas, on November 5, 2009; a Nigerian man attempted to bomb an airliner arriving in Detroit on December 25, 2009; and a Connecticut Pakistani-American man tried to bomb Times Square on May 1, 2010 (Mazzetti, Tavernise, and Healy 2010). Groups associated with Al Qaeda were also active in Iraq, Mali, Somalia, and Yemen (Aboudi and Evans 2013; Associated Press, June 18, 2010; Lewis and Prieur 2013; Omar 2013).

US intelligence services continuously searched for top Al Qaeda and allied Islamic extremist leaders and killed many of them with missiles launched from unmanned drone aircraft (Ahmed and Sahak 2013). However, innocent civilians were also killed or injured. On May 1, 2011, US Navy SEALs killed Osama bin Laden at his walled compound in Abbottabad, Pakistan (Tapper 2012; Wilson, Whitlock, and Branigin 2011). Information discovered there revealed a plan to kill President Barack Obama and General David Petreaus.

Taliban of Afghanistan

The development of the Taliban (religious students or students of the Book, the Qur'an) movement, its military victories in Afghanistan between 1994 and 1996, and its four-year rule over 90 percent of the country were due to several simultaneously occurring factors.

In the years before 1994, tens of thousands of young men were educated in fundamentalist-oriented Islamist schools, *madrasas,* affiliated with the Deobandi form of Islam. Deobandi Islam, apparently originating in northern India, advocated a purified form of Islam similar to that of the Wahhabis of Saudi Arabia. The intellectual father of the Deobandi movement, Shah Waliullah, was said to have been inspired by the founder of Wahhabism, Muhammad ibn Abdul Wahhab (Rubin 1999, 82). Although from different *madhabs* or legal schools of Sunni Islam (the Deobandi are of the Hanafi school, and the Wahhabi are of the Hanbali school), the Deobandis were "sympathetic to the Wahhabi creed" (Rashid 2000, 90). This was also partly due to Saudi Arabian funding for many *madrasas* in Pakistan and Afghanistan, often run by Deobandi clergy.

The billions of dollars that the Saudis spent spreading Wahhabi Islam around the world through thousands of Wahhabi missionaries and supporting religious schools and mosques served several functions for the royal family. It helped secure the Wahhabi clergy's support of the Saudi monarchy, despite its cooperation with and dependence on the United States; it exported to other countries many young Saudi Wahhabi clergy who might otherwise have caused problems for the regime at home; and it helped counter the international influence of Shia fundamentalism, which had increased following its victory over the US-backed Iranian monarchy in 1979. Some educated at the Deobandi *madrasas* fought against the Soviet occupation of Afghanistan. Many younger students, filled with religious zeal from their years in the *madrasas*, would fill the ranks of the Taliban (Gill 2006; Rashid 2000).

A second key element in the Taliban's rise and victory was the terrible civil war conditions, banditry, lawlessness, and economic disruption that afflicted Afghanistan after the departure of Soviet forces in 1989. This situation created a popular demand for public security to deter and punish criminals, ensure a stable environment for commerce, and unify the country under honest government. When the Taliban displayed these characteristics, many people welcomed the movement and the new Taliban regime.

Finally, Pakistan provided assistance to the Taliban (Rubin 1999), which was extremely important, especially for its early military victories. These gave the Taliban the opportunity to demonstrate its other capabilities to people in the areas it secured, causing support to develop for the movement in other regions, which helped to bring about new Taliban triumphs. The Pakistanis reportedly promoted the Taliban for two major reasons. First, Pakistan hoped to benefit from energy resources and resource transportation from countries to the north of Afghanistan, such as the natural gas of Turkmenistan. But building pipelines required stopping the fighting and an end to the multiple tolls different militias and criminal groups charged trucks on the roadways. The Taliban were supposed to accomplish these goals. Second, since Taliban members were mostly from the Pashtun ethnic group, the largest in Afghanistan at about 45 percent of the population (also a significant component of Pakistan's population), and since a future Taliban government would be grateful for Pakistan's assistance, the Pakistan government probably anticipated that it would have a friendly Afghan regime to its west. This would be helpful to Pakistan in any future conflict with its much bigger longtime rival, India.

The Taliban began its military campaign by taking Spin Baldak, a transportation depot town near the Afghanistan-Pakistan border, in October 1994. Then the Taliban demonstrated that it could ensure clear passage along the length of road it controlled from Pakistan. In November the Taliban took Afghanistan's second largest city, Kandahar. In the words of Ahmed Rashid (2000, 29), "the Taliban immediately implemented the strictest interpretation of Sharia (Islamic) law ever seen in the Muslim world. They closed down girls' schools and banned women from working outside the home, smashed TV sets, forbade a whole array of sports and recreational activities and ordered all men to grow long beards." The Taliban enforced laws and punished criminals, collected firearms from the population to suppress armed conflict among tribal or ethnic groups, and reestablished conditions for businesses and commerce to function. Subsequently the movement's popularity grew among many Afghanis.

The Taliban took the capital, Kabul, in September 1996 and imposed their extremely restrictive form of Sharia rule. They established a government under Mullah Mohammad Umar, the leader of the group of *madrasa* teachers and students that had created the Taliban movement. Eventually the Taliban controlled approximately 85 to 90 percent of Afghanistan. Only the Tajik-populated area in the northeastern part of the country, under the Northern Alliance led by Ahmed Shah Massoud, continued to effectively resist the Taliban. On September 9, 2001, two men posing as journalists interviewing Massoud, assassinated him with a bomb concealed in a camera. This was likely an Al Qaeda attempt to weaken the Northern Alliance before expected retaliation from the US after the planned September 11 attacks.

In May 1996 Osama bin Laden returned to Afghanistan. The Taliban allowed him to set up training camps for hundreds of Islamic volunteers who came to prepare for Al Qaeda–inspired attacks against the US and other nations.

Following the September 11, 2001, attacks, President Bush gave an ultimatum to the Taliban to turn over bin Laden and Al Qaeda members. When the Taliban leadership refused, the US military used air attacks, special forces, and the anti-Taliban Northern Alliance in its assault on Taliban and Al Qaeda forces in October 2001. The Taliban were driven from major cities, but bin Laden and Mullah Umar escaped capture. Certain rural and mountainous areas of Pashtun-populated sections of Afghanistan and Pakistan continued to support the Taliban and oppose the US-assisted government in Kabul. While the United States focused its resources on securing Iraq, Al Qaeda regrouped, and the Taliban rebuilt. US authorities began to refer to distinct Afghan and Pakistani Taliban organizations. Out of all Taliban fighters, 5–10 percent were thought to be volunteers from nations such as Chechnya, Uzbekistan, Iraq, and Jordan. The Khost suicide bomb killings of CIA agents referred to earlier was carried out by a Jordanian linked to Al Qaeda in retaliation for the August 2009 US missile attack that killed one of the Pakistani Taliban's major leaders.

By 2010 the Taliban intensified its war against US forces in Afghanistan, which had increased to 94,000, and their NATO allies. The Taliban received financing from private contributors in Saudi Arabia, Pakistan, and some Persian Gulf countries; opium trafficking; and other criminal activities, such as extorting protection payments from businesses in Taliban-controlled areas and kidnapping for ransom (*New York Times*, February 18, 2010). Several key members of the US-supported Afghan government, however, were also accused of corruption and criminal activities. Those thought to be involved in drug operations or using their positions to enrich themselves included members of Afghan President Hamid Karzai's family (Shanker and Schmitt 2010).

The US war in Afghanistan was further complicated by the abrupt dismissal of the commander of American forces there, General Stanley A. McChrystal, on June 23, 2010, after comments critical of US government officials attributed to him or his aides appeared in an article in *Rolling Stone* (Hastings 2010). President Obama replaced McChrystal with General David H. Petraeus, who had worked with Mc-Chrystal in designing counterinsurgency strategy for the Afghan war similar to the approach Petraeus used in Iraq. Petraeus's counterinsurgency strategy in Iraq included clearing successive areas of enemy fighters, protecting residents and also monitoring movements in and out of cleared areas, establishing beneficial services and construction projects within secure areas as part of the process of winning public support, and recruiting enemy fighters to switch sides through various means, including the offer of jobs. A former Petraeus aide was quoted as describing the approach as "make everyone feel safer, reconcile with those who are willing and kill the people you need to" (Rubin and Filkins 2010). The Obama administration was reportedly divided over whether to use this labor-intensive method versus relying on smaller numbers of special forces troops and high-tech missile strikes to keep Al Qaeda and the Taliban in check by continuously eliminating key leaders and their military resources. Another problem for the Obama administration's Afghan policy was declining popular support for the war, which had dropped below 50 percent by the end of June 2010.

During the 2012 presidential campaign, President Obama promised to withdraw US combat troops from Afghanistan by the end of 2014. But as the departure date neared, many in the US government believed that Afghan government forces were not prepared to take on full responsibility for fighting the Taliban and Al Qaeda. The solution proposed was a status of forces agreement (SOFA) with Afghanistan that would permit the US to keep an estimated 6,000 to 9,000 US troops in Afghanistan to train Afghan soldiers and conduct antiterrorism operations long after 2014 (Bowman and Siegel 2013).

The War in Iraq

On March 20, 2003, US and British-led forces invaded Iraq. Reasons offered to justify the invasion included claims that Iraq possessed weapons of mass destruction and, despite the fact that Osama bin Laden had disapproved of Saddam Hussein and Iraq's relatively secular government, that the Iraqis had somehow been involved in the September 11, 2001, Al Qaeda attacks. Later investigations indicated the claims were false (DeFronzo 2010). But in the post–9/11 atmosphere in the US, with the focus on the "war on terrorism," these charges played a role for the Iraq War similar to that played by the Gulf of Tonkin incident for the Vietnam War. Both helped stampede the US Congress into passing a resolution that provided the legal basis for the president to take the country to war (see Chapter 4).

US companies were awarded contracts in occupied Iraq while the country's oil seemed to be, in effect, under US control. The post-invasion justification for the military occupation was to help establish a stable democratic system rather than withdrawing while the insurgent, inter-religious, and interethnic violence that followed the invasion continued. The resistance insurgency to foreign occupation was multifaceted, varying in motives, ideology, goals, and tactics. The estimated number of active insurgents ranged "from a few thousand to more than 50,000" (Finer 2006). Approximately 90 percent were Sunni, and 90 percent or more were Iraqi rather than foreign volunteers.

The primary reasons offered by Sunni insurgents for their armed resistance was either "patriotism or Salafi . . . religious fervour" (Guidère and Harling 2006). In addition to the mostly Sunni insurgents, there were many thousands in Shia militias attempting to protect Shia neighborhoods or engage in sectarian conflict with Sunni groups. The US-led invasion removed the Saddam Hussein regime and ended decades of Sunni domination of government (about 35 percent of the population is Sunni, while more than 60 percent of Iraqis are Shia).

Iraq War: Nationalist Insurgents

Virtually as soon as the US-led occupation of Iraq began, so did insurgent resistance. Many of the original insurgents were members of Saddam Hussein's Baath Party, including former military and intelligence officers. Some of these may have hoped to reinstall a Baath Party government. But after Saddam Hussein was captured on December 13, 2003, former Baathists who continued to participate in the insurgency shifted to the nationalist goal of fighting to establish conditions for what they would consider a government that was the product of Iraqi self-determination rather than a creature of the foreign occupation. They also tried to punish foreign corporations, which they viewed as stealing Iraq's oil for the benefit of the invading powers and Israel. Other nationalists fought because they had family members or friends who had been killed as a result of the invasion or the actions of occupation forces against insurgents. The nationalist insurgents targeted US forces and non-Iraqi contractors in the large majority of their attacks (Lehrer 2006).

Iraq War: Sunni Islamic Insurgents

Some Iraqi Sunnis were members of the Iraqi branch of the Muslim Brotherhood, which advocated that Iraq should be freed from non-Islamic influences, should adopt the authentic form of Islam that the Brotherhood believed existed early in Islam's history, and should be transformed into an Islamic republic.

In addition to indigenous Iraqi Salafi Sunni insurgents, hundreds of foreign Islamic volunteers crossed into Iraq from Syria, Libya, Jordan, and Saudi Arabia, many of whom were Wahhabi-schooled Saudis. One of the Jordanians was Abu Musab al-Zarqawi, who led a major group of foreign Islamist volunteers that identified itself as a branch of Al Qaeda. Whereas the nationalist-oriented insurgents and Iraqi Sunni Islamic insurgents tended to attack occupation forces with roadside bombs, ambushes, mortars, and rifle-propelled grenades, the foreign Islamic fighters were more prone to suicide bombing attacks (martyrdom missions) than other fighters. The Zarqawi-led group was blamed for some of the most brutal acts of violence of the insurgency, including bombing attacks killing many Shia civilians.

Many nationalist and Islamic Iraqi insurgents strongly condemned the bombings of civilians, and the brutal beheadings of captured hostages as unjustified and counterproductive. Even the leaders of Al Qaeda criticized these actions. Some Iraqi insurgents attacked and killed a number of foreign fighters to prevent them from carrying out bombings or executions of civilians or to punish them for such brutality. As the insurgency continued, Al Qaeda–linked groups appeared to include mostly indigenous Iraqis. Despite their criticisms, both top leaders of Al Qaeda, Osama bin Laden and Ayman al-Zawahiri, issued audio recordings praising Zarqawi as a martyr after he was killed by a US air strike on June 7, 2006. The divisions among insurgents played a major role in the reduction of violence in Iraq after mid-2007, when the US, promising to eventually withdraw its combat forces, in effect hired tens of thousands of former Sunni insurgents to help fight Al Qaeda–linked groups (DeFronzo 2010, 231–232).

Iraq War: Shia Fundamentalists

Juan Cole (2006) argues that the Bush administration's invasion of Iraq and overthrow of the Baath Party government may have set in motion a second Shia Islamic fundamentalist revolution (the first being the Iranian revolution of 1979). Ayatollah Khomeini had called on the Iraqi people to overthrow Saddam Hussein's regime and establish an Iraqi Islamic republic. Some members of the Shia Iraqi Dawa Party, which had formed in the 1950s to counter the appeal to Shia young people of both the Baath Socialist Party and the Iraqi Communist Party, were accused of organizing a fundamentalist rebellion against the Iraqi government. This appears to be one of the reasons Saddam Hussein invaded Iran in 1980. Although the invasion did not overthrow the Iranian Islamic Republic, Iraq's military effort was thought to have slowed the spread of Shia Islamic revolutionary movements to other countries. The economic consequences of that war contributed to Iraq's invasion of Kuwait in 1990. This action, in turn, led to the first Gulf War and later, coupled with the US reaction to the September 11, 2001, terrorist attacks, to the Bush administration's decision to invade and occupy Iraq.

The end of the secular Baath Party regime in Iraq unleashed the revolutionary potential of Iraq's Shia majority and encouraged Shia movements in other countries. Throughout much of southern Iraq as well as in other Shia-populated areas and sections of Iraqi cities, Shia men formed armed militias. The Shia militias were often under the authority of one of three Shia organizations—the Dawa Party, the Supreme Council for Islamic Revolution in Iraq (SCIRI, renamed the Islamic Supreme Council of Iraq [ISCI] after May 2007), or Shiite cleric Moqtada al-Sadr's Mahdi Army. Ultimately these three groups entered into an electoral alliance (Finer and Fekeiki 2005), the United Iraqi Alliance, in the US-sponsored Iraqi elections of December 2005. This Shia alliance won 128 of the 275 seats in the national assembly, the Council of Representatives, and was able to form a coalition government. Shia alliances also won in eleven of the country's eighteen provinces in the January 2006 provincial elections.

An elected constitutional assembly wrote a constitution that "stipulated that Islam is the religion of state and that civil parliament could pass no legislation that contravened established Islamic laws" (Cole 2006, 21). To some observers this represented the achievement of the central fundamentalist goal of the integration of church and state in Iraq and the ultimate triumph of Khomeini's ideas. However, the constitution also states that no law may contradict the principles of democracy (De-Fronzo 2010, 201–202). The new Shia-dominated government in Iraq served as an inspiration to other Shia groups in the Middle East, such as the Shia Lebanese Hezbollah Party; the Shia minority of Saudi Arabia, which resides primarily in its oil-rich Eastern Province; and the Shia majority of Bahrain, ruled by a Sunni monarch.

Iraq War: The Future of Iraq?

The US-led invasion of Iraq in 2003 may ultimately have any of several consequences:: a civil war, in particular between segments of the Sunni and Shia populations for reasons such as the unwillingness of Sunnis to accept a state dominated by Shia religious groups or what they might view as rule by an Iranian-allied regime; the fragmentation of Iraq into separate Arab and Kurdish countries or into Kurdish, Sunni Arab, and Shia Arab states; or the existence of Iraq as a partial or "guided" democracy in reality controlled by the US. Another possible future for Iraq could be its emergence as a fully independent democratic nation. But such an outcome could only be verified if foreign troops totally left the country, including any occupation forces masquerading as employees of private security firms or under other covert identities, and if a completely democratically elected Iraqi government was allowed to formulate its domestic and foreign policies free from foreign coercion or intimidation. Such an achievement would only be likely if permitted by the internal political conditions in other powerful nations, especially those that invaded Iraq in 2003.

Many Iraqis were inspired by the wave of pro-democracy uprisings in Arab countries against authoritarian regimes that began in late 2010. (See Chapter 11 on the Arab revolution.) In February 2011, limited demonstrations occurred in parts of Iraq against things like the enormous level of corruption (Transparency International ranks Iraq as the fourth most corrupt nation in the world; Sly 2011), inadequate electric service, high unemployment, and restrictions on freedom of the press and assembly. In 2012 and 2013 new protests broke out in mainly Sunni-populated areas like Anbar Province (Ruhayem 2013). Sunni activists claimed that the Iraqi prime minister Nouri al-Maliki was biased against and repressive towards Sunnis and more loyal to Iran than Iraq. One issue many Sunnis were concerned about was the continued legal discrimination against former members of the Baath Party that dominated Iraq under Saddam Hussein. Thousands of former party members were barred from government jobs on the theory that anyone who was a party member at a specified level of party rank or higher must have committed significant violations of human rights. However the latent function of the anti-Baath law may be to prevent the resurrection of an Iraqi political party that is truly nationalist and could unify Iraqi Sunnis and Shias in a political movement that could end the domination of Maliki's sectarian Shia alliance.

Violent political and religious conflict among Iraqis climbed to levels not seen since the 2006–2007 period of intense sectarian strife that followed the US-led invasion. In 2013, over 7,000 civilians and 950 security personnel were killed in bombings and other violent attacks (Associated Press 2013). Some observers feared the country faced increased internal violence or even all-out civil war (Pollack 2013).

HEZBOLLAH AND THE WAR WITH ISRAEL

The Iranian revolution contributed to the 1982 formation of a militant Islamic organization, Hezbollah (Party of God), among the 35–40 percent of Lebanon's population that is Shia. The immediate impetus for its creation was the Israeli occupation of southern Lebanon. The Israeli Defense Forces (IDF) entered Lebanon in 1982 to stop attacks into northern Israel by PLO guerrillas. Eventually Israel occupied much of the country, including the territory around Beirut, and drove PLO forces from Lebanon. However, the IDF then allowed a Lebanese Christian Phalange militia to enter the Palestinian Sabra and Shatila refugee camps on September 16 to search for remaining PLO fighters. The Phalangists reportedly killed somewhere between 460 and 3,500 people, depending on the source, including women and children. This massacre of unarmed Palestinians enraged many Lebanese against both the Christian extremists and the Israeli occupying forces.

Israel occupied southern Lebanon until 2000, and in the process employed a Christian-Druze militia, the South Lebanon Army (SLA), accused of torture and murder, in efforts to control the area. The Israeli occupation, while ousting the PLO, resulted in the creation among Lebanese Shia of a new threat to Israel, Hezbollah. With the aid of an estimated 1,500 to 2,000 Iranian Islamic Revolutionary Guards, who came to Lebanon to train Lebanese Shia volunteers to fight the Israeli occupation, Hezbollah's armed wing engaged in violent actions against the SLA, Israelis, and other foreign forces viewed by Hezbollah as hostile to Lebanon's Islamic residents or allied with Israel.

Hezbollah was thought to be responsible for kidnapping US citizens during the 1980s, including several who were apparently released through Iranian influence as part of the Iran-contra deal (see Chapters 6–7). Hezbollah members were also thought to have carried out suicide attacks against Americans in Lebanon, including the April 18, 1983, bombing of the US embassy in Beirut, which killed sixty-three people, and the October 23, 1983, barracks bombing, which killed 241 US Marines. US forces later withdrew from Lebanon. During the 1982–2000 Israeli occupation of south Lebanon, Hezbollah, believed to have received major assistance and funding from Iran and Syria, became the most effective Lebanese force resisting Israeli occupation. The links between largely Sunni Syria and Shia Hezbollah and predominantly Shia Iran may in part be due to the fact that Syria's top governing elite is disproportionately Alawi, a form of Islam closely related to Shiism.

When Israel agreed to withdraw from Lebanon, most observers thought continuous casualties sustained by the IDF from Hezbollah attacks played a role. Many viewed Hezbollah as the first Arab army to ever accomplish such a victory against the Israeli armed forces. As a result, its popularity increased. Hezbollah, however, was far from just a military organization. Its civilian sector provided educational and social services to tens of thousands of grateful Lebanese. For some time Hezbollah advocated transforming Lebanon into an Islamic republic like Iran. But in the face of opposition from the large Christian minority, about 39 percent of the population, most Hezbollah leaders seem to have abandoned this goal. Hezbollah developed significant electoral support and in 2005, as a political party, won 23 of 128 seats in the Lebanese parliament. Two Hezbollah members were appointed to cabinet positions.

Under the leadership of Sheik Hassan Nasrallah, Hezbollah was strongly critical of both Osama bin Laden's September 11, 2001, attack on the US (because it resulted in the deaths of many innocent people) and the Al Qaeda–linked bombings and executions in Iraq, which took the lives of civilians after the 2003 US-led invasion. Hezbollah also condemned the Afghan Sunni Taliban regime as a repressive and "very hideous example of an Islamic state" (Wright 2006).

Hezbollah, however, cooperated with Sunni Hamas and other Palestinian organizations. Hezbollah did not accept the Israeli state and referred to it with expressions such as "the Zionist entity." Hezbollah (Westcott 2002) indicated that it was "ready to open a second front against Israel" in support of the Palestinians. After several Palestinians tunneled their way from Gaza to an Israeli outpost, killed two Israeli soldiers, and captured a third, Israeli forces invaded Gaza at the end of June 2006 and seized many Hamas members of the Palestinian government. Possibly in response (Erlanger 2006a) and also apparently to force the return of a number of Lebanese from Israeli captivity, Hezbollah guerrillas crossed into Israel on July 12, killed eight Israeli soldiers, and captured two others. Israeli forces then carried out air and artillery bombardments of Hezbollah positions and a ground invasion of southern Lebanon. Hezbollah launched about a hundred fifty or more rockets into Israel almost each day of the conflict. Hezbollah's popularity surged within much of the Islamic world. During the conflict Israel destroyed much of Lebanon's infrastructure, which elicited criticism from a number of nations.

After thirty-three days, the violence subsided on August 14, when a cease-fire negotiated by the United Nations went into effect. Approximately 1,150 Lebanese, mainly civilians, had perished, while about 150 Israelis, mostly soldiers, died (Erlanger 2006a). The Israeli military estimated it killed about five hundred Hezbollah fighters, but Hezbollah claimed the number was lower.

Both sides claimed victory. Israel believed it had significantly weakened Hezbollah and anticipated that the Lebanese government would be strengthened and come under international pressure to disarm Hezbollah or at least prevent Hezbollah from operating as an armed force between the Litani River and the Israeli border. This area, according to the cease-fire agreement, was to be patrolled by both the Lebanese army and United Nations troops.

To many observers, however, Hezbollah seemed to emerge politically strengthened. Hezbollah's prowess in battle and ability to launch several thousand rockets into Israel damaged the myth of Israeli military invincibility and bolstered the pride of millions of Arabs and Muslims. The popularity of Hezbollah leader Sheik Hassan Nasrallah soared internationally, while anger over the collective punishment Israel inflicted on Lebanon was widespread. Hezbollah's war with Israel likely accelerated the growth of political Islamic movements and motivated thousands of young Muslims to join Hezbollah or similar organizations. According to Slackman (2006), "the lesson learned by many Arabs from the war in Lebanon is that an Islamic movement, in this case Hezbollah, restored dignity and honor to a bruised and battered identity."

In the Lebanon election of June 9, 2009, the coalition led by Hezbollah won 57 of 128 seats in the National Assembly and received 10 of 30 cabinet positions (Worth 2009). The government allowed Hezbollah to retain its weapons (Associated Press, June 18, 2010). Hezbollah claimed it needed them to deter future attacks from Israel. The US suspected Iran and Syria of providing rockets to Hezbollah (*Albuquerque Express*, April 28, 2010).

In a world in which the technology of war available to perceived imperialist nations continues to improve and existing elites in Islamic countries are viewed as corrupted by collaboration with those powers or with international profit-driven corporations, among the most effective resistance movements possible may be those whose participants are religiously driven. Such soldiers are relatively unafraid to die, their ranks are soon replenished by highly motivated volunteers, and their leaders' religious commitment makes them less susceptible to the financial inducements offered by foreign interests.

Summary and Analysis

The Salafi movement, which advocated returning to an early, pure form of Islam that would protect Islamic peoples from the corrupting influences and domination of non-Islamic nations, developed in the nineteenth century in response to European military conquest and technological superiority. Another religious movement with similar ideas had been formulated earlier by Mohammad Wahhabi. A modern manifestation of the Salafi perspective is the Muslim Brotherhood, founded in Egypt in 1928. A member of the Egyptian Muslim Brotherhood, Sayyid Qutb, opposed the notion that Muslims should endure unjust rulers. In contrast, Qutb defined such regimes, especially those serving non-Islamic imperialist countries, as non-Muslim governments that true Muslims were required to overthrow. Branches of the Muslim Brotherhood were established in a number of Sunni Islamic countries. Some groups that split off from or were inspired by the Muslim Brotherhood engaged in violence, such as the Egyptian Islamic Holy War and the armed wing of Hamas, the Izzadin al-Qassam Brigades.

A form of Shia fundamentalism was put forth by Ayatollah Khomeini, whom some believe was inspired in part by the writings of Qutb. Khomeini viewed secular republics and monarchies as un-Islamic forms of government and, similar to

Qutb and the Sunni Salafi fundamentalists, rejected separation of church and state. The 1978–1979 Khomeini-led Iranian revolution resulted in the establishment of the first modern Islamic republic in which religion and state were integrated under clerical leadership. The success of the Iranian revolution in overthrowing a US-supported monarchy encouraged Islamic fundamentalists, both Shia and Sunni.

The next major victory for Islamic fundamentalism occurred when Sunni Islamic fighters defeated the Soviet occupation of Afghanistan. Foreign Islamic volunteers in the Afghan war against the Soviets, including Osama bin Laden and Ayman al-Zawahiri, organized a communications network among the thousands of volunteers in 1988 that came to be called Al Qaeda. After large US forces were deployed to Saudi Arabia in the early 1990s, Al Qaeda and allied Salafi movements launched what they called a global holy war on behalf of Islam, one that included many violent acts, such as the September 11, 2001, terrorist attacks in the US.

Another consequence of the Afghan war was the formation of the Taliban and its repressive Islamic regime. Because the Taliban provided bases for Al Qaeda in Afghanistan, the United States drove them from power at the end of 2001. But while Taliban rule was overthrown, another Sunni fundamentalist movement, Hamas, gained power through the Palestinian parliamentary election of 2006.

As part of its response to the September 11, 2001, terrorist attacks, the George W. Bush administration invaded and occupied Iraq. The US ousted Saddam Hussein and his Baath Party government and then held elections for a new legislature in December 2005. Violence in Iraq temporarily declined after 2007 but reached a high level in 2013.

While the US was preoccupied with Iraq, the Taliban and Al Qaeda reorganized and launched new attacks. In 2010 the US dramatically increased its forces in Afghanistan and conducted numerous missile strikes to eliminate Taliban and Al Qaeda leaders.

The Israeli invasion and occupation of southern Lebanon in 1982–2000 led to the creation of Hezbollah, a Shia Lebanese military, political, and social welfare organization. War broke out between Hezbollah and Israel on July 12, 2006. Its ability to resist the new Israeli invasion of southern Lebanon and to attack Israel with thousands of rockets bolstered the pride of many Arabs and Muslims around the world and enhanced the attractiveness of politically oriented Islamic movements. Hezbollah continued to be a major political and military force in Lebanon.

The five factors crucial to the development of revolutionary movements can be applied to Islamic revolutionary movements.

Many people in Muslim nations suffered from poverty, economic exploitation, and political oppression. Mass discontent in some of these societies was heightened by foreign invasion and occupation, which made people receptive to revolutionary ideologies that might offer a solution to their plight. Many Afghan people whose nation was occupied by the Soviets, then devastated by years of war, followed by more years of fighting and lawlessness, became attracted to the Taliban since it at least restored some level of social order. Arab Palestinians, many of whom suffered long-term poverty and occupation by a foreign power, turned to Hamas and voted the fundamentalist movement into power.

A prerequisite for the development of revolutionary ideologies and organizations within Islam is the existence of a dissident elite. Dissident elites were often religious scholars or clergy who responded to social injustice, moral corruption, and imperialism with Salafi-like revolutionary ideologies. These called for the restoration of the form of Islam that existed in the early decades of the Islamic faith. Such a religiously based ideology could, and in some cases did, provide the unifying motivational factor necessary to unite people of different social classes in a revolutionary movement.

For a number of pre-revolutionary Muslim societies, the fourth and fifth factors of state collapse and world permissiveness are interrelated. Some Muslim countries, in particular those governed by monarchies, relied significantly on foreign support from non-Islamic nations to resist revolutionary movements seeking their overthrow. As noted in Chapter 7, the Carter administration's human rights policy, which required the Iranian monarch to improve the treatment of Iran's people as a condition of continued US aid, weakened the shah's government, contributing to its ultimate collapse and the victory of a Shia fundamentalist revolution. In Afghanistan the Soviet-backed government that preceded the Taliban's Sunni Islamic revolution could not survive the Soviet withdrawal. Islamic revolutionary movements in a number of countries have not succeeded in part because of the support provided to existing governments by the US and other nations. The election of another US administration with foreign policies similar to those of the Carter administration might weaken certain regimes enough to permit new victories for Islamic revolutionary movements.

ISLAMIC REVOLUTIONARY MOVEMENTS: CHRONOLOGY OF MAJOR EVENTS

571–632   The life span of the Prophet Muhammad, whose leadership and teachings inspire one of the greatest religious movements in history

632–661   The Rashidun, or era of the Rightly Guided Caliphs, the period from the death of the Prophet to the death of Ali, the last of the four leaders of Islam who had personally known Muhammad

680   Death of Hussein, son of Ali, in battle at Karbala; some adherents of Islam, the Shia (Shiat Ali, or "Partisans of Ali") come to believe

that only certain male descendants of Ali and his wife, the Prophet's daughter, Fatima, should rule Islam; by the twenty-first century, it is estimated that Shia are less than 20 percent of Islam, while Sunni are over 80 percent

1744 Saud family allies with Muhammad ibn Abdul Wahhab, the religious leader of an Islamic purification movement; the alliance helps the Saud family conquer what becomes known as Saudi Arabia and leads to Wahhabi Islam, a conservative form of Islam, becoming dominant there

1798 Napoleon conquers Egypt, shocking the Islamic world with the reality of European technological superiority

1860s Jamal al-Din al Afghani begins the Salafi movement, which emphasizes the idea that the Islamic world could modernize and successfully confront European nations by first returning to the culture and concepts of the *salaf* ("ancestors"), the original version of Islam of the Rashidun period

1917 British Balfour Declaration supports the Zionist movement to create a homeland for the Jewish people in then overwhelmingly Islamic Palestine

1928 Hassan al-Banna creates the first modern Islamic political movement, the Ikhwan Muslimin (Muslim Brotherhood), in Egypt

1947–1948 United Nations supports creation of the state of Israel

1948 First Arab-Israeli war results in hundreds of thousands of Arab Palestinian refugees

1967 Israel's victory over Egypt, Jordan, and Syria in the Six Day War

1979 Iranian revolution ousts the pro-US monarchy

1979–1989 Soviets occupy Afghanistan, and in response tens of thousands of volunteers, including Osama bin Laden, from dozens of countries join Afghan Islamic fighters in combating the army of the leftist Afghan government and Soviet military, which is forced to withdraw in 1989

1981 Islamic extremists assassinate President Sadat of Egypt

1982 Israeli army invades Lebanon to evict Palestine Liberation Organization forces there, but in reaction Shia Lebanese create Hezbollah to resist the occupation and force the Israeli military to withdraw from the country

1987 Hamas (Islamic Resistance Movement), inspired by the Muslim Brotherhood branch in Palestine, is founded among Palestinian Arabs by Sheikh Ahmed Yasin

1988 Osama bin Laden and his associates create Al Qaeda, "the base,"
an organizational and communications network among Islamic
foreign volunteers in Afghanistan

1989 Soviets withdraw from Afghanistan

1990 Iraq invades Kuwait

1990–1991 United States increases its military deployment to Saudi Arabia

1991 Iraq defeated by the United States, Britain, and their allies

1993 Islamic extremists use a truck bomb to attack the New York World
Trade Towers

1994–1996 Taliban emerges in Afghanistan and wins control of most of the
country

1996 May—Osama bin Laden returns to Afghanistan

1998 February—Al Qaeda leaders form global jihad alliance
August—US embassies in Kenya and Tanzania are attacked by Al
Qaeda associates using vehicle bombs

2001 September 11—Al Qaeda attacks the New York World Trade Towers
and the Pentagon in Washington, DC
October 7—The United States and its allies begin military operations
against Al Qaeda and the Taliban in Afghanistan and soon oust the
Taliban regime

2003 March 20—US, British, and allied forces begin an invasion and occupation of Iraq

2004 Israel assassinates Sheikh Ahmed Yasin, founder of Hamas

2006 January—Hamas wins control of the Palestinian parliament in the
legislative election
July 12—War breaks out between Hezbollah and Israel
August 14—Hezbollah-Israel cease-fire with both sides claiming
victory

2007 Civil war among Arab Palestinians between Hamas and Fatah; Israel
establishes blockade of Hamas-controlled Gaza

2009 Barack Obama becomes president and attempts a more conciliatory
approach to Islamic nations with historic disagreements with the US

2010 Resurgence of the Taliban in Afghanistan; US commits more troops
to the Afghan war

2010–2011 The Arab revolution (Arab Spring) leads to Islamist political campaigns and rebellions in several Arab Nations; Islamists win Tunisian election

2012 Muslim Brotherhood wins elections in Egypt

2013 Democratically elected President Morsi of Egypt overthrown

REFERENCES AND FURTHER READINGS

Aboudi, Sami, and David Evans. 2013. "North Yemen Fighting Kills More Than 120." Reuters, December 1. www.reuters.com/article/2013/12/01/us-yemen-fighting-idUSBRE 9B00CI20131201?feedType=RSS.

Ahmed, Azam, and Sharifullah Sahak. 2013. "Drone and Taliban Attacks Hit Civilians, Afghans Say." *New York Times,* September 8. www.nytimes.com/2013/09/09/world /asia/two-deadly-attacks-in-afghanistan.html?_r=0&pagewanted=print.

Albuquerque Express. April 28, 2010. "Gates Accuses Iran and Syria of Providing Weapons to Hezbollah." story.albuquerqueexpress.com/index.php/ct/9/cid/c08dd24 cec417021/id/628334/cs/1.

Associated Press. June 18, 2010. "11 Killed As Militants Storm Yemen Jail." www.nytimes .com/2010/06/20/world/middleeast/20yemen.html.

―――. 2013. "2013 Iraq Death Toll Passes 8,000, Return of Death Squads Feared." *New York Post,* December 2. http://nypost.com/2013/12/02/2013-iraq-death -toll-passes-8000-return-of-death-squads-feared.

Baer, Robert. 2010. "The Khost CIA Bombing: Assessing the Damage in Afghanistan." *Time,* January 8. www.time.com/time/nation/article/0,8599,1952531,00.html.

Berman, Paul. 2003. "The Philosopher of Islamic Terror." *New York Times,* March 23.

Bowman, Tom, and Robert Siegel. 2013. "Afghan Elders Will Decide Future of US Troops After 2014." NPR, November 19. www.npr.org/templates/story/story.php ?storyId=246201816.

Cole, Juan. 2006. "A 'Shiite Crescent'? The Regional Impact of the Iraq War." *Current History* 105 (January): 20–26.

Crenshaw, Martha. 2001. "Why America? The Globalization of Civil War." *Current History* 100 (December): 425–432.

DeFronzo, James, ed. 2006. *Revolutionary Movements in World History: From 1750 to the Present.* 3 vols. Santa Barbara, CA: ABC-CLIO.

―――. 2010. *The Iraq War: Origins and Consequences.* Boulder: Westview.

Erlanger, Steven. 2006a. "Lebanon Cease-Fire Begins After Day of Fierce Attacks." *New York Times,* August 14.

―――. 2006b. "Seizures Show New Israel Line Against Hamas." *New York Times,* June 30. www.nytimes.com/2006/06/30/world/middleeast/30palestinians.html.

Euben, Roxanne L. 2002. "Jihad and Political Violence." *Current History* 101 (November): 365–376.

Finer, Jonathan. 2006. "Iraq's Insurgents: Who's Who." *Washington Post,* March 19.

Finer, Jonathan, and Omar Fekeiki. 2005. "Iraqi Shiite Groups Form Election Alliance." *Washington Post,* October 28.

Fisher, Ian. 2006. "Women, Secret Hamas Strength, Win Votes at Polls and New Role." *New York Times,* February 3. www.nytimes.com/2006/02/03/international/middleeast /03women.html.

Gill, Jungyun. 2006. "Student and Youth Movements, Activism and Revolution." In De-Fronzo, ed., *Revolutionary Movements in World History*, 3:848–854.

Goldstone, Jack A., ed. 1998. *The Encyclopedia of Political Revolutions*. Washington, DC: Congressional Quarterly Press.

Guidère, Mathieu, and Peter Harling. 2006. "'Withdraw, Move on, Rampage': Iraq's Resistance Evolves." *Le Monde Diplomatique*, May. mondediplo.com/2006/05/02irak.

Halliday, Fred. 1998. "Islamic Fundamentalism." In Goldstone, ed., *Encyclopedia of Political Revolutions*, 263–265.

Hamas (Islamic Resistance Movement). 1988. The Covenant of the Islamic Resistance Movement. August 18. avalon.law.yale.edu/20th_century/hamas.asp.

Hastings, Michael. 2010. "The Runaway General." *Rolling Stone*, June 22. www.rolling stone.com/politics/news/17390/119236.

Huntington, S. P. 1993. "The Clash of Civilizations." *Foreign Affairs* 72:28–50.

Joffé, E. G. H. 2006. "Islamic Fundamentalist Revolutionary Movements." In DeFronzo, ed., *Revolutionary Movements in World History*, 2:452–464.

Kifner, John. 1996. "Aims and Arms: Tactics in a Holy War." *New York Times*, March 15.

Lehrer, Jim. 2006. "Who's Behind the Violence in Iraq?" *NewsHour Extra*, June 12.

Lewis and Prieur. 2013. "Revival of Islamists in Mali Tests French, U.N. Nerve." Reuters, November 14. http://uk.reuters.com/article/2013/11/14/uk-mali-islamists-insight -idUKBRE9AD0NJ20131114?feedType=RSS&feedName=worldNews.

Lewis, Bernard. 2002. *What Went Wrong? Western Impact and Middle Eastern Response*. London: Weidenfeld & Nicolson.

Mazzetti, Mark, Sabrina Tavernise, and Jack Healy. 2010. "Suspect, Charged, Said to Admit to Role in Plot." *New York Times*, May 4. www.nytimes.com/2010/05/05/nyregion /05bomb.html.

New York Times. February 18, 2010. "Taliban."

Omar, Feisal. 2013. "Somali Islamists Take Responsibility for Mogadishu Hotel Bombing." Reuters, November 9. www.reuters.com/article/2013/11/09/us-somalia-blast -islamists-idUSBRE9A803S20131109.

Pollack, Kenneth M. 2013. "Iraq Faces the Brink Again." *Current History*, December, 349–355.

Rashid, Ahmed. 2000. *Taliban: Militant Islam, Oil, and the New Great Game in Central Asia*. New Haven, CT: Yale University Press.

Rinehart, James F. 2006. "Millenarianism, Religion and Revolution." In DeFronzo, ed., *Revolutionary Movements in World History*, 2:570–574.

Rose, David. 2008. "The Gaza Bombshell." *Vanity Fair*, April. www.vanityfair.com /politics/features/2008/04/gaza200804.

Roy, Sara. 2003. "Hamas and the Transformation(s) of Political Islam in Palestine." *Current History* 102 (January): 13–20.

Rubin, Alissa J., and Dexter Filkins. 2010. "Petraeus Is Now Taking Control of a Tougher

Fight." *New York Times,* June 23. www.nytimes.com/2010/06/24/world/asia/24 petraeus.html.

Rubin, Barnett R. 1999. "Afghanistan Under the Taliban." *Current History* 98 (February): 79–91.

Ruhayem, Rami. 2014. "Protests Engulf West Iraq as Anbar Rises Against Maliki." BBC, January 2. www.bbc.co.uk/news/world-middle-east-20887739.

Schmitt, Eric. 2010. "American Strike Is Said to Kill a Top Qaeda Leader." *New York Times,* May 31. www.nytimes.com/2010/06/01/world/asia/01qaeda.html.

Shanker, Thom, and Eric Schmitt. 2010. "US Intelligence Puts New Focus on Afghan Graft." *New York Times,* June 12. www.nytimes.com/2010/06/13/world/asia/13intel.html.

Sherwood, Harriet. 2010. "Israel Eases Gaza Blockade." *Guardian,* July 5. www.guardian .co.uk/world/2010/jul/05/israel-eases-blockade-gaza-list.

Skocpol, Theda, and Ellen Kay Trimberger. 1978. "Revolutions and the World Historical Development of Capitalism." *Berkeley Journal of Sociology* 22:101–113.

Slackman, Michael. 2006. "And Now, Islam Trumps Arabism." *New York Times,* August 20.

Sly, Liz. 2011. "Egyptian Revolution Sparks Protest Movement in Democratic Iraq." *Washington Post,* February 12. http://www.washingtonpost.com/wp-dyn/content/article/2011/02/12/AR2011021202100_pf.html.

Tapper, Jake. 2012. "Papers Show Osama Bin Laden Plot to Kill President Obama and David Petraeus." ABC News. http://abcnews.go.com/blogs/politics/2012/03/papers -show-osama-bin-laden-plot-to-kill-president-obama-and-david-petraeus.

Westcott, Kathryn. 2000. "Who Are Hamas?" BBC News, October 19. news.bbc.co.uk/1 /hi/world/middle_east/978626.stm.

———. 2002. "Who Are Hezbollah?" BBC News, April 4. news.bbc.co.uk/1/hi/world /middle_east/1908671.stm.

Wilson, Scott, Craig Whitlock, and William Branigin. 2011. "Osama bin Laden Killed in US Raid, Buried at Sea." *Washington Post,* May 2. http://articles.washington post.com/2011-05-02/national/35264963_1_surgical-raid-al-qaeda-leader-osama -bin-laden.

Worth, Robert F. 2009. "Impasse Over, Lebanon Forms Cabinet." *New York Times,* November 10. www.nytimes.com/2009/11/10/world/middleeast/10lebanon.html.

Wright, Robin. 2006. "Inside the Mind of Hezbollah." *Washington Post,* July 16.

SELECTED DVD, FILM, AND VIDEOCASSETTE DOCUMENTARIES

See "Purchase and Rental Sources" at the end of this volume for information on how to obtain the following resources and for full names of media companies and other organizations listed here as abbreviations.

Afghanistan Unveiled. 2004. ITVS. The lives of women under Taliban rule.

Al Qaeda in Yemen. 2012. PBS. http://video.pbs.org/video/2240574561.

The Arming of Saudi Arabia. 1993. 60 min. Video. PBS. US policy toward Saudi Arabia.

*Battle for the Holy Land.*2002. 60 min. PBS. Perspectives of Israelis and Palestinians.

Behind Taliban Lines. 2010. 60 min. PBS.

Blood and Oil. 2008. 52 min. Amazon.com.

Bush's War. 2008. 270 min. DVD. Amazon.com. Bush administration invasion of Iraq.

Fighting for Bin Laden. 2011, 54 min. PBS Frontline. Fighting against Al Qaeda and the Taliban and forces opposing the US in Afghanistan. http://video.pbs.org/video /1908468892.

Hunting Bin Laden. 2001. 60 min. Video. PBS. Describes bin Laden, the Al Qaeda leader.

The Insurgency. 2006. PBS Frontline. Investigation of aspects of the Iraqi insurgency including interviews with insurgents.

Jihad: The Men and Ideas Behind Al Qaeda. America at a Crossroads. 2007. 120 min. PBS.

The 9/11 Hijackers: Inside the Hamburg Cell. 2007. DVD. Amazon.com.

Kill/Capture. 2011. 54 min. PBS Frontline. US fight Against Al Qaeda and the Taliban. http://video.pbs.org/video/1917910631.

Obama's War. 2009. 60 min. PBS. War in Afghanistan.

Opium Brides. 2012. 54 min. PBS Frontline. Secret war and opium in Afghanistan. http:// video.pbs.org/video/2183223771.

Osama Bin Laden. 50 min. BIO.

Party of God. 2003. PBS Frontline. Hezbollah.

*Return of the Taliban.*2006. 60 min. PBS Frontline. Taliban resurgence following the 2001 US-led overthrow of the Taliban regime.

Saudi Time Bomb. 2001. 60 min. PBS Frontline. Saudi Arabia and Wahhabi international activities.

Soldiers of God. 1998. 46 min. CNN Cold War Series, Episode 20. Truman Library. Islamic revolutionaries and fighters in Iran and Afghanistan.

The War Against Al Qaeda. 2006. 50 min. AETV.

Women of Hezbollah. 2000. 49 min. FRIF. Women activists in Hezbollah.

9

South Africa

The Russian, Chinese, Vietnamese, Cuban, Nicaraguan, and Iranian revolutions aimed to overthrow dictatorships, foreign imperialism, and unjust economic systems. Efforts for social change in southern Africa, however, confronted the further obstacle of institutionally and culturally embedded racism. In the late twentieth century only one major nation claimed the distinction of awarding political rights on the basis of race: the Republic of South Africa. The white minority had confirmed its control of the mineral-rich country through the passage of a set of laws during the years 1948–1960 reinforcing race separation under the label "apartheid." In the 1950s peaceful protests against white minority rule were severely repressed, as were attempts at rebellion from the 1960s on. In the 1990s movements opposing apartheid finally achieved access to state power through the national elections of 1994. But after the death of Nelson Mandela, the legendary leader of the anti-apartheid movement, inequality and widespread poverty remained enormous problems that challenged a new generation of South African activists and leaders, despite the end of white minority rule and apartheid, and even though significant progress had been made in some areas.

GEOGRAPHY AND POPULATION

South Africa has a land area of 471,008 square miles (1,219,912 square kilometers) bounded by the Atlantic on the west, the Indian Ocean on the south and east, Namibia in the northwest, Botswana and Zimbabwe in the north, and Mozambique and Swaziland in the northeast. The independent kingdom of Lesotho is an enclave totally encompassed by South African territory in the southeast. Much of the interior is a high plateau or veld, half of which averages 4,000 feet (1,219 meters). The

Drakensberg Mountains rise to 11,000 feet (3,350 meters) in the east. The longest river is the Orange, which begins in Lesotho and flows westward 1,300 miles (2,092 kilometers) to the Atlantic. South Africa possesses large deposits of platinum, gold, diamonds, uranium, chromium, titanium, and other important minerals. The country's population was estimated at about 48.6 million in 2013, of which approximately 79 percent was of indigenous African ancestry, 9.6 percent European, 2.5 percent Asian (mostly persons of Indian ancestry), and 8.9 percent of mixed racial ancestry (identified as "colored" in South African society before 1994) (CIA 2014a). About 62 percent of the population lived in urban areas.

Prior to the establishment of a Dutch settlement at the Cape of Good Hope in 1652, a number of African peoples inhabited the territories that eventually became the Republic of South Africa. The San (whom the colonists called Bushmen) were located in the Cape area. The San had a hunter-gatherer economy based on the abundant game, fish, vegetables, and fruits of the region. They roamed parts of southwestern Africa in bands as small as twenty-five to as large as three hundred. The San, like the other major group in the area, the Khoi (whom the colonists called Hottentots), spoke a "click language" (characterized by clicking sounds). The Khoi, however, made use of domesticated animals, sheep, and large herds of cattle. They lived in villages varying in size from 500 to 2,000 over a large territory that stretched from the Cape as far as 500 miles (800 kilometers) to the east and 190 miles (300 kilometers) to the north.

Other peoples in southern Africa were technologically more advanced than the San and the Khoi in that they used iron tools and engaged in agriculture as well as cattle and sheep herding. Most of these groups have been classified by linguists as Bantu speaking. In this sense the expression "Bantu" was used to refer to an African language category that had several major subdivisions. *Bantu* appears to have been derived from the Zulu word *abantu*, which means "people." White colonists later applied the expression in a derogatory sense to all indigenous Africans (Danaher 1984; North 1985).

In the area from the Drakensberg Mountains to the Indian Ocean lived the Nguni-speaking groups of the Bantu linguistic category. These included the Xhosa and the Zulu. Much of the territory of southern Africa north of the Orange River was inhabited by the Sotho-Tswana groups, whose Bantu dialects were mutually intelligible. In addition, a number of smaller groups whose languages were included in the Bantu family inhabited various parts of South Africa.

DUTCH AND BRITISH COLONIZATION

After the Dutch East India Company set up a naval refreshment facility at the Cape of Good Hope in 1652 for their ships in transit to and from Asia, some of the company's employees were encouraged to establish farms and cattle herds to help provision the trading vessels. Early white settlers were overwhelmingly Dutch but also included some Germans and significant numbers of French and Belgian Huguenots (Calvinist Protestants). Although the Huguenots constituted about one-sixth of the late-seventeenth-century white settler population, they adopted the Dutch language and affiliated with the Protestant Dutch Reformed Church. Over time, the colonists sharing the Dutch culture added some African expressions and other modifications to their speech, which came to constitute a new Dutch dialect called Afrikaans, and referred to themselves as Afrikaners. The colony's farmers were called Boers. These people obtained land and cattle from the surrounding Khoi, initially through purchase and trade. But when the Khoi resisted, the settlers resorted to warfare. After several decades many of the San and the Khoi had been transformed into a destitute class whose members could only survive through accepting the role of servant or slave to the white colonists (Magubane 1979; Magubane and Mandaza 1988; Omer-Cooper 1987).

In 1806, Great Britain, to facilitate trade with its Asian interests, seized Holland's Cape Colony. About 5,000 English settlers arrived in 1820. Many Afrikaans-speaking inhabitants resented British domination and the increasing use of English in the colony. Furthermore, young Afrikaners who sought to establish large farms—of 1,000 or more acres—found their goal to be less attainable as the Cape became more heavily populated. Finally, in 1834 many Afrikaners were outraged when the British abolished slavery. Thousands decided to head for other territories as yet free from British control. A series of large settler expeditions, collectively referred to as the Great Trek, set out from the Cape from 1836 to 1856. The heavily armed wagon trains generally avoided the most densely populated areas and well-organized African groups, such as the Xhosa along the coast, and turned into the interior to regions that had recently been partially depopulated by warfare among the Africans. English merchants provided equipment, weapons, and ammunition the trekkers used to defeat, dispossess, and subjugate the inhabitants of the territories they invaded (Magubane 1979).

Eventually the Afrikaners who trekked (most had stayed at the Cape) established two landlocked Afrikaner states independent of British rule: the Orange Free State, between the Orange and Vaal rivers, and the much larger Transvaal Republic (also called the South African Republic), to the north of the Vaal. The British, in part discouraged by the potential cost of subduing and then administering the republics, tolerated their existence. The discovery of diamonds at British-controlled Kimberley, near the border between Cape Colony and the Orange Free State, in 1867 and the economically more significant discovery of vast gold deposits in the Transvaal in 1886 prompted Britain's leaders to seek to incorporate the Afrikaner republics into a united South Africa, along with the Cape Colony and the colony of Natal on the eastern coast, under a pro-British regime.

Thousands of Britons arrived in the Transvaal to mine gold. The ore, though abundant, was of moderate to poor quality, meaning that enormous quantities had to be extracted and processed. Furthermore, much of the gold was located far below the surface, necessitating the construction of expensive deep mines. Exploiting the gold would require major capital investments and cheap, plentiful labor to ensure large profits.

British miners and businesspeople, who by the 1890s were generating most of the Transvaal's export income, were termed "outlanders" and were not allowed to vote. British authorities rejected a compromise for an eventual extension of the vote to British residents of the Transvaal and provoked war with the republics in 1899. Mounted Boer guerrilla fighters numbering up to 40,000 waged an effective resistance, forcing the commitment of a quarter of a million British troops to the conflict. British authorities forcibly removed Afrikaner farm families to concentration camps, where 25,000 women and children perished from disease, and destroyed many farms to deprive guerrillas of sustenance. The British also detained the Boers' African servants and workers in separate concentration camps, where similar numbers died (Omer-Cooper 1987).

Many Africans denied provisions to Boer troops and even at times attacked Boer commandos, anticipating that British victory would result in the extension of political rights to nonwhites. African opposition was instrumental in forcing the Boers to accept British peace terms (Omer-Cooper 1987; Warwick 1983). But in an attempt to convince the Boers to agree to the 1902 peace proposal, the British promised not to grant political equality to nonwhites, thus betraying African wartime sacrifices (the Boers often executed Africans who aided the British). British authorities even arrested native Africans for violating the Transvaal's laws by burning their mandatory work passes and obliged them to continue working at low wages in the mines, owned largely by British interests (Magubane 1979; Omer-Cooper 1987).

In 1905 the Liberal Party won control of the British Parliament from the Conservatives and proposed a policy of reconciliation with the Boers in which the formerly independent republics would quickly be returned to self-government within the framework of a union with the Cape and Natal colonies. The constitution of the Union of South Africa, approved by 1910 by the legislatures of the four states and the British Parliament, limited the vote to white males except in the Cape, where certain economically prosperous nonwhite men retained the franchise (these constituted at the time about one-seventh of all Cape voters). British Liberals adopted the optimistic view that the Cape would serve as a model to the three other members of the union. Instead, white South African leaders eliminated nonwhite Cape voting rights by denying the vote to Cape indigenous Africans in 1936 and Cape residents of mixed race in 1956 (Radu 1987). Thus the measures taken by the British in resolving the Boer War resulted in the establishment of a virtually all-white state structure, which both constituted a major continuous cause for nonwhite mass discontent and provided a motivation for overthrowing the white regime, a motivation that conceivably could unify nonwhite population groups in a revolutionary effort.

When the Union of South Africa was formed, mining and other developing industries, along with the professions, were dominated by whites of British ancestry. Although some Afrikaners were involved in trades or other businesses, they were predominantly farmers. But as a result of the devastation of the Boer War and later taxation, thousands of Afrikaners were forced to sell or abandon their farms, often to expanding agribusiness interests, and seek employment in the mines or in the urban industries. This massive movement of thousands of former Afrikaner farmers from the countryside to the mining and urban areas after the Boer War was called the Second Great Trek. Thus much of the Afrikaans-speaking majority of the white population (approximately 60 percent of whites) became an impoverished working class. These Afrikaners maintained their ideology of racial superiority both as a source of psychological status and as a justification for preventing nonwhites from competing economically on an equal footing with whites or from having access to political power (Magubane 1979; Omer-Cooper 1987; Thompson 1985). Afrikaner leaders attempted to gain control of South Africa's new government by convincing all Afrikaners, who were a majority of the white voters, to support the (Afrikaner) Nationalist Party, founded in 1914.

The British tended to be more liberal than the Afrikaners, as reflected by the extension of the vote to some nonwhites in the Cape Colony. British missionaries converted many Africans to Christianity and provided educational opportunities for limited numbers. But certain British colonial authorities not only held a personal belief in white racial superiority but also took actions at various points to crush nonwhite opposition and capacity for self-sufficiency. These included the British-precipitated Zulu War in the 1870s, which (though later condemned in England, especially after initial Zulu victories resulted in the deaths of many British soldiers) led to the subjugation of the Zulu and their availability as laborers for various white-owned industries. British authorities imposed taxes that coerced hundreds of thousands of indigenous Africans to seek employment in mining, industry, or other jobs to earn money to pay taxes and survive in the new economic environment (Omer-Cooper 1987).

THE UNION OF SOUTH AFRICA

After 1910 a national parliament elected exclusively by whites, except in the Cape Province, governed South Africa as a member of the British Commonwealth. Early parliaments were dominated by parties that generally promoted reconciliation among the nation's whites. However, during World War I thousands of Afrikaners protested against South Africa's alliance with Britain and its seizure of German-occupied Southwest Africa (Namibia). After the war, which drew many more black South Africans into the industrial labor force and, consequently, into competition with whites, many white workers, objecting to their own poor working conditions and to advances by nonwhites, staged strikes and violent protests. Government forces killed scores of white workers. As a result, the white workers' Labor Party formed an alliance with the National Party (then supported largely by Afrikaner farmers and businesspeople) and during the 1920s helped pass a series of laws further restricting the rights of nonwhites. The Labor Party, however, was soon weakened by internal conflict between members who proposed cooperation with nonwhite workers and those who refused. The National Party continued to gain support under the leadership of a former official of the Orange Free State, J. B. Hertzog.

Hertzog's government (first elected in 1924) took measures to improve employment opportunities for Afrikaner whites, such as the creation in 1928 of the state-owned Iron and Steel Corporation (ISCOR), and assisted other Afrikaner-controlled industries by imposing protective tariffs. These and other businesses were required to reserve certain types of jobs for whites only and employ specific quotas of white workers. Many Afrikaners, believing that continued political association with Britain would gradually erode Afrikaner culture and perhaps even lead to racial equality, favored withdrawal from the Commonwealth. Afrikaner nationalism was embodied in the growth of a covert Afrikaner organization called the Broederbond, which set up secret cells in economic, cultural, and governmental institutions, including the armed forces (Giliomee 1980; Omer-Cooper 1987).

The worldwide Great Depression devastated South Africa. In 1934 Hertzog's National Party and the party supported by many whites of British descent, the South Africa Party, led by a moderate Afrikaner, Jan Smuts, joined forces to form the United Party, which then enjoyed a large majority in the parliament. English-speaking whites who opposed the United Party organized the Dominion Party, whereas Afrikaners objecting to unifying politically with British interests formed the much more important Purified National Party (later known simply as the National Party), under D. F. Malan (Omeara 1983; Omer-Cooper 1987).

As World War II began, the United Party experienced internal conflict. Hertzog and many of his Afrikaner followers favored neutrality. But Smuts, with his Afrikaner associates and the English-speaking members of the United Party, supported by the smaller Dominion and Labor parties, obtained a majority in the parliament in favor of entering the war on Britain's side. As a result, thousands of South Africans of all races served in the war, although only whites were allowed to bear arms (nonwhites performed support functions). Some Afrikaners supported Germany because they approved the Nazi doctrine of Aryan racial superiority. A number sabotaged military facilities, and some were incarcerated for the duration of the conflict.

MAP 9.1 South Africa (Before 1994)

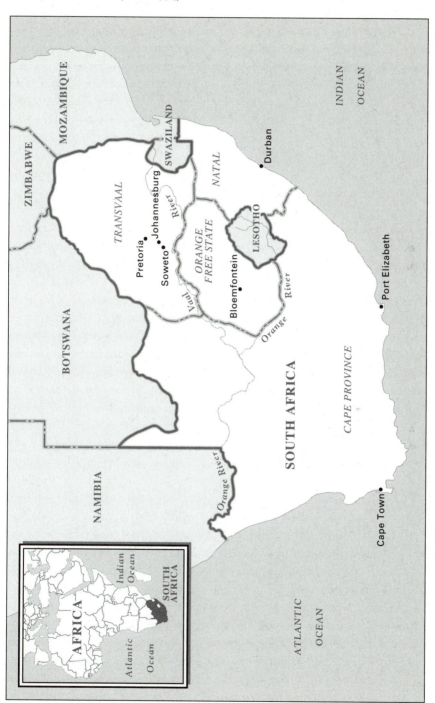

The war caused a tremendous boom in and transformation of the economy. At the onset of the conflict South Africa's wealth was derived primarily from mining. But at the conclusion manufacturing was foremost. The war stimulated South Africa to develop the capacity to build much of the machinery and equipment it had formerly imported. Furthermore, in the absence of the many whites serving in the armed forces, a massive influx of indigenous Africans into mining and urban industry occurred.

After World War II the United Party, under Smuts, expected victory in the 1948 election for parliament. However, most Afrikaners and some English-speaking whites had become dissatisfied over certain issues. United Party leaders had proposed permanent urban residency for Africans, who by that point were extensively employed in industry. Thousands of returning whites feared not only racial integration but also increased economic competition from blacks if the United Party retained power (Lazerson 1994; Omeara 1983; Omer-Cooper 1987). Also, Afrikaner farmers blamed the United Party for a shortage of low-cost African agricultural laborers. Others were concerned with the wartime growth of groups opposed to the racially based political system; they were especially wary of the South African Communist Party, which had gained influence in the labor movement.

All these factors combined to heighten the popularity of the concept of continued and increased apartheid (separateness of the races) championed by Malan's National Party. According to apartheid doctrine, each race and nation has its own distinct cultural identity and has been created to achieve a unique destiny laid down by God. Therefore each race must be kept pure and allowed to develop along its own lines because "excessive contact between races, above all interbreeding, would corrupt and destroy the inner potential of both races" (Omer-Cooper 1987, 190). Whites fearing liberalization of racial policies provided the National Party with a narrow victory in the momentous 1948 election.

THE APARTHEID STATE

Malan's new National Party government immediately moved to implement a series of laws intended to increase and systematize separation not only among the four official racial categories of white, colored, Asian (Indian), and black, but also among the major ethnic, or tribal, groups within the huge indigenous African majority. Legislation formalizing apartheid included the Population Registration Act (mandating official racial classification of all South Africans) and the Prohibition of Mixed Marriages Act. The Suppression of Communism Act, passed in 1950, not only banned the South African Communist Party but also permitted the punishment of anyone working to implement the supposedly communist doctrine of racial equality (Davis 1987; Omer-Cooper 1987). Thus the government created a powerful tool to protect the white-controlled state by severely punishing opponents of apartheid as communists and traitors.

The 1952 Native Laws Amendment Act restricted indigenous Africans' right to permanent residency in towns and urban areas largely to those who had previously resided and worked in a particular town for fifteen or more years. Africans in this category, though, could not move to any other urban area and could be removed from the town if authorities determined they were unemployed for long periods or were judged harmful to the public good. All other indigenous Africans were permitted to reside only temporarily in urban areas (in designated locations usually remote from the white cities) as long as they were employed and had the necessary clearance. But they officially held permanent residency only in their tribal homelands.

The South African government had previously, through the 1913 Native Land Act and the 1936 Native Trust and Land Act, allotted 13.5 percent of South Africa's territory as tribal homelands or Bantustans, which were the only permanent residences available to most of the country's population. The ten homelands, which on average had close to half of their supposed populations living in the white 86.5 percent of South Africa, included Basotho-Qwaqwa of the Southern Sotho, Bophuthatswana of the Tswana, Ciskei of the Xhosa, Gazankulu of the Shangaana, KaNgwane of the Ngwane, KwaNdebele of the Ndebele, KwaZulu of the Zulu, Lebowa of the Northern Sotho, Transkei of the Xhosa, and Venda of the Venda (Magubane 1979; Omer-Cooper 1987). Most Bantustans possessed little mineral wealth or industrial or transportation infrastructure. They functioned primarily as sources of cheap labor for white industry, business, and domestic service, and depositories for the elderly, the infirm, and surplus labor. Many migrant workers were not permitted to bring their families with them to white areas and were often required to live in barracks-like conditions that fostered alcohol abuse and crime. Hundreds of thousands of indigenous African women were forced to surrender care of their own children to others as a condition of employment as domestics in white homes, where, ironically, they played a major role in raising and tending to their employers' children.

The 1952 Pass Law required indigenous Africans to carry in a single passbook a personal photograph and information on place of birth, employment, tax payments, and record of police contacts.

The 1956 Native Resettlement Act helped re-segregate blacks after years of urban expansion left certain black areas surrounded by white residential developments. Many indigenous Africans were uprooted from these enclaves and forced to take up residency in new government-built townships, such as those southwest of Johannesburg (known by the acronym for South Western Townships, Soweto, eventually inhabited by more than 1 million people).

Other laws restricted education for nonwhites so that they would be trained only in the skills necessary to serve their tribal kin in the Bantustans and "perform the labouring roles which might be required of them by whites" (Omer-Cooper 1987, 201). By 1961 the National Party government had enacted into law all the measures that constituted its original white supremacist form of apartheid. This system not only perpetuated separation of the races but also guaranteed the lion's share of the nation's growing wealth to the white minority, eventually virtually eliminating poverty among whites. The National Party also renamed the nation in 1960 the Republic of South Africa and withdrew it from the British Commonwealth. These events, in a sense, reversed the outcome of the 1899–1902 Boer War.

CHANGES IN THE APARTHEID SYSTEM

After 1959 the apartheid system underwent several modifications. As former African colonies achieved independence from European domination, South Africa attempted to influence the emerging states through offers of technical assistance and trade. One purpose of the new tactic was to deflect criticism and increasing anti-apartheid animosity emanating from the United Nations. As newly independent African and Asian nations were admitted to its ranks, that body was becoming less dominated by European nations (which in the past had seemed relatively tolerant of South African racism). The white regime also sensed that good relations with other nations on the continent would provide nearby markets for the exports generated by South Africa's growing manufacturing sector.

Greater reliance on manufacturing and increasing technological sophistication, along with white social mobility out of the working class and into white-collar occupations, changed the nature of the demand for nonwhite labor. Previously, mining and industry had utilized mainly unskilled or semiskilled nonwhites. Now the economy needed larger numbers of skilled nonwhite workers who could reliably carry out their jobs over an extended period. Finally, the increasing internal protests against apartheid since World War II, progressing from peaceful campaigns of defiance to armed resistance, and punctuated by internationally condemned episodes of violent repression, also prompted significant policy alterations (Danaher 1984; Omer-Cooper 1987).

The three major innovations engineered by the white regime between 1960 and 1990 included pursuing political independence for the tribal homelands, developing a skilled, stable nonwhite labor force, and in 1983 enacting a new constitution intended to co-opt Indians and South Africans of mixed racial descent (coloreds) into an alliance with whites against the indigenous African majority (Danaher 1984; Omer-Cooper 1987).

Prior to 1959, the South African government intended that the native homelands would develop local self-government along tribal lines but would remain under the

MAP 9.2 South African Tribal Homelands (Before 1994)

jurisdiction of the white republic. However, theoreticians within the National Party eventually won support for the argument that South Africa could both achieve wider international acceptance and divide internal opposition by pushing a policy of full independence for the homelands. Publicly the white regime began to assert that it now recognized indigenous Africans' capability to govern modern nation-states. But establishing the homelands as independent states would transform the basis for economic and political discrimination against indigenous Africans from racism to citizenship. The millions of indigenous Africans employed in South African industries, businesses, and households would in the future be classified as foreign migrant labor; their lack of entitlement to the rights of South Africans would be based on nationality, not race (Danaher 1984; Magubane 1979; Omer-Cooper 1987).

Furthermore, National Party leaders anticipated that the development of independent homeland government administrations, service bureaucracies, and economic enterprises would provide opportunities for social mobility for educated indigenous Africans blocked from participating in the republic's government or from playing major roles in other institutions, thus minimizing African elite discontent. Additional benefits to the white community included the probability that blacks would in the future target their own homeland governments for protest actions rather than white authorities. Granting independence along tribal lines was also thought likely to heighten competitiveness and hostility among ethnic groups, thereby presenting whites with a divided and more easily controlled black population, whose tribal animosities might override the motivation to unite against apartheid. As most of the homelands lacked both industrial infrastructure and known significant mineral wealth and some were actually composed of several noncontiguous parcels separated by the republic's territory, they would remain economically dependent on the white-controlled state and could be easily intimidated by South Africa's powerful military.

Business leaders reacted to the growing shortage of skilled workers by pressuring the government to open many previously restricted jobs to nonwhites. Furthermore, in seeking a stable, skilled workforce, the white regime by the 1980s granted many Africans virtual permanent residency outside the homelands by successively allowing them the right to lease houses in segregated urban townships for thirty years and then ninety years, and finally permitting them to purchase homes. Furthermore, to promote emotional stability among African skilled workers, the regime allowed many to have their families live with them. In 1970, before the worker stabilization program had begun at the Kimberley diamond mines, 86 percent of the workforce was composed of migrants, whereas in 1979, after seven years of the new program, 62 percent of the mine workers were stabilized (Omer-Cooper 1987).

The need to reduce wildcat strikes and provide mechanisms through which business and government could communicate with the increasingly skilled and difficult-to-replace workforce prompted the government to legalize black labor unions after 1979, provided they did not engage in political activity (Davis 1987; Kerson 1987). To meet the demand for highly trained technicians of all races, segregated nonwhite universities were expanded, and white universities were opened to those needing courses not available at nonwhite institutions. In 1986 the white regime abolished the Pass Law and permitted freer movement of African workers to black urban districts (*New York Times,* June 27, 1988, A1).

In 1983 white voters approved a new multiracial constitution that supposedly offered a share of power to coloreds and Indians, to the exclusion of the indigenous African majority. The three-part legislature included a white House of Assembly, with 166 members; a colored House of Representatives, with eighty-five members; and an Indian House of Delegates, with forty-five members. The president of the republic, selected by an Electoral College of eighty-eight (fifty elected by the white parliament, twenty-five by the colored, and thirteen by the Indian), enjoyed greatly expanded executive powers under the new constitution. Individual parliaments were to deal with matters particular to their racial groups and jointly with matters of common interest (Danaher 1984, 23), as determined by the president. Many considered this constitution a mechanism for preserving white domination. Large numbers of mixed race and Indian South Africans refused to register to vote under the new constitution. The new political system infuriated many members of the totally excluded black population and precipitated the most widespread protests since the 1976 Soweto uprising (Danaher 1984; Davis 1987; Omer-Cooper 1987).

Opposition to Apartheid

The defeat of Chief Bambatha's 1903 rebellion against taxation and white-supported collaborationist tribal leaders was the last traditional war of resistance against white domination. But in 1912, following the rejection of political equality for nonwhites by the victorious British, an important African movement opposed to white domination was organized, the African National Congress (ANC), originally called the South African Natives' National Congress. This group, established largely by Western-schooled black professionals, businesspeople, and prosperous farmers, whose education was often the product of Christian missionary efforts, was the "first modern, nontribal organization of blacks formed to discuss black interests under white rule" (Davis 1987, 3). The early ANC was resigned to the at-least-temporary reality of white rule but was committed to working against laws promoting racial discrimination and for an extension of the benefits of modern education and technology to the larger population. The group supported a future nonracial political system in which all South Africa's peoples would enjoy equal rights in a European-style democratic state. ANC leaders originally hoped that peaceful protest and legal efforts,

coupled with anticipated international pressure from Britain, other democratic nations, and the worldwide Christian church, would bring about a reorganization of
South Africa along nonracial lines. But during its early years the ANC remained
largely an elitist, middle-class group, somewhat isolated culturally from the traditional lifestyles of the majority of Africans (Davis 1987; Omer-Cooper 1987).

During World War II, as South Africa joined the Allies against Nazi Germany
and its doctrine of racial supremacy, ANC leaders supported the war effort in the
expectation that victory would result in a reduction of racism and an extension of
political rights at home. The 1948 election, which brought the Afrikaner National
Party to power, reversed wartime liberalization and led to the passage of laws that
reaffirmed and systematized racial segregation. It also precipitated the more militant younger generation's ascendancy to leadership of the ANC. Youthful activists
favored mass protest movements instead of negotiating and making moral appeals
to white leaders, who seemed primarily concerned with appeasing the racially biased elements within their existing electorate.

On June 26, 1952, the ANC, together with the anti-apartheid South African Indian Congress (SAIC), launched the Defiance Campaign. Volunteers would violate
segregation laws in several cities and then passively submit to arrest. The campaign
quickly generated large-scale popular support among nonwhites, and ANC membership, which had been 4,500 in 1947, rapidly increased to 100,000. But among
the many recruits were scores of paid government agents (some motivated by opposition to the ANC's nontribal orientation), whose information regarding the
movement's leadership helped the white government's repression. In August and
September the white regime arrested ANC and SAIC leaders and accused them of
violating the Suppression of Communism Act. Then in mid-October in response,
spontaneous riots broke out in several cities that were violently crushed. As a result
of the mass arrests of leaders and the smashing of riots, the Defiance Campaign
collapsed (Davis 1987; Omer-Cooper 1987). In reaction, Nelson Mandela, a young
lawyer of Xhosa ancestry who was an architect of the Defiance Campaign, began
constructing a secretive cellular network within the ANC, the elements of which
in the future would continue to provide leadership at the local level regardless of
whether top leaders or any components of the overall organization were eliminated
(Davis 1987).

The ANC and the SACP

The ANC received instruction in organizing its internal underground network
from members of the illegal South African Communist Party (SACP). The SACP
had been founded among exploited white workers in 1921 and initially avoided
working with blacks, reflecting the racist attitudes of many whites. But well before

the 1950s the SACP had committed itself to organizing black laborers and working for racial equality. SACP activists played significant roles in some labor unions and in protests against the regime. They perceived that the ANC had the capability to organize and guide the development of a mass movement to bring an end to white rule. In the original SACP view, this would lead to a second revolutionary transition to "a socialist South Africa, laying the foundations of a classless, communist society" (Davis 1987, 10). The SACP's estimated membership of 2,000 in 1950 included 150 whites and 250 Indians (Davis 1987; Karis 1986/1987; Lazerson 1994).

The ANC's attitude toward the SACP shifted over time. From the 1920s through the 1940s many ANC members opposed working with the SACP (Karis 1986/1987; Mandela 1994). But the post–World War II National Party government's apartheid program and, in particular, its implementation of broad repressive policies under the Suppression of Communism Act of 1950, which mandated that anyone working for racial equality could be punished for advocating communism, tended to promote cooperation between the ANC and the SACP.

When the ANC was outlawed in 1960, it became more dependent on assistance from the SACP. SACP members helped establish the critically important secret leadership network of ANC militants inside South Africa, obtained financial and military aid for the ANC from the Soviet Union and other Communist Party–dominated states, and provided information on the South African government, military, and economic installations that was gathered either by SACP members or by the Soviet Union (Davis 1987; Karis 1986/1987; Magubane 1979). The SACP's characterization of South Africa's system as a form of European imperialist exploitation of Africa appeared increasingly valid to many ANC members, whose peaceful efforts at change were crushed within the country while many capitalist nations cooperated with the white government and refused to help the ANC.

British historian Stephen Ellis, working with information from people who had been in the SACP and other data, concluded in a paper published in 2011 that Nelson Mandela joined the SACP around 1960 and had actually become a member of the party's central committee (Keller 2013; Freeman and Flanagan 2012). Immediately after Mandela's death on December 5, 2013, the SACP (2013) confirmed that Mandela had been a member of the party and its central committee. Active membership could only have been short-lived since, as described below, Mandela was arrested and imprisoned in 1962.

By the end of 1969 the ANC began to accept nonindigenous South African Communists into its ranks, and in 1985 the ANC National Executive Committee was opened to all races. At that time the number of SACP members on the thirty-three-person ANC Executive Committee was estimated to be at least three to as many as twenty-three (Karis 1986/1987; *New York Times*, Nov. 11, 1990, A15; Radu 1987). However, ANC leaders asserted that the ANC represented a broad coalition of interests and ideologies within South Africa, was not controlled by Communists, and publicly called for a multiparty, nonracial democracy.

The ANC and the Freedom Charter

The ANC and other groups participated in a Congress of the People at Kliptown in June 1955, involving a mass meeting of 3,000 people of all races. Those present voted to adopt a Freedom Charter, which asserted that the wealth of South Africa belonged to all its inhabitants and demanded the elimination of apartheid and the establishment of a nonracial democracy. In addition to calling for a more equitable distribution of land, resources and profits, and equal access to education and employment opportunities, further goals proclaimed in the charter included:

> The mineral wealth beneath the soil, the banks and monopoly industry shall be transferred to the ownership of the people as a whole; . . . other industries and trade shall be controlled to assist the well-being of the people. . . . The police force and army shall be open to all on an equal basis and shall be helpers and protectors of the people. . . . Free medical [treatment] and hospitalization shall be provided for all with special care for mothers and young children. . . . Peace and friendship amongst all our people shall be secured by upholding the equal rights, opportunities and status of all. (Congress of the People [1955] 1987, 209, 210, 211)

The white regime reacted harshly to the Freedom Charter. On December 5, 1956, after months of gathering information on activists, the government arrested scores of leaders of participating groups and accused them of treason. The so-called Treason Trial continued until November 29, 1961, with all the defendants found not guilty. However, the government had succeeded in imprisoning key leaders for extended periods and in harming those apprehended, financially and occupationally, to deter future potential activists.

The ANC and the PAC

Long-standing controversies within the ANC over multiracial cooperation to end white domination, the role of the SACP, and reliance on funding from non-African countries dominated by communist parties resulted in a major defection from the ANC and the establishment in April 1959 of the Pan-Africanist Congress (PAC). The PAC, like the ANC, supported the establishment of a nonracial government. But the PAC argued that South Africa must be freed from apartheid primarily through black militancy, not through the ANC multiracial cooperation approach, which, according to the PAC, was being subverted by ANC communist members and was too greatly influenced by the non-African nations from which it obtained much of its funds and weapons. The PAC advocated the black nationalist view that the psychology of black South Africans, crippled by decades of oppression and humiliation at the hands of whites, could only be rejuvenated by having the nation's blacks "act alone in reclaiming South Africa from white domination" (Davis 1987, 11). The PAC's ideology gained popularity because it enhanced feelings of pride and importance among many young Africans and engendered a special sense of mission.

Both the ANC and the PAC planned to launch a campaign against the Pass Law in spring 1960. PAC leaders, however, decided to begin their protest on March 21, ten days before the scheduled start of the ANC antipass drive. At Sharpeville on the morning of March 21, a large number of people gathered without their pass documents to await arrest. Some police, possibly fearing for their own safety, opened fire on the crowd, killing sixty-seven, most shot in the back as they tried to flee. Police shootings at other locations also resulted in deaths and scores of injuries. The killings precipitated riots by tens of thousands in the black townships outside the white cities and industrial centers they served. On April 8 the South African government outlawed both the ANC and the PAC. Because the ANC had built an underground network, it was less devastated than the PAC, which had virtually no clandestine organizational structure and was almost eliminated (Adam 1988; Davis 1987; Schlemmer 1988).

The ANC and Armed Resistance

Elements of the ANC, under the leadership of Nelson Mandela, made one last attempt to convince the white government to accept peaceful change. They demanded a national convention of all races to draft a new nonracial constitution. When the white regime rejected this, ANC militants reluctantly abandoned the organization's long-held commitment to nonviolent protest and began a campaign of selective sabotage. Because older and more moderate members of the ANC resisted the shift in tactics, the younger activists formed a semi-independent military organization, Umkhonto we Sizwe (Zulu for "Spear of the Nation"), which was affiliated with the ANC. The aim of Umkhonto was to sabotage important transportation, communication, and industrial facilities in order to damage the nation's white-owned economy and frighten off foreign investors, thereby pressuring the government into serious negotiations with the ANC (Davis 1987; Mandela 1994; Omer-Cooper 1987). SACP members with military experience began to train young South Africans in the use of bombs, grenades, and other weapons and obtained military assistance from the Soviet Union. Western countries dependent on South Africa for important minerals, such as platinum and chromium, and favorably influenced by South Africa's strong anticommunist stance, refused to provide military aid to the ANC, although by the 1980s several Western European nations were assisting through cash donations and in other nonmilitary ways.

The Umkhonto sabotage campaign began on December 16, 1961, to counter the Afrikaner celebration of an 1838 Boer victory over a Zulu army at Blood River during the Great Trek. Over several months scores of targets were hit by dynamite bombs, but the damage was usually slight. In August 1962 Mandela was captured, reportedly with the aid of information supplied to the South African government by the CIA (*New York Times*, June 10, 1990, A15), and later tried for attempting violent overthrow of the government; he was given a life sentence. By the end of 1963 the Umkhonto sabotage effort had been largely crushed. A sabotage-assassination campaign by PAC extremists was also smashed. The ANC leadership concluded that before they attempted another large-scale armed assault, the ANC underground "would have to be purged of counter-espionage agents and made secure" and that a military command center outside South Africa would have to be established to plan, coordinate, and order operations "without fear of capture" (Davis 1987, 21).

Revolutionary Changes Among South Africa's Neighbors

In the mid-1970s major changes north of South Africa improved the chances for anti-apartheid movements and certainly had the effect of encouraging nonwhite militancy and alarming the white minority. After more than a dozen years of attempting to repress nationalist guerrilla movements in its Angola and Mozambique colonies, Portugal experienced its own revolution. Leftist-oriented Portuguese soldiers, disillusioned by decades of right-wing military dictatorship and the futile and wasteful colonial wars, and in part inspired by the ideology of the African revolutionaries they had struggled against, overthrew their nation's authoritarian regime. The new left-leaning Portuguese government soon granted independence to Angola and Mozambique. In both nations leftist-oriented movements, extremely hostile to the apartheid state to the south, achieved dominance (Mabeko-Tali 2006; Newitt 2006). For the first time, countries geographically close to South Africa appeared ready to support a large-scale revolutionary effort.

Within a few more years nationalist guerrilla movements in another nearby country, Zimbabwe (formerly called Rhodesia, after the wealthy white British expansionist Cecil Rhodes), succeeded with the aid of international pressure in forcing a negotiated end to the rule of its then approximately 4 percent white minority (Rubert 2006). In the April 18, 1980, election for a national parliament, The ZANU (the Zimbabwe African National Union) party of the self-proclaimed Marxist and "most radical of the contenders," Robert Mugabe, won a resounding victory (Omer-Cooper 1987, 234). The new government declared its commitment to helping to overturn white minority rule in South Africa.

The Black Consciousness Movement and the Soweto Uprisings

Prior to the changes in Angola, Mozambique, and Zimbabwe, a new activist movement had been organized by young blacks at Bloemfontein in August 1971. Steve Biko was selected as leader of the new black consciousness movement. The BCM, inspired in part by the black power movement in the United States, was mainly influenced by earlier African nationalist ideology, such as that formulated by PAC leaders. The militants of the BCM asserted the need for blacks to lead the anti-apartheid movement but relied on legal means to attain their goals. This meant that the BCM was to avoid the ANC and PAC campaigns of civil disobedience and their later armed struggles. BCM leaders began "a scrupulously law-abiding education and community action campaign designed to work at the grass-roots level toward building a psychology of self-reliance among blacks" (Davis 1987, 25).

The BCM asserted that the pressure of a politically aroused, unified, and determined black majority, the anticipated result of the BCM program, would persuade the white government to negotiate a restructuring of South African society. Wherever the BCM set up local organizations, whether community action groups, labor unions, or political education seminars, only blacks were allowed to participate. Because the BCM advocated strict legality and seemed to employ its own form of apartheid rather than embrace the supposedly communist method of multiracial cooperation to attain a nonracial state, the white regime temporarily tolerated the movement (Omer-Cooper 1987). The apartheid government may have hoped that the BCM would draw potential recruits away from the more radical ANC and PAC. But the BCM failed to build a significant mass-organization network, relying instead on a relatively small elite of educated middle-class individuals for guidance. The BCM raised expectations through its leaders' public speeches eliciting black pride and self-confidence and by instilling a belief that sweeping change could be accomplished through the legal structures existing within the apartheid state. Since the group rejected the extralegal confrontational approach, it was not prepared to coordinate the protests generated by mass frustration when white authorities ignored peaceful demands for change (Davis 1987).

The efforts of the ANC, PAC, and BCM helped motivate a new defiance campaign by schoolchildren in the massive black township of Soweto in 1976. The protest was directed against a law requiring that black students "not only learn Afrikaans as a language as well as English but accept it as the media of instruction through which they would have to learn other key subjects like mathematics." Many viewed this rule as constituting "an intolerable, artificial obstacle to their struggle for advancement" (Omer-Cooper 1987, 224). In June 1976 Soweto schoolchildren began large-scale protests. When police used force to suppress the demonstrations, rioting broke out and spread to other towns in the Transvaal as well as to cities in Natal, the Cape, the Orange Free State, and the homelands.

The wave of riots constituted the largest black rebellion in twentieth-century South Africa. Unlike earlier outbreaks, the Soweto rebellion was not quickly crushed, despite vicious police and military violence, but continued for months. At least six hundred people, mostly young students, were shot to death by state forces. The white regime arrested hundreds of suspected protest leaders, dozens of whom died in police custody from supposed suicides, hunger strikes, and unexplained causes (Brewer 1986). In September 1977 the BCM leader, Steve Biko, was arrested and beaten to death by police. Thousands of young people, however, fled South Africa, and many joined ANC guerrilla forces organized in the anti-apartheid states to the north (Brewer 1986; Davis 1987). The Soweto uprisings infused the ANC with a new generation of radicalized youth and intensified mass frustration with the white regime and support for violent revolution.

Other young militants were drawn to the PAC, which shared the black nationalist orientation of the shattered black consciousness movement. They formed the Azania People's Liberation Army. Many members were quickly arrested, as the PAC had been infiltrated by government agents. The post-Soweto repression crushed all major contenders for leadership of the black opposition—except the longer established and more secretively organized ANC—and persuaded many more nonwhite South Africans "of the futility of above-ground, peaceful opposition" (Davis 1987, 33).

After 1978 "the story of the black military opposition in the Republic is largely the story of the ANC and its allies" (Davis 1987, 33). The ANC in the early 1980s was able to commence a sustained guerrilla effort, beginning with bombings of major South African oil facilities. The dominant view within the ANC was that although armed resistance could not result in a military victory in the near future, given the strength of the white regime's army and security forces, it could increase the costs of maintaining apartheid and, along with other factors, help pressure Pretoria into serious negotiations toward establishment of a nonracial democracy (Adam 1988).

Opposition to White Domination in the 1980s

The 1983 multiracial constitution, widely interpreted as an attempt to co-opt the colored and Indian minorities while maintaining white control, precipitated a massive intensification of protest. To protest the white referendum on the multiracial constitution, a new, initially legal, anti-apartheid organization was established in August 1983, when 12,000 delegates convened in Cape Town to form the United Democratic Front (UDF, after 1988 referred to as the "Mass Democratic Movement" in an effort to circumvent government repression). The UDF sought to link together the many local anti-apartheid groups through a countrywide board of directors that would set national policy objectives, suggest tactics, and offer coordination. "By the end of 1986, some seven hundred community bodies had affiliated with the umbrella-like UDF," including civic organizations, "women's groups, labor unions, youth leagues, and religious councils" (Davis 1987, 87).

Although the UDF declared itself independent of the illegal African National Congress, the UDF's goals for the future of South Africa appeared almost identical to those of the ANC. Most UDF member groups supported the ANC and accepted the Freedom Charter, and several national and local UDF leaders acknowledged past membership in the ANC. The UDF differed from the ANC in terms of its publicly accepted range of tactics, which excluded violence. However, in 1988 the white government declared the UDF, then claiming 3 million members, illegal (*New York Times*, February 25, 1988, A1). In addition to the UDF, a major new union federation, the Congress of South African Trade Unions (COSATU), was established at Durban in December 1985. Similar in structure to the UDF, COSATU also declared its independence of the ANC while expressing many of the same goals, and "announced socialist aims and principles" (Davis 1987, 102). Within several months thirty unions, representing 600,000 workers, had joined COSATU (membership would reach approximately 1 million by 1990), the largest union association in South Africa's history. The pro-PAC National Council of Trade Unions, in comparison, had about 150,000 members (*New York Times*, March 4, 1990, A14).

ANC leaders decided that rather than attempt the difficult task of organizing large numbers of South Africans directly into the illegal ANC, they would federate with like-minded legal organizations. In return for the cooperation of the UDF, COSATU, and associated groups, the ANC accepted the significant degree of ideological variation characterizing the allied organizations and a decentralized authority structure. But federation meant genuinely united, massive participation in a coordinated effort to overthrow white domination through measures including labor strikes, boycotts of white businesses, and sabotage of key economic installations as well as violent attacks on the military instruments of white oppression.

The ANC also called on nations trading with South Africa to boycott the republic and to convince or coerce their citizens to remove their investments from South Africa or from companies doing business in South Africa to help damage the economy and force change. The ANC hoped that its supporters would make the black townships ungovernable for the white-approved, often collaborationist township councils (whose members achieved power through elections in which generally less than 20 percent of those eligible voted) and that the townships could be turned into relatively secure bases for ANC activities. By 1986 many councils had been effectively replaced by local popular committees favorable to the ANC. The African National Congress and allied groups in the 1980s enjoyed the backing of about 50 percent of the black population (40 percent of South Africa's population), making it the single most widely supported political group in the nation (Davis 1987).

Another indication of popular allegiance to the ANC was that an estimated 70 percent of indigenous African workers participated in the nationwide strike called by the Mass Democratic Movement (the renamed UDF) to protest the 1989 South African elections (*US News & World Report*, September 18, 1989, 52).

Support for the ANC was motivated not only by opposition to apartheid but also by economic hardships. In the 1980s white per capita income was more than four times that of Indians or individuals of mixed racial ancestry and over eight times that of indigenous Africans (Seedat 1987a; 1987b).

Inkatha

A major rival to the ANC among the Zulu in Natal Province was Inkatha yeNkululeko yeSizwe (National Cultural Liberation movement). Its leader was Chief Gatsa Buthelezi, head of the most populous homeland, KwaZulu, to which more than 6 million black South Africans were assigned, even if working in white areas. Inkatha, a Zulu cultural organization revived by Buthelezi in 1975, had 100,000 members by 1977 and claimed 1.7 million by 1990. Inkatha attracted mostly Zulus living in rural areas in KwaZulu or other parts of rural Natal. Inkatha's "political culture was dominated by the personality cult surrounding Buthelezi's populist leadership, and by the traditions of Zulu power" (Davis 1987, 107).

While opposing apartheid, Buthelezi and other Inkatha leaders criticized the ANC for advocating socialism as opposed to free enterprise; for demanding a one person, one vote democratic political system instead of being flexible enough to consider other forms of sharing power with whites; and for resorting to armed resistance rather than continuing to utilize nonviolent means to pressure the white regime to accept reforms. Buthelezi also rejected ANC calls for other nations to disinvest in South Africa; instead, he promoted foreign investment in order to develop the nation's economy and thereby provide more jobs for nonwhites. In opinion surveys conducted during the 1980s, the KwaZulu chief's followers, much to the pleasure of the white government, reflected their leader's views. Only small percentages of pro-Inkatha blacks favored the use of strikes, divestiture, or violence against the white regime in comparison to large majorities among ANC-UDF supporters (Bernstein and Godsell 1988; Davis 1987).

In KwaZulu, where unemployment was high, the jobs and opportunities for advancement that Buthelezi could provide to thousands, both through his control of the homeland administration and through his influence over Inkatha's staff hiring, constituted a major patronage-dispensing base of his power. Unlike several other homeland leaders, however, he had refused to accommodate white demands that he accept full independence for the several geographically separated territories that constituted KwaZulu. Instead he proposed an experiment in which Zulus, Natal

Indians, and coloreds would have some role, along with whites, in governing Natal Province. Buthelezi's opposition to total independence for KwaZulu partially shielded him from being perceived as a puppet of white rulers. His prestige was further enhanced by the coverage his public statements received in the white media, which portrayed him as a relatively responsible and reasonable advocate of black aspirations.

Comparatively favorable white attitudes toward Buthelezi in part resulted from his rejection of ANC violence. He instructed his followers to "avoid at all costs being made cannon fodder by people who want to use our corpses to stand on in order to be seen as leaders" (Davis 1987, 108). But in contrast to his condemnation of armed attacks directed at the white regime or its agents, Buthelezi's Inkatha members became widely known for using violence against supporters of the ANC (*New York Times*, April 22, 1990, A3; August 22, 1990, A7). Inkatha's influence in the 1980s and early 1990s was limited primarily to Natal Province and other locations with large numbers of Zulu immigrants from rural backgrounds, whereas the ANC and its allied organizations enjoyed wide support in nonwhite urban areas throughout South Africa. In July 1990 Buthelezi announced that Inkatha was being reorganized as a political party, the Inkatha Freedom Party, anticipating its participation in a reformed South African political system (*New York Times*, July 15, 1990, A5).

White Opposition to Apartheid

Several white groups opposed aspects of the apartheid system. Elements of the white business community, responding to the economy's need for an expanded, stable, skilled workforce, convinced government officials to alter legal codes in order to achieve this goal. The changes included opening new occupational categories to nonwhites, legalizing indigenous African labor unions, and the 1986 repealing of the Pass Laws (Bernstein and Godsell 1988). Some business leaders asked the government to negotiate with the ANC, and several called for establishing a nonracial democracy.

The Progressive Federal Party, which drew support disproportionately from middle- and upper-middle-income whites, had spent thirty years fighting for greater civil and political rights for the nonwhite majority. In April 1989 this group joined with two smaller political parties to create a united left-wing opposition to the National Party government. The result was the Democratic Party, which in the 1989 national election won about 20 percent of the vote and 33 seats in the 166-seat white parliament (*New York Times*, September 8, 1989, A8). The Democratic Party advocated "a true democracy which rejects race as its basis and protects the human dignity and liberty of all its citizens" (*New York Times*, April 9, 1989, 6).

A third element of white society, the South African Dutch Reformed Church, which long helped provide ideological justifications for white domination, decided to oppose apartheid. In 1986 leaders of the church, which at that time included 80 percent of white legislators among its 1.7 million members, declared racism to be a sin "and opened its membership to Christians of all races" (Berger and Godsell 1988b, 298).

COUNTERINSURGENCY STRATEGIES OF THE REGIME IN THE 1980S

White leaders developed a comprehensive strategy to cope with democracy movements. This included coordination of governmental policy, the economy, mass media, the military, and police to sustain or increase divisions among the black majority, co-opt nonwhite elite elements by providing them with channels of economic and social mobility, and selective violence against rebellious groups and individuals.

The 1983 constitution vested potentially dictatorial powers in the president, who was authorized to act decisively in emergencies regardless of any divisions within the white establishment. A major split within the white elite existed between the moderates (mainly members of the National Party, which had engineered the 1983 supposedly power-sharing multiracial constitution and won 48 percent of the vote in the 1989 election and ninety-three seats in the white parliament) and the conservatives (largely associated with the Conservative Party, the product of a schism in the National Party), who were generally opposed to any concessions to nonwhites (Brewer 1986; Davis 1987). The Conservative Party obtained 31 percent of the vote in 1989 and thirty-nine parliamentary seats. The Conservative Party drew support from lower-middle-class and lower-income whites, many of whom felt their economic interests and status would be threatened if the apartheid system was weakened (Schlemmer 1988). The primary disagreement among white leaders during the 1980s was not over the issue of whether to prevent black majority rule but rather of how to prevent it: through the co-opting reforms advocated by the moderates or through the repression stressed by the conservatives. In general, the white elite recognized the necessity of reducing apartheid barriers in the labor market in order to ensure economic growth, but "in the social domain, and more emphatically in politics, racial division and white racial hegemony" were to be maintained (Berger and Godsell 1988b, 281).

The South African Defense Force (SADF) could quickly mobilize more than 70,000 men, and more if necessary, from its reserves (almost all white men were required to undergo military training). About 5 percent of the SADF were nonwhites, often organized into units separated on the basis of tribal membership. This ensured that military service reinforced ethnic identities. Recruits for nonwhite units, carefully screened to admit only those with anti-leftist views, strong tribal identification, or other antirevolutionary attitudes, were attracted to military service by financial incentives within the context of high nonwhite unemployment rates (Davis 1987). The South African Defense Force was supplemented by 75,000 police, about half of whom were nonwhite (*New York Times*, January 6, 1991, A9).

After signs of nuclear blasts were detected in the South Atlantic during South African naval exercises, followed by evidence of radioactive fallout, many observers concluded that South Africa possessed nuclear weapons. Military pressure against neighboring black revolutionary states, including incursions by South African troops and support for groups opposing leftist African governments, contributed to forcing several pro-ANC countries to deny the ANC bases on their territories (Davis 1987; Nolutshungu 1988). In return South Africa pledged to cease its hostile actions and reduce aid for counterrevolutionary forces.

The white regime counted on the six homeland armies it had trained and staffed, in part with white officers, not only to help repress ANC activities but also to control political developments within the homelands. Homeland constitutions often granted the rulers, initially selected by the white regime, the right to appoint much of the homeland's parliament or in other ways reserve a large number of seats for individuals willing to collaborate with Pretoria. This resulted in elections in which the candidate favored by the white regime lost as much as 70 percent of the homeland vote but continued to rule because he still controlled the homeland parliament (Davis 1987).

REFORMING APARTHEID

By 1991 some aspects of the apartheid system had been eliminated (*New York Times*, March 12, 1989, E2). Modifications included the 1983 measure allowing residents of black townships to buy rather than rent their homes, the 1985 acceptance of the right of individuals of different racial designations to marry or live together, the 1986 retraction of the Pass Laws, and the 1990 opening of public hospitals to patients of all races (*New York Times*, May 17, 1990, A1). Many movie theaters, sports events, restaurants, and airline flights were made accessible to all people who could afford them. Many skilled job categories were opened to indigenous Africans. But white workers still earned considerably more than blacks, and the largely segregated educational system spent 5.5 times more on a white child than on a black child. About 10 percent of previously all-white public schools admitted at least some nonwhite students during January 1991 (*New York Times*, January 10, 1991, A3).

The ANC, supported by the Organization of African Unity nations, called for "negotiations and elections leading to majority rule in South Africa" (*New York Times*, August 22, 1989, A8). ANC conditions for talks with the white government included Pretoria lifting the state of emergency, releasing political prisoners, legalizing all anti-apartheid political organizations, withdrawing troops from the black townships, and halting trials and executions.

President F. W. de Klerk announced that the National Party intended to gradually alter the political system toward wider power sharing among racial groups (*African News*, August 1989, 14). But he also said this would not lead to indigenous African majority rule (*New York Times*, July 23, 1989, E2).

Many South Africans, however, demanded absolutely equal rights of political participation and ending exclusive white control of the security forces and major economic institutions. This could have opened opportunities for nonwhites in state-owned industries as happened when the government used employment in state corporations to raise the economic status of Afrikaners following the Boer War.

The South African government, however, began to sell state-owned corporations to private businesses, including its Iron and Steel Corporation (ISCOR) in 1989. The process would place in the hands of affluent whites industries and other capital that would have been owned collectively by all South Africans. The ANC, COSATU, and other major anti-apartheid organizations vigorously condemned the regime's privatization of state property; it was viewed as an attempt to deprive a future, democratically elected, nonracial government of the ability to distribute resources and economic opportunities more equitably (*New York Times*, November 13, 1990, A10). Some anti-apartheid activists feared that white leaders would co-opt middle-class indigenous Africans into a new ruling coalition that would then economically and politically dominate the almost exclusively nonwhite industrial and agricultural working classes.

Dismantling apartheid laws would mean little to impoverished people unless accompanied by governmental measures to redistribute resources. For example, the repeal of the Land Acts of 1913 and 1936, which had given 87 percent of the land to the white minority, was of questionable value to millions of people who did not have the means to buy property. The majority could only benefit if the government provided them with land either free or at very low cost. The opponents of white domination, however, had to confront the dilemma of improving the condition of the nation's majority without alienating large numbers of whites who possessed technical knowledge, managerial skills, and investment capital essential to the nation's future development.

In February 1990 the government took a major step toward resolving South Africa's civil conflict by releasing the famous ANC leader Nelson Mandela, after more than twenty-seven years of imprisonment (*New York Times*, February 12, 1990, A1). The government also legalized the previously banned ANC, the SACP, and other anti-apartheid organizations. In March 1990 Namibia, the country between South Africa and Angola, achieved independence after seventy-five years of South African occupation (*New York Times*, March 21, 1990, A1).

ANC officials elected Mandela deputy president of the organization (the president was the ailing Oliver Tambo). Mandela called for continued international economic sanctions against South Africa until democracy was established with equal rights for all. Mandela was also demanding a restructuring of the economy, but he noted, especially during his June 1990 visit to the United States, that economic reform need not necessarily involve extensive nationalization if other measures would improve the welfare and protect the interests of the nonwhite majority (*New York Times,* June 22, 1990, A20; June 27, 1990, A11).

Mandela reconfirmed the ANC's friendly relations with Cuba and the ANC expressed gratitude for Cuban efforts in aiding the ANC and in combating white South African intervention in Angola and in helping Namibia achieve independence. As talks with the white government progressed, the ANC in August 1990 suspended its armed struggle (*New York Times,* August 12, 1990, E4). But de Klerk and other National Party leaders consistently refused to accept the ANC's demand for a totally nonracial, one person, one vote democracy.

Dismantling Apartheid

During years of negotiations for a new political system the participating parties pushed for often conflicting goals (Grundy 1993; Jost 1994). The ANC demanded a nonracial democracy and a strong central government capable of carrying out policies to provide dramatic improvements in educational, housing, and economic opportunities for the country's majority. The National Party, Inkatha, die-hard Afrikaner nationalists, and tribal homeland authorities wanted a federal system characterized by relatively strong provincial governments capable of defending local and minority interests. These groups also pushed for dividing the country into a larger number of smaller provinces in which locally concentrated ethnic minorities could exercise influence.

Inkatha leaders demanded and received continuation of the Zulu hereditary monarchy as part of the price for their participation in elections. All parties to negotiations appeared concerned with safeguarding the economic benefits enjoyed by privileged groups, classes, and elites, evidently as a way of deterring any large elite segment from either organizing significant mass opposition to a final agreement or leaving the country and depriving it of their valuable resources and skills (*New York Times,* May 15, 1994, 14; June 4, 1994, 1; May 8, 1995, A19).

During the negotiation process, protests and violence continued. Thousands died in lethal exchanges between Inkatha and ANC supporters. Evidence arose that elements within South Africa's white military and police leaderships helped Inkatha extremists massacre ANC sympathizers and then escape punishment (*New York Times,* March 19, 1994, 1; March 20, 1994, 10; February 20, 1995, A7). White nationalist fanatics planted bombs and assassinated ANC leaders, in particular Chris Hani in 1993, who had led the ANC guerrilla group, Spear of the Nation, and was serving as chairperson of the South African Communist Party.

The ANC's policy objectives and the future of South Africa may have been significantly affected by the loss of these leaders. However, its negotiating position
was strengthened by the popular support it enjoyed and by economically damaging
strikes that the Congress of South African Trade Unions led in support of ANC
demands (Jost 1994).

Negotiations finally resulted in a temporary five-year constitution. It ensured
that the 1994 elections would result in a government of national unity that would,
ideally, be capable of moving toward significant social change while reducing internal domestic conflict and avoiding extreme measures. The constitution divided
the country into nine provinces from the original four, primarily by subdividing
the former Transvaal and Cape Provinces. The new legislature consisted of a National Assembly with four hundred members and a National Council of Provinces
of ninety. National Assembly seats were awarded on the basis of the proportion of
popular vote received by each political party (Jost 1994). The citizens of each of the
nine provinces elected ten members of the National Council of Provinces. The National Assembly was to select the president. The constitution provided for multiple
deputy presidents, one for each political party that received at least 20 percent of
the popular vote.

Tribal homeland governments, including the supposedly independent homelands, were eliminated, and their bureaucracies incorporated into the new government. Similarly, the anti-apartheid guerrilla armies were merged with the much
larger South African Defense Force (Nathan 1994). Constitutional amendments
or a whole new constitution had to be approved by either a two-thirds vote of the
legislature or a 60 percent approval by direct popular vote.

In the 1994 election the ANC received about 63 percent of the popular vote, the
National Party 20 percent, Inkatha Freedom Party 10 percent, and other parties 7
percent, including 1.5 percent for the PAC. The parliament selected Nelson Man-
dela as president; Thabo Mbeki, also of the ANC, as first deputy president; and
F. W. de Klerk of the National Party as second deputy president (*New York Times*,
May 3, 1994, A1; May 11, 1994, A1).

President Mandela and his government, facing massive inequality and over 40
percent unemployment among indigenous Africans, proposed a five-year reconstruction and development plan. It called for providing a minimum of ten years free
education for all children, creation of 2.5 million public works jobs, building 1 million new homes, electrifying 2.5 million residences, and redistributing 30 percent
of the arable land (*New York Times*, April 21, 1994, A10; July 29, 1994, A6; August 19,
1994, A3).

To accomplish these goals through peaceful democratic methods within the
context of the post–cold war international environment, the ANC encouraged foreign investment and even entertained the possible economic and efficiency benefits

MAP 9.3 South Africa (After 1994)

of privatizing certain state industries. This policy shift reflected the new reality. By the mid-1990s virtually all the advanced nations South Africa traded with and received assistance from were committed to capitalist economic systems and trade relations. South Africa, therefore, even though governed by the ANC with SACP participation, structured its economy according to the rules of capitalist economic development.

The modifications in the ideology of the liberation movement and the moderation of its construction and redistribution plans led some critics within the ANC to question whether the anti-apartheid movement had taken over white South Africa or whether white South Africa and the international capitalist system had taken over the liberation movement.

On May 8, 1996, more than 85 percent of South Africa's national legislators voted to adopt and implement over a three-year period a new constitution that retained several major features of the 1994 constitution, such as the four-hundred-member National Assembly and the ninety-member National Council of Provinces (*New York Times*, May 9, 1996, A1). Provincial governments were given exclusive control over provincial planning, sports, recreation, and roads. But the new charter provided for a strong presidency and central government. The new constitution included a bill of rights guaranteeing freedom of speech, movement, and political activity and banned discrimination on the basis of race, gender, sexual orientation, age, pregnancy, or marital status. It also supported every citizen's right to adequate housing, food, water, education, and health care.

South Africa After Apartheid
Economy

South Africa possessed not only enormous natural resources but also energy, transportation, communications, and financial sectors similar to those in the most developed nations. However, much of the economy resembled that of poor developing societies. South Africa had the second highest Gini index of income inequality in the world (0 = total equality and 1 = total inequality), .631, in 2005 (CIA 2014a). The Gini index had actually been lower in 1994, .593, when the ANC came to power. The average person in the top 10 percent of the population by income had forty-three times more income that the average person in the bottom 10 percent (CIA 2014a,b). About 31 percent of the population lived in poverty (CIA 2014a) and the vast majority were nonwhite (Kenny 2013). Some South African sources state that the percentage of poor is really around 47 percent (Bhorat 2013) and that more than half of South Africa's children live in poverty (Laing 2012). Unemployment in 2012 was about 25 percent (CIA 2014a). GDP growth was estimated at 2.5 percent in 2012. The neoliberal capitalist economic system inherited from the apartheid era and basically continued under the ANC government seemed incapable of reducing inequality. According to Antoinette Handley, in 2004 "Black Africans, who made up 75 percent of the population, are generally considered to own between 2 percent to 7 percent of capitalization in terms of stock shares" (2004, 200).

The ANC governments after 1994 attempted to alleviate the worst economic sources of misery and social discontent. They tripled the number of people receiving social grants (child support, old age assistance, disability aid) and established seven hundred new health clinics (Lawson 2005, 159–160). They also increased housing, electricity, and clean water. According to Handley (2004, 198–199), "the percentage of households with access to clean water rose from 60 percent in 1996 to 85 percent in 2001 and those with sanitation from 49 percent in 1994 to 63 percent in 2003. The proportion of households with electricity rose from 32 percent in 1996 to 70 percent in 2001." Households with electricity increased to 84 percent by the end of 2013 (Cohen 2013). The South African government also provided free medical care to pregnant women and to children under the age of five.

One of the most important antipoverty measures enacted in the 1990s was initiated by the white National Party shortly before the first democratic election in 1994 to attract votes from poor nonwhite people. The National Party government carried out racial equalization of pensions for elderly persons, raising those of nonwhites to the level that whites received. This act immediately boosted state pensions for elderly indigenous Africans to about "$90 per month, or roughly twice the median black income" (Handley 2004, 199). This dramatic increase also benefited nonelderly persons assisted by their older relatives and contributed to improving the nutrition and health of millions of children. But the cost of the state pension system and also coping with the enormous AIDS problem threatened to overwhelm the government's budget.

The AIDS Catastrophe

Life expectancy in 2013 was 49.5 years (CIA 2014a). Poverty and the flawed educational system contributed to the AIDS epidemic, simultaneously a gigantic medical problem, a huge drain on resources, and an immense human rights disaster. An estimated 11.5 percent of South Africa's population was infected with the HIV virus in 2009, the highest percentage of any country in the world (CIA 2014a). Research indicates that low income persons are much more likely to be HIV positive than higher income persons (Wabiri and Taffa 2013).

Handley (2004) suggested the response to AIDS was slow because the disease appeared just as the ANC was defeating apartheid. Gaining control of the state, ANC leaders were focused on launching reforms to benefit millions of poor people. There was reluctance to heed warning signs of the AIDS problem because early government recognition of the disease could have meant an immediate diversion of funds to combat the medical emergency rather than dealing with the people's pressing economic and social needs. Victims of AIDS included Chief Buthelezi's son, who died of the disease in 2004, and Nelson Mandela's son, who died in 2005.

Crime

South Africa has one of the highest homicide rates in the world. The homicide rate reached its highest recorded level of about 68 (number of homicide victims per 100,000 residents) in 1995 (Wild and Mbatha 2013). Then it generally declined. By 2012 the homicide rate was about 30.9 (South African Police Service 2013) but in 2013 went up slightly to 31.1 (Wild and Mbatha 2013). This was about six times the US homicide rate. The homicide rate may have declined due to expanded welfare measures alleviating the worst miseries of poverty and improved medical services saving the lives of wounded people.

Property crime rates in South Africa, unlike violent crime rates, were not notably higher than in other countries. This may have been partly due to affluent homes being residentially segregated from poor areas and typically well-protected, often by private guards. CNN (April 6, 2006) reported that there were almost three private security personnel for every one publicly employed police officer.

Political Developments

To reduce the likelihood of continued conflict after the end of apartheid, the democratically elected government created the Truth and Reconciliation Commission. It convened for the first time in January 1996. One of its main purposes was to reveal the truth about murders, disappearances, and bombings committed by defenders as well as opponents of apartheid in the hope that this process would help bring about reconciliation among all South Africans. Many persons who committed acts of violence during the conflict were offered immunity from criminal prosecution if they confessed their actions. Those confessing included members of the former white security forces. According to Lawson (2005, 169), about 7,000 people applied to the commission for amnesty from criminal charges.

In the 1999 election, the ANC's share of the vote increased to 66.4 percent. But so many people were disappointed by the failure of the ANC-led government to do more to improve the situation of the poor that the total number of voters declined by 3.5 million. Thabo Mbeki of the ANC replaced Mandela as president.

In the 2004 election, the ANC's percent increased to 69.7 percent. President Mbeki was reelected. Public opinion surveys showed people were least satisfied with the government's performance in creating jobs and combating crime but somewhat more satisfied with improvements in health care and education. The percentage of votes going to the National Party declined to about 1.7 percent, leading to its disbanding in 2005.

Within the ANC serious divisions arose over AIDS policy, inequality, unemployment, and further privatization of state-owned enterprises. Some opposed what they viewed as the emergence of a new ruling alliance between the small minority of well-to-do indigenous Africans and wealthy whites, who overwhelmingly possessed the shares of South Africa's privately owned companies and dominated the economy. Under the neoliberal economic model, rather than having the state own and operate major companies to bring more jobs and benefits to the poor, small numbers of nonwhites were allowed to acquire partial ownership in private corporations (IRIN, November 11, 2004). COSATU criticized this so-called empowerment as doing nothing to improve the well-being of the majority of South Africans, but instead enriching a small percentage of black South Africans, including certain members of the ANC. President Mbeki was accused doing little to help South Africa's workers, who were so essential to the creation of the democratic system, and of ignoring and then ineptly responding to the AIDS crisis.

In September 2008, the ANC-dominated legislature replaced Mbeki with former trade union leader Kgalema Motlanthe (Bearak 2008) as interim president until the 2009 national election. In this election many members of COSATU and the SACP favored Jacob Zuma, an ANC leader of Zulu ancestry, who, they hoped, would do more to create jobs and reduce poverty. But many other South Africans considered Zuma, who had been accused but not convicted of corruption and rape, a flawed leader. Some Mbeki supporters and others started a new party called the Congress of the People (COPE). In the 2009 election, the ANC received 65.9 percent (264 seats in the National Assembly), the Democratic Alliance 16.7 percent (67 seats), COPE 7.4 percent (30 seats), the Inkatha Freedom Party 4.6 percent (18 seats), and other parties 5.4 percent (21 seats) (CIA 2014a). Zuma became president.

Continuing Economic and Social Problems

Although Zuma promised to rapidly address the concerns of labor unions and the poor, his government was hindered by the worldwide recession emanating from the US and Europe (Dugger 2009b). In June 2009 the government announced that between April 2008 and April 2009 factory output declined 21.6 percent. Hundreds of thousands lost their jobs. Some of Zuma's supporters urged him to extend social assistance programs, even though more than a quarter of the population already received welfare aid (Dugger 2009b). Many favored a new emphasis on expanding job opportunities for South Africa's millions of unemployed poor rather than simply trying to increase black presence in management positions. The jobs shortage was viewed as a major reason for violence between poor South Africans and refugees from other African nations such as Zimbabwe (Dugger 2009a).

Another problem is the so-called brain drain as highly educated South Africans leave the country. As often occurs with significant sociopolitical change, people uncomfortable with the new circumstances seek to leave. This potentially damages a nation's economy because investments in developing highly skilled individuals are lost to other societies. A significant minority of skilled white South Africans left the country after 1994, often for destinations such as the US, the United Kingdom, Canada, Australia, or New Zealand. However, because of limited job opportunities or concern over crime, corruption or other problems, many well-educated black and Indian South Africans also left. Mattes and Mniki (2007) reported results of a national survey of 4,784 highly educated South African young people showing that many were considering emigrating to have better lives. A 2010 survey of 900 South African young people found that while about 33 percent of white and Indian youth wanted to leave the country, 42 percent of black middle-class youngsters also wanted to leave (Naidoo 2010).

Another concern was the employment of many former members of South Africa's armed forces by private military or security firms around the world, perhaps 2,000–4,000 in Iraq alone (Nullis 2006). In response, the South African National Assembly on August 30, 2006, passed the Prohibition of Mercenary Activity and Regulation of Certain Activities in Areas of Armed Conflict Bill, which required that all South Africans wanting to work abroad in military-type jobs to get government permission (BBC News, August 30, 2006).

Despite serious ongoing problems, South Africans celebrated their country's hosting of the 2010 World Cup, in which the top thirty-two men's soccer teams competed for the world championship. Many hoped that this time in the global spotlight would lead to increased foreign investment, trade, and tourism and provide a boost to economic development.

THE PASSING OF MANDELA AND THE FUTURE OF SOUTH AFRICA

On December 5, 2013, Nelson Mandela, main leader of the anti-apartheid struggle and the first post-apartheid president of South Africa, passed away. Ninety-one world leaders, including US President Barack Obama, attended the memorial for Mandela on December 10 in Johannesburg to honor his amazing courage, determination, and achievements (Gumuchian 2013). But some South Africans interviewed at the time said major socioeconomic goals of the revolution Mandela led had yet to be achieved despite significant development of the economy, increases in services like electricity, and expansion of welfare assistance to the poor. These measures, though, probably at least temporarily limited economic protest (Zuern 2013).

While income inequality between whites and native Africans declined some-what, overall income inequality remained the highest in the world (except possi-bly for Lesotho), partly because income inequality grew among native Africans (Van der Berg and Louw 2004). In other words, the end of apartheid appeared to allow some native Africans to improve their economic situation to a significantly greater extent than many other native Africans. Analyses of household data indi-cates that intragroup income inequality was significantly greater a decade after the end of apartheid among indigenous Africans, than among South Africans of Indian background and mixed racial ancestry and much greater than among whites (Leib-brandt, Woolard, Finn, and Argent 2010), the large majority of whom were in the top income fifth of the population (Statistics South Africa 2012).

While the average white household income in South Africa was close to six times the average native African household income (Statistics South Africa 2012), *wealth* inequality between whites and native Africans was much greater. Using as-sets (land and other physical property, bank accounts, stocks, bonds, etc.) own-ership data provided by Benjamin (2013) and population composition data (CIA 2014a), the average white household in South Africa appeared to have 12.5 times the assets of the average indigenous African household. Despite the end of racial apartheid, an economic apartheid continued to exist with a fraction of indigenous Africans living in the walled affluent areas once reserved for whites while the vast majority of indigenous Africans had very little. To many it seemed that those at the top of the indigenous African socioeconomic pyramid collaborated with affluent whites to maintain an economically oppressive system.

This perception led to major protests (Zuern 2013). One tragic confrontation occurred between police and 3,000 striking miners at the Lonmin company's Mari-kana platinum mine. Several persons, including two police officers, were killed during the first seven days of the strike. On the eighth day, August 16, 2012, police opened fire on striking miners, many of whom were carrying sticks or machetes. Thirty-four miners were killed and seventy-eight were wounded (McClenaghan and Smith 2013; South African History Online 2013). To make matters worse, pros-ecutors attempted to use an apartheid-era law to charge 270 miners with murder in the deaths of their fellow strikers rather than the police who shot them (*Daily Mail* 2013). On September 19, 2012, the strike finally ended when the Lonmin Company agreed to a 22 percent pay increase for the miners (Selebi 2012).

Dissatisfaction grew among many South Africans over persisting poverty, job-lessness, and corruption, and the perception that some ANC leaders were content to reap huge financial benefits for themselves by collaborating with largely white owned corporations rather than fulfilling the promise of the apartheid revolution to the poor. Significant divisions widened within the ANC and within its allies COSATU and the SACP between right-wing and left-wing factions. The rightists appeared to believe that continued privatization of businesses and industries and the neoliberal approach would generate enough economic growth to reduce the unemployment rate and improve the lives of the poor. The leftists pushed for policies such as nationalization of large industries and financial institutions, and government action to decrease unemployment and economic inequality, including taking land and other property from the wealthy and using the confiscated wealth to provide new opportunities for the millions of poor South Africans.

One focal point of the left-right conflict existed within the ANC-allied CO-SATU. The leftist-oriented general secretary of COSATU, Zwelinzima Vavi, criticized some ANC leaders by stating, "We are heading rapidly in the direction of a full-blown predator state in which a powerful corrupt and demagogic elite of political hyenas increasingly controls the state as a vehicle of accumulation" (Kadalie 2012). After the passing of Mandela in December 2013, it appeared possible that a number of left-leaning unions in COSATU would organize a new leftist worker-based Labor Party to challenge the ANC in elections. It was also possible that the unions in COSATU might split into two separate union federations, reflecting the conflict within the ANC. A recent opinion poll found that 65 percent of COSATU members would vote for a new Labor Party if one was formed, while only 28 percent would vote for the ANC (Plaut 2013; Sparks 2013). It appeared likely that South Africa was headed for a new period of political conflict.

SUMMARY AND ANALYSIS

The white-dominated state in South Africa had its origins in Dutch settlement of the Cape in the seventeenth century. Afrikaners justified confiscating the wealth of indigenous peoples as a religious mission: Whites were acting to fulfill God's plan for a Christian South Africa. After gold deposits were discovered in the Transvaal, the British conquered the Boers and unified South Africa into a single white-dominated state.

Afrikaners, many impoverished by the effects of the Boer War, constituted the bulk of the white working class, which intensely feared social and economic integration with the country's nonwhite masses. Inflamed by the migration of tens of thousands of blacks to urban areas during World War II and into jobs previously reserved for whites, Afrikaners voted the National Party into power in 1948. Over the next twelve years the apartheid system was formally established. It confirmed past segregationist policies and reversed much of the limited integration that had previously occurred. Despite numerous internal and external pressures, the white regime continued to endure because of several factors: the support of the large majority of whites; a well-trained, technologically advanced military; a successful policy of selectively co-opting, dividing, or repressing elements of the nonwhite majority; and the cooperation, sometimes covert, of major Western powers in need of South Africa's important mineral resources.

South Africa's system of white domination motivated the nonwhite majority to join together to establish a truly representative, nonracial government. But achievement of the necessary degree of unity was impeded by divisions over issues such as whether goals should be pursued violently or through nonviolent methods; or whether the movement should demand a one person, one vote democracy or should settle for some form of power sharing that would allow whites to retain disproportionate control of government. Another factor interfering with unity was ethnic rivalry among indigenous Africans.

Mass discontent among the majority of South Africans had its origin in the European conquests and seizure of the nation's wealth. Traditional forms of rebellion against white invaders were unsuccessful. Although European exploitation of the country's resources improved the living conditions of many nonwhite South Africans relative to the residents of other African states, the distorted levels of inequality between whites and nonwhites and the humiliation imposed by various aspects of the racially oriented political, economic, social, and cultural systems constituted powerful sources of modern discontent.

South Africa was distinguished in part by the fact that its educated elites were separated along racial and ethnic lines. Although by the time of the 1989 parliamentary elections the majority of white political leaders (those of the National and Democratic parties) at least publicly supported an end to the 1950s-style apartheid system, an even larger majority of white political leaders (those of the National and Conservative parties) resisted the creation of a political system that would allow the possibility of indigenous African majority rule.

Nonwhite educated elites organized a series of movements to end white minority rule. Virtually all of these, inspired by varying ideologies, initially attempted to use legal means or at least nonviolent methods like civil disobedience to motivate whites morally to negotiate change. When they appeared to be gaining strength, such movements were crushed by the white regime, convincing many that South Africa could only be changed through revolutionary violence. In the 1960s and the 1970s leaders of the black nationalist PAC and BCC argued that only the black population acting alone could result in a simultaneous dismantling of the racist system and a restoration of psychological strength (pride and positive self-esteem) among indigenous Africans.

The ANC was the strongest, best organized, and most widely supported of the anti-apartheid groups. It developed into an interracial organization advocating a nonracial, one person, one vote democracy. The tactics employed by the ANC until the 1950s were generally peaceful, legal, and nonconfrontational. But following the 1948 victory of the pro-apartheid National Party, the younger generation of ANC militants, led by Nelson Mandela, organized campaigns of mass civil disobedience in defiance of racist laws. After several such efforts were repressed in the 1950s, the ANC developed an underground network and organized a revolutionary armed force to employ selective violence against the white regime.

Foreign involvement in South Africa primarily assisted the white-dominated state. Throughout most of the twentieth century Britain and the US continued to trade with South Africa and overtly or covertly supply weapons to the white regime in exchange for strategically important minerals and its anticommunism (Cran 1979). Until the late twentieth century, only some Communist Party–dominated states and a few Western European and African nations provided significant aid to anti-apartheid revolutionary forces.

At the beginning of the 1990s several factors precipitated a rapid political transformation of South Africa. The end of the cold war and the disintegration of the USSR reduced fear of the ANC both among leaders of the white South African National Party and among foreign powers that once dreaded the possibility that South Africa's critical resources might fall into unfriendly hands. Trade restrictions imposed by many nations against South Africa's white government and strikes by large numbers of nonwhite South African workers economically pressured the business community and state officials to enter into an agreement with the ANC to democratize the country.

After the end of apartheid, nonwhite South Africans had the legal right to enjoy previously denied freedoms. But millions lacked the economic means to do so to any substantial degree. ANC-led governments significantly expanded electrical and sanitation services and the availability of education, health care, and housing. But even after the fourth post-apartheid election, between one-third and one-half of the population lived in poverty, about one-quarter lacked jobs, and economic inequality was enormous.

Significant divisions developed within the ANC. Various groups criticized the neoliberal economic policies pursued after the end of apartheid, the high inequality, persisting high levels of unemployment, widespread corruption of public officials, and inept handling of the AIDS crisis. In particular, the strategy of empowering blacks by giving small numbers high-paid managerial positions or allowing them to obtain ownership shares in private companies seemed to accomplish little more than make a tiny proportion of indigenous Africans rich. COSATU called for reducing unemployment and inequality. Some COSATU unions seriously considered creating a new workers or labor party to the left of the ANC to compete in elections.

Around the world people continue to be inspired by South Africa's anti-apartheid movement and the dedication and sacrifice of its central leaders, especially Nelson Mandela, and look forward to new efforts to address the country's ongoing challenges.

South Africa: Chronology of Major Events

1652 Dutch begin settlement and conquest of South Africa

1806 Britain assumes control of the Dutch settlement

1836–1856 Great Trek inland as Afrikaners establish independent Boer republics

1899–1902 British wage and win Boer War

1910 Union of South Africa established

1912 African National Congress founded

1913 Native Land Act limits access to land for large majority of South Africans

1914 Afrikaner National Party founded

1948 National Party wins elections and begins process of reinforcing separation of races, which it calls "apartheid"

1950 Suppression of the Communism Act and the Group Areas Act (limiting people's residences and businesses to their racial areas)

1952 ANC and South African Indian Congress launch Defiance Campaign

1955 Congress of the People proclaims Freedom Charter

1959 Pan-Africanist Congress (PAC) established

1960 Sharpeville Massacre; ANC and PAC declared illegal

1961 ANC organizes Spear of the Nation and launches armed resistance

1962 Mandela arrested and eventually sentenced to life in prison

1976 Soweto uprisings

1983 Multiracial constitution approved by white voters; United Democratic Front organized

1984 Sustained protests against constitution begin

1985 Congress of South African Trade Unions organized

1989 F. W. de Klerk becomes president of South Africa and pledges to end apartheid

1990 Mandela released from prison; anti-apartheid organizations relegalized; ANC ends violent resistance to South African regime; government leaders announce plans to develop a new constitution; repeated violent conflict between ANC and Inkatha supporters

1994 ANC wins first fully democratic elections in South Africa; Nelson Mandela elected president

1996 New South African constitution adopted

1999 Second post-apartheid election won by the ANC; Thabo Mbeki of the ANC succeeds Nelson Mandela as president

2004 Third post-apartheid election won by the ANC; Thabo Mbeki reelected president

2005 National Party disbands

2008   Thabo Mbeki replaced; Kgalema Motlanthe becomes interim president

2009   ANC wins election; Jacob Zuma becomes president

2010   South Africa hosts the World Cup

2012   South African police kill dozens of striking platinum miners

2013   Nelson Mandela dies; Some COSATU leaders consider creating a
new political party to the left of the ANC

References and Further Readings

Adam, Heribert. 1988. "Exile and Resistance: The African National Congress, the South
African Communist Party, and the Pan African Congress." In Berger and Godsell,
eds., A Future South Africa.

African News. August 1989. "We're Changing, Government Says," 14.

BBC News. August 30, 2006. "MPs Approve New SA Mercenary Bill." news.bbc.co.uk/2
/hi/africa/5297704.stm.

Bearak, Barry. 2008. "South Africa Picks President, but Uncertainty Remains." New York
Times, September 26.

Benjamin, Chantelle. 2013. "White People Still Earn the Most." Mail and Guardian, January 25. http://mg.co.za/article/2013–01–25-white-people-still-earn-the-most.

Berger, Peter, and Bobby Godsell, eds. 1988a. A Future South Africa: Visions, Strategies, and
Realities. Boulder: Westview.

———. 1988b. "South Africa in Comparative Context." In Berger and Godsell, eds., A
Future South Africa.

Bernstein, Ann, and Bobby Godsell. 1988. "The Incrementalists." In Berger and Godsell,
eds., A Future South Africa.

Bhorat, Haroon. 2013. "Economic Inequality Is a Major Obstacle." New York Times, December 6. www.nytimes.com/roomfordebate/2013/07/28/the-future-of-south-africa
/economic-inequality-is-a-major-obstacle-to-growth-in-south-africa.

Brewer, John D. 1986. After Soweto: An Unfinished Journey. Oxford: Clarendon.

Cauvin, Henri E. 2002. "H.I.V. Survey in South Africa Suggests Plateau in Infections."
New York Times, June 11.

Central Intelligence Agency (CIA). 2014a. "South Africa." In World Factbook. www.cia
.gov/library/publications/the-world-factbook/geos/sf.html.

———. 2014b. "Household Income or Consumption by Percentage Share." www.cia
.gov/library/publications/the-world-factbook/fields/2047.html.

CNN. April 6, 2006. "Crime, Private Security Boom in South Africa." www.cnn
.com/2006/WORLD/africa/04/06/safrica.crime.reut/index.html.

Cohen, Mike. 2013. "The Threat to Mandela's Economic Legacy." Bloomberg Business Week, December 12. www.businessweek.com/articles/2013-12-12/mandelas
-economic-legacy-under-threat.

Congress of the People. [1955] 1987. "The Freedom Charter." In Mermelstein, ed., *Anti-Apartheid Reader*.

Cran, William. 1979. *Hot Shells: US Arms for South Africa*. Boston: WGBH Transcripts.

Daily Mail. 2013. "South African Police Ordered Enough Mortuary Vans to Carry 32 Bodies Hours Before Shooting Dead 34 Striking Miners, Inquiry Hears." November 25. www.dailymail.co.uk/news/article-2513189/Marikana-miners-strike-South-African-police-ordered-vans-carry-32-bodies-shooting-34.html.

Danaher, Kevin. 1984. *In Whose Interest? A Guide to US–South Africa Relations*. Washington, DC: Institute for Policy Studies.

Davis, Stephen M. 1987. *Apartheid's Rebels: Inside South Africa's Hidden War*. New Haven, CT: Yale University Press.

DeFronzo, James, ed. 2006. *Revolutionary Movements in World History: From 1750 to the Present*. 3 vols. Santa Barbara, CA: ABC-CLIO.

Dugger, Celia W. 2009a. "Rising Anger at Other Africans Fuels South Africa Attacks." *New York Times*, December 21.

———. 2009b. "South Africa's Jobless Hope Zuma Delivers Work." *New York Times*, June 11.

Freeman, Colin, and Jane Flanagan. 2013. "Nelson Mandela 'Proven' to Be a Member of the Communist Party After Decades of Denial." *Telegraph*, December 14. www.telegraph.co.uk/news/worldnews/nelson-mandela/9731522/Nelson-Mandela-proven-to-be-a-member-of-the-Communist-Party-after-decades-of-denial.html.

Giliomee, Hermann. 1980. "The National Party and the Afrikaner Broederbond." In Price and Rosberg, eds., *Apartheid Regime*.

Grundy, Kenneth W. 1993. "South Africa's Tortuous Transition." *Current History* 92 (May): 229–233.

Gumuchian, Marie-Louise. 2013. "Obama, World Leaders Praise 'Giant of History' at Mandela Memorial." CNN, December 10. www.cnn.com/2013/12/10/world/africa/nelson-mandela-memorial/index.html.

Handley, Antoinette. 2004. "The New South Africa, a Decade Later." *Current History* 103 (May): 195–201.

Integrated Regional Information Networks (IRIN). November 11, 2004. "South Africa: Anger Over Enrichment of Black Elite." UN Office for the Coordination of Humanitarian Affairs. www.irinnews.org/Report.aspx?ReportId=52020.

Jost, Kenneth. 1994. "South Africa's Future." *Congressional Quarterly Researcher*, January, 24–48.

Karis, Thomas. 1986/1987. "South African Liberation: The Communist Factor." *Foreign Affairs*, Winter, 267–287.

Keller, Bill. 2013. "Nelson Mandela, Communist." *New York Times*, December 7. www.nytimes.com/2013/12/08/opinion/sunday/keller-nelson-mandela-communist.html?_r=0&pagewanted=print.

Kenny, Charles. 2013. "Remembering Nelson Mandela's Unsung Economic Legacy." *Business Week*, December 5. www.businessweek.com/articles/2013-12-05/remembering-nelson-mandelas-unsung-economic-legacy.

Kerson, Roger. 1987. "The Emergence of Powerful Black Unions." In Mermelstein, ed., *Anti-Apartheid Reader.*

Laing, Aislinn. 2012. "More Than Half of South Africa's Children Live in Poverty." *Telegraph*, May 21. www.telegraph.co.uk/health/healthnews/9280481/More-than-half-of-South-Africas-children-live-in-poverty.html.

Lawson, George. 2005. *Negotiated Revolutions: The Czech Republic, South Africa and Chile.* Burlington, VT: Ashgate.

Lazerson, Joshua N. 1994. *Against the Tide: Whites in the Struggle Against Apartheid.* Mayibuye History and Literature 50. Boulder: Westview.

Leibbrandt, Murray, Ingrid Woolard, Arden Finn, and Jonathan Argent. 2010. "Trends in South African Income Distribution and Poverty Since the Fall of Apartheid." OECD Social, Employment, and Migration Working Papers, no. 101. OECD Publishing. http://dx.doi.org/10.1787/5kmms0t7p1ms-en.

Mabeko-Tali, Jean-Michel. 2006. "Angolan Revolution." In DeFronzo, ed., *Revolutionary Movements in World History*, 1:61–70.

Magubane, Bernard. 1979. *The Political Economy of Race and Class in South Africa.* New York: Monthly Review Press.

Magubane, Bernard, and Ibbo Mandaza, eds. 1988. *Whither South Africa?* Trenton, NJ: Africa World Press.

Mandela, Nelson. 1994. *Long Walk to Freedom: The Autobiography of Nelson Mandela.* Boston: Little, Brown.

Mattes, Robert, and Namhla Mniki. 2007. "Restless Minds: South African Students and the Brain Drain." *Development in Southern Africa* 24 (1): 25–46.

McClenaghan, Maeve, and David Smith. 2013. "The British Mine Owners, the Police, and South Africa's Day of Blood." *Guardian*, November 24. www.theguardian.com/business/2013/nov/24/lonmin-mine-shooting-police.

Mermelstein, David, ed. 1987. *The Anti-Apartheid Reader: The Struggle Against White Racist Rule in South Africa.* New York: Grove.

Naidoo, Subashni. 2010. "South Africa's Black Brain Drain." *Times Live* (Johannesburg), April 25. www.timeslive.co.za/sundaytimes/article418948.ece/South-Africas-black-brain-drain.

Nathan, Laurie. 1994. "Merging the Military." *Work in Progress* 95 (February/March): 3–4.

Newitt, Malyn. 2006. "Mozambique Revolution." In DeFronzo, ed., *Revolutionary Movements in World History*, 2:575–582.

New York Times. February 25, 1988. "South Africa Bans Most Anti-Apartheid Activities," A1.

———. June 27, 1988. "Pretoria Pass Law Dies, but Spirit Lives," A1.

———. March 12, 1989. "Apartheid Frays at the Edges, but Its Core Is Unchanged," E2.

———. April 9, 1989. "New Party Meets in South Africa," 6.

———. July 23, 1989. "Seeing Change, Apartheid's Foes Seek a Path of Less Resistance," E2.

———. August 22, 1989. "South African Rebel Blueprint Is Backed by Continent Group," A8.

———. September 8, 1989. "Pretoria Leader Sees Mandate for a Change in Racial Policy," A8.

———. February 12, 1990. "Mandela Freed, Urges Step-up in Pressure to End White Rule," A1.

———. March 4, 1990. "Rival Congress Wants No Talks with Pretoria," A14.

———. March 21, 1990. "Namibia Achieves Independence After 75 Years of Pretoria's Rule," A1.

———. April 22, 1990. "Neutrality Has Its Dangers in the Blood Feuds of a South African Province," A3.

———. May 17, 1990. "South Africa to Admit All Races as Patients to Its Public Hospitals," A1.

———. June 10, 1990. "CIA Tie Reported in Mandela Arrest," A15.

———. June 22, 1990. "Mandela Says Movement Does Not See Socialism as the Only Route," A20.

———. June 27, 1990. "Mandela Invokes Struggles of US, Rousing Congress," A11.

———. July 15, 1990. "Zulu Chief Turning Movement into Political Party," A5.

———. August 12, 1990. "Who Speaks for Whom in South Africa?" E4.

———. August 22, 1990. "In South Africa, Joint Plea to End Black Strife," A7.

———. November 11, 1990. "South Africa: A Communist Looks Ahead," A15.

———. November 13, 1990. "Pretoria Retreats on Privatization," A10.

———. January 6, 1991. "Crime Overwhelms Pretoria's Police," A9.

———. January 10, 1991. "South Africa Integrates Some Schools," A3.

———. March 19, 1994. "Inquest Finds South Africa Police Aided Zulus in Terror Campaign," 1.

———. March 20, 1994. "War to Keep Apartheid Spawned Terror Network," 10.

———. April 21, 1994. "Blacks and Whites Wonder, Will Apartheid's Wrongs Now Be Reversed?" A10.

———. May 3, 1994. "Mandela Proclaims a Victory: South Africa Is 'Free at Last'!" A1.

———. May 11, 1994. "South Africans Hail President Mandela; First Black Leader Pledges Racial Unity," A1.

———. May 15, 1994. "Mandela's Inheritance: Bloated Bureaucracy," 14.

———. June 4, 1994. "Same Old Bureaucracy Serves a New South Africa," 1.

———. July 29, 1994. "Back to the Land: South African Blacks Walk a Legal and Economic Maze," A6.

———. August 19, 1994. "Mandela's First 100 Days: 'On Course,' He Says," A3.

———. February 20, 1995. "A Glimpse of Apartheid's Dying Sting," A7.

———. May 8, 1995. "How Mandela Wooed Businessmen," A19.

———. May 9, 1996. "A New Charter Wins Adoption in South Africa," A1.

Nolutshungu, Sam C. 1988. "The South African State and Africa." In Magubane and Mandaza, eds., *Whither South Africa?*

North, James. 1985. *Freedom Rising.* New York: Macmillan.

Nullis, Claire. 2006. "South African Assembly OKs Mercenary Bill." Associated Press, August 29. www.zimbabwesituation.com/aug30_2006.html.

Omeara, Dan. 1983. *Volkskapitalisme: Class, Capital, and Ideology of Afrikaner Nationalism, 1934–1948.* Cambridge, UK: Cambridge University Press.

Omer-Cooper, J. D. 1987. *History of Southern Africa.* London: James Curry.

Plaut, Martin. 2013. "Birth Pangs of a New South African Worker's Party." *New Statesman,* November 29. www.newstatesman.com/world-affairs/2013/11/birth-pangs-new-south-african-worker%E2%80%99s-party.

Price, Robert M., and Carl G. Rosberg, eds. 1980. *The Apartheid Regime: Political Power and Racial Domination.* Research Series 43. Berkeley: University of California Press.

Radu, Michael. 1987. "The African National Congress: Cadres and Credo." *Problems of Communism,* July/August, 58–75.

Rubert, Steven C. 2006. "Zimbabwean Revolution." In DeFronzo, ed., *Revolutionary Movements in World History,* 3:984–994.

Schlemmer, Lawrence. 1988. "South Africa's National Party Government." In Berger and Godsell, eds., *A Future South Africa.*

Seedat, Aziza. 1987a. "Health in Apartheid Africa." In Mermelstein, ed., *Anti-Apartheid Reader.*

———. 1987b. "Poverty in South Africa." In Mermelstein, ed., *Anti-Apartheid Reader.*

Selebi, Mogomotsi. 2012. "Lonmin Miners Accept Pay Rise to End Strike." *Sowetan,* September 19. http://www.sowetanlive.co.za/news/2012/09/19/lonmin-miners-accept-pay-rise-to-end-strike.

South African Communist Party (SACP). 2013. "Cde Nelson Mandela: Hamba kahle Mkhonto!: SACP Statement on the Passing of Madiba, 6 December 2013"; "Life and Contribution of Comrade Nelson Rolihlahla Mandela"; and "We seize the spear fallen from his hands: The Young Communist League of South Africa mourns the loss of Comrade Nelson Mandela, declaring: Hamba kahle Mkhonto! It is now our turn to fight! *Umsebenzi,* December, 2–5. www.sacp.org.za/pubs/umsebenzi2/2013/dec.pdf.

South African History Online. 2013. "Marikana Massacre 16 August 2012." *South African History Online,* December 15. http://www.sahistory.org.za/article/marikana-massacre-16-august-2012.

South African Police Service. 2013. "Murder: 2009/10 to 2011/12." www.saps.gov.za/statistics/reports/crimestats/2012/downloads/crime_statistics_presentation.pdf.

Sparks, Allister. 2013. "A Weakening ANC: Coalition Governments to Rule South Africa Soon." *African Globe*, December 11. www.africanglobe.net/africa/coalition-governments-rule.

Statistics South Africa. 2012. "Income and Expenditure of Households, 2010/2011." *Statistics South Africa*. November 6. www.statssa.gov.za/Publications2/P0100/P01002011.pdf.

Thompson, Leonard. 1985. *The Political Mythology of Apartheid*. New Haven, CT: Yale University Press.

———. 2001. *A History of South Africa*. 3rd ed. New Haven, CT: Yale University Press.

Thomson, J. D. S. 2004. "A Murderous Legacy." *South Africa Crime Quarterly* 7 (March): 9–14.

US News & World Report. September 18, 1989. "No Time to Dawdle," 52.

Van der Berg, S., and M. Louw. 2004. "Changing Patterns of South African Income Distribution: Towards Time Series Estimates of Distribution and Poverty." *South African Journal of Economics* 72 (3): 546–572.

Wabiri, Njeri, and Neguisse Taffa. 2013. "Socio-economic Inequality and HIV in South Africa." *BMC Public Health* 13, 1037. www.biomedcentral.com/1471-2458/13/1037.

Warwick, Peter. 1983. *Black People and the South African War 1899–1902*. Cambridge, UK: Cambridge University Press.

Wild, Franz, and Amogelang Mbatha. 2013. "South Africa's Murder Rate Increases Amid Surge in Protests." *Business Week*, September 19. www.businessweek.com/news/2013-09-19/south-africa-s-murder-rate-increases-amid-surge-in-protests.

SELECTED DVD, FILM, AND VIDEOCASSETTE DOCUMENTARIES

See "Purchase and Rental Sources" at the end of this volume for information on how to obtain the following resources and for full names of media companies and other organizations listed here as abbreviations.

Apartheid's Last Stand. 1993. 60 min. Video. PBS. Dismantling of apartheid.

Biko: Breaking the Silence. 1988. 52 min. Video. AFSC, SAMC. Steve Biko and the impact of the black consciousness movement he led.

Changing This Country. 1988. 58 min. Video. SAMC. How South African labor unions organized to combat exploitation and became the most powerful internal force against apartheid.

Classified People. 1987. 55 min. Video. AFSC. Explains how racial classification in South Africa affected many aspects of how people lived and interacted.

Cry of Reason: An Afrikaner Speaks Out. 1987. 58 min. Video. AFSC, SAMC. Describes the extraordinary transformation of a clergyman who, after living and preaching among South Africa's pro-apartheid wealthy elite, left his affluent congregation to join the anti-apartheid movement and establish a new nonracial ministry.

Countdown to Freedom: Ten Days that Changed South Africa. 2009. 98 min. DVD. Amazon. com. The days leading to the election of Mandela as president.

The Deadline. 1996. 52 min. FRIF. Development of the 1996 South African constitution.

Dear Mandela. 2012. 94 min. Amazon.com. Young activists attempt to defend low-income persons' rights in post-apartheid South Africa.

Good Guys, Bad Guys. 1998. 46 min. CNN Cold War Series, Episode 17. Truman Library. Cold war conflict in Angola, as well as South African and Cuban military involvement.

Long Night's Journey into Day. 2000. 95 min. Amazon.com. Four cases before the Truth and Reconciliation Commission.

The Long Walk of Nelson Mandela. 120 min. PBS. Life of the legendary anti-apartheid leader and first president of post-apartheid South Africa.

Maids and Madames. 1986. 52 min. Video. AFSC, Filmmakers. Describes the relationships between white women and the more than 1 million indigenous African women who worked for them as domestic servants, typically forced to leave their own children to others while caring for their employers' offspring.

Mandela's Fight for Freedom. 1995. 150 min. DCTV.

Mandela: Son of Africa, Father of a Nation. 1997. 118 min. Indie or Amazon.com.

Nelson Mandela: Journey to Freedom. 50 min. AETV.

Samora Machel, Son of Africa. 1989. 28 min. FRIF. Interview with Samora Machel, leader of the Mozambique revolution.

Spear of the Nation: History of the African National Congress. 1986. 50 min. Video. SAMC. Documents the development of the ANC and its changing and varied means of opposing apartheid.

White Laager. 1978. 58 min. DVD. AFSC. Documentary on the white settlement of South Africa, the development of Afrikaner nationalism, and the establishment of the apartheid system.

10

Revolution Through Democracy

In the past thirty years dozens of countries have shifted from authoritarian to democratic government, amazing many observers. Some believed that the advent of democracy in nations with high inequality would soon be followed by other major changes. They anticipated that once poor people had the right to vote, the majority would support parties pledging to dramatically redistribute resources and opportunities. Thus democracy was expected to greatly reduce inequality. Until recently, however, this generally did not occur. In fact, it is highly likely that the ease with which many nations democratized was precisely because ruling elites built in mechanisms to prevent change detrimental to their interests or were otherwise convinced that such change would not be possible. Thus, even the election of socialist candidates did not seriously threaten the wealth or power of elites who had dominated the previous authoritarian regimes or the prerogatives of foreign corporations allied with them.

Beginning in 1998, however, with the election of Hugo Chávez as president of Venezuela, a new model began to emerge. Chávez, the son of schoolteachers, admired Fidel Castro and believed the Cuban revolution brought major benefits to Cuba's people. He advocated a new form of socialism blending the best features of Communist Party–dominated states with those of capitalist democracies. But capitalism in Venezuela would have to be humane capitalism, manifesting constructive, creative, and competitive features, not the profit maximization at all costs (savage capitalism) characteristic of the neoliberal economic model. Chávez launched what he termed the "Bolivarian revolution," which aimed to free Venezuela's economy and resources from foreign control and reduce the power of elites allied with foreign interests. These goals would be achieved through state intervention in the economic system and state ownership of major enterprises. In addition, the state would help individuals and small companies compete more effectively with large businesses. Moreover, the movement intended to politically empower the poor, expand educational and job opportunities, and permit people to share more equitably in their nation's wealth. The Bolivarian revolution was international. Venezuela worked to establish a multination commercial and aid network based on mutual cooperation, elimination of poverty and illiteracy, free health care, ending discrimination against indigenous people, and becoming self-sufficient agriculturally and industrially.

Revolution to Democracy

There was considerable speculation that when democracy came to countries characterized by high inequality and poverty, voters would choose leaders who would bring about a more equitable distribution of educational and income opportunities. Some observers anticipated that elected governments would pursue such goals through vigorous intervention in the economy, including state takeovers of privately held businesses and resources. In virtually all cases of recent democratization, the reality was quite different. The new governments basically maintained neoliberal economic policies and limited change to attempting to improve social services. Major neoliberal policies include privatization of state enterprises and services (including water and sanitation), a free market system with minimal state intervention or economic regulation, and elimination of broad government subsidies for items such as food and fuel. According to Schmitter (2010), it is likely that the ease with which many nations democratized was precisely because democratization had fewer consequences than originally anticipated. After initial democratizations did not result in changes that seriously threatened wealthy interests, the elites of other societies believed they had little to fear from shifting to at least limited democratic systems.

There are several reasons why democratization from conservative dictatorships did not have major economic consequences. First, right-wing authoritarian governments had domestic economies linked to the international capitalist system, which continued to inhibit significant change. Second, wealthy elites used their power, including influence over mass media, to support candidates protecting their interests. Third, those who had committed human rights abuses to suppress opponents were often amnestied as part of agreements to shift to democratic political systems. The fear of unpunished human rights abusers and the previous pattern of military overthrows of democratic systems likely discouraged some people from voting for political parties or individuals proposing major changes. The end of the cold war is a fourth factor. The dismantling of state-dominated economies in Eastern Europe and the former Soviet Union suggested to voters in many countries that capitalist economic systems were inherently superior. Furthermore, the option of adopting a socialist economic system appeared doomed, given the power of capitalist nations and multinational corporations and the scarcity of international support.

For revolution—that is, real structural change—to be accomplished through elections, the same five critical elements described in Chapter 1 must be present in some way in democracies: mass frustration, elite dissidence, unifying motivations joining different groups in a massive revolutionary alliance, a severe political crisis, and a permissive world context. In the late twentieth and early twenty-first centuries, only a few democracies were characterized by the simultaneous occurrence of these factors.

REVOLUTION THROUGH DEMOCRACY:
THE VENEZUELAN EXCEPTION

As noted in Chapter 5, democratically elected leaders attempted to bring about sweeping economic changes to benefit lower-income groups in Guatemala in the early 1950s and in Chile in the early 1970s. These governments were the targets of destabilizing economic pressure from the United States and were violently overthrown. They were replaced with right-wing military dictatorships that established policies favorable to US and other foreign corporations.

In 1998, however, the election of Hugo Chávez in Venezuela (approximately 27 million people; land area 912,050 square kilometers, more than twice the size of California), launched a new effort to bring revolutionary change through democracy. The Chávez government benefited from unique opportunities and strengths that allowed it to survive. First, the major existing political parties had been thoroughly discredited. Second, much of the armed forces turned against the policies of previous political leaders. Furthermore, Hugo Chávez had been an army lieutenant colonel and member of a revolutionary movement within the armed forces and therefore had allies in the military. Third, Chávez enjoyed the support of most Venezuelans. He was elected with a substantial majority in 1998. The new constitution was approved by voters in 1999. He was reelected in 2000, survived a recall election in 2004, and was reelected again in 2006 with more than 60 percent of the vote (*USA Today*, December 4, 2006). In February 2009, Venezuelans voted to eliminate term limits, permitting Chávez to run for reelection indefinitely. And in 2012, Chávez was reelected president with an 11 percent margin over his main opponent (Devereux 2013). Fourth, the government controls the country's enormous energy resources. This provides the means to improve the well-being of millions of Venezuelans and assist other nations seeking to pursue domestic and foreign policies similar to those of Venezuela.

MAP 10.1 Venezuela

FEDERAL STATES OF VENEZUELA

1	ZULIA	13	VARGAS
2	TACHIRA	14	MIRANDA
3	MÉRIDA	15	GUÁRICO
4	BARINAS	16	ANZOÁTEBUI
5	TRUJILLO	17	NUEVA ESPARTA
6	PORTUGUESA	18	SUCRE
7	LARA	19	MONAGAS
8	FALCÓN	20	DELTA AMACURO
9	YARACUY	21	BOLÍVAR
10	COJEDES	22	APURE
11	CARABOBO	23	AMAZONAS
12	ARAGUA		

Emergence of the Bolivarian Revolution

Led by Simón Bolívar, the "Liberator," Venezuela declared independence from Spain in 1811. This was followed by a fifteen-year, wide-ranging conflict that ended with the capture of the final Spanish enclave at Callao, Peru, in 1826 (Fowler 2006). Bolívar failed to unite Spain's colonies in one great republic. Chávez revived Bolívar's vision when he attempted to create new ways to link the nations of South and Central America and the Caribbean economically and politically.

In the nineteenth century, when the economy was based on farming and cattle raising, Venezuela was characterized by civil wars as political-military leaders (caudillos) contended for power. One striking contrast to the typical caudillos was Ezequiel Zamora, a commander of federal forces during the 1840s and 1850s (Gott 2000, 118–124). Zamora expressed intense hostility toward the landed oligarchy and supported land reform and resource distribution to benefit the poor, but without success. Between 1899 and 1945 military dictatorships controlled the country.

Oil exploration began in the Lake Maracaibo area in 1914, and by 1929 Venezuela became the world's leading exporter, with operations dominated by subsidiaries of Royal Dutch Shell and Standard Oil of New Jersey. During the Juan Vicente Gómez dictatorship (1908–1935), a new generation of leaders emerged amid the 1928 pro-democracy student protests. One of the noncommunist student activists, Rómulo Betancourt, played the primary role in founding Acción Democrática (AD), a social democratic party, in 1941, one of the two main political parties between 1958 and 1998. Another activist, Rafael Caldera, became a leader of a Christian anticommunist student movement during the 1930s, which evolved into Venezuela's Christian Democratic Party, COPEI, founded in 1946. Finally in 1958 a new civilian-military alliance established a democratic system based on an agreement between the AD, COPEI, and military leaders, called the Pact of Punto Fijo. In 1961 a constitution based on representative democracy was created; it stayed in effect until the 1999 constitution enacted early in the Chávez presidency. From 1958 to 1998, the so-called Punto Fijo period, elections brought either AD or COPEI presidential candidates to power.

Betancourt was elected to be president from 1959 to 1964; in 1960, in order to protect Venezuela's petroleum resources, he made Venezuela a founding member of the Organization of the Petroleum Exporting Countries (OPEC). But in the early 1960s young Marxist rebels, dissatisfied with the high level of inequality and encouraged by the success of the Cuban revolution, launched a guerrilla war. In 1969 Christian Democrat president Rafael Caldera successfully ended the conflict by offering amnesty to guerrillas who gave up armed struggle, with former guerrillas forming two left-wing parties, Movimiento al Socialismo and La Causa Radical (or La Causa R).

AD President Carlos Andrés Pérez nationalized oil operations in 1976 and created the state-owned oil company Petróleos de Venezuela, Sociedad Anónima

(PDVSA, Petroleum of Venezuela Company). During his first term, 1974–1979, Pérez displayed a leftist orientation by criticizing US policies and sending aid to Sandinista revolutionaries trying to overthrow the pro-US Nicaraguan dictatorship of Anastasio Somoza. But when he regained the presidency a decade later, his views and policies shifted to the right, contributing to the development of widespread discontent and political upheaval.

Caracazo and the Revolutionary Movement in the Armed Forces

Between 1974 and 1982, when world oil prices were high, significant benefits flowed to Venezuela's poor. But oil prices dropped quickly and remained low from 1983 to 1999 (WTRG Economics 2010). The rapid fall in oil revenues eroded gains the poor had made, and presidents of both major parties imposed austerity measures demanded by the International Monetary Fund (IMF) as a condition of helping Venezuela cope with its soaring debt. Corruption among government officials and business elites became less tolerable after the economy deteriorated, and lower-class families suffered increasing hardships.

Carlos Andrés Pérez of the AD, promising to restore aid to the poor, was elected president again from 1989 to 1993. But Perez adopted neoliberal policies to repay foreign loans. He raised what had been state-controlled prices on widely used services and goods, sparking extensive outrage. A flashpoint was the 100 percent increase in the cost of public transportation, essential for millions to get to work, school, or stores (Gott 2000, 47). The dramatic increase occurred because in February 1989 the Pérez government doubled the cost of fuel in order to increase government revenue. Many bus owners then doubled fares to cover their increased fuel costs. To poor workers and their families it seemed that overnight the government had made it impossible for them to survive. On Monday morning, February 27, as people first encountered the doubled bus fares, spontaneous protests developed in Caracas and other major cities. Buses were overturned and set on fire, followed by looting of stores, supermarkets, and central business districts. The government called in the armed forces to suppress the rebellion, called the Caracazo ("Caracazo" is derived from "Caracas" combined with the suffix "azo," which signifies a blow or a strike, in this context an explosion of social protest). According to Gott (2000, 45), on the day the protests began, then-lieutenant Hugo Chávez had been diagnosed with a contagious illness and ordered home to recover so that he would not infect other soldiers.

Most soldiers were from low-income families. Some identified with the rioters and acted with restraint. But others were brutal. Estimates of the number killed ranged from hundreds to thousands. The Caracazo had major impacts on the future of Venezuela. The neoliberal policies that led to the rebellion and were continued afterward seemed to demonstrate to citizens and soldiers that the established political parties, the government, and the international economic system all protected the corruption, greed, and incompetence of those who had plunged the country into debt while making the poor bear the burden of coping with economic crisis.

In 1982 Hugo Chávez and other young officers secretly organized a revolutionary group, Movimiento Bolivariano Revolucionario-200 (MBR-200), at the military academy. (The "200" was added in 1983 to refer to the two hundredth anniversary of Bolivar's birth in 1783.) Discontent in the armed forces resulted from several factors. One was the huge wealth gap between the affluent and poor Venezuelans from which many enlisted soldiers were drawn. Another was racial stratification. The top levels of government and business were occupied by persons largely of European ancestry, while much of the general population and the armed forces were of mixed racial background, like Chávez, who is of Amerindian, African, and Spanish descent. Rampant corruption and the legal and structural characteristics of society favoring the rich outraged soldiers as well as civilians. This discontent was intensified by government actions leading to the Caracazo and by requiring the armed forces to engage in its suppression. Military men were receptive to the ideology of the leftist guerrillas they had fought, and many listened to Chávez's revolutionary interpretation of Bolivar's ideas. MBR-200 aimed at achieving just social, economic, and political policies and eliminating corruption. The revolutionary organization grew within the armed forces but was not prepared to act when protests exploded in 1989. Many officers were appalled at being forced to help repress the rebellion, and some would have preferred to fight alongside the people against the government (Gott 2000, 48). The Caracazo motivated revolutionary officers to speed up plans to topple the government.

The Attempted Military Coups of 1992

Chávez's ability to move against the government was greatly enhanced when he was given command of a parachute battalion in 1991. He and his associates organized a coup. He believed that around 10 percent of the military, including units in the air force, were firmly committed to the plan (Gott 2000, 66–73), and thus the coup could only succeed if Chávez's forces captured President Pérez and the top generals in Caracas, obtained communication equipment to coordinate rebel military groups, and gained access to television and radio stations to broadcast to the entire country. But other military units learned of the coup shortly before it was launched, and Chávez's soldiers failed to achieve any of these objectives. Consequently there was no way to rally support from sympathetic civilians, and most of the armed forces would likely continue to obey the president.

During the coup attempt, which was launched on February 3, 1992, fourteen soldiers were killed and fifty wounded (Gott 2000, 68, 73). Eighty civilians were wounded in the cross fire. Realizing the coup could not succeed, Chávez asked permission to address the nation and the officers and soldiers participating in the coup, particularly the parachute regiment holding the town of Aragua and the tank brigade holding Valencia. In his one-minute television broadcast Chávez called on his comrades to "lay down your arms" but also stated that the goals of their Bolivarian revolutionary movement were being postponed only temporarily and that "new possibilities will arise again and the country will be able to move definitively towards a better future" (Gott 2000, 71). He also declared, "I alone shoulder the responsibility for this Bolivarian military uprising." While ending the violence, the broadcast introduced Chávez to the entire nation. Many were impressed by his charisma, sincerity, and courage and began to look to him as the potential leader of a movement to change Venezuela through elections rather than force of arms.

Following the coup, about 1,000 officers and soldiers, including Chávez, were put under detention. In November 1992 a second coup involving units of the navy and air force attempted, unsuccessfully, to overthrow the government. But in May 1993 the Venezuelan congress removed President Pérez from office on a charge of corruption. He was replaced by two interim presidents until the Pérez term expired in 1994. In the election that year, Rafael Caldera won a four-way race with about 30 percent of the vote; he served as president from 1994 to 1999. Caldera had abandoned COPEI, and his victory was credited to a widely publicized speech to the Venezuelan congress in which he blamed neoliberal economic policies and corruption for provoking Chávez's coup attempt. Caldera referred to "exaggerated increases in the cost of living" and "the terrible round of corruption that has eroded the institutional legality of the country" (Gott 2000, 72). (As president, however, Caldera also adopted the neoliberal approach; Ewell 2006, 906.) Caldera ordered participants in both 1992 coups released from prison. On March 27, 1994, Chávez was released from Yare prison and began his successful campaign to become Venezuela's next president.

The Presidential Election of 1998 and the Constitution of 1999

During the 1980s and 1990s income inequality and the percentage of people living in poverty increased (World Bank 2001). Chávez became convinced that he and his movement could achieve power through elections and gain approval for a new constitution supporting a more valid form of democracy—a blend of representative and direct participatory democracy—that gave voters the ability to recall elected leaders before their terms ended. Since Venezuelan law forbad the use of Simón Bolívar's name for any party, and since Chávez intended to replace the existing fourth Venezuelan republic with a fifth republic based on the new constitution, his movement changed its name from the Bolivarian Revolutionary Movement to

Fifth Republic Movement (MVR) in July 1997 (the V being the Roman numeral five). The movement expanded beyond armed forces personnel to include civilians from leftist parties, such as Movimiento al Socialismo and La Causa R, who infused MVR with a more comprehensive socialist ideology. In the campaign for the December 1998 election, Chávez pledged to fulfill Bolivar's ideals. He would end "savage neoliberal" policies that inflicted so much harm on the poor, foster a humane form of capitalism, and reduce inequality by increasing health care, educational opportunities, and the minimum wage. Chávez also pledged to promote unity, beneficial trade, and mutual aid among the peoples of the Americas. He won with 56.2 percent of the vote and was sworn in as president on February 2, 1999.

Chávez declared that a referendum be held to decide whether a national constituent assembly should be elected to write a new constitution. In this April 1999 vote, the yes option received 88 percent (Gott 2000, 154). In July the assembly was elected, with pro-Chávez delegates taking 119 of 131 seats. The assembly convened on August 3. The new constitution it produced renamed the country the Bolivarian Republic of Venezuela, transformed the legislative branch from a bicameral to a unicameral assembly of 167 seats (members elected by popular vote to five-year terms with three seats reserved for representatives of indigenous peoples), and extended the president's term from five to six years. It expanded presidential powers but also provided for the possibility of a recall election to remove a president from office before the term was completed, and created a two-term limit for the presidency. The constitution also integrated participatory democracy (direct citizen participation in the democratic processes of government) with representative democracy. And it provided for land reform, greater state intervention in the economy, better protection for the rights of indigenous peoples, and a stronger social security system. In the December 1999 national referendum the new constitution was approved by 71 percent of the voters (Gott 2000, 154).

The 2000 Election and the 2002 Right-Wing Coup Attempt

The 1999 constitution required new elections for the congress (National Assembly) and the presidency in 2000. Chávez was elected again, with about 60 percent of the vote, and began his second term on January 10, 2001. Chávez developed ties with many Venezuelans through speeches, television programs, and a radio call-in show called *Hello President!* (Ewell 2006, 907). Like Simón Bolívar and Ezequiel Zamora, Chávez appealed to the people to support him against the domination, injustices, and attempts to distort history and control ideas and culture by oligarchs and their allies. Among these he included the conservative business association Fedecámaras, executives of the PDVSA who resisted new policies, the Bush administration, and elements of the private mass media that "maintained an unremitting hostility toward him" (Ewell 2006, 907). "Many Venezuelans saw [in Chávez] a man of color who looked and talked like them, and they resented the racialized epithets the opposition used to refer to Chávez" (Ewell 2006, 907).

One early Chávez goal was to bring PDVSA firmly under the state, which owned it on behalf of the Venezuelan people. Ewell (2006, 907) reports that before Chávez's reforms, "oil executives were delivering only 20 percent of PDVSA's profits to the nation, had minimized cooperation with OPEC, and dealt independently with foreign companies." Many executives favored privatizing the company. Some PDVSA profits were invested outside Venezuela, were channeled into payments to foreign businesses, or were used for high managerial salaries.

Chávez's land reform alarmed high-income Venezuelans concerned about government confiscation of privately owned corporations. As Chávez vilified, angered, and marginalized traditional elites who were used to being masters of the country, he also antagonized the United States by attempting to strengthen OPEC, raise oil prices, and persuade other countries to oppose the US Free Trade Area of the Americas (FTAA). In addition, Chávez's friendship with Fidel Castro and expressions of admiration for Cuba's achievements concerned the George W. Bush administration. Likely anticipating they would face no opposition from the US, conservative military leaders and businessmen launched a coup against Chávez on April 11, 2002. Chávez was captured. The Bush administration, unlike most governments of the Americas, did not condemn the removal of the democratically elected president (Ewell 2006, 908). Businessman Pedro Carmona of Fedecámaras was selected to lead a new government. Hundreds of thousands of people, however, protested the coup and demanded the release of Chávez and his reinstatement as president. Furthermore, pro-Chávez sectors in the armed forces made similar demands. Civil war seemed a possibility with potentially dire consequences for the coup plotters. The coup leaders gave up and released Chávez after about two days. Chávez claimed that "the Venezuelan oligarchy had conspired with US imperialism to disrespect the will of the Venezuelan people and overthrow the democratically elected government" through a fascist coup involving "more than 100 traitorous generals and admirals" (Janicke 2010). But when hundreds of thousands poured into the streets of the capital to oppose the coup, "the soldiers not only refused to commit a massacre, but placed themselves and their guns on the side of the people."

The 2004 Recall Vote and Later Elections

The failed coup attempt was followed in December by a strike involving thousands of PDVSA executives and workers opposed to Chávez's plans. The strike damaged the economy. After about two months, the government fired some 18,000 primarily administrative, management, and professional employees (Kozloff 2008, 21).

Apparently hoping that the wounded economy and the conflict over the PDVSA had significantly undermined Chávez's support, the opposition decided to use the recall provision of the new constitution to remove Chávez from the presidency. This required getting 20 percent of registered voters to sign a recall petition, approximately 2.4 million people. The National Electoral Council determined that the required number of signatures was obtained. The recall election was held on August 15, 2004. When 59 percent of voters opposed the recall, Chávez maintained the presidency. He ran for reelection in 2006 and won about 63 percent of the vote (CIA 2010b).

While a 2007 referendum on eliminating the presidential term limit and making other constitutional changes was defeated, in 2009 another referendum eliminating term limits for all elective offices, including the presidency, was approved by voters. In 2007 Chávez's Fifth Republic Movement united with several other parties to form the United Socialist Party of Venezuela (PSUV). In 2010, 156 of the 167 seats in the Venezuelan National Assembly were held by members of the PSUV. Herrera (2008) noted that in a 2007 Latinobarómetro survey, Venezuelans ranked their country second only to Uruguay in level of democracy in the region and in the top position on dimensions such as equality of opportunity, concern for the poor, opportunities for employment, gender equality, social security, and even protection of private property.

The Leftward Shift of the Bolivarian Revolution

According to Ewell (2006, 907), Chávez's policies through mid-2005 were "to redistribute power and wealth within Venezuela's capitalist system; to empower the poor to take political action; to construct a nationalism that drew on Venezuela's past history; and internationally, to encourage the emergence of a multipolar world that would depend less on the United States." Chávez's Bolivarian revolution, however, appeared to shift left over time. Likely he moved cautiously at first in pursuit of his long-range goals to avoid provoking right-wing elites and anti-Chávez elements in the armed forces until he had consolidated popular and military support. His movement's achievements—winning the 1998 election, passing a new constitution, winning the 2000 elections, defeating the right-wing coup and the recall vote, winning the 2006 elections, and getting approval for amending the constitution in 2009—bolstered his confidence and that of his supporters.

IDEOLOGY, POLICIES, AND SOCIAL CHANGE

Chávez's ideology combined his interpretation of the ideas of Bolívar and other Venezuelans, such as Ezequiel Zamora, with those of more recent Latin American revolutionaries such as Fidel Castro and Che Guevara and the Chilean democratic socialist Salvador Allende. Bolivarianism includes anti-imperialism and the intent to bring about a more equitable distribution of opportunities, resources, services, and income; a more socially responsible form of capitalism and international trade; elimination of corruption; and economic self-sufficiency. At his third presidential inauguration in 2007 (Associated Press 2007), Chávez used a famous Fidel Castro expression, "Toward victory always! Fatherland, socialism, or death! We shall prevail!" He also referred to Jesus Christ as the greatest socialist in history and pledged to use his new term to build a socialist Venezuela. An Associated Press–Ipsos survey carried out just before the December 2006 election found that 62 percent favored nationalizing companies when it was in the nation's interest (Associated Press 2007), indicating significant popular support for Chávez's twenty-first-century socialism.

Domestic Policies

Chávez and his associates studied past leftist revolutionary movements to understand their achievements and avoid their mistakes. The Chávez government implemented policies intended to improve the well-being of low-income Venezuelans. According to Gott (2000, 172), in 1995 the top 10 percent of Venezuelans received half of all income. Despite the country's vast energy resources, its economic system channeled export revenue very disproportionately to a small minority.

To bring quick assistance to the poor, Chávez began "using the armed forces in the provision of social services" (Gott 2000, 178). Thousands of soldiers were put to work constructing schools, health centers, and roads. Assistance was provided to new farming settlements and rural revitalization efforts. The government created new programs called Bolivarian Missions to provide literacy education, health care, and job training to the poor. Thousands of Cuban doctors, health care workers, and teachers helped staff clinics and schools.

Early in the Chávez administration, thousands of local organizations, called Bolivarian Circles, were formed to provide a means for workers and poor people to participate in political discussions, make their views known to government, and carry out local improvement programs. In 2006 the National Assembly enacted the Law of Community Councils, which established a new mechanism of participatory democracy that largely took the place of Bolivarian Circles. The law offers funding to neighborhoods after they democratically organize councils and "submit feasible projects to state agencies" (Ellner 2009). In 2009 approximately 20,000 such community councils, each generally including "between 200 and 400 families in urban areas and upward of 20 families in rural areas," were formulating and carrying out community development projects (Irazábal and Foley 2010, 103).

According to Ellner (2010, 85), the Chávez government had three central goals for the economy. First, increase Venezuela's independent productive capacity, in particular by reducing its reliance on advanced capitalist nations for technology and capital investment. Second, expand and diversify trade relationships in order to decrease dependence on the US oil market. Third, reduce the economic domination of a small number of companies by providing opportunities for more competition. Ellner (2010, 87) notes that although Chávez advocated "state management of basic industry" before becoming president, he largely postponed moving on this goal until he had won his third presidential election. Beginning in 2007, Chávez nationalized several foreign-owned companies, including the National Telephone Corporation (CANTV), a number of electrical companies, the Orinoco Steel Company (SIDOR), several cement companies, and the Bank of Venezuela. The government through PDVSA also took over at least 60 percent ownership of the Orinoco Oil Belt.

To help diversify oil production, territories in the Orinoco Belt were opened to mainly state-owned companies from Argentina, Belarus, Brazil, China, Iran, Russia, Uruguay, and Vietnam. In general, nationalizations were carried out mainly to achieve greater economic self-sufficiency, national development, and social benefits. For example, control of the cement companies could keep a greater percentage of cement production in Venezuela, where it is needed for construction projects rather than going to the world market, where it might earn higher profits. CANTV offered 820,000 low-income customers 10–15 percent price discounts (Ellner 2010, 87).

Military

Pro-Chávez military officers were appointed to government positions. The 1999 constitution gave the executive branch exclusive control over the promotion of officers. The Chávez administration concluded that a government attempting to bring about significant social change perceived as threatening the interests of wealthy groups or powerful foreign interests must have firm control over the armed forces. This became even more clear after the attempted right-wing coup in 2002. There were indications that the Venezuelan armed forces became increasingly politicized in support of the Bolivarian movement. A retiring general stated that Cuban personnel were active in training and advising Venezuelan soldiers who began accompanying their salutes with the slogan "Socialist Homeland or Death!" (Associated Press 2010). Cubans reportedly trained Venezuelan troops in communications, intelligence, sniping, and other areas. Sources indicated that Cubans were helping the armed forces prepare to resist a potential US invasion (GlobalSecurity.org 2010). In addition to at least 80,000 active troops, the government was developing a reserve force of about 100,000 and distributing arms to tens of thousands in civilian Bolivarian militias (Janicke 2010). Chávez spent several billion dollars for new equipment, including modern fighter planes, helicopters, radar systems, missiles, laser guided bombs, ships and submarines, assault and sniper rifles, and night vision devices from Russia, China, Belarus, and other nations.

Health, Education, Inequality

According to the Central Bank of Venezuela, government spending devoted to social purposes increased from 38.6 percent in 1997 to 44 percent in 2007 (Herrera 2008). The fact that low-income voters continued to strongly support Chávez and his movement in elections and referendums indicated that the large majority of the poor believed that they were benefiting significantly from Chávez policies.

The percentage of children attending school between 1998 and 2006 increased at all levels. Nine times as many children gained access to free meals at school (Herrera 2008). A special Chávez administration program designed to help dropouts complete high school, Misión Ribas, graduated 450,000 by 2008 (Ellner 2010, 90), although in many cases the quality of education did not measure up to the standards of the private or regular public high schools. The government also attempted to expand educational opportunity at the university level through Misión Sucre and the associated Universidad Bolivariana (Ellner 2010, 90). In addition the government asked public universities to drop their individual internal entrance examinations; created the National Experimental University of the Armed Forces (UNEFA), which in ten years grew from 2,500 to 250,000 students at thirty-nine campuses; and planned to build eighteen new public universities (Janicke 2010). With the help of thousands of Cuban physicians and health care workers, medical services in low-income and rural areas increased significantly, and from 1999 to 2007 the number of public sector primary care doctors in Venezuela increased from 1,628 to 19,571 (Weisbrot 2008, 6).

Herrera (2008) claims that from 1998 to 2006 the income of the poorest Venezuelans rose 445 percent, while the wealthiest had an increase of 194 percent. The CIA *World Factbook* for Venezuela indicates that inequality in family income declined significantly (2014c), with the country's Gini index measure of family income inequality dropping from .495 in 1998 to .39 in 2011. Weisbrot (2008, 2) presented data from Venezuela's National Statistical Institute indicating that in the first half of 1999, 50 percent of the population was living in poverty, whereas in 2007 it was under 34 percent. By 2011, it was less than 32 percent (CIA 2014c). The country's high oil revenue through the first decade of the Bolivarian revolution meant that the well-being of the poor could be improved without reducing the income of the wealthy.

Challenges

Despite efforts to reduce inequality and poverty and increase opportunity, certain forms of crime increased after Chávez's 1998 election. The national homicide rate was 8 per 100,000 residents in 1987. In 1998, the year before Chávez took office, the rate had climbed to 19. When the economy was devastated by the national oil strike in 2003 and the poverty rate soared, the homicide rate grew to 44. The Venezuelan government indicated that in 2012 the homicide rate was 56 (Wells 2013), one of the highest in the world. The number of kidnappings followed a similar, though not identical pattern. In 1998, fifty kidnappings were reported in the country, but 277 were reported in 2003. After declining somewhat, the kidnappings reached 382 in 2007 (Pontón, Villacrés, and Guevara 2010, 6). Anti-Chávez politicians criticized the government for not combating crime more effectively, and the more extreme opposition figures argued that Chávez actually encouraged "the poor to steal from the rich" (Lown 2009, 3). Government officials hoped that increasing opportunity would soon lower crime rates.

Chávez critics, including some socialists who formerly supported him, feared that despite his repeated election victories, his government was making Venezuela less democratic. Chávez may have believed that he had unique qualities that made him essential to the Bolivarian revolution. This constituted a potential weakness of the Bolivarian movement and raised the question of what would happen after Chávez was gone. The success of the movement in the long run requires a strong, well-organized, and popularly supported political party that can field appealing political candidates and programs and continue to win elections without Chávez. The United Socialist Party attempted to achieve this goal.

Another potential limitation of the Bolivarian revolution is that currently it is dependent on the international price of oil. If the price of oil falls significantly, the government would be hard-pressed to maintain benefits and might be forced to begin redistributing wealth from the affluent to the poor, which could provoke intense conflict. Grinberg (2010, 199) suggests that much of the revenue flowing to countries such as Venezuela should be invested in improving domestic industrial production to the extent necessary to create new technologies capable of effectively competing on the world market.

International Policy: ALBA—
Revolutionary Infrastructure Instead of Guerrilla Foco

As described in Chapter 5, Che Guevara tried to spread revolution internationally through armed struggle using the guerrilla *foco* concept. Chávez and his allies created an alternative approach, an international infrastructure to provide support for governments attempting transformative change. On December 14, 2004, Venezuela and Cuba signed an agreement initiating the Bolivarian Alternative for the Americas (ALBA, a word meaning "dawn" in Spanish, changed to the Bolivarian Alliance for the Americas in 2009) to counter international neoliberal policies and in particular the US-sponsored Free Trade Area of the Americas. In 2006 Bolivia, following the election of Evo Morales, joined ALBA. Ecuador, a nation of about 15 million (CIA 2014b) led by Rafael Correa, became a member of ALBA in 2009. By 2010 ALBA also included Antigua and Barbuda, Dominica, Nicaragua, and Saint Vincent and the Grenadines.

ALBA opposes privatization of essential public services and policies that perpetuate unfavorable trade relations causing poor countries to fall further into debt to wealthy nations. According to ALBA policy statements, government provision of public services such as water, health care, education, libraries, energy, public transportation, and fire and police services is indispensable for overcoming social inequality. The alliance intends to serve as a framework for uniting all Latin American and Caribbean countries into a cooperative economic network. A major aim is to lessen dependency on the US and other advanced capitalist nations or their multinational corporations, and to work toward the creation of a multipolar world in which no single nation dominates.

Venezuela's fuel assistance efforts extended beyond ALBA member nations. By 2013, Venezuela's Petro Caribe program was supplying low-cost oil (peaking at an average of about 196,400 barrels per day in 2009) to Cuba, the Dominican Republic, Jamaica, and ten other Caribbean islands (Pearce 2013). Venezuela also provided low-cost oil to lower-income communities in the US. Cuba received about 90,000 barrels a day in exchange for Venezuela getting some 30,000 Cuban medical personnel and experts in areas such as education and sports. Thousands of Venezuelans were flown to Cuba for specialized medical treatment, and ALBA's Operation Miracle (Operación Milagro) conducted nearly 850,000 operations to improve the eyesight of people from twenty-eight countries in Latin America and the Caribbean (Azicri 2009).

ALBA claims its goals include establishing trade based on mutual cooperation; eliminating poverty, illiteracy, and discrimination against indigenous people; and making health care available free to those who can't pay. ALBA supporters assert that the alliance is the beginning of a new hope for the world's poor in the context of global economic problems caused by greed and profit maximization. ALBA proposes more self-sufficiency in food production. The weakest nations are to be helped to develop essential economic infrastructure so that they become less dependent on foreign corporations. Venezuela is crucial to ALBA because its oil can provide members with energy independence and can bankroll development programs and the acquisition of advanced technologies.

Chávez's animosity toward the Bush administration's foreign policy was demonstrated when he addressed the United Nations on September 20, 2006, the day after the US president had spoken there. Chávez said, "Yesterday, the devil came here.... As the spokesman of imperialism, he came ... to try to preserve the current pattern of domination, exploitation and pillage of the peoples of the world" (Stout 2006). Chávez also implied that the United States under the Bush administration was "the gravest threat looking over our planet, placing at risk the very survival of the human species. We appeal to the people of the United States to halt this threat, like a sword hanging over our heads."

Whereas Chávez appeared to view Bush as an irredeemable imperialist, his attitude toward President Barack Obama seemed more hopeful. At a meeting of South American presidents on April 18, 2009, Chávez met Obama, posed for a picture with him, and gave Obama a book, *Open Veins of Latin America: Five Centuries of the Pillage of a Continent,* by the Uruguayan author Eduardo Galeano (1997), instantly turning the book into a best-seller (ABC News, April 18, 2009). The book describes and critically evaluates the forms and impacts of five hundred years of European and US intervention in South and Central America and the Caribbean. Galeano asserted that at first gold and silver were the most sought after resources. But Europe and the United States also wanted the region's agricultural products; its industrially important minerals such as copper, iron, and oil; and also its cheap labor. He believed that the relationship between powerful foreign nations and Latin America maintained the poverty of most of the continent's people while making the rich countries ever richer. Chávez believed that if President Obama developed an understanding of history, the behavior of the US would change for the better and the future of Latin America and the Caribbean would be much brighter.

Venezuela After Chávez

Shortly after Hugo Chávez was reelected president in October 2012, his health deteriorated. He flew to Cuba for cancer treatment. Chávez succumbed on March 5, 2013, before he could be inaugurated, and a new presidential election had to be held. The two main candidates were Chávez's vice president, Nicolás Maduro, candidate of the PSUV, and Henrique Capriles Radonski, candidate of Justice First. Maduro comes from a working class background and worked as a bus driver and a union leader before being elected to the Venezuelan legislature. He was elected speaker of the National Assembly in 2005 and was appointed minister of foreign affairs in 2006 (Venezuela Solidarity Campaign 2013). In 2012 he became Chávez's vice president and then acting president in 2013 after Chávez died. Capriles is from one of Venezuela's wealthiest families (Correo Del Orinoco International 2013). He was educated as a lawyer and eventually elected mayor of the wealthy Caracas suburb of

Baruta from 2000 to 2008 and then governor of the Venezuelan state of Miranda in 2008. In the October 2012 presidential election, Chávez won about 55 percent of the vote and Capriles about 44 percent.

In the campaign for the special election, Capriles appealed to Chávez supporters by stating he would preserve benefits for the poor that Chávez had implemented but do a better job of running the country than Maduro. Maduro pledged to continue Chávez's Bolivarian revolution and socialist transformation of Venezuela. On election day, April 14, 2013, Maduro won a narrow victory, receiving 50.6 percent of the vote to 49.1 percent for Capriles (a difference of about 223,000 votes) (National Electoral Council 2013). In December municipal elections, however, Maduro's PSUV defeated the main opposition party by 6 percent of the vote (Mogollon and Kraul 2013).

CHÁVEZ'S ACHIEVEMENTS AND PERSISTING CHALLENGES

Hugo Chávez's leadership brought about major changes domestically and internationally (Grandin 2013; Rosen 2013). During his presidency, assistance to and opportunities for the poor increased dramatically. The percentage of the population living in poverty declined significantly. Chávez intervened in the economy to give the people a more prominent role. In particular, his administration regained effective control over Venezuela's oil. Venezuela then used some of its oil revenue to aid poor people in the Caribbean and other nations and to significantly increase the economic autonomy of Latin American countries. Politically, Chávez's policies vastly expanded the political power and participation of the poor and in the process created and maintained majority electoral support for his twenty-first-century socialism program.

Venezuela, however, experienced significant problems which threatened future economic development as well as voter support for the PSUV. One problem was the continued high level of crime. Much of this was committed by low-income males, many of whose victims were also low-income males, often rival gang members (Carroll 2013). Many high- and middle-income persons were victims of kidnappings for ransom. The fear of crime undermined the increased benefits and improved opportunities for many low-income persons. Other troubling economic problems were a high inflation rate, around 21 percent in 2012, and lagging productivity in some nationalized enterprises (CIA 2014c).

THE MADURO PRESIDENCY

President Maduro pledged to protect the achievements of the Bolivarian revolution, continue the process of socialist transformation, and combat economic difficulties like high inflation (Ellner 2013). In September 2013, Venezuela's finance minister, Nelson Merentes, stated that although Hugo Chávez's economic policies had improved the lives of many Venezuelans, serious economic problems existed (BBC 2013). Inequality and poverty had been significantly reduced, but inflation was unacceptably high and there were shortages of certain goods. Although Chávez's critics blamed mismanagement of public revenues and reduced productivity in nationalized industries, President Maduro and his supporters believed that many private businesspersons, in collusion with hostile foreign powers, were purposely sabotaging the economy. They were accused of doing things like slowing down production, withholding essential goods from stores to create scarcities and discontent, and charging customers excessively high prices (which contributes to inflation).

To deal with economic difficulties, President Maduro requested, and on November 19, 2013, received, emergency decree powers from the Venezuelan legislature (Rueda 2013). This measure, granted four times to President Chávez and used to increase government influence over the economy, allowed Maduro to enact laws without seeking approval from the legislature for up to a year. In the days leading up to the emergency decree vote, Maduro had ordered the military to seize dozens of appliance stores, reduce prices on imported electronics items, and arrest more than a hundred business owners for charging excessive prices. These actions were very popular with many-working class Venezuelans and even appealed to some of the opponents of the PSUV government. Following the legislature's approval of presidential emergency power, Maduro repeated his promise to limit profit levels to a maximum of 30 percent for all businesses and industries. He further stated that the government would launch a major offensive against corruption and against the country's high homicide rate about which the public became even more concerned after the January 6, 2014, robbery-related murder of a former Miss Venezuela, Monica Spear, and her ex-husband Thomas Berry (Mogollon and Kraul 2014).

REVOLUTION THROUGH DEMOCRACY: BOLIVIA

The characteristics of the five factors necessary for revolution through democracy in Venezuela, though historically unique, are similar for Bolivia. Mass frustration intensified because of the perception that neoliberal policies were increasing economic inequality and undermining the well-being of millions, that people of mixed race and Amerindian background were the victims of racial discrimination, and that many of the privileged power holders in government and business were corrupt and greedy. The existence of pro-revolution charismatic leaders among officers in the armed forces and among indigenous or mixed-race groups, as well as highly educated leaders of leftist social movements, constituted elite dissidence.

Unifying motivations for revolution were rejection of neoliberal economic policies, abhorrence of corruption, anti-imperialist feeling, and opposition to racism. State collapse in the case of Bolivia (as in Venezuela) was actually the collapse of the legitimacy of the previously dominant political parties and leadership (generally purveyors of neoliberalism with ties to foreign powers) and a form of government dominated by economic oligarchs, coupled with domestic military support for, or at least tolerance of, democratic revolutionary movements. Growing world commitment to democracy and US preoccupation with the wars in Iraq and Afghanistan constituted the permissive world context. The election of Barack Obama likely reduced the threat of US military intervention against democratically elected leftist revolutionary governments.

When Evo Morales, a union activist of Aymara Amerindian ancestry and candidate of the Movement Toward Socialism (MAS), was inaugurated president on January 22, 2006, Bolivia became one of Venezuela's staunchest allies and partners in ALBA. In the nation where Che Guevara was executed after failing to bring revolution to the South American continent through guerrilla warfare, a new revolutionary movement gained power through elections. Morales won almost 54 percent of the 2005 vote, the largest percentage since civilian rule resumed in 1982. His government quickly nationalized privately owned hydrocarbon companies, abandoned neoliberal economic policies of previous administrations, increased social services, expanded rights of the indigenous majority, and established ties to Venezuela, Cuba, and other countries with leftist or anti-imperialist governments. His support increased as overwhelming majorities of voters rejected recalling him from office, approved the new constitution he favored, and reelected him president in 2009.

Two centuries earlier, an anticolonial insurrection of indigenous Bolivians, led by a sexton calling himself Túpaj Katari, laid siege to Spanish-controlled La Paz from March to October 1781 (Hylton and Thomson 2004). The rebellion ultimately failed, but before he was executed by Spanish colonists, Túpaj Katari stated, "I may die alone, but I will return and I will be millions" (NACLA 2004, 14). Many Bolivians believe this prophecy was fulfilled in a series of later indigenous-led political mobilizations, including the campaign to elect Evo Morales.

Emergence of the Bolivian Revolution

Bolivia, named for Simón Bolívar, gained independence from Spain in 1825. Its political history was characterized by almost two hundred coups and countercoups until civilian rule was reestablished in 1982. Totally landlocked and bordering Argentina, Brazil, Chile, Paraguay, and Peru, the country has a territory of 1,098,581 square kilometers. It has vast natural resources, including significant reserves of natural gas and deposits of precious metals and lithium. In 2009 its population was

MAP 10.2 Bolivia

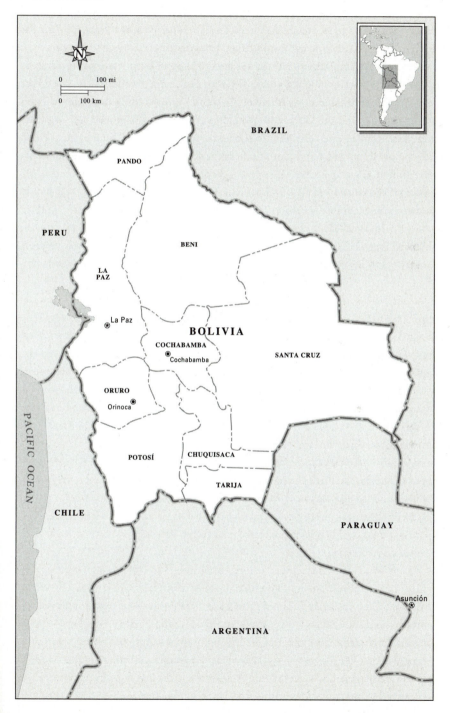

estimated at 9,775,246. Ethnic composition is about 30 percent Quechua, 30 percent mestizo (mixed white and Amerindian ancestry), 25 percent Aymara, and 15 percent white. In 2006, an estimated 60 percent of the population lived below the poverty line (CIA 2010a), but this declined to 50 percent in 2010 (CIA 2014a).

Following independence, Bolivia was governed by military leaders and members of the country's economic elite of largely European ancestry. The majority indigenous population was impoverished and generally limited to manual labor such as mining and agricultural labor, with virtually no access to education. Wars cost Bolivia much of its original territory. In the devastating War of the Pacific (1879–1884), Bolivia lost its seacoast and a mineral-rich area to Chile. A conservative Bolivian government, seeking a river route to the Atlantic Ocean and a new source of oil, provoked the Chaco War (1932–1935) with Paraguay, fought it incompetently, was defeated, and lost more territory. These events discredited traditional elites and led to a surge in socialist movements among workers and some in the middle class, as well as indigenous demands for full political rights. Leftist-oriented military officers seized power in 1936 but were replaced by a conservative civilian government in 1939.

National Revolution of 1952

In the early 1940s a new political party formed, the National Revolutionary Movement (MNR). Initially including some right-wing elements, the leadership and ideology shifted left. Faced with the growing popularity of the MNR, the protests of socialist-oriented workers, and the increasing mobilization of the indigenous majority, Bolivia's conservative leaders resorted to military repression and suppression of election results to hold on to power, leading the MNR and its allies to consider armed revolution. When the government refused to honor the results of the May 1951 presidential election, which the MNR won with about 72 percent of the vote (Klein 1998, 45), the MNR launched an uprising on April 9, 1952. Miners using dynamite and other civilians armed with weapons from captured armories defeated the army in three days of intense combat in which about six hundred died. Once in power, the MNR began to respond to the demands of its supporters with new laws and policies.

People were given the right to vote without regard to literacy or property ownership. Universal suffrage increased the number of eligible voters from 200,000 to 1 million (Klein 1998, 45; Thomson 2009, 22). Free public education for all was established. A national labor federation was formed, the Bolivian Workers Central (COB), which demanded the nationalization of mines. In October the MNR government took over the three largest mining companies and then combined them into the state-owned Bolivian Mining Corporation. Six percent of property holders had owned 92 percent of the cultivated land (Thomson 2009, 22). Following the successful April rebellion, peasants spontaneously seized the lands of the big agri-cultural estates (haciendas) in 1952 and early 1953, destroyed records, and expelled or killed landlords and overseers (Klein 1998, 46). In response, the government approved an agrarian reform law that gave the lands of big estates to indigenous workers through their communities or unions. As the hacienda system was abol-ished, "a new class of communal peasant owners was established" (Klein 1998, 46). However, MNR leaders were more moderate than the workers and peasants who constituted their major popular support.

Apart from nationalizing tin mines and land reform, the government protected private property and tried to attract foreign investment. The MNR allied Bolivia with the US against the USSR in the cold war. In return, the US provided aid for Bolivian social programs. According to Klein (1998, 46), in 1960 Bolivia was the highest per capita recipient of US foreign aid in the world, much of which included food shipments that helped Bolivia cope with shortages caused by disruption of agriculture during the land reform process. In 1964, in the context of the growth of armed revolutionary movements in Latin America inspired by the successful Cu-ban revolution, the Bolivian military seized power and began repressing the most militant workers and middle-class leftists. Similar right-wing military takeovers oc-curred in other Latin American countries, such as Brazil (1964), Argentina (1966), Peru (1968), Chile (1973), and Uruguay (1973).

Neoliberal Shift

Following a massive strike of workers against the military government, the armed forces, discredited by accusations of corruption, finally returned the country to civilian rule in 1982. In 1985 the MNR, more conservative and with far less support than in 1952, won the presidency. The national legislature selected its candidate from among the top three vote getters in the direct popular election in which no one received more than 50 percent. The MNR government quickly responded to the country's problems, which included a large debt from the period of military rule, extensive damage to highland agriculture from a major drought, and a decline in the price for a key Bolivian export, tin, by adopting neoliberal economic restruc-turing favored by the US and international financial institutions. The new policies included privatizing state enterprises; deregulating prices, salaries, and markets; undermining the power of unions; and removing protections for domestic agricul-ture and industry (Arze and Kruse 2004; Cusicanqui 2004).

In 1988 the government gave in to US pressure to cooperate in eradicating much of the country's coca agriculture, which had cultural as well as economic repercus-sions (Farthing and Ledebur 2004). The Aymara and Quechua have chewed coca leaves for centuries as an appetite suppressant during food shortages, and in the mountains brewed coca tea is used as a cure for altitude sickness. Coca also plays a role in some indigenous religious ceremonies and historically has been part of ritual exchange practice. Since growing and consuming coca is an important part of indigenous culture, and since the government made inadequate efforts to introduce substitute crops, discontent among Bolivia's Amerindian population increased. In addition, state finances suffered because income from previously state-owned companies was lost, while the level of revenue from private businesses predicted by proponents of neoliberalism failed to materialize. Thus a crisis of state legitimacy accelerated. Government policies had simultaneously surrendered economic sovereignty by privatizing state companies and making them available for foreign ownership; increased unemployment; undermined the welfare of the poor and the unions that represented worker and peasant interests; and trampled on indigenous culture and livelihood by attacking coca farming. The European ancestry of many government officials accentuated the racial and cultural divide between them and the large majority of the people. As discontent surged, a new leader and movement emerged to rally and unify insurgent sectors of the population.

Evo Morales and MAS

Juan Evo Morales Ayma was born in 1959 in a poor Aymara village in rural Orinoca, Oruro Department. His parents had seven children but only three survived to adulthood, an experience common among poor indigenous families (Morales 2010). As a child he worked as an agricultural laborer and a llama herder. In order to pay for schooling, he later took jobs as a baker, a bricklayer, and a trumpet player in a band, and he fulfilled mandatory military service. He did not receive formal education beyond the eleventh grade. In the early 1980s, Bolivia's high plateaus were hit by a severe drought that destroyed 70 percent of crops and killed half the farm animals. The Morales family, like many others, moved to the Chapare lowlands of Cochabamba Department and began raising crops such as bananas, oranges, papaya, grapefruits, and coca.

In 1985 Morales became a member of the local coca farmers (*cocaleros*) union. Despite being the victim of beatings by opponents of his activism, he was persistent, and by 1996 he became the president of the coordinating committee of six Cochabamba union federations. In 1997, he was elected to the lower house of the Bolivian legislature as a candidate of an alliance of leftist parties, including his Political Instrument for the Sovereignty of the Peoples–Movement Toward Socialism (IPSP-MAS), a coalition of social movements (Kozloff 2008, 11). In the 1999 election Morales's movement participated using the logo MAS for the first time (Obarrio 2010, 92, 105). MAS called for Bolivian—rather than foreign—ownership of resources, equal rights for indigenous people, the right to cultivate coca, and nationalization of major industries to achieve economic sovereignty and increase state revenues for use in expanding health care, education, and job opportunities.

In 2002 Morales was expelled for asserting that coca farmers had the right to defend themselves against soldiers in the government's coca crop eradication efforts, but later the same year he was reelected with over 80 percent of his district's vote. And as the MAS candidate for president, he also received 20.9 percent for that office, second to the 22.5 percent obtained by the MNR candidate, Gonzalo Sánchez de Lozada (Morales 2010). MAS also finished second in the vote for legislators, obtaining twenty-seven seats in the lower house and eight senate seats. Between 2002 and 2008 support for MAS and Evo Morales continued to surge dramatically, spreading from the Chapare region of Cochabamba Department in central Bolivia to much of the country, but especially to the heavily indigenous western departments, where the percentage of the vote for MAS reached or exceeded 80 percent in many areas (Obarrio 2010, 91–106). Beyond Morales's spectacular personal popularity and the intense discontent generated by neoliberal policies and the anticoca campaign, two particular government actions provoked major popular mobilizations against the political establishment.

The 2000 Water War and the 2003 Gas War

The first of the two sensational mass mobilizations followed the government's 1999 decision, apparently the result of pressure from international financial institutions, to privatize SEMAPA, the public water system in Bolivia's third largest city, Cochabamba (population about 600,000). The water service was taken over by Aguas del Tunari, a company owned in great part by US, Italian, and Spanish corporations. The company was reportedly even given control of water from wells dug by local cooperatives. Rates promptly increased by as much as 200 percent, meaning poor families could end up paying 20–30 percent of their income for water (Chávez 2006). Protests began early in 2000 and intensified in April when citizens, organizing themselves into the Coalition in Defense of Water and Life, set up roadblocks, organized strikes, and essentially shut down the city.

The rebellion against water privatization forced the government to reverse itself and return water operations in Cochabamba to public control. The victory of the popular uprising in the Cochabamba water war inspired similar protests against water privatization elsewhere in Bolivia and in other parts of the world, damaged the legitimacy of the existing government and political elites, brought more support for Evo Morales and MAS, and fostered a confidence in civil insurrection that would be unleashed in more dramatic fashion over natural gas policy.

In 1996 the government passed a new hydrocarbons law that eliminated the state energy company, "setting the stage for the transnational takeover of Bolivia's rich oil and natural gas resources" (Hylton and Thomson 2004, 17). Neoliberal policies were supported by government elites, wealthy oligarchs, technocrats influenced by conservative US economists, and many people in the eastern lowland departments, especially Santa Cruz, where much of the energy extraction and agribusiness operations were located. While some Bolivians prospered, many others remained in dire poverty and inequality grew. The CIA (2010a) reported that Bolivia's Gini index of family income inequality grew to .592 in 2006 (the seventh highest inequality score in the world) from .447 in 1999. (After Evo Morales won the presidency in 2005, the Gini index of income inequality declined to .53 in 2010; CIA 2014a.)

As tensions increased over the impact of neoliberal policies, MNR president Sánchez de Lozada approved a plan allowing British and US companies to build a pipeline to transport Bolivian natural gas to a port in Chile, where it would be liquefied for shipment to California. Many Bolivians considered the share of gas profits for their country far too low and suspected the deal would involve bribes for corrupt government officials, greater wealth for already rich businesspeople, and little or no benefits for most Bolivians. From their point of view, this would be another enormously unjust process in hundreds of years of foreign exploitation through which Bolivia, one of the most resource-endowed countries in the world, became one of South America's poorest nations. Another cause for outrage was that the pipeline would economically benefit Chile, which in the Pacific war of 1879–1884 had deprived Bolivia of its coastline. If Chile would not restore at least part of the coast, many Bolivians preferred shipping the gas through a longer pipeline to a port in Peru.

In September and October 2003, protests over the gas deal intensified. Hundreds of thousands demonstrated in the capital, La Paz, and other cities demanding its cancellation and the removal of President Lozada. In clashes between government forces and protestors, dozens were killed. Finally, on October 17, Lozada resigned and flew to Miami; his former vice president, Carlos Diego Mesa, assumed the presidency. Evo Morales and MAS, however, were not satisfied with Mesa's reformulation of the gas deal and demanded at least a 50 percent share of revenues for Bolivia. These demands were supported by massive protests in May and June 2005, which called for a fairer natural gas export policy and a national election as soon as possible for a new government to formulate it. Mesa resigned on June 6. On June 10, the legislature selected the head of Bolivia's supreme court, Eduardo Rodríguez, to serve as president until new elections could be held in December.

Elections 2005–2009

Most Bolivians hoped a new government would reject neoliberal policies and dramatically increase the country's revenue from natural gas and oil. On December

18, 2005, with about 85 percent of registered voters participating, Evo Morales won a five-year presidential term, receiving about 54 percent of the votes cast, beating his nearest competitor by more than 20 percent. In the lower house of the national legislature MAS took 72 of 130 seats and in the senate twelve of twenty-seven seats (Obarrio 2010, 97). Morales identified the victory with historic indigenous struggles against colonialism and racial and cultural repression, Simón Bolívar's fight against foreign domination, and Che Guevara's quest for socialism (Postero 2010, 18). After being sworn in on January 22, 2006, Morales fulfilled his promise to hold an election for a Constituent Assembly to write a new Bolivian constitution. The Constituent Assembly would provide the Bolivian people with the potential to accomplish revolutionary structural change in their political and economic system without violence. In July 2006, with again approximately 85 percent of registered voters participating, MAS won about 54 percent of the seats in the assembly, which convened in August. Once the lengthy process of constructing the new constitution was finished, it was approved in a national referendum in January 2009 by approximately two-thirds of those voting (Regalsky 2010, 36).

In response to demands from opposition groups, Morales had agreed to a recall election for August 10, 2008, which he won with 67 percent voting to maintain him as president (Obarrio 2010, 96, 101). Then in December 2009, a national election was held in accordance with the new constitution. Morales received 64 percent of the vote for a new five-year term as president. His MAS party took 89 of the 130 seats in the lower house of the legislature, the Chamber of Deputies, and twenty-six of thirty-six seats in the Senate (expanded to thirty-six seats by the 2009 constitution). This series of votes between 2005 and 2009 represented a new political era in Bolivia. The poor indigenous majority hoped the new government controlled by MAS would more effectively use Bolivia's resources for the benefit of all the country's people.

Given that opponents of MAS had powerful resources in the form of capital and energy wealth, control of departmental and municipal governments in eastern Bolivia, and ties to foreign governments and corporations, the transition to Bolivarian socialism could not occur overnight. It is nevertheless significant to recognize what dramatic changes in Bolivia's government and political system were achieved through democratic means. The next section is a brief description of several key elements of Bolivia's new constitution.

Constitution of 2009

The new constitution changed the country's name from the Republic of Bolivia to the Plurinational State of Bolivia, signifying that Bolivia is peopled by diverse ethnic and racial groups all entitled to equal rights. The constitution attempts to

"decolonize" the politically excluded and racially and culturally oppressed indigenous peoples. The traditional cultivation of coca is permitted, and indigenous
courts are allowed some jurisdiction. The state is declared independent of any particular religion. The document condemns "all forms of dictatorship, colonialism,
neocolonialism, and imperialism" (Constitution of the Plurinational State of Bolivia 2009).

The constitution states that Bolivia's natural resources are owned by the Bolivian people; "hydrocarbons" are the "inalienable" property of the Bolivian people;
and the state, "on behalf of the Bolivian people," owns "all hydrocarbon production
in the country" and controls hydrocarbon marketing. The constitution guarantees
access to water and sanitation as human rights, not subject to privatization, and free
health care and education at all levels. The government is responsible to work to
eliminate poverty, reduce inequality in access to productive resources, and reduce
inequality among regions. The constitution, however, also protects private or collectively owned property and business activity regulated by the state and in conformity with the constitution; it requires safe working conditions and decent wages.
Bolivians are to be taxed "in proportion to their economic capacity. . . . All forms
of violence against children and adolescents, both in the family and in society," are
prohibited and punished. The constitution also promotes participatory democracy
through giving citizens the right to initiate legislation, vote on proposals through
referendums, and vote to recall any elected officials except judges.

Ideology, Policies, Changes, and Challenges

The Bolivian Constitution of 2009 describes a series of continuing goals under
broad categories such as decolonization, socialism, and participatory democracy.
One important aspect of decolonization is achieving national economic sovereignty by reclaiming resources taken from the people during colonization and
more recently during the period of privatization and increased foreign ownership.
MAS characterizes national economic sovereignty as gaining state control of resources and major enterprises on behalf of the people, developing industry so that
raw resources are transformed into valuable products rather than just exporting
resources to other countries, and also diversifying both export markets and sources
of foreign assistance.

Domestic Policies

As president, Morales increased government participation in the economy and
introduced new health care, education, and social security programs (Kohl and
Bresnahan 2010). He resurrected the state energy company that had been broken

up and privatized during the 1990s. Before 2006, foreign corporations controlled the extraction of natural gas, when, where, and how much to sell, and what price to sell it for. Nationalization involved taking 51 percent ownership of the private companies that had been formed from the old state energy company and gave Bolivia control of its extracted hydrocarbons all the way to the point of sale with the ability to decide how much to sell, to whom, and at what price. The state's share of revenue generated by the sale of hydrocarbons was increased through a combination of royalties and taxes from 18 percent to 50 percent (Kaup 2010, 129). Under nationalization, the government in effect hires companies, both private and state-owned, to extract hydrocarbons and deliver them to the point of sale in return for, in general, half the revenue. Between 2005 and 2008, the price Brazil paid for Bolivian natural gas increased by more than 40 percent, and the rise for Argentina was even greater. Increasing both price and percentage share meant that Bolivia's income from its hydrocarbons climbed from $287 million in 2004 to $1.572 billion in 2007 (Kaup 2010, 129), a rise of over 400 percent.

While the hydrocarbon nationalization and other nationalizations were generally opposed by traditional elites, a number of social movements that had supported Morales criticized them as too mild and called for total expropriation of private companies and properties. Despite the steady progressive thrust of the MAS government, some observers viewed its early polices as more reformist than revolutionary and too conciliatory overall. Right-wing opponents, especially those in the resource-rich and agriculturally and industrially productive Santa Cruz Department, opposed Morales and pushed for greater autonomy or even secession from the rest of Bolivia. Meanwhile, the armed forces remained loyal to the central government. Morales admitted indigenous people to the armed forces officer training college for the first time, increased military salaries, and purchased new equipment. Furthermore, imbued with nationalism, the armed forces generally supported Morales's efforts to redirect the main benefits of the county's resources to Bolivians rather than foreigners.

Bolivia continued further nationalizations "in order to fulfill the new constitution," in the words of President Morales (BBC News, May 2, 2010). On May 1, 2010, for example, Bolivia nationalized four electric companies created from the privatization of the state electric company in the 1990s in an effort to place all electrical production under state control.

The issue of building of a 182-mile highway through the Isiboro-Secure National Park (TIPNIS) sparked opposition from some indigenous people as well as environmentalists (Achtenberg 2013). The Morales administration believed that the highway could be built with minimal impact on the environment and would fulfill a longtime goal of linking the people and economies of Bolivia's Amazonian and Andean regions. It would also bring needed services to the relatively isolated people of the TIPNIS communities. Opponents argued that the highway would lead to colonization of the TIPNIS by Bolivians from other parts of the country and to major deforestation as land was cleared for new farms and other enterprises. Furthermore, they claimed that the decision to build the highway violated the Bolivian constitution, which requires prior consultation with the communities directly affected by such an enormous project.

Following a major protest march against the highway, the government canceled the project. But soon large numbers of people who believed in the benefits of the highway began to demonstrate in favor of the project. Ultimately the Morales government allowed the communities of the TIPNIS to vote on the highway. Results indicated that a sizable majority favored going forward with the highway. But the entire episode indicated that public vigilance is crucial in bringing pressure to bear on the officials of even a self-proclaimed revolutionary government to abide by the new revolutionary constitution.

The Morales government continued efforts to improve the well-being of lower-income Bolivians and to reduce inequality. One measure requires that annual wage increases keep pace with inflation. Another law requires all employers to pay their employees a second monthly paycheck in December of each year. But President Morales, emphasizing the need to more equally distribute Bolivia's wealth and reduce poverty, decreed on November 20, 2013, that since the economy was doing well each salaried worker in the country should receive a third December paycheck (Valdez 2013). In other words, pay should be tripled for the month of December each year as long as the growth rate for country's gross domestic product is at least 4.5 percent (it was around 6.4 percent in 2013).

Foreign Policy

Evo Morales's efforts to achieve economic sovereignty through nationalizing foreign-owned companies, reducing the need for imports by developing domestic industries, diversifying international sources of investment, shifting from relying on privately owned foreign hydrocarbon companies to state-owned companies from Venezuela, Russia, and China (Kohl 2010, 117), rejecting neoliberal economic globalization, and refusing to fully cooperate with US drug suppression efforts have obvious foreign policy implications. Bolivia's foreign policy under Morales had much in common with that of Chávez's Venezuela, which Bolivia joined in ALBA in 2006. The Morales government claimed that between 2006 and 2008, the US ambassador to Bolivia, Philip Goldberg, met repeatedly with leaders of opposition groups, and it expelled Goldberg in September 2008 on the grounds that he was attempting to destabilize the Bolivian government (Kohl and Bresnahan 2010, 13). The United States then expelled Bolivia's ambassador, and Bolivia then expelled

US drug enforcement agents. The Bush administration decertified Bolivia for not meeting US coca eradication standards and in December 2008 increased duties on Bolivian goods (Kohl and Bresnahan 2010, 13). Kohl notes (2010, 118) that in comparison to US strategy, European efforts to reduce coca production in Bolivia put greater emphasis on reducing the poverty that leads many Bolivians to grow coca.

The Bolivian government has developed a relatively peaceful approach to limit the cultivation of coca and reduce the manufacture and sale of cocaine. Bolivia now allows the licensed and satellite-monitored farming of coca for traditional use, as long as a farmer does not exceed the set maximum of acreage for coca cultivation (Neuman 2012). The cultivation of other crops for the international market, like bananas, is encouraged. The program seems to have had some success, since the United Nations Office on Drugs and Crime estimated the land devoted to coca cultivation in Bolivia declined by around 12 percent in 2011.

Relations between Bolivia and the US were damaged when a plane carrying President Morales home from a visit to Moscow was forced to land in Vienna. Bolivia accused the US of convincing France and Portugal to deny Morales's plane permission to fly through their air space as required by the flight plan. The US government apparently suspected, erroneously, that Edward J. Snowden, the former US security contractor who had been exposing covert US actions, was on the plane seeking asylum in Bolivia (Gladstone and Newman 2013). Bolivian officials were outraged at the US and the other countries involved for interfering with the flight and the president's freedom of movement.

ELECTIONS IN OTHER NATIONS

Following the election of Chávez in Venezuela and Morales in Bolivia, leftist candidates were elected or reelected in other Latin American nations, including Brazil, Chile, Ecuador, and Nicaragua in 2006, Argentina in 2007, Paraguay in 2008, and El Salvador and Uruguay in 2009. Of these, Nicaragua and Ecuador joined ALBA in 2007 and 2009, respectively. Rafael Correa, the leftist president of Ecuador, an economist with a PhD from the University of Illinois, rejected neoliberalism and, like Venezuela and Bolivia, sought to increase state control over his country's energy resources and realize a higher share of revenues from foreign oil companies (Kozloff 2008, 13–15, 52).

Nevertheless, in 2009 in Honduras a right-wing military coup removed formerly center-right President Manuel Zelaya after he shifted dramatically to the left and was preparing Honduras to join ALBA. The ouster of the democratically elected president of Honduras indicated that military intervention was still a viable method to block change. Furthermore, the Honduran coup may have inhibited the policies of the new leftist president of nearby El Salvador, Mauricio Fuentes, who ran as the candidate of the Farabundo Martí National Liberation Front (FMLN), the political arm of the former FMLN guerrilla alliance that had fought the army during the country's brutal civil war from 1980 to 1991. It was possible that government policies in El Salvador could shift to the left following the election of one of the FMLN's top guerrilla commanders, Salvador Sánchez Cerén, as president in March 2014 (Partlow 2014).

A number of the governments elected on leftist platforms pursued policies far less change-oriented than those of Venezuela or Bolivia. Brazil, for example, continued predominantly neoliberal economic policies and did not join ALBA. In some cases, the ideologies of left-wing parties had moved in a more conservative direction, especially when economic growth levels had been high under previous right-wing governments. In other cases, conservative military leadership and armed forces as well as mass media controlled by economic oligarchs functioned to prevent change detrimental to the interests of traditional elites or their foreign corporate allies. Furthermore, the ability of some nations to defy neoliberal globalization was limited by the nature of their exports to the world market. For example, a heavy reliance on agricultural exports that must be sent to foreign markets within a limited time frame to prevent spoiling, as is the case with Chile, is more vulnerable to foreign economic pressure than the hydrocarbon exports of Venezuela or Bolivia.

Summary and Analysis

Movements attempting to bring about revolutionary change through democratic means, like other revolutionary movements, can be analyzed in terms of the five factors necessary for success.

A number of elements contributed to generating high levels of mass frustration. One was the experience of exclusion and discrimination based on race, ethnicity, and class. In the case of Bolivia, the majority Amerindian population was denied the vote until relatively recently. In Venezuela, the pattern of racial discrimination was less explicit but no less real. Before Chávez, who is of Amerindian, African, and European descent, persons of exclusively European background tended to dominate government, the economy, media, and entertainment imagery. White elites benefited from extreme inequality in patterns of income and wealth distribution. Discontent grew when, in order to cope with economic problems often caused by their own greed, incompetence, and/or corruption, power holders adopted neoliberal economic policies that placed great burdens on the poor.

Elite dissidence developed as many well-educated people became morally alienated from the tremendous inequality and conservative and often racially tinged ideologies of their societies. Some participated in revolutionary guerrilla movements in the 1960s and 1970s before engaging in electoral politics. What is unique about

Venezuela and Bolivia is that the key leaders of the revolutionary movements in each case, Hugo Chávez and Evo Morales, arose from the lower-income classes. The Morales case is more unusual since he had no elite role in the government, military, or economy, while Chávez had risen to the rank of lieutenant colonel in the army, where he and fellow officers organized a revolutionary movement in the armed forces.

As was the case in South Africa, where race played a role in uniting many different indigenous African ethnic groups, the experience of being members of groups who were discriminated against helped motivate people of color to unite behind Chávez and Morales. Other unifying motivations bringing some members of relatively privileged groups into the revolutionary alliances included nationalism and anti-imperialism against perceived foreign exploitation or interference and moral concern for rectifying extreme social injustice.

In revolutions through democracy in Venezuela and Bolivia, the political crisis factor involved the previous structure of elite domination being weakened to the point of becoming vulnerable to emergent popular movements. Older political parties were undermined by adopting neoliberal policies that forced great hardships on those least responsible for the mistakes or circumstances causing economic problems. Corruption and ties to foreign powers further alienated many people from establishment political figures and their parties. In Venezuela the development of a significant revolutionary movement within the armed forces also weakened the control of traditional elites. In both Venezuela and Bolivia disillusionment with the old political system led to the formulation and popular approval of new constitutions shortly after the election of revolutionary leaders.

Why have the revolutionary movements elected or reelected to power in the early twenty-first century survived as long as they have, when leftist reform movements in Latin America such as those of Arbenz in Guatemala and of Allende in Chile lasted only a few years (see Chapter 5)? One important factor seems to be that the world context became more permissive of such movements. With the end of the cold war, the United States did not view leftist movements in the Western Hemisphere as the phalanx of a threatening communist superpower. In addition, the security of the democratic process in Latin America appeared reinforced by the increasing acceptance by societies around the world of democracy as the preferred form of government. ALBA gave member nations increased resources to resist economic pressures from both multinational corporations and antagonistic foreign powers. Furthermore, after the September 11, 2001, attacks, the United States focused its attention elsewhere. The US-led wars in Afghanistan and Iraq, which began in 2001 and 2003 respectively, reduced the likelihood of US military action in Latin America. With the election of Barack Obama, who had opposed the Iraq War, the chance of US intervention against elected leftist revolutionary governments appeared to diminish further. In Venezuela the effort to ensure that the military was committed to the Bolivarian revolution made it increasingly difficult for a foreign power to use Venezuela's armed forces to overthrow the elected revolutionary government.

The Bolivarian revolution was significantly weakened by the unexpected death of the charismatic Hugo Chávez in 2013, shortly after he was reelected to the presidency. The new candidate of the PSUV, Nicolas Maduro (Chávez's vice president), won the special election for the presidency and pledged to continue the revolution.

CHRONOLOGY OF MAJOR EVENTS

1982 Chávez revolutionary group formed in Venezuelan armed forces
1989 Caracazo: explosion of social protest in Caracas and other major Venezuelan cities
1992 Chávez attempts coup
1997 Formation of Chávez revolutionary party
1998 Hugo Chávez elected in Venezuela
1999 New Venezuelan constitution
2000 Chávez reelected
2002 Defeat of attempted right-wing coup in Venezuela
2004 Formation of ALBA; Chávez wins recall vote
2005 Evo Morales elected in Bolivia
2006 Chávez reelected; Bolivia joins ALBA; Correa elected in Ecuador
2008 Morales wins recall vote
2009 New Bolivian constitution; Morales reelected; Ecuador joins ALBA
2010 President Morales nationalizes four electricity companies and declares state control of 80 percent of Bolivia's electric power generation
2011–2012 While poverty and inequality decline, Venezuela's homicide rate and inflation rate remain high
2012 Hugo Chávez again elected president by a wide margin
2013 President Hugo Chávez dies; Chávez's vice president, Nicolas Maduro, narrowly elected president as PSUV candidate; Maduro granted emergency power to deal with economic difficulties and to clamp down on businesses accused of withholding goods from the market or excessive profit making; President Evo Morales of Bolivia declares that as long as Bolivia's economy continues to make strong gains, workers should receive two extra monthly paychecks every December to reduce poverty and economic inequality

References and Further Readings

ABC News. April 18, 2009. "Chavez Gifts Obama with Book That Assails US for Exploiting Latin America." blogs.abcnews.com/politicalpunch/2009/04/chavez-gifts-ob.html.

Achtenberg, Emily. 2013. "Contested Development: The Geopolitics of Bolivia's TIPNIS Conflict." *NACLA* 46 (Summer): 6–11.

Arze, Carlos, and Tom Kruse. 2004. "Bolivia Fights Back: The Consequences of Neoliberal Reform." *NACLA Report on the Americas* 38 (November/December): 23–28.

Associated Press. 2007. "Chavez Promises a Socialist Venezuela as He Starts New Six-Year Term." *USA Today*, January 10. www.usatoday.com/news/world/2007-01-10-chavez-venezuela_x.htm.

———. 2010. "Ex-General: Cubans Involved in Chavez's Military." *Boston Globe*, April 22. www.boston.com/news/world/latinamerica/articles/2010/04/22/ex_general_cubans_involved_in_chavezs_military.

Azicri, Max. 2009. "The Castro-Chávez Alliance." *Latin American Perspectives* 36 (1): 99–110.

BBC News. May 2, 2010. "Bolivia Takes Over Energy Firms." news.bbc.co.uk/2/hi/americas/8656644.stm.

Carrol, Rory. 2013. *Comandante: Hugo Chavez's Venezuela.* New York: Penguin.

Central Intelligence Agency (CIA). 2010a. "Bolivia." In *World Factbook.* https://www.cia.gov/library/publications/the-world-factbook/geos/bl.html.

———. 2010b. "Venezuela." In *World Factbook.* https://www.cia.gov/library/publications/the-world-factbook/geos/ve.html.

———. 2014a. "Bolivia." In *World Factbook.* https://www.cia.gov/library/publications/the-world-factbook/geos/bl.html.

———. 2014b. "Ecuador." In *World Factbook.* www.cia.gov/library/publications/the-world-factbook/geos/eg.html.

———. 2014c. "Venezuela." In *World Factbook.* https://www.cia.gov/library/publications/the-world-factbook/geos/ve.html.

Chávez, Franz. 2006. "Cochabamba's 'Water War,' Six Years On." Inter Press Service, November 8. ipsnews.net/print.asp?idnews=35418.

Constitution of the Plurinational State of Bolivia. 2009. pdba.georgetown.edu/Constitutions/Bolivia/bolivia09.html.

Correo Del Orinoco International. 2013. "Presidential Candidate Henrique Capriles." *Venezuelan Analysis*, April 7. http://venezuelanalysis.com/analysis/8515.

Dangl, Benjamin. 2007. *The Price of Fire: Resource Wars and Social Movements in Bolivia.* Oakland, CA: AK Press.

DeFronzo, James, ed. 2006. *Revolutionary Movements in World History: From 1750 to the Present.* 3 vols. Santa Barbara, CA: ABC-CLIO.

Devereux, Charlie. 2013. "Chavismo Set to Outlive Chavez as Venezuela Braces for Elections." Bloomberg, February 7. http://www.bloomberg.com/news/print/2013-02-08/chavismo-set-to-outlive-chavez-as-venezuela-braces-for-elections.html.

Ellner, Steve. 2009. "A New Model with Rough Edges: Venezuela's Community Councils." *NACLA Report on the Americas* 42 (May/June): 11–14.

———. 2010. "Hugo Chavez's First Decade in Office: Breakthroughs and Shortcomings." *Latin American Perspectives* 37 (1): 77–96.

Ellner, Steve. 2013. "Just How Radical Is President Nicolas Maduro." *NACLA* 46 (Summer): 45–49.

Ellner, Steve, and Daniel Hellinger, eds. 2003. *Venezuelan Politics in the Chavez Era: Class, Polarization, and Conflict*. Boulder: Lynne Rienner.

Espin, Patricia Rondon. 2010. "Ex-General: Venezuelan Army Secrets in Cuban Hands." Reuters, April 27. www.reuters.com/article/idUSTRE63S3CO20100429.

Ewell, Judith. 2006. "Venezuelan Bolivarian Revolution of Hugo Chavez." In DeFronzo, ed., *Revolutionary Movements in World History*, 3:903–912.

Farthing, Linda, and Kathryn Ledebur. 2004. "Bolivia Fights Back: The Beat Goes On: The US War on Coca." *NACLA Report on the Americas* 38 (November/December): 34–39.

Fowler, Will. 2006. "Spanish American Revolutions of Independence." In DeFronzo, ed., *Revolutionary Movements in World History*, 3:810–824.

Galeano, Eduardo. [1971] 1997. *Open Veins of Latin America*. New York: Monthly Review Press.

Gladstone, Rick, and William Neuman. 2013. "New Rumor of Snowden Flight Raises Tensions." *New York Times,* July 2. http://www.nytimes.com/2013/07/03/world /europe/snowden.html.

GlobalSecurity.org. 2010. "Venezuelan National Armed Forces." www.globalsecurity .org/military/world/venezuela/fan.htm.

Gott, Richard. 2000. *In the Shadow of the Liberator: Hugo Chavez and the Transformation of Venezuela*. London: Verso.

Grinberg, Nicolas. 2010. "Where Is Latin America Going? FTAA or 'Twenty-First-Century Socialism'?" *Latin American Perspectives* 30 (1): 185–202.

Hellinger, Daniel. 2003. "Political Overview: The Breakdown of Puntofijismo and the Rise of Chavismo." In Steve Ellner and Daniel Hellinger, eds., *Venezuelan Politics in the Chavez Era: Class, Polarization, and Conflict*, 27–53. Boulder: Lynne Rienner.

Herrera, Bernardo Alvarez. 2008. "How Chavez Has Helped the Poor." *Foreign Affairs,* July/August. www.foreignaffairs.com/articles/64459/bernardo-alvarez -herrera-and-francisco-rodr%C3%83%C2%ADguez/revolutionary-road.

Hylton, Forrest, and Sinclair Thomson. 2004. "Bolivia Fights Back: The Roots of Rebellion: Insurgent Bolivia." *NACLA Report on the Americas* 38 (November/December): 15–19.

Irazábal, Clara, and John Foley. 2010. "Reflections on the Venezuelan Transition from a Capitalist Representative to a Socialist Participatory Democracy." *Latin American Perspectives* 37 (1): 97–122.

Janicke, Kiraz. 2010. "Venezuela Celebrates 'Day of the Bolivarian Militias, the Armed People and the April Revolution.'" *Venezuelan Analysis*, April 14. venezuelanalysis .com/news/5276.

Kaup, Brent Z. 2010. "A Neoliberal Nationalization? The Constraints on Natural-Gas-Led Development in Bolivia." *Latin American Perspectives* 37 (3): 123–138.

Klein, Herbert S. 1998. "Bolivian National Revolution (1952)." In Jack A. Goldstone, ed., *Encyclopedia of Political Revolutions*, 44–47. Washington, DC: Congressional Quarterly Press.

Kohl, Benjamin. 2010. "Bolivia Under Morales: A Work in Progress." *Latin American Perspectives* 37 (3): 107–122.

Kohl, Benjamin, and Rosalind Bresnahan. 2010. "Bolivia Under Morales: Consolidating Power, Initiating Decolonization." *Latin American Perspectives* 37 (3): 5–17.

Kozloff, Nikolas. 2008. *Revolution: South America and the Rise of the New Left.* New York: Palgrave Macmillan.

Lown, Zachary. 2009. "Violence and Transformation in Venezuela's Public Universities." *Venezuelan Analysis*, July 8. Venezuelanalysis.com/print/4604.

Mogollon, Mery, and Chris Kraul. 2013. "Venezuela's Ruling Socialists Survive Electoral Test." *Los Angeles Times*, December 9. www.latimes.com/world/worldnow/la -fg-wn-venezuela-election-20131209,0,2692862.story#axzz2sTOqxX6y.

———. 2014. "Venezuelan Officials Identify 7 Suspects in Slaying of Beauty Queen." *Los Angeles Times*, January 9. www.latimes.com/world/worldnow/la-fg-wn-venezuela -actress-beauty-suspects-20140109,0,173509.story#axzz2sTOqxX6y.

Morales, Evo. 2010. "Evo Morales." www.evomorales.net/paginasEng/perfil_Eng_intro .aspx.

NACLA. 2004. "Bolivia Fights Back: Introduction." *NACLA Report on the Americas* 38 (November/December): 14.

———. 2009. "A New Day in El Salvador: The FMLN Victory and the Road Ahead." *NACLA Report on the Americas* 42 (November/December): 15.

National Electoral Council. 2013. Divulgación Presidenciales, 2013. http://www.cne.gob .ve/resultado_presidencial_2013/r/1/reg_000000.html.

Neuman, William. 2012. "Coca Licensing Is a Weapon in Bolivia's Drug War." *New York Times*, December 26. http://topics.nytimes.com/top/news/international/countries andterritories/bolivia/index.html.

Obarrio, Fernando Oviedo. 2010. "Evo Morales and the Altiplano: Notes for an Electoral Geography of the Movimiento al Socialismo, 2002–2008." *Latin American Perspectives* 37 (3): 91–106.

Partlow, Joshua. 2014. "Former Guerrilla Commander Wins El Salvador Presidential Election." *Washington Post*, March 14. www.washingtonpost.com/world/former -guerrilla-commander-wins-el-salvador-presidential-election/2014/03/14/ddaa0 dda-b77c.

Pearce, Stephanie. 2013. "Chavez in the Americas: Increasing Autonomy in Latin America and the Caribbean." *NACLA* 46 (Summer): 40–44.

Pontón, Daniel C., Pamela Villacrés, and Pahola Guevara. 2010. *Seguridad Pública y Privada: Venezuela y Bolivia*. Organization of American States: Department of Public Security. www.oas.org/dsp/documentos/Publicaciones/Seg%20Publica-%20Venezuela %20y%20Bolivia.pdf.

Postero, Nancy. 2010. "Morales's MAS Government." *Latin American Perspectives* 37 (3): 18–34.

Regalsky, Pablo. 2010. "Political Processes and the Reconfiguration of the State in Bolivia." *Latin American Perspectives* 37 (3): 35–50.

Rueda, Jorge. 2013. "Venezuelan Congress Grants Maduro 'Emergency Decree Powers.'" Huffington Post, November 19. www.huffingtonpost.com/2013/11/20/maduro-decree -powers_n_4309521.html.

Schmitter, Phillipe C. 2010. "Twenty-Five Years: Fifteen Findings." *Journal of Democracy* 21 (1): 17–28.

Sivak, Martin. 2010. *Evo Morales: The Extraordinary Rise of the First Indigenous President of Bolivia*. New York: Palgrave Macmillan.

Stout, David. 2006. "Chávez Calls Bush 'the Devil' in U.N. Speech." *New York Times*, September 20. www.nytimes.com/2006/09/20/world/americas/20cnd-chavez.html.

Suggett, James. 2009. "Latin America's Bolivarian Alliance Grows." *Green Left Weekly*, June 27. www.greenleft.org.au/node/41933.

Thomson, Sinclair. 2009. "Bull Horns and Dynamite: Echoes of Revolution in Bolivia." *NACLA Report on the Americas* 42 (March/April): 21–27.

USA Today. December 4, 2006. "Venezuelan President Hugo Chavez Wins Re-Election by Wide Margin." www.usatoday.com/news/world/2006-12-03-chavez-election_x .htm.Venezuelan Constitution. 1999. venezuelanalysis.com/constitution/title/4.

Weisbrot, Mark. 2008. "Poverty Reduction in Venezuela: A Reality-Based View." *ReVista: Harvard Review of Latin America* 8 (1): 36–39.

Wells, Miriam. 2013. "Venezuelan Government Recognizes Record Murder Rate." InSightCrime, March 4. www.insightcrime.org/news-briefs/venezuelan-government -recognizes-record-murder-rate.

World Bank. 2001. "Bolivarian Republic of Venezuela Investing in Human Capital for Growth, Prosperity and Poverty Reduction." March 30. www-wds.worldbank.org /servlet/WDSContentServer/WDSP/IB/2001/04/27/000094946_0104140845140 /Rendered/PDF/mutiopage.pdf.

WTRG Economics. 2010. "Oil Price History and Analysis." *Energy Economist Newsletter*. www.wtrg.com/prices.htm.

Valdez, Carlos. 2013. "Bolivia's Leader Decrees Special Christmas Bonus." Associated Press, November 21. http://abcnews.go.com/International/wireStory/bolivias-leader -decrees-special-christmas-bonus-20956099.

Venezuela Solidarity Campaign. 2013. "Nicolas Maduro: A Profile." http://www.venezuela solidarity.co.uk/nicolas-maduro-a-biography.

Selected DVD, Film, and Videocassette Documentaries

See "Purchase and Rental Sources" at the end of this volume for information on how to obtain the following resources and for full names of media companies and other organizations listed here as abbreviations.

Bolivia: Leasing the Rain. 2002. PBS Frontline World.

Bolivia: My Five Years with Evo. 2010. 24 min. PBS Frontline. http://www.pbs.org/wgbh /pages/frontline/2010/12/bolivia-evo-morales-video.html.

Chavez: Inside the Coup. 2003. 60 min. Amazon.com.

Cocalero. 2007. 94 min. Documentary on the first successful presidential campaign of Evo Morales. FRF.

Crude. 2009. 105 min. Ecuador versus a foreign oil company. FRF.

The Hugo Chavez Show. 2008. 60 min. Amazon.com.

Inside the Venezuelan Revolution: A Journey into the Heart of Venezuela. 2009. 65 min. Alborada Films.

Listen to Venezuela. 2009. 125 min. Inside Film.

South of the Border. 2010. 78 min. DVD. Amazon.com. Oliver Stone documentary. Includes interviews with the leaders of Argentina, Bolivia, Brazil, Cuba, Ecuador, Paraguay, and Venezuela.

Venezuela: Revolution in Progress. 2005. 50 min. DCTV. President Hugo Chávez and conflict over his policies.

11

The Arab Revolution

The concluding chapter of this book's fourth edition (which went to press in the fall of 2010) viewed the Middle East as a likely site for future revolutions. The Arab revolutionary wave (also known as the Arab Spring and the Arab Awakening) that began on December 18, 2010, resulted in the overthrow of dictators in Tunisia, Egypt, Libya, and Yemen, massive uprisings in Bahrain and Syria, and major protests in Jordan, Morocco, Algeria, and Iraq. But the resulting changes varied greatly in degree. Libya experienced the most significant upheaval: the pre-revolutionary armed forces were defeated and the old political system and old ruling elite eliminated. In Egypt, however, changes were ultimately far more limited. Although several pre-revolutionary officials were ousted, the military and economic power structures remained intact. Many persons who had served under the pre-revolutionary dictatorship continued to control government bureaucracies. When large-scale protests broke out against Egypt's first post-revolution democratically elected president, military leaders removed him on July 3, 2013, and suspended the constitution. The central conservative dictatorship in the region, Saudi Arabia, was minimally affected by the democratic revolutionary movement. Instead, it became the main regional driving force behind a counterrevolution, helping to crush the uprising in Bahrain and providing billions of dollars to support and protect other conservative regimes. The revolution for democracy and social justice in Arab countries continues in the face of enormous and often brutal opposition.

THE PRE-REVOLUTIONARY POLITICAL TERRAIN
The starting point for understanding the Arab revolution is an overview of the political and economic characteristics of pre-revolutionary Arab societies. Most Arab

nations have authoritarian governments. Students of the region attribute this pervasive authoritarianism to the policies of powerful non-Arab nations, in particular Great Britain and later the US. Before World War I, a number of Arab societies were controlled by the Ottoman Empire (Ibrahim 2006). After the war, Great Britain dominated most of the Arab territories previously under Ottoman control and played a major role in determining that going forward they would be monarchies rather than republics (Gelvin 2012). The monarchies that received British support had vast oil and natural gas resources, like Saudi Arabia, Iraq, Kuwait, Bahrain, Oman, Qatar, and what became the United Arab Emirates. The monarchies of Egypt and Jordan, which also received British support, were not as well endowed with oil.

Why would a democracy like Great Britain support dictatorial monarchies in Arab countries? Many analysts believe that the monarchies which owed their existence and security to Great Britain tended to be very cooperative in providing access to crucial energy resources at reasonable prices and supporting Britain's global policies. Democratic governments were considered less reliable. Many residents of these countries were hostile to British policies and would likely have elected governments less obedient to Britain if the people had the vote. The same was true in the late twentieth century and the twenty-first century after the US replaced Britain as the prime supporter of the Arab monarchies. Neither Great Britain nor the US nor other democracies reliant on Middle Eastern oil acted as if they wanted Arab monarchies to become democracies. Instead, they assisted the monarchs who denied their people the very political and human rights Britain and America claimed to champion as worldwide goals. This is one reason why Arab populations viewed American and British claims of supporting democracy as blatant hypocrisy.

Arab republics also tended to be authoritarian despite being led by presidents instead of kings. Some scholars suggest that discipline was needed to fend off foreign imperialism and resist the monarchies that were perceived as tools of foreign imperialists. The histories of Egypt and Iraq illustrate this. When the British mandate to administer these countries expired, they left pro-British monarchies in control. Many Egyptians became concerned with the situation of the Arab Palestinians administered by Britain after World War I. They believed the Palestinians were being denied the right of self-determination and that their land was being taken over by Zionist settlers aiming to create a homeland for the Jewish people. The British 1917 Balfour Declaration favored the creation of a Jewish homeland in Palestine.

When war broke out between the new state of Israel and several Arab nations in 1948, many Egyptians believed that the Egyptian monarchy, following British orders, refused to mount an effective military effort against Israeli forces. The war and Israel's victory prompted hundreds of thousands of Arab Palestinians to flee from their homes, and many became impoverished refugees. Believing that the Egyptian king collaborated with imperialist Britain, especially in the establishment of Israel and the devastation of the Arab Palestinians, many Egyptians became enraged, including young officers in the armed forces. In addition, inequality appeared to be increasing between businessmen and workers and between landowners and peasants (Gorman 2006). In 1952 a secretly organized group within the armed forces, the Free Officers, led by General Muhammad Naguib and Colonel Gamal Nasser, overthrew the monarchy and established a republic. The revolutionary leaders proclaimed the goals of anti-imperialism, anti-feudalism, social justice, breaking up business monopolies, strengthening the armed forces, and democratic government. Nasser and his supporters, however, believed that a one-party system was necessary to achieve the first five revolutionary goals and their plans for Arab socialism and uniting all Arabs in single state. Thus Egypt became an authoritarian republic.

In 1958 officers in the Iraqi military, motivated by similar factors, followed the Egyptian example and overthrew the pro-British Iraqi monarchy (Al Qazazz 2006). Fears of foreign intervention and concerns over internal conflict led to the eventual establishment of an authoritarian republic under the Baath Party and Saddam Hussein (DeFronzo 2010). Anti-imperialism, opposition to monarchies viewed as imperialist puppets, and fear of threats from Israel and Persian-dominated Iran helped justify authoritarian governments in most Arab republics.

A major economic factor that facilitates authoritarianism in some Arab states is economic reliance on exporting oil and natural gas for funding rather than on citizen taxes. This can strengthen the power of the governing elite in several ways. First, since the regime is not dependent on a flow of taxes from individuals, government leaders tend to be less concerned with public opinion (Gelvin 2012). Second, since the government regulates energy exports and obtains income directly from the payments for these resources, it plays a more central role in the economy than in countries with more diversified economic systems. And third, regime control of income from resource exports provides the means for the governing elite to protect its power by rewarding supporters with patronage and by selectively buying off individual dissenters or discontented sectors of the population.

Authoritarian Arab republics such as Egypt under Nasser, Iraq under Saddam Hussein, and Libya under Qadafi often opposed US and British policies. But the Arab monarchies generally supported the US and Britain regionally and globally. The economic, political, and geographic pattern that imperialism structured in the Middle East put enormous energy resources, and therefore energy income, in the hands of Arab royal families. With the military and technological assistance provided by Britain and the US, the monarchies effectively resisted the democratic aspirations of their own citizens as well as international pressure to improve human rights. Oil-rich monarchies used their billions to help preserve monarchies in Jordan and Morocco and to influence the policies of resource limited republics,

MAP 11.1 The Middle East

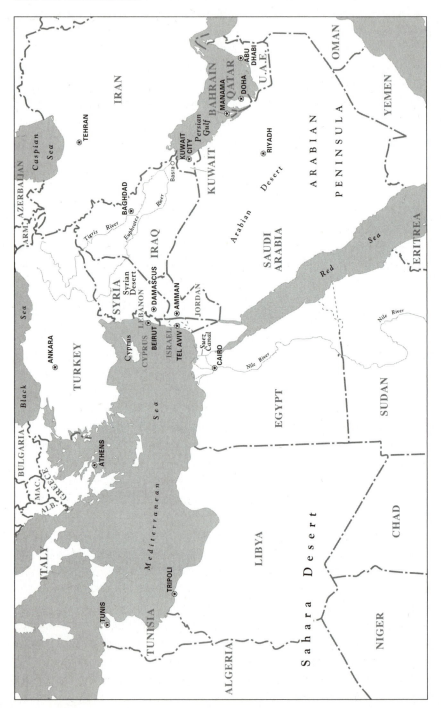

especially Egypt after the death of Nasser in 1970. Oil monarchy money also influenced the course of the Arab revolution and the counterrevolution that largely
suppressed it.

THE ARAB REVOLUTION AND THE
FIVE ESSENTIAL REVOLUTIONARY FACTORS

We can broadly assess the elements that led to the Arab uprisings of December 2010
and 2011 in terms of the five general factors crucial for the development and success
of revolutionary movements.

Mass Discontent

A number of economic, political, and moral factors contributed to the development
of mass discontent. The geography of the Arab world that imperial rule left behind
contributed to ongoing economic problems. The British played a major role in determining which territories would become individual states, what their boundaries
would be, and that their governments would be or remain monarchies. Virtually all
of the Middle Eastern nations with significant oil or other energy resources were
monarchies that depended on British support. This guaranteed that Britain would
have access to oil at low cost and that its oil companies could profit from selling
Middle Eastern oil on the world market. But it also meant that poor Arab countries,
like populous Egypt, could be strongly influenced by Britain indirectly through
the pro-British oil-rich monarchies making assistance contingent on supporting
polices acceptable to Britain and later also to the US.

By 2010, many Arab nations had high unemployment rates, even among university graduates. Consequently young adults remained dependent on their parents
and lacked the means to marry. Many people lived in poverty as economic inequality increased and social services deteriorated. Pressured into adopting neoliberal
economic policies, poor Arab nations cut public assistance, even for basic foods,
to millions of people. Impoverishment and economic hopelessness made dictatorship, brutality, and corruption even more intolerable and increased people's frustration. Most Arabs were angered at having to live under dictatorships and, just like
most other people around the world, sought to enjoy the human rights inherent in
democratic political systems.

Another major cause of discontent among Arab peoples was their government's
perceived collaboration with British and US foreign policies. First, Arab governments, including Mubarak's regime in Egypt and the Saudi Arabian monarchy,
were accused of abandoning the cause of a Palestinian state, regardless of what
they said in public. Second, while a number of Arab regimes publicly or privately

supported the US-led war against Iraq in 1991 and the invasion and occupation of Iraq in 2003, most of their people strongly opposed these military actions. Anger over Arab governmental collaboration with US and British foreign policy was one of the strongest reasons why so many Arabs supported a revolution to democracy (Lynch 2012, 63). Democracy would give the people a say in politics and allow them to end support for American and British policies.

Concern for morality and religion also motivated discontent with the corruption plaguing the economies and governments of the dictatorial regimes. This factor spurred the growth of Islamist movements that came to see revolution to democracy as a way to transform society morally.

Public frustration reached explosive levels following a series of events perceived to prove the corrupt and repressive nature of existing regimes. One was the December 17, 2010, self-immolation of a poor Tunisian street vendor, Mohamed Bouazizi, after the police confiscated his equipment. The resulting Tunisian rebellion provoked Egyptians to take to the streets to protest their own corrupt government and officials. Police violence against protesters infuriated more people and multiplied the number turning out for protests.

Dissident Elites

As in other revolutions, educated young people played a prominent role in organizing the protests and in proclaiming the goals of removing dictators and establishing democracy. But their tools now included the Internet and cell phones and social media websites like Facebook and Twitter. In Egypt, the early vanguard of youthful and relatively secular organizers was soon joined by labor leaders, members of professional organizations (doctors, lawyers, and engineers), and later by leaders of the Islamist Muslim Brotherhood.

New information technologies played a significant role in the Arab revolution. The Internet, cell phones, and social media undermined dictators' control of the communication systems they used to protect their power (Cockburn 2012; Lynch 2012). It's important to note, though, that only a minority of citizens in these countries used the Internet. Only 20 percent of Egyptians, for example, had Internet access (Gelvin 2012). And some of them opposed the uprising. But many knowledgeable young Egyptians did play an important role in coordinating protest actions and providing information to those who lacked Internet access.

Coverage by the Al Jazeera satellite television network (based in the monarchy of Qatar) also played a significant role in the spread of the Arab revolution. However, Al Jazeera appeared selective in what it chose to report. It seemed strongly influenced by the interests of the Qatar regime. Cockburn (2012) states that while Al Jazeera covered the actions and proclamations of Libyan rebels whom Qatar supported, it provided much less coverage of the mass protests against the Bahraini monarchy and the monarchy's brutal repression of pro-democracy activists.

Advanced personal communications technology helped bring about the Arab revolution in combination with other factors. Its availability and use was far from decisive and alone could not bring success. Several uprisings, including that in Bahrain, failed despite the availability and use of these technologies. More decisive was whether the international context would permit an uprising to succeed or prevent it from succeeding. In Tunisia and Egypt, other nations permitted the overthrow of dictators, and in Libya and Syria the US and some European powers actually assisted rebels. But in other cases the uprisings were crushed because foreign powers seemed to prefer maintaining dictatorships.

Unifying Motives for Revolution

Several goals united diverse categories of people in the Arab revolutionary uprisings. One was the desire to get rid of a particular dictator. But most also appeared united behind the goal of removing, not just a single dictator, but the entire oppressive regime that was the basis of dictatorship and replacing it with democracy. Many protestors used slogans that demanded the end of a dictatorial regime system, not just the overthrow of a particular ruler. Secularists supported democracy because they wanted a free political system, the ability to participate in politics, and protection of human rights. Many Islamists supported democracy for some of the same reasons, but also because they perceived they could win free elections. Another unifying motive in some uprisings was anti-imperialism. The monarchies and the Mubarak regime in Egypt were widely perceived, as noted earlier, to be cooperating with US and British foreign policies that the large majority of Arabs opposed. So shifting to democracy was a way to combat imperialism.

The Weakening of the Pre-Revolutionary State

The authoritarian Arab republics were generally more vulnerable than the monarchies because they supposedly relied on the consent of the people to remain in power. And in general the strongly pro-American and pro-British monarchies were better protected by these foreign powers. Although the authority of some Arab regimes deteriorated because of country-specific factors, a general weakening of perceived legitimacy resulted from several events that helped establish a precedent for mass protests. The first was the Palestinian intifadas (uprisings) against Israel. The first intifada began in 1987 and continued into 1991 (Lynch 2012). For more than a decade before this, Arab governments had been unable or unwilling to effectively confront Israel over the plight of the impoverished, stateless Palestinians.

But beginning in December 1987, the Palestinians themselves launched a sustained series of mass participation protests against Israeli occupation. The protests drew international attention to the desperate conditions under which most Palestinians lived. At the time, the movement provided hope that international pressure on Israel could lead to an independent Palestinian state. It also seemed to demonstrate that the courage and actions of ordinary people pouring into the streets to confront injustice could bring positive change. It reignited concern for the Palestinians in many Arab countries, and local populations staged repeated demonstrations in support of the Palestinian cause. And the intifada raised questions about why Arab regimes appeared to neglect the Palestinians while accepting seemingly permanent Israeli occupation of the land that was supposed to become a Palestinian state.

As the intifada continued, Iraq invaded Kuwait in August 1990. Most Iraqis considered Kuwait a part of their country that Britain had set up as a separate state for Britain's own interests. Kuwait, having approximately 10 percent of the world's known oil reserves, an indigenous population of about 1,305,000, and a workforce that is about 80 percent foreign, is similar to other pro-British monarchies that control vast energy resources (DeFronzo 2010). Iraqis believed the Kuwait monarchy was over-producing oil beyond OPEC guidelines to drive the price down and reduce Iraq's income. Having recently concluded a devastating war with Iran, Iraq needed money to repair its damaged economy and infrastructure. The governments of most nations condemned Iraq's invasion of Kuwait and demanded immediate withdrawal. The US and Britain organized a huge army in Saudi Arabia and forced the Iraqis to leave Kuwait. But most people in Arab countries actually opposed the US-British led attack on Iraq and demonstrated against it. In contrast, Arab dictators generally backed it and ignored their people's protests. This represented another huge gap between Arab peoples and their rulers, which further undermined regime legitimacy. Most Arabs also opposed the harsh economic punishment and trade restrictions imposed on Iraq by the US, Britain, and the UN.

As Arab regimes collaborated with US pressure on Iraq, and hopes for an independent Palestinian homeland dwindled, Palestinians launched a new uprising against Israeli occupation, the Al Aqsa intifada or second intifada, on September 28, 2000. This proved far more violent than the first intifada and hundreds died in suicide bombings and Israeli military actions. Once again Arab rulers appeared unable or unwilling to help the Palestinians. Protests in Arab countries on behalf of Palestinians shifted quickly to demonstrations against Bush administration plans to invade Iraq after 9/11. Most Arabs viewed allegations that Iraq had a role in 9/11 or possessed weapons of mass destruction as excuses to thinly disguise military aggression against a relatively defenseless nation. The real goals were believed to be an American-British takeover of Iraq's energy resources.

The claim by Republican neoconservatives that the US wanted to bring democracy to the Arab world was widely viewed as false. Arabs who craved democracy simply asked why the Americans and British continued to arm and protect Arab monarchies instead of forcing them to democratize. And how could neoconservatives really want Arab peoples to have democracy when the policies they pursued, like extreme one-sided support for Israel's repression of the Palestinians and harsh economic penalties and then the invasion and occupation of Iraq, outraged the overwhelming majority of Arabs. If democracy really came to Arab countries, the people would vote in governments much less pro-American than most Arab dictatorships. (This is what happened when Hamas won the 2006 Palestinian elections and the Muslim Brotherhood won the 2012 Egyptian parliamentary and presidential elections.)

In sum, Arab regimes' collaboration with or passive acceptance of US, British, and Israeli policies were vehemently opposed by most of their citizens and undermined their legitimacy before the Arab revolution. Some regimes were also weakened by the perception that their economic policies caused corruption, unemployment, poverty, and economic inequality to increase dramatically.

Arab regimes' legitimacy was further diminished by the ability of Hezbollah, a Shia Lebanese militia, to effectively fight a thirty-three-day war with Israel in 2006. This conflict occurred after Israeli forces invaded Gaza in retaliation for an attack on Israeli forces. While the armies of Arab states stood by and did nothing, Hezbollah's readiness to support the Palestinians reminded Arabs how unwilling or unable authoritarian Arab states were to help the Palestinians.

Permissive World Context

Possibly the most crucial factor for the Arab revolution is the presence or absence of a permissive world context. Will powerful nations, in particular the United States, permit or repress the Arab revolution? The answer so far seems to depend on which Arab nation and how much of a revolution.

The George W. Bush administration (2001–2009) proclaimed support for expanding democracy around the world, in particular in the Middle East. But this rhetoric could hardly be taken seriously by most Arabs. After the 9/11 attacks in 2001, the Bush administration appeared to provide more, not less, assistance to dictatorial Arab leaders who pledged to fight Al Qaeda. The US government could not satisfactorily explain why, if it really favored democracy, it continued to fortify Arab monarchal dictatorships instead of forcing them to democratize. Also, as noted earlier, American policies toward the Palestinians and Iraq infuriated most Arabs, so it was not credible that the US really wanted the Arab people to be able to elect their own leaders.

The Bush administration's main achievement in creating "democracy" in the Middle East was to invade Iraq and, under US military occupation, oversee the creation of a new Iraqi government. The new political system allowed the predominately Kurdish area of the country to act essentially as an independent state and

---

Iraq as a whole was to function under a constitution consistent with both democracy and Islam (DeFronzo 2010). Although the US military withdrew in 2011, it remained close by in neighboring Kuwait and Saudi Arabia in easy range of redeployment to Iraq. And thousands of private military contractors stayed behind. The US invasion dramatically increased conflict between Iraq's Shia and Sunni Arabs and the government was plagued by corruption and gridlock, although Iraqi oil flowed onto the world market. The mess that the Bush administration's war left in Iraq may have discouraged, rather than encouraged, democracy movements in other Arab countries. In sum, the Bush administration provided no convincing evidence that it was truly permissive of revolution to democracy. Its unjustified invasion of Iraq and its unwavering support for pro-US Arab monarchies indicated just the opposite.

Barack Obama took office in January 2010 and seemed to provide real permissiveness for revolution to democracy. Since Obama had opposed the Iraq War, he was not tarred with the perceived hypocrisy of the Bush administration and all the hatred that Bush's aggressive foreign policies generated internationally. Within months of his inauguration, President Obama on June 4, 2009 delivered a major speech in Cairo to Islamic peoples:

> I do have an unyielding belief that all people yearn for certain things: the ability to speak your mind and have a say in how you are governed; confidence in the rule of law and the equal administration of justice; government that is transparent and doesn't steal from the people; the freedom to live as you choose. Those are not just American ideas, they are human rights, and that is why we will support them everywhere . . . America respects the right of all peaceful and law-abiding voices to be heard around the world, even if we disagree with them. And we will welcome all elected, peaceful governments-provided they govern with respect for all their people. This last point is important because there are some who advocate for democracy only when they are out of power; once in power, they are ruthless in suppressing the rights of others. No matter where it takes hold, government of the people and by the people sets a single standard for all who hold power: you must maintain your power through consent, not coercion; you must respect the rights of minorities, and participate with a spirit of tolerance and compromise; you must place the interests of your people and the legitimate workings of the political process above your party. Without these ingredients, elections alone do not make true democracy.

A year before the first pro-democracy uprising of the Arab revolution in Tunisia, there was reason to believe that under the leadership of President Obama, the US, in the past one of the biggest supporters of dictatorships in the Arab world, was becoming more permissive of revolution to democracy.

The Counterrevolution

Once the Arab revolution was under way, however, this permissiveness proved limited and selective. The US was slow to back the pro-democracy uprising against the Mubarak dictatorship in Egypt and later stood by as Egypt's first democratically elected parliament and then its first democratically elected president were removed and a new military dictatorship established. The most permissive stance by the US government was toward two regimes seen as troublesome. The first was the uprising against the Qadafi dictatorship in Libya. In fact, the stance went well beyond permissiveness to military intervention on the side of the rebels by several US-allied NATO air forces. This appeared decisive in the rebel victory. The US also favored the rebels in Syria.

But when the Bahrainis rebelled against that country's monarchy and were brutally repressed, the US was almost totally silent and appeared to do nothing to protect pro-democracy activists. The Obama administration seemed to back only those rebels fighting against regimes that opposed US policies or those of Saudi Arabia, or other US allies.

The Arab revolution stalled in great part because the window of world permissiveness was shut by an international counterrevolution that appeared led most directly by Saudi Arabia. The Saudi royal family, controlling a nation of about 27 million, including some five and a half million non-nationals (CIA 2014d), undoubtedly fears the spread of democracy primarily because it threatens its wealth and power. The US indirectly assisted the counterrevolution by continuing to back and arm Saudi Arabia and other pro-US monarchies. The International Institute for Strategic Studies reported that in 2013 Saudi Arabia was the world's fourth largest defense spender after the US, China, and Russia, acquiring immense quantities of military hardware (Reuters 2014).

Tunisia

The Tunisian revolution was the first uprising of the Arab revolution. Within Tunisia, a North African nation of almost 11 million people (CIA 2014f), the revolution is often referred to as the Sidi Bouzid revolution, after the city in central Tunisia where the rebellion began in December 2010. Discontent with the repressive political dictatorship of President Zine El Abidine Ben Ali was high leading up to the outbreak of the revolt because of government and police corruption and high unemployment.

The powder keg of discontent was ignited when a twenty-six-year-old vegetable vendor, Mohamed Bouazizi, fatally burned himself as an act of protest against economic desperation, and what he viewed as police harassment, and corruption. Bouazizi's meager income had supported several family members. But on the morning of December 17, 2010, police confiscated his cart and produce because he supposedly did not have a required permit. When he was refused a hearing at the provincial headquarters or the return of his property, he poured flammable liquid on himself at the headquarters and then set it alight. He was taken to a hospital where died on January 4, 2011, from his injuries. People in Sidi Bouzid immediately began protesting the injustice done to him and the corruption of local police. When police tried to stop the initial protests, more people joined in.

Observers and participants posted images of the protests and clashes with police on Facebook and YouTube. People in other Tunisian communities also began to protest against government corruption and economic conditions. Confrontations with police resulted in several deaths, sparking increasing participation in the up-rising. The developing movement demanded not only improved local conditions but the removal of President Ben Ali, the disbanding of his ruling Constitutional Democratic Rally (RCD) Party, and the creation of a genuinely democratic polit-ical system. Strikes by blue-collar workers were soon joined by strikes of lawyers and teachers. Protests spread to the nation's capital, Tunis. On January 14, 2011, the Tunisian army deserted the Ben Ali government and seized control. Ben Ali and his family were given asylum by Saudi Arabia. On February 6, 2011, the new Tunisian government suspended the RCD and officially dissolved it on March 9.

On October 23, 2011, a multiparty democratic election was held for a new single house national legislature. A moderate Islamist party, Ennahda (al-Nahda), won 37 percent of the popular vote for the assembly and a leader of this party became the new president. The regime overthrow in Tunisia in January 2011 encouraged young Egyptians to launch protests against the Mubarak dictatorship.

EGYPT

The Egyptian revolution began on January 25, 2011. People in this nation of 85 million (CIA 2014b) were inspired by the ability of Tunisians to rise up and end the twen-ty-four-year rule of Ben Ali. Many Egyptians had in preceding years participated in mass demonstrations that were implicitly or explicitly critical of the Mubarak regime.

Preceding Mobilizations

A wave of demonstrations took place to protest the US-British led invasion and oc-cupation of Iraq in 2003. Many objected when Mubarak blamed Saddam Hussein for the war rather than the invading nations. Mubarak was seen as siding with the Americans and British instead of the majority of Egyptians, who saw the invasion as the seizure of Iraq's oil. Many demonstrators shouted "Leave, Mubarak, leave!" as Mubarak's security forces moved to suppress the protests (Hassan 2003).

The anti–Iraq War protests soon evolved into the Keyfaya (Enough!") move-ment in 2004 and 2005 (Gelvin 2012; El-Ghobashy 2005). This movement protested against Hosni Mubarak's continuation in power as well as what appeared to be a plan to have his son Gamal Mubarak succeed him as president. Activists demanded that Mubarak resign and that the political system be democratized.

The April 6 movement was another important mobilization leading up to the 2011 revolution. This protest initially involved a few individuals in their twenties, including Esraa Abdel Fattah Ahmed Rashid and Ahmed Maher, both twenty-seven. This apparently was the first movement to use social media to call for mass demonstrations against economic conditions and lack of democracy in Egypt. On March 23, 2008, the activists set up a Facebook page to support textile workers striking in the city of Mahalla al-Kobra on April 6 to protest high food prices and low pay (PBS 2011a). They invited three hundred others to link with their page, but within a day the number shot up to 3,000 and grew to 70,000 in a few weeks. But police suppressed the April 6 protests, killing four persons and arresting about four hundred. Despite this repression, the movement survived. Its members learned valuable lessons from their experiences and also from studying the nonviolent revolutionary tactics of Serbian and Ukrainian youth movements that had helped overthrow regimes in their countries (PBS). April 6 movement activists would play an important role in organizing the early phase of the Egyptian revolution.

Egypt's Emergency Law

In addition to widespread dissatisfaction with the Mubarak regime's collaboration with US foreign policy, lack of democracy, government corruption, and the perception that Hosni Mubarak intended to have his son Gamal succeed him in the presidency, other issues inflamed many Egyptians.

One was Egypt's Emergency Law, which had been in effect almost continuously since Israel defeated Egypt, along with other Arab countries, in the Six Day War (1967). This law permitted the government to suspend basic constitutional rights of citizens, limit street demonstrations, censor media, detain people indefinitely without charge, and spy on personal communications (BBC 2012a). On the grounds of protecting national security or fighting terrorism, Mubarak's regime used the law to limit who could run for political office and in general prevent democratic elections. The April 6 movement targeted removal of this law as necessary to creating a democratic republic.

Demography, Unemployment, Poverty, and Elite Corruption

Egypt's relatively high birth rate led to a so-called youth bulge, with over 50 percent of the population under twenty-five (CIA 2014b). The economy has not grown fast enough to provide employment to young adults, except at low-income jobs. The adoption of neoliberal economic policies in Egypt limited the number of government jobs that previously absorbed the country's college graduates. This has meant that tens of thousands of young adults with higher educational degrees found it difficult to get jobs in the professions they trained for. The unemployment rate for young Egyptian college graduates was estimated at almost ten times that for persons with primary educations (Noland and Pack 2011). Discontent generated by unemployment and poverty was heightened by the perception that elite families in Egypt had become multibillionaires through political connections and corruption while so many of their country folk could barely get by.

Police Corruption and Brutality

Poor and middle-class Egyptians feared police brutality. US government sources reported that police brutality is "routine and pervasive" (Harding 2011). Torture appeared to be used not only on suspected criminals but also on arrested Islamists and activists and bloggers critical of authorities and the political and economic system. In 2007 the Egyptian Organization for Human Rights claimed it had documented 567 cases of torture in police custody since 1993, which resulted in 167 deaths (BBC 2007). One notorious alleged case of police brutality led to the creation of a Facebook page that became one of the social media organizing tools leading to the 2011 uprising.

Wael Ghonim, a computer engineer with an MBA in marketing and finance, became head of marketing for Google Middle East and North Africa. He was passionate to liberate Egypt from the Hosni Mubarak dictatorship and help establish democracy. Wael became a cyber activist and worked on pro-democracy Internet websites. After Khaled Said, a young businessman who had exposed police corruption online, was reportedly dragged from an Internet café by police and beaten to death on June 6, 2010, Wael created a Facebook page, "We are all Khaled Said." Wael used the page to mount a campaign against police corruption and brutality through posting news stories, photos, and videos. This rapidly became one of Egypt's most popular activist websites (BBC 2011; Jensen 2013).

The Tunisian Revolution and the Police Day Protest

Egyptians were finally shocked into action by the uprisings in Tunisia. When Tunisia's dictator was overthrown on January 14, 2011, Wael, then thirty years old, believed the time was right to begin Egypt's own revolution. He used his website to call for mass demonstrations for democracy and against tyranny, corruption, torture, and unemployment on January 25, Egypt's National Police Day (Loveluck 2013). Hundreds of thousands of Egyptians turned out for protests in Cairo, Alexandria, and elsewhere. Wael was arrested by security forces and on January 27 the government shut down the Internet in an effort to stop the growing revolution.

Google demanded Wael's release, and he was set free following twelve days of detention. He became a heroic symbol of the developing revolution. For weeks the police tried to evict protestors from key areas of major cities.

The Egyptian Muslim Brotherhood (see Chapter 8) did not openly endorse the uprising on January 25 (Hamid and Brooke 2011), although some younger members participated. The Brotherhood leadership had long preferred incremental change over a disruptive and potentially risky revolution. But as hundreds of thousands joined the protests, the Brotherhood endorsed the movement on January 28. It did not lead the movement, but chose to be part of it and benefit from it. However, as hundreds of thousands from the Brotherhood joined the protests in various cities, the secular, pro-democratic leaders of the initial uprising became concerned that their movement might be taken over by Islamists (PBS 2011b). Instead of the democratic system so many Egyptian revolutionaries aimed for, secularists feared that the outcome could be a type of Egyptian Islamist state, a result similar to what happened in the Iranian revolution described in Chapter 7. As the protests intensified, concern about the Muslim Brotherhood's expanding role was partially eclipsed by growing outrage at the Mubarak regime.

On February 9, hundreds of thousands of workers struck around the country. In response to the popular uprisings, the Egyptian military forced Mubarak to resign on February 11. Millions of Egyptians celebrated. But despite the euphoria, little had changed except a few faces at the top of the regime. The basic power structure remained in place. Mubarak, a former military officer, was replaced by a council of military commanders publicly promising to restore civilian rule and allow the establishment of democracy. The armed forces, rather than simply being an organization of professional soldiers, also controlled a large section of the economy. High-ranking officers had their own economic interests to protect from any future elected government and might intervene if they felt those interests were threatened. The government bureaucracy and the high courts were dominated by people appointed by the Mubarak regime. They were unlikely to cooperate willingly with an anti-Mubarak government. And the old structure of economic power remained in place. Essentially the revolution up to that point had succeeded only in removing Mubarak and a few of his cronies, temporarily restraining the violence-prone security forces, and winning a questionable commitment of military leaders to democratization. The new "democratic" future was very uncertain.

The Military in Control

Following the removal of Mubarak from the presidency, the armed forces leadership exercised direct control over the country. As noted above, Mubarak era appointees still held most important positions in the government bureaucracy and the courts. This created the potential for the military to experiment with different possible courses of action and then rely on the courts to "legally" justify or other-wise assist any policy changes the armed forces leadership believed were necessary to protect its interests or those of its allies.

Fear of an Iranian-Type Outcome

Both military leaders and pro-democracy Egyptians feared that the Egyptian revo-lution could give Islamists an opportunity to take power, as happened in the Iranian revolution in 1979. In Iran the nonfundamentalist components of the revolutionary alliance, including nonsectarian democracy advocates, Islamic modernists, Islamic leftists, and Marxists, were overwhelmed in elections by Islamic fundamentalists (see Chapter 7). Instead of a secular democracy, a limited Islamic democracy was established with ultimate authority invested in the hands of a supreme religious leader. The pre-revolution Iranian military leadership was decimated during the revolution, with many top officers executed or forced to flee the country.

After Mubarak was removed, the only organization in Egypt capable of trans-forming into a political party to quickly field candidates against former Mubarak supporters was the Muslim Brotherhood. Of course, a key difference in the Egyp-tian revolution was that while the Iranian army had attempted to crush the revo-lution and was virtually destroyed as an effective independent force, the Egyptian army had acted preemptively to save itself by ousting Mubarak and in that sense seemed to support the revolution. This also allowed no opportunity for Egyptian Islamists to form their own revolutionary militia, as happened in Iran, which might have acted to protect elected Islamist leaders. In other words, in Egypt the pre-revolutionary army maintained a monopoly on military force after the old regime was ousted so that whoever was elected in the post-revolution period was left de-fenseless against potential military intervention.

The Initiation, Subversion, and Overthrow of Democracy

Elections for a post-Mubarak parliament were held in stages from November 28, 2011, through January 21, 2012 (Doucet 2011; El-Din 2012). Islamist political parties won over two-thirds of the seats. One of the parliament's main tasks was to select a one-hundred-person assembly to write a new constitution. Secular democrats, leftists, remnants of Mubarak's old National Democratic Party, and the military all appeared to fear that Islamists would dominate the process of writing a constitu-tion. On June 14, 2012, the Egyptian Supreme Constitutional Court ruled that the procedure for electing the new parliament was invalid under the old constitution because persons running on political party slates had been improperly allowed to run for the one-third of seats reserved for independents (CBS 2012). The court said that therefore the elected parliament had to be dissolved immediately. The ruling Supreme Council of the Armed Forces (SCAF) then disbanded the parliament.

Egypt's First Democratically Elected President

Shortly after the elected parliament had been disbanded by the court and the armed forces, Mohammed Morsi, candidate of the Muslim Brotherhood, became Egypt's first democratically elected president on June 17, 2012, after winning almost 52 percent of the popular vote (Fox News 2012). Morsi was born in northern Egypt where his father was a farmer. He earned bachelor's and master's degrees in engineering from Cairo University and a PhD in material sciences from the University of Southern California (Driggs 2012). He served on the faculty of California State University at Northridge from 1982 to 1985. Morsi then returned to Egypt and became a professor at Zagazig University until 2010. In the presidential election, he defeated the candidate favored by many in the military, the wealthy class, and the Mubarak era establishment, Ahmed Shafik, the former air force commander who had briefly served as Mubarak's last prime minister.

Domestic Opponents

President Morsi defied the armed forces and the Mubarak-appointed judges by recalling the elected parliament and refusing to abide by restrictions the military had imposed on the presidency before the election. Morsi also replaced several of the top generals who had led SCAF after Mubarak was removed. Besides top military leaders (who feared that an elected civilian government would gain effective control over the armed forces and its economic enterprises) and the Mubarak appointees who dominated the courts and government bureaucracies, Morsi faced opposition from other sources. The young, well educated, secular male and female activists who had initiated the revolution against Mubarak feared Morsi and the Muslim Brotherhood would impose an Islamic state, effectively end real democracy, and curtail women's rights in the name of religion. Coptic Christians feared for their religious freedom and personal safety. In addition, members of Egypt's economic elite feared that a democratically elected government could endanger their wealth and economic dominance.

Foreign Opponents

The Morsi government also had foreign opponents. The Saudi Arabian monarchy had supported the Mubarak regime and reportedly its accommodative policy toward Israel and was distressed when the Obama administration withdrew its support from Mubarak. The advent of a truly democratic government in Egypt, the most populous Arab nation, was a profound shock to the Saudi regime and all the other Arab monarchies that had previously enjoyed US support and military assistance. The success of democracy in Egypt, especially if followed by the election of a government that would promote democracy elsewhere in the region and significantly change Egypt's foreign policy, threatened the royal families' power and the mutually supportive network of Arab elites.

Israel also feared the loss of the cooperative Mubarak regime, which had tried to assist in stopping the flow of arms from Egypt to Hamas-controlled Gaza. Mubarak favored the more moderate Palestinian Authority faction that dominated the West Bank.

Geographic Vulnerability

Another weakness of the Morsi government had to do with the geography of its popular support. Morsi's main strength was in the countryside and outlying cities and towns, not in relatively cosmopolitan and secular Cairo. In the 2012 presidential election, Morsi received only 44 percent of the votes in Cairo (Egyptian Independent 2012). This meant that in the event of a military coup against his government in the capital city, his supporters would likely be overwhelmed by his opponents.

The Development of a New Constitution

Members of parliament selected a one-hundred-member Constituent Assembly to write a new constitution. But many people voiced concern that it, like the parliament that selected it, was dominated by Islamists. The constitution that emerged attempted to appease different interest groups while proclaiming support for human rights and democracy. For example, while banning arbitrary arrest and torture, it preserved the military's autonomy and independent power by continuing to permit military trial of civilians. While not incorporating Sharia law as Islamic fundamentalists desired, it proclaimed that the articles of the constitution could not contradict the principles of Sunni Islam. While banning discrimination against people on the basis of gender, race, or religion, it did not, in the eyes of critics, go far enough in providing protections for religious minorities and did not explicitly state that women were equal to men. The new constitution stated that government should be consistent with Islam (something not very different from the previous constitution). But that, coupled with the fact that democratic elections had resulted in an Islamist president and an Islamist-dominated parliament, provoked concern among many secular Egyptians that under Morsi Egypt would eventually become a nondemocratic conservative Islamic state. Such a system could mean extreme punishments for "offenses" like adultery and religious dissent, or common crimes and define the government's power as deriving not from the people but from God. This might result in placing ultimate government power in the hands of the religious leadership, as occurred in Iran after the 1978–1979 Iranian revolution.

These fears were exacerbated when Morsi proclaimed, on November 22, 2012, that the courts—dominated by Mubarak appointees—could not interfere with the Constituent Assembly's drafting of the new constitution or his own actions until after the new constitution was approved by a nationwide referendum. Morsi's opponents claimed he was establishing a new authoritarian regime. On the other hand, Morsi's supporters could argue that allowing the former dictator's judges and the old nondemocratic constitution to control the writing of a new constitution and the actions of the country's first democratically elected president made no sense. Once the new constitution was ratified by popular vote throughout Egypt, judges would then have to determine the constitutionality of any government actions, including those of the president, according to the post-revolution constitution. Some secular and liberal members of the Constituent Assembly abandoned the process of writing the new constitution out of concern that the Islamist majority, unrestricted by the courts, might incorporate rigid Islamic rules into the constitution.

Human Rights Watch and Amnesty International criticized Morsi's declaration, and tens of thousands of anti-Morsi protestors took to the streets to demand that he renounce it. They also wanted the Constituent Assembly drafting the new constitution to be replaced. Morsi reportedly agreed to a compromise: he would again be subject to Supreme Court rulings but the Constituent Assembly would be allowed to complete formulating the new constitution. The April 6 movement and other liberal groups that had participated in the uprising against Mubarak, however, remained critical of both Morsi and the Constituent Assembly.

At the beginning of December the Constituent Assembly presented President Morsi with the proposed new constitution, and a national vote to approve or reject it was held over several days beginning on December 15, 2012. A little over 30 percent of those eligible participated in the referendum, with about 63 percent voting to approve it (BBC 2012b). Through the first half of the 2013, economic conditions failed to improve. Electricity outages occurred, gas shortages developed, and unemployment stayed high. Critics claimed this proved that Morsi was incompetent while many of Morsi's supporters blamed lack of cooperation or even sabotage by pro-Mubarak holdovers in the government bureaucracies. International financial institutions put pressure on Egypt to reduce food subsidies as a condition of getting desperately needed foreign credit. In addition, sectarian conflict increased between Muslims and Christians and between Sunnis and Egypt's small Shia population.

Military Seizes Power

In June, anti-Morsi street demonstrations reached massive levels as did counter-demonstrations by his supporters. Opponents urged removal of the elected president for several reasons: incompetence causing continued economic hardships and social turmoil that further hurt the economy by scaring away foreign investment and tourists (a major source of income for Egypt); plotting to turn Egypt into a theocratic Islamic state in which conservative religious authorities would rule, harsh Sharia punishments would be mandated for religious violations as well as crimes, religious minorities would be crushed, and democracy would cease to exist; and election fraud in that Morsi had portrayed himself as a religious moderate representing all Egyptians equally in order to get votes and win the presidency.

On July 1 the military presented an ultimatum to all political parties stating that they should resolve their disputes within forty-eight hours or the military would intervene and impose a solution. But President Morsi rejected the generals' ultimatum the next day, stating that he and other civilian political leaders should work out an agreement to resolve the crisis.

Then on July 3, the armed forces arrested President Morsi and seized power. In the weeks that followed, hundreds of thousands of Morsi supporters took to the streets to demand Morsi's release and return to the presidency. Hundreds of them were killed. The armed forces maintained control and later announced that Morsi would be tried for inciting his supporters to murder demonstrators against his policies in December 2012 (Associated Press 2013). Fourteen other members of the Muslim Brotherhood were to be tried along with him. Two thousand Brotherhood leaders and another six thousand ordinary members were reportedly being detained in October 2013. The military officers who overthrew the elected government and the courts labeled Morsi and many of his supporters criminals. This appeared to be an attempt to redefine the armed forces coup not as an overthrow of democracy but rather as the removal an outlaw regime that had wronged and alienated most Egyptians. The military also appeared to be engaging in an effort to destroy the Muslim Brotherhood as an effective organization and treat anyone who resisted through the use of violence as terrorists. In April 2014, 683 alleged Morsi supporters were sentenced to death in one of a series of mass trials (Press Association 2014).

The Obama administration hesitated to call the military takeover a coup but eventually cut off some military assistance as repression continued (Labott 2013). While Obama called for the rapid restoration of democracy, Saudi Arabia, the United Arab Emirates, and Kuwait reportedly put together a $12 billion assistance package. This was about four times the funding Egypt had been receiving from the US and the EU combined. The Saudi regime appeared to be backing a restoration of the power structure that existed in Egypt before the 2011 revolution, minus longtime Saudi ally Hosni Mubarak.

Some observers believed that the Saudi royal family feared the revolution in Egypt and the democratic election of a member of the Muslim Brotherhood as a grave danger to its rule. Bush administration statements favoring democratization in the Middle East were simply not credible and were not viewed as a serious threat. Democracy would mean that populations outraged by Bush's policies could vote out the very regimes collaborating with his administration and elect leaders hostile to Republican neoconservative policies. But the Obama administration was actually siding with revolutionaries attempting to bring democracy to Egypt. And then the first democratic elections brought to power the Muslim Brotherhood, a movement that like other Islamist movements, apart from the Saudi Arabian Wahhabis, opposed the monarchy form of government. According to Herbst (2013), the Saudi royal family worked to destabilize the elected Egyptian government by providing support to groups and TV stations opposing President Morsi. Rather than confront this activity publicly, Morsi tried to ignore it because some 2 million Egyptians were working in Saudi Arabia and their remittances to families in Egypt was a significant lifeline for that nation's struggling economy.

The Egyptian revolution fell victim to a counterrevolution supported by foreign dictatorships, domestic secularists who feared the election of a government set on creating an Islamic state, and the military and economic power structures that were left virtually untouched when Mubarak was removed. The military's attempt to criminalize and imprison Egypt's first democratically elected leaders and to bar the Muslim Brotherhood from effective political participation indicates a high probability that nothing resembling real democracy will emerge from Egypt's so-called second revolution (the military takeover) of July 2013.

Libya

Libya, a nation with a population of about 6 million (CIA 2014c), was ruled by Muammar Qadafi since the 1969 Libyan revolution when then Colonel Qadafi led a military overthrow of the monarchy (Ahmida 2006). Following the Tunisian and Egyptian uprisings, protests against Qadafi's regime began on February 15. Within days, rebels controlled most of the country's second largest city, Benghazi, located in the eastern coastal region. The regime's forces were unable to recapture the city. Protests against Qadafi's rule also broke out in the largest city and capital, Tripoli, but were repressed by government security units. Qadafi made some offers of compromise, but the insurgents demanded that Qadafi and his family give up power and leave the country. Rebels seized control of a number of smaller cities and towns along the coast, but many of these were retaken in a counteroffensive. Then on March 17 the fifteen-member United Nations Security Council voted for UN Security Council Resolution 1973, which authorized international military intervention in Libya to protect civilians. This included establishing a no-fly zone over all of Libya to prevent the Libyan air force from operating on behalf of Qadafi's ground forces. Ten security council members voted in favor of international intervention, including three permanent members, the US, Britain, and France. Five nations abstained, including Russia and China, the other two permanent members, either of which could have vetoed the resolution. On March 19, Britain and France attacked Libyan military assets from the air. Other nations, including the US and Italy, assisted efforts against the Qadafi regime. It appeared that the foreign planes and missiles went beyond depriving Qadafi's military of air power and in reality became the air offensive force of the rebels, ultimately tipping the conflict decisively in favor of the rebels.

In late August 2011, after Libyan military and government sites in Tripoli were attacked from the air, rebel groups seized control of the city. Qadafi one of whose sons had already been killed in combat, fled with another of his sons and some government officials to his hometown of Sirte. There in October, after repeated air attacks, father and son were captured and executed by rebel forces, effectively ending the civil war.

The rebels were deeply divided along ideological, religious, and tribal lines. The new central government appeared to exercise little control over much of the country, including Benghazi. Many post-Qadafi government officials and military officers were assassinated (Steven 2013), and mini civil wars broke out periodically among factions that had previously been allied in the effort to oust the Qadafi regime. Disruption, sabotage, and a major strike by oil workers caused oil production to fall drastically. Large armed militias operated beyond the control of the new regime (Mohamed 2013). Libya appeared in danger of experiencing a new civil war and/or fragmenting with Al Qaeda–affiliated groups becoming securely entrenched in parts of the country.

An additional consequence of the Libyan conflict was that a number of nations accused the countries that militarily intervened in Libya of violating the UN resolution that authorized the implementation of a no-fly zone to protect civilians and bring about a cease-fire. Critics asserted that the foreign air attacks handed victory to the rebels. This action went beyond providing a permissive world context for revolution to actually winning the revolution for the rebel side. It's possible that some of the other four conditions for the success of a revolution were not sufficiently present in Libya for it to succeed. In particular it is not clear whether the pre-revolutionary state was weakened enough or the rebels unified enough to win without foreign military intervention. In response to perceived deception by the US, Britain, and France, Russia and China were reluctant to cooperate with the US and its allies regarding the civil war in Syria.

Syria

Military officers loyal to the Syrian Baath Party won a struggle over other military factions in the 1960s. In a further military coup, Baathist air force general Hafez al-Assad (father of Bashar al-Assad) and his allies seized control in 1970 (Lawson 1998). Support for the Baath Party came mainly from workers who favored its socialist policies, nationalization of banks and insurance companies, and agricultural reform. Al-Assad, however, allowed many private businesses to operate and encouraged foreign investment. He remained in power in an essentially one-party state until he died in 2000 and was succeeded by his son Bashar al-Assad.

After protests broke out in Tunisia, Egypt, and Libya, significant demonstrations against Bashar al-Assad's regime began in March 2011. But unlike Tunisia and Egypt, where the ruling dictators were ousted, al-Assad was able to hang on to power and retain control of much of the country. As in Libya, a civil war broke out, but unlike that country, where the rebels won with major military assistance from Britain and France, these nations did not directly intervene and the civil war persisted, resulting in more than 100,000 deaths by the fall of 2013 (CNN 2013).

The first major protest in Syria, a 90 percent Arab nation of about 22 million (CIA 2014e), occurred when a group of children and teenagers in the town of Daraa were arrested by police after writing political graffiti. Parents and other people protested and dozens of people were reportedly killed in the conflict between demonstrators and security forces.

As protests spread, the Syrian regime announced measures to bolster its supporters and calm its opponents. These included a pay raise for state employees, lifting Syria's forty-eight-year state of emergency, and a proposal to permit the operation of new political parties.

Opponents of the regime, although deeply divided among themselves, generally ignored reform offers and demanded that al-Assad be removed from power before negotiations for a new political system began and that he not participate in any new government. A number of nations accused the Syrian government of using excessive force against protestors and insurgents, resulting in mounting civilian casualties. Significant numbers of government soldiers and officers and some officials defected to the opposition. There was also evidence of human rights abuses on the rebel side (Maguire 2013).

As civil strife intensified, the US and the EU banned the importation of Syrian oil. In October 2011, several groups opposing the Syrian regime endorsed the goal of establishing a democratic political system. But in the United Nations Security Council, permanent Security Council members China and Russia displayed their willingness to use their vetoes to block any resolutions authorizing military action against the Syrian government.

In November, most Arab nations voted to suspend Syria's membership in the Arab League and to impose, along with Turkey, economic sanctions against Syria (CNN 2013). Then in February 2012 a large majority of UN member nations voted for a nonbinding resolution asking Bashar al-Assad to leave office. On March 27, 2012, the Syrian government accepted a plan proposed by UN envoy Kofi Annan to cease fire, allow free movement for providing humanitarian relief, and begin negotiations to bring reforms and peace. But in June a plan to send hundreds of unarmed UN observers to monitor the supposed cease-fire was scrapped amid increasing violence.

In August, the Syrian prime minister Riyad al-Hijab resigned from al-Assad's government and left with his family for Jordan. Then in November an announcement was made that Syrian opposition groups would form an alliance—the National Coalition for Syrian Revolutionary and Opposition Forces. Al-Assad referred to the armed opposition as terrorists. In mid-May 2013, the UN stated that more than 1.5 million refugees had left Syria to escape the conflict and later in the month European Union nations permitted the sale of weapons to Syrian rebels (CNN 2013). By the end of August, the UN was investigating whether chemical weapons had been used in the civil war and examining evidence of the execution of captured Syrian soldiers and civilians by opposition forces. During the civil war, the Syrian government used air power against the rebels, and rebel factions were accused of using dozens of suicide bombers and vehicle bombs to kill people in government-controlled areas.

By mid-2013, the Syrian civil war had become a more complex conflict than at the outset. Within Syria a branch of Islam linked to the Shia, the Alawites, makes up about 12 percent of the population and tends to support the government. The al-Assad family is Alawite, as reportedly are a disproportionate number of top government officials and military officers. Approximately 74 percent of Syrians are Sunni (CIA 2014e). Relatively secular Sunnis appear divided between supporting the government or participating in the rebellion. But conservative Sunni Islamists seem mainly on the rebel side. Many among the minority of Syrians who are Christians reportedly lean towards supporting the government because, like the Alawites, they fear brutal repression if the rebels win and Sunni Islamic fundamentalists gain control of the country. Although the government forces were largely under a unified central command, the rebel forces were composed of several groups and many local militias with a great deal of independence and they occasionally even engaged in violent conflict with one another. A major division among the rebels concerned whether the al-Assad regime should be replaced with a genuinely democratic government with religious freedom and protections for minorities and women's rights or whether a strongly Islamic post-revolutionary system should be established based on implementation of strict Islamic law.

Militarily on the government side, in addition to the regular armed forces and reserves, there were thousands in local pro-government militias, including some organized within particular population categories like the Alawites. In addition, a significant number of Shia Hezbollah fighters from neighboring Lebanon crossed into Syria to help al-Assad's forces fight the rebels. Furthermore, some Iranian Revolutionary Guard personnel were believed to be assisting the al-Assad regime. Shia from other countries, such as Iraq, were also reported to have fought on the government side. Iran and Russia sold or otherwise provided weapons and other assistance to the Syrian government.

Armed forces on the rebel side were divided, generally less well armed, and lacked air power. Some were soldiers and officers who had defected from the Syrian army. There was disagreement regarding how much of the rebel forces was Islamist or linked to Al Qaeda, but some estimates were as high as 50 percent. It did seem, though, that Islamist rebel forces were responsible for dozens of suicide and other mass casualty bombing attacks against the Syrian government and its supporters. Thousands of foreigners crossed into Syria, often through Turkey, to join in the fight against the Assad regime and set up a Syrian Islamic state. These included Sunni Islamist fundamentalist volunteers from as many as twenty-nine countries, such as Saudi Arabia, Libya, Iraq, Jordan, Tunisia, the United Arab Emirates, Pakistan, and Afghanistan (Maguire 2013). Particular rebel factions appeared to receive help from Saudi Arabia and other Sunni Arab monarchies, several European countries, and the United States.

At the end of August 2013, the US reported evidence that 1,429 people, including 426 or more children, were killed in a chemical attack suspected to have been carried out by the Syrian military. President Obama then asked Congress to authorize US air attacks against Syria's armed forces. However, the Syrian government denied using chemical weapons. Furthermore, public opinion polls indicated that a majority of Americans opposed any US military action in Syria and Congress appeared likely to refuse to give permission for an attack on Syria.

In September Russia proposed allowing international observers, with Syria's permission, to locate and destroy or remove all the country's chemical weapons and chemical weapons–making equipment. Evidence indicated that Syria began destroying its chemical weapons, including chemical armed bombs and missile warheads, and by the end of October 2013 the Organization for the Prohibition of Chemical Weapons announced that Syria had destroyed all its disclosed chemical weapons production facilities.

Peace negotiations proved difficult in part because of rebel disunity and contrasting goals for the future of Syria (Dorell 2013). In addition, Russia demanded that Iran be a party to the negotiations, while the US opposed Iranian participation. At the time of this writing, the Syrian civil war continued.

Bahrain

Bahrain is an archipelago nation in the Persian Gulf with about 1,281,000 residents (including approximately 235,000 foreigners, mainly male workers) (CIA 2014a); it is connected by a causeway to Saudi Arabia. A democratic uprising there began in February 2011. Bahrain and its monarchy are important to the US because the US Fifth Fleet is stationed in the Bahraini capital, the port city Manama. As in other Arab countries, protests were in part sparked by the Tunisian and Egyptian uprisings. But in Bahrain the royal family is Sunni while approximately 70 percent of Bahraini citizens are Shia (Erlich 2013). The armed forces are also reportedly disproportionately Sunnis. In fact, according to analysts, many members of the Bahrain security forces are hired Sunni non-nationals from countries including Pakistan, Jordan, Iraq, Syria, and Yemen (Black 2011). Critics often referred to them as mercenaries. Both Shia and Sunni Bahrainis have participated in numerous pro-democracy demonstrations, some involving as many as 100,000 to 150,000 demonstrators. Some protestors publicly called for greater political freedom, but many others went beyond this to demand the overthrow of the monarchy and the establishment of a democratic republic. But opponents of the democracy movement portrayed it as inspired by or even controlled by Shia Iran. They claimed its real goal was not democracy but the establishment of a Shia Islamic fundamentalist system in Bahrain similar to that in Iran. This pro-monarchy strategy terrified many non-Shia residents and instigated a sectarian division between Sunni and Shia Bahrainis.

Demonstrations

In an attempt to convince people not to participate in the impending antiregime demonstrations, the Bahraini monarchy indicated it would increase social spending and release some Shia young people being held by security forces. Then on February 11, 2011, King Hamad bin Issa al-Khalifa announced that each Bahraini family would receive 1,000 dinars ($2,650) (Al Jazeera 2011a). Despite these actions, large pro-democracy protests began in Bahrain on February 14. They were quickly countered by regime security forces. One demonstrator was reported killed and another thirty injured. Later the same day protestors established a tent camp at the Pearl Roundabout monument in Manama. But on February 17, security forces raided the camp. Six protestors were killed and dozens injured (Al Jazeera 2011b). Outraged by the killings and the repression, approximately 100,000 to 150,000 Bahrainis staged a huge demonstration at the Manama Pearl Roundabout on February 22. Then on February 25 as many as twice that number marched through the streets of the capital demanding democracy and an end to the repression (Slackman and Audi 2011).

Large antigovernment protests developed in multiple locations. The king of-fered minor modifications like removing some cabinet ministers and opening discussions on a number of issues important to the protestors such as democratic elections for parliament and Shia concern over the regime's policy of granting citi-zenship to foreign Sunnis to increase the size of the Sunni minority. But as protests continued and Bahraini forces experienced difficulty controlling the large num-bers of protestors, the regime decided to call for military intervention by troops of other Sunni Arab monarchies. The foreign forces were apparently to protect key installations while Bahraini security personnel suppressed the protests. On March 14, a Saudi-led Gulf Cooperation Council (GCC) peninsular shield force of about 1,500 crossed the causeway from Saudi Arabia to Bahrain and occupied key posi-tions (BBC 2011; Bronner and Slackman 2011). Bahraini forces then intensified a sweeping suppression of protestors and on March 18 demolished the Pearl Mon-ument, which had served as a central rallying point for pro-democracy activists (Bronner 2011). The regime arrested thousands, including hospital personnel who treated beaten or wounded protestors, and several activists reportedly died in cus-tody from mistreatment (Bassiouni, Rodley, Al-Awadhi, Kirsch, and Arsanjani 2011; Jones, Marc Owen 2013). Richard Sollom, deputy director of Physicians for Human Rights, stated that after more than two decades of human rights investiga-tions in some twenty countries, he had never seen such extensive and systematic vi-olation of medical neutrality as took place during the Bahrain regime repression of the pro-democracy protests (2011). He said doctors, nurses, and other medical staff as well as hospitals, clinics, and ambulances were targeted. The Bahraini regime may have seized and prosecuted medical personnel for aiding wounded demon-strators because in the process of giving medical care they obtained evidence of re-gime violence against and mistreatment of protestors. A number of physicians were reportedly charged with trying to topple the monarchy (Fisk 2011). Thousands of people, including labor union leaders participating in a general strike in support of the pro-democracy protests, were reportedly fired from their jobs. Pro-democracy activists were arrested and imprisoned, yet protests continued.

RESULTS OF THE ARAB REVOLUTION

The uprisings revived pan-Arab consciousness with the hope that Arab dictator-ships could be swept away in a democratic revolutionary wave. But as of spring 2014, the results of the Arab revolution have amounted to far less than participants aimed to achieve. A more democratic government was established in Tunisia with an elected president. Qadafi's rule was ended through a civil war and large-scale foreign military intervention on the side of the rebels. But the new Libya appeared on the verge of another civil war and/or permanent fragmentation while its oil was exploited by foreign powers. Numerous uncontrolled militias and their often lawless violence seemed to constitute a state of institutionalized terrorism with pro-democratic Libyans intimidated into passive submission.

In much more populous Egypt, the 2011 uprising ousted the Mubarak regime. Democratic elections eventually took place. But entrenched economic, government, and military elites supportive of the old regime, and some leaders of the initial rebellion began to fear the policies of those who had been elected. As a result, the military seized power and imprisoned the democratically elected president. The pre-revolution Mubarak system (minus Mubarak) appeared virtually untouched and protected by a military dictatorship.

In Syria a brutal ongoing civil war developed with international participation. There, as in Libya, groups allied with Al Qaeda gained control of some areas. Uprisings and demonstrations in other countries resulted in limited changes such as the replacement of Ali Abdullah Saleh, the man who had ruled Yemen for more than three decades, by his former vice president, Abd Rabbuh Mansur al-Hadi. In some oil-rich monarchies grants of money were dispersed to citizens in an apparent attempt to inoculate them from the democratic tide and convince them not to engage in protests.

A crucial turning point in the Arab revolution occurred when Saudi-led GCC forces entered Bahrain and the Bahraini monarchy brutally repressed the democratic movement. And Britain, the US, and other democracies stood aside and let it happen. This seemed to demonstrate that their support for revolution to democracy was only real when the revolution would oust an unfriendly government and replace it with one favorable to their interests. Their inaction appeared to green-light an acceleration of the antidemocratic counterrevolution.

SUMMARY AND ANALYSIS

Most Arab nations are monarchal dictatorships or authoritarian republics. One reason Arab nations have lagged behind the rest of the world in democratizing is the major role that oil and natural gas exports play in their economies and the world economy. Despite rhetorical support for the concept of democracy, neither the US or Britain have consistently displayed believable interest in supporting really democratic political systems in strategically important Arab countries (those with large energy resources or key military-security significance).

Control of energy resources has put enormous power into the hands of Arab dictators. But the major reason that the Arab world is dominated by dictatorships appears to be that Britain and the US tolerated or supported authoritarian governments. The most powerful capitalist democracies seem to have preferred co-operative dictatorships in the oil rich Arab states rather than pressuring them to democratize. Since US and British policies have generally been abhorrent to most Arabs, allowing Arab peoples to elect their own leaders would almost certainly result in new governments more independent of foreign influence and less obedient to US and British policies. Democratically elected Arab governments would likely be more supportive of the Arab Palestinians and use their energy resources more for beneficial development and addressing inequality and social problems rather than purchasing expensive weapons from British and American arms suppliers.

The claims of the George W. Bush administration and its neoconservative advisers that they aimed to democratize the Middle East lacked credibility for most Arabs and virtually any unbiased student of the history and power structures of the region. It seems clear that the only governments the Bush regime wanted to "democratize" were those highly critical of US policy. The Bush administration hypocritically backed the cooperative monarchies while using false claims of weapons of mass destruction to justify seizing control of Iraq.

There was some hope that US policy would genuinely shift to supporting democratization under the new leadership of President Barack Obama, who had opposed the Iraq War. Obama's 2009 Cairo speech encouraged pro-democracy activists in the Middle East and North Africa. By 2010, revolutionary situations were emerging in several Arab countries.

Economic, political, and moral factors contributed to the development of mass discontent. Large foreign debts motivated a number of oil poor Arab nations to adopt neoliberal economic policies resulting in cutbacks to social services, food subsidies, and government employment. As a result, joblessness, poverty, and other hardships increased. Economic hopelessness made dictatorship, brutality, and corruption even more frustrating. Another major cause of discontent among many Arabs was the perception that their governments were collaborating with British and US foreign policies that they strongly opposed.

Educated pro-democracy young people organized initial protests using multiple means, including cell phones and social media, to circumvent regime attempts to cut off communication. Once protests picked up support, leaders of professional organizations, labor unions, and Islamist groups began to join in and encourage their members to participate in demonstrations.

Several goals united diverse categories of people in the uprisings. Almost all wanted to remove a particular long-term dictator. But many also wanted to change the form of government to democracy. Anti-imperialism was another unifying motive in some cases, since leaders were often viewed as being paid off (through military and police equipment and training to maintain power) to do the bidding of foreign powers. Establishing democracy was widely viewed as a way ordinary people could prevent Arab governments from collaborating with imperialist powers.

The legitimacy of Arab governments in the eyes of their people was weakened in several ways. One was that they often acted against the wishes of the majority of their citizens by supporting unpopular US policies such as its wars against Iraq. The poorer Arab dictatorships, such as Egypt, unlike those that were oil rich, did not have the resources to buy off their citizens with gifts of money when discontent over government policies, lack of democracy, or economic inequality rose too high.

Massive street protests by Palestinians in their intifadas against Israeli occupation, despite overwhelming odds, seemed to contrast with how submissive and accommodating the materially comfortable Arab rulers had become. And when a popular uprising in Tunisia in December 2010 forced that country's dictator to flee, the Egyptian Mubarak dictatorship and others in the region were shaken as seldom before.

Possibly the most crucial factor influencing the course and fate of the Arab Revolution was the presence or absence of a permissive world context. The United States and other powerful nations permitted uprisings to enjoy some limited success, at least temporarily, in certain Arab countries, but not at all in others.

The Obama administration had little difficulty accepting the overthrow of the Tunisian dictatorship. But the Mubarak dictatorship in Egypt was a different story. Egypt is the most populous Arab nation, borders Gaza, and has a history of cooperating with both Israeli and US policies in the Middle East. Ultimately, the US encouraged the Egyptian military to permit relatively democratic elections, to the dismay of Saudi Arabia, which had backed the Mubarak regime. But when Bahrainis rose up against that country's monarchal dictatorship and were repressed by Bahraini and other Gulf monarchy troops, the Obama administration was almost totally silent. Instead of aiding the rebels, as it did in Libya and Syria, it continued to assist and remain allied with the antidemocratic monarchies.

And when the Egyptian military overthrew the elected president Mohammed Morsi in July 2013, the US did little more than cut off some funding and feebly implore the Egyptian generals to restore some type of democratic process (but not the democratically elected president they had overthrown).

A central underlying dynamic of the counterrevolution appears to be the Saudi royal family's desire to continue its domination and hold on to its wealth. In an otherwise democratizing world, the undemocratic, anachronistic regime in Saudi Arabia ultimately depends on the support of the US and Great Britain. Saudi oil money, as well as that of several other oil-rich monarchies, props up the privileged elites and economies in other Arab nations that endorse US, British, and Saudi policies. This underlying structure of money and power and the network of cooperating elites appears to be the key to understanding why the Libyan regime was overthrown with massive foreign assistance and why the Egyptian military was permitted to overthrow the elected government. It appears that currently no revolution to democracy will be permitted if it threatens the interests of the US, Britain, or allied powers in the Middle East or the ability of the region's royal families to hold on to power.

After a few months of exuberance and rising expectations, the Arab revolution was side-tracked in some places and brutally repressed in others. It has stalled in great part because the window of world permissiveness has been shut down by an international counterrevolution. While the transnational reactionary movement's main geographically proximate leader appears to be Saudi Arabia, the US assists the counterrevolution by continuing to back Saudi Arabia and other monarchies. For now, the Arab revolution has been largely stalled by a conservative counterattack permitted by the advanced capitalist democracies that are dependent on the perpetrators' energy resources and apparently unwilling to risk sharing democracy with the peoples of many Arab nations.

CHRONOLOGY OF MAJOR EVENTS

2009   President Barack Obama delivers a speech in Cairo on June 4 supporting democracy in all countries

2010   December—The Arab revolution begins in Tunisia

2011   January 14—Tunisian military ousts Ben Ali

January 25—The Egyptian uprising begins

February 11—Hosni Mubarak resigns as president of Egypt

February 14—Pro-democracy protests in Bahrain begin

February 15—Protests against the Qadafi regime in Libya

March 14—Saudi-led Gulf Council forces enter Bahrain as Bahraini forces suppress pro-democracy activists

March 15—Major protests begin against the Syrian regime

March 17—Foreign military intervention in the Libyan civil war

June 3—Longtime president of Yemen injured in bomb blast

August—Libyan rebels capture Tripoli, capital of Libya

October—Qadafi and one of his sons executed by rebels; multiparty election for the new government of Tunisia

2012   February 27—President of Yemen replaced by vice president

June 24—Mohammed Morsi of the Muslim Brotherhood wins the Egyptian presidential election

November 22—Large protests against Egypt's first democratically elected president, Mohammed Morsi, because he barred judges from interfering with the writing of a new constitution or his actions as president until the new constitution is in place

2013 July 3—Egyptian military overthrows the elected president, Morsi, and takes control of the country

August—High level of international participation in Syrian civil war; charges of use of chemical weapons in Syria

September—Syrian regime agrees to give up its chemical weapons

2014 January—Geneva peace talks between opposing sides in the Syrian civil war begin

March–April—Mass trials in Egypt of Morsi supporters

REFERENCES AND FURTHER READINGS

Ahmida, Ali Abdullatif. 2006. "Libyan Revolution." In DeFronzo, ed., *Revolutionary Movements in World History*, 538–544.

Al Jazeera. 2011a. "Bahrain Doles Out Money to Families." February 12. www.aljazeera .com/news/middleeast/2011/02/20112125185485792.html.

———. 2011b. "Clashes Rock Bahraini Capital." February 17. www.aljazeera.com/news /middleeast/2011/02/201121714223324820.html.

Al-Qazzaz, Ayad. 2006. "Iraq Revolution." In DeFronzo, ed., *Revolutionary Movements in World History*, 427–440.

Associated Press. 2013. "Egypt's Muslim Brotherhood Facing Wave of Trials." October 19. www.nytimes.com/aponline/2013/10/19/world/middleeast/ap-ml-egypt-prosecuting -the-brotherhood.html?adxnnl=1&adxnnlx=1382329585-X8KQsaL6DB5rYSSvnJ /kuQ&pagewanted=print&_r=0.

Bassiouni, Rodley, Al-Awadhi, Kirsch, and Arsanjani. 2011. *Bahrain Independent Commission of Inquiry.* www.bici.org.bh/BICIreportEN.pd.

BBC (British Broadcasting Company). 2007. "Egypt Police Sued for Boy's Death." August 13. http://news.bbc.co.uk/2/hi/africa/6943704.stm.

BBC. 2011. "Gulf States Send Forces to Bahrain Following Protests." March 14. www.bbc .co.uk/news/world-middle-east-12729786.

BBC. 2012a. "Egypt's Ruling Generals to Partially Lift Emergency Law." BBC News, Middle East, January 24. www.bbc.co.uk/news/world-middle-east-16704551.

BBC. 2012b. "Egyptian Constitution 'Approved' in Referendum." December 23. www .bbc.co.uk/news/world-middle-east-20829911.

Black, Ian. 2011. "Bahrain Security Forces Accused Of Deliberately Recruiting Foreign Nationals." *Guardian*, February 17. www.theguardian.com/world/2011/feb/17 /bahrain-security-forces-sunni-foreign?INTCMP=SRCH.

Bronner, Ethan. 2011. "Bahrain Tears Down Monument as Protesters Seethe." *New York Times*, March 18. www.nytimes.com/2011/03/19/world/middleeast/19bahrain .html?_r=0.

Bronner, Ethan, and Michael Slackman. 2011. "Saudi Troops Enter Bahrain to Help Put Down Unrest." *New York Times,* March 14. www.nytimes.com/2011/03/15/world /middleeast/15bahrain.html?pagewanted=all&_r=0.

Brown, Nathan J. 2011. "The Palestinians' Receding Dream of Statehood." *Current History* 110 (740): 345–351.

CBS. 2012. "Egyptian Court Rules Entire Parliament Illegally Elected, Orders Body to Dissolve After Unconstitutional Vote." June 14. www.cbsnews.com/8301-202_162 -57453035/egypt-court-rules-entire-parliament-illegally-elected-orders-body-to -dissolve-after-unconstitutional-vote.

Central Intelligence Agency. 2014a. "Bahrain." In *World Factbook.* www.cia.gov/library /publications/the-world-factbook/geos/ba.html.

———. 2014b. "Egypt." In *World Factbook.* www.cia.gov/library/publications/the -world-factbook/geos/eg.htm.

———. 2014c. "Libya." In *World Factbook.* www.cia.gov/library/publications/the -world-factbook/geos/ly.html.

———. 2014d. "Saudi Arabia." In *World Factbook.* www.cia.gov/library/publications/the -world-factbook/geos/sa.html.

———. 2014e. "Syria." In *World Factbook.* www.cia.gov/library/publications/the -world-factbook/geos/sy.html.

———. 2014f. "Tunisia." In *World Factbook.* www.cia.gov/library/publications/the -world-factbook/geos/ts.html.

CNN. 2013. "Syria Civil War Fast Facts." October 31. www.cnn.com/2013/08/27/world /meast/syria-civil-war-fast-facts/index.html.

Cockburn, Patrick. 2012. "After the Euphoria." *The Nation,* November 5, 27–28, 30–31.

DeFronzo, James. 2006. *Revolutionary Movements in World History.* Santa Barbara, CA: ABC-CLIO.

———. 2006. Introduction. In *Revolutionary Movements in World History,* xix–xxii.

———. 2010. *Iraq War: Origins and Consequences.* Boulder: Westview.

Dorell, Oren. 2013. "Syrian Peace Talks Postponed in Blow to Obama." www.usatoday .com/story/news/world/2013/11/06/syria-peace-talks-canceled-again/3453463.

Doucet, Lyse. 2011. "Egyptian Election: Long Queues in First Post-Mubarak Vote." BBC, November 28. www.bbc.co.uk/news/world-middle-east-15914277.

Driggs, Alexis. 2012. "Egyptians Elect USC Alumnus." *Daily Trojan,* June 26. http://daily trojan.com/2012/06/26/egyptians-elect-usc-alumnus.

Egyptian Independent. 2012. "Al-Masry Al-Youm's Count: Morsy Wins Presidency with 51.13 Percent of Poll," June 18. www.egyptindependent.com/news/al-masry -al-youms-count-morsy-wins-presidency-5113-percent-poll.

El-Din, Gamal Essam. 2012. "Egypt's Post-Mubarak Legislative Life Begins Amid Tensions and Divisions." Ahramonline, January 23. http://english.ahram.org.eg

/NewsContentPrint/33/0/32384/Elections-/0/Egypts-postMubarak-legislative
-life-begins-amid-te.aspx.

El-Ghobashy, Mona. 2005. "Egypt Looks Ahead to Portentous Year." Middle East Research and Information Project, February 2. www.merip.org/mero/mero020205.

Elshinnawi, Mohamed. 2013. "Economic Issues Plague the Arab Spring." Voice of
America, March 26. www.voanews.com/content/arab-spring-economies/1628898
.html. Accessed September 5, 2013.

Erlich, Reese. 2013. "In Bahrain, a Growing Sunni-Shia Rift." *Global Post,* March 18.
http://www.globalpost.com/dispatch/news/regions/middle-east/130315/bahrain
-growing-sunni-shia-rift.

Fisk, Robert. 2011. "I Saw These Brave Doctors Trying To Save Lives: These Charges Are
a Pack of Lies." *Independent,* June 14. www.independent.co.uk/voices/commentators
/fisk/robert-fisk-i-saw-these-brave-doctors-trying-to-save-lives-ndash-these-charges
-are-a-pack-of-lies-2297100.html.

Fox News. 2012. "Muslim Brotherhood-Backed Candidate Morsi Wins Egyptian Presidential Election," June 24. www.foxnews.com/world/2012/06/24/egypt-braces
-for-announcement-president.

Gelvin, James L. 2012. *The Arab Uprisings.* New York: Oxford University Press.

Gorman, Anthony. "Egyptian Revolution of 195." In DeFronzo, ed., *Revolutionary Movements in World History,* 246–253.

Harding, Luke. 2011. "US Reported 'Routine' Police Brutality in Egypt, WikiLeaks Ca-
bles Show." *Guardian,* January 28. www.theguardian.com/world/2011/jan/28/egypt
-police-brutality-torture-wikileaks.

Hassan, Abdalla F. 2003. "As War Continues, Tensions Rise in Egypt." Worldpress.org,
March 31. www.worldpress.org/Mideast/1029.cfm.

Herbst, David. 2013. "Why Saudi Arabia Is Taking a Risk by Backing the Egyptian Coup."
Guardian.com, August 20. www.theguardian.com/commentisfree/2013/aug/20
/saudi-arabia-coup-egypt.

Ibrahim, Ahmed H. 2006. "Arab Revolt." In DeFronzo, ed., *Revolutionary Movements in
World History,* 70–77.

Khouri, Rami G. 2011. "The Arab Awakening." *The Nation,* August 24. www.thenation
.com/print/article/162973/arab-awakening. Accessed September 5, 2013.

Labott, Elise. 2013. "US Suspends Significant Military Aid to Egypt." CNN, October 9.
www.cnn.com/2013/10/09/world/meast/us-egypt-aid/index.html.

Lawson, Fred H. 1998. "Syrian Revolution (1963)." In Jack A Goldstone, ed., *Encyclopedia
of Political Revolutions,* 473–475. Washington, DC: Congressional Quarterly.

Leverett, Flynt, and Hillary Mann Leverett. 2013. "The Real Challenge from Iran." *The
Nation,* February 25, 22–25.

Loveluck, Louisa. 2013. "Why Egyptians Don't Care About Khaled Said, Whose
Death Began Their Revolution." *Christian Science Monitor,* October 3. http://

www.csmonitor.com/World/Middle-East/2013/1003/Why-Egyptians-don-t-care
-about-Khaled-Said-whose-death-began-their-revolution.

Lynch, Marc. 2012. *The Arab Uprising.* New York: Public Affairs.

Maguire, Mairead. 2013. "Report on Syria–Noble Prize Laureate Mairead Maguire: "The Syrian State Is Under a Proxy War Led By Foreign Countries." Global Research, May 27. http://globalresearch.ca/report-on-syria-nobel-peace-laureate-mairead-maguire
-the-syrian-state-is-under-a-proxy-war-led-by-foreign-countries/5336569?print=1.

Mohamed, Esam. 2013. "Militias Pull Out of Libya's Capital, Tripoli." *Washington Post,* November 21. www.washingtonpost.com/world/militias-pull-out-of-libyas-capital
-tripoli/2013/11/21/52f25b3a-52e3-11e3-9fe0-fd2ca728e67c_story.html.

Noland, Marcus, and Howard Pack. 2011. "Arab Revolutions of Rising Expectations." *Real Time Economic Issues Watch,* February 1. www.piie.com/blogs/realtime/?p=1998. Accessed October 7, 2013.

Obama, Barack. 2009. Full Text of Obama's Speech in Cairo. NBCNEWS.com, June 5, 2009. www.nbcnews.com/id/31102929/ns/politics-white_house/t/full-text-obamas
-speech-cairo.

Press Association. 2014. "683 Semtenced to Death in Egypt." MSN News World, April 29. http://news.uk.msn.com/world/683-sentenced-to-death-in-egypt.

Public Broadcasting Service (PBS). 2011a. *Frontline.* "April 6 Movement." www.pbs.org
/wgbh/pages/frontline/revolution-in-cairo/inside-april6-movement.

PBS. 2011b. "Revolution in Cairo." *Frontline.* http://www.pbs.org/wgbh/pages/frontline
/revolution-in-cairo.

Reuters. 2014. "Saudi Arabia Named World's Fourth Largest Defense Spender," February 5. www.arabianbusiness.com/saudi-arabia-named-world-s-fourth-largest-defence
-spender-537534.html.

Slackman, Michael, and Nadim Audi. 2011. "Protestors in Bahrain Demand More Changes." *New York Times,* February 25. www.nytimes.com/2011/02/26/world/middle
east/26bahrain.html?_r=0.

Sollom, Richard. 2011. "The Shocking Thing Is That Bahrain Abuse Is Systematic." *Independent,* April 21. www.independent.co.uk/voices/commentators/richard-sollom
-the-shocking-thing-is-that-bahrain-abuse-is-systematic-2270678.html.

Stephen, Chris. 2013. "Assassination Pushes Libya towards Civil War Two Years After Gaddafi's Death." *Guardian,* October 19. www.theguardian.com/world/2013/oct/19
/assassination-libya-civil-war-gaddafi-benghazi.

Selected DVD, Film, and Videocassette Documentaries

The Battle for Syria. 2012. 54 min. PBS Frontline. http://video.pbs.org/video/2280715740.

Egypt in Crisis. 2013. 54 min. PBS Frontline. The overthrow of President Morsi and its aftermath. http://video.pbs.org/video/2365080516.

Revolution in Cairo. 2011. 54 min. PBS Frontline. Two stories: the youth movement and the Muslim Brotherhood. http://video.pbs.org/video/1810338755.

Syria Behind the Lines. 2013. 54 min. PBS Frontline. http://video.pbs.org/video /2364993210./

12

Conclusions

The opening chapter presented five major factors that have played essential and interdependent roles in the success of revolutionary movements throughout history: the development of mass frustration, the existence of elite dissident movements, the presence of a unifying motivation that brings together different classes and social groups in support of revolution, a severe political crisis that erodes the administrative and coercive capacity of the state, and an international environment permissive of revolution. The revolutions and the revolutionary conflicts covered in this volume illustrate the importance of the five factors in varied contexts. Internal societal characteristics and the interrelationship between the subject societies and other nations of the world helped determine which factors were most central to the success of individual revolutionary movements.

COMPARISONS AMONG THE CASE STUDIES

In the case of the 1917 Russian Revolution the deterioration and collapse of the state was of primary significance. Lenin and other Bolsheviks correctly anticipated that a Russian defeat in World War I would create a crisis of legitimacy and competency for the czarist regime much greater than what occurred after Russia's loss to Japan in 1904. Taking advantage of the disintegration of czarist authority and mass military mutiny, the revolutionists bypassed the stages of historical development described in Marx's model and established a socialist society.

In comparison to the Russian situation, Chinese revolutionaries, following the overthrow of the Manchu dynasty, confronted a stronger antirevolutionary state based on an alliance among former imperial officers, warlords, landlords, and coastal commercial elites. China's revolution won last in the centers of state power, the cities. The Chinese revolution, once under the leadership of Mao and like-minded associates, succeeded primarily because of the profound discontent of China's people, reflected in centuries of peasant rebellions against landlord avarice or excessive taxation and in uprisings against humiliating foreign invasions and occupations. Intensification of mass frustration in the twentieth century resulted from hardships caused both by the increasingly impersonal and exploitive relations between landlords and poor peasants under the Guomindang and by the Japanese invasion, which further inflamed nationalist passions. The course of the war displayed the incompetence, moral shallowness, and even collaboration of pre-revolutionary elites with Japanese authorities and helped propel the Chinese revolution to victory.

Vietnam's revolution was distinguished by the dominant theme of resistance to centuries of foreign invasion and exploitation. Nationalism unified diverse social groups in the revolutionary effort. In Vietnam only one of many anticolonial movements displayed the capacity to organize a successful revolution, the communist-led Viet Minh. This group's assets included a revolutionary policy of redistributing wealth, especially land, to the poor and the general independence of the revolutionary movement from foreign sponsorship. Noncommunist Vietnamese leaders or groups that aspired to play a nationalist role had relatively narrow bases of support and typically depended on substantial foreign assistance, thereby betraying any believable claim to genuine nationalism. Furthermore, the members of such groups tended to display the material concerns characteristic of the upper classes of their sponsoring countries, rather than the spirit of self-sacrifice essential to a successful revolutionary effort.

The Cuban, Nicaraguan, and Iranian revolutions, like the Vietnamese, were viewed as national liberation movements by their participants. Whereas the Vietnamese revolution opposed colonial French control, the other three were directed against neocolonialist governments: technically independent but perceived to be instruments of foreign exploitation. Revolutionaries in all three countries appealed to their fellow citizens to rally behind efforts to oust notorious personalized dictatorial regimes.

Unlike Vietnam, however, leadership for the revolutions in Cuba, Nicaragua, and Iran was not provided by the existing pre-revolutionary communist parties, all of which had limited appeal and initially opposed armed rebellion as a means of political transformation. The Cuban revolution benefited from a situation in which the pre-revolutionary regime lacked legitimacy, having seized power in 1952, and was largely unprepared for the rural guerrilla tactics employed by Castro's forces. Cuba was further distinguished by the existence of a clearly identifiable and towering revolutionary leader whose concepts dictated the country's future course of development.

Nicaraguan revolutionary leaders faced a military opposition specially trained in counterinsurgency warfare and at first unconditionally backed by the United States. Experiencing more than a decade of failure in its attempts to overthrow Somoza, the FSLN temporarily fragmented over future strategy and tactics. One faction, the so-called FSLN Third Force (Christian Wing), developed the approach best suited to Nicaragua's strong religious culture and to taking advantage of the popularity of liberation theology. The Third Force transformed the FSLN into a broad coalition of anti-Somoza, socially progressive, and reform-minded Nicaraguans. After the victory the revolutionary government, profiting from knowledge of early mistakes made by Cubans after their 1959 revolution, maintained a strong private sector in the economy and contributed to the development of a pluralistic democratic political system.

Iran's nationalistic, anti-shah revolution was, like the Cuban, ultimately dominated and shaped by a charismatic and commanding revolutionary leader, Ayatollah Khomeini. Khomeini mobilized the single major Iranian social institution, Shia fundamentalism, that could unquestionably be perceived as free from foreign ideological taint or assistance and, consequently, be recognized by the large mass of strongly religious Iranians as a legitimate nationalist force (although Khomeini vehemently argued the revolution was religious, not nationalist). Reminiscent of the Russian czar's overthrow, the shah's military and government disintegrated in the face of repeated urban demonstrations and insurrections. The ayatollah, having guided the revolution to victory, was then in position to influence greatly the formulation of the nation's post-revolutionary political, social, and economic systems.

The success of the Iranian revolution encouraged Islamic movements, both Shia and Sunni, in other societies. Modern Sunni fundamentalist movements often derived their theological and social principles and revolutionary concepts from one of three similar bodies of thought: Wahhabism, Salafism, and the philosophy of the Muslim Brotherhood. All of these traditions advocated revitalizing Muslim societies by returning to the pure form of Islam thought to have characterized the earliest historical period of the Islamic community. The momentous conflict in Afghanistan following the 1979 Soviet military intervention ultimately gave rise to two related Sunni fundamentalist revolutionary movements—the Taliban and Al Qaeda. The Taliban movement developed in and directly affected one nation, Afghanistan. The Taliban victory in 1996 gave rise to the most conservative and repressive Islamic regime in modern times. The other fundamentalist movement arising out of the Afghan War, Al Qaeda, first organized among the thousands of foreign volunteers from many countries who came to fight in Afghanistan, was by its nature and its ideology internationalist or "transnational." Its leaders sought to wage a global jihad against what they viewed as the enemies of Islam and Islamic peoples. The response of the United States, Britain, and a number of other nations to attacks by Al Qaeda led to new wars in Afghanistan and Iraq, attempts to construct more democratic political systems, and insurrections against foreign occupation.

Of all the societies covered in this volume, South Africa was the one character-ized by the deepest social divisions and the one in which the revolutionary move-ment was in greatest need of mass commitment to a unifying revolutionary goal, the creation of a nonracial political system. Barriers to the sufficient realization of this element of the revolutionary process included ethnic and class differences within the nonwhite population. But the most important impediment had been the unwillingness of a majority of white South Africans, who had constituted the basis of the pre-revolutionary state and armed forces, to support the transformation to a nonracial society. As anticipated in the first edition of this book, this conversion required continuous pressure and encouragement from internal as well as external opponents of apartheid coupled with negotiations in which the emergent revolu-tionary leadership attempted to assure South Africans of European ancestry that they would not be persecuted or severely penalized in an open democratic system by the nonwhite majority.

In 1994 this process led to the first national elections in which all South Africans could vote, the election of a nonwhite majority in the new parliament, an indige-nous African president, and a government of national unity. By 1995 South Afri-ca's new government had opened public schools to all groups and abolished laws requiring the social segregation of different races. But the abolishment of socially restrictive apartheid laws and the ascendancy of indigenous Africans and other nonwhites to national political leadership was not accompanied by sweeping so-cioeconomic restructuring. Instead post-apartheid leaders largely continued the neoliberal economic policies of the previous apartheid regime. While a small mi-nority of nonwhites were permitted to enter the nation's economic elite, about half the population remained below the poverty line, and income inequality actually appeared to increase in the post-apartheid era. As a result of this and other issues, conflict increased among the leaders of South Africa's ruling African National Congress party, with leftists demanding new policies to benefit industrial workers and miners and the poor.

In the twenty-first century, an alternate revolutionary pattern developed in which voters in democratic elections empowered parties and leaders promising to bring about drastic economic and social change. When such a process had been attempted decades earlier in the context of the cold war, powerful nations inter-fered to help crush democracies attempting revolutionary transformations through elections. But following the end of the cold war and the entrenchment of new democratic systems, this model of revolution reemerged. Because of unique cir-cumstances and the extraordinary leadership of Hugo Chávez, Venezuela played a leading and very significant role in this trend. Bolivia soon followed with the election of Evo Morales, whose goals included not only political and economic transformation but also empowering the country's previously excluded indigenous majority. In both nations early policy initiatives of the self-proclaimed revolutionary governments were rewarded with majorities of the vote in later elections. This seemed to reinforce commitment to revolutionary change and encourage similar movements in other democratic nations.

In the fourth edition of this book, the nations of the Middle East were described as likely to experience revolutions. Starting on December 18, 2010, in Tunisia, a revolutionary wave of protests for democracy began sweeping across the region. The longtime Tunisian president was removed and a more democratic political system created. In Egypt, the armed forces responded to huge demonstrations by ousting the president, Mubarak, who had ruled the country for three decades. But after eventually allowing democratic elections for parliament and the presidency, the military again seized power. Libyan protests against the Qadafi regime developed into a full-scale civil war. Other nations not only permitted the rebellion in Libya but intervened militarily to help the rebels win. The new Libyan government appeared weak and unable to control armed militias and Islamic extremists. A brutal civil war also developed in Syria, but in this case international support and volunteer combatants entered the conflict on all sides. As in Libya, many of the antigovernment rebels in Syria were Islamic fundamentalists. When protests occurred in Bahrain, the US and other self-proclaimed supporters of democracy stood by while the regime's security forces, supported by military intervention from other Gulf monarchies, brutally suppressed the pro-democracy movement. A powerful counterrevolution, closing the window of world permissiveness, emerged to block the Arab revolution for democracy in many countries. This development once again illustrates the crucial importance of world permissiveness in the success of revolutions.

Inadequacies in the Theories of Revolution

Chapters 2–11 explored the five essential factors affecting the success of revolutionary movements in different societies. Since the importance of these elements has been repeatedly demonstrated, it may be instructive to assess the capabilities as well as the limitations of general theories of revolution to account for their development. Chapter 1 described the core features of the Marxist, frustration-aggression, systems, modernization, and structural theories of revolution and noted that the first four theories neglected the necessary unifying motivation factor for revolutionary success. The Skocpol and Trimberger structural theory, though concerned primarily with explaining the factor of state deterioration, implicitly identified a logical basis for the development of a unifying motivation for revolution, international conflict and competition, which could provoke heightened feelings of nationalism among all classes in a society threatened by more powerful countries. All five theories, however, ignored the world permissiveness aspect of successful revolutions.

The reasons for these serious oversights may include the fact that the internal logical structure of several of the general theories implies an overly rational and materialistic basis for revolution. The Marxist, frustration-aggression, systems, and modernization theories suggest that the major cause of frustration is a lack of satisfaction of material needs or expectations. This emphasis, however, tends to promote theoretical omission of the necessary unifying element because such a factor must transcend economic considerations in order to bond together social groups whose economic interests are often nonidentical and sometimes even in conflict. Analyses of past revolutions indicate that key unifying factors have been nonrational in a strict economic sense and appealed for movement support on moral and emotional bases. For the majority of revolutions examined in this volume, a major unifying element was nationalism. This is a sentiment not necessarily identical to the gratification of economic aspirations, but rather one that involves a passionate need to rally in solidarity with one's country folk and to fulfill that part of one's self-identity and self-esteem that derives from membership in a particular national group.

The Skocpol and Trimberger structural theory, in contrast, does provide a logical framework for explaining the development of nationalism by focusing on the role of competition and conflict among countries at different levels of technological and economic strength. According to this structural theory, just as a society's government, often the most immediate target for revolutionary transformation, is not defined as an entity reducible to the interests of an individual economic class, similarly the driving engine of revolution, mass participation, is not exclusively the expression of a single class's aspirations. Rather, popular involvement and support for revolution can be viewed in part as a manifestation of most of the population's mobilization against a foreign adversary. The effort to overthrow a domestic government perceived as either unable or unwilling to defend the nation against exploitation by a foreign power can be interpreted as functionally the central component of the war against the external enemy itself. Thus, unlike the more limited Marxist, frustration-aggression, systems, and modernization theories, the Skocpol and Trimberger structural perspective provides a possible explanation for the occurrence of the necessary unifying motivation for revolution. As noted in Chapter 8, the Skocpol and Trimberger structural theory can also be applied to a group of nations sharing the same religious tradition. In that case common religious identity (such as Islam), rather than nationalism, can play the role of uniting not only people of different classes but also people of different countries in a transnational revolutionary effort.

Lack of theoretical inclusion of the world permissiveness factor has probably resulted from the difficulty of identifying a scientific basis for predicting this element
of the revolutionary situation. In modern history the willingness of major powers,
such as the United States and the Soviet Union, to stand aside and allow revolutions
to occur appeared very dependent on the idiosyncrasies and personal philosophies
of top government leaders, in particular Jimmy Carter (Nicaragua and Iran) and
Mikhail Gorbachev (Eastern Europe). In other cases, powerful nations have chosen not to intervene effectively or to stop interventions and allow revolutions to
succeed because of lack of popular support for such interventions; fear of provoking war with or economic sanctions by disapproving countries; military, economic,
or other internal strife that made effective intervention impossible; or, in some
cases, opposition to the government a revolution seeks to overthrow. Just as some
students of revolution have argued that the circumstances giving rise to individual
revolutions are too unique to particular societies to be validly depicted in any general theory of revolution, it might also be argued that the causes of international
permissiveness toward revolution have been so varied as to defy incorporation into
any existing theoretical framework.

REVOLUTIONS OF THE FUTURE?

The great reduction in East-West hostility from the 1990s on constituted a far-
reaching increase in international permissiveness for revolutionary change. Many
societies had been characterized by both mass and elite discontent, but until the
1990s proponents of revolution were restrained by the perception of a high probability of external intervention, as well as internal repression, justified by the need to
counter the threat of communist or capitalist aggression. Without the restraint of
the previously intense East-West conflict, many peoples were at least temporarily
freer to consider significant or even sweeping economic, political, or other social
change as a means of coping with serious social problems.

There are a number of sites with potential for revolution. Many nations are dominated by authoritarian governments or are characterized by extreme levels of economic inequality, or both. The motivation for revolutionary change has spurred the
development of social movements within some of these societies. Participants often
envisioned differing forms of political and/or social transformations. Some aspired
to create European-style democracies and others Islamic republics. In Iran, the first
modern Islamic republic, millions struggle for greater freedom of assembly and democracy and some for an end to clerical domination of the state.

In Asia tens of millions confront the task of democratizing China, Myanmar,
North Korea, Thailand, Vietnam, and other nations. Many Latin American, African,
and Caribbean peoples face the monumental problems of dealing with enormous

foreign debts, reducing poverty, accomplishing the genuine democratization of political systems, and, in some cases, dealing with powerful drug-trafficking organizations. Given the chance, those experiencing such problems may opt for radical change.

The repression of several pro-democracy movements in the context of the Arab revolution that began in December 2010 shows international permissiveness for revolution, even for revolution to achieve democracy, does not exist everywhere. In the Middle East oil-rich monarchies appear to fear the establishment of democracy and democratically elected governments in Arab nations. This also seems to be true of some political elites in the US and Europe. There is concern among these entities that democratically elected governments in Arab nations, reflecting popular sentiment, would be less favorable toward US and British policies in the region. Without strong, unconditional support from at least the United States, revolutions to democracy in the Middle East appear unlikely to succeed in the face of domestic and regional opposition.

Genuine democracy, unrestrained and free from intimidation by other nations or external economic forces, has the potential to be an instrument of popular revolution in countries where people suffer from limited opportunity and exploitation. In the twenty-first century, rejuvenated political democracies in several Latin American nations, including Venezuela, Bolivia, and Ecuador, led to the election and reelection of leaders committed to sweeping change on behalf of their nations' poor and to curbing what they viewed as socially and morally destructive neoliberal economic policies. Revolution—meaning, according to our definition, structural social change—may be carried out in more and more cases through the ballot box. This appears to be the main reason why the peoples of so many Arab nations, despite widespread participation in pro-democracy uprisings that began in December of 2010, have at least temporarily seen their aspirations frustrated by antidemocratic forces.

Social movement leaders who formulate themes of moral and community renewal and devise new forms of society that combine the equal opportunity and freedom from want historically emphasized by socialism with the individual fulfillment stressed by capitalism will likely continue to inspire many people with the call to revolutionary change.

REFERENCES AND FURTHER READINGS

DeFronzo, James. 2006a. Introduction. In *Revolutionary Movements in World History*, xix–xxii.

———, ed. 2006b. *Revolutionary Movements in World History: From 1750 to the Present*. 3 vols. Santa Barbara, CA: ABC-CLIO.

Foran, John. 2005. *Taking Power: On the Origins of Third World Revolutions*. Cambridge, UK: Cambridge University Press.

Foran, John, David Lane, and Andreja Zivkovic. 2008. *Revolution and the Making of the Modern World*. New York: Routledge.

Goldstone, Jack A., ed. 1998. *The Encyclopedia of Political Revolutions*. Washington, DC: Congressional Quarterly.

———, ed. 2002. *Revolutions: Theoretical, Comparative, and Historical Studies*. 3rd ed. Beverly, MA: Wadsworth.

Goodwin, Jeff. 2001. *No Other Way Out: States and Revolutionary Movements, 1945–1991*. Cambridge, UK: Cambridge University Press.

Katz, Mark N. 1997. *Revolutions and Revolutionary Waves*. New York: St. Martin's.

Selbin, Eric. 2001. "Same as It Ever Was: The Future of Revolution at the End of the Century." In Mark N. Katz, ed., *Revolution: International Dimensions*, 284–297. Washington, DC: Congressional Quarterly Press.

———. 2010. *Revolution, Rebellion, and Resistance: The Power of Story*. London: Zed.

Skocpol, Theda, and Ellen Kay Trimberger. 1978. "Revolutions and the World Historical Development of Capitalism." *Berkeley Journal of Sociology* 22:101–113.

PURCHASE AND RENTAL SOURCES

AEMS: Asian Educational Media Service, www.aems.uiuc.edu

AETV: Arts and Entertainment Television, www.aetv.com

AFSC: American Friends Service Committee, 2161 Massachusetts Ave., Cambridge, MA 02140; 617–497–5273; www.afsc.org/resources/video-film.htm

Alborada Films: www.alborada.net/alboradafilms

Amazon.com: www.amazon.com

BBC: British Broadcasting Company, www.bbc.co.uk/worldservice/documentaries/

BFF: Bullfrogfilms, www.bullfrogfilms.com/catalog/cubas.html

BIO: Biography, www.biography.com

BU: Boston University, Krasker Memorial Film Library, 985 Commonwealth Ave., Boston, MA 02215; 617–353–8112; www.bu.edu/media/krasker.html

Cine Las Americas: www.cinelasamericas.org/2009/documentary-shorts/91-american sandinista

CNR: California Newsreel, www.newsreel.org

CWU: Central Washington University Media Library Services–IMC, Ellensberg, WA 89826; 509–963–2861; www.lib.cwu.edu/media/

DCTV: Discovery Times Channel, www.dctvny.org

EMC: Educational Media Collection, www.css.washington.edu/emc/index.php

Filmakers: Filmakers Library, 124 East 40th St., New York, NY 10016; 212–808–4980; www.filmakers.com

Films Inc.: Films Incorporated, 5547 N. Ravenswood, Chicago, IL 60640; 800–323–4222

FRF: First Run Features, The Film Center Building, 630 Ninth Ave., Suite 1213, New York, NY 10036; 212–243–0600; firstrunfeatures.com

FRIF: First Run Icarus Films, www.frif.com

HC: History Channel, www.historychannel.com

Indie: Indie Docs, www.indiedocs.com

Inside Film: insidefilm@btinternet.com

ISU: Iowa State University Media Resource Center, 121 Pearson Hall, Ames, IA 50011; 515–294–8022

ITVS: Independent Television Service, www.itvs.org

IU: Indiana University Audio Visual Center, Bloomington, IN 47405

KSU: Kent State University Audio Visual Services, 330 University Library, Kent, OH 44242; 330–672–3456

LVC: Library Video Company, www.libraryvideo.com

NAATA: National Asian American Telecommunications Association, www.capaa .wa.gov/naata.html

PBS: Public Broadcasting Service, 1320 Bradock Pl., Alexandria, VA 22314; 800–344–3337 and 800–328–7271 (for ordering videos); www.pbs.org

PSU: Pennsylvania State University Audio Visual Services, Special Services Building, University Park, PA 16802

PTTV: Paper Tiger Television, http://papertiger.org/node/650

PU: Purdue University Audio Visual Center, West Lafayette, IN 47907

SAMC: Southern African Media Center, Resolution Inc./California Newsreel, 149 Ninth St. #420, San Francisco, CA 94103; www.newsreel.org

SEG: Sterling Entertainment Group, www.sterlingentertainmentgroup.com

SUN: Sunrise Media LLC, www.sunrisemedia.tv/films

SUNY-B: State University of New York at Buffalo, Educational Communications Center, Media Library, 24 Capen Hall, Buffalo, NY 14260

SYRU: Syracuse University Film Rental Center, 1455 E. Colvin St., Syracuse, NY 13210; 315–479–6631; library.syr.edu/information/media/film/main.htm

Truman Library: www.trumanlibrary.org/educ/video.htm

UARIZ: University of Arizona Film Library, 1325 E. Speedway, Tucson, AZ 85721; www .library.arizona.edu

UC-B: University of California/Berkeley, Extension Media Center, 2223 Fulton St., Campus Box 379, Berkeley, CA 94720; www.lib.berkeley.edu/MRC

UI: University of Illinois/Urbana, University Film Center, 1325 S. Oak St., Champaign, IL 61820; www.library.uiuc.edu

UIOWA: University of Iowa Audiovisual Center, C-5 East Hall, Iowa City, IA 52242; www.uiowa.edu/~avcenter

UMINN: University of Minnesota Audio Visual Services, 3300 University Ave. S.E., Minneapolis, MN 55414; www.classroom.umn.edu/cts/avrental

UMISSOURI: University of Missouri/Columbia, Academic Support Center, 505 East Stewart Rd., Columbia, MO 65211; www.missouri.edu/~ascwww

UMONT: University of Montana Instructional Materials Services, Missoula, MT 59812; www.libcat.lib.umt.edu

UNEV-R: University of Nevada/Reno, Film Library, Getchell Library, Reno, NV 89557; 775–784–6037; www.innopac.library.unr.edu/search/X

USF: University of South Florida, Film Library, 402 Fowler Ave., Tampa, FL 33620; www .lib.usf.edu

UT-A: University of Texas/Austin, Film Library, P.O. Box W, Austin, TX 78712; www.lib .utexas.edu

UT-D: University of Texas at Dallas, Media Services, P.O. Box 643, Richardson, TX 75083; www.utdallas.edu/library

UWASH: University of Washington Instructional Media Services, Seattle, WA 98195; www.lib.washington.edu

UWISC-M: University of Wisconsin/Madison, Bureau of Audio-Visual Instruction, 1327 University Ave., Madison, WI 53701; www.library.wisc.edu

UWY: University of Wyoming, Audio Visual Services, Laramie, WY 82071; 307–766–3184; www-lib.uwyo.edu

WMM: Women Make Movies, www.wmm.com

WSU: Washington State University, 4930 Academic Media Services, Pullman, WA 99164–5604; 509–335–4535; www.wsulibs.wsu.edu

ABOUT THE AUTHOR

James DeFronzo is emeritus faculty of sociology at the University of Connecticut. His books include *The Iraq War: Origins and Consequences* (Westview Press) and the award-winning three-volume encyclopedia *Revolutionary Movements in World History*, now available in more than sixty nations around the globe. He is also the author of numerous articles on political sociology, revolutionary movements, criminology, and social policy related to crime.

INDEX